NORMAL WOMEN

PHILIPPA GREGORY

NORMAL WOMEN

900 YEARS OF MAKING HISTORY

WILLIAM
COLLINS

William Collins
An imprint of HarperCollins*Publishers*
1 London Bridge Street
London SE1 9GF

WilliamCollinsBooks.com

HarperCollins*Publishers*
Macken House, 39/40 Mayor Street Upper
Dublin 1, D01 C9W8

First published in Great Britain in 2023 by William Collins

1

A catalogue record for this book is
available from the British Library

HB ISBN 978-0-00-860170-6
TPB ISBN 978-0-00-860171-3

Set in Adobe Garamond Pro
Printed and bound in the UK using 100%
renewable electricity at CPI Group (UK) Ltd

Contents

Part 4: 1485–1660 Becoming a Weaker Vessel

Part 5: 1660–1764 Locked Out and Locked In

Part 6: 1765–1857 Making a Lady

Part 7: 1857–1928 Separate Spheres

Part 8: 1928–1945 Into the World

Part 9: 1945–1994 A Woman Today

Introduction

I first had the idea for this book around the time that I wrote *The Other Boleyn Girl*, when I found a woman, Mary Boleyn, who made her own remarkable life but enters history only as the sister to the more famous Anne. She made me think of all the other women whose names and stories are lost, and even the stories my mother told me: about growing up during the war years, of her mother who did not dare to be a suffragette, of her aunt, a scholar who could not graduate from an English university, of the letters she edited, written by her kinswoman – an eighteenth-century feminist. This book is about them, and all the women who 'lived faithfully a hidden life, and rest in unvisited tombs'.[1]

The first schools in England were church schools and the first scholars were priests, so the first historians were men like the Venerable Bede who wrote the *Ecclesiastical History of the English People* in AD 731, naming only 18 women in their own right from a population of about 1 million: 0.0018 per cent – statistically invisible. There are only six chronicles surviving from the early medieval period – all written by men, mostly about the kings and their wars, and these are the basis of all the histories of the period.

They set a tradition. *A History of the English-Speaking Peoples* by Winston Churchill, published in the twentieth century, is a description not of the 'peoples' but of English-speaking men: 1,413 named men, and just 98 named women. What we read as a history of our nation is a history of men, as viewed by men, as recorded by men.

Is 93.1 per cent of history literally 'His Story' because women don't *do* anything? Are women so busy with their Biology that they have no time for History, like strict timetable choices – you can't do both? The only women of interest to the male record keepers were mothers, queens, taxpayers and criminals. The records are all written by men – mostly men of the church – and they have little or no interest in women. Women are there, making fortunes and losing them, breaking the law and enforcing it, defending their castles in siege and setting off on crusades; but they're often not recorded, or mentioned only in passing by historians, as they were just normal women living normal lives, not worthy of comment.

Medieval women only enter the records when the record keepers complain of them: when they are accused in the church courts of adultery or promiscuity, when they are named in the records as gossips, when they appear in the criminal courts charged with thieving or usury or fraud, when they are registered as prostitutes or kidnapped. They're often named as rioters: every time land was enclosed, women in England broke fences, trespassed, poached, reclaimed the common land. Every hungry year they broke into bakers, corn mills, or the barns where grain was stored for export, and divided it among the crowd and paid the right price. Sometimes the local priest or magistrate would arrive and oversee the weighing and the selling. If the baker or the merchants resisted, windows might be broken and food might be stolen, but usually everyone understood that the poor women – women whose names were not even recorded – were price-setting and rationing food. But then, in the eighteenth century, the mood changed: merchants and the landowners stopped appeasing the crowd and the women were named as troublemakers, identified in the court records and their harsh punishments recorded. Part of my work in writing a history of Normal Women has been recognising the normality of women, however they are named: rioting women, power-mad women, manipulative women, viragoes, angels, witches.

Poor medieval women had a sense of themselves: supporting each other, employing each other, naming other women as their heirs, holding other women to a standard of behaviour – but legally they were owned by their fathers or husbands and bound to stay in their communities. Only in work gangs and guilds could they have a sense of themselves as a group with a distinct shared female life. They did not record themselves as a group, they did not define themselves, describe themselves nor publish, nor are there are many diaries of individual women's lives: until the English civil wars in the middle of the seventeenth century drove women into writing petitions and demanding rights from the men-only parliament, keeping journals of their experiences, recipes for their medicines, private letters to keep families together and businesses intact, and then – finally publishing, so that women could read about themselves.

They asked why women were not in the Creation story as an equal to Adam? In the explosion of women writing fiction in the eighteenth century, they asked: 'How is a woman different to a man?' About 1860, they asked, 'Why can't we get a divorce on the same grounds as men?' Around 1890, they started to ask, 'Why can't we vote?' Around 1950, they asked, 'Why are we not in History?' – and women historians began the process of rereading the historical records to find out what the women were doing in their dark and silent past while men were shining a spotlight and amplifying themselves. These are the historians who produced the first great histories of women, succeeded by biographers of heroines and of the family, social historians of movements and then the editors of lists of 10 memorable women or top 20 names. All these publications help put women into history. But the biographies emphasise exceptional individuals, histories of the family see women as daughters and mothers – Biology again! The histories of groups speak of witches or suffragettes or midwives – focusing on bizarre or campaigning groups, not the normality of women's lives, and the shortlists of women are too short – only 20 women in history? Even Winston Churchill counted 98!

Indebted to all these authors, what I wanted to write was a *huge* book about women – those engaged in unusual practices and those living uneventful lives, those who were up against their society and those gliding along the top of it, the few we have heard of and the millions that we have not. And I wanted to show that murderers and brides, housewives and pirates, whores and weavers, farmers and milliners, female husbands, hermits, the chaste, the jousters, painters, nuns, queens, witches and soldiers – are all part of women's history, all part of our national history – even though they lived and died without a man noticing them for long enough to write down their names.

And finally – here is just one, very dear to me:

Elaine Wedd, around 20 years old, a member of the First Aid Nursing Yeomanry. This picture reminds me that when we write normal women into the history of our country, we restore ourselves: our sisters, our friends and our foremothers. And this is my mother – a normal woman, like all heroines.

Part 1

1066–1348
Doomsday

Doomsday

The invasion of England by the Norman army in 1066 – Duke William of Normandy versus King Harold of England – would be far more than a regime change for the women of England. It was the hardening of a tyranny by men who captured the kingdom and its fortune, passed it father to son excluding women, created laws enslaving women, composed religion and philosophy to denigrate women; men whose violence was directed at women, and whose need for cash and greed for profit would underpay and overwork women for centuries.

The account book compiled to establish the value of lands for royal taxation could be challenged no more than Judgment Day itself, and was named in the twelfth century as the Domesday Book. For the women of England, the Norman invasion was indeed a day of doom.

The Bayeux Tapestry, a near-contemporary 70-metre long embroidered linen panel, shows an invasion of men: 632 of them. Nearly 200 horses are depicted, 55 dogs, 500 other animals and birds – but only five women, all of them threatened or suffering violence. Anglo-Saxon Queen Edith mourns her husband Edward the Confessor; another woman (probably Ælfgifu, the wife of King Cnut – or Ælfgyva as it is on the tapestry) is being touched by a clerk or priest; a woman flees a burning building with her son; and, in the margin, a naked woman runs from a nude man with an erect penis, and another naked woman defies a naked man who holds an axe.

There are more penises than English women in the tapestry: 88 on the horses, five on the men. The expert designers, weavers and embroiderers

– probably English women themselves working for a Norman lord[1] – showed allowable male sexual violence arriving with the Normans and tolerated by them.

William of Normandy was a notoriously aggressive leader, who had already brutally conquered his homeland with a battle-hardened army. Their arrival marked the end of an England that had settled into relatively peaceful rule under Anglo-Saxon lords, inspired by a concept of 'good lordship', where women had legal rights, some owned land and their own fortune, ruled over their tenants, could marry or separate freely and could choose their heirs.[2]

A third of the surviving pre-conquest wills were written by women, signing their own names. Wynflæd, grandmother of King Edgar, left a fortune on her death (*c*.950), and a special bequest to her daughter Æthelflæd of favourite jewellery and an estate: 'Her engraved bracelet and her brooch, and the estate at Ebbesborn and the title deed as a perpetual inheritance to dispose of as she pleases; and she grants to her the men and the stock and all that is on the estate.'[3]

The 'men' would have been the villeins attached to the land with tenancy and employment agreements, the landless serfs who worked for free and were housed by the lord, and the slaves, who made up as much as 10 per cent of the population,[4] captured in war or purchased. They too were landless, unpaid and unfree, mostly white workers. Wynflæd ordered that her slaves be freed, for the benefit of her soul; but two highly skilled among them, 'a woman-weaver and a seamstress', she left to her daughters; a cook (probably a slave) was left to her granddaughter Eadgifu, who also inherited two chests, her best bed-curtain, her best tunic and cloak, her old filigree brooch and a long tapestry.[5] Other children were to receive a 'red tent', a double badger-skin gown, tapestries, bed linen and books.[6]

Wynflæd was not the only wealthy woman landowner in Anglo-Saxon England. In East Anglia and the town of Oxford, about one in every seven landowners was a woman, and 14 per cent of the tenants on royal lands were named as women.[7] The Domesday Book – a snapshot of England at the moment of William's invasion – listed 16,667 male landowners and 479 women.[8] Among these were some extremely wealthy women: Gytha Thorkilsdottir, Countess of Wessex, mother of King Harold, owned massive estates in southern England stretching over 11 modern counties. Harold's influential and wealthy wife Edith Swan

Neck held vast lands. Two of the greatest women landowners of 1086 were not even named in the Domesday Book – they were referred to as the *wife* of Hugh, son of Grip, and the *mother* of Robert Malet.[9]

A woman named Asa, a small landowner in Yorkshire, appeared in the Domesday records claiming her lands after separating from her husband. The jury in the case followed the old Anglo-Saxon law: Asa won and held her land in her own right. She was lucky to come under Anglo-Saxon law – the new Norman laws would rule that no wife could own land or keep it after marriage without a specific settlement. No woman would annul a marriage or divorce without permission from the church courts or Parliament for the next eight centuries.

Another woman tenant, Widow Leofgeat, held 400 acres in Knook in Wiltshire, probably a pension from the Anglo-Saxon royal court where she made the gold fringe to trim royal robes.[10] The widow of Manasses, the royal cook, held her dower lands in her own name.[11] There was a woman landowner and brewster in Chester and a woman jester or musician-poet – Adelina – who held lands in Hampshire.[12] A skilled sempstress, Æflgyd, was paid in land at Oakley in Buckinghamshire for teaching the sheriff Godric's daughter gold embroidery work.[13]

The Domesday Book had been commissioned to show the invader the state of the land that he claimed as all his own. As the *Anglo-Saxon Chronicle* described: 'After this had the king a large meeting, and very deep consultation with his council, about this land; how it was occupied, and by what sort of men. Then sent he his men over all England into each shire; commissioning them to find out "How many hundreds of hides were in the shire, what land the king himself had, and what stock upon the land; or, what dues he ought to have by the year from the shire."'[14]

All the lands belonged to the king by right of conquest, and he favoured his chiefs of staff with grants of land. Female ownership all but died out. In 1066, there were 25 women landholders recorded in Essex but only 9 recorded in 1086. Yorkshire listed 19 women in 1066 and 4 in 1086. Suffolk listed more than 50 women owners in 1066 but 43 of them vanished in only 20 years. The great landowners were now all Normans, all male. William did not grant any land to women except kinswomen and a few nunneries.[15]

Anglo-Saxon women who refused to accept Norman rule found themselves landless. Edith Swan Neck, widow of King Harold Godwinson, lost her widow's dower of Walsingham Manor and the famous shrine associated with her. Gunnhildr, King Harold's own daughter, lost all her lands and hid in a nunnery to escape a forced marriage to a Norman lord.[16] Lower-class Anglo-Saxon women were robbed, assaulted and raped by the invading soldiers. Although William commanded the nobles to 'restrain themselves', the 'Penitential Ordinance' ruled that rapists and fornicators should pay nothing more than a fine, and William's vice-regents – Odo of Bayeux and William FitzOsbern – protected their men when they were accused of plunder or rape. English women were abducted and sold into slavery.[17]

William's 15 chiefs of staff were given huge estates to hold for the new king. In turn, they granted land to their officers: 170 tenants-in-chief.[18] It took only a few years for the Anglo-Saxon aristocracy to be completely replaced by a Norman, French-speaking elite, which protected itself so successfully that it has survived to this day.[19] The top tier of landowners in England remains Norman: 70 per cent of the country is owned by 10 per cent of the people,[20] most of them descendants of Norman invaders.[21] The Grosvenor family, headed by the Duke of Westminster, descend from William of Normandy's master huntsman, Hugh le Grand Veneur, and are the richest family in England after the monarchy, owning around 140,000 acres of land in Britain, including much of Mayfair and Belgravia in London.[22] Asked the secret of his success, the late duke said that it helped to arrive with William the Conqueror.

The Anglo-Saxons had an elective monarchy – their king was chosen by a parliament of lords – but William won the throne in battle and then left it to his sons. His lords copied him: lands were inherited by male heirs, however distant, however incompetent, overlooking all daughters. The Normans brought patriarchy to England, formalised it in law and kept women from the throne for five centuries.

One of the few women to be given land was William's niece Judith. She was endowed with properties and married to a defeated Anglo-Saxon lord: Waltheof, Earl of Northumbria. The attempt to lock the earl to the invaders failed: Waltheof rebelled against William in the 'revolt of the earls' and was executed, leaving Judith a wealthy widow. When she defied King William, refusing to marry his next choice, he took her lands back.

The most powerful woman in England, Queen Matilda, the wife of William, was less honoured than Anglo-Saxon queens, who had been anointed with special holy oil and crowned as monarchs in their own right. Matilda was only crowned in 1068, nearly two years after William, and she was not consecrated with holy oil.[23] She did get the work: her husband gave her huge royal lands and fees and the title of regent, relying on her to rule the Duchy of Normandy when he was in England, and England as regent in his frequent absences. Lords' wives also devoted their lives to managing the lands and houses, workers, industries and communities for the men of their family to inherit. Wives became unpaid managers, tenants for life, not owners.

William's great demand of England proved to be money to pay his army and to send back to Normandy. But the England he invaded was a subsistence economy with little use for coins or precious metals. Goods produced locally were bartered and exchanged; people only needed cash for luxuries or rarities that could not be made or grown locally. William tried to stimulate a cash economy, encouraging Jewish merchants from Rouen to settle in England from 1070. Under church laws against usury, Christians were not allowed to loan money and charge interest, and the work was given to Jewish people. Their reliability and honesty led to Jewish financiers managing huge state and private debts, essential to the European economies but hated by their debtors. In London, Jewish men and women settled in the district called 'Old Jewry' close to the Guildhall, and by the twelfth century had expanded to other towns, specifically protected by the king as his wards, with the freedom of the highways, so that they could travel the kingdom on business.[24] At the end of the century, the Jewish population of England would be less than 0.25 per cent but contributing 8 per cent of taxes, and English people found themselves deep in debt to Jewish moneylenders – their resentment sowed the seeds of antisemitism.[25]

After the invasion, everyone had to earn coins to pay taxes. This hit women food producers who fed their family and bartered surplus produce for other goods in the community. As cash became the only measure of value, women's domestic production looked as if it were done for free and women's work at home appeared to be unpaid.

Such a woman was Juliana Strapnel, a tenant renting her cottage and lands in the manor of Ingatestone, in Essex, in 1275. She paid most of her annual rent in labour: she had to do two days of ploughing and one and a half days of weeding, and one and a half days of harrowing the manor fields. She had to help with haymaking and reap one acre at harvest time. Three times a year, she had to work on projects for the manor – like road repair or ditching – and join in nut gathering in autumn.[26] She also worked for herself: ploughing, sowing, weeding and harvesting her own strips of land in the common fields, growing her own food and cooking it, raising her own animals, collecting firewood, cutting turves and gleaning after the harvest. She probably brewed her own ale and baked bread and pies in the communal village oven. She was self-sufficient, highly productive, bartering for the things she needed. The new taxes changed this economy. Juliana had to earn cash, selling her surplus food – not bartering – in the market, spinning for a fee for a manufacturer or working for another employer for cash.

William I kept a fifth of the entire lands of England for himself, as the royal estate, and decreed new laws to preserve vast areas for royal hunting, as much as a third of southern England. 'Forest law' became one of the most hated consequences of the invasion – excluding men and women from the land that supported them. *The Rime of King William*, written in 1087, probably by an Anglo-Saxon cleric, names forest law as one of the worst sins of the king, second only to taxation:

He had castles built
and poor men terribly oppressed.
The king was severe
and he took many marks of gold and
hundreds of pounds of silver from his underlings …

… He established many deer preserves
and he set up many laws concerning them
such that whoever killed a hart or a hind
should be blinded …

His great men complained of it,
and his poor men lamented it;
but he was so severe
that he ignored all their needs.

But they had to follow above all else
the king's will,
if they wanted to live
or hold on to land …[27]

This land grab took thousands of acres from previous owners and from community use as 'common land' and made them the private preserve of the king. The forest law that applied in these huge areas of England was the will of the invading king; there was no other law or courts. Anglo-Saxon kings had hunted for food and for sport, but they had never created royal forests for their exclusive use, nor banned people from the land. For women, who specialised in harvesting and gathering, the countryside that surrounded their villages offered a free source of wild fruits, herbs, nuts and mushrooms, firewood, turves and grazing land. They fished in streams and rivers, gathered rushes for making baskets and to scatter on floors. They took game and wild birds, collected eggs and put beehives on meadows and moorland. On the coast, they made salt, fished and gathered crabs, lobsters and shellfish. The medieval women lived off the land that was all around them, some of it named as 'common land' for all to share in grazing and harvesting rights, some as 'waste' where anyone could build a shelter and take up residence. To the women, whose first occupation was food production, the English countryside was both home and larder.

But by the end of the 1100s, about a quarter of England had been closed to the English people: a third of all southern England and all of the counties of Essex and Huntingdonshire. There was frequent, probably daily resistance against the forest laws, and opposition to the expansion of the hunting preserves resulted in the Forest Charter of 1217, which restored some rights to the people and limited the expansion of the protected lands. Hunting and trespass were recorded, prosecuted and punished with deaths and fines, but the women and children who carried out daily minor incursions and pilfering were rarely caught and rarely punished. Women's defiance of forest law became a civil resistance that would be seen again and again in the following centuries, as women defended their rights, their communities, their food, their markets and traditions.

One such defence was recorded in the late 1100s at a Suffolk abbey, where the chronicler Jocelin of Brakelond made a rare mention of women who came to the aid of a cottager who had fallen behind with his rent. When the abbey cellarer arrived to collect payment or take goods and food in lieu of rent from a tenant near Bury St Edmunds, he and his men were set upon by 'old women brandishing their saucepans, threatening and abusing them'.[28] The village women won the battle, frightened the bailiffs away, and the cottager kept his furniture for another day.

The Normans defended their land grab by building castles: more than 535 of them were thrown up in a hurry in the 30 years after the invasion, by a patriarchy that knew they could only keep their new territory by force. People took to arms to oppose the Norman invaders, and the medieval poet Baudri of Borgeuil described the English resistance: 'In a pathetic effort at defence, an unwarlike legion of girls, old men and boys gird up the city walls with whatever they can find.'[29]

Other rebellions were led by Anglo-Saxon women. Gytha, mother of the dead king Harold, organised a revolt at Exeter, before taking a group of women into voluntary exile from the new rulers.[30] There were uprisings on the Welsh borders from 1067 and a year later in the north of England, where an army of 900 Normans were massacred. This would provoke the 'Harrying of the North' by William that devastated Yorkshire, causing famine and depopulation, and prompted guerrilla warfare in the east of England led by Anglo-Saxon rebel Hereward the Wake in 1070.

In 1075, Emma de Gauder (1059–99) defied William I to marry the man of her choice, Ralph, Earl of East Anglia, and recruited him into the 'revolt of the earls' with her brother against William's rule. When the rebellion collapsed and her husband fled, Emma – aged only 16 – held William's own castle of Norwich against him for three months, forcing the king to make a truce with her, granting her and her troops safe passage to Brittany, where she rejoined her husband. She died while travelling with him on the First Crusade.

One of the other leaders of the revolt, Anglo-Saxon Waltheof, Earl of Northumbria, became a focus for female disobedience when the nuns of Romsey Abbey declared him a saint and his execution by William a martyrdom. Abbess Athelitz proclaimed his tomb to be the source of miracles, causing Archbishop Anselm to write to the abbess to order her silence, without success. He had to threaten to suspend Romsey Abbey's right to celebrate mass before Abbess Athelitz bowed to the greater force, ended the cult and asked Waltheof's son to leave Romsey village.[31]

Country

England was a rural country with a small population of about 1.5 million people speaking Scandinavian languages, different regional English dialects and overnight about 6,000 new Norman invaders speaking Old French. Most of the country remained empty, called 'waste': coastal plains, floodland or moorland, mountains and fens, forests and heath. Small wooden-built villages nestled around the stone-walled old manor houses, or sprang up around the new castles, where the ex-military commanders lived. Strips of common land, farmed by each family, petered out into moorland, heath or forest, where packs of wolves and wild boar roamed, and charcoal burners – often teams of women – set up little camps. Vast areas were unknown to anyone but the few poor families who scraped a living from hovels at their edges, or the vagrants or outlaws who used them as hiding and meeting places. Higher lands were used as pasture for flocks of sheep, or left as wild desolate moorland, unmapped and untouched except for the occasional mines or quarries worked by families: husbands, wives and children digging side by side. It was cold and damp, thanks to a 'little ice age' in the last quarter of the 1200s. Travellers needed a guide to take them from one village to another, and most poor people never left their village except to go to the nearby market. People could drown in the fords or even in the deep puddles that had opened up on the old Roman highways built centuries before. But the pilgrim ways linked one hospitable abbey to another, beacons of culture and wealth, often run by elite women, offering healthcare, education and a bed for the night. The inns and alehouses of the bustling and lively market towns, run by women who brewed and baked, were busy with men and women visiting for the day, or making the journey of a lifetime to the holy shrines in churches, monasteries and co-ed abbeys and women-only convents – unique places where women could hold power, manage wealth, study and create a life independent of men.

Abbeys and Convents

The only Anglo-Saxon women to retain their wealth and power through the conquest were the women of the convents and abbeys. To buy support for his invasion, William I gifted a quarter of all the agricultural land to the church and as the religious houses flourished, so did the elite group of women who managed them. They did not answer to any man in England but reported directly to the pope in Rome, with status equal to a bishop or lord. They created the great religious houses of Wilton, Romsey, Barking, Shaftesbury, St Mary's Winchester and Wherwell, which were famous for their wealth, landholdings, culture and prosperity.[32]

There was a rush of women to enter the safety of the convents after the invasion. Seven or eight new houses for women were founded after 1066 and in the next century, the new cult of Mary, Mother of God, inspired another 100 new houses, offering places for 3,000 women.[33] Theodora, in 1096 Huntington, broke her betrothal promise and, disguised as a man, ran away from home before her parents could force her to marry. Once safe, she discarded her disguise, became an anchoress – a female hermit – and took her vows.

In the twelfth century, the new doctrine of 'purgatory' – the belief that sinful souls must wait in discomfort before ascending to heaven – created a new business for enclosed, or 'cloistered', women. Patrons hoping for a fast track to heaven left rich endowments in their wills, to buy masses to be sung by the chantry choirs, creating a new income stream for the chantry and careers for musician nuns.

Under Norman rule, English abbesses improved their wealth, power and status, and some became advisors to the new royal court. In England as in Europe, abbesses were drawn from upper-class families and moved easily between church and court. Abbess Jean de Valois was authorised by the pope himself to leave her post at Fontenelle Abbey to arrange a peace between her son-in-law Edward III of England and her brother Philip VI of France. Mother superior Hildegard of Bingen advised four popes, two emperors and several kings and queens. Queens endowed nunneries, and sometimes retired to them; junior royal daughters might take the veil. Young Matilda, who would marry Henry I, proved an unruly postulant at Romsey, pulling off her black veil and stamping on it. But when crowned queen, she chose her ladies-in-waiting from her convent friends, and after her death they returned to a religious life at the Kilburn convent.[34]

Nunneries increased their wealth and influence by charging high fees to novices – they could demand the full dowry of a noble-born girl. This became such a successful way to raise funds that in 1257 it was noted as an abuse by the general church council. Senior nuns could rise to be brilliant administrators: managing employees, working many acres of land and running a huge nunnery as a big business. A class of professional women accountants and managers served as priors, sub-priors and treasurers. Choir mistresses organised the complex music of the church services, while the sacrist cared for the precious vestments, and the fratress was responsible for the tables and linen. An almoner took charge of donations to the convent or abbey and the overall finances; a chamberer looked after the beds and bedding; a cellarer supervised the food and often ran the home farm; a kitchener oversaw the kitchens; an infirmarian managed the hospital, where nuns worked as surgeons, physicians and nurses, diagnosing, prescribing and treating the sick of both sexes. A novice mistress supervised and taught the novice nuns; scholars copied, translated and wrote books; and artists illuminated manuscripts, carved sculptures and painted murals. The buildings themselves were huge mansions, almost palaces, the lands extensive.

Some enclosed women became famous scholars, musicians, theologians, mystics, philosophers or saints. Euphemia (?1100s–1257), the abbess of Wherwell in Hampshire, was an architect, builder and gardener. Elected to her post on the death of the previous abbess her aunt, Euphemia doubled recruitment at the abbey from 40 to 80 nuns. She built a mill, a hall, rebuilt two manor houses at Middleton and Tufton, planned and built a homestead, a hospital, a dormitory and latrines with a fully working sewage system. When the old abbey bell tower collapsed, she designed a new one, and conceived and built a new sanctuary with 12-foot-deep foundations. She created a landscape garden with a meditation area – all this before the profession of architecture was invented or any theoretical training was available.

Before the arrival of the printing press, the nunneries were centres of research and writing, book-copying, illustrating, book-making, publishing and book collecting in their great libraries. They were places of education for girls, teaching novices and pupils reading, writing and in some cases mathematics, music and languages. Convents became so successful as schools that the first written instructions for hermit women forbade them the distraction of teaching and told them to study alone. Enclosure and solitude developed into a female speciality after the Norman invasion, and the first instruction for all hermits by Aelred of Rievaulx was addressed exclusively to women.[35] More women than men lived as hermits in England from 1100, until the Reformation of the church ended the practice.[36] Julian of Norwich was one of them.

Some women outside the church chose to live and work together in communities called 'beguinages', sometimes following the hours of the convent but without taking religious vows or submitting to the control of the church. The Maison Dieu at York in the 1300s may have been one of these – more like a spiritual female commune than a convent.[37] Some widows chose to become 'vowesses', taking a vow of celibacy on the death of their husband and following the hours of a convent, and some even separated from living husbands and managed their secular households according to convent hours and nunnery vows.

Women were prepared to die for their faith: in 1285, eight women and 55 men were burned for heresy against the Roman Catholic Church in Yorkshire.[38] Not all enclosed women were so committed: some postulants were given to the church as an act of thanksgiving by their families, or to avoid the costs of raising a daughter; these girls were probably unwilling recruits. Nuns escaped from their orders, and some of the reported rapes and kidnaps of nuns were women staging their escape from the convent with the help of a friend or lover. Agnes Sheen, a nun of Godstow Nunnery, was apparently kidnapped in 1290 – but an inquiry revealed she had been escaping the nunnery, not taken against her will.[39] Another discontented nun, Agnes de Flixthorpe, ran from her religious house at Stamford and hid out in Nottingham. She was dressed as a man when she was recaptured in 1309. The nunnery put her in chains and punished her for five years, until she convinced them of her penitence in 1314 ... when she ran away again. This time she was not recaptured.[40] Another nun, Joan of Leeds, faked her own death to get away from her Benedictine nunnery at St Clement's, York, to the town of Beverley. The Archbishop of York, William Melton, wrote to the dean of Beverley in 1318, telling him to 'warn Joan that she should return to her house'. He complained that Joan had persuaded her friends to help her make a dummy to pass off as her dead body and be buried in her place, in consecrated ground. According to the archbishop, she 'perverted her path of life arrogantly to the way of carnal lust and away from poverty and obedience. Having broken her vows, and discarded the religious habit, she now wanders at large to the notorious peril to her soul and to the scandal of all her order.'[41] But the archbishop did not order the dean to arrest Joan and send her back to her convent, only to reprove her. Perhaps both men thought it was easier to scold than to capture a woman who was determined to be free.

Towns

There were only 18 towns in England in 1066, each a sprawl of unplanned houses with big gardens, drying greens for laundry, grazing greens for the town's animals, orchards, market gardens and parkland for hunting, as well as workshops for craft industries. Here, just as in the surrounding farmland, raising livestock and growing food was essential. The country people brought their produce for sale in the daily or weekly markets, driving the animals on the hoof down long-distance drovers' roads to urban markets and slaughterhouses. Urban women entrepreneurs went out to the country, taking raw materials to women pieceworkers in their cottages: textiles for spinning, weaving or finishing; cloth for tailoring; leather for saddlers and cobblers; metals for blacksmiths and goldsmiths.

Most people were born in the rural areas, and many would return to them, particularly girls who would go into town for a few years in domestic service before going back to their villages for marriage, to take up a partnership in the family business, inherit family land and rights, or a tenancy. Town and country life merged – every countrywoman went to market, and townswomen would head out into the countryside for seasonal work during harvesting and haymaking.[42] Despite the hard work of tenant farmers like Juliana Strapnel, there were hungry years: in the great famine of 1315–18, about 10 per cent of the population starved.[43]

The towns offered people economic opportunities and freedom from the strict rules of the lord of the manor. A Sussex town like Lewes could be a magnet for country girls: women outnumbered men there in 1378.[44] Towns presented work opportunities for women as well as for men: Stratford-upon-Avon listed 60 different recognised occupations, Bristol more than a hundred.[45] By 1300, there were at least 30 towns and cities in England, each with a good-sized church, a regular market and stone-built buildings. Most settlements had originally formed around a castle, and spilled beyond the old defensive walls, around the castle gates, which might still be closed at sunset every day.

As the towns grew bigger and more prosperous throughout the century, they became increasingly independent of the local Norman lord in his castle. They sought royal charters to be self-governing: electing a mayor, aldermen and bailiffs to enforce rules on public behaviour, safety and hygiene, and to represent civic interests to important visitors or in disputes with the church or neighbours. Once independence was won, the little towns guarded it fiercely, obeying their own charter and defying requests from lord, church or king.[46] They raised local taxes to pay for the few urban services like street sweepers, watchers and gate keepers, and these civic jobs were open to women.

Life in the urban areas proved so unhealthy, especially for women and children, that towns had to be repopulated from the countryside, especially during plague years or epidemics. Elite people suffered from the dirt and disease almost as much as the poor did: a lady in a castle would use a privy that voided into a moat that was rarely cleaned; townswomen's houses had a pit dug for waste, which was occasionally dug out; and poor people would use a dung heap or defecate in the muddy streets, which were already fouled by animals. People drew their water from the rivers or from the local pump or well, all contaminated by the waste dumped by households into watercourses and the pollution from industries like leather works, textiles and metal works. With no understanding of how infections spread, there was little interest in cleanliness and hygiene, except as a luxury.

Small manufacturing industries flourished alongside residential areas. Leather works, with their poisonous dyes and disgusting smells from freshly skinned hides, would be sited on streams and rivers, and women worked in these hard environments, as they did everywhere else: Petronilla Ballew was a tanner in Shrewsbury in the early 1300s.[47] Foundries and metalworks were sited in their own, high fire-risk areas, and women worked with metal: forging heavy pieces like ploughshares, skilled pieces such as armour and delicate work like jewellery.

The guilds became the leading organisations in towns and cities, setting apprentices to masters, admitting male and female members, maintaining standards, excluding 'foreigners' (even artisans from nearby towns) and supporting members who had fallen on hard times. They organised celebrations, feast days and holy days, and sometimes put on events for the public. The Guild of Tailors of Lincoln showed its care for men and women members – promising to pay for masses for any deceased brother or sister, at home or away, a sort of after-life insurance.[48] No one could set up a workshop and open for business unless he or she was a member of the relevant guild. Women could be guild members, but generally not officers, and there were very few trades without women workers as 'masters' or partners. Usually, a man would only join a guild after he had completed his apprenticeship and married, so that he could set up a workshop with a working wife as a full partner.

Some guilds only admitted women who were related to guildsmen, such as the London Girdlers', which ruled in 1344 that members could only employ women who were family members.[49] Female guild members could claim townsmen status and the freedom of the town: the obligation to pay local taxes and the right to vote for the officers. Other women could claim the freedom of a town if they were independently wealthy or inherited their husband's townsman status on his death. Some towns were well aware that they needed a female workforce and attracted women with an offer of the status of a 'freeman' or 'townsman' with legal rights – whatever her status. Women were valued for their money-making abilities, and in many towns even a poor woman who had run away from her home or her feudal lord would be granted 'freeman' status if she could show that she had supported herself in the town for a year and a day. Such women – working for themselves and keeping their own wages – usually chose to marry later than those living in the country, and some never married at all, creating a group so numerous and so distinct that historians call them 'singlewomen'.[50]

London

Prior to 1066, the capital of England was Winchester. It provided the administrative centre for a royal court that moved seasonally, from castle to palace around the country. In 1200, the royal documents were moved to a permanent home in the palace of Westminster, then a small town outside the walled City of London. Westminster and London grew side by side: the City as the centre of trade and Westminster as the home of the royal court and government. In 1100, the population of all the parishes of London was little more than 15,000. By 1300, it had grown to about 80,000.

There was steady demand for women domestic servants in all the towns, especially in London, where many servants were needed to manage and maintain the great town houses and their market gardens, with their own cows, hens or pigs. Servants also worked in the businesses that were sited at home – manufacturing, retail, catering and crafts – with little distinction being made between work for the family and production for sale.

Women dominated many London trades; the textile trade was almost entirely run by women, and in the early 1400s the London Brewers' Company had 39 women members.[51] Women formed the majority in retail marketing, especially in second-hand goods, small loans and the pawn business of trading goods for credit or cash: Mariotta Convers was a successful pawnbroker in London in the 1300s.[52]

Londoner Emma Hatfield inherited and ran her own chandlery business, making and selling candles. Goda a Gablere was a London moneylender to merchants and shippers in the 1200s.[53] She confessed to the crime of being a Christian engaged in the sin of usury, repented and lived out the rest of her life as a nun.[54] With no trades closed to women, their industry powered London's prosperity.[55] Women who partnered with their husbands in a trade and then at his death married a fellow guild member consolidated two successful businesses, unifying capital and keeping experienced management in the business. Some widows united and developed multiple businesses over their lives, using their inheritance from husbands to reinvest. Many master widows married their apprentices, giving the business continuity and solving the problem of succession.

Girls were apprenticed to trades as well as boys, working in skilled and well-paid jobs and gaining a place in the guild on their graduation. In 1276, Marion de Lymeseye was apprenticed to Roger Oriel in his business as a paternoster-maker – a creator of rosaries for Roman Catholic prayers.[56]

Many London parishes had their own local guild, an association of prosperous parishioners to provide charity and social control in their area, open to any successful male or female master in the parish, regardless of their trade. The guild of Holy Trinity at St Botolph's near Aldersgate listed 274 women members and 530 men in the late 1300s.[57] Women were equal members in the parish guild of St James, Garlickhithe, in London, and paid the substantial sum of 20d each for the compulsory annual feast – about four or five day's pay for a skilled worker – suggesting women members were working full-time at skilled artisan level and getting paid the full rate.[58] Some parish guilds provided dowries for poorer young women members, for marriage or entry to a nunnery. Pilgrims formed into guilds, as did devotees of some saints and worshippers at certain churches, and some people joined a guild to provide for funeral expenses.[59]

Women's Status

All Englishwomen lived in a society that accepted without question the judgement of the ancient Greeks and the wisdom of the church fathers: that women were 'naturally' inferior to men, physically, mentally and spiritually.[60] The incoming Normans enshrined this into law. Every woman lived under her father's name. On marriage, she became a 'femme couvert' – everything she already owned or earned in future became the property of her husband. The children she birthed were his alone. She had no official legal existence and was assumed to act under her husband's direction. He had to answer for her crimes. If she were kidnapped or raped, it was a crime against her husband or father, who were compensated for damage to their property.

As always, women were quick to take advantage of their oppression. If a woman had no presence in law, she could run up debts for her husband or father to settle, and he would be sued – not her. He might be held responsible for her criminal behaviour too, such as taking part in public unrest. This became an increasingly difficult question for the courts when women rebelled – for seven centuries after the Norman invasion, judges were afraid that women believed they were free to riot, and were terrified that they were right.

Women accepted the dogma of inferiority but lived as if they were healthy, strong, intelligent, spiritual and sexual. They were told, and some may have believed, that they were inferior to men; but many lived as equals, getting on with their real lives, ignoring the lawmakers, creating their own businesses, making their own fortunes and keeping them, leaving money and lands to their chosen heirs – often kinswomen. They played as well as worked alongside men, dancing, dicing, competing at chess and other games, as witnessed by Ipomydon, a twelfth-century poet:

> When they had dyned, as I you saye,
> Lordes and ladyes yede to playe;
> Some to tables, and some to chesse,
> With other gamys more or lesse.[61]

In 1276 in the London Eyre, a game of chess turned violent: 'David de Bristoll and Juliana wife of Richard le Cordwaner were playing chess together in Richard's house, with several others present; a quarrel arising between them, David struck Juliana in the thigh with a sword, so that she died forthwith.'[62]

In the game of chess, the queen was a piece of authority, essential to the survival of the king – whose death marked defeat and the end of the game. But she was not yet able to move in all directions. She could only move one diagonal square at a time, until around 1300, when she was allowed to move two squares in her first move and became one of the key pieces for victory.[63]

Some women married late, or never married at all, and were single women, owing fealty to no man, economic managers of their own individual lives.[64] To cope with women like these, the feudal law had to invent a category known as 'femme sole' – a woman alone. Such a woman could enter into a tenancy in her own name, run a business, borrow, lend and even earn freeman status, equal to men. Many widows also declared themselves femmes sole and even married women could claim the status if their husbands allowed. Some towns insisted on giving women traders femme sole status to prevent them hiding behind their husbands' names, dodging taxes and shirking their civic responsibilities.

Noble Norman women took their husband's status as their own – often deputising for him. Some queens assumed full regency powers in the absence of the king: William I's wife Matilda took on a heavy share of the work, ruling in his absence as a duchess in the Norman lands and as queen regent in England, where she was the first female consort to be named 'Queen of England'. She established herself as an active ruler in both of her territories, travelling between the two countries to enforce her rule and, as shown in the Domesday Book, sitting as a judge on legal cases and granting charters.[65]

Her son's wife, Queen Edith Matilda (1080–1118), served as regent during Henry I's frequent absences from England, initiating a programme of church-building and signing laws and treaties with her own name. Their daughter, Empress Matilda, would invade England at the head of her own army against the usurper to the English throne, her cousin Stephen.[66] Eleanor of Aquitaine (1122–1204), famous for her independence, sexual freedom and unconventional behaviour, acted as regent during the absence of Henry II, and as an old lady served as regent for her son Richard I, negotiating for his release after he was captured while returning from the Third Crusade in 1190.[67] Isabella, queen consort of Edward II, planned and executed an invasion of England in 1326, deposed her husband the king and ruled as regent for her son Edward III.[68]

Most great Norman estates, gifted to Norman lords by the king in return for a vow of loyalty, were managed by their wives and, after their deaths, their widows. Slowly, women moved into positions of power. These women employed hundreds of workers, farming thousands of acres, managing many houses – some of them castles or palaces. These upper-class women behaved as lords, deputising for their absent husband or young son, on the land and in the manor court, sometimes drawing an income, some making a fortune and leaving wealth and goods to their chosen heirs. Women's authority was so normal that it was rarely a topic for comment.[69] While the noble husbands represented the family at the royal court and in the wider political world, competing with other great men, summoned by the king to serve in his army or even called by the church to crusade, the women ran the great homes and lands, ordered the servants, managed the workers, commanded the peasants, sat as judges in the manorial courts, and recruited and even led fighting forces. On the lord's death, his widow would manage the estate for a young son – like the thirteenth-century Margaret de Lacy, later de Quincy, Countess of Lincoln, who inherited the title of Countess of Lincoln from her mother and never handed over power and fortune to her son, who died before her.[70]

As poet and author Christine de Pisan (1363–c.1430) wrote: 'Because barons and still more commonly knights and Squires and gentlemen travel and go off to the wars, their wives should be wise and sound amid wars and manage their affairs well.'[71] Lady Isabel Berkeley was clearly worried to leave her home with her husband in charge. She told him to do absolutely nothing: 'Keep well all about you till I come home, and treat not without me, and then all things shall be well.'[72]

Bridget of Sweden, who founded the order of nuns known as the Bridgettines in 1344, would only appoint women to run the abbeys that housed both monks and nuns in co-ed houses, believing leadership to be a natural quality for women because the Virgin was 'head and queen of the apostles'.[73]

Walter de Bibbesworth's treatise on gardening in 1230 urged women to be good gardeners – he meant food producers.[74] When Bishop Robert Grosseteste wrote his French manual in 1241 on managing a great household, estate and farming, he addressed it to the English heiress Margaret de Lacy, who may have been the bishop's patron and may have commissioned the book.[75]

Upper-class women served as legal authorities and were sometimes appointed to formal office – their status outweighed their 'female defect'. In 1257, the lady of the manor Angareta de Beauchamp sat as judge in her own manor court and sentenced criminals to be hanged on her own gallows. Nichola de la Haye, who held Lincoln Castle through two sieges, was appointed sheriff of Lincoln in 1216. Ela, who inherited the title of Countess of Salisbury from her father, requested and was awarded the post of sheriff of Wiltshire in 1231.[76] One lady even reprimanded the king himself. Isabella, Countess of Arundel, with a dignity 'more than that of a woman', complained to Henry II that he was extorting money and breaking his word in 1252. According to chronicler Matthew Paris, she told the king, 'You govern neither us nor yourself well.'[77]

The Magna Carta – the 1215 agreement forced on a reluctant King John by the leading lords of the land – accidentally gave women new rights. In promising that there should be no arbitrary arrest and guaranteeing a trial by jury for freemen, the charter also gave rights to women who had the freedom of a town or city. Covered by Magna Carta under the status of freemen, they assumed a new legal existence.

Two clauses of the Magna Carta benefited widows. The lords wanted to free their own families from the control of the king so that a wealthy widow's lands could be managed by her family – not sold by the king to the highest bidder or given to a favourite. This proved a win for the widows who, as acting heads of families, might now control their dower lands. In addition, Clause 8 of Magna Carta ruled that 'No widow is to be distrained to marry while she wishes to live without a husband, as long as she gives security that she will not marry without our [royal] consent.'[78]

For the first time since the arrival of the Normans, a widow could refuse a second husband; no one – not the king, not her family – could force her to the altar. This was a huge real-life gain for many individuals, since about a third of all women were widowed – now they could suit themselves. For all, it offered the possibility of a future state of freedom.

Common women assumed authority too, appointed by town and church councils to be the principal inquirers into crimes like false paternity claims, abortion or witchcraft. In almost every market, it was women who were appointed to inspect food and ale production and women officials who approved licences. Often women led the hue and cry – pursuing named individuals or suspected criminals, policing the community before there was an official force. It was the duty of all to chase after the criminal. In the village of Warboys, there were 124 hues from 1290 to 1353 – 33 of them raised by women.[79]

Without legal status, women seldom served as reeves or constables – legal officers – and were only rarely called as witnesses at the manor criminal courts.[80]

In 1195, under Richard I, some knights were sworn to keep the peace on their lands, and by 1344 an Act required 'two or three of the best reputation in the counties' to be assigned keepers of the peace by the King's Commission – there was no specific request that the keepers be men. In 1361, an Act entitled 'What sort of persons shall be Justices of the Peace; and what authority they shall have' specified that 'one lord and with him three or four of the most worthy in the county with some learned in the law' should become justices of the peace, able to arrest, hear and punish.[81] Again, no sex is specified and ladies would deputise for their lords as justices. Manor courts would be judged by the lady of the manor in the absence of the lord.

Many women represented themselves in the civil courts. In 1344, Idonea de Hukestere successfully sued William Simond for butchering her sow. Isabella de Worstede, a house owner, took builder William Grene to court for poor work on her chimney.[82] In 1328, Alianore Wormenhal represented herself before the councillors of Oxford to ban her husband's heir from tenement buildings that she had bought jointly with her spouse and now claimed as exclusively hers. Despite the explicit law that a wife's property belonged to her husband or his heirs, and that she had no rights, the Oxford council listened to Alianore Wormenhal and consulted London councillors. They reported that in London a woman could hold land – and buildings – in her own right. Oxford decided to follow suit and Wormenhal, representing herself, won her case, kept her property and set a precedent.[83] There were even women attorneys practising law in London in the thirteenth century, one of whom was Avice de Gardebois, an attorney at law who pursued her husband's debtors.

Women were complainants in nearly half the cases of slander in the church courts, often representing themselves, to insist on their virtue as wives or daughters, or their reliability and honesty as businesswomen.[84] A woman's 'good name' not only affected her status in the community and her marriage prospects – her business depended on it. While officially she had no legal existence – her name on a contract meant nothing – in real life she could run a business if her word was known to be completely reliable. A 'good name' was not just a woman's dowry, it was her capital.

Women's Work

Many women worked in the business of credit – lending money in small amounts to each other, and pawning clothes and household goods for cash to redeem later.

Specialist moneylenders were always Jewish: a woman's name as good as that of a man, licensed equally by the church to undertake the so-called sin of usury, offering large credit and international banking businesses. Jewish bankers took bonds – promises to pay – and issued tokens to be redeemed by other Jewish moneylenders, backed by their own gold reserves and guaranteed by their word. Bankers were so badly needed for national and international trade that they were specifically protected by the monarchs in all the European countries.

A Jewish woman, Licoricia, lent money on her own account and in partnership with other lenders in the 1230s. The death of her first husband, Abraham, made Licoricia one of the richest women of

Winchester as she consolidated his business with hers. The estate of her second husband, David of Oxford, held such great debts that they had to be sealed and taken to the Jewish Exchequer in London, and Licoricia was imprisoned until the assessment was complete. After the debts had been calculated, she was offered the chance to buy his debt book at a price of 5,000 marks – the equivalent of £3.8 million in 2022.[85] Licoricia bought back her husband's debt book with her own money, to become one of the country's greatest financiers, meeting with King Henry on his visits to Winchester, using royal support against her bad debtors, and liaising with king, court and other Jewish moneylenders to manage royal and even international loans.

Licoricia ran a successful business of moneylending for thirty years, financing the royal family, the aristocracy and even the church, travelling from her home in Winchester all around England. Her name, and that of her son, was often recorded in the Calendar of the Rolls of the Jewish Exchequer over disputes when she pursued bad debts. She died in 1277, murdered with her maid, Alice of Bicton, apparently during a robbery at her house, and was probably buried at the Jewish cemetery in Winchester.[86]

Licoricia's success in supporting the national finances, like other Jewish businessmen and women in England and Europe, caused envy and suspicion. Individual lords who owed more than they could afford to moneylenders encouraged outbreaks of antisemitic hatred by their tenants to rip up debt books and cancel debts. An English Benedictine monk, Thomas of Monmouth (1149–72), accused the Jewish people of Norwich of murdering a Christian boy, inventing the 'blood libel' against them, in order to create a profitable shrine for the boy, adding a fake legend to the increasing antisemitism.

The Second Crusade against non-Christians in Europe and Muslims in the Middle East, the taxes and the debt to finance the crusade, all stoked feelings against Jewish people. When Jewish representatives attended the coronation of the new crusader king, Richard I (the 'Lionheart') in 1189, it caused antisemitic riots at the ceremony and in other English towns. Two York moneylenders, Benedict and Joceus, were attacked on their journey home and Benedict was killed. Months later, a mob broke into his house, killing everyone and looting his papers, including his debt book. Joceus led the Jewish people of York to royal protection in the king's tower in York Castle, but royal troops left their posts to join the mob in a siege of the tower. A few Jewish families who accepted safe passage and baptism into Christianity left the refuge and were killed. Those still inside – about 150 men, women and children – took the decision to die. The men killed their wives and children, and set fire to their possessions, before killing themselves. The mob then raided York Minster and destroyed the Jewish debt books that were kept there.

While York was the most notorious of massacres, attacks also took place in London, Norwich and King's Lynn. A papal decree requiring Jews to wear a white or yellow badge came into force in England, where it was ordained that 'every Jew shall wear on the front of his dress tablets or patches of cloth four inches long by two inches wide, of some colour other than that of the rest of his garment'.[87]

Richard's successor, King John, desperate for money, imposed crushing taxes on English Jews and imprisoned families and communities – men, women and children – when they could not pay. In 1275, Jewish people were even forbidden to lend money.[88] The royal debts, and finance for the corn and wool trade, were taken over by Italian bankers authorised by the pope.[89] In 1290, Edward I, urged on by his wife Eleanor of Castile and his mother Eleanor of Provence, executed 300 Jewish heads of household and expelled Jewish families from the kingdom. It was estimated at the time that more than 16,000 families went into exile, perhaps as many as 8,000 women refugees. Those families who professed Christianity and remained in England struggled to survive.[90] Many converted, denied their religion or hid their identity by changing their names, a decision that fell especially hard on Jewish women, who traditionally passed down their religion to their children. While Italian bankers controlled the profitable areas of moneylending and finance, further down the social scale the poorer debts came to be serviced by English people – often women – who concealed the crime of 'usury' by not charging interest but adding a 'gift' to the repayment.

Women's work in the country remained a necessity: 'A household will survive without the husbandman; but not without the goodwife.'[91] So declared a peasant proverb, recognising that the labour of a woman proved indispensable: her husband's was not. Everything that a man did, his wife would do alongside him, in their shared family business, and she would give birth, plant, harvest, cook, feed and raise the family as well.

A woman was so essential that few men entered into the rental of a cottage and land until they were married. Sometimes a bachelor tenant

Women trapping rabbits with a ferret in the Queen Mary Psalter, *c.*1316–21

would resign his tenancy to renew jointly with his wife, acknowledging the equality of their partnership.[92] In the village of Cuxham in Oxfordshire, a man marrying a bride with her own land would take her name. When Joan Chyld wed her husband, he shared her inheritance and took her name to became Henry Chyld at Chertsey.[93] Cristina Penifader's father gave her grants of land from 1313 until her marriage in 1317 in the village of Brigstock, in Northamptonshire, where up to a quarter of land was inherited by daughters.[94]

A woman could pay her own feudal entry fee for the right to inherit the cottage and the land and, at her death, she could leave the cottage and fortune to her heirs.[95] Widowers tended to ignore the church's traditional mourning period of a year, to remarry a new wife at once.[96] But a widow would be expected to observe mourning and run her house and business alone for a year; many continued to do so – avoiding a second marriage. Despite the Norman laws that ruled that a man leave everything to his son, widows inherited. From the 1200s, a peasant couple tended to own land 'in jointure' so that when the husband died it passed automatically to his equal partner: his wife.[97] Agnes Kateline, a widow, was a tenant in her own right when she was fined for not keeping her ditches properly dug in Broughton village in 1309. Her son was also a tenant in the village, but he did not represent his mother, who answered for herself to the manor court as an independent landowner.[98] In most areas of the country, widows of tenant farmers took over their husband's tenancy as a right, paying a fee only if the man had been a villein.[99]

The oldest son might be named as sole heir in order to keep the land-holding together, but daughters were traditionally given an inheritance, and if there was no surplus land or money to be divided, daughters usually had the right to live on the family tenement, a resident partner in the family home and business.[100] Sometimes women were gifted land in return for caring for their elderly parents; some villages allocated land to single women or widows in return for their care of elderly members of the community.

In the gardens outside the cottages, tenants grew vegetables and fruit, and grazed hens or a pig or a cow, mostly in the care of the women.[101] Dairy produce, 'puddings', fruit, grains and vegetables were women's speciality: 'housewifely made' meant it was of high quality.[102] No real distinction was made between food production for the family table and food production for barter or cash. They were the work of women and self-evidently valuable. Women found time for recreation as well, wrestling, running and playing ball games such as 'stool ball', which traditionally used three-legged milkmaid stools as bats.

In the early 1300s, men and women in labouring jobs seem to have earned about 3d a day: equal pay for equal work, and a set rate for the task, with employers paying for the skill, not for the sex of the worker.[103] Casual work – hired by the day or for the task – paid better than contracted work; urgent, seasonal and temporary work was the best paid.[104] This proved a huge advantage for women workers who could fit highly paid short seasons of intense work around their usual work of farming, producing and maintaining the home. The value of a woman's daily work in her own fields set the rate for seasonal work outside the home: any cash offered by an outside employer had to be worth more than her domestic work or pay more than the value of her home produce, for a woman to take the job.

Some countrywomen chose to leave their gardens and fields to become wage labourers: as live-in servants in a gentry household in town or country. Service was not demeaning; servants were often family friends, or children from a neighbour's household. Upper-class families sent sons and sometimes daughters to stay in other households to learn manners and management of land and home. Apprentices might be put by their parents with a family friend to work alongside the employer's children. Wards, godchildren and friends might be first employed and then married into employers' families. Servants were described as 'family' and often remembered with affection in employers' wills.[105] Some servants even left their savings to their employers as a recognition of a loving long-term bond.

Most countrywomen preferred casual work, picking up seasonal jobs, like sheep-shearing in spring or reaping or gleaning in a gang in summer to supplement the money they earned working in their homes.[106] In the towns, women gangs would work on big buildings or on repairing roads and bridges. Sometimes they were engaged on large projects like drainage or enclosures. Gangs of women dominated the charcoal business: going into the forests to cut or gather firewood, turning it into charcoal by controlled burning, working in day and night shifts over the smoking heaps of smouldering wood, before selling it to the industries that needed high heat: the metal forges and glass-making workshops, and the saucepans in the kitchens of the great houses.

The business of textiles, especially wool production, was done by women in their own homes and workshops in city, town and country. Women were shepherdesses, managing the flock; all-women shearing gangs travelled around the country in early summer; and almost every woman spun as she went about her working day, her spindle twisting as she walked, her distaff stuck in her belt. Women dyed wool – sometimes employing their little children to trample the fabric in the dye tub – and some set the thread for their husband's loom or wove on their own looms in their homes. Women in nunneries and abbeys had textile departments, spinning, dyeing, weaving, finishing and embroidering. Finished fabric would go on sale in England, while unfinished fleeces became the biggest English export to Europe. Women also spun flax for linen, hemp for ropes and strong thread, and dominated the luxury textiles.

The rich silk trade was almost wholly owned, managed and staffed by women, and the women masters represented themselves in appeals to the aldermen of London and to the king to block the import of cheap finished silks that threatened English production and trade. The craftswomen imported raw silk and silk thread and spun and wove a heavy silk yarn.[107] The work they did was so superior that Queen Matilda, wife of William I, bought religious vestments made in Winchester by Helisenda, the wife of Alderet, and presented them to the cathedral at Caen. Helisenda, famous as the best orfrey worker in England – a specialist sewing technique that blended colours and complex patterns – was poached by Queen Maud of Scotland.[108] English women textile artists invented the Opus Anglicanum, which overlaid threads of silver and gold with embroidery incorporating precious stones. In 1239, Mabel of Bury St Edmunds made a chasuble and altar veil that so impressed Henry III that he commissioned an embroidered standard for Westminster Abbey. Roesia Burford made a cope with coral for Queen Isabella in the 1300s.[109]

All medieval clothing was designed to be re-made: women's gowns' sleeves, skirts and bodices were detached and laced together in different combinations. No stigma attached to something being 'second hand': the royal wardrobe maintained and supplied clothes for successive monarchs, and a queen could wear a gown created for her predecessor. Gifts of used clothing between equals signalled favour; clothing was left in wills and given to servants as a benefit. Items of clothing circulated as trade goods, while the mending, redesigning, cleaning and reselling of clothes was a profitable and legitimate women's occupation, one that overlapped with the market in stolen goods. Women became lenders and pawnbrokers, swapping goods or paying cash against an item of clothing or household equipment, and also dominating the business of 'fencing' – buying and reselling stolen goods.

Almost every woman sold wool from her own sheep, used it herself, or spun it for sale as yarn in the local market or for a woman wool merchant. Many women did piecework for cash, spinning for contractors who supplied them with fleeces or flax and collected the finished yarn. Many of these contractors were women, some of them rising to great prosperity in the wool business: England's greatest export and women's special trade. A spindle was easily made: it was nothing more than a weighted hook, which span around, twisting the thread, and the distaff was a pole, rather like a broom handle that held the raw wool. The work could take place anywhere, often while the woman was doing another task like travelling to market or waiting for water at the well.

The change from the little hand-spindle to a spinning wheel, slowly adopted in England from the 1300s, moved the work from a portable cheap technology into a piece of larger, heavier equipment that confined women in isolation in their homes, where they had to sit at the wheel and work on their own. Spinning was faster with a wheel, but few women in the cash-poor subsistent-farming households had enough savings to buy a spinning wheel, and without official legal status could not borrow. If a woman spinner did borrow a spinning wheel she had to devote herself to it, to pay off the debt. She was more productive; but now she had added costs of debt, and lost time for her other productive work. Her labour became invisible – disappearing behind the closed door of the home – and her true wage also became invisible, some of it vanishing in debt before she even saw the cash.

No longer was she producing the whole product for sale at the price she could get for it: she had become a pieceworker, paid according to the employer's terms. And, crucially, she was no longer visible in the village and community, taking her place in field and market, pooling knowledge and exerting influence, enforcing laws and traditions. Her rate of pay, the value of her work, was no longer visible either. She was not working alongside other women doing the same work, and they could no longer set a price in the public market or collectively agree the rate for the job.

Other trades like the brewing and bakery business were also the business of women. Women bakers sold baked goods and rented space in their bread ovens for householders to bake their own home-made dough and pies. In 1310, Sarra Foling, Goedieyva Foling, Matilda de Bolingtone, Christina Prochet, Isabella Sperling, Alice Pegges, Johanna de Caunterbrigge and Isabella Pouveste, all 'bakeresses' of Stratford, were called up before the mayor and aldermen, who weighed their half-penny loaves and found them light. Since the bread was weighed cold (contrary to tradition), the bakers did not have to forfeit it, but they had to sell three half-penny loaves for one penny – three for the price of two.[110]

Some of the bakers developed their business using the yeast left over from brewing ale – always a women's speciality. Alice de Lye, who was also a weaver in Shrewsbury, brewed ale in 1370,[111] and Agnes de Broughton of Broughton village paid occasional fees to her lord for brewing from 1297 to 1302.[112] The light ale – 'small ale' – of the medieval period, which was safer to drink than the polluted water, went 'off' after a few days and so most households had their own malting house, brewed every week and sold the surplus. In the country, the lord of the manor took a fee from women tenants for brewing; in the towns, ale wives paid a levy on their profits. Towns monitored the quality of ale on sale, preferring women inspectors to taste it and maintain standards. The Oxfordshire village of Cuxham appointed only women as ale tasters to ensure the quality and set the prices.[113]

Many ale wives developed their business from selling surplus ale at their door to opening an ale house. Women innkeepers appeared in the records under their own names as hostellers and some developed their ale houses into property portfolios, turning their inns into rented rooms and then buying houses to let.

Laundering cotton and linen chemises and undergarments was strictly women-only work, as paid servants in the laundry rooms of the big houses, where additional casual women labourers would be hired for a monthly or quarterly 'wash day', when all the household linen would be washed, dried and sometimes pressed. In the country, women would often wash their household linen collectively at a pool in the stream or river, helping each other with heavy items. Women-only laundries also operated in the towns. It was hard, dirty work and even dangerous – washing women could fall into rivers and lakes and drown fetching water or struggling with heavy wet washing. A hot wash at home was done as infrequently as possible; it was a huge task to boil up a washing copper and the whole family would help.

A woman blacksmith in the Holkham Bible, c.1327–35

Women assisted in the public bathrooms, washing and sponging bathers; female perfumiers supplied imported oils and herbs, scented powders and cosmetics, dusting powders for cleaning clothes, scented soap for washing. Poor women made their own soap from wood ashes and lye, wiping themselves down with damp cloths, bathing in rivers or washing in a half-barrel or tub.

No business was closed to women in these centuries. The widow of Peter the Potter inherited his business and ran it herself.[114] Marriott Ferrars became a successful horse-trader in the 1100s, supplying the best-quality horses and equipment to Henry II.[115] The Bristol Company of Soapmakers recorded women masters training apprentices. In Shrewsbury, the Drapers' recorded 'brothers and sisters' in the guild. The Tailors' of Exeter allowed any paid-up widow of the guild to expand her business with a limitless number of workers.[116] Women butchers were named in the records of medieval York, accused of leaving dung and entrails in the streets. In York – as in every town – women were foremost in cooking meat, making sausages, black puddings and other dishes from entrails.[117] Women also ran the fresh fish trade.

Some women remained in control of the price for their home-produced goods, taking them to the weekly and bi-weekly markets in a nearby town for sale directly to consumers. Some women sold in the streets – dairymaids with buckets of milk, flower girls with posies, cheese-makers, buttermakers, ballad sellers, pedlars with ribbons, haberdashery, chapbooks and little goods. In Coventry in the 1300s, nearly half of all the hawkers were women.[118]

Townswomen went into the country to buy up seasonal produce or craft products from rural producers. Long-distance travelling saleswomen went further afield, carrying luxuries from town to town, or from great house to great house. Travelling women poets and composers – trobairitz (female troubadours) and jongleurs – sang and played instruments, recited poems or stories, or composed them. Women entertainers travelled from festivals and fairs to private shows, perhaps in a troupe, sometimes as soloists. They would juggle, walk on fire, do tricks, tell fortunes and report news, even perform a handstand on the blades of swords.[119]

Troupes of strolling players, men and women, put on masques or dramas, or were hired for the 'morality plays' or 'passion plays' staged by the churches or guilds for church festivals and on saints' days.

Some women poets and writers lost their language as Anglo-Saxon fell out of fashion after the Norman invasion and Old French became the language of the conquerors and the elite. Anglo-Saxon women poets and storytellers may have resisted changing their oral tradition to that of a written culture, especially in the foreign language of the invaders, and their poems have been lost. The old language became the speech of the common people, rarely written down. The new Norman-French was the script of the monastery-trained literate clerks.[120] Some women writers were fluent in their own language, in Latin and in the new language of the elite. At Barking Abbey – one of the greatest centres of female literacy – women authors wrote and published. They included Clemence of Barking, who wrote a *Life of St Catherine of Alexandria* in the twelfth century,[121] and one woman, a nun of Barking Abbey, who wrote a plea that rings out down the centuries: 'It is asked of all who hear this work that they do not revile it because a woman translated it. That is no reason to despise it, nor to disregard the good in it.'[122]

The work was a verse history of the last Anglo-Saxon king, Edward the Confessor, translated by the author from the Latin into Anglo-Norman French, which may have been her third language. Hers was an idiosyncratic interpretation: she took the male historian's original account and added a female character – Edward's wife – restoring a 'normal woman' into the all-male history in an extra section.[123] She was the first recorded English woman historian and one of the first English women to be published ... but we don't even know her name.[124]

All nunneries and abbeys provided women's education as 'she-schools', and from 1179 cathedrals were ordered to teach poor scholars – including girls – for free. The nuns of St Rhadegund in Cambridge were paid in meat for educating a butcher's daughter. As culture and ideas of learning spread, the quality of girls' schooling improved. Gilbert of Sempringham established an order of nuns – the Gilbertines – in 1131 that specialised in the education of women. Queen Philippa founded Queen's College, Oxford, in 1341 for male scholars. Marie de St Pol, widow of the Earl of Pembroke, taught the younger daughter of Edward II, founding Denny Abbey to educate nuns and, in 1347, Pembroke College, Cambridge, for men. The fictional heroine of the 1300s romance 'Guy of Warwick' was an idealised female figure boasting a wide education. Felice was learned in grammar, logic, rhetoric, geometry, arithmetic, astronomy and music, and also studied sophistry, wit, rhetoric and other clerkly learning.[125]

Most ladies in secular households saw themselves as heads of the family, responsible for the safety, health, education and religious observances of everyone in the large households, whether kin, guests or employees. They were responsible for the education and training of young apprentices at every level of their industries and in their homes. Some of these were children working in the kitchen, stables, laundry, dairy or brew rooms; some were trainee servants of the body; and some were the children from other aristocratic houses, learning courtly behaviour by serving as page boys or maids-in-waiting, provided with an education by the lady of the household, alongside other noble children often in a schoolroom in the castle, with a female tutor for younger children and a male tutor for the boys and older girls.

Some female philanthropists founded schools for village children. Wealthier women established colleges or provided scholarships for training priests; many ladies engaged a priest for the family chapel who would also read and study with them and teach the children. These women often organised and supervised a local hospital or funded it jointly with the church, which they also supported, contributing to its upkeep and paying tithes for the priest. Some ladies were patrons of the arts, and some were scholars and artists in their own right. Ela, Countess of Salisbury (1187–1261), sheriff of Wiltshire for two years, founded Lacock Abbey, was a patron of the outstanding poet Marie de Compiègne and finally retired to the abbey she had established as abbess.[126]

Ladies rode, hunted and were expert falconers. John of Salisbury (1120–80) conceded that women excelled at hunting with hawks and falcons, which indicated to him that the sport was 'effeminate and not worth the pains spent on it'.[127] Women often led hunting parties of their own.

Lower-status women had little education: they might attend the few convent or church schools, but most would only learn to recite the Latin responses for church services – perhaps not even understanding the words. Some might learn to sign their name, a few to read, even fewer to write. But they would pick up enough arithmetic to calculate prices and costs: they were in charge of marketing, buying and selling, and managing household transactions. Girls would learn from their mothers the essential skills of farming, food preparation and processing, ale-making, spinning and animal husbandry, and daughters of specialists would be taught by their mothers or grandmothers, or even apprenticed to follow in their footsteps.

Medicine, herbalism, nursing, midwifery, toothdrawing, bone setting, blood letting, laying out of the dead, all were women's work at every level of society, noble and common at this time. It was widespread and profitable employment. Female physicians were accepted into the

Fourteenth-century women hunting in open fields: winding the horn and hunting with arrows – see the accurate shooting!

barber-surgeon guilds and the apothecary guilds. Women could train as doctors, serving apprenticeships in their specialities, and they set up as physicians, surgeons, apothecaries and healers.[128] Agnes Medica was working in Huntingdonshire in 1271, her name suggesting she was a doctor, surgeon or apothecary. Matilda le Leche, a 'sage femme', earned a living as a wise woman in Berkshire in 1232.[129] Katherine, known as 'la surgiene', worked in London in 1286 with her father and brother.[130] Cecilia of Oxford was 'surgeon' to Queen Philippa of Hainault, wife of Edward III. The court records show that the court surgeon was paid 12d a day.[131]

Most elite women had their own laboratories for distilling and drying herbs, the 'still rooms' where they experimented and produced herbal remedies, sometimes following recipe books, sometimes making their own notes and handing down the books to their daughters or heiresses. Women who developed their expertise as herbalists, physicians and surgeons took care of the health of their own children, family and household, and cared for their communities, their neighbours and their labourers. In the frequent accidents and injuries of the medieval world, the presence of a skilled physician able to treat burns, set bones and attend to injuries could make the difference between life and death. Women's medical skills proved vital during the many years of warfare and violent unrest.

In the twelfth century, nuns were invited to run the hospitals for the Knights Hospitallers – the military order set up to guard and assist pilgrims and crusaders on their way to Jerusalem. The sisters had responsibility for the care of children and the organisation of the Hospitaller priories while the brothers supervised the medical staff. A large priory was established by Henry II at Clerkenwell in 1185 with a Benedictine nunnery.

The lesser-paid work of nursing, midwifery, gynaecology and end-of-life care was always the work of women practitioners. Only women were allowed to attend women in childbirth or deal with gynaecological problems; some midwives were practising surgeons and could undertake a Caesarean operation, delivering the baby from its dead mother. Women nurses cared for newborns and babies, influential and well-paid work in a society where noble women were discouraged from caring for their own children. Lactating women could find well-paid and well-fed and perhaps enjoyable work, breast-feeding noble and gentry babies, though it might mean they had to leave their own baby. All the nursing for the terminally ill – including victims of the plague – was done by women practitioners, locked up with their dying patient, hoping to emerge after the death and collection of the body – unless they contracted the disease themselves. Women laid out the dead and prepared the bodies for burial and were sometimes paid to attend funerals.

Women traditional healers held a respected and valued place in a society with no understanding of germ theory or even accurate knowledge of anatomy. Only the very wealthy could afford to call in university-educated male physicians and these men – basing their work on completely imaginary and pre-scientific theories of disease – were no more likely to prescribe a successful cure than experienced women practitioners.

Midwives gained additional pay and status in their community when they served as public inspectors on sexuality and legitimacy issues: advising the church and later the civil courts on law suits concerning virginity, impotence, sexual assault and the parenthood of illegitimate babies. They were called as witnesses in witchcraft trials because of their experience with women's bodies. As 'searchers' – women appointed to search a suspect witch for marks or moles or any signs of satanic contact – they held official posts with high social prestige.[132]

Every medieval community had a 'wise woman', some of them acknowledged midwives and healers, some heirs to a family tradition, the daughter of a cunning woman or a herbalist. Some might enter the trade by a lucky moment of insight or a guess that was reported as a 'gift'. Some were confidence tricksters preying on gullible and superstitious people. In the towns they might be well paid in cash, while in the villages and rural communities they might work for favours or barter goods. The skilled women were hired by everyone, from the most educated and wealthy families who feared bewitching and cursing and would employ a 'cunning woman' for defence, to the very poor people who had no way to distinguish between the Latin prayers of the priest and the baptismal water in the font and the abracadabra gabble of the wise woman and the water from a sacred spring. At a time when folklore was taught alongside Christianity, when there was no scientific research in the Western world, anything was possible: natural phenomena were alarming and ominous, and wise women were rewarded, for apparently knowing more than anyone else.

Women who were poor, in dispute with their neighbours or regarded as malicious might be accused of using their powers for evil and could be cruelly punished. They would be denounced to the priest or local lords by their fellow citizens or enemies. Many neighbourhood quarrels escalated into cursing that could be denounced as witchcraft. But at this time, before the Great Pestilence of 1348, it was mostly men who were accused of witchcraft: 70 per cent of the witchcraft accusations were made against them. These may have been men who troubled the community peace with disorderly behaviour and threats, or were seen as heretics (who were thought to be in league with witches). The relative absence of women from witchcraft accusations may have been because women claiming expertise were less feared, and poor women rudely demanding charity were better tolerated in the years before the Great Pestilence.

Women of the emerging 'middling classes' sometimes lived as mistresses of noble or royal men, attending the great houses and royal court and enjoying good treatment, money and gifts while they were in fashion. Most common women who were paid for sex were supplementing a low income, or under coercion. They sold sexual experiences to men either 'on demand' on the street, took them to a room, or worked in 'bawdy houses' or 'bath houses' where a man could rent a woman for a short time or hire her for the whole night. Women who worked in bawdy houses were often hired and paid as domestic servants, handing over all or some of the money they were paid for acts of sex.

Several medieval cities banned prostitutes; others required that they wear a striped hood to identify them as immoral women. In 1344, the city of Bristol banned prostitutes and lepers in the same decree, blaming both for epidemic illness.[133] Many other towns required women selling sex to wear identifying yellow hoods.[134] Forty Exeter women were accused of being whores in 1324, when about 1 per cent of the town's population of women were thought to be selling sex.[135]

London's specialist areas for the sex trade were in the City of London, where legal brothels traded on Cock Lane (or Cokkes Lane), and outside the City boundaries, south of the river in the parish of Southwark: convenient for courtiers and politicians, a short boat ride from Westminster where the 'stews', often bath houses, had been regulated by the crown since 1161 when, in an attempt to prevent the spread of sexually transmitted diseases, Henry II ruled that they might not 'keep any woman that hath the perilous infirmity of burning'.[136] By 1374, 18 'stews' in the borough of Southwark were offering baths, dining and sexual acts, all run by women from Flanders.[137] The area was owned by the Bishop of Winchester, and the women were known as the 'Bishop's chickens' and expected to wear clothes that identified them as prostitutes. They could not be seen wearing aprons or spinning, like respectable housewives, and they were not to harass men in the streets.[138]

From the earliest centuries, the church viewed prostitution as an inevitable part of society. Thomas Aquinas believed that paid women should satisfy men who otherwise would turn to sodomy: 'Take away prostitutes from the world and you will fill it with sodomy.'[139] The church said that those who made a profit from the prostitution of women were condemned, but women themselves should be encouraged to repent.[140] From about 1300, ecclesiastical acceptance led to an open trade in sex, partially regulated for the safety of clients and the women workers.[141] There was no condemnation of the clients, yet Thomas of Chobham, a twelfth-century theologian, believed that prostitutes should not receive mass or take communion but be encouraged to confess.[142] Any man who married a prostitute was offered a remission of his sins by the church, which believed he was doing a 'good deed'.[143]

Prostitutes were socially accepted. Most women working in the recognised whore houses in the bigger towns were included in community events. They could join sewing and spinning circles; they almost always took other work in addition to prostitution, and participated in community and even church rituals, and could testify in court as witnesses or pursue their own civil cases. When they were cash-rich, they might loan money and goods and be integrated into community life as respected donors to charity. Some also worked as 'fences' for stolen goods, or in criminal gangs or with their families.

Few women made a good living from selling sex; most were driven to it by hunger or poverty and might take food or drink for a sexual act and make no money. Working casually on the streets, they were especially vulnerable to abuse. A prostitute could bring an accusation of rape, but no jury would convict a man on the word of a lone woman, and even if they did they would not think that she had suffered any damages, as her chastity and good name were already gone.[144]

Women at War

There was no peace after the 1066 invasion but constant uprisings, local battles between landowners, feuds among lords and armed conspiracies against the monarchs. Women of all classes participated as leaders and foot soldiers. After 1135, when Empress Matilda tried to regain her throne, there were nearly 20 years of civil war between her and her cousin, the usurper Stephen. The daughter and only direct heir to Henry I, Matilda (1102–67) was the first Norman woman to inherit the English throne, and forced to be the first queen militant – raising her own army and leading it into battle for two years of skirmishes, until her victory at the Battle of Lincoln in 1141.[145] She imprisoned the pretender Stephen and ignored a demand from his wife, Queen Matilda of Boulogne. Matilda of Boulogne then mustered her own army to plunder the country around London, persuading Londoners to ally with her against the empress, who moved her forces to Winchester and besieged the bishop's castle. Matilda of Boulogne pursued Empress Matilda and defeated her. For six years Empress Matilda led her own troops, her own vassals and knights, and paid mercenaries to follow her into battle. Eventually Stephen acknowledged his defeat and made peace, but even then he did not hand over the throne. He named Matilda's son as his heir, and the boy became Henry II.[146]

In 1173, Eleanor of Aquitaine led her sons in a revolt against their father Henry II. In 1215, the English barons revolted against King John, and in 1264 against Henry III. Local boundary disputes were settled by raids and violence: all English border lands with Wales and Scotland were raided constantly from both sides, and English kings marched on both unruly neighbours. The English fought wars in Europe and went on a series of crusades to the Holy Lands with women in the lead and among the troops.

Since all lords held their lands under the agreement that they would raise a certain number of soldiers and lead them into battle, women deputies for feudal lords, and female lords themselves – heiresses and widows – were also obliged to raise troops for the king. The abbess of Barking Abbey was one of four abbess-barons who were required to perform military service and called upon to provide fighting men by Henry III and Edward I.

Lady Hawis of London (1211–74) held the manor of East Garston in Berkshire and was bound by the terms of her tenancy to Edward I in 1250 to 'conduct the vanguard of the king's army as often as he should go into Wales ... and in returning to bring up the rerward of the said army'.[147] She had to lead from the front, be the first into Wales which was being colonised by the English, and the last out – the most dangerous positions.

Another royal tenant, Elene la Zouche (1228–*c*.1345), who could pay a fee to send a knight in her place, chose to ride with the army. The record of the Exchequer said: 'She did her Service with the King (*habuit servicium suton cum Rege*) in the Army of Wales, according to the King's Precept or Summonce, as appeared to the King by the Rolls of the Marshalsy of his Army.'[148]

All feudal tenants including women had to offer military service to their lord for a number of days every year in the lord's army. Some women volunteered and dressed as men; some used the army as a way to live as men. Women also followed armies in support of soldiers, finding or buying food, cooking, cleaning and doing laundry, and in battle, loading and arming guns, and rescuing and nursing the wounded. Some followed their family members or lovers and found themselves in dangerous and historic events, but rarely in the records. Some women, especially those living in port towns, who were experienced sailors, volunteered or were 'pressed' – forced – to serve at sea.

Working women were almost always involved in defence when their own town or castle came under siege; unlike the ladies, they could not get away. During the Scots invasions of northern England in 1136–8, entire towns were put to the sword and women were killed or kidnapped.[149] Women prisoners were often raped or even enslaved as an act of war.

Aristocratic women acted in joint command with their husbands, often the only advisor and assistant that a nobleman could trust.[150] Petronella, Countess of Leicester, was said to have dressed in armour, carried a shield and lance, and fought as a knight at the Battle of Fornham in October 1173.

Most ladies took responsibility for fortifying their castles against attack when their male family members were away. Bamburgh Castle, a major point of defence on the north-east coast, was held by Matilda de l'Aigle against siege from the king, William II, in 1095, only surrendering when the royal forces captured her husband Robert de Mowbray and threatened to blind him.[151] In 1139, Matilda of Ramsbury commanded the stronghold of Devizes and held it against King Stephen.[152] Countess Mabel, Robert of Gloucester's wife, held King Stephen in captivity after his capture at the Battle of Lincoln in 1141.[153]

Richenda de Longchamp (c.1145–?) was sister to William de Longchamp, the unpopular justiciar and chancellor of England under Richard I, who was in dispute with Geoffrey, Archbishop of York, the king's illegitimate brother. Things came to a head when Geoffrey tried to return from France to England in 1191 and William demanded that he renew his oath of loyalty to the absent King Richard before returning. Geoffrey found himself blocked from England by an alliance of three women loyal to William de Longchamp: his sister Richenda de Longchamp, governess of Dover and castellan of Dover Castle, and her allies the Countess of Flanders and the Countess of Boulogne – all three in sole charge of their lands while their husbands were on crusade.

When Geoffrey got past his two enemy European countesses and arrived in Dover, Richenda had her men demand that he repeat his oath of loyalty before she would admit him to England. The archbishop refused, and Richenda's men were ordered to arrest him; but he galloped to St Martin's Priory and demanded sanctuary. Invoking the authority as the most senior archbishop of England, he sent a message to Richenda demanding to know if she was aware of how her men had treated him.

Richenda cheerfully replied that she was following the instructions of her brother William de Longchamp, the lord chancellor, and 'in order to put an end to idle speech', the archbishop should be aware that if her brother sent her word to burn her own castle to the ground, she would do so.[154] She added that she would burn down the entire city of London if her brother wished.

The archbishop excommunicated her on the spot – banning her from confession, forgiveness and mass, and permitting any faithful Christians to disobey her. Nobody did. Richenda ordered her men to break sanctuary and arrest Geoffrey, but when they entered the church and found him seated on his throne before the altar, wearing his alb and stole and holding a golden cross, they did not dare. Memories of the sainthood of Thomas à Beckett were too strong for Richenda's men, if not for her.

When Richenda's husband Matthew de Cleres returned from crusade, he was appalled to find his wife in the middle of this dramatic stand-off with a royal archbishop. He dashed to the priory to propose a compromise. While her husband was apologising for her, Richenda seized the archbishop's horses and sent them as a gift to her brother. For five days there was stalemate: Richenda's men did not dare to break the sanctuary of the church; Geoffrey would not repeat his oath of loyalty to the king; and Richenda's husband could not command her.

Finally, her men – fearing the wrath of Richenda more than that of God – broke sanctuary and dragged the archbishop to her castle through the outraged town of Dover. Richenda's husband Matthew, in tears, fell on his knees to the archbishop at the castle gate and would not rise until he was forgiven. But Richenda made no apology – once again she demanded Geoffrey swear an oath of loyalty to the king or leave the kingdom. Once again he refused. She threw him into the castle vault.

There he stayed for eight days, refusing food from her excommunicated hands, so that she told him to send out to the bakehouses in Dover and buy his own dinner. Finally, Archbishop Geoffrey's supporters forced William de Longchamp to order Richenda to free her prisoner. William fled the country, to his king Richard I, and was partially forgiven and restored by him. Richenda kept her post as castellan of Dover Castle, and may have held it till her death.[155]

Nichola de la Haye (c.1150–1230) inherited the right to be castellan of Lincoln Castle and was there alone when her husband's enemy, William de Longchamp (Richenda's brother again), attacked Lincoln in 1191. She held out for more than a month before a truce was called. After the death of her husband, she held her inheritance in her own right, until offering to retire in her sixties, but King John refused to let such a powerful and loyal woman leave the castle and appointed her sheriff of Lincolnshire. When the king died the following year, in 1217, the French army invaded England and took the city. By now about 67 years old, Nichola held out in the castle as Louis of France's army brought up siege machinery and reinforcements, bombarding it from the south and east for three months, until the English royal army arrived to lift the siege.

Despite Nichola de la Haye's loyal service to King John, he granted her castle and the city of Lincoln to the Earl of Salisbury, William de Longespée. So Nichola mounted her horse and rode 150 miles to the new king Henry III, to demand the return of her castle. He conceded to her and when she died as the castellan in 1230, aged about 80, she left her fortune to her sole surviving heir: her granddaughter.[156]

Alice de Montfort, wife of Simon, was 'one of his most trusted lieuten-
ants', delivering reinforcements, advising in his war council and
commanding Narbonnais Castle in his absence in 1217.[157] Another
woman castellan at Bamburgh – Isabella Beaumont de Vescy – was
appointed in 1304 by Edward I. She proved to be so successful that when
the king died, his son renewed Isabella in her post.[158]

In 1321, Isabella of France, queen consort to King Edward II of
England, at the head of her force, was denied entry to Leeds Castle by a
rebel woman – Lady Badlesmere. The queen forced an entry, and Lady
Badlesmere's archers opened fire on the queen's men, killing six and
forcing the queen to retreat.[159]

While campaigning in Scotland in 1335, Edward III entrusted the
defence of his kingdom to three women. He commanded Margaret,
widow of Edmund, Earl of Kent, and Marie, wife of Aymer de Valence,
Earl of Pembroke, and Joan Botetourt, wife of Thomas, to gather trusted
advisors together in London and to 'arm and array your people … to
repel powerfully and courageously the presumptuous boldness and
malice of our same enemies … if those enemies invade.'[160]

Agnes Randolph, Countess of Dunbar and March (1312–69),
defended Dunbar Castle in 1338 against the English forces led by
William Montagu, 1st Earl of Salisbury. Agnes held the castle with only
a small garrison force against the English army with the powerful and
experienced general, and is supposed to have said:

Of Scotland's King I haud my house,
I pay him meat and fee,
and I will keep my gude auld house,
while my house will keep me.[161]

She did keep her good old house, defeating the Earl of Salisbury, who
abandoned the five-month siege and retreated.

The Crusades – so-called 'holy wars' mustered by successive popes to
try to recapture the Christian sites in the Middle East – took men from
their farms and castles. But the image of a wife helplessly abandoned for
years while her husband was on crusade, is the opposite of the reality. The
men were only able to go because they could trust their wives or mothers
to manage their lands in their absence. It was the leadership qualities of
the women that freed their husbands to go to war or on crusade.[162]

Working women went on crusade as soldiers in great numbers, obeying the call from the Vatican to raise money for the church, fight a so-called holy war and capture the city of Jerusalem from the Muslim Arab kingdoms. Women as well as men were inspired by the cause, the opportunity for adventure and profit, and the chance to get away from English life. Not all went to fight. One English chronicler claimed that the prostitutes travelling with Richard I's army on the Third Crusade made so much money that they lived better than the French king's brother.[163]

Bernold of Constance wrote that 'innumerable' women wore male clothes to march with the crusader army and engage in battle.[164] Muslim chroniclers reported women armed and fighting. One crusader ship had a passenger list of 453 on board, 42 of them women, half of whom were travelling without a male companion.[165] A woman might go on crusade as a supporter of the armies, or as a supporter of an individual crusader or pilgrim. Or she might go as a pilgrim herself, travelling with the crusading army.[166] Women were admitted to the Order of St John, a hospital order founded to support crusaders, and established their own centre at Minchin Buckland in Somerset.[167] So many women and children went on the First Crusade in 1096 that Pope Urban II specifically banned them.[168] Nothing discouraged the women crusaders, and in 1213 Pope Innocent III bowed to their perseverance and decreed that women as well as men could take the crusader vow.[169]

Some upper-class English women accompanied their husbands, and some may have been the crusader – persuading their less enthusiastic husbands to join them. Emma of Hereford, Countess of Norfolk who held her castle under siege, travelled on crusade with her husband, Ralph I of Gael, and died on the way to Jerusalem. Edith, daughter of William de Warenne, the 1st Earl of Surrey, accompanied her husband Gerard of Gournay-en-Bray with both the armies of Hugh the Great and Robert Curthose. Eleanor of Aquitaine took the crusader cross in her own right, recruited her ladies-in-waiting as royal guards, and led her own army of feudal vassals in the unsuccessful Second Crusade, accompanying her then husband King Louis of France in 1147. Eleanor of Castile accompanied her husband Edward I of England on the Eighth Crusade to the Holy Land while pregnant in 1271 and had her baby, Joan, in the city of Acre. Returning home, she rode out again with Edward to invade Wales and gave birth to their son Edward on 25 April 1284 while Caernarvon Castle was being built around her.

Crime and Punishment

The feudal Norman law of femme couvert created a loophole for law-breaking women to hide from justice and claim that their husbands were responsible for their actions. In Salle in Norfolk, in 1321, two sisters from a well-known family of thieves named Waraunt were accused of stealing and escaped punishment by claiming they were femmes couvert so could not be charged for their crimes. Another sister later charged with theft was also released. When their cousin John was apprehended for stealing clothes and household goods valued at 8s, he had no such defence and was hanged. Four years later, the sisters were all imprisoned – and released again; a year after that, two sisters were once more accused of theft and again escaped punishment.[170] The family criminal unit was not unusual: a third of all gangs were families, often headed and organised by the mother of the group, experienced in avoiding the attention of the courts.[171]

London bakers Alice de Brightenoch and Lucy de Pykeringe ran an ingenious fraud on customers who brought in their own dough to bake in the women's oven in the early 1300s. The table for the bread dough to rise on was prepared with holes and the two women's husbands hid under it, tearing pieces of dough from the waiting loaves. The bakers were accused of working 'falsely, wickedly, and maliciously; to the great loss of all [their] neighbours and other persons living near'.

While the husbands who had helped them were set in the pillory, with dough hung around their necks, the women pleaded femme couvert status, saying 'said deed was not their deed'. They were spared the pillory as wives under the control of their husbands.[172]

Businesswomen who were femmes sole were easier to prosecute for infractions of trading law as they could not put their husbands forward for punishment. In the Wakefield court rolls of 1348–50, most women appeared for offences relating to brewing and selling ale. Alice, daughter of Adam, dug her own pit for iron in Yorkshire and was charged for mining without permission.[173] Mabel the Merchant was charged with stealing ash trees by the Chalgrave court of 1294.[174] Country women were often accused of illegal gleaning – taking more than the agreed share of leftovers after the harvest of cereal crops – or of stealing fruit and vegetables from gardens.

Women could be violent in a violent world: in Wakefield around 1348, Matilda, wife of Robert of Combirworth, attacked Magota, daughter of John, and drew blood – she was fined 3d. Agnes, wife of William Walker, drew blood in her attack on William de Pudsay and was fined 12d. Amabel the Cowkeeper fractured a man's skull while defending her herd.[175] Amicia, the daughter of Hugh of Wygenale, was the official watchwoman – guarding the fruit crop – when she tackled Cecilia, wife of Richard le Gardyner, who was stealing.[176]

The older women of the village and towns were sometimes officially appointed to make inquiries into sexual misconduct, pregnancies or witchcraft, but they kept a constant surveillance over everyone and maintained the social standards of communities. They would denounce women as 'scolds' – argumentative women – and a woman would be punished.

Women community leaders could summon neighbours to make 'rough music', clattering pans outside their targets' windows, or organise a 'skimmington ride', when local people would perform a pantomime of insult. Cuckolds would be visited by a man wearing horns; a disorderly household would be shamed by a horse led past their house, with riders seated backwards, or insulting symbolic gifts left on the doorstep.

Occasionally, the women of the community would side with an abused woman and publicly shame a violent, drunken or adulterous husband; but it was mostly women who bore the brunt of scrutiny and censure from other women. Women who offended against community standards or traditions might be taken to the church or manor court and punished, sometimes by time on the cucking stool.

The early cucking stools were little more than ordinary seats. The local lord or the priest or community leaders would order that an offending woman be strapped down and left on the stool for some hours or even the whole day. Some seats could be raised and held up using a lever – like being stuck at the top of a see-saw. Sometimes the woman would be left so long that she soiled herself; sometimes the stool was a chamber pot. Since the term 'cucking stool' comes from the Latin *caccare* – 'to defecate' – it may have been intended that the woman soil herself in public as part of her humiliation. The Domesday Book records a cucking stool in Chester to punish the sellers of short measures or bad ale.[177] From 1216 onwards, every parish was ordered to provide a cucking stool: legal institutionalised violence for women who had done nothing more than offend their neighbours or argue with their husbands. Later stools were developed into 'ducking stools' to drop a woman into water. The town ordinance for Glamorgan in 1330 ruled that: 'If any woman be found guilty by six men of scolding or railing any townsman or his wife, or any of their neighbours, then she is to be brought at the first fault to the Cucking Stool there to sit one hour, at the second fault two hours. And at the third fault to let slip …'[178]

People who missed church services would be brought before the church court, while people who failed to work the common-held lands, perform their feudal duties or pay their fees would be brought before the manor court of the lord. Women said to be unchaste would be formally charged in either court. Unmarried women caught having sex would pay a 'leyrwrite' – a fine – but sexually active bachelors faced no such punishment: the double sexual standard was justified because a woman might give birth to a bastard and the cost of the child might fall on the manor. Agnes Chilyonge had to pay her feudal lord 2d for being found guilty of 'adultery' at Manningham in 1350.[179]

Every parish had to have a 'cucking seat' from 1216. The seats would later become 'ducking stools'

Violence Against Women

Domestic violence was probably so common as to be rarely reported and no commentators complained of it for centuries. A husband could legally use so-called 'reasonable force' on his wife and children, usually understood to be a beating with a whip or stick no wider than his thumb. In practice, women only reported violent husbands to the authorities if they feared for their lives, and then a husband might only be 'bound over' to keep the peace. Only if domestic violence disturbed the community would he be prosecuted or reproved by community action – a violent prank against the abuser or an official public shaming. Usually, the senior women of the community would warn a violent husband against going too far – sometimes they violently attacked him. Since most of daily life took place in public, and women entered each other's homes for communal working sessions, cooking and support in illness and childbirth, village women had an inside view of local marriages. This was not always helpful: most of the court actions against women were accusations of 'slander' – complaints that others had been commenting on their private lives.

Rape by a husband was no crime – the wedding oath was consent once and for all, and both husband and wife were considered to have consented for the life of the marriage to sex on demand.

Sex without consent outside marriage was first outlawed in the law codes of Alfred, 200 years before the Norman invasion, written in the late ninth century. A sliding scale of compensation charged seizing the breast at 5 shillings, throwing a woman down without penetration at 10s and penetration by force at 60s, and the fines were paid to the woman's family or even to her personally.[180]

'Rape' under Norman law was understood both as the kidnap of the woman from her family and damage to their property. A 'rapist' would be prosecuted by a woman's father or brother for stealing their property: 'If anyone carry off a maiden by force, [he is to pay] the owner 50 shillings and afterwards buy from the owner his consent [to the marriage]. If it be rape of a maiden, seven half-cumals for it.'[181]

A cumal was a value – about 3 ounces of silver. The rape of the maiden cost about three times as much in a fine as the kidnap, because her virginity had been stolen and could not be restored.[182] There was great anxiety about the kidnap and abduction of wealthy women – mostly widows – as a forced marriage handed her fortune to her abductor.[183] A study from 1100 to 1500 revealed 1,198 allegations of kidnap.[184] Some apparent victims may have been escaping unwanted marriages by arranging their own abduction with their lovers. Some unwilling nuns freed themselves from the nunnery with a male accomplice-lover.[185]

The stringent conditions for reporting rapes, and the scepticism of the all-male judge and jury, meant that few prosecutions were initiated by women themselves.[186] To prosecute a rape, wrote Henry de Bracton in 1235, the woman had to have lost her virginity during the rape; she had to raise a public hue and cry against her rapist the moment it was over; she had to immediately report to men of good repute showing them bloodstains and torn garments; she must explain the circumstances to the local official (the reeve), to the king's sergeant and to the sheriff; and she had to appeal for justice at the county court. What she said at each point must agree exactly with what she first said, since any variation would prove that she was lying. If she successfully managed all of these unlikely encounters immediately after a violent assault, and the courts found the rapist guilty, he would be blinded or castrated – unless she agreed to marry him.[187] This would save his life or his sight, and her good name, since the man who had raped her had taken her 'honour' and could restore it with marriage.

Throughout the thirteenth century, the laws changed and changed again to define rape either as a crime of violence, punishable by death, or merely a trespass that could be punished with fines, exile or beatings. The decision was sometimes left to local communities, who could call for execution or mutilation if they felt strongly in a particular case.[188] The law was reformed in 1285 to establish that rape against nuns or virgins was a crime punishable by death; but rape of a woman who was not a virgin was a trespass and her husband or father might be compensated for damage to his property. In 1300, rape was clarified as a crime against property, damaging a woman's value, affecting her marriageability, her status and her family's wealth. The new law required that the woman receive a payment into her dowry, so compensating any future husband for his loss. The sentence for rape was reduced from hanging, drawing and quartering to hanging (a similar punishment as for theft), but the raped woman was again given the option to marry her rapist and save his life and her good name.[189]

If an accusation of rape ever got to court, a woman's word was not as good as a man's word – he had legal status and she did not. There are few records of accused rapists making any defence. Mostly, an accused man simply denied the accusation.

Henry, son of Fullar of Shelfield in Walsall, denied raping Maud, daughter of Henry Spurnall, in 1221, 'word for word', according to the court record. He told the court that Maud's father was an accused murderer and that he had caught Henry Spurnall with Maud, her sister and 15 sheep in the woods. Henry claimed that Maud accused him of rape 'in grudge'. The jury of 12 men from four villages ruled that he was not guilty.[190]

One woman, abducted, raped and imprisoned for two years, could not get her rapist punished as she had failed to report her rape within the permitted period. John raped Rose, a virgin of Irchester, in Northamptonshire. When she tried to raise the hue and cry, he kidnapped her, took her to Oxfordshire and held her prisoner for two years. After she escaped, raised the hue and cry, and brought her rapist-kidnapper to court, his defence was a technical one – that she had not named 'a definite day or a definite year or a definite place when he had raped her'.

The court agreed and John walked free. But on this rare occasion, the intervention of the king called John back to court and a second trial convicted him of rape and fined him £10. The fine was paid to the king, as the complainant – not Rose.[191]

If a woman conceived a child as a result of a rape, her claim of rape was automatically discounted, because it was believed (from Aristotle) that a woman would only conceive a child if she had experienced an orgasm: conception proved an orgasm, and an orgasm proved consent. That was what the judge told Joan of Kent, who claimed she had been raped and made pregnant. His judgment was recorded in the year books of Edward II.[192]

About a quarter of rape accusations were successfully prosecuted. In one study of thirteenth-century records, of 108 rape accusations 15 per cent yielded guilty verdicts, 12 per cent were settled out of court and in 33 per cent of the cases charges were dismissed.[193] None of the guilty men were sentenced to death as the law provided, not even those who pleaded guilty. Agnes of Westwode said that Roger of Cheveral in Wiltshire was guilty of 'rape and the violation of her body', and he admitted to the coroner that he had 'raped her with violence'. The jurors' verdict confirmed that Roger was guilty of rape. The court fined him 4s and outlawed him.[194]

The difficulty of making an accusation, the almost impossible requirements of proof and the lenient punishments deterred women from making complaints.[195] The shame of sexual intercourse with a stranger – even a rape – was a lasting stain on a wife's reputation and a raped single woman would have to find a husband who would accept a dishonoured bride. Some reigns passed with no recorded allegations of rape at all, like those of Richard I (1189–99) and John (1199–1216).[196]

A study of all the surviving records of rape accusations between 1208 and 1321, from different parts of the country, shows that 21 per cent of men accused of rape were found guilty. Of these 31 men found guilty, 24 of them were punished. Two men were hanged, and about a third of the guilty men were imprisoned, a third were outlawed, and the rest compensated or even married the woman complainant. Some men probably ran away and became outlaws to avoid their trial.[197]

But 71 women – nearly half of those complaining of rape (49 per cent) – were arrested for false accusing or failing to attend court, or failing to complete the procedures. These were easy counter-accusations – given the complex requirements for a successful complaint and the fact that almost all rape victims were working poor women, social inferiors to their rapists who were almost all tradesmen, clerks or churchmen.[198] The literate men could easily defend themselves to a male jury of their peers. The common women were in a court of their masters without representation.

The visiting judge, on a circuit from a distant town, was more concerned with imposing correct court procedure on an unruly area than on the rights of rape victims. His principal task was to raise money from the court by setting fines, and it was easier to fine a woman complaining of rape than to pursue and prosecute the man she had accused.[199]

Jurors were drawn from the villages of the accused and the accuser, and there may have been a desire for community peace. Since a woman was automatically an object of desire – whatever her intentions – she was traditionally held responsible for crimes that were committed against her. In the church's view, the sin of raping a beautiful woman was a lesser sin than that of raping an ugly woman, because the temptation to assault a beautiful woman was so much greater.[200]

Convicted rapists could attract a royal pardon. Henry III's Dictum of Kenilworth of 1266 gave a general amnesty to his supporters, whatever crimes they had committed – including rapes.[201]

Marriage

A wedding was a verbal promise that could be made anywhere – it did not even need to be on holy ground, with or without a priest, or any other witness. From the 1100s, the desire of the lords to control heiresses and their dowries prompted a new tradition that required promises to be made before witnesses, ideally a priest. The cleric would be responsible for making sure that the bridal couple were not closely related and that neither had a live previous spouse. From the twelfth century, canon law tried to prevent marriages forced on young people, or kidnapped brides, by making consent an essential element of a valid wedding.[202] But a priest who owed his place and income to a powerful patron was unlikely to oppose him.[203]

A private promise to marry in the future – a betrothal – was considered as binding a commitment as a wedding oath. Theodora, born to a wealthy merchant family around 1096 in Huntingdon, was betrothed to a lord, despite her wish to become a nun. Her parents complained that her attempt to break her betrothal made them the 'laughing stock of their neighbours'.[204] The support of a hermit, who recommended Theodora's vocation to the Archbishop of Canterbury, encouraged the young woman to escape from her family and she ran away from home dressed as a man, to join a woman hermit: Alfwen, at Flamstead. Theodora changed her name to Christina and supported herself by her art – she worked in silk, embroidering and weaving pictures often based on illuminated manuscripts. The *St Albans Chronicle* records her beautifully worked sandals and mitres, which she made as a gift for the pope.[205] Two years later, her fiancé released her from the betrothal and the Archbishop of York annulled the oath. Christina took her vows at St Albans Abbey and lived in the hermitage at Markyate, where a priory was established around her. She served as prioress and was joined by other devout women. She befriended and advised the abbot of St Albans, Geoffrey de Gorham, who recorded his feelings for her in the St Albans Psalter, in which there is a letter 'C' for Christina at Psalm 105, the psalm that celebrates the power of God to protect his people.

A betrothal could be converted into a binding marriage by a wedding ceremony – ideally before a priest and witnesses – or merely by a sequence of rituals: the payment of a token, the gift of a ring and consummation of the marriage: penile penetration. After that, the couple were fully married and the wife might be considered as her husband's responsibility, both for her behaviour and for her debts. A bride did not even speak in the wedding service. In the *Bury St Edmunds Missal* of the 1100s, only the husband has a voice. He was to say:

> With this ring I thee wed,
> this gold and silver I thee give,
> with my body I thee worship,
> and with this dowry I thee endow.

Then the bride, having received the gold and silver and the dowry, falls to the feet of her husband.[206]

She heard the almost idolatrous description of their union: 'with my body I thee worship'. It's a potent line, for marriages that we generally think of as 'arranged' and even 'loveless'. She accepted the substantial gifts: the ring that proved the marriage, the ceremonial coins that represented the lifelong financial partnership, and her contribution – her dowry. She knelt, like a feudal tenant before a lord, like a lord before a king, to her superior.

Marriages for love took place – especially when there were no great fortunes to be settled. A church deacon in England met a young Jewish woman in Oxford while he was being taught by her father, a Jewish scholar. The two fell in love and the deacon proposed marriage and promised to convert to her religion. He took circumcision and converted to Judaism to marry the woman he loved. He was accused of apostasy by the church and burned at the stake at Osney in 1222.[207]

Agnes Nakerer fell in love with a travelling minstrel, John Kent, and married him in secret in the early 1300s. Her parents forced her to the altar with a more valuable son-in-law, but John the Minstrel took them to the church court at York and won his wife back.[208]

Common women tended to marry after they had worked for some years. Some Lincolnshire women married after 21 years of age, or even later in the thirteenth and fourteenth centuries, when both husband and wife had saved enough money to start a home.[209] Women at Wakefield,

Spalding and in some manors in Huntingdonshire were required to pay a feudal fee to the lord of the manor for the right to marry the man of their choice, and they often used their own money.[210]

Marriages among the upper classes were made by parents and guardians for young people, as they were used to transfer property between families, resolve quarrels and even end local wars. The old Anglo-Saxon word for wives was 'peace-weavers'.[211] Any happiness that might follow the wedding proved a lucky bonus. Considerate and loving parents might choose a partner likely to suit their child; but others might be only concerned with the finances.

Most marriages ended in an early death: one in 40 medieval women died in childbirth in England in the 1500 and 1600s.[212] The average age at death for medieval men and women was 40 years. There was no divorce but a marriage might be declared invalid because the spouses were closely related or the marriage forbidden by canon law. Causes for annulment could be leprosy, flagrant adultery by the wife, malicious abandonment, the couple being of different faiths, or a forced wedding. A marriage could be annulled if either of the couple were unable to conceive children or the man was declared impotent. The judgment of experienced women was called on in such cases. A jury of 12 Canterbury women in 1292 examined Walter de Fonte and testified – after trying and failing to arouse him – that his 'virile member' was 'useless'.[213] Neither husband nor wife could refuse sex, having given consent at their wedding day once and for all – but there were many days off: the church ruled no sex on saints' days, nor on feast days, holy days and days of penitence. Altogether, no-sex days took up about a third of the year, and sex was discouraged during menstruation or breast-feeding.[214]

Misbehaviour in marriage was punished – but the marriage would not be dissolved. In Rochester in the 1300s, any wife guilty of adultery was whipped three times around the churchyard and three times around the market – the same punishment as for an adulterous husband.[215]

Roman Catholic churches in Europe hosted same-sex marriages of women to women in the eighth century. These were legitimate marriages undertaken by parish priests who recorded the marrying women's names in parish records in the usual way. As England came under the same papal jurisdiction, women-only marriages probably took place in English churches too. The wording of English marriage services from the tenth century speaks of a 'wife' and a 'bride' and blesses future children of the marriage but does not define the marriage as heterosexual. The wedding service used in the twelfth century, the *Bury St Edmunds Missal*, refers to a bride and bridegroom, but not specifically to a man and woman. It was not until the sixteenth century that the *Sarum Manual* wedding service specifically referred to a man and a woman in the marriage vows.[216]

Women's Love and Sexual Desire

In medieval England it was widely believed that women had an active sexual appetite for both male and female partners, sought sexual intercourse and experienced orgasm – the 'Eve' view of women as creatures of strong sexual desires. Since medical practitioners believed that orgasm released a female seed – just as it released male seed – a husband who wanted heirs had to give his wife sexual pleasure.

Sexual intercourse, with the intention of conceiving a child, was to act with God. It was a sin to try to prevent this in any way – including masturbation and nocturnal emissions, or contraception and abortion. Low pregnancy rates in the early medieval period suggest that people sought sexual pleasure without penetrative intercourse. 'Bundling' – erotic cuddling, and non-penetrative sexual touching, was a tradition, especially among unmarried lovers – and herbal contraceptions and practices were so widespread that the church included advice to parish priests in the handbook on suitable penances. Aborting before the baby had 'quickened', or been felt to move, was considered an equal sin to contraception, since the fetus had no soul before quickening. Women who confessed to causing a miscarriage by taking herbs would be given a 40-day penance – the usual punishment for a minor sin.[217] Wise women and herbalists had recipes for spermicides and herbs that were supposed to cause abortions. Hildegard of Bingen (1098–1179), the mother superior and future saint, recorded recipes for abortion and instructed that abortions should be performed if the mother's life was endangered by a pregnancy.[218] Unwanted babies were sometimes killed by a risky surgical abortion with a knife or needle, and reported as still births. Newborn babies were killed or abandoned to die and this was defined as the greater sin of murder, and the mother was always the first suspect; she had to prove her innocence and might be hanged if found guilty.

Church leaders were opposed to any form of sexual intercourse other than penile penetration, face to face, with the husband on top, for the sole intention of conceiving a child. Orgasm was essential but sexual pleasure for its own sake was a sin. In the thirteenth century, Thomas Aquinas provided a helpful list of sins, from the bad to the worst: masturbation, bestiality, sodomy and – worst of all – heterosexual intercourse using contraception or in any position other than male dominant. Masturbation was a worse sin than rape, since it prevented God giving a life.[219] Sodomy, at this time, was defined as any act that put a penis into anywhere but a human vagina, or put anything *but* a penis into a human vagina.

Both church and manor courts could hear evidence against women accused of fornication or adultery, and both set penances and punishments. Occasionally men were tried and punished. Three women in Worcestershire in 1270 were fined for 'fornication' – with no accusation against their male partners. In 1247 in Norfolk, a group of five women paid fines for losing their virginity, but no men were accused or fined.[220]

Concern about the chastity of nuns led Pope Boniface to issue a decree in 1298 that all nuns should be strictly enclosed in their religious houses and forbidden from receiving guests or entertaining. This was supposed to encourage the women 'to serve God more freely, wholly separated from the public and worldly gaze and, occasions for lasciviousness having been removed, may most diligently safeguard their hearts and bodies in complete chastity'.[221]

But the new rules were not welcomed by women. In 1300, Bishop John Dalderby visited Markyate Priory with the new regulations and reported that the nuns 'hurled the said statute at his back and over his head'. Meaux Abbey nuns rejected the new rules, claiming they were not bound to obey anything stricter than their original vows.[222]

In any case, the building of walls and gratings in convents was irrelevant – the few nuns who were having sex with men had lovers inside the enclosures: co-sited monks, religious visitors, workers or guests. The raising of walls and the bolting of doors and the installing of grilles in convents showed the deep-rooted fear of women's 'propensity for sinful behaviour'. Not even women who had taken vows to be 'Brides of Christ' could be trusted to control their sexual desires. Nuns pointed out that imprisoning them elevated the vow of chastity above the other vows of poverty and obedience. Surely, praising God was more important than making sure that nuns did not have sex?[223]

Nuns who sinned with men were assigned penances of diet, or beaten by their superiors or peers, or imprisoned. In the story of the Nun of Watton, as told by Aelred of Rievaulx in 1160, a young nun who had been enclosed from childhood in Watton Priory, in Yorkshire, met a young monk from the co-sited monastery and conceived a child with him. The nuns beat her, tore the veil from her head, had to be restrained from flaying and branding her, and chained her in her cell, feeding her only bread and water. The co-sited monks captured her lover and forced the nun – his lover – to castrate him, and his severed genitals were pushed into her mouth. The young man was returned to his monastery, and the young woman imprisoned in her cell. There she had a vision of Henry Murdac, Bishop of York, who took away her baby and cleansed her of sin. Next morning the nuns found her alone in her cell, without her baby and with no signs of pregnancy. Church fathers agreed that this was a miracle, and the young woman was forgiven. There is no indication in the story that the life-threatening punishments for the young man and woman were excessive or inappropriate.[224]

Penalties for same-sex relationships in the convent were far less harsh than those for heterosexual intercourse. In the seventh century, Theodore, Archbishop of Canterbury, published a 'penitential' – a list of possible sins and their appropriate punishment. A woman who 'practices vice with another woman' should be given a penance for three years. This was a lesser penance than that recommended for a married woman who committed adultery with a married man.[225] Historian and theologian the Venerable Bede agreed: there should be a penance of three years for women lovers, but ten years if the women used a 'device'.[226]

In the eighth century, the punishment was reduced. Nuns who had participated in 'intimacy' (Constantine V's word) were ordered a brief penance of a diet of bread and water. This punitive diet was to be extended for 40 days if one woman 'rode' another, but there was no suggestion that the nuns having sex with other nuns should be beaten.[227] The papal ban on 'intimacy' was not concerned with emotional relationships between nuns. When, in the twelfth century, Hildegard of Bingen acknowledged her intense feelings for her assistant Richardis, this was seen as a problem of favouritism, damaging the discipline of the convent, not a sin of sexuality.[228]

Sexual activity between women had been known and named in the Christian world since the second century. The word 'lesbia' for a woman marrying a woman was recorded in the margins of a manuscript from the time.[229] St Paul had described both female desire and perversity as God's punishment for idolatry: 'For this cause God gave them up to vile affections: for even their women did change the natural use into that which is against nature.'[230]

Since medieval theologians named the penetration of anything but the penis into anywhere but the vagina as 'sodomy', women using a fake penis for penetration would be guilty of sodomy: a sin and a serious crime that could be charged in a church or civil court. In reality this was very rare – there are only 12 known trials of women using objects to penetrate other women in medieval Christendom, and none in England.[231]

Women kissing together are shown as an example of the 'sin of the mouth' – not as a sin of same-sex intimacy – in a French illustrated Bible of the thirteenth century. There are men embracing nearby. The illustration to a poem from *The Romance of the Rose* by Guillaume de Lorris (1200–40) shows two girls kissing in an imaginary garden of pleasure, an idyllic scene of women's happiness, where women dance, argue, do handstands and kiss.

A thirteenth-century female troubadour, the trobairitz Bieiris de Romans, described her passionate love for a woman in her poetry:

Lovely woman, whom joy and noble speech uplift,
and merit, to you my stanzas go,
for in you are gaiety and happiness,
and all good things one could ask of a woman.[232]

Centuries of scholarship have been devoted to explaining that Bieiris de Romans is adopting a male voice or writing in the tradition of male troubadours to a non-existent woman, or that since women are not erotic lovers it is a poem about sentimental affection and not physical.[233]

Or maybe she was a woman writing a love poem to a woman she loved.

The Nature of Women

Medieval male philosophers learned from Aristotle (384–322 BCE) that there was one basic human body type, with the same sexual organs – external in men and internal in women, one human form, differently arranged, though men were more visible, understandable and healthy than the mysterious and hidden female. All the classical texts since Plato, from about 400 BCE onwards, agreed that there was an ideal wholeness, in which all the possible variations of genders were unified and united in one: a spectrum of sexes, with highly masculinised men at one end and highly feminine women at the other, and a vast variety between the two extremes.[234]

Later, in the second century, Aurelius Galen proposed that every human body was controlled by 'humours' that were combined differently in each individual. Where an individual sat on the spectrum depended on the mixture of the humours: women should be moist and cold, men dry and hot; but individuals differed in their composition and could be adjusted to the desired mixture. Because a person's nature depended on the mixture of the humours, an infinite variability was possible inside the one sex; cold and moist caused femininity in men and women, hot and dry caused masculinity.[235] The classical model of one sex, one flesh dominated thinking until the seventeenth century.[236]

Both theories were clear that there was one human body shared by men and women. Hermaphrodites – with both male and female genitals – were believed to be a normal and frequent occurrence.[237] A woman could turn into a man. If she masturbated, her clitoris might grow into a penis;[238] or a penis might pop out of its normal position tucked inside as a vagina through physical exertion, such as jumping a ditch.[239] It was generally understood that exertion, sexual activity or excessive heat frequently turned women into men, and both Greek philosophers and church fathers agreed that would be an improvement.

Medieval churchmen believed that to be 'in Christ' was to be gender free, in a state of spiritual awareness, above bodily differences, beyond biology. St Paul said: 'There is neither Jew nor Greek, there is neither bond nor free, there is neither male nor female: for ye are all one in Christ Jesus.'[240]

Changing from one sex to another is described in the apocryphal gospel of St Thomas. The last 'saying' of the collection is from Jesus, of

Mary his mother: 'I, myself, shall lead her, in order to make her male, so that she too may become a living spirit resembling you males. For every woman who will make herself male will enter the kingdom of heaven.'[241]

Although women dressing as men was banned in the Bible, there were warmly approving medieval ballads, poetry and stories about women acting like men or transforming into men.[242] An early medieval heroine in the song 'Yde et Olive' performed chivalric quests dressed as a knight and at the end was rewarded by transforming into a fully functioning man capable of fathering children.[243] More than thirty-five legends named cross-dressing women saints where holy women dress as men as a permanent choice.[244]

Womanhood was not a different and opposite sex to men, it was a different status to men. Medieval male philosophers who spent their lives pondering the question 'Why *are* we so superior to women?' answered that inferiority was the 'nature of women'. They spoke of the 'female defect': the law cited the lack of female existence unless specifically defined, the church banned women from the priesthood, the crown preferred male heirs, and the culture knew of the natural inferiority of women.

The church council of Mâcon in 585 discussed whether women could be considered as 'man' in the sight of God and concluded that they could. This was mischievously misreported through the centuries as a synod decision that women did not have souls.[245] They certainly did not have status. St Paul wrote that women should be 'under obedience': 'Let your women keep silence in the churches: for it is not permitted unto them to speak; but they are commanded to be under obedience as also saith the law. And if they will learn anything, let them ask their husbands at home: for it is a shame for women to speak in the church.'[246] Henry de Bracton, the legal expert, defined female inferiority in 1235: 'Women differ from men in many respects, for their position is inferior to that of men.'[247]

But a new definition of female nature was emerging from the art forms around 'courtly love'. A literary tradition in the Arab world, the idea of 'courtly love' had been introduced to France from Muslim Spain, and when Eleanor of Aquitaine came to England in 1152, to marry Henry II, she brought this new version of the 'nature' of women with her. The poems were love stories about a closely guarded heroine and the noble young man who adores her. Their love, expressed in poetic dialogue and courageous acts, attains a high level of spirituality and, finally, union with God. The woman of the courtly love stories was nothing like the earthy, fallible woman that philosophers said was naturally inferior to man. The woman of the courtly love stories was perfect, without sin, capable of a deep and sinless passion modelled on Mary, mother of Jesus, whose cult was developing in every European country, with great cathedrals and shrines such as Our Lady of Walsingham in England. Courtly love provided the secular version of the cult of Mary, with a heroine whose nature was nearly divine.

The hero was often a poor poet, free to love, without ties, able to dedicate his life to her service. She was always a noble or royal wife, in an arranged and loveless marriage – available for fin'amor, 'fine love'.

The theme of courtly love expanded from the patrons of travelling poets – male troubadours and female trobairitz – into other forms: paintings, plays, jousts and masques, spreading countrywide, far beyond the great houses. The popular masques – performed by professionals and nobility before huge audiences of common people – retold the courtly love stories; the tales were referenced during jousts, which were often dedicated to courtly love romances. 'Courts of Love', hearing interesting dilemmas of love, loyalty and courtesy, were said to be judged by noble ladies sitting in authority over men. Eleanor of Aquitaine and her daughter may have held such tribunals, and the rulings of the women judges – fictional or real – were published, describing how courtly love should be expressed and regulating the behaviours appropriate to the lowly lover and his demanding lady-lord. Marie de France's '*lais*' were enjoyed by Eleanor of Aquitaine and her court. They told of aristocratic ladies suffering for love.

The noble heroines took active roles in the early stories. In the earliest tales they defended their husbands or lovers and physically fought against their enemies. They could disguise themselves as knights, go adventuring and even court other women while disguised as a man. In the *Roman d'Enéas*, the heroine, Camille, leads a troop of women in battle against the Trojans; in the German tale *The Ladies' Tournament*, the women joust with each other; in Chaucer's 'The Knight's Tale', the women are Amazons, fighting men before they join the court; and in the *Chanson de Guillaume*, two women of authority appear, one maintaining a castle in a war zone and managing its defence, the other a queen who advises her husband. These commanding, active, powerful heroines were a complete contradiction to the inferior women described by the classic writers and the early churchmen.

As courtly love came to dominate the arts and entertainment of the medieval world, the two contradictory versions of the nature of women – bawdy, earthy woman and ethereal lady – were affirmed and retold until they became universally accepted, even by women themselves, who then tried to live up to them. Any idea of sisterhood, even womanhood, was riven by this division of women. No longer could a woman merely 'do' or merely 'be': she must choose one role or another and then stay within it. From now on, a woman must be either 'naturally' a frigid lady, superior to all others and above earthly desires, or 'naturally' an obedient, inferior, sexually active commoner – and the biggest and most significant indicator of a woman's nature was whether or not she was readily available for sex with a man.

Part 2

1348–1455
Women Rising

The Great Pestilence

A deadly virus, later named 'the Black Death' but known at the time as 'the Great Pestilence', arrived in England in 1348. The epidemic started in East Asia and spread across all of Europe along the trade routes. It was a form of bubonic plague, but to those it afflicted the cause was a terrifying mystery and there was no known cure. The first outbreaks proved the worst: bringing the Hundred Years' War with France to a halt, destroying cultural life, severing connections between England and Europe, emptying villages and fields, damaging the church – which had neither doctrine nor priests to offer hope. Every aspect of life in England was transformed by widespread deaths, as the population halved: from 5 million people in 1300 to 2.5 million in 1400,[1] with 30–40 per cent dying in the first year alone.[2] In the towns the workshops stood empty, as masters and apprentices fled to the country if they could or died in their thousands. In the country people died alone in their cottages; villages tried to exclude travellers, but the plague seemed unstoppable. The impact was extraordinary – scientists have even suggested that so many farmers died that agricultural land reverted to forest, cooling the climate and creating the later 'Little Ice Age' of the seventeenth century.[3]

The most important consequence of the plague for women is not remarked in the histories. In these desperate years, women were called on to serve the church as if they were ordained male priests. In January 1349, Ralph of Shrewsbury, the Bishop of Bath and Wells, ordered dying Christians to confess their sins to a layman if no priest was available; and if no layman was available, the patient might confess and receive the last rites from a woman. He said:

> The plague ... has left many parish churches ... without parson or priest to care for their parishioners ... Therefore, to provide for the salvation of souls ... you should at once publicly command and persuade all men that, if they are on the point of death and cannot secure the services of a priest, then they should make confession to each other ... if no man is present, then even to a woman.[4]

'Even to a woman'! It was an extraordinary, almost-forgotten break-through into the men-only priesthood. The significance is that by allowing women (as a last resort) to hear the confession of a dying man, Bishop Ralph implied that women could intercede with God – just like men. Women had a voice that God could hear – they were not the 'second sex'; they could intercede with God as well as a man. This extraordinary transformation of women from inferior creatures, into God-blessed beings, did not last beyond the plague years, and Bishop Ralph's admission of female spiritual equality would never be repeated by the Roman Catholic Church. Six hundred years later, the Church of England finally agreed that women could be ordained as priests.

As the plague took its toll, the deaths overwhelmed the church. Life in convents and abbeys collapsed, with no one to farm their fields, nor run their industries, nor collect their rents. Their infirmaries had nothing to offer; patients died, and nurses and physicians contracted the disease. Orphan children and the poor were abandoned by the religious houses that could not feed themselves. The smaller convents fell into abject poverty.[5] Women leaders, skilled practitioners and labourers died, and surviving nuns deserted failing nunneries and never returned. By 1500, only two large houses survived, at Shaftesbury and Syon. More than 100 had closed. Many of the convents – especially those of Benedictines – shrunk into small domestic groups of four or five women; other nuns returned to their parents, married or tried to fit into the secular world.[6]

But surviving women in town and country found new opportunities. Those in the country were freed from the supervision of the lord of the manor or his agents. Taxpayers could refuse to pay taxes, many collectors were dead and the government recognised the breakdown of the system by reducing taxes in the post-plague years. Rent collectors were dead and surviving tenants could not be forced into onerous leases; they might walk away to a better lord in an empty manor or even find an abandoned farm.[7] Women survivors in the towns might be the only ones able to continue a business or the only heirs to property. There were not enough workers to fill vacancies; male and female labourers could set their own wages.

Olivia Cranmer, in the village of Walsham le Willows, Suffolk, rose from the lowest class – the daughter of a serf and so even lower status than a serf – a single mother who was probably ordered to marry to force the father to support her bastard. When the Great Pestilence came to her village, 119 men died in the two months of May and June 1349, as did unrecorded numbers of women and children. Olivia's grandfather, father, brother and husband all died, leaving Olivia as the only surviving heir to the family plot of land and the tenancy. As the feudal system collapsed around her, she was no longer named as a serf, and new freedoms opened up for her. She farmed her own plot, made a profit, expanded her business and even rented or bought land, increasing her landholding to such an extent that she could lease surplus land to a tenant of her own. Her tenant's rent paid her for her old age. She never remarried and lived into her seventies, a farmer, businesswoman and entrepreneur.[8]

The pestilence created a nationwide shortage of labour. There were not enough workers even to harvest the crops in the fields. Surviving women labourers probably made up as much as 50 per cent of the workforce and were so much in demand that they earned equal pay with men.[9] Wages were still paid by the task, not according to the sex of the worker, and women in skilled arduous trades such as thatching and reaping worked alongside men, equally productive and paid at the same rate.[10]

Higher wages drew women from working in home production into wage work and into trades and business.[11] The next 200 years saw them taking home equal pay with men, competing with men for casual work, continuing with their own domestic production of food and textiles, entering apprenticeships and training and so rising into higher-paid work. Women moved from rural tenancies into urban areas to seize entrepreneurial opportunities: in some towns they outnumbered men.[12] Women stepped into businesses or fortunes of dead husbands or parents, like Agnes Ramsey who inherited her father William's design and building business in London in 1349 and became a leading architect:

contracted by Queen Isabella to design her £100 tomb in Greyfriars Church in the capital.[13]

Mathilda Penne ran her husband's business as a skinner for 12 years after his death; she trained her own apprentices and employed male servants and, possibly, a female scrivener to keep the accounts. Johanna Hill (d. 1441) inherited the bell foundry at Aldgate from her husband. She trained four male apprentices and the daughter of a fellow bell-founder, as well as employing two female servants, 10 male servants, a specialised bell-maker and a clerk.[14]

Successful women entrepreneurs used the law in their own names: in 1368, Emma Saltere of London sued Thomas Blankowe and Alice Breton for a huge debt of 52 shillings. When they did not appear in court to answer for their debt, she gained 32s 6d in goods: a fur-trimmed blue coat, a chest and a mattress with coverlet tester and linens. Maud Ireland traded as a femme sole silkwoman even though her husband Thomas was so successful that he was a London alderman in 1380. She represented herself when she was sued by an Italian silk merchant in a dispute over some white silk.[15]

The numbers of girls taking up trade apprenticeships soared in the decades after the pestilence – a third of the names in the surviving records are those of girls. Most were bound to masters by their fathers, planning a career for their girls. Robert de Ramseye, a fishmonger who died in 1373, left 20 shillings to his daughter, Elizabeth – for her marriage and for 'putting her to a trade'. One woman made her own apprenticeship agreement, travelling from Sussex to London to enter a contract with a woman master.[16]

These were genuine apprenticeships to genuine trades, entered in the guild rolls, supervised by the guilds, providing a training of seven years to learn the skills of the craft and graduation as a registered craftsman with guild membership. Many of the women apprentices entered the textile business, especially highly paid silk and embroidery work. The girl apprentices, like the boys, 'lived in' with their male and female masters and were in some cases treated like members of the family.

Rural women successfully took up the extra work needed in food production. After 1375, there were no regular, frequent national famines, thanks to the reduced population and the increased productivity of women in market gardening, farming, food production processing and distribution.[17]

Women who took up work in all occupations, at rates of pay that had previously been unobtainable, chose to marry later or even stay single.[18] Older wives with smaller families caused a decline in the birth rate and so maintained a smaller population with a shortage of labourers, which in turn kept wages high, encouraging women to prolong their single years.

With few male tenants, landlords leased land and houses to single women – those women living without husbands, renting in their own right and negotiating for themselves. In 1380, Joanna de Boneye, a widow without supportive children, provided for her old age with an agreement with her neighbour John Attestyle of Radcliffe. She gave him the bulk of her land in Bunny and Bradmore, Nottinghamshire, and he housed her for the rest of her life, as attested by a deed between them recorded in Latin on 29 July that year:

> John is to give the said Joanna a competent living for herself from the next Feast of St Michael into the future for the whole of her life, and sufficient land for annual sowing of one fernedel of flax seed from John's own lands, and also annually the sustenance for one cow with her own calf, and one room in John's own house below the fire and also she may take one key to the hostium celavi [probably larder] of the said John, with liberty to enter and exit for her victuals or necessities in the absence of the wife of the said John.[19]

Elite families – the nobility or upper gentry – also depended on women survivors. In some families a widow ran the estate and headed the family until the infant son could grow up and take his inheritance. Male guardians and male executors left wills giving women fortunes and authority. Some families were left with only female heirs. Entire dynasties and fortunes depended on the competence of the female head of the family.

Employers and landowners struggled to stop the changes. In Sussex, a relatively poor area of England in 1349, a ring of landowners held down wages and casual labourers and the poor faced hardship.[20] Women were pressured to marry and have families to restore the population. Those choosing to live as single women fell under suspicion of the authorities, and the church taught that women should not take on the work of God by deciding who was born and when: contraception became a serious sin. Women who confessed to causing their own miscarriage were given heavier punishments by their confessors, and birth control methods in the published medical texts were hidden in Latin – the language exclusive to the upper classes.[21] Midwives were discouraged from teaching birth control methods to their clients.[22]

The trauma of the plague years changed household charity. No longer were large numbers of the poor fed at the kitchen door, or even at regular feasts at the lord's table. Lordly giving ceased to be a tradition of the upper classes, with lords no longer demonstrating their wealth and their 'good lordship' by generosity to their own people. Laws preventing workers from leaving their parishes meant that travellers were not welcomed. Gifts of food and goods were more controlled, scaled down and directed to employees, not to the local poor, nor vagrants and beggars.[23]

The plague brought a new twist to misogyny. Some diseases were already blamed on women – it was thought leprosy in a man was caused by having sex with a menstruating women and that sexual diseases were generated by women in their bodies. Now people theorised that women had caused the Great Pestilence. The *Westminster Chronicle* declared that women had caused the plague because

> women flowed with the tides of fashion in this and other things even more eagerly, wearing clothes that were so tight that they wore a fox tail hanging down inside their skirts at the back, to hide their arses. The sin of pride manifested in this way must surely bring down misfortune in the future.[24]

New laws emphasised the status of husbands by naming the crime of 'husband-killing' as the gravest of murders. Only killing a king was worse. The Treason Act of 1351 ruled that a woman who killed her husband committed a crime as serious as that of a priest killing his bishop or a servant killing his master. Establishing the horror of husband-killing and legally defining the subservience of wives, this law reserved a special punishment for murderous wives until 1828 – for nearly 500 years.

A new tax was introduced, specifically aimed at married women. Previous 'poll' taxes had counted man and wife as one economic unit – they paid one tax. But the new levy offered no deduction for a wife. Now a married woman had to pay as much as a man or a single woman. While in law she remained under her husband as a femme couvert, tax was now to be levied on her as if she were single. The nationwide resistance created a series of rebellions that would become known as the Peasants' Revolt of 1381, or even Wat Tyler's Rebellion: almost all of the histories ignore the fact that the tax that triggered the uprising was a tax on wives – and it was led by women.

The Peasants' Revolt

The first acts of insurrection were staged by two Kent women: Joan Hampcok and Agnes Jekyn, in the spring of 1381. They were arrested and imprisoned. On 7 June that year in Larkfield, Kent, Margaret Stafford was accused of 'helping people to rise up'. A day later, Wat Tyler staged an attack on Canterbury Castle to free Joan Hampcok and Agnes Jekyn, finding them in hand and leg cuffs, treated as the most dangerous prisoners. The rebels broke open the jail and the three leaders, Hampcok, Jekyn and Tyler, led the march of the Kent rebels to London. The next day Maidstone jail was raided and torn to the ground by rebels led by another woman: Julia Pouchere.[25]

When the rebels invaded London on 13 June, another woman, Johanna Ferrour, led the revolutionaries to the Savoy Palace, stealing a chest of gold from the hated advisor to the king, his uncle John of Gaunt, Duke of Lancaster. Ferrour and her supporters burned the Savoy Palace to the ground and loaded a boat with stolen gold, sending it across the river to Southwark, where she divided the profit between herself and other rebels.

Two other women were named as leaders in official documents:

> Londoners Matilda Brembole, and her daughter Isabella, were at the firing of the Savoy Palace, they tore to pieces cloth of gold and silver and rich tapestries, broke up the rich furniture, crushed the Duke's plate, and ground his jewels and precious stones under foot. All that could not be destroyed was thrown into the river. When the work of destruction was over, the Savoy lay a smouldering ruin.[26]

After the looting of the palace, Matilda and Isabella Brembole led the rioters to the fabulously wealthy Priory of Clerkenwell, the headquarters of the Knights Hospitaller of St John of Jerusalem and sacked and fired that too. Another woman, Katherine Gamon, intercepted the rescue boat that had been sent by the authorities to save Chief Justice Cavendish from the mob, setting it adrift. It floated downriver as he dashed towards it, leaving him to be caught by the pursuing mob and beheaded.[27]

The day after the burning of the Savoy Palace, King Richard II met Wat Tyler to agree a ceasefire. While the peace talks were being held, Johanna Ferrour, who had led the attack, marched at the head of rebels to London's citadel and pulled the Archbishop of Canterbury and the Lord High Treasurer out of their refuge: 'She went as the chief leader to the Tower of London and she laid violent hands on Simon, recently Archbishop of Canterbury, and then on Brother Robert Hales ... and she dragged them out of the Tower and ordered that they be beheaded.'[28]

As Ferrour was murdering the most hated advisors of the court, Tyler believed he was making progress in negotiations with the 14-year-old Richard II and his advisors. The king promised to suspend the hated tax and end serfdom. But the following day, when Richard met the rebels again, this time at Smithfield, a scuffle broke out and the royal party killed Wat Tyler. The London militia dispersed the rebels and the king reneged on his promises and the royal forces captured the city. The rebellion did not end with the death of Wat Tyler – uprisings took place all around England and the king had to deploy soldiers from East Anglia to Yorkshire. Contemporary reports name some uprisings as criminal acts, not part of the rebellion – but attacks and looting were probably motivated by both protest and profit. Women led their families thieving in shops and markets, and from private homes. They assaulted, abducted and robbed their victims, sometimes working with prostitutes to rob or blackmail upper-class clients. The wife of Richard Carter led and maintained a criminal gang with her husband, seizing goods in Essex in the revolutionary month – June 1381.[29] Women were also charged with violent attacks on neighbours, sometimes with raiding people who owed them money, sometimes leading their families in attacks upon rivals or debtors.

One uprising in Cambridge, directed against John of Gaunt's college, Corpus Christi, was led by an old woman: Margery Starre. The rebels broke into the college buildings and seized the charters and letters patent, setting fire to them in the marketplace. Starre flung the ashes into the air and cried out, 'Away with the learning of the clerks! Away with it!'[30] The colleges of the town submitted themselves to the civic authorities and came under the control of the borough.

As late as 1386, a peasant uprising took place at Romsley in Worcestershire led by a woman: Agnes Sadeler. Overall, about 1,500 rebel leaders were killed, women and men. In the pardon roll issued by Richard II to offer amnesty to the rioters, 30 of the names were women applicants, a small minority of those who had taken part. Excluded from pardon were murderers – especially the women who had burned the Savoy Palace or Clerkenwell Priory – and those who had escaped from prison or were from certain named towns where the riots had been especially violent.[31] Those women who could not afford the expensive cash payments for pardons found themselves charged in the criminal courts – 70 women rebels from the county of Suffolk alone.[32]

The 30 women applicants for pardon were both literate and wealthy: they understood the value of a written document giving them immunity against later accusations. They must have had substantial cash reserves, enough to pay the heavy fine of about £1 each.

Upper-class women were robbed during the uprisings: Joan Atdenne, a widow, lost 28 ox cows and silver and jewellery – worth £20 – when her own family, Henry and Thomas Atdenne, came at the head of 'a mob' against their mother and stole from her. Many women landowners lost their rent records: Lady Alesia Nevile at Wethersfield was robbed of her documents, which were burned; the king's own mother, Joan of Kent, lost her manorial records in the North Weald of Kent and she was assaulted in the raid on London. Margaret de Enges, the prioress of Norwich, was forced to give up the rent rolls of the house for burning by the mob in June, and Joan Colbrand's records room was plundered and she was beaten by a mob.[33]

In 1428, a women-only riot took place against Duke Humphrey of Gloucester when he put aside his first wife, Jacqueline of Hainault, to marry his mistress, Eleanor Cobham. Identified as 'the first known women's protest in England', the women were demonstrating in defence of a deserted wife and in support of unbreakable marriage vows, which they believed should hold a man just as much as they held his wife.[34]

Women also supported a 1450 rebellion of about 5,000 people led by Jack Cade (1420/30–50) from Kent to London to complain about the corrupt leadership around Henry VI. Welcomed at first in the capital, the rebels set up trials and executions of the despised royal advisors, but once looting started, they were driven from the city by the citizens and tricked with false pardons. Cade went on the run and was found and killed, and his followers were executed in their villages. In July that year, more than 140 women were granted royal pardons by name for their part in the rebellion and 3,308 men. The most senior woman listed was the abbess of the Monastery of St Mary, Katherine de la Pole – probably the sister of the murdered William de la Pole and head of the most important abbey in England at Barking. She was pardoned for raising her tenants, household and servants to support Cade, and allowed to continue to lead one of the greatest religious houses in the land.

Single women pardoned for supporting Cade were named as Joan Triblere, Agnes Poleyn, Alice Permantre, Anne Cherch, Joan Smyth, Joan Webbe, Katharine Rye and Agnes Southlond; and there were two widows: Alice, late the wife of William Broun, and Joan, late the wife of John Kent. One woman, Joan Marchall, was listed as a wife but may have turned rebel without her husband – who was not listed. Other women supporters were listed alongside their husbands in the pardon. More unrecorded women may have died in the fighting at Sevenoaks, Kent, and London Bridge, and some may have been executed in their villages after the rebellion was crushed.[35]

Women led and supported these first large-scale rebellions, two of which were inspired by women defending the rights of women. In the case of the Duke Humphrey protest, the women violently rose up to support an innocent wife against a deserting adulterous husband. In the biggest uprising of the period – the Peasants' Revolt – the women rose against a tax that burdened wives. Single women and widows joined the rebellion to defend married women from unfair taxation. These actions were an extraordinary show of female solidarity against male tyranny, both domestic and national, private and legal. And they were effective – the shocked written accounts following the Peasants' Revolt hid the fact that the uprising achieved its objective. The feudal hierarchy thrown into turmoil by the Great Pestilence would never be successfully restored. From 1400, serfdom was ended in England. Labourers remained bound to the land, and they still owed rents and service to the landowners, but the system of feudalism brought in by William I, which had defined everyone in their place from slaves to lords, was gone forever.

Gone forever for men, that is. A woman was still defined by her relationship to a man – as a widow, wife or daughter. He gave her his social status, his name and his presence under the law. Even after the uprisings, a woman had no legal identity. She could not officially own property – a woman still gifted everything to her husband on her wedding day without any return. A woman could only make a will with her husband's permission, and wives lost everything if they left their homes. A runaway wife could take nothing with her, not even her children. A wife had no rights over her own body: rape by a husband was not a crime; physical punishment by him was allowed as long as he used no more than 'reasonable' force. If a man murdered his wife, he was not guilty of 'petty treason' and burned to death, he was charged only with murder, and he might successfully argue to an all-male jury and a male judge that it had been an accident or even a legal punishment that went wrong. Juan Vives, writing in the fifteenth century, 100 years after the apparent 'end of feudalism', wrote that a wife should behave to her husband, 'as though she had been bought into the house as a bond and handmaid'.[36]

Women Rising

As always – despite the laws, despite the theories – women seized opportunities. Women tenants applied for the many vacant properties and negotiated for better terms. By 1390, women were buying land as well as leasing.[37] In Sussex in the 1400s, husbands and wives bought land together as recognised equal partners: Juliana Greenstreet acquired two cottages and half an acre with her husband William and used one of the cottages as her ale house to run her own brewery business.[38] A renewed tenant shortage in 1440 created even more opportunities for working women to buy and inherit land.[39]

Some empty towns wanting the economic dynamism of independent women offered the status of 'freemen' to encourage single women seeking an alternative to the restrictions of life on the manor. Some towns even allowed married women to become 'free' with or without their husbands' consent. York saw increased numbers of women voting as 'freemen' of the city, including master weaver Isabella Nonhouse, who was given freewoman status in York in 1441, two years after the death of her husband.[40] Throughout the fifteenth century, more households came to be headed by single women, and more women's wills appear.[41] The guild of St George of Norwich enlisted 'brothers and sisters' on equal footing in 1418. The fraternity of St John the Baptist in Winchester commanded 'brothers and sisters' to the feast in 1411.[42]

Women expanded their traditional work in the textile trade: Emma Erle was one of the many successful women entrepreneurs. Margaret de Knaresburgh made so much money from her tailoring business that she left two gold rings and six silver spoons in her will – a fortune in 1396.[43] Elena Couper was a pin-maker, and Isabella de Copgrave was a brick-maker till her death in 1400 in Wakefield. Margery Moniers, a widow, inherited the family property development business and owned an entire street of houses.[44] Joan Hille ran the family metal foundry and taught four male apprentices after her husband's death in 1440. Alice Byngley, a widow, ran the family business of shearing sheep till her own death in 1464. In the first half of the fifteenth century, women increasingly moved into the trades that had been regarded as men's jobs: skilled, well-paid work.[45]

The population of London had been halved by death and flight during the years of pestilence, and in 1465 the city fathers opened the right of being 'free of the city' to the widow of any citizen, wealthy or poor, creating at a stroke a city of financially independent women.[46] Married women also registered themselves as femmes sole to trade independently of their husbands. A 1363 regulation already permitted women to take on as many trades as they wanted, even though men were allowed to pursue only one.[47] The city exerted itself to create opportunities for dynamic businesswomen, some of whom were women of colour. An excavation of a burial pit for 634 victims of the Great Pestilence found that 29 per cent of those buried had non-white DNA. Four women had African ancestry, and other bodies were of Asian ancestry. One woman had both African and Asian heritage: analysis of her teeth and bones suggested that she had been born and raised in pre-plague medieval England.[48]

Agnes Asser was a master cooper with her own mark in London in 1400. Emma Huntyngton survived her husband and kept the marital home and apothecary business in 1362. In 1370, Emma Bayser worked as a barber alongside her husband in the city, performing small surgical procedures.[49]

A third of the members of the Brewers' Guild of London in 1418–25 were women registered under their own name and in their own right.[50] Alice Holford was bailiff of London Bridge from 1433 to 1453, and Agnes Forster (widow of the London mayor, Stephen) rebuilt and reorganised Ludgate prison. Agnes Gower announced that she practised the art of a silkwoman and wanted to trade independently of her husband John, and to answer 'sole for her own contracts according to city custom', in October 1457.[51] A London furrier, Agnes de Bury, fell the wrong side of the regulations for her trade when she was imprisoned for dyeing old furs and selling them as new.[52]

The influence of wealthy women in London created a boom in the city. It was a tradition in the capital that an entrepreneur's fortune would be left to his widow, not to his sons; nor would he insist that his widow return her inheritance to his family on her remarriage. A widow could go on to remarry inside her late husband's guild, creating a 'horizontal' line of inheritance, and she might do this more than once, combining the two original fortunes with a third. Most London widows remarried (57 per cent between 1309 and 1458) and by marrying wealthy second husbands, widowed women could concentrate the family fortunes, with themselves as the head of the family.[53] Much of the prosperity of the city in these years came from widows forging takeovers and mergers by marriage, consolidating fortunes inside their guilds.

Some women living in the country were well paid for their work. A professional woman gardener worked in the garden of Durham Priory's cell at Monkwearmouth in 1360, and Alice Payntour was paid 6s 8d a year for keeping the gardens of Lady Margaret and Sir William Cromwell at Tattershall in Lincolnshire in 1417. Two other 'garthwomen' working under her supervision received 5s each.[54] Some wealthy women made their own fortunes: Eleanor, Countess of Arundel, left more than £100 of wool at her manor at Heytesbury in 1453. Dame Eleanor Townshend owned 8,000 sheep.[55]

Women were essential to the small local markets and village economies. But when a woman-owned small business needed capital to expand or invest in new technology, or better transport or distribution systems, she experienced a barrier to getting credit. With no banking system, personal loans could only be raised from usurers at high rates or by going into partnership with someone in a similar business. A woman's word – unenforceable in law – provided no guarantee, and she had no network of female entrepreneurs to call upon.[56] Many women who headed large business enterprises entered them as an heir, joined a husband in partnership or inherited his business as a widow. Women could succeed; but they were prevented from launching.

The possibility of education for girls was enshrined in law when the Statute of Artificers ruled in 1406 that 'every man or woman, of what estate or condition that he be, shall be free to set their son and daughter to take learning at any manner of school that pleaseth them within the realm'.[57] This did not make education compulsory, nor did it make it affordable, but it sanctioned the education of girls. Increasing numbers of them from yeoman and merchant families might attend girls' schools in a convent, church or secular establishment.[58]

Noble girls were mostly educated at home and some would be offered a classical education the equal of their brothers' – until the boys left the home tutor for university. Often girls' tutors would be women: Mary Hervey taught the daughters of Henry IV, Blanche and Philippa, to read and write in 1390 using an alphabet book.[59] Some wealthy elite women were highly educated. Alice de la Pole, the granddaughter of the poet Geoffrey Chaucer, owned a large library including books on theology. A patron of the arts, Alice used her huge fortune to commission tapestries, especially those of religious scenes with women. Interestingly, one of her tapestries shows a scene of female scholarship: St Anne teaching the Virgin Mary to read.

Landed women continued to found schools and the chaplain to Philippa of Hainault established the 'Hall of the Queen's scholars of Oxford' in 1341 and named it after his royal patron.[60]

A new group of people called the middling classes – emerging from wealthy working people such as the yeomen, farmers and merchants – valued management skills in women, and they and some noble women were trained in property law to represent themselves and their families. When widows were summoned to court they often demonstrated a familiarity with the law and a comfort in speaking for themselves without an attorney, or a second husband, to pursue a case. Alice and Matilda Shaw, orphan sisters, were apprenticed to a notary public, Master Peter Church, in 1420. The general rule was that every freeman of the city could apprentice his son or his daughter to another freeman, guaranteeing the rise of literacy and education among these middling townspeople. Although girls made up a minority of apprentices (40 out of 200 in the London court rolls), many women won their own 'free' status by other routes, and pursued their own trades and trained others.[61]

The importance of trade grew as people moved from rural self-sufficiency to buying produce and foods in urban areas. By the fifteenth century, even the poorest family did not wholly live off the land, but needed cash. The burden of buying essentials fell largely on women. Goods such as salt, cooking utensils and pots, household equipment, clothing and tools could still sometimes be bartered in local markets for household production, but were increasingly bought with money. Poor families in cities could not farm or forage in a forest for goods to trade. Small urban homes had no kitchens or bathrooms – families had to pay for bathhouses and to use space in a baker's oven. Such town families might pawn goods for cash and redeem them later, sometimes on a weekly basis. Earning money and credit, foraging and collecting, borrowing and trading, pawning, fencing stolen goods and stealing were overlapping techniques for survival for many poor women.

Noble and gentry families living in the country might visit London once or twice a year for social contact and shopping. Mary de Bohun, wife of Henry of Derby, came to the capital in 1387–88 to go shopping in Bread Street with her sister Eleanor, Duchess of Gloucester, and visited her mother.[62] Even these women were limited by strict dress regulations, which ruled what colours, furs and fabrics could be worn by which class of people. The regulations were designed to support English industry, and to identify status. Known as the 'sumptuary laws', they limited the choice available to consumers and even limited the consumers themselves. Diamonds became popular in the fourteenth century, but jewellery was restricted to nobility – excluding knights, who were forbidden from wearing rings.[63] Luxury goods and textiles were imported from distant producers – silks and damasks overland from Japan and China, ivory from Africa and India, all subject to specific high import duties – but they were only available to consumers of the right class.

Even households run by the wealthiest women relied on credit with tradespeople and upper-class women ran the credit arrangements. Elizabeth, Lady Zouche, wrote to her receiver in London every month in the spring and summer of 1401, asking him to buy damasks and silks, a gold rosary with a paternoster and a pipe of white wine. Ladies could order craftspeople to send goods on approval. Dame Edith St John ordered a woman London jeweller, Ellen Peryn, to bring a gold frontlet (a forehead band) to her house for approval before buying.[64] As coins were in short supply, the ladies of the great houses would have a 'treasure room' where valuables and coins would be kept, to be given to trusted servants for shopping errands.

It is too simple, and too optimistic, to talk about a 'golden age' for women. But in the years after the plague had killed so many and women's riots had broken down the feudal restrictions, equal opportunities were there to be had for the surviving men and women. Entrepreneurial women, married and single, seized their chances. Large numbers of them entered training, professions and business in London in 1400–25.[65] But by 1450 the economy was deteriorating, markets were contracting and women were squeezed out of the jobs they had entered.[66] If there ever was a 'golden age' for some women, in some trades, in some areas – for sure it didn't last very long.

Pushback

Just a generation after the plague came a pushback against all workers, men and women, by landowners and by employers who introduced the first laws on labour, to force wages back down and create a pay gap between men and women workers. The 1388 Statute of Labour ruled that men were to be paid more than women: not an enormous pay gap – only a penny a month – but a sign of things to come.[67] A ploughwoman's wages were legally capped at 1 shilling a year less than those of a ploughman.[68] Some other trades had their own sex differential written into law in order to underpay women. The landowning lawmakers saw they would reduce their wage bill by cutting women's wages and that men would not protest.

New laws were passed to prevent labour mobility, to stop workers moving from their parishes to find work or better wages. Landowners were forbidden to accept new tenants and employers were forbidden to poach workers.

Single women found themselves specifically targeted by the new legislation. Women's mowing, harvesting and sheep-shearing gangs were banned from travelling together and women forbidden to leave their villages unless they could show an address and work at another place.[69] Parishes could refuse entry to poor single women or send them back home. With no escape from their home villages, women had to accept onerous leases and bad wages.

Respect towards women eroded as the memory of the plague years faded, and women now bore the brunt of community discipline, held to a higher standard of behaviour, summoned to church or manor courts for social and personal offences, under surveillance by the community – especially by other women. Women were named for sexual misconduct more often than men, and they were mostly accused by other women. Common insults against a woman accused her of promiscuity, while common insults to men accused them of bastardy – even when a man was being insulted, it was his mother's reputation that was endangered. The insult 'harlot' was applied to men and women like the word 'knave' – but by the late fifteenth century it had come to mean only a sexually promiscuous woman.[70] The crime of 'scolding' was a uniquely female offence.

In 1422, the men of Queenhythe, London, decided that a woman could not be trusted in a responsible position – the measuring of oysters – which was the job of John Ely, who had subcontracted his work to women 'who know not how to do it; nor is it worship to this city that women should have such things in governance'.[71]

The failure of folk medicine to protect against the plague inspired a general doubt of the ability of practitioners, especially the women healers who worked in small communities where failures were particularly visible, deaths were grieved and blame was allocated swiftly. The religious reformation spreading from Europe into England named almost all traditional and folklore traditions – herbalism, spell-casting, predicting, fertility work, finding lost things and cunning work – as a heresy and a sin.[72] As the status of traditional healing and cunning fell, it came to be seen as women's work. Most of the accused witches in the 1300s had been men; but by the 1500s, 90 per cent of accused witches would be women.[73] As suspicions and punishments grew more severe and the pay deteriorated, men deserted the craft, creating instead new guilds and professional associations of healers, herbalists and apothecaries with entry requirements that excluded women. A woman healer could not join the new men-only guilds: if she wanted to continue to practise, she had to take the risk of being named as a witch, without a professional association to defend her, as the new men-only associations boosted their reputations by slandering folklore remedies and women healers.

At the same time, increasing numbers of single women – initially without partners because of plague deaths, and now refusing to marry – became more visible in town and country. When financially successful in their own businesses, they were envied; when poor, they had to beg from increasingly unfriendly neighbours. Single women, especially those practising folklore traditions, begging and borrowing from their neighbours, quarrelling with their communities and threatening their enemies, became objects of suspicion, which from 1450 soured into a small 'moral panic' against women witches.

Marriage

For the upper classes, marriage remained a business contract, arranged by parents or guardians, the bride and bridegroom rarely consulted, though the church increasingly required their consent. Shared interests, respect, affection and even love might follow, but these were not the purpose of elite marriage. Union was an arrangement for family finances – even more necessary in the hard years after the plague, when an able unpaid woman manager was needed to run the business and produce an heir.

Wifely trustworthiness and ability might be rewarded by a husband's affection. William de la Pole named his wife Alice Chaucer as the sole executor for his massive fortune on his death in 1450: 'For above al the erthe my singular trust is moost in her'.[74]

Marriages for the children of tradesmen and artisans were also arranged by their parents for the benefit of the family fortune, often paired with fellow guildsmen to consolidate skills and fortunes, and to ensure that the incoming bride understood the business of which she would be a partner, might inherit as sole heir and must teach to her children.

Lower-class women were free to choose their partners. Parents or even the lord of the manor might insist on a wedding if a woman was pregnant, but most working women chose both their husband and the time of their wedding. After the Great Pestilence there was even less control over women who chose their husbands and saved their own dowries. Ramsey Abbey's documents for the early 1400s show that a third of peasant women chose their own husband and paid their own fees for doing so, 22 per cent chose to marry a neighbour, but 28 per cent looked further afield and married townsmen.[75]

It was not possible for a working woman to get a bad marriage annulled and she could not divorce him. A minority ran away from husband, home, family and manor, to the towns that welcomed single women without enquiry. Some submitted to the ritual of 'wife sale', when a wife would be taken to market by her husband, sometimes with a halter around her neck or waist, and 'sold' by him. The most open sales saw the husband parade his wife around the market as he would show an animal and auction her to the highest bidder. More discreet sales took place with the wife holding a rope around her waist, perhaps partly hidden by her gown. The sale would be made by the passing of the rope for a coin or even a token to the new 'husband' and the agreement was sometimes sealed with a farewell drink. Some communities accepted this as a legal and valid end to the marriage, and some wives colluded in the ritual to end an unsatisfactory marriage. The ritual of the wife sale could also be used to demonstrate a second marriage, the husband performing the transfer of his wife to another man, perhaps to her choice of a future spouse.[76] Some women were expelled from the marital home by an abusive husband. Wife sales date from 1073,[77] are recorded in 1302,[78] and become widely known, with increasingly disapproving comment, until the practice dies out in the nineteenth century.

Upper-class marriages could be ended at great expense by the church on very limited grounds. A few husbands managed to persuade and bribe the church to provide an annulment; very few wives were successful. Maud Clifford had her 1406 marriage to John Neville, Lord Latimer, annulled on the grounds of her husband's impotence. In the eyes of the church law, an impotent man had not given his consent to marriage, since he could not consummate it.[79]

A more troubled family were the Cantilupes. Katherine Cantilupe (née Paynell), wife of Nicholas, won an annulment by claiming her husband had no male genitals at all. Nicholas imprisoned his wife and travelled to Avignon to appeal to the pope to reverse the decree of annulment. Katherine was released by her father, Sir Ralph Paynell of Casthorpe, and her husband died in Avignon, possibly poisoned by his own brother and heir, William. William inherited the title and estates after a royal inquiry but was himself later murdered, probably by his wife – who escaped charge.[80]

Many so-called abductions were runaway wives escaping with their lovers. About two-thirds of the women reported as kidnapped between 1100 and 1500 were probably escaping bad marriages.[81] The courts recognised a distinction between genuine unwilling kidnap and an elopement – though the charge for both might be a 'ravishing'. Defendants, the woman herself and jurors sometimes declared that the so-called abduction was, in fact, a consensual departure of a woman with her lover.

In January 1356, the prioress of Haliwell, in Middlesex, complained that Thomas Mott, a textile seller, along with three other drapers, a shearman and others unnamed, had broken into the priory, carried off Joan Coggeshale of London and arranged her marriage to her kidnapper, Mott. The young woman Joan had been placed with the nuns by her guardian, Henry le Galeys, after the prioress had agreed to protect his ward's chastity. The loss of Joan Coggeshale meant the loss of her fees to the prioress and the loss of her inheritance to her guardian. When the case was heard at the court of the King's Bench a few months later, only Thomas Mott was required to answer. Henry le Galeys claimed his ward had suffered ravishment and demanded £200 compensation for the damage to his charge. While the jury agreed that Mott was guilty – 'Thomas abducted the same Joan with her assent and her permission … against the will of the same Henry' – Joan's readiness to leave with him diminished her value to her guardian. The jury judged that Thomas owed Henry 20 marks in compensation – two-thirds of the original claim.[82]

The abduction of Eleanor West from her mother's care by an armed band led by Nicholas Clifton – her father Sir Thomas's former friend, comrade and household retainer – was reported by Sir Thomas as a rape; but Eleanor may have been eloping with her chosen lover, with the consent of her mother. Sir Thomas's interest is revealed in the new rape law that he demanded in 1382, which was not designed to free an abducted girl, nor return her to her parents, but only to ensure that she could not take her fortune to her husband. Eleanor's outraged father was mainly concerned with her dowry.[83] Her mother signalled her approval by leaving the young couple part of her fortune.[84]

The laws were designed to protect the parents of heiresses against the loss of their daughter's fortune on her kidnap, to compensate them for the loss of her future value as a bride if she was restored to them, to compensate the woman herself for the loss of her virginity, and to prosecute a man for violently penetrating a woman without her consent, and set a punishment of maiming and death.[85] A convicted rapist could escape the death sentence by pleading the benefit of clergy (that he was literate) or by marrying his victim if she consented to this compensation for the injury to her honour.[86] Women who had been abducted or raped could also take a case for damages to the civil courts, which avoided a criminal trial for the rapist.[87]

There were about 1,198 'allegations of female seizure' in the 400 years from 1100 to 1500, including abductions, elopements and rapes. Between 1334 and 1441, the crown pardoned 42 convicted rapists.[88] Some rapists may have paid compensation privately.[89] Women were well aware that it was almost impossible to make a correct complaint and get a prosecution and a verdict of guilt. They rarely made an official accusation.

Isabella Gronowessone and her two daughters took the law into their own hands in Shropshire in 1405 when they ambushed their rapist, Roger de Pulesdon, stole his horse, tied a cord around his neck and cut off his testicles. They were pardoned for the assault – which suggests that that they were attacking a known rapist, inflicting the traditional punishment of castration. It seems that the court accepted they had the right to take the law into their own hands.[90]

Single Women

Widowed, fatherless and in some cases made homeless by the Great Pestilence, the numbers of single women grew: both those expecting to marry in the future and those reluctant to marry or remarry. Almost a third of English women were single, far more than in Europe (where the figure was 10–20 per cent).[91] Many of these women had no surviving families to support and were free to compete with male workers for jobs, training and education away from home.

For local authorities – the city fathers, village elders and lords of the manor – such single women could be a mixed blessing: a force for change and development but, away from the control of the lord of the manor and without a father or husband at home, potentially unruly. Female ability and female energy made single women a fearsome competition for men returning to work. New ideas from courtly love about women's frigidity, and the rise of the cult of Mary, suggested that women could be seen as people with an independent will who might refuse male advances and choose their own futures. It became clear that if women were not held back by a sense of deference, held down by laws, held up to shame for boldness and held at home by a controlling husband, they might seize the new opportunities of the post-plague years.

Town authorities began to regulate all single women under the city codes for prostitutes, a move they justified by the overlap between single women and prostitutes. Neither answered to a resident man, often neither had a registered legal identity. Many single women exchanged sex for cash or food.[92] A London priest paid a woman known as 'Prone Joan, who lives with Spanish Nell' four pence for sex at their first meeting, but the second time he only gave her cake and beer.[93] By registering all single women as prostitutes, the town authorities could set them specific rules, including identifying dress codes, and could inspect them and their homes, register them, and charge them fees and taxes. Men, alarmed by independent-minded skilled women competing for work, explained their success by attributing it to sexual manipulation, linked single women to prostitutes and welcomed legislation against single women competition.

Prostitution

The Great Pestilence increased suspicion of prostitutes as vectors for disease. In England and Europe, urban zones were created for municipal brothels, supervised by town officials, for the profit of the town, the convenience of male clients and to isolate prostitutes from ordinary civic life. In their desire to create controlled sex areas, local authorities ignored how and when women offered sex. The local laws created an artificial divide between women whose chastity was supervised and those who were not. Amid 'growing concern that prostitutes could corrupt good women', the sisterhood of wives, widows, single women, daughters and prostitutes meeting in the sewing circle, the church guild and the parish charities was ended.[94]

New regulations to manage prostitutes made it illegal to beat prostitutes from the 1400s, or for brothel owners to make them do extra housework in the bath-house brothels. Women could not be held there against their will, and officials of the Bishop of London himself were licensed to inspect brothels.[95] It was widely believed that single men needed prostitutes to serve their appetites for sex. English church guidance for priests instructed: 'There are many that commit fornication with strumpets because they have no wives.'[96]

One Westminster brothel in 1409 was run by two women in partnership – Elizabeth Warren, the wife of a skinner, and her partner, Stephen Essex's wife – and specialised in servicing the 'monks, priests and others'. A poll of 1381 recorded seven married couples in Southwark working as 'stewmongers' – professional full-time brothel-keepers.[97] In York, Margaret Philips was accused of procuring sex for five priests, and in 1424 Elizabeth Frewe and Joan Scryvener were both summoned for providing prostitutes for priests.[98] One York woman, 40-year-old Isabella Wakefield, was repeatedly charged with prostitution, procuring and brothel-keeping. She was said to be in a long-term relationship with a priest, Peter Bryde, and it may be this relationship that caused her to be singled out for accusation.[99] She was charged nine times with prostitution but always managed to find respectable citizens to speak for her and win her discharge: defended by a community.[100]

Women Loving Women

A rare medieval example of the recognition and celebration of a loving partnership between two women can be seen in the Church of St Nicholas and St Mary at Etchingham in East Sussex. This memorial brass plate shows two women together, standing as a married couple would be portrayed, facing each other, holding their hands as in prayer. Both have uncovered heads – a sign that they were unmarried. They are turned towards each other, looking into each other's eyes in a far more intimate and warm pose than the usual marital brass memorials.[101]

The woman portrayed as very small, Elizabeth Etchingham, died first, in 1452, nearly 30 years before her friend Agnes Oxenbridge, who died in 1480. The brass memorial was made in a London workshop commissioned by the women's brothers, who must have agreed that they be buried together in Elizabeth's parish church. It may have been Agnes who said that she wanted to be buried beside her friend and memorialised with her, but the heirs to both women and the church authorities agreed. Clearly there was a bond, still profoundly felt nearly three decades after they had been parted by death, and respect for their love – both from their families and the local church – and no anxiety that this love had been carnal. Intimate touching between women was still defined as a sin, but the greatest concern was reserved for a woman who was assertively

Elizabeth Etchingham (?–1480) and Agnes Oxenbridge (?–1452) were buried together at the Church of St Nicholas and St Mary at Etchingham, East Sussex, and memorialised in this brass plate

sexual. A contemporary poet described the sin: 'Women who exercise their lust on other women and pursue them like men.' In 1400, another theorist recommended that an 'active' or so-called 'male' partner in a female couple should be tried and condemned to death.[102] But these were European complaints. In England, no such complaint was heard, and there are no records of women being executed for same-sex love.

The Nature of Women

In 1348, Henry Knighton, an Augustinian canon in Leicester who wrote a chronicle called *Knighton's Leicester Chronicle*, recorded that beautiful ladies from wealthy families and noble lineage would regularly take part in jousting competitions:

> In these days a rumour and a great complaint arose among the people that when tournaments were held, in every place a company of ladies appeared … in the diverse and marvellous dress of a man, to the number sometime forty, sometimes fifty … in divided tunics, that is, one part of the one kind and the other of another kind, with small hoods and liripipes flying about the head … even having across their stomachs, below the middle, knives which they vulgarly called daggers placed in pouches from above. Thus they came, on excellent chargers or other horses splendidly adorned, to the place of the tournament. And in such manner they spent and wasted their riches and injured their bodies with abuses and ludicrous wantonness that the common voice of the people exclaimed.[103]

When Agnes Hotot (b. 1378) put on full jousting armour and entered the lists as her father's champion in a battle of arms, after he had fallen sick before a fight with another lord in a duel, she fought a 'stubborn encounter' and won – unhorsing her father's enemy. Only then, as he lay on the ground, did she remove her helmet, let down her hair and take off her breastplate to show her breasts and prove that he had been defeated by a woman. When she married into the Dudley family, they celebrated her victory with a crest showing a woman wearing a military helmet with loosened hair and her breasts exposed, commemorating their female champion.[104]

Some people born as men lived as women and undertook women's work. A woman calling herself Eleanor was arrested in 1395 and accused of 'detestable unmentionable and ignominious vice' with a man. The mayor of London interrogated her and her answers were translated into Latin by his clerk, who recorded that Eleanor may have been born John Rykenor and was introduced into prostitution as a child by a woman named 'Anna'. Eleanor and Anna apprenticed themselves to Elizabeth

Agnes Hotot in the Dudley family crest created to celebrate her victory when she took her father's place in the joust

Brouderer – probably Elizabeth Moring, who was accused in the 1380s of running a brothel and recruiting girls as apprentice embroiderers, to use them as prostitutes. Eleanor worked as a seamstress and a prostitute in Oxford and Beaconsfield in 1394 and admitted having sexual intercourse with many partners: three scholars of Oxford, two Franciscan monks, six foreign men, a woman called Joan in Beaconsfield and – when dressed as a man – with 'many nuns'. The crime that brought Eleanor to court was that of having sex with a man, a Yorkshireman – John Birtby. They were caught together breaking curfew after 8 p.m.[105]

Birtby told the mayor's inquiry that he thought he was hiring a female prostitute – which would mean he was guilty of nothing but breaking curfew. If Eleanor was a woman prostitute, she was guilty of breaking curfew and of infringing the ban the city had imposed on prostitutes in a campaign of moral purity after the plague years. If she were a man, they were both guilty of sodomy – a sin and a crime. The clerk did not report the decision and sentence of the court, and Eleanor disappears from the record.

John Tirell was arrested in London in June 1425 for 'walking around' – meaning soliciting as a prostitute in women's clothing. Tirell took an oath for future good behaviour and was released.[106]

In *The Canterbury Tales* (published in 1392 but possibly written before then), Geoffrey Chaucer struggled to define the sex of one character: 'I trowe he were a geldyng or a mare.'[107] A 'gelding' is a castrated male horse, a 'mare' is a female horse. The Pardoner wears his blond hair long, spread over his shoulders, his big eyes 'like a hare', a spray of Veronica, the flower of love and fidelity, in his cap. He has a voice as light as a goat, and he is beardless and smooth-faced:

A voys he hadde as smal as hath a goot.
No berd hadde he, ne nevere sholde have;
As smothe it was as it were late shave.
I trowe he were a geldyng or a mare.[108]

Discussion continued about the definition of women, the many sorts of women, the fluidity of sex and about women's nature. As the stories of 'courtly love' were retold and developed, spreading across Europe, the description of the heroines changed. The women of the epic poems had been active, powerful women in the world, sometimes fighting their own battles, like the women of Leicester who fought in jousts, those who went on missions and crusades, and those who were said to sit in judgement in 'Courts of Love', ruling on chivalry and the etiquette of fin'amor – fine love.[109]

Chaucer offered another active version of womanhood in 'The Wife of Bath', where the heroine describes using her 'instrument' – her genitals – freely, night and morning. She has rights over her husband's body and he has to pay the debt of marital intercourse:

In swich estaat as God hath cleped us
In such estate as God has called us
I wol persevere; I nam nat precius.
I will persevere; I am not fussy.
In wyfhod I wol use myn instrument
In wifehood I will use my instrument
As frely as my Makere hath it sent.
As freely as my Maker has it sent.

If I be daungerous, God yeve me sorwe!
If I be niggardly, God give me sorrow!
Myn housbonde shal it have bothe eve and morwe,
My husband shall have it both evenings and mornings,
Whan that hym list come forth and paye his dette.
When it pleases him to come forth and pay his debt.
An housbonde I wol have – I wol nat lette –
A husband I will have – I will not desist –
Which shal be bothe my dettour and my thral,
Who shall be both my debtor and my slave,
And have his tribulacion withal
And have his suffering also
Upon his flessh, whil that I am his wyf.
Upon his flesh, while I am his wife.
I have the power durynge al my lyf
I have the power during all my life
Upon his propre body, and noght he.
Over his own body, and not he.
Right thus the Apostel tolde it unto me,
Right thus the Apostle told it unto me,
And bad oure housbondes for to love us weel.
And commanded our husbands to love us well.
Al this sentence me liketh every deel" –
All this sentence pleases me every bit"–[110]

The Wife of Bath is not an exceptional character in medieval stories. Cautionary tales, comedy stories, bawdy poems, plays, ballads and court cases showed medieval women as sexually active and indeed enthusiastic. The Wife of Bath promises exclusive fidelity to her husband, warning him that she could prostitute herself and 'walk as fresh as is a rose', but if he will love her 'pretty thing' – her genitals – she will reserve herself for his exclusive pleasure.

What eyleth yow to grucche thus and grone?
What ails you to grouch thus and groan?
Is it for ye wolde have my queynte allone?
Is it because you want to have my pudendum all to yourself?
Wy, taak it al! Lo, have it every deel!

Why, take it all! Lo, have it every bit!
Peter! I shrewe yow, but ye love it weel;
By Saint Peter! I would curse you, if you did not love it well;
For if I wolde selle my bele chose,
For if I would sell my 'pretty thing,'
I koude walke as fressh as is a rose;
I could walk as fresh (newly clothed) as is a rose;
But I wol kepe it for youre owene tooth.
But I will keep it for your own pleasure.
Ye be to blame, by God! I sey yow sooth.'
You are to blame, by God! I tell you the truth.'[111]

Women in real life were similarly sexually assertive and enthusiastic. The mystic preacher Margery Kempe (1373– after 1438), who sold her brewery and milling business in Lynn to go on a pilgrimage, spoke of her adulterous desire for another man as well as her enjoyment of sex with her husband when she dictated her spiritual autobiography, *The Book of Margery Kempe*. Her description of her imaginary marriage with Jesus was consciously passionate and sexual. She persuaded her husband to accept a sexual ban so that she might concentrate on her spiritual mission, but she made it clear that giving up sex was hard for her.[112] Clearly, this was a woman (a mother of 14 children) who understood female sexuality and chose her own sexual expression.

Chaucer also describes a completely different sort of woman – the woman that was emerging in the courtly love stories – no longer sexually assertive, no longer militant. In 'The Knight's Tale', he writes of Emelye – the sister of the queen of the Amazons, who returns with Theseus to Athens after he has defeated her country and married her sister. The lady is seen by two imprisoned knights, Arcite and Palamon, on May Day morning – the morning celebrated for love and witchcraft.

That Emelye, that fairer was to sene
That Emelye, who was fairer to be seen
Than is the lylie upon his stalke grene,
Than is the lily upon its green stalk,
And fressher than the May with floures newe –
And fresher than the May with new flowers –
For with the rose colour stroof hire hewe,

For her hue vied with color of the rose,
I noot which was the fyner of hem two –
I do not know which was the finer of them two –[113]

The two knights are instantly in love, ready to die of love:

And but I have hir mercy and hir grace,
And unless I have her mercy and her grace,
That I may seen hire atte leeste weye,
So that I can at least see her,
I nam but deed; ther nis namoore to seye."
I am as good as dead; there is no more to say."[114]

After years of suffering by the two rival knights, of which Emelye is completely unaware, a joust is arranged between them to decide who will marry her. Emelye decides she will marry neither and prays to the goddess Diana:

Chaste goddesse, wel wostow that I
Chaste goddess, well knowest thou that I
Desire to ben a mayden al my lyf,
Desire to be a maiden all my life,
Ne nevere wol I be no love ne wyf.
Nor never will I be no lover nor wife.[115]

The joust is won by Arcite, and Emelye, abandoning her oath of chastity at speed, signifies her consent by smiling on him, but he is injured in a fall and dies, with her name on his lips, after recommending his cousin Palamon as her husband. Emelye collapses in near-fatal grief and performs the rituals of a widow. But in the last seven lines of the poem she cheers up and marries Palamon, at the command of Theseus. The happiness is described as his:

For now is Palamon in alle wele,
For now is Palamon in complete happiness,
Lyvynge in blisse, in richesse, and in heele,
Living in bliss, in riches, and in health,
And Emelye hym loveth so tendrely,

And Emelye loves him so tenderly,
And he hire serveth so gentilly,
And he serves her so gently,
That nevere was ther no word hem bitwene
That never was there any word between them
Of jalousie or any oother teene.
Of jealousy or any other vexation.

Inside the one collection of tales, Chaucer describes both the idealised 'lady', seen from a distance, apparently unobtainable who hopes to remain chaste but then agrees to marry, and an accessible bawdy woman who loves sex and demands pleasure from her husband and – if he refuses her – says she would not be ashamed to sell sex on the street. The women are opposites, both in nature and in class position. The bawdy sexually available woman is a labouring woman; she makes her own demands, bluntly, in cheerful ordinary language. Her story is set in everyday England, among ordinary people.

Emelye, the lady in 'The Knight's Tale', is a subject of the story, not a narrator. She does not even speak till 2,000 lines in, and then it is a prayer to keep her maidenhood. She is far from England, set in a legendary past, sister to a queen, guest of a classical hero – Theseus. She is incomprehensible because she is unexplained – a foreign princess from a strange land, turning up to spectate at the heroes' adventures, with no report of her life before or after her scene with them. She changes her mind from a commitment to lifelong chastity to consent to marry a victorious knight, experiencing near-fatal grief at his death, and then marriage to another, with no process of decision-making or even sustained thought. She is an object, seen and desired and given as a reward. She is not an agent – making her own story; she is a lady doing nothing.

Courtly Rape

Over time, the courtly love stories became more sexually explicit, more realistic and more violent, and the heroines became less active – even failing in self-defence. The metaphor of a noble youth finding his way into a castle and picking the rose in the walled garden changed to become a realistic fiction about a siege of a castle, a breaking down of doors and entering without consent. The heroine was no longer icily commanding his service; the hero was no longer pleading for a glance, satisfied with a lifetime of service. Now he was a bold housebreaker. He no longer found a rose in a walled garden, he found a vulnerable woman in her bedroom and he had sex with her – despite her protestations. What had begun as an elite art form playing with the idea of worshipping an unobtainable, idealised woman developed into stories of violent entry.

The 'nature of women' in the courtly love tales took a dark turn. Women still demanded to rule but they could be thrown down. They said 'no' to men who were deaf to their commands. They claimed their castles were invulnerable, but a man could break in; they claimed to be above and beyond sexual desire, but they could be persuaded or forced. Apparently, the nature of women was self-contradictory – saying one thing but doing another. Women were unpredictable – they might take any action in any way. Women were irrational – maddened by their own contradictions. The unpredictability of women, the irrationality of women, the inscrutability of women, the unreliability of women was proclaimed and glamourised in the stories; their attack was glamourised too.[116]

The fictional assault of the lover on his lady offered a new vocabulary and a way of thinking about real-life rape. The crime had been defined as the theft or kidnap of a woman in order to win her fortune. The Latin word *rapere* was used in thirteenth- and fourteenth-century courts for the crimes of both abduction and forced heterosexual intercourse.[117] Neither were crimes against a person – they were theft of, or damage to, another man's property. But in the courtly love stories, the metaphor of plucking the rose represented both stealing a guarded treasure and sexual satisfaction for the man. In the *Romance of the Rose*, the pilgrim has to break down the defensive fence before he can put his staff in the hole and win the rosebud. 'I had to assail it vigorously, throw myself against it often.'[118]

Earlier lovers had threatened to die of love; now they demanded pleasure. His lady was no more the commander of his fate, she was an involuntary assistant to his satisfaction. The will of the lady – her refusal – was broken in the act of rape. No longer was the lady an agent of her own story with intention and action that steers the narrative. Now the story was about seduction or rape – the story became the lover's adventure. The lady is diminished to an object on which the act of sex is done.

This introduction of male sexual desire as the prime motive for the crime of rape has enormous consequences. It suggests that rape sits at the far end of a scale of male sexual activity that extends from permitted intimacy … through refusal … to beyond. Rape becomes seen as the act that takes place when seduction has failed. Rape becomes an act of sex with a person, not an act of theft or damage to a property, but an act of sex driven by desire, now categorised as uncontrollable. This belief seeps into society's consciousness and even appears in law courts, even modern law courts where men explain that they 'could not stop', as if the scale of male sexual intimacy is not a scale after all, but a helter-skelter slide that once launched cannot be halted.

Once rape is seen as an involuntary physical response, it can be excused. It is hardly a crime at all. The man can claim he is not a criminal who decided to commit a crime – he is just a body experiencing an involuntary reaction, which he 'couldn't stop'. Once rape is seen as a point on the scale of male sexuality, it is easy to suggest that it is also on a scale of female sexual activity, just beyond 'no'. For her too, sex can follow refusal. A million jokes, not one of them funny, were inspired by the idea that a woman's 'no' does not mean 'no'. If rape is a possibility, only one step beyond female refusal, then refusal does not indicate 'stop'. The end of the male sexual helter-skelter is his satisfaction – whatever she may have said during the slide. The act can only be defined as a rape by the woman before it is completed, and the definition is only meaningful if she repeats the 'no' after the act, and takes it onwards, and says it again, to others, over and over, and convinces them that she said it at the time, loud enough for him to hear, and that she says it still. The victim of the crime becomes the one who names it as a crime, and she has to name it as a crime before he does it – so that it is knowingly done. If she does not name it as a crime – before it is done – there is no crime. So the victim is the one who is interrogated, who has to prove – not that sex happened (which is agreed) – but what she said before it happened, and after it happened.

No other crime requires a victim definition before and after the act; the wildly illogical understanding of rape comes from the stories of courtly love glamourising rape as an irresistible act by an attractive man, raising doubt over his ability, and her intention, to stop.

It did not take long for even the most squalid assault in real life to get a sprinkle of courtly glamour. A Sussex court in January 1481 summoned

William Pye of Lewes, a 'clerk' – a low-level churchman – on the '12th day of September in the 20th year of the reign of King Edward the Fourth after the Conquest [that is, 1480]'. The court accused William Pye of two assaults. The first was on his 'mistress', Alice Martin, in her marital home. The court was told that William Pye 'by force and arms, viz. with sticks and knives, broke and entered the close and house of Thomas Martin of Southover near Lewes in the said County, and then and there made an assault on Alice, wife of the said Thomas'.

The clerk of the court, writing in Latin, described the assault: 'and with his stones stoned her and struck her', and then adopted the language of poetry: 'with his carnal lance wounded and maltreated her'. The poetic language conceals the violence of the attack. William Pye may have stoned his former lover, or he may have sexually assaulted her with his 'stones' his testicles. He certainly violently raped her; his penis romantically described as his 'carnal lance' ('*ipsam cum lancea sua carnali vulnerabat*'), and she was so severely injured, 'so that her life was despaired of'.

A second assault by William Pye – a violent attack on members of the jury – was not enhanced with any metaphors at all. As a physical assault on a man it required no poetic description. The court heard that Pye 'made an assault on Thomas Piper, one of the said jurymen, by force and arms, viz. with sticks and knives, and struck, wounded and maltreated him, against the peace of the lord King'.[119]

Between the clerk, William and Alice, the wife of another man, now stretch centuries of deliberate confusion over whether men can stop before satisfaction and if a woman's 'no' does indeed mean 'no', only to find it heralds a rape which is described in court in the language of love poetry.

Part 3

1455–1485
Women at War

Women at War

Women stepped into roles of military leadership and civil authority during the disruption of the thirty years of civil war between the two rival families who descended from the sons of Edward III – the houses of York and Lancaster. Later named the 'Wars of the Roses', after the emblem of the red rose of Lancaster and the white rose of York, the long struggle could equally well have been named 'the Mothers' Wars', given that the royal houses were headed by determined women who plotted, spied, suffered imprisonment and mustered armies to get their sons on the throne.

Queen Margaret of Anjou (1430–82) led her army into battle, fighting for her comatose husband and his heir, their son. Jacquetta, Duchess of Bedford, rode with the Lancaster army supporting Margaret and was with her queen when she was defeated at the Battle of Blore Heath in 1459, when Margaret was said to have turned the horseshoes on her horse so that no one could track her escape. Later, Jacquetta would famously change sides to support her daughter Elizabeth Woodville, who married the newly victorious young king, Edward IV of York, in a secret ceremony on May day morning.

During one of the York reverses, King Edward fled into exile, and Elizabeth hid in sanctuary with her daughters. Jacquetta was arrested, charged, tried and found guilty of bewitching the king and causing her daughter's marriage using magic charms – even producing the enchanted figures as evidence in court. Jacquetta was only saved from imprisonment or execution for witchcraft by the triumphant return of her son-in-law, Edward, who ordered her release.

Elizabeth Woodville, the first common-born woman to take the throne as a queen of England, fought through years of warfare, once in sanctuary, once in the Tower of London during a siege, before finally enjoying years of peace. On the death of her husband Edward, she fled into sanctuary again as Richard III claimed the throne and was crowned with his wife Anne in a joint ceremony. Elizabeth Woodville launched a rebellion to free her sons, bribing Margaret Beaufort – the sole surviving heiress to Henry VI and the House of Lancaster – with a promise that her son Henry Tudor should marry Elizabeth's daughter Princess Elizabeth of York as reward for her support.

Henry Tudor took the crown after the victory of his mother's husband's army and through his mother's right. He married the princess that his mother had chosen and he governed the country with his mother's advice. Margaret Beaufort invented a new title for herself, 'My Lady, the King's Mother', and signed her name 'Margaret R.', which could have meant Margaret of Richmond (her title) or Margaret Regina – Margaret the Queen. Carefully, she never defined the initial. After using her husband to get her son the throne, Margaret put him aside and became a 'vowess' – a secular woman, living by monastic hours – and led an independent life as a celibate woman, the greatest landowner after her son the king, and the uncrowned queen of his court, where she dominated her daughter-in-law Elizabeth of York.

The wars – really a series of battles, fought intermittently over 28 years, between the royal houses of York and Lancaster – were sometimes no more than local fights between rival lords sometimes represented by the women. Alice Knyvet defended Buckingham Castle at Norfolk against Sir Gilbert of Debenham in 1461. Perhaps raising a siege was the lesser of two evils: she shouted from the battlements that she would rather die in battle 'than be slayne when my husband cometh home, for he charget me to kepe it'.[1]

Margaret Paston defended, but lost her manor at Gresham in Norfolk.[2] With men away at war (or, like John Paston, regularly absent on business), it fell to aristocratic and ordinary women to defend their communities from passing armies and to run their landholdings in difficult times. Elizabeth Treffry held her house, Place, at Fowey in Cornwall in 1457 against Breton pirates, mustering her workers from the corn, tin and wool business to defend the house from attack and looting. She is credited with the technique of pouring molten lead on the raiders.[3]

That pirate siege was an exception to the usual skirmishes of the Cousins' Wars, as battles were usually encounters in open country or outside towns, so few women landowners had to defend their homes against siege. Disruption to civil and political society was local and temporary and did not give elite women much opportunity to move into leadership roles, as men were not absent for very long.[4]

The disruption of wartime and the absence of protective men from their homes may have increased violence against women from strangers. Incidents of abduction, kidnap and rape of wealthy women for forced marriage were increasingly feared and reported.[5] A new act in 1487 made it clear that the law was to protect the property of the woman, not the woman's person.[6]

The absence of labouring men from home, even for a short time, threw families into poverty and left the woman as sole breadwinner; some moved into trades during the wartime labour shortage. Some women travelled with armies to support their husbands and some saw the passing army as an entrepreneurial opportunity, offering cooking, laundry and sexual services as ancillary workers. Probably some women enlisted and fought; but left no records.

The end of the wars came as a relief to most women, who had suffered from the social disruption, damage to property and finances, and from personal loss. Wives and widows of defeated men often shared their punishment, going into exile or paying fines.[7] With the injury, death or disappearance of their partner, many women faced hardship and many children were orphaned – creating extra numbers of the poor.

Women's Work

In the years of peace, the Plantagenet courts aspired to be as centralised, ritualised and grand as the famously sophisticated court of Burgundy. Upper-class women were educationalists: Margaret of Anjou founded Queens' College, Cambridge – exclusively for men. Elizabeth Woodville continued the patronage and encouraged Thomas Caxton, the printer, to come to England in 1476 with the first printing press, which caused a revolution in book and pamphlet production. Elizabeth herself helped translate and edit the *Histoire des Philosophes*, and may have encouraged publication of *Le Morte d'Arthur*, the retelling of the Arthurian courtly love legends. Courtly love rituals and jousts were famously undertaken at her court. Margaret Beaufort also supported Queens' College and endowed lectureships in theology at both Oxford and Cambridge, and founded St John's College, Cambridge.[8] Aristocratic women copied the elegance of the queens' courts, educating and training young kinswomen, visiting women, apprentice girls and servants, creating domestic institutions under female leadership.[9]

Luxury work for the court encouraged craftspeople all around England as the retinue moved from one palace to another. Courtiers needed specialist clothing skills such as laundry, tailoring, embroidery, starching and headdresses, creating business for women entrepreneurs who visited court and took commissions back to their workplaces. Women weavers were introduced to a new textile when Margaret of Anjou encouraged silk weavers to come to London from Lyon, in her native France, and settle at Spitalfields. She founded the 'Sisterhood of Silk Women' to enter the trade.[10] Ellen Landwith (d. 1481) was a London silkwoman who trained three female apprentices in her first husband's workshop, which was a cutler's business. She bought gold thread and raw silk direct from Venetian merchants, and in 1465 supplied the saddle decorations and silk banners for the coronation for Queen Elizabeth (Woodville). Ellen Landwith was so successful as a silkwoman that she was invited to join both her first husband's guild, the Cutlers' Company, and her second husband's guild, the Tailors' Company.[11]

In 1469, Margaret Cobb, Elizabeth Woodville's midwife, received a life pension of £10 a year, as did Alice Massey, who attended Elizabeth of York in 1503.[12] Margaret Cotton cared for the nieces and nephews of Queen Elizabeth of York from 1502–3 while their mother, Katherine Courtenay, attended court.

In 1400, widows were responsible for about a third of all property transactions in London, but by 1474 this had changed and the market was dominated by men, who had increased their share from 65 per cent in 1374 to 85 per cent.[13] Some widows continued the pattern of making a fortune from good inheritances and well-judged second marriages. Guild widows in particular concentrated wealth in families by marrying inside the guild. Thomasine Bonaventure (1470–c.1530) made a remarkable transition from Cornwall shepherdess to highly wealthy London widow. She joined the household of the city's bridgemaster Thomas Bumsby as a servant and married him. On his death, she married his colleague Henry Gall; on his death, she married Sir John Perceval, Lord Mayor of London, in 1498; and when he died, she enjoyed the widow's dower from three city fortunes. She was one of the many wealthy widows who consolidated London wealth, merged businesses under one experienced management and solved succession problems. Thomasine, now Lady Percival, used her considerable fortune to pay for a bridge, a school and a library in her home of Week St Mary, Cornwall, where she is still honoured today.[14]

Some women entrepreneurs continued their success in all industries and trades. Alice Shevyngton, a London servant maid, cured her master and built up a clientele for her remedy for sore eyes in 1480; London widow Joanna Rowley imported sugar from Lisbon in 1479, and in 1480 shipped oil and wax from the Portuguese capital and wood and wine from Spain. Ship-owner Margery Russel in Coventry seized two Spanish ships as legal compensation for the loss of her own ship to Spanish pirates.[15] In 1495, the Holy Cross guild's annual feast in Stratford-upon-Avon bought massive amounts of cream (8½ gallons), curds and milk from five local suppliers, four of them women.[16]

A woman's word still had no legal weight unless she were registered as a femme sole. In 1496, in the consistory court held by the prior and convent of Durham, Christina Fressell complained that Joan Lambert, wife of Nicholas, had slandered Christina saying that she had caught her having sex with Nicholas. Christina brought a defamation case against the married couple to defend her good name.

Three weeks later, when the court sat again, Christina stood in the dock: accused of the 'crime of fornication with Nicholas Lambert'. The claim of slander that she herself had raised had been turned against her. The court believed Joan Lambert and punished Christina Fressell for having sex with Nicholas. She was given a day to 'purge' herself – confess and take a church punishment, probably a fast. Nicholas Lambert – guilty either of slander or adultery – went unpunished.[17]

Marriage

Marriages of propertied families were mostly arranged with a view to consolidating fortunes and providing a reliable wife and mother for the family and their business. But there were marriages for love. The royal marriage of Edward IV and Elizabeth Woodville was undertaken so quickly and secretly that it would be evidenced at a trial for witchcraft and provide the basis for a legal challenge from Richard III. Jacquetta Rivers's second marriage was a love match and she had to pay a fine for wedding the man of her choice. The Pastons were unlucky when Margery Paston (1449–79) fell in love with the family land manager. Her parents tried to send her away from her home to separate the young couple. Her mother reported in 1469, 'we be ... wary of other'.[18]

Despite the family's best efforts, Margery, an heiress, and the family land manager, Richard Calle, exchanged binding vows in secret. Summoned before a bishop and questioned, Margery stood by her betrothed, and the secret promise could not be overruled. Her mother expelled her from the household and disinherited her. Her brother gloomily predicted that she would end up selling 'mustard and candles' – since her new husband's family were grocers.[19] But he himself found love with his wife, Margery Brews, who wrote the world's first valentine poem to him:

> And yf ye commande me to kepe me true wherever I go,
> I wyse I will do all my myght yowe to love and never no mo
> And yf my freends say, that I do amys,
> Thei shal not let me so for to do,
> Myne herte me bydds ever more to love yowe
> Truly over all ertheley thing
> And yf thei be never so wroth
> I tryst it schall be better in tyme commyng.[20]

Some women chose their husbands in defiance of their families or their vows. Joan Portsmouth and Philippa King, two nuns at Easebourne Priory, Sussex, conceived children with their lovers – the chaplain of the priory and a servant of the Bishop of Chichester – and staged a 'kidnap' by their men in the summer of 1478.[21]

Prostitution

Elite mistresses and prostitutes were accepted at the court of Edward IV. Jane Shore, the ex-wife of a London goldsmith who appealed for the annulment of her marriage due to her husband's impotency, took the eye of Edward IV and was praised by him as his 'merry whore'. After the king's death, she was publicly humiliated by his brother Richard III, who forced her to walk around the city walls wearing only a shift and carrying a lighted taper to show her shame and penitence. The London crowds were said to have been so sympathetic to her that they refused to watch her walk. King Richard himself later relented to allow Jane to marry no lesser person than the king's solicitor general, Thomas Lynom.

Prostitutes and brothel-owners were mostly tolerated, with London and other cities and towns licensing brothels. The port of Sandwich had a municipal brothel supervised by the town authorities, run by a married couple, offering four resident prostitutes who paid 16d a week for bed and board. They could not be beaten or overcharged for their ale. Southampton's town-regulated brothel faced the same restrictions. Some women made a good living. Alice Stapledon, a convicted brothel-keeper from Suffolk, died in funds, leaving bequests to women friends and to charities.[22]

Some towns occasionally tried to be more restrictive: in 1467, Leicester required townsmen to report any prostitutes to the authorities so that they could be expelled from the town. In Ipswich, 'disorderly houses' were targeted by the authorities during a plague outbreak, and in 1470 'harlots and bawds' were expelled. In London, under new harsher rules, women accused of prostitution had their heads shaved for a first offence, were forced to stand in the pillory for a second offence and were banished from the city for a third. In 1473, a new mayor, William Hampton, ordered prostitutes to be publicly shamed. He demanded 'diligent and sharp correction upon Venus' servants, and caused them to be garnished and attired with ray [striped] hoods, and to be shown about the city with their minstrelsy before them by many and sundry market days'. He may have had little effect. In the 45 years of London commissary court records from 1471, 377 women were charged with prostitution, but only 10 confessed. The landlord of the Bell Tavern in Warwick Lane was accused of 'harbouring suspected women' and being a house of 'whoredom' in 1485, but 14 years later, tapster Joan Blond was charged with being a whore and Agnes Thurston, another employee, as a bawd.[23]

Part 4

1485–1660
Becoming a Weaker Vessel

Religious Change

In 1535, Henry VIII ordered a state examination of religious houses called the *Compendium Compertorum*, to justify their closure. Thomas Legh, one of the king's commissioners, visited Crabhouse Nunnery, at Wiggenhall, and found four nuns, all in poverty. He accused them of being sexually incontinent and of bearing children, including the prioress, Margeria Studefeld. He said one nun, Cecilia Barnesley, had given birth to two children, one fathered by a layman and one by a priest. Legh reported to Henry's chief minister Thomas Cromwell that it was a 'lewd nunnery' and claimed the nuns were selling nunnery goods for their own profit. A later inspection cast doubt over Legh's assessment, reporting that the house was in good repair, with valuables kept safe and bells hanging in the church: 'Ther name ys goode ... goode name and manner of life.'[1]

Some abuses did take place. A visitation to the Benedictine priory of Littlemore found mismanagement in the 1400s and again in 1517. It was a small religious house of only seven nuns. The visitors claimed that the prioress, Katherine Wellys, was supporting her bastard daughter from convent funds, even paying her dowry for marriage. The girl's father was said to be a local priest, Richard Hewes, who regularly visited the abbey, staying overnight with the prioress. The prioress put one nun, Elisabeth Wynter, in the stocks for 'incorrigibility'. Three nuns, perhaps her sisters Juliana and Johanna Wynter, with another nun Anna Willye, helped Elisabeth escape, breaking a window to get out. The three were absent for three weeks and later, Johanna Wynter gave birth to a child. Prioress

Wellys put Anna Willye in the stocks and physically attacked Elisabeth Wynter, punching and kicking her. Another nun, Juliana Bechamp, begged the bishop to move her into a different convent: 'I am ashamed to [be] here off the evil ruele off my ladye.'[2]

Many reports claim that not all nuns maintained their vows of celibacy. Alice Longspey, a nun at the Benedictine abbey of Godstow, was sentenced to a year of strict confinement for her affair with a priest named Hugo Sadylere. Agnes Smyth of Crabhouse Nunnery confessed to giving birth, but lost only her rank within the cloister hierarchy for a month and had to perform the psalms of David seven times. Most of the relationships with men were long term, usually with churchmen, some of them loving as well as lasting. Denise Lowelych, the prioress at Markyate Priory, conducted a love affair with a chaplain for five years, ceasing only at his death. Some affairs were only revealed by pregnancy – an exposure that sinning monks escaped. Margaret Mortmere, a nun at St Michael's Priory in Stamford, was known to have left the priory to give birth and returned. The inquiring bishop could not discover the child, or the father. The concern of the church was sometimes more about the public scandal than the sin: when Bishop William Gray of Lincoln learned of nun Mary Browne's pregnancy at Godstow Abbey, his main concern was to keep her out of sight.[3]

Actual numbers of nuns reported for having sex with men were few: in the diocese of Lincoln and Norwich in the century after 1430, 16 nuns were identified by church investigations in the 9 women's houses, amounting to 2.8 per cent of the cloistered women being investigated – compared to 4.19 per cent sexually active monks.[4]

The disruption of the national church was of unprecedented significance to the women of England, as Henry VIII broke with the Church of Rome, which would not grant him a divorce from his first wife, Catherine of Aragon, and joined the European-wide Reformation. Some women changed their faith with the king, some defended it, some died for it; but every woman felt the lack of respect for women when an innocent queen died in poverty, as Catherine of Aragon did, and when the closure of women-only religious houses meant there were no high-status, respected women choosing celibate lives, independent of men.

In his quest to claim the wealth of the Roman Catholic Church, Henry VIII would close 900 religious houses and expel about 10,000 men and 2,000 religious women. It is almost impossible to list the women-only traditions that were lost in the dissolution: the women and girls' schools, the female scholars working in the famous library collections archived and curated by women experts, the great women gardeners, agronomists and herbalists, the women architects and designers, great diplomats and theologians. Lower-class women, too, lost their place in the day-to-day running of the nunneries, convents and abbeys

Priests and monks could transfer into the Church of England and some could even continue in their old parishes. Men like Bartholomew Fowle, who was prior at St Mary Overie, Southwark, 'surrendered' in 1539 to Thomas Cromwell, then served as a priest, and was paid by Dame Joan Milbourne to pray for her soul in 1543 – several years after his house had been dissolved and chantries closed. His fellow canons from St Mary Overie also found posts in the reformed church.[5] But there was no place for gifted, spiritual, well-educated women in the national church of England for 400 years, and no welcome for them in society. A biased observer, Eustace Chapuys, ambassador for Charles V at the English court, saw the impact on men and women in 1536, and said: 'It is a lamentable thing to see a legion of monks and nuns who have been chased from their monasteries wandering miserably hither and thither seeking means to live.'[6]

Women exiles from the religious houses returned to their parents, found refuge with sympathetic host families or lived alone, or recreated their communities, called beguinages, keeping the tradition of working, praying and living together. There were beguinages in York, Ipswich and Norwich. Some ex-nuns chose to live in religious solitude as anchoresses. Katherine Manne lived in a cell attached to the Dominican Friary church in Norwich, and may have remained there after the dissolution. She owned Reformation texts: a copy of William Tyndale's translation of the Bible and his book *The Obedience of a Christian Man*.[7] Ex-nuns and churchmen were granted small pensions, and expected to maintain their vows of celibacy until 1549 under Edward VI. Only about 19 per cent of nuns chose marriage (and about 17 per cent of monks). Isabel Lynley, who had been a nun at Heynings Priory, survived on the small one-off payment of £1.10s, and never married.[8]

The closure of the great religious houses marked the end of professional religious women in England. Virginity or celibacy was no longer a highly regarded, well-paid choice. The image of women in society became secularised and sexualised – every woman was apparently available for seduction or marriage. Women no longer represented celibacy: they represented temptation. Bishop Longland, an English Roman Catholic confessor to Henry VIII, warned the monks of Westminster in tones of paranoid misogyny: 'Avoid everywhere the company of women, lest a silent wound enter your breast, if their faces adhere to your heart. Among women, the most splendid flower of chastity withers, and the lily of modesty perishes. Why therefore … why would you seek conversations with women, why in the cloister, why at home, why in sacred and profane places, why in any place would you allow yourself to stay with them?'[9]

Even Elizabeth I's brand of virginity did not restore female celibacy to its previous high regard. Most subjects would have preferred her to provide a stable line of heirs. Protestant reformer Martin Luther defined virginity as an unnatural state, and virgins as 'not women'.[10] In his view only a woman who had experienced intercourse with a man could be a true woman; any other female was either a child or a being without sex. A celibate woman, such as an ex-nun or a woman who did not marry, was to be regarded as a strange creature: an unfulfilled character, a non-person.

For secular women the changes to their parish church and its ritual would be immense. The churches lost their independence of the throne and women lost their church roles. They no longer had a lady chapel dedicated to women, and no powerful female figure in the church iconography.[11] Saints' days were no longer observed and women's rituals were banned. The state religion of England would change three times over the course of four reigns from 1525, when Henry VIII started to suppress the great religious houses, to the queenship of Elizabeth I, the 'Protestant Princess'. Each time a form of religion was banned, it became a 'fortress religion' defended principally by women in secrecy in their homes.[12] Since husbands were legally obliged to keep their wives from heresy and to report all defiant women – even a wife – to the authorities for punishment, many women had to choose between obedience to their husband or to their God.

Religious Protest

Few women rebels were recorded by name in the popular uprisings against Henry VIII and the Reformation. The Pilgrimage of Grace – the 1536 uprising of the north and east of England – mustered an army of 30,000, which included women and depended on their support. At the head of the troops, soldiers held aloft banners of the five wounds of Christ, crafted by supporters with the skills and the materials – elite women. The most detailed histories of the pilgrimage describe women as 'ardent supporters'.[13]

Certainly it was Henry VIII's intention that punishment not be restricted to named male leaders. He ordered his commander to 'cause such dreadful executions upon a good number of the inhabitants hanging them on trees, quartering them, and setting the quarters in every town, as shall be a fearful warning'.[14]

Margaret Pole, Countess of Salisbury, was executed without trial on 27 May 1541, charged with owning a banner of the five wounds of Christ – the rebel standard. Margaret Cheyne (born Stafford) died because she was said to command her husband. Her own parish priest called her 'a strong and arrant whore'. Cheyne and her husband Sir John Bulmer had mustered their neighbours and encouraged their tenants to rise against Henry VIII's religious changes. After being arrested, sent to London and pleading guilty, Sir John was hanged and his head put on a spike on London Bridge, but Margaret's punishment was worse – dragged on a hurdle from the Tower of London through the streets to Smithfield Market[15] and 'there burned according to her judgment, God pardon her soul, being the Friday in Whitsun week; she was a very fair creature, and a beautiful.'[16] Her cruel death was intended as a warning about the proper behaviour of women: not to rebel, but of equal importance, not to dominate their husbands.[17]

As the Roman Catholic religion was declared illegal by Henry VIII and his Protestant heirs, aristocratic women turned their houses into religious refuges, hiding priests, creating family chapels, sending children to religious schools abroad, marrying them inside the faith and keeping the family together with letters.

Poor and ill-educated women had always played an important role in the medieval Roman Catholic Church as visionaries and mystics. The lower the status of a women mystic, the more convincing she was when speaking in tongues or reporting visions.

Elizabeth Barton, the 'Nun of Kent', added a powerful voice against the Reformation and the marriage of Henry VIII to Anne Boleyn. Accepted as a true prophet by the poor people who flocked in their thousands to her, and even by the great churchmen, including Thomas More and John Fisher, she met with ambassadors from Rome and wrote directly to the pope.[18] Her enmity to the Reformation and to Anne Boleyn personally was finally silenced by her trial and execution for treason. Her enemies reported that she admitted fraud before her death on 20 April 1534.

Some royal women were famous upholders of their own faiths: Catherine of Aragon was supported by Roman Catholic women of her court, including the king's sister, Queen Mary of France. In contrast, Anne Boleyn supported reform and it was the Boleyn family chaplain Thomas Cranmer – the great theologian of English reform – who, with Henry's last wife, Kateryn Parr, herself a theologian, scholar and convinced reformer, co-wrote the beautiful translation of Latin ritual that would become the Book of Common Prayer. Parr maintained the reform party at court, at great risk when her husband was veering back towards the papacy. Kateryn Parr's friend Anne Askew was arrested and tortured even after she confessed her faith, in an attempt to make her name the queen as a fellow heretic. Even at the stake, ready for burning, she was offered a pardon if she would name the queen; but she died without betraying her friend.

The king signed a warrant for Kateryn Parr's arrest for heresy – which carried a sentence of death. Previous doomed queens had panicked, but Parr went to the king and told him she was 'But a poor silly woman accompanied by all the imperfections natural to the weakness of her sex'.

The king disagreed. As his courtiers waited for the trap to be sprung, he accused his wife: 'You are become a doctor, Kate, to instruct us, as we take it, and not to be instructed or directed by us.'

Kateryn saved herself, and the Reformation party at court, by assuming female inferiority: 'If your majesty take it so then has your majesty very much mistaken me for I have always held it preposterous for a woman to instruct her Lord. If I have presumed to differ with your Highness on religion, it was partly to obtain information for my own comfort regarding nice points on which I stood in doubt.'[19]

Henry forgave her and when they walked together in the garden the next day he dismissed the arresting guards who came for her. Kateryn survived the old wife-killer to publish her own prayers and thoughts under her own name: the first woman to publish under her own name in the English language.

When Henry VIII's daughter, Roman Catholic Mary I, succeeded in 1553, after the brief reign of her Protestant brother Edward VI, many reformers and Protestants found themselves ordered to recant publicly or face punishment for heresy. Margaret Geoffrey of Ashford, Kent, was sentenced to attend mass holding rosary beads. Elizabeth Poste from Kent was forced to declare before the congregation that 'in the sacrament of the altar is the very body and blood of Christ really'.[20]

Fifty women and 230 men would be burned for declaring their reformist faith during the final four years of the reign of Mary I.[21] Mary Tudor has been nicknamed 'Bloody Mary' by generations of Protestant historians, but they are wrong to suggest that she persecuted reformers because she was made mad by an unsatisfactory husband and gynaecological problems – though both can be very irritating. She was the granddaughter of Isabella of Castile and Ferdinand of Aragon, who founded the Inquisition in Spain, which executed between 2,000 and 5,000 people. Both her family and her wider culture believed their religion could and should be improved by violence.

Lady Katherine Willoughby, wife of Charles Brandon, was closely knit into the Parr-Askew reform circle. She almost singlehandedly reformed religion in the county of Lincolnshire. Willoughby appointed Hugh Latimer as a preacher and later helped him and Nicholas Ridley when they were imprisoned by Mary I. She was so influential and daring that in March 1554 the powerful anti-reform Archbishop Gardiner summoned her new husband Richard Bertie and warned him to silence his wife. The couple fled into religious exile, only to return when the Protestant Princess Elizabeth came to the throne.[22]

Elizabeth inherited the throne in 1558 and passed the Act of Supremacy the following year; England's official religion swung back to the Reformation, and the queen ruled that everyone should attend the national church, which was now Protestant. Elizabeth did not believe that someone could be loyal to both foreign pope and Protestant queen, and she acted against Roman Catholics as if they were all traitors. The maintenance of Roman Catholic faith fell mostly on women, who created the priest holes and fed and hid visiting clergymen.

The Northern Rising of 1569 was led by the women of two great noble northern families: Anne Percy, Countess of Northumberland, and Jane Neville, Countess of Westmorland. They marched under the familiar banner of the five wounds of Christ to rescue Elizabeth's cousin, the Roman Catholic heir to the throne, Mary, Queen of Scots – held under house arrest by the Earl of Shrewsbury and his formidable wife Bess of Hardwick. This hugely popular uprising led by women, included women as supporters and possibly even soldiers. Certainly, women suffered for the revolt. Elizabeth demanded 700 hangings in northern villages, to punish communities where individuals could not be identified. Jane Neville spent the rest of her life under house arrest. Anne Percy's husband Thomas was executed for his part in the rebellion, while Anne fled to exile leaving her daughters behind. She spent her remaining days plotting for the restoration of Roman Catholicism to England.

The greatest challenge to Protestant authority came from the Roman Catholic wives of loyalist Protestant husbands. Claiming to obey God before their husbands, they denied the monarch's right to rule the church, and challenged the status of men as head of the household. Some husbands physically dragged their wives to church; others threatened them with divorce or disgrace; and some surrendered to their wives and paid their fines. Magistrates up and down England were faced with the problem of wifely disobedience. They solved this by sending persistently offending wives to jail until 1620, when the government chose to fine and tax the great Catholic landowners to produce a revenue, and ignore heretic poor women.[23] The defiant lower-class wives successfully resisted both their husbands and the state.

Women Who Died for Their Faiths

The courage and determination of English women in defence of their faiths challenged the traditional view of women as sinful Eve. Their holy resolve replaced the idea of easily tempted women with an idea of women as highly spiritual and courageous. Spiritual – but not powerful. Women who suffered persecution and death for their faith were seen not as

'Christian soldiers' but as victims and martyrs, sacrificing themselves for their beliefs. The old model of Eve as ready for temptation was exchanged for a new model of a victim-woman – ready for self-sacrifice.

The earliest female death recorded by the Protestant martyrologist John Foxe[24] is that of an 80-year-old: Joan Boughton, burned for heresy in 1494 at Smithfield, the butchers' market and the capital's site for burning. A later victim was a Dutch Anabaptist burned at Smithfield in 1538. Anne Askew, the gentlewoman illegally tortured to make her incriminate Kateryn Parr, was burned there in 1546. Joan Boucher smuggled Bibles in English into England, even supplying the radical reformists around Kateryn Parr. When arrested, she proudly confessed to reform beliefs. Archbishop Thomas Cranmer, a reformer himself, failed to persuade her to recant, and she was burned at Smithfield in May 1550.

Under the Roman Catholic Queen Mary I, it was the Protestants and the reforming sects who were persecuted: Margery Polley was burned in Tunbridge in 1555, Rose Pencell at Bristol in the same year. Elizabeth Warne was taken at a prayer meeting, examined and burned at Stratford Bow in 1556, her daughter the serving maid Joan Warne or Joan Laysh was martyred the following year. Mrs Isabel Foster, wife of a cutler, was burned at Smithfield in January 1556. Widow Agnes Snoth, Joan Sole, Anne Albright and Joan Catmer, the widow of an executed reformer, shared two stakes and were burned together at Canterbury. According to *Foxe's Book of Martyrs*, they died singing hosannas. Agnes Potten, the wife of a brewer, and Joan Trunchfield, wife of a shoemaker, were captured after refusing to desert their husbands and children, and burned together at Ipswich in 1556. Joan Beach, widow, was burned at Rochester that year, refusing to accept that the Roman Catholic Church was her mother or agree to the doctrine of transubstantiation. Katherine Hut, a widow, was burned with Elizabeth Thackvel, Margaret Ellis and Joan Horns, all maids, after the three defended their reform beliefs at Smithfield in 1556. Elizabeth Pepper, a weaver's wife, and Agnes George were burned at Stratford Atte Bowe by the especially cruel method of making them walk in the fire, which was built around the 11 stakes of their male co-religionists. Pepper was pregnant but refused to 'plead her belly' and be released, claiming that 'they knew it well enough'.

Catherine Cauchés, also spelled Katherine Cawches, with her two daughters, Guillemine Gilbert and Perotine Massey, was burned at St Peter Port, Guernsey, in 1556. Perotine Massey went into labour and delivered a baby boy as she was being burned, and the bailiff ordered him to be thrown back into the flames. 'Mother' Anne Tree was burned at East Grinstead that year. In Derby, Joan Waste, a 22-year-old woman, blind from birth, who worked as a knitter and a rope-maker, was prosecuted for objecting to church services in Latin, buying a New Testament in English and paying for it to be read to her. Her twin brother led her by the hand to her death. She was executed by being hanged until the rope burned through and dropped her in the flames. Margaret Hide and Agnes Stanley were burned together at Smithfield in 1557. Five of the seven 'Maidstone' martyrs of that year were women: Joan Bradbridge, Petronil Appleby (burned with her husband), Katherine Allin (burned with her husband, a miller), Joan Manning and Elizabeth (surname possibly Lewis), a blind maid.

Widow Bradbridge was one of the seven 'Canterbury' martyrs burned in 1557 – the other women were 'Wilson's wife', Barbara Final, and Alice Benden, who was denounced by her own husband. Ten Protestants were burned in one fire at Lewes, including Thomasina Wood a maidservant, Margery Morris who was burned alongside her son, Ann Ashdon and Mary Groves. Maidservant Elizabeth Cooper, the wife of a pewterer, withdrew her recantation and chose instead to die for her faith by burning at Norwich. Ten reformers were killed at Colchester Castle for their faith in 1557, five of them women: Agnes Silverside, Helen Ewring a miller's wife, Elizabeth Folk a young maiden and servant, and Alice Munt burned with her husband, and her spinster daughter Rose Munt. Two women, originally scheduled to die with them – Agnes Bengeor and Margaret Thurston – died later in the same year. The sister of George Eagles was burned at Rochester, with an unnamed woman. Agnes Prest, a 54-year-old Devon woman 'of very little and short stature, somewhat thick with a cheery countenance', who had left her Roman Catholic husband to support herself by spinning, was arrested when she returned to him and burned at Southernhay. Mistress Joyce Lewis was a gentlewoman converted by the martyrdom of Laurence Sanders. She was arrested for irreverent behaviour in church and burned at Lichfield. Margery Austoo was burned with her husband at Islington in 1557. Cicely Ormes, a tailor's daughter and the wife of a worsted weaver, retracted her recantation and was burned after delivering a spirited sermon from the stake at Norwich. Margaret Mearing refused to recant and was burned at Smithfield. Christian George, the second wife of

Richard George of Essex, whose first wife was also martyred, was burned at Colchester in 1558. Alice Driver, a 30-year-old ploughwoman, the wife of a husbandman, was arrested for hiding a Protestant martyr, Alexander Gouch, in a haystack, argued with her interrogators and was burned at Ipswich. Katherine Knight/Tynley, an aged woman, was burned at Canterbury.

Three women died in prison: Margaret Eliot (or Ellis) was imprisoned in Newgate in 1556 and may have died in jail or been burned at Smithfield that year; William Dangerfield's wife, imprisoned with him, died after he did; their baby was sent away and died of cold and hunger. Alice Potkins died during her imprisonment in Canterbury Castle in 1556. Lady Jane Grey was beheaded in the Tower of London in 1554 ostensibly for treason, but partly for her refusal to accept the Roman Catholic doctrine.

Roman Catholic women died for their faith in the next reign: professing Roman Catholicism under Elizabeth I. Margaret Clitherow, the daughter of a Protestant York wax chandler and wife of a York butcher, refused to plead when accused of hiding Roman Catholic priests in 1586. Although pregnant with her fourth child, she was executed by being crushed to death, under a door piled with seven hundredweight of stone.[25] Margaret Ward, a maidservant to a London family, visited a priest in prison and smuggled in a rope so he could escape. She refused to reveal his hiding place, and refused to attend a Protestant church in exchange for a pardon. She was hanged in August 1588.[26] Alice 'Anne' Line had a priest hole built in her house and was hosting a Candlemas service, with a priest in attendance, when her home was raided. The priest went into hiding and escaped, but Anne Line and her friend Margaret Gage were arrested. Gage was released and pardoned but Line was sent to Newgate Prison and sentenced to death by hanging on 27 February 1601. She spoke from the scaffold: 'I am sentenced to die for harbouring a Catholic priest, and so far I am from repenting for having so done, that I wish, with all my soul, that where I have entertained one, I could have entertained a thousand.'[27]

Religious Exiles

Some reformers escaped Mary I's England. Of the 788 recorded religious emigrants, 131 are known to have been women. One of these was a Jewish woman: Beatriz Fernandes, the wife of a physician, Henrique Nuñes, a leader of her community, holding sabbath services in her house, keeping up with new Jewish literature, baking Passover bread and eating a kosher diet. The Jewish community in London and Bristol had posed as Calvinist – a safe cover under Edward VI, but it made them heretics under Mary I. The Fernandes family fled to France in 1555, leaving some better-hidden members of the community in England.[28] The Italian-Jewish family the Bassanos were arrested in 1541, but released. Their daughter Aemilia Lanyer would go on to be a courtier and poet under Elizabeth I and, after another expulsion of Jews in 1610, she wrote a poem, 'Salve Deus Rex Judæorum' (1611), which blames all men for the death of Jesus – not specifically Jewish men.[29]

Anne Locke (1530–90) was born to a Calvinist family of London merchants who housed John Knox until he went into exile in Geneva. Locke and her husband followed him, and she studied with the Protestant reformer Calvin, translating and publishing his sermons. On her return to England on the death of Mary I in 1558, Anne married her second husband, a reformist preacher, and her money and influence put them in a circle of literary, Puritan and reformist women, including Lady Mary Mildmay, Lady Golding, Mrs Mary Honeywood, Mrs Barnett of Bray and Mrs Catherine Killigrew, who connected them to the Elizabethan court.[30] Anne Locke was the first writer to compose in sonnet form. She published a 26-sonnet series on Psalm 51 called 'A Meditation of a Penitent Sinner'.

Many women fled into exile when the national religion was changed. Catherine Carey, daughter of Mary Boleyn, went into exile on the accession of Mary I in 1553. Her cousin Princess Elizabeth wrote in her diary 'Cor Rotto' ('broken heart') at Catherine's leaving. Catherine and her husband Sir Francis Knollys would return when Elizabeth took the throne and become favoured members of her court. Rose Hickman preached the reformist word to a small congregation hidden in her own rooms before fleeing, like other reformers, to Europe.[31] They were acknowledged during the crisis as religious leaders in their families and in

One of the five women pictured in the Bayeux Tapestry. This may be King Harold's wife, Edith Swan Neck fleeing with her son Ulf from a house torched by the Norman invaders.

One of the 93 penises; a naked man with an erection is reaching for a naked woman who cowers from him.

Opposite: A glorious woman acrobat balancing on sword tips as musicians play. From the *Smithfield Decretals, c.*1340

This illumination in the *Bible moralisée*, (*c.*1220, Paris) illustrates a 'sin of the mouth' with two pairs of same-sex lovers kissing. The female couple, on the left side, are assisted by devils.

'A garden of pleasure': an illustration to the poem *The Romance of the Rose* by Guillaume de Lorris (1200–40) includes two girls kissing, women dancing, debating, and one doing a handstand.

Mean wages in pence per day of unskilled men and women

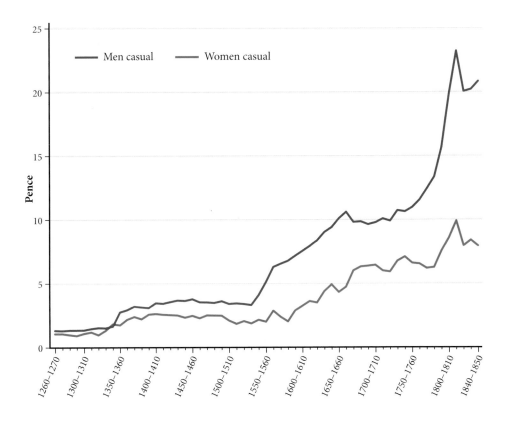

The mean wages of women in England from 1260 to 1850 shows the equality of pay between men and women until the late 14th century, and then the widening gap as legislation held down women's wages but male workers improved their pay.

their communities. Their contribution to religious scholarship and commitment in danger and in exile kept the Reformation alive in England. But on their return they were not rewarded for their fidelity to the church. No longer seen as heroines and leaders, they lost the equality that had been forged in equally shared danger. The church in Elizabethan England became moderate and turned its back on radical revolutionary theology and the women who had risked their lives for it.[32]

Equally determined English women of the opposing faith also chose exile, fleeing Elizabethan England into Roman Catholic havens. In Europe, 17 houses in eight orders were established for English women who preferred to be enclosed abroad, rather than live in Protestant England.[33] In the 100 years after the death of Elizabeth, as many as 4,000 English women would take the veil in 21 convents in Flanders and France.[34]

Englishwoman Mary Ward (1585–1645) created a new Roman Catholic order of teaching and conversion for women, modelled on the work of the Jesuits. She claimed to have created ten religious houses for 500 women in Europe, and established a foundation near Fountains Abbey in Yorkshire, with the reluctant permission of the pope.[35] The convent was later removed to Mickelgate Bar, York, where a convent boarding and day school was created and survived constant harassment from religious opponents and mobs.

Ward was a feminist Christian – claiming equality in the sight of God:

wherein are we so inferior to other creatures that they should term us 'but women?' For what think you of this word, 'but women?' but as if we were in all things inferior to some other creature which I suppose to be man! Which I dare to be bold to say is a lie; and with respect to the good Father may say it is an error … There was a Father that lately came into England whom I heard say that he would not for a thousand of worlds be a woman, because he thought a woman could not apprehend God. I answered nothing, but only smiled, although I could have answered him, by the experience I have of the contrary. I could have been sorry for his want – I mean not want of judgment – nor to condemn his judgment, for he is a man of very good judgment; his want is in experience.[36]

Preachers

Reformation women seized the chance given them by their religion's emphasis on personal prayer and revelation, to give witness to their faith. Women reformers preached in the open air, in secular spaces or in private rooms in houses. They may even have preached inside radical churches. Lollards – a group pressing for the reform of the Roman Catholic Church – included women in their meetings on equal grounds to men and were taught by women preachers.[37]

Dorothy Kelly married a reformist preacher, and her marital home in Bristol became a centre of reformist thinking and a refuge for religious migrants fleeing to New England. Women were invited to give birth in secret, with Kelly attending as midwife, to avoid the 'papist' ceremonies of churching and baptism. Dorothy, in 1640, on her way to her husband's church, filled with doubts, opened her Bible for guidance and found Revelation 14: 9–11, 'If any man worship the beast'. Inspired, she formed her own separatist church and preached to a growing congregation of up to 160 Puritans in private houses and, when barred from houses, in the open air. Dorothy protested the 'false sanctification' of Christmas Day, claiming, as did many Puritans, that it was not defined as a holy day in the Bible. She defied the Bristol city fathers to keep her grocery shop open on the 25th.[38]

English translations of the previously Latin or Greek Bible provided key work for the reformers, since it made the Bible accessible to everyone who could read; the word was no longer the exclusive property of elite, mostly male, scholars. Many poor people learned to read from the parish Bible – left open in the church – the only text that was available to them for free, perhaps the only book that they would ever be allowed to read.

The Reformation freed women from ignorance, inspired them to literacy and promised spiritual equality before God. This view – of an accessible God and an individual private conscience – was of tremendous importance to all Christians but, for Christian women, who had been taught that they could not approach God without the mediation of a male priest, it was a special liberation. Though the Bible said that man had been made in the image of God, it nowhere ruled that a male priest stood at the gateway to God. When working women could read this in their own language, the rituals and traditions of the church, which had grown up over more than 1,000 years, were challenged. Women read that they could pray to God without the permission of a priest – without even a priest hearing their prayers. Women argued that a priest was not even needed for baptism. Now that God understood English, any English woman could speak to Him.

English women, inspired by this direct relationship with God, now claimed equality with men before God. A civil war pamphlet complained of the false pride of at least six women preachers, who were said to demonstrate a logic and grasp of theology that was superior to that of men preachers. The pamphlet accused the women of wanting to dominate male preachers.[39]

Women whose sexuality was repressed by the teaching of the church might find emotional and even physical release in personal private prayer. One Puritan preacher, Nathaniel Ranew, recommended that a devout woman should imagine: 'Her Beloved the Lord Christ, his pure Colours white and Red, his most rare features and exact proportions of every part, his Head, Looks, Eyes, Cheeks, Lips, Hands, Legs and all his glorious perfections … he is altogether lovely'.[40]

No wonder that Mary Rich, Countess of Warwick (1625–78), confided in her diary: 'While I was thinking of Godes great love I fond my heart was warmed with a peaculior and transcendent deagree of love.'[41] Rich's transports of religious feeling coincided with the unhappy periods of her marriage with an extremely sick husband. At his death, when she became a wealthy widow and executor of his will, she enjoyed the work and profits of being a great landlord and gave up ecstatic prayer.

No longer could God's favours be bought. Everyone could examine their own conscience, and everyone – man or woman – might recognise in themselves the signs of Grace: the certainty of salvation. It was a matter of individual revelation, and a woman's epiphany was as valid as any man's. If a believer understood from God that she was saved, that was between her and God. Everyone was freed from the authority of the priesthood, and, especially and radically, women were free from the spiritual authority of men.

John Foxe himself, the great historian of reformist martyrs, explicitly linked reformist faith with equality, telling women: 'Ye were redeemed with as dear a price as men, yet be you all his flesh, so that also in the case and trial of your faith towards God, ye ought to be as strong.'[42]

'Weaker Vessel'

A successful queen on the throne (Elizabeth I, 1558–1603), women in authority especially in country estates, women in business especially in the growing towns, and a new state religion that authorised women to speak directly to God without the intervention of a male priest, suggested the equality of women in the world and before God. But a new translation of the Bible contradicted this. The translation of 1525–36 by William Tyndale invented a damning metaphor for women. He called them a 'weaker vessel'.

Here is the passage, as translated by John Wycliffe, in the medieval Wycliffe Bible of 1382–95:

> Also men dwelle togidre, and bi kunnyng yyue ye onoure to the wommanus freeltee, as to the more feble, and as to euen eiris of grace and of lijf, that youre preieris be not lettid. (1 Peter 3:7)[43]

> Also men dwell together, and by knowing give ye honour to the woman's frailty, as to the more feeble, and as to even-heirs of grace and of life, that your prayers be not hindered.[44]

The woman is more 'feeble' but she is equally to inherit. She is an even-heir to grace and life.

The verse goes on: '… (Also men together dwelling, after science, or knowing, giving honour to the woman's vessel, or body, as to the more sick, as and to even-heirs of grace of life, that your prayers be not letted.)[45]

Two centuries later, William Tyndale in 1522 introduced – for the first time – the phrase of 'weaker vessel' into the first passage:

> Lyke wyse ye men dwell with them accordinge to knowledge gevinge honoure vnto the wyfe as vnto the weaker vessell and as vnto them that are heyres also of the grace of lyfe that youre prayers be not let.[46]

> Likewise ye husbands, dwell with them as men of knowledge, giving honour unto the woman, as unto the weaker vessel, even as they which are heirs together of the grace of life, that your prayers be not interrupted.[47]

The new translation of the Bible changed women from being 'more feeble' but 'even heirs' to a 'weaker vessel' and an 'also' heir. It was a huge and extraordinary alteration by Tyndale, robbing women of their identity as individuals: describing a woman as a household object – I imagine a leaky water-pot – a different thing altogether from a man, the householder who owns the pot. Tyndale's Bible became the text from which all other Bibles descended, even the famously poetic King James Version.

William Tyndale expanded his definition of women as a 'weaker vessel' in his book *The Obedience of a Christian Man*, writing that the weak vessel contained lusts and wanton appetites: 'God, which created woman knoweth what is in that weak vessel (as Peter calleth her) and hath therefore put her under the obedience of her husband to rule her lusts and wanton appetite.'[48]

By 1563, the official Elizabethan sermon, the 'Homily of the State of Matrimony', which was read in every church by law, spoke of the 'weaker vessel' without further explanation – Tyndale's condensed words became an accepted synonym for women, one still in dictionaries even today. The Homily spoke of the superiority of husbands and the feeble nature of all women.[49] Every parish priest, in every church in England, was ordered to preach the new definition of women to his congregation: 'The woman ought to haue a certaine honour attributed to her, that is to say, shee must bee spared and borne with, the rather for that she is the weaker vesell, of a fraile hart, inconstant and with a word soone stirred to wrath.'[50]

Extraordinarily, under a queen militant, a church that had been defended by women saints, martyrs and militants, now defined women as weak and volatile: 'A weake creature, not indued with like strength and constancie of minde, therefore they be the sooner disquieted and they be the more prone to all weake affections and dispositions of mind, more then men bee, and lighter they bee, and more vaine in their fantasies and opinions.'[51]

The Elizabethan state sermon followed Tyndale in urging men and wives to live lovingly together as help-meets and partners, but (you will be amazed) most of the instruction was aimed at women, telling them to be obedient to their husbands and that they should endure domestic violence without complaint. The Homily tried to persuade men not to beat their wives, however badly behaved. This is the royal government, declaring from the pulpit, to a congregation whose attendance was compulsory, that women were inferior to men and should be gently taught rather than beaten: 'honest natures will sooner bee reteined to doe their dueties, rather by gentle words, then by stripes'.[52] 'Stripes' meaning the weals made by a whip.

Women were ordered to subject themselves to their husbands and told how to apologise for defiance: 'Let them acknowledge their follies, and say, My husband, so it is, that by my anger I was compelled to doe this or that; forgiue it me, and hereafter I will take better heede.'[53]

Tyndale argued that if a husband was violent to his wife, she must patiently bear it, both for the improvement of her marriage and for the order of society:

> Euen so think you, if thou canst suffer an extreme husband, thou shalt haue a great reward therefore: ... if wee be bound to hold out our left cheeke to strangers which will smite vs on the right cheeke: how much more ought wee to suffer an extreme and vnkind husband?
>
> But if by such fortune thou chancest vpon such an husband, take it not too heauily, but suppose thou, that thereby is laid vp no small reward hereafter, & in this life time no small commendation to thee, if thou canst be quiet. But yet to you that be men, thus I speake, Let there bee none so grieuous fault to compell you to beat your wiues.[54]

The imaginary difference between the sexes had to be learned by everyone and the imaginary features of woman's nature had to be coached into people, who had not observed that women were weak, uncertain, indecisive and volatile in real life.

Sexist training had to begin. But traditional child-rearing was an obstacle. The sex of a newborn baby was only rarely recorded; medieval babies were swaddled, without any identifying signs as to boy or girl, wrapped up tightly and carried around on a board, sometimes hung up out of danger. When babies started to walk, they came off the swaddling board, and boys and girls would be dressed in similar gowns and put in the care of older children or their mother – or, in aristocratic families, sent away to a wet nurse until they were about four years old. The 'blank slate' theory of child psychology proposed by John Locke in the middle of the seventeenth century argued that children had no innate tendencies – they must be trained for their future role in the world and appropriate behaviour for their sex from the age of about six years old. In castles and cottages this was done: girls were coached in 'girlish' behaviour, put into small versions of their mother's dress and expected to help with her work; sometimes they were sent away from home to be mentored by an admired woman friend. Around the age of ten years old, an elite boy would be 'breeched' – taken out of petticoats and dressed in breeches – and removed from the care of his mother, sent to a tutor or school or to another family, and expected to learn 'manly' behaviour. The young people would live in mostly same-sex groups, learning appropriate behaviours and mixing for courtship and friendships.

This was not easy for all boys: in 1639, grandmother Anne North wrote that the breeched boy is to 'act his part':

> You cannot believe the great concern that was in the whole family here last Wednesday, it's being the day that tailor was to help dress little Frank in his breeches … Never had any bride that was to be dressed upon her wedding night more hands about her … when he was quite dressed he acted his part as well as any of them.[55]

In labouring families the girls learned to spin, sew, keep house and grow food, do agricultural work or whatever work their mothers and female kinswomen did, including perhaps skilled craft work, from a very early age. They might be apprenticed to a craft. Boys worked with their fathers and, if in a trade, might take an apprenticeship with a neighbour, kinsman or in the family business when they were twelve years old or older. Ballads and chapbooks – the only literature for working people – focused on the apparently complex task of becoming that superior being: a man. There were no advice books for lower-class girls[56] – they copied their mother, naturally inferior to men, bound for marriage, when they would promise obedience to their husband.

In the traditional wedding rite, the *Sarum Manual*, used from about 1540, the bride promised obedience but also to be 'Bonoure and buxom in bed and at borde'.[57] The church confirmed that women could be sexually aroused, indeed they must climax during marital sex if children were to be conceived. The danger lay in the delicate balance between the virginal appropriate modesty before marriage and appropriate arousal (with their husband only) thereafter. Widespread fears that women were insatiable continued: 'Of women's unnatural insatiable lust what country, what village does not complain?'[58] Robert Burton fretted in 1621.

Courtly love was still highly fashionable, and the most popular theme of all entertainments and arts. It had been sexualised; the story was no longer about reaching unity with God, but about sexual satisfaction. Heroines must appear sexually cool at first; but this was a stage in the love story not a permanent inviolable state. The heroines either melted or were overwhelmed by male force in the stories. Their oaths of chastity were an obstacle for the hero to overcome. But – though frail – it was a core virtue. In some readings of women's nature, it was their only virtue. Whether women were bonny and buxom in bed or unawakened, virtue in women meant chastity or modesty. All the other virtues belonged naturally only to men.

Pressure on women to enact modesty increased. A female commentator – Jane Anger – pointed out the perennial contradiction for women who want to be sexually attractive and encourage courtship but know that to encourage flirting is unattractive: 'If our honest natures cannot away with that uncivil kind of jesting, then we are coy. Yet if we bear with their rudeness and be somewhat modestly familiar with them, they will straight make matter of nothing, blazing abroad that they have surfeited with love, and ... telling the manner how.'[59]

Anger lost the debate about the nature of women, which grew more toxic from the 1600s. It saw an entirely new genre of literature develop: 'women-hater' writings.[60] *Against Lewd, Idle, Froward and Unconstant Women*, first published in 1616, went through ten editions and was still selling well in 1634. The genre complained generally of women, not only of those who did not conform to the impossible requirements of courtly love virtues, but also any independent women who were outside male control: single women, widows and disobedient wives. In 1632, a clergyman, Daniel Rogers, wrote balefully to his women readers: 'Remember thy sex is crazy ever since Eve sinned.'[61]

Then – just as things were going moderately badly for women – there was a national emergency: after nearly five centuries of male rule, three queens came along one after another.

It was a disaster. The theologian John Knox wrote:

For who can denie but it repugneth to nature, that the blind shal be appointed to leade and conduct such as do see? That the weake, the sicke, and impotent persones shall norishe and kepe the hole and strong, and finallie, that the foolishe, madde and phrenetike shal

gouerne the discrete, and giue counsel to such as be sober of mind?
And such be al women, compared vnto man in bearing of authoritie.
For their sight in ciuile regiment, is but blindnes: their strength,
weaknes: their counsel, foolishenes: and judgement, phrenesie, if it be
rightlie considered.[62]

Young King Edward, son of Henry VIII, crowned at nine and dead by
15, named his cousin and fellow Protestant Jane Grey as his heir – queen
of England. Bullied by her in-laws and her own ambitious parents, the
15-year-old girl claimed the crown for nine days in July 1553, before
her cousin, the rightful heir, Mary I, was acclaimed queen and marched
at the head of her troops into London. Jane would have been spared
execution but for her own determined refusal to convert to Roman
Catholicism. She wrote to her sister, Katherine Grey: 'Laborre alway to
lerne to dey, deney the world, defy the devell, and disspyse the flesh,
delite yourselfe onely in the lord' – 'Always work at learning to die, deny
the world, defy the devil and despise the flesh – delight only in the
lord.'[63]

Victorian historians (who love nothing better than a doomed young
woman) celebrated Jane Grey's martyrdom, and her story was told as that
of an innocent pawn trapped by ambitious men.

This 1833 portrait, by Paul Delaroche, woefully inaccurate on many
counts, shows Jane in the virginal colour of white, slumping into silence
while a sensible man supports and advises her (mansplaining death), and
the executioner displays yards of leg and codpiece in skin-tight red stockings. Delaroche specialised in the melancholic: he also painted the
famous pictures *The Princes in the Tower*, *Young Christian Martyr* and
Strafford on his way to Execution. Jane Grey's own words show she was no
helpless victim nor anyone's pawn. She was a young woman determined
on death rather than life as a Roman Catholic, who chose death as a religious and political act of great power, enforcing the image of women's
nature as spiritual, even martyred.

Her nine days named as queen were succeeded by two successive
reigning queens with only female heirs – a crisis for patriarchy. How
could a man be subject to a woman? How could men submit to the rule
of a woman since women were incapable of even governing themselves?
The line of Mary I, Elizabeth I and their heir, Mary, Queen of Scots,
threatened the monarchy itself. Coincidentally, women regents also ruled

A woefully inaccurate depiction of Lady Jane Grey, painted in 1833 as a doomed young woman

Scotland and France, and these five women were enough to frighten John Knox into declaring that the world faced a 'monstrous regiment of women' – an unnatural government by the blind, weak, sick, impotent, foolish, mad and frantic.

Mary I (1516–58) took the throne in July 1553, surviving a siege and marching on London. Her decision to marry Philip of Spain provided a husband to rule her, but challenged her primacy as queen. The English lords tried to square the circle, saying she was superior to her foreign husband in England only, but he ruled her everywhere else. All official documents were to be signed first by him, but they would summon Parliament and reign jointly. He could not take her out of the kingdom, nor have custody of their children and he could not inherit the throne and reign alone. English advisors and lawyers tied themselves in knots trying to maintain a husband's authority who 'owned' his wife, his children and all her possessions, while keeping her country and an heir independent of Spain.

Luckily for them, Philip showed little interest in Mary, nor even in ruling her in England, and she died childless, succeeded in 1558 by her half-sister Elizabeth (1533–1603) who – having lived through the murder of her mother, her stepmother, the divorce of two stepmothers and the desertion of her half-sister's husband – was understandably sceptical about marriage.

Manly Qualities

Elizabeth started her reign denying feminine weakness: 'Though I be a woman, yet I have as good a courage, answerable to my place, as ever my father had.'[64]

Her speech at Tilbury, on the eve of the Armada, reassured her followers that she had the courage of a king: 'the body but of a weak and feeble woman but the heart and stomach of a king, and of a king of England too'. And later in life she referred to herself as a king, the 'husband' to England as well as a virgin queen.[65]

Elizabeth's own male supporters believed that the task of reigning over a country was too much for a woman. Her advisor and secretary Sir William Cecil hesitated to put a report before her because it was 'a matter of such weight, being too much … for a woman's knowledge', and the hostile Spanish ambassador to England remarked in 1559 that she was 'troublesome … naturally changeable … a spirited and obstinate woman'.[66]

Mary Cleere of Ingatestone, Essex, was burned at the stake in 1576 for daring to say that a woman had not the power to bestow knighthood, like a king.[67] Only in triumph did Elizabeth celebrate her womanhood. The Armada medal, struck to celebrate the English victory against the Spanish in 1588, had the motto *Dux femina facti*: 'Under a woman's command'.[68]

The idea that everyone was one flesh and a blend of different characteristics – the ancient Greek belief – meant that a woman of power could be thought of as 'manly'. The previous Plantagenet queen Margaret of Anjou was described by diplomat Polydore Vergil as 'A woman of sufficient forecast, very desirous of renown, full of policy, council, comely behaviour, and all manly qualities'.[69] The interrogator who failed to break Margaret Pole in 1539 said, 'We may call her rather a strong constant man, than a woman.'[70]

Lady Anne Berkeley ruled Gloucestershire for two decades from the 1530s and was described as 'a Lady of a masculine spirit, over-powerful with her Husband'. When Lady Berkeley's rights as a widow were attacked by her brother-in-law, who had expected to inherit instead of her, she sat as judge, empanelled a jury, called witnesses, ruled in her own favour and fined him for bringing the case against her. She was notorious for her litigious aggression: 'seldom at rest with herself, never wanting matter of suit or discontent to work upon'.[71]

Elizabeth I's tutor, Roger Ascham, confirmed that the clever girl had a male mind: 'Her mind has no womanly weakness, her perseverance is equal to that of a man.'[72] Thomas Howard, Duke of Norfolk, complained that his daughter Mary was 'too wise for a woman', telling Henry VIII's advisor Thomas Cromwell that he had not plotted with her: 'In all my life I never commoned with her in any serious cause … and would not have thought she had been such as I find her, which as I think, is but too wise for a woman.'[73]

The Countess of Westmorland (c.1533–93), who raised armies against Elizabeth I, was said by Sir Thomas Tempest to 'rather playeth the part of a knight than a lady'. Writer Aphra Behn explained her talent by saying that it was her masculine side: 'All I ask is the Priviledge for my Masculine Part the Poet in me.'[74]

Some women went even further than thinking like men – they chose to look like men, borrowing men's clothes and offending against the sumptuary laws that ruled what class might wear what clothes. Queen Elizabeth might wear a man's jacket to symbolise her power, but when non-royal women started to do so, it frightened men who feared a woman taking on the mantle of male authority. Concern about women's vanity and extravagance, an ancient complaint, took on a new urgency when fashionable women started to adopt men's clothing. Elizabethan women wore Spanish or French ruffs – decadent foreign fashions – and a long doublet like a man. They adopted high crowned hats with a proud waving feather instead of the modest coif-type headscarf that hid their hair.[75] The gorgeous fabrics, rich colours and billowy tailoring of men's clothes topped with great wigs of lustrous ringlets of the late Tudor and Stuart courts caused no concern to anyone but the few Puritan commentators when it was men peacocking about; but when women gloried in them, there was a clampdown by the crown, which triggered arrests in the 1470s, 1490s, 1550s and 1570s.[76]

The city fathers of Chester were disturbed that women were wearing a variety of caps that did not show their marital state, 'which disordering and abusing of apparrell, is not oncly contrary to the good use and honest facion used in other good cities and places of the realme … but also is verrey costly, more than necessary charges conveynyently requireth, and ageynst the common welthe of this city'.[77]

King James I – notorious for his favours to men – was hugely offended by ladies at the court wearing men's clothes. He ordered sermons be preached 'against the insolencie of our women, and theyre wearing of brode brimd hats, pointed dublets, theyre haire cut short or shorne, and some of them stilettoes or poniards, and such other trinckets of like moment'.[78]

The clergy obligingly hammered the point that women cutting their hair and wearing hats like men were immodest, unwomanly and an offence against God. The campaign against 'Men's Shee Apes' spread to plays, ballads and pamphlets.

The Puritan preachers agreed. William Prynne, the influential Puritan writer, was as offended as the Bishop of London. The offence was only partly of appearance: women in men's clothing were behaving in ways that breached the standards of conduct imposed upon them: they were noisy, public, playful and carrying weapons. It was also an offence against national pride: the women were wearing foreign fashions and behaving in an un-English manner. And it was an offence against class: fabrics and colours were reserved for different classes of society, and the women were wearing whatever they chose. The worst offence was that by dressing like men, the commentators claimed that they had made themselves into a 'hermaphrodite' or 'monster':

I have met with some of these trulls in London so disguised that it hath passed my skill to discern whether they be men or women. Thus it has now come to pass that women became men and men transformed into monsters.[79]

Commentators in 1583 agreed that women who dressed as men were making themselves into 'monsters of both kinds', Puritan pamphleteer Philip Stubbes said: 'Our apparel was given us as a sign distinctive to discern betwixt sex and sex and therefore one to wear the apparel of another sex is to participate with the same and to adulterate the verity of his own kind. Wherefore these women may not improperly be called hermaphrodites, that is monsters of both kinds, half women, half men.'[80]

Disguising for entertainment, wearing costumes for plays and performances, dressing as another gender or class had been a tradition of public play, part of 'misrule' undertaken on high days and holy days. Hocktide (the Monday after Easter Monday) was celebrated in Hexton, Hertfordshire, by women dressing as men and challenging a men's team to a tug of war. The defeated team would be pushed in a ditch and smeared with mud.[81]

Dressing as the wrong class was probably as provocative as dressing as the wrong sex, and highly erotic for people in a rigidly class-bound society. According to a fifteenth-century playscript, and reports in the courts, sex workers in brothels or ale houses might entertain clients with a dance in which they dressed as men in breeches, as 'matrons' – respectable elite women – or naked.

The London courts recorded frequent accusations.[82] A German or Dutch woman dressed in men's clothing was caught having sex with a man named 'Charles of Tower Hill' in September 1471; and in the same year a man named Thomas a Wode in the parish of St Peter Westcheap was reported for giving a German or Dutch woman a man's silk doublet to wear. No punishment was recorded for either of these two women; but in 1473, 'Trude Garard' was recorded as a 'common strumpet', street-walking in men's clothing. The court ordered that she be marched by minstrels to the pillory, carrying a white rod and wearing the striped hood that identified a prostitute, and that after standing in shame, she be expelled from the city for life.

Thomasina, a corse-weaver, was accused in March 1493 of taking a woman dressed as a man to her rooms and holding her there. The Latin of the court record calls the woman Thomasina's 'concubine' but it is not clear whether she was kidnapped or was visiting by choice. Thomasina was not charged – she could produce three witnesses to her good character, and she only had to pay a fine. In 1495 in the Parish of St Mary, a woman named Alice was arrested for dressing as a man to follow her lover to Rochester, where she lived with him 'for a long time'. The man was a priest, and Alice was cited in court as a common prostitute who specialised in sex with priests. There was no punishment as the fine was paid.

Elizabeth Chekyn, who had been seen in bed with two priests in 1516, was arrested for walking around in a priest's gown and her punishment was to wear a picture of a woman in a priest's gown on her shoulder and a yellow 'H' to make it clear that her offences were both 'Harlotry' and dressing as a priest, as she was led through the streets from the prison at Newgate to the pillory at Cornhill. She had to stand there in shame, and then go to Aldgate, to be expelled from London for life. In July 1519 – as part of a general sweep of the 'idle vagrant and suspicious persons' in the capital – four women were arrested as strumpets and common harlots. Three of them – Margery Brett, Margery Smyth and Margery Tyler – were said to have 'Cut their here like unto mennys hedes to theunt [the intent] to goo in mennes clothing at tymes whan their lewde pleasure is'. The three women, wearing both men's bonnets and the striped hoods of prostitutes, were led by minstrels to the pillory, where they stood holding white rods, before being expelled from the city.

In March 1534, a woman named Alice Wolfe was arrested, disguised as a man, escaping from the Tower of London the night before her execution for murder, with the help of her jailer John Bawde. She was caught when a watchman identified her as a woman. Her execution, along with her husband John Wolfe, for the murder of two Italian merchants went ahead – the couple were chained on the bank of the Thames and drowned by the rising tide, the usual punishment for pirates and sea-robbers, suffered by Alice Wolfe perhaps because her accomplice-husband was a Hanseatic merchant and their victims had been merchants.

In 1537, Agnes Hopton was punished in Hertfordshire for dressing as a man and living with her male lover, John Salmon, who 'kept her in manne's rainment'. Their punishment was like that of a skimmington ride, a public denouncing. They were both seated on a horse. John Salmon was dressed as a minstrel playing an instrument and forced to ride facing the tail of the horse, so that he was face to face with Agnes, to the amusement of the neighbourhood. They were banished for a year.

In 1576, Margaret Bolton and her daughter went abroad in men's clothes, and Dorothy Clayton wore men's clothes for her work as a prostitute, and Alice Young aged only 17 disguised herself 'lewdly' in men's apparel. Jane Trosse was arrested in 1577 for wearing clothes 'more manlike than womanlike'.

Margaret Wakeley was charged with giving birth to a bastard and going about in men's apparel in 1600; Helen Balsen, a prostitute, dressed as a man to please a client in 1601. Elizabeth Griffin was punished for lewdness and going about in men's apparel in October 1601, and in June 1602 a vagrant couple, Rose Davies and John Littlewood, were both arrested for dressing as the opposite sex.

'Moll Cutpurse' – real name Mary Frith – became widely known, thanks to a sensational biography published about her in 1662. She was born in the 1580s to an artisan family – her father was a cobbler – and while she was still a girl, her uncle, a minister, tried to send her to New England, probably as an indentured worker sworn to serve a master for a number of years without pay. Before the ship sailed, she jumped overboard and swam to the shore and went into hiding. Mary became Moll and made her living from thieving, earning her name 'Cutpurse' as a pickpocket, cutting the strings that tied the wallet or purse to the victim's belt. In August 1600, she was found guilty in a Middlesex court for stealing 2s 11d. It was the first of several arrests, and she was branded on the hand as punishment for thieving. She gained fame in 1610 when John Day wrote a play, *The Madde Pranckes of Mery Mall of the Bankside*. A second play in 1611, by Thomas Dekker and Thomas Middleton, celebrated her under the title *The Roaring Girl*.

The playwrights made their heroine a single woman and though dressed in men's clothes she was chaste. But the real-life Moll Cutpurse was known as a 'libertine' – a sexually active woman. She worked as a highwaywoman and held up General Fairfax, on Hounslow Heath outside London, stealing a huge sum of 250 jacobuses (each worth 25s). According to the *Newgate Calendar*, a scandal sheet based loosely on the court hearings at Newgate Prison, Moll shot at the Cromwellian general, killed two horses under his servants and rode away. Fairfax reported the attack at Hounslow and a party of military officers chased her for six miles, until Moll's horse failed her at Turnham Green. Some histories recorded her as being a Royalist soldier, attacking Fairfax as a last stand for the king; however, she was arrested not for warfare, but for a criminal attack and condemned to die. She escaped the gallows by buying a pardon, paying General Fairfax £2,000 – a fortune.[83]

In public she wore a man's doublet and breeches and smoked a pipe, and she once won a bet to ride from Charing Cross to Shoreditch in London dressed as a man carrying a banner and blowing a trumpet. She appeared with the famous horse trainer William Banks and his 'counting horse' Marocco.

The title page of Thomas Middleton and Thomas Dekker's play *The Roaring Girl*, based on and starring Mary Frith – also known as 'Moll Cutpurse'

Mary Frith took to the stage as herself in 1611 at the Fortune Theatre, in London, where, dressed as a man, she sang songs, played the lute and exchanged jokes with the audience, one of the earliest women on stage, the first recorded stand-up comedienne. She was charged with indecency of her dress in December that year and accused of being involved in prostitution. A few months later, in February 1612, she was also ordered to perform a public penance, wearing only a sheet, during the Sunday morning sermon at St Paul's Cross, when according to a witness she wept bitterly and was very penitent.

Despite her reputation as a cross-dressing bawdy single woman, she married Lewknor Markham in 1614, perhaps to gain the legal invisibility of being a wife. But by 1620 she admitted receiving stolen goods and procuring sexual partners: young women for sex with men, and male lovers for middle-class women. She may have been taken into Bethlem Hospital (Bedlam) diagnosed as insane. There is a record that she was released from the hospital in 1644. She died in Fleet Street of dropsy in 1659.

A woman who sometimes identified as a man, Thomasina Hall, lived as a woman in London until 1595 when, dressing as a man and going by the name of Thomas, Hall joined the expedition to Cadiz. Surviving the disaster of the expedition and returning to London, Hall assumed the name Thomasina again and became a seamstress, then took ship to Virginia as 'Thomas', but on arrival in the colony took work as a chambermaid. Summoned by the General Council of Virginia and accused of being a man dressing as a woman, Thomas/Thomasina told the council: 'I go in women's apparel to get a bit for my cat.'

The court ruled that Thomas/Thomasina could wear men's clothes but must wear a woman's apron over the breeches and a woman's headdress.[84]

Katherine Jones was arrested in Fleet Street in January 1624 dressed as a man, 'for merriment'; Margaret Willshire, armed with a dagger and a pikestaff, her sister, her female employer and her woman neighbour all dressed in men's clothes and went out into the streets of Chaceley in Worcestershire, at Christmas in 1610, and gave a constable a written message to raise the hue and cry. The offence, so like the old tradition of 'misrule', was brought to court in a sign that the practice – dressing in the wrong clothes for class and sex, partying with a superior and teasing the authorities – was no longer accepted.

Three young women like Katherine Jones, dressing up for fun, were taken to a church court in Essex, accused of going 'a-mumming' and dressing as men in 1596. But it was their father who had to answer for allowing the girls to dress as men.[85] The eccentric Margaret Cavendish, Duchess of Newcastle (1623–73), wore both theatrical costume and male clothing. In her writing she sometimes used a male authorial voice, and sometimes female.[86]

Anxiety about women dressing as men escalated into moral panics, one lasting a decade from 1620. It was believed that women who cut off their hair and wore men's clothes were challenging the authority of men, leaving their sex and changing their nature. Exceptional 'manly' women had been explained away, but women disguising as men, women living as men, women becoming men, not only disrupted the control of women but made it impossible to define them.

Since the Norman law of inheritance ruled that a man should inherit, it was essential to know the sex of an heir and that sex must be unchanged throughout life. Sir Edward Coke, the Elizabethan law expert, ruled that legally there were three sexes: everyone was either male or female or hermaphrodite. Hermaphrodites must choose the sexual identity 'that prevaileth'[87] and retain it permanently, for fear of having sex with the 'wrong' gender and so fall into sodomy.[88] If someone chose to be a man, and inherited property, he could not then change sex, as that would disrupt patrilineal inheritance and put a woman in charge of a man's true inheritance. If someone chose to be a woman, they would not inherit in the male line.

An Unkingly King

The inheritance of a male monarch – James I – succeeding Elizabeth after 50 years of female rule was expected to mark a return to normal authority: a king leading the country, a man leading his household; male authority dominant in public and private, kingdom and hearth. But James I of England proved little help in restoring virile male authority.[89] James's wife, Anne of Denmark, defied him by converting to Roman Catholicism and refused to attend Protestant communion – even at her own coronation in England. She smuggled priests into her royal household and celebrated mass with her Roman Catholic ladies. The royal couple lived apart, separated.[90] She refused to give James control of their first son, Henry, and defied his specific order by travelling with Henry from Scotland to their new kingdom of England.[91] Queen Anne's study of architecture, her patronage of artists and her love of the masque were criticised by James as extravagant, and his verdict that she was 'stupid' was repeated by gossips and then historians.[92] James's own preference for handsome young men led to murderous rivalry and corruption at his court. The king indulged his second son Charles, who was in turn besotted with his father's favourite, the dashing George Villiers.

Everyone knew that the greatest buttress against female disorder was a dominant male head of the household, and James clearly failed. He was blamed for the disorder, extreme favouritism, sex scandals and law-breaking at his court.[93] But his dislike of educated assertive women showed itself in a pushback against female power and education. The eulogy he ordered for Elizabeth's tomb praised her as learned 'beyond her sex'.[94]

James encouraged a rising suspicion and fear about women that peaked in a frenzy of witch-hunting in his first kingdom of Scotland, and imported it to England. The return of male rule to the throne of England became a disaster for the women of England – especially the poor and friendless.

The understandable absence of the cultured and educated Anne of Denmark from her husband's court left a gap where a queen should be. When their son Charles I took the throne with his wife, Queen Henrietta Maria, her love of the masque and courtly love presentations restored the image of a woman as a passive object of male admiration[95] – and invigorated courtly love in the court masques and imagery. It was only when the civil wars broke out that Henrietta Maria dropped the 'beautiful lady' act and emerged as a formidable leader and an aggressive soldier, typical of many of the elite women who took up arms to defend their own homes, smuggled and spied on both sides of the conflict, and kept their lands safe through years of war. After the defeat and execution of Charles I, Henrietta Maria led the royal court into exile, but she could not maintain a coherent opposition nor threaten a return. Many of her former subjects despised her and – as a Roman Catholic widow dependent on the king of France – Henrietta Maria could not be a model for female power for many English women.

She-soldiers

Mary Ambree adopted men's clothes to be a soldier in Belgium in 1584, fighting against Spain, as recorded in a popular later ballad:

> When the captain courageous whom deeth could not daunt
> had roundly besieged the City of Gaunt
> and manly they marched by two and by three
> but the foremost in battle was Mary Ambree.[96]

Long Meg of Westminster also wore men's clothes to serve as a soldier against the French at Boulogne, returning to petticoats after the war was over – she was said to have been a tall woman who married an exceptionally tall man, promising obedience in her marriage vows.

Put mee on [a] man's attire,
Give mee a Souldier's coat,
'I'll make King Charles's foes,
Quickly to change their note![97]

So sang the heroine of a popular royalist ballad, as she signed up to be a she-soldier, a woman recruit for the army of King Charles. How many women marched as recruited soldiers for each side was difficult to calculate for commentators at the time, but several reports survive. A soldier captured at Evesham who proved to be a woman said: 'her selfe and three more sufficient men's daughters came out of Shropshire, when the King's forces commanded there, and to get away, came disguised in that manner, and resolved to serve in the Warre for the Cause of God'.[98]

Sir Thomas, Lord Fairfax, claimed to have captured a 'regiment' of Royalist women in January 1644 in Cheshire. A woman named Jane Ingleby rode in the Royalist cavalry charge at Marston Moor. Another Royalist woman, serving under General Lindsey in the cavalry, was captured by Parliament forces; and Oliver Cromwell himself, who thinking he had captured a young Royalist soldier, was surprised to hear a woman's soprano voice when he ordered the youth to sing. At least one of the Royalist corporals was known to be a woman in 1645; Charles I believed that 'she-soldiers' were so numerous in his army that he issued an edict against women taking up arms, saying it was contrary to tradition and God.[99]

A woman named 'Molly' survived the wars to run the Mad Dog pub at Blackheath and was said to have been a she-soldier. 'Mrs Clarke' was celebrated in a ballad when she took up arms and wore breeches to accompany her husband into battle. A female gunner's mate was blamed for the loss of the frigate *Duncannon*.

Women of Lyme Regis defended the port from a Royalist siege in April 1644. Prince Maurice of the Rhine brought his army of 6,000 men against the town's militia of 4,000 – which included Lyme Regis's women, who dressed as soldiers in hats and jackets to fool the besieging force into thinking that there were more men under arms. Local vicar Reverend James Strong of Bettiscombe celebrated their courage in a poem entitled: *'Feminine valour; eminently discovered in Western women; as well by defying the merciless enemy at the face abroad, as by fighting them in the Garrison towns, sometimes carrying stones, anon tumbling of the stones over the Works on the enemy, when they have been scaling them, some carrying powder, others charging pieces to ease the soldiers, constantly resolved for generality, not to think any one's life dear, to maintain that Christian quarrel for the Parliament.'*[100]

Prince Rupert met the same sort of female opposition when he set siege to Bristol. Dorothy Kelly, the midwife-preacher, Mistress Joan Batten and others blocked the Frome gate with woolsacks and earth, repaired the walls with sandbags and stood behind the gunners, reloading and maintaining the fire.[101]

Women were the principal defenders of their own communities in the absence of men. Some women organised themselves and reproduced the discipline and rituals of male troops. In Coventry, companies of women marched behind a drum led by 'Goodwife Adderley with a Hercules club on her shoulder and drew off from work by one Mary Herbert with a pistol in her hand that she shot off when they were dismissed.'[102]

The mayoress of Coventry mustered her own troop of women and led them out of the town, to pursue and capture the baggage train of a local Royalist troop.[103] Parliamentarian and writer Lucy Hutchinson said that the wife of the mayor of Nottingham in the besieged city was 'a woman of great zeal and courage and more understanding than women of her rank usually have'.[104]

At the siege of Worcester, 400 women citizens served as cannoneers and some as snipers; at the siege of Pontefract, a woman was shot bringing ale to the sappers who were repairing the town walls. Chester women shot the guns from the ramparts of their besieged town. At Leicester in 1645, Parliamentary women did not surrender when the town fell, but continued fighting from street to street.[105]

Elite women and their women servants found themselves defending their houses and lands from the enemy troops, some of them resisting long sieges of their property. In the blockade of Basing House in Hampshire, it was the women who held off the Parliamentary troops by stoning the besieging forces from the parapets. When the siege was broken, many women died, including the daughter of the doctor, Dr Griffiths, who rushed to defend her father and was smashed in the head.[106]

Many ladies became famous for the defence of their houses, such as Lady Mary Winter at Lydney House, Gloucestershire. Lady Mary Bankes held Corfe Castle with her daughters and 80 soldiers for a six-week siege.

She refused rescue and when the castle fell to Parliamentary troops and was razed to the ground, they allowed her to keep the keys and the seal as a gesture of respect for her generalship. Her epitaph claimed that she had 'a constancy and courage above her sex'.[107]

Lady Brilliana Harley refused to surrender Brampton Castle for three months in August 1643, commanding with 'a masculine bravery both for religion, resolution, wisdom and manlike policy'.[108] Lady Portland said that she would fire the cannon herself rather than surrender Carisbrooke Castle on the Isle of Wight, and Lady Charlotte Derby, embroidering a bed hanging while organising the siege, swore that she would fight to the death. In fact she did not die; she broke out of Lathom House, seized the enemy mortars and won the battle in February 1643. Lady Cholmley stayed with her husband throughout the siege of Scarborough Castle, and Elizabeth Twysden nursed the wounded. Blanche Arundell held Wardour Castle.[109] The queen herself, Henrietta Maria, came under fire in 1643 when she landed in England and marched at the head of her troops, and was fired on again when she sailed from Falmouth.

Some local people banded together to enforce peace in their own community, ready to fight against any marauding troop of either side, to keep their town or county free of warfare. They were called 'clubmen', but some of the bands were proudly female, 'maiden' bands: troops of women who defended their homes and their communities, and armed, drilled and fought for their locality. The 'Virgins of Norwich' commissioned and paid for their own troop. On the opposing side, the Parliament army women recruits and followers were known as 'Leaguer Ladies'.[110]

In addition to serving as soldiers, women followed the armies as auxiliary troops, scavenging, cooking, providing laundry and medical and support services, frequently close to battles and sometimes caught up in them: the capture and plunder of the baggage train proved a highlight of victory for both sides. Some of these women would have been the wives of individual soldiers, travelling with their husbands and perhaps fighting at their sides. All women followers risked capture and attack from the opposing side, and even being abused by the army they were supporting. Sergeant Wharton in Denzil Holles' Parliamentary regiment put his own women camp followers in the pillory and then threw them into the river.[111]

Both sides complained that camp followers were exploiting the situation, accusing women of accompanying the armies for profit rather than loyalty, and both armies protested that the other side was a magnet for women sex workers.

Thousands of women were caught up in the wars and suffered for their affiliation. Lady Ann Fanshawe and her sister followed their father to Royalist Oxford, and Lady Ann then travelled with her husband, in royal service all around Britain and to Europe, at enormous personal cost. Her children died during the family's exile, and she buried a child in Lisbon, Madrid, Paris, Oxford, Yorkshire, Hampshire and Kent.[112] Lady Filmer was trapped in her house and searched by suspicious troops ten times; Lady Anne Clifford, a Royalist, was held under house arrest in her London home for months; Margaret Eure reported that she was 'exposed to all villainies'. Joyce Jeffreys had to pay protection money to Royalist troops;[113] Mrs Atkyns travelled from Oxford to London to find her house looted and vandalised, and then miscarried her child and nearly died herself. Lady Anne Saville gave birth during the siege of York. In April 1644, Alderman Taylor's laundry maid was killed while hanging out washing, and a maid was killed by accident at Wendover.[114]

Women were targeted for attack when towns were sacked by both sides, part of the plunder of a siege and punishment for the defenders. Some incidents were brutal; but some perpetrators were punished by their officers. In September 1644, after the Parliamentary surrender of Fowey to the king, a Lostwithiel woman who had given birth only three days before died after being stripped naked and thrown in the river. Charles I ordered the hanging of her murderers – his own soldiers. The terrible abuse of women and the civilian population by Oliver Cromwell in Ireland – 200 women were murdered at the Market Cross in Wexford in one incident alone on 11 October 1649 – was one of many savage imperialist crimes; not typical of Parliamentary troops nor of Cromwell's behaviour in England.

Women made significant contributions to both sides as spies, agents and informants.[115] Catherine Howard Lady d'Aubigny, served as a royal agent, hiding messages under her ringlets. She delivered the royal orders to Edward Waller, whose name not hers was given to the 'Waller Plot'. Lady Isabella Thynne spied for and advised on royal strategy. Jane Whorwood, the highly active, highly skilful Royalist spy, planned Charles I's escapes from imprisonment in Carisbrooke Castle and Hampton Court, and carried thousands of pounds of funds for him. From 1642–4 she moved more than £83,000 in gold for the Royalist cause, possibly hiding it in her soap barrels. Elizabeth Wheeler carried the king's messages, as did Lady Mary Cave, who was caught trying to get to Charles, imprisoned at Holdenby, with a ciphered letter. The cipher alone meant that she would face charges of treason, punishable by death – and there are no records of her after her arrest.

Susan Hyde, sister of Edward Hyde, later Earl of Clarendon, spied for the Royalist conspiracy group the Sealed Knot, taking messages directly to the king, operating at the centre of the Royalist spy system for four years from 1652 to 1656. Arrested for spying by Parliament agents, she was imprisoned and possibly tortured. She died a fortnight after her arrest. Her brother, who wrote the definitive history of the English civil wars, never even mentioned her service: such was his shame at a lady in espionage; or perhaps it was sibling rivalry from a less courageous brother.

Elizabeth Carey and Elizabeth Murray were also lady members of the Sealed Knot. Catherine Murray (Elizabeth's sister) financed the wartime court at Oxford and came under suspicion for spying throughout the war. Martha Parratt lost her property in 1650, accused of spying, riding with Sir John Byron's troop and paying Captain Ashley £100 for horses for the king. Elizabeth Mordaunt worked with her husband John to spy for Prince Charles. When he went to England, she remained in Calais to send and receive secret messages. Anne Halkett was in the service of the young James Stuart, Duke of York, later James II, and she managed his disguise and his escape to the Dutch republic in 1648, and served the Royalist cause spying in London. The novelist and playwright Aphra Behn may have worked as a spy for the Royalists, or she may have forged false intelligence and her reports. A woman spy caught in the Earl of Essex's camp before the Battle of Newbury was shot in the head and thrown in the river to die. Another female Royalist spy who confessed that she was paid 14s a week to spy for Prince Rupert was also killed and thrown in the water. The punishment of women spies by drowning suggests that men liked to duck them like scolds or 'swim' them like witches as a special punishment for disobeying male rule.

Working women also served the Royalist cause. Charles's correspondence with his wife Henrietta Maria in France, while he was held captive at Carisbrooke Castle, was hidden and carried by Mrs Dowcett, the wife of the clerk of the kitchen, Abraham. The royal laundress Elizabeth Wheeler and her assistant Mary also risked their lives to save the royal prisoner. Women booksellers took secret messages for the Royalist spy Richard Royston. His brother, Peter Barwick, said they were 'faithful and honest Messengers ... in circumstances not much to be envied, and were consequently, through the Mediocrity or rather Meanness of their condition, less conspicuous and more safe'.

He noted: 'These women used frequently to travel on Foot like Strowlers begging from House to House and loitering at Places agreed-upon to take up Books ... it was easy to sew Letters privately within the Cover of any Book and then give the Book a secret Mark to notify the Insertion of Letters therein.'

Women spied for Parliament too. Lucy Hay, Lady Carlisle, leaked the news that the king was on his way to arrest the five leading Parliamentarians in 1642 in time for them to escape. Working women too, some out of conviction, some for money, as the spy business became more professional. The Parliament books of 28 May 1652 show a payment of £100 to a woman whose identity is hidden 'for the good service done by her in gieving intelligence to the Armies of this Commonwealth at Worcester'.

As the reward indicates, the unknown woman made a significant contribution to one of the most important battles of the civil wars – the last, in 1651, a Parliamentary victory.

In 1650, Susan Bowen was paid £10 for intelligence; Elizabeth alias Joan Alkyn got £2 for 'several discoveries'. Alkyn worked as a propagandist and journalist under the name of 'Parliament Joan', publishing pro-Parliament news books but also for the Royalist press such as the *Mercurius Anglicus*, fulminating against the monarchy.

When the king's eldest son Prince Charles escaped from England after defeat at the Battle of Worcester, he was famously smuggled and hidden by women royalists. Ann Wyndham, wife of Colonel Francis Wyndham, helped him escape from Worcester, as did her niece Juliana Coningsby; Anne Bird was 'instrumental' in the king's escape, and other women like Catherine Gunter, Joan Harford, Eleanor Sampson and Ann Rogers were later given pensions for their service. Jane Lane, a young Roman Catholic woman, forged letters and passports and rode for two weeks, with the prince disguised as her servant, from Bentley Hall in Staffordshire to Lyme Regis on the south coast, where he took ship into exile.

A Parliamentary woman, Jane Bradley, a barmaid at the Heaven Tavern in Westminster, overheard men plotting against the government in 1679. She reported them and was paid a gold coin and recruited as a spy. She reported on a second plot against a nobleman and was charged with being part of a conspiracy, but was acquitted.[116]

Hard Times for Poor Women

There was a succession of disasters after the Tudor invasion: the start of a 'Little Ice Age', which caused bitterly cold weather and poor harvests; and an epidemic of a new illness – called the 'Sweat'. The Reformation closed the religious houses that had provided charity, medicine and employment. The increasing profits of the wool trade and developments in agriculture tempted landlords to exclude tenants from common land in a fresh wave of 'enclosures', which made the elite richer and the poor poorer. The remains of lordly giving in the old-fashioned large households – supporting the local poor with gifts and loans, paying fair wages and supporting local markets – continued to decline under these pressures.

Anxiety about the poor, and especially the itinerant poor who were not controlled by parish or lord, increased pressure on homeless and travelling people. People known as 'gypsies' were ordered out of the country by Henry VIII; 'gypsy' immigrants could be removed within 15 days of their arrival; and there were mass expulsions to the then English port of Calais of people named as 'gypsies' in 1544, and to Norway from Boston, Hull and Newcastle. In 1562, an Elizabethan law declared that travelling with or joining 'gypsies' was illegal. In 1596, nearly 200 'gypsies' (some of them women) were put on trial at York and 106 were sentenced to death. Nine were executed and the rest reprieved and sent to their home parishes. A woman in 1601 Middlesex was hanged for living with a 'gypsy' family, while a second was sentenced to death and only reprieved for her pregnancy.[117]

The Tudor poor laws formed a complex set of measures punishing beggars and vagrants, restricting beggars' licences to those considered deserving, forcing people to stay in their parishes and registering the poor. They were set to work in purpose-built workhouses on low wages, financed by a compulsory poor rate paid by landowners to their parishes. This was supposed to replace lordly giving at the kitchen door; but avoided as a tax and meanly distributed by local middling men, it was almost impossible for the poor to get adequate support: the Norwich Census of the Poor in 1570 refused payment to Janis House, a widow of 85 years old, ruling that she was 'able to keep herself, by her spinning'. The poor laws were not passed to assist the poor but to control and contain them, and used almost exclusively against poor women.[118] The Statute of Artificers of 1563 forced any adult without their own property to take the work they were offered, regardless of pay or conditions.[119] A London law at the same time put any woman without a male guarantor aged 14–40 into service at the whim of the 'Burgesses' or aldermen. Any single woman could be bound 'to serve and be retained by yeare, weeke, or day, in such cost and for such wages as they shall thinke meete, and if she refuse, they may commit her to prison, till she shall he bound to serve'.[120]

The Statute of Artificers of 1601 ruled that the magistrates of an area – all of them landlords and employers – should be the ones to set the wages for everyone. Unsurprisingly, they set them as low as they dared. It was a crime for a neighbouring farmer to set better rates. New regulations for the guilds favoured employers: making all apprentices under the age of 21 serve for a new minimum of seven years, usually unpaid.[121]

The Elizabethan labour and poor laws of 1597–1603 were hard on all women, especially independent women living and working alone. A single woman could only leave her home parish if she could prove she had a lodging at her destination, though working men could still move for better pay – increasing the gulf between the wage for men and women.[122] Women labouring gangs who followed the harvest, women shearing gangs who travelled and worked as a group, women pedlars, travelling merchants and entertainers, all were banned from the roads. Even travelling saleswomen with good businesses had to get a licence. A poor single woman could be legally forced into an apprenticeship by the parish authorities, or set to work in a workhouse. A pregnant single woman could be driven out of the parish. Single women on the streets were harassed, assaulted and abused, and there was an informal but widely observed curfew for women after dark.[123]

In Southampton in the 1600s, the city fathers demanded proof that a single woman living alone could support herself, and even when she demonstrated her business, they could still order her into employment of their choosing. If they put her into domestic service, she came under the rule of the male head of the household. In 1609, Elizabeth Green was ordered either to go into service or leave the city. In Norwich, women who lived alone could be sent to a house of correction, whipped and put into domestic service. Young single women were targeted by the authorities, who were increasingly afraid of them: conventional men frightened of disorder.[124] The wealthy merchants and rising yeomen who aspired to be magistrates, and took the parish overseer jobs, opposed the old spontaneous charity of lordly giving. John Pike was summoned to the ecclesiastical court of Little Bedwyn in Wiltshire in 1610, charged with 'harbouring a stranger in his house that came to him from Gloucester, great with child'.[125]

The court put pressure on the woman to name the father of her child – and so take the cost of the infant off the local rates: 'We desire that the said Pike and the woman concerned, may be cited in court that the father of the child may be known, and the parish discharged.'[126]

Some women felt a sense of sisterhood: Anne Frie of Broad Hinton defended herself to the magistrates, telling them that she found 'a walking woman … in travail of child in the open street and took her in for womanhood's sake'.[127]

The Bastardy Act of 1610 imprisoned an unmarried mother for up to a year if she could not support her child. There was a moral panic about infanticide in Parliament in 1606, even though actual prosecutions remained low: in nearly 150 years in Surrey (1663 to 1802), only 11 per cent of women accused of murders were found guilty of infanticide (34 of 318).[128] In Essex, it was the charge in 20 per cent of murder cases against women (84 cases). Most women sentenced to death were executed for infanticide – killing their babies – until the Restoration of Charles II in 1660 that signalled more merciful sentencing. Later prosecutions would have to prove that a woman had deliberately planned the death of her baby, until the repeal of the law in 1803.

Elite women landlords joined in the oppression of working people. Joan Thynne (1558–1612) warned her husband in 1601 to take legal action about his 'common': 'It were not amiss if you did serve Tap with process for your common, or else you shall have but little by his goodwill. For he doth put in so many sheep and other cattle, that you shall have no common there, as I hear they say unto others. But I hope you will not let it pass so carelessly.'[129]

Margaret Cavendish, Duchess of Newcastle, ordered her steward to enclose land and overcharge rents on the lands she managed as her husband's widow. Her exploitation of the local poor people became so extreme that even her heirs complained.[130]

The poor men and women who suffered under the poor laws, excluded from the land by enclosures, understood completely what was happening. This ballad, from the sixteenth century, is called 'The Poore Man Paies for All':

Me thought I saw how wealthy men Did grind the poore men's faces,
And greedily did prey on them, Not pittying their cases
They make them toyle and labour sore For wages too-too small.

Even as the mighty fishes still Doe feed upon the lesse;
So rich men, might they have their will, Would on the poore men cess
It is a proverbe old and true –
That weakest goe to th' wall;

Rich men can drink till th' sky looke blue,
But poore men pay for all.[131]

Many ballads like this, sung all around England, referred to an earlier better world, where the elite cared for their household, and even for their community, as their family. Whether such a world ever existed was not important – this was not a revolutionary call for change, but an appeal for a return to an imaginary past with the lord as a good father to a harmonious community.[132]

Violence Against Women

Women found themselves not only targeted by the poor laws, but also under tighter community control and censure. Judge Anthony Fitzherbert published a book on legal procedures in 1510, which confirmed a husband's right to govern and chastise his wife and beat her to a 'reasonable' degree. She had some legal defence – a wife threatened with murder could ask the court for protection. In the Essex, Hertfordshire and Sussex Assizes of 1559 to 1625, women were victims in almost three-quarters of marital murders.[133] From the 1550s, community cruelty to women was made legal and spontaneous abuse of women a legitimate punishment. The cucking stool that hoisted a woman into the air to shame her was widely developed after 1597 into a 'ducking stool', a more solid chair for a life-threatening punishment of holding a woman underwater, with every parish ordered by law to have a working version. The magistrates or community leaders would rule how often or for how long the woman should be ducked – sometimes women drowned; sometimes they died of shock.

Ann Bidlestone was walked through the streets by an officer of Newcastle, recorded by the brewer Ralph Gardiner

In Newcastle in 1655, Ann Bidlestone was put in a scold's bridle – the town's preferred punishment for argumentative women. The cage around her head had an iron skewer that she had to hold in her mouth which cut her and made her mouth bleed. This helmet-like torture device with a tongue depressor, to publicly gag the woman, was legal and commonly used from 1567.[134] Some courts ruled that a guilty woman stand alone in church or in the market square, sometimes wearing only her shift or carrying a taper (a candle) as her punishment of public shame, especially for sexual misconduct. Women might be set in the stocks in the market or churchyard for the neighbours to stone or abuse.

Women found guilty of serious crimes could escape execution if they were pregnant. Edith Sawnders, a single woman of London, caught thieving silver, 'pleaded her belly' in August 1565. She was not inspected by a jury of matrons until December, by which time she was pregnant and received a royal pardon. Catherine Longley was charged, with three other women, of stealing clothes in 1579. All but one were pregnant by the time they were inspected, and so pardoned. Occasionally a woman refused to shame herself. Agnes Samuel, accused of witchcraft in 1593, refused to plead her belly: 'This I will not do. It will never be said that I was both a witch and a whore.'[135] The magistrates hanged Agnes and her mother, who was also accused of witchcraft.

The question of rape and who suffered from the crime changed in 1576 to recognise that it was a personal attack on a woman, not theft or damage of property owned by her husband, father or guardian.[136] It was separated from charges of kidnap and defined as penile penetration of an unwilling woman, a definition that would be unchanged over the next 200 years. As a personal crime of violence, it was punishable by death,[137] but this probably made juries reluctant to bring in a guilty verdict, for fear of executing an innocent man. The new law seemed to recognise a woman's right to safety, but by making the crime one of unwanted sexual intercourse rather than a theft or damage to property, it defined rape, for the first time, as a sexual encounter motivated by desire. The victim was no longer a man whose property had been stolen away and damaged by a thief. The thief was no longer pursued by the man for compensation to be awarded by a judge and jury of similar property owners. Now the victim was a person notorious for unreliability. She – the last person anyone would trust – was obliged to define the act as rape by an audible, preferably violent, resistance during the act, coherent complaint afterwards, and production of witnesses and evidence. The woman faced sceptical interrogation from her social superiors long before anyone went to find the rapist. And since no woman could be trusted, she faced automatic doubt.

In the past, everyone had agreed that female sexuality was voracious. Eve was easily tempted; a woman would have sex with almost anyone if her father or husband did not guard her. Thinkers influenced by the ideas of courtly love believed that women were initially cool but female refusal could be followed by seduction, and rape was only a degree of force beyond that. In a society that held these opinions, rape conviction rates were vanishingly low: less than 1 per cent of all indictments recorded on the total Home Assize Circuit between 1558 and 1700.[138] In three Elizabethan counties of Kent, Surrey and Essex, 63 men stood trial for rape, and 19 were found guilty, a conviction rate of 30.15 per cent.[139] This was high because in Surrey, 25 of its 32 trials had been for the rapes of under-age girls, and since young girls could not consent, any intercourse was a rape.

Prostitution

Prostitutes came under increasing criticism and control as sexually transmitted diseases were blamed on them. Syphilis, an incurable and fatal sexual disease, was first seen in England in early 1490. Every country in Europe named it after their enemy. To the Russians, it was the 'Polish disease'. But in Shrewsbury in 1493, a chronicler gloomily recorded the 'French pox': 'About thys tyme began the fowle scab and horrible sickness called the freanche pocks.'[140]

However named, everyone agreed that promiscuous women provided the source of the illness. Even previous plague outbreaks had been blamed on sexually active women, as God's punishment for fornication.[141] Leprosy was believed to be carried by women without any sign, and transmitted by sexual intercourse during menstruation. Syphilis was thought to spontaneously generate in the bodies of promiscuous women, who gave it to healthy men, who might suffer from it but were not themselves infectious.[142]

Venereal disease came into England in the late 1500s, the first case recorded in Romford in 1578. Joan Callowaie told the church court that she had intercourse with five men and one 'did burn her very pitifully'. An enterprising brothel-keeper of Romford, Widow Agnes Newman, became a surgeon to sufferers.[143] Other theorists took the view that since venereal disease was caused by unchaste women, it would be cured by a diseased man having sex with a virgin.[144]

Licensed brothels, which had protected prostitutes from abuse, were closed in most towns from 1546.[145] Sex work became illegal and prostitutes faced arrest, while clients were mostly ignored. Part of the clampdown came only for the sake of appearances. Some towns fined prostitutes as a way of taxing their profits. At the port of Winchelsea, sex workers had to pay a fine of 6s 8d every quarter – in effect a fee to trade – and in York, sex workers rented their rooms in St Andrew's churchyard from the church.[146]

For many women prostitution was not a permanent job but a resource in an emergency, according to their personal difficulties. Some single women exchanged sex acts for gifts or financial support but were not considered prostitutes. The Norwich Census of the Poor of 1570 categorised women as single, married, widowed, deserted, and as 'grass wenches' – sexually active unmarried women, sometimes with bastard children. Six grass wenches were named.[147]

In London, women walking in the streets could be sent to the prison for criminal women and orphans at the old Palace of Bridewell, accused of prostitution on nothing more than the word of the magistrates. Provincial women found themselves punished by their community. Those who were on the streets for any reason, away from workplace, home or church, faced public censure. By the 1600s, women had been all but enclosed: even meeting places like ale houses or the new coffee shops were barred to them unless they were working there.

Puritans in power from 1649 to 1660, during the Commonwealth years, again attempted to close brothels. One prosecution of a St Clement Danes' bawdy house named the prostitutes, including Anne Cobbie, who was well regarded and popular. The court records described her as a 'tawny Moor' with famously 'soft skin'. The brothel owners were imprisoned and the house closed. Cobbie may have retired and married a local haberdasher, Richard Sherwood.[148]

The restoring of the permissive court of Charles II allowed the return of public prostitution. It was clear that some of the ladies of the court, indeed women favoured by the king himself, were rewarded with money, goods, land and titles. Charles II's English mistress, actress Nell Gwynn, endeared herself to the crowd by saying she was not one of his disliked Roman Catholic mistresses but she was the 'Protestant Whore'.

Women Enslaved

From the 1560s onwards, increasing numbers of kidnapped people were brought from Africa to England and sold as slaves to owner-employers. More than half a century before, Catherine of Aragon had brought a slave in her retinue when she arrived in England to marry Arthur, Prince of Wales. She was named after Catherine – Catalina – and she worked as a domestic servant in the queen's chamber: 'She had to make the Queen's bed and attend to other secret or private services of her Highness's chamber.'[149]

Catalina attended both of Catherine's wedding nights in 1501 and 1509, before returning to Spain to marry and have children. She was later described as 'esclava que fue' – 'the slave that was', suggesting that she had been released from slavery.

A baby girl described as 'a negro' was baptised with the name of Mary in Plymouth in 1594, and her father was said to be a Dutchman.[150] 'Lucy Negro' played a part in the Gray's Inn revels of Christmas 1594. She had been a dancer at the court of Elizabeth and was cast in the masque in the role of 'the Abbess of Clerkenwell' – probably a brothel-keeper.[151] A census of 'Strangers' in Barking, around 1598, lists five 'negras' including two women: one named Clare who lived at the house of Widow Stokes, and Maria who lived at Olyver Skynnars. The census in the next year shows Clare still living at Widow Stokes', but Maria – written as Marea – had moved to Richard Wood's house. Men and women slaves kidnapped from Africa became fashionable status symbols as servants to the aristocracy. In 1599, Dennis Edwards wrote to the Earl of Hertford's secretary, 'Pray enquire after and secure my negress: she is certainly at The Swan.'[152]

The number of African people kidnapped and brought to England prompted an announcement from Elizabeth I in 1596 that they should all be transported again – out of the country. In 1601, a German slave taker was authorised to kidnap 89 slaves from their owners, ship them to Spain and Portugal, and exchange them for white prisoners who had been enslaved by Barbary pirates.[153]

Some enslaved women created strong bonds with their owner/employers, who remembered them in their wills. Frances – an 'African maid' – received £10 in the 1600 will of her London merchant employer, and Joane 'the blackemore' was given £3 in her employer's will in 1612.[154] A former slave, Helenor Myou was wealthy enough to own household goods in Middlesex in 1612. She witnessed against thieves who had stolen her property: collars or ruffs, a pillowcase and other 'divers goods'. Another woman who may have been enslaved but managed to gain both freedom and prosperity was Cattelena – a single African woman living in Almondsbury, Gloucestershire. The only surviving record of Cattelena is the inventory of her possessions at her death in May 1625, when she left a cow (worth £3 10s), a bed, a bolster, a pillow, a pair of blankets, a sheet, a quilt, four little pots, one pewter candlestick, one tin bottle, a dozen spoons, three earthen dishes, two dozen trenchers, one table cloth, all her wearing apparel, and one coffer and two little boxes.

Some women found freedom but not prosperity. Unknown numbers died of poverty in the streets with no parish to claim as home. One, named Marie, was found in the capital in 1623, 'a poor woman being a Blacke Moor, Named Marie, who died in the street in Rosemary Lane'.

A very few slaves were freed by baptism, following the dwindling belief that a Christian could not be enslaved by Christians. Mary Fillis (1577–?1631) arrived as a child slave from Morocco aged about six years old and worked for a London merchant, John Barker. On his death, Mary Fillis was inherited by his widow, until she was bought or hired by Millicent Porter – a widowed seamstress in the village of East Smithfield. Here Mary Fillis converted to Christianity and was baptised at St Botolph's Aldgate on 3 June 1597, her owner/employer Millicent Porter acting as her godmother. The two women may have regarded baptism as setting Mary free, and she may have married Christian Peters of the parish. Mary Peters, a 'poor blackamore woman', was buried at Tower Hill in 1631.[155]

Most of the slaves in England won freedom for themselves by running away and making a life among escaped slave communities, or finding shelter with white working-class people. Augustina Patra, a 'blackamoor servant', was punished in 1601 by the London Bridewell 'for running away in diverse times' from a noble household.[156] Mary – 'a Black moore servant to Captain Sallanova of Weymouth and Melcombe Regis' – was caught at Dorchester after running away from her owner and sent back to him in 1633.

The slave-owners had not yet invented a theory of different races each with different status. Most people thought – as the ancient Greeks, and indeed as modern gene scientists[157] – that there was one human race with variations and no meaningful constant differences between one variant and another. But by the 1500s, the word 'fair' was used interchangeably with whiteness, as well as its earlier meaning of beauty; and the opposite of 'fair' was not only 'foul' but also 'dark'.[158] 'Blackness' and 'Jewishness' were sometimes used interchangeably.

Even elite white women did not have control over their lives. Frances Coke, daughter of the jurist Edward Coke, known as the 'father of English liberties', was kidnapped by her own father, tied to a bedpost and whipped until she agreed to marry the man of his choice, Sir John Villiers, who was said to have gone insane three years after the marriage.

Upper-class Women's Work

Ladies of the centralised and growing Tudor courts were career courtiers, providing continuity during the change of a monarch – especially important during the revolving door of the Henry VIII years. Four ladies of the Henrician court became queens themselves – promoted from being ladies-in-waiting. Ladies represented their country at diplomatic meetings and parties, created a stylish and cultured ambience that was part of the identity of the monarchy, prepared and performed in devotional acts and secular entertainments, and assisted in the smooth running of the court – consuming and creating etiquette, culture, fashion and art.[159]

The development of the masque into a complicated and lengthy musical dance-drama, calling for many performers and audience participation, reinforced the courtly love image of passive women, but created a serious art form for women as writers, choreographers, designers, prop-makers, costumiers, musicians, artists, stage technicians and managers.

Women painters benefited from the fashion for portraits and murals for the court and the elite. There were 24 women painters registered with the Painter Stainer's Guild, which numbered 2,600. Famous women court painters include Susanna Horenbout (1503–54), who was a 'gentlewoman' and 'illuminator' at the courts of Anne of Cleves and Kateryn Parr. Her sister-in-law Margaret Holsewyther, another elite woman painter, may have inherited her brother Lucas Horenbout's workshop on his death, and continued his work. Levina Teerlinc (1510–76) was the only court miniaturist at the court of Henry VIII, and received commissions for hundreds of miniatures. Paid an annual pension by the king and his successors, she may have trained the more famous Nicholas Hilliard. Anne Gulliver, widow of the Serjeant Painter to the Crown, John Brown, inherited his equipment and possibly his post on his death in 1532. He left her his tools 'for as long as she occupyeth mine occupation'.[160]

Audrey Beene inherited her painting shop in 'the Exchange' and a stock of paintings from her professional painter husband Thomas, himself the son of a painter mother and father. Susannah Penelope Rosse painted with the more famous Samuel Cooper and most of the miniatures in the so-called 'Samuel Cooper pocket book' were painted by her.[161] The fashion for portraits spread to the provinces. Katherine Maynor of Ampthill, Bedfordshire, was the widow of a painter and may have taken over his artwork business. Alice Hearne, a painter in her own right, inherited her husband's equipment and continued in the business. The records of the Painters' Guild of Chester from 1575 to 1640 show seven women painters in the town who inherited their husbands' shops and freeman status. If they did not paint, they ran the business: training apprentices and hiring journeymen. The widows of the painters Gerlach Fliche and Robert Pilgrim were executors of their husbands' wills.[162] Alice Gammedge of Saffron Walden in Essex left painting supplies and frames to her son in 1591.[163]

As the Tudor court grew bigger than its predecessors, more paying and pensioned roles were created for elite women. Elizabeth Woodville of York (queen from 1464 to 1483) had five ladies-in-waiting, seven maids of honour and two female servants. Two generations later, Catherine of Aragon had 33 women in her household.[164] The reigning queen Mary I had up to 36 and Elizabeth I had 38.[165]

Elizabeth's privy chamber consisted of a semi-professional corps of women: 16 paid and six or more honorary. Some were permanent appointments: Blanche Parry and Mary Radcliffe never married and served for almost the entire reign. Some were family members from the Boleyn and Carey side. They supervised her linens, wardrobe and jewels, assisting with dressing and washing, serving food and nursing her during illness. One woman usually slept with the queen as her 'bed-fellow', for company and security. The constantly changing young maids-of-honour served as companions, dancers, entertainment and as an attractive back-drop to Elizabeth when the court was on show.[166] Many of the relationships were long-lasting and affectionate.

Women visitors attending court on special occasions might catch royal favour, be rewarded with gifts or fees, and they might be co-opted into court roles, appointed to places or make political marriages.[167]

Alice Montague, the royal silkwoman, pioneered a technique in 1561 for knitting stockings from sheer silk instead of the baggy wool used previously, and in 1564, Dinghen van der Plasse invented a form of linen starch that created the famous stiff ruff of Elizabethan courtiers. When a Tudor knitting machine was invented by William Lee in 1599, Elizabeth I refused to grant the inventor a licence in an early recognition that mechanisation would destroy the craft skills and livelihoods of women: 'I have too much love for my poor people who obtain their bread by the employment of knitting to give my money to forward an invention that will tend to their ruin by depriving them of employment and thus making them beggars.'[168]

A townswoman, Katherine Fenkyll, inherited a substantial drapers' business and properties on the death of her husband, and was named as executor of his will. She had a share in a fleet of ships to export the cloths and the will gave her a continuing interest in the ships and a life interest in their London home.[169]

A Lyme Regis woman, Sara Sampford, sold her ship the *Diamond* in 1611 to two local merchants, witnessed by two seamen. She performed the sale by taking the buyers on to her ship moored at the Cobb and handing them a rigging or mooring rope.[170]

In the country, elite women were responsible for running the great houses and agricultural businesses in the frequent absence of their husbands. The ambition of Plantagenets, Tudors and Stuarts to create a large royal court, supported by an organised, centralised administration, summoned lords to Westminster who left the management of their houses and lands to their wives and widows, often in leadership and executive roles that – as women – they were not officially allowed to perform. During the wars the men might be fighting or in exile. Wives and widows of the gentry and aristocracy were often the only constant competent managers and landlords. The vast majority of knights and noblemen predeceased their wives (69 per cent), so widows were frequently left in charge of houses, much land and often several industries. During the Reformation many great houses of Tudor England were suddenly and dramatically enriched by church lands and church funds, creating new lands and industries for the ladies to manage, and extra domestic space, where women studied, worked textiles, produced art and medicine, and sometimes prayed – rather as they had in convent life.[171]

Women landowners made knowledgeable, hard-working stewards of the family business. Joan Thynne of Caus Castle and Longleat took on all of the day-to-day work of running the estates. In September 1600, she reported in detail to her absent husband:

> I have received the wheat which is very little, and not so much as we shall need at this time, not by forty bushels, for this will not serve one of your fields, and for the sacks, they shall be presently returned to you again. They demand much more than you write that I should give them for the carriage of the millstone, but he shall have no more than you have set down. I have received one hundred and four score pounds five shillings and four pence, there is a great part of it owing, of the rest I will make what spare I can. I know your travail to be both great and troublesome, for the which I am heartily sorry, wishing that it lay in me any way to ease it. For sending of beefs thither, they must be fat and very forward in fat before they come hither, for here is very little grass to feed any here, by the reason of the great wet which hath been here very lately, for all the Lord's Meadow is covered with water so that there can be no feeding of any beast till there be frost to dry it up, and the rest of the grounds are not much for feeding, considering how many are here already.[172]

Another Elizabethan landowner, Lady Margaret Hoby (1571–1633), ran the house and the family business outside Scarborough, Yorkshire, in the frequent absence of her husband on parish and judicial business. She kept a journal, one of the earliest women's records. It is a chronicle of relentless spiritual exercises, ill health and work: 'I walked to see som wheat; walked about to workmen and was bused setting som wheat, was sometime at the plowers and had sowen of rye five pecks; was busy about setting corne; delivered corne, walked forth and received in corne, measured corne to see what prouision we had; was busie seeing som rooms made handsome for corne.'

Thomas Knyvet (1596–1658) told his wife Katherine, left to manage his lands in the English civil wars, 'I know I cannot have a better steward than thyself to manage our affairs.'[173]

Bess of Hardwick (c.1521–1608) is sometimes described as a successful widow who rose from minor gentry to countess by four judicious upwardly mobile marriages – but she would not have been married by successive wealthy men, if she had not had a proven record of land stewardship, entrepreneurial and political skills. She was married while very young to a young bridegroom, which earned her a small widow's dower, and her second marriage was to a much older man, Sir William Cavendish, royal treasurer, who was probably guided by her to sell his lands in the south of England and buy the Chatsworth estate near her home in Derbyshire. On his death he settled his fortune on their heirs and Bess took control of the family assets, next marrying William St Loe and managing his business so well that he left his fortune away from his family, entirely to Bess. Her final marriage was to George Talbot, Earl of Shrewsbury, and she consolidated their fortunes by marrying his heirs to her own. The marriage was a happy one, with Bess running the large estates, including mines, shipbuilding yards and glass-making industries, while George served Elizabeth I, until the exiled Mary Queen of Scots, under house arrest in their care, proved to be a ruinously expensive and divisive guest, demanding to be served as a queen while conspiring to escape, for 15 years.

Under these strains, Bess and her husband George Talbot separated and there were bitter disagreements about the fortune that Bess had managed. She lost her house and built a new one – Hardwick Hall – which she had topped with her initials in stone – ES – as if to make sure that no one could take it from her. Her solo management of her own funds meant that she died the richest woman in England after the queen, aged 80, leaving her children heirs to great fortunes and provided with great connections – arranged marriages into four ducal families and one royal line, the Stuarts.[174]

Women's superior knowledge of land values was demonstrated after the wars when Royalist families were forced into exile and their estates valued by the victorious Commonwealth government. Local women were preferred to men as valuers in sequestration cases.[175]

Despite their lack of official legal status, elite women inherited offices of state, and increasingly moved into roles of authority. In 1503, senior judges ruled that women, married or single, could serve as magistrates. Two sisters inherited the office of high constable in 1551.[176] Women used the courts as litigants, as well as defendants. About 25 per cent of chancery cases (dealing with wills and settlements) were brought by women, and 13 per cent of the common pleas.[177] Women of property, especially widows and single women, often assumed the same rights and duties as men.[178] Elite women served in public offices and cast a vote in local elections, especially if there was a local tradition of female authority or if they had inherited the right from a man and would leave it to a man.[179]

The small community of Jewish immigrants in London and Bristol were led by a woman, Beatrice da Luna, also known as Gracia Mendes, a hugely wealthy woman who financed and organised escape routes out of Spain and Portugal for Jewish people during the Inquisition. She directed some of them to England, where – though Jewish people had been banned since 1290 – the Protestant authorities ignored them, as long as they posed as Christians. Beatrice da Luna visited England in 1535 with her family.

Women entrepreneurs and inventors registered for patents. In the late 1630s, three women patented their processes for woodworking and one invented a technique for distilling and storing flower essences.[180]

Middling-class Women's Work

As England recovered from the invasion of the Tudors and the Sweat, the disease that followed them, the changes to agriculture and the growth of industries led to increased prosperity for the upper levels of working people. Yeomen farmers, merchants, traders, proto-industrialists and professionals established fortunes, not as great as the upper classes', but far wealthier than the uneducated labourers. They were called at the time 'middling' people – it was their enterprise, hard work and religious fervour that increased profits and expanded their numbers.

The middling classes drove a demand for servants who could be hired cheaply and provided a clear sign of a family's rising status. Aspirational families preferred to have women servants on show 'waiting' in their domestic homes. Servants would no longer be drawn from family and friends, as they had been previously, and their labour no longer added value to their employers' businesses; instead they looked like a luxury and appeared as a cost.[181] Of course, they attracted less affection and respect as they became a status symbol for their employers.[182] Women servants were paid an average of 10s a year and male servants were paid 15s a year in 1444. Fifty years later this gap widened – men had risen to 16s 8d but women were still on 10s.[183]

Middling-class women took up the work of management and accounting in family enterprises. The 'casting of accounts' was women's work, traditionally done by wives and daughters of businessmen from the 1500s onwards.[184] Middling-class women moved into leadership roles in their community, serving in such positions as churchwarden until as late as 1600,[185] and as sexton into the 1700s.[186] Women served as overseers of the poor and some middling-class women continued a tradition of public service throughout the civil wars and after. Some of them were paid civil servants like Anne Rolfe, a tithing woman in Wiltshire who failed to punish vagrants in her parish, or Sarah Cave in Hertford in 1645, who ran the house of correction. There were women postmasters at St Albans and Waltham, and women teachers, jurors of matrons and women executrixes.[187]

Labouring Women

Labouring women in the country continued to do the same work as men and jobs like thatching and reaping were paid at the same rate as men until 1500, but women's work and production at home for their families remained cash free.[188] As cash became more necessary and barter and credit less common, domestic services and domestic production were not valued unless they could be sold for cash. Since no money changed hands when a woman cleaned her own house, made the family clothes, fed or nursed them, people behaved as if domestic women's labour was free.

The Tudor food industries continued to be supplied and often run by women, selling ale or food from their front doors, in the streets or from stalls in markets. Women moved into brewing ale commercially and became the landladies of ale houses, dominating the hospitality and entertainment trades. 'Mrs Harrison' and 'Mrs Barker' contributed food to the Smiths', Cutlers' and Plumbers' Guild entertainments in 1561. Widow Percevall paid 3s towards the costs of putting on a guild play in 1566 and Widow Robinson paid with her in 1567. In 1567–68 in Chester, the Painters', Glaziers', Embroiderers' and Stationers' paid Richard Chalewodde's wife 17d for haggis, bacon, a calf's head, bread and ale for the Whitsun plays. In the same year, the Guild of Smiths paid Griff Yeuans' wife for washing the curtains. The records show at least five women blacksmiths working in the city. Women were also involved in procuring performance scripts. In 1574–75, the Coopers' spent 2d 'on margery gybban to get our regynale' – to make a performance copy from the original or master text kept in the Pentice, Chester's central civic building.[189]

Women ale wives put on entertainments in their houses, using the central courtyard for bear-baiting, cockfighting, prize fights and travelling players. Some of the ale houses specialised in plays and became known as theatres; the landladies commissioned playwrights and formed their own theatre companies, becoming women impresarios. Margaret Craythorne owned or leased the Bell Savage from 1568 until her death in 1591; Alice Layston owned the Cross Keys from 1571 until her death in 1590; and Joan Harrison was the proprietor of the Bull from the death of her husband Matthew in 1584 to her own death in 1589.[190] Anne Farrant inherited 'the Leaze of my howse in the blacke ffriers in London' from her husband Richard on his death in the early 1580s, the first Blackfriars playhouse. The first standalone theatre in England was built by Ellen Brayne, who brought her husband James Burbage into partnership with her brother, John Brayne. Together with Brayne's wife Margaret, they built the Red Lion in Stepney in 1567, an ale-house theatre, and in 1576 they built a specialist standalone theatre: the Theatre, in the liberty of Holywell, Shoreditch. The Curtain Theatre, built on land owned by Alice German, opened nearby in 1577 and operated as a sister-theatre.[191] When the partnership broke down, Margaret Brayne sued her brother-in-law for her share of the profits of the Theatre. There was a fist fight and James Burbage called Margaret Brayne a 'murdering whore'. John Alleyn of the Admiral's Men acting company took Margaret Brayne's side and the Admiral's Men left the Theatre. When the lease on the land expired, Cuthbert Burbage, son of the founder Ellen, salvaged the structural beams from the site, shipped them across the River Thames under cover of darkness and built the Globe Theatre, owned jointly by six partners, including his brother Richard Burbage (William Shakespeare's muse and leading man) and William Shakespeare himself.[192]

Labouring women were drawn more and more into domestic service for the middling classes, where wages were poor and treatment deteriorated. A pamphlet signed by Rose, Jane, Rachell, Sara, Philumias and Dorothie complained of a 1547 publication that insulted London's domestic servants. Their missive, 'A Letter sent by the Maydens of London', claims to be a collective response from London maids arguing that employers and maids need each other: 'For as ye are they that care and provide for our meat, drinke and wages, so we are they that labor and take paines for you: so that your care for us, and our labor for you is so requisite, that they can not be separated: so needful that they may not be severed.'[193]

Isabella Whitney wrote 'A Modest Meane for Maids', advising her sisters and other young women how to keep their place and exposing the certainty of exploitation and abuse from their employers. She warned against taking revenge on abusive employers, who would be judged and punished by God.

Murderous women servants were punished as severely as murderous wives. Two female poisoners were boiled in oil during the reign of Henry VIII: Margaret Davy was boiled alive at Smithfield for multiple murders in March 1542, and a maidservant was boiled in the marketplace of King's Lynn for poisoning her mistress. In 1560, a maidservant escaped burning for poisoning her master because he had survived the attempt. Instead, she was pilloried: both her ears were cut off and she was branded on the forehead. In 1590, a young woman was burned to death at St George's Fields, London, for poisoning her mistress.[194]

Education

Only upper-class girls received an education in the fifteenth century. They might be taught their brothers' classical curriculum at home, but they were banned from schools, colleges or universities. However, women often bought books, which were published cheaply in greater numbers by the new presses of the day, aimed, for the first time, at a female readership. Books were a favourite gift and inheritance from one woman to another.[195] Female literacy increased from about one in a 100 women in

1500 to about ten in a 100 in 1600 – still lower than male literacy (25 per cent in 1600) but showing a similar increase.[196] An essay on hunting in *The Book of Saint Albans* was probably written by Juliana Berners, the prioress of Sopwell Nunnery near St Albans.

Ladies studied household and estate management and learned enough property law to defend their estates against claims, to pursue defaulting tenants or rival landlords, and to serve as executors for dead husbands. They knew enough criminal law to sit as JPs. They had to practise skilful management and read and write, in order to manage multiple distant houses. Many studied herbalism and medicine, leaving written receipts, or published medical books and left them to their daughters.[197]

Ladies were expected to be literate in English and in French, understand arithmetic and study music, sometimes performing on instruments. Latin became part of the scholarly lady culture during the reign of the three highly educated queens of Henry VIII. Two of them – Catherine of Aragon and Anne Boleyn – were fluent in other languages, and created schoolrooms, hired tutors and devised curricula for their daughters. The third renowned scholar, Kateryn Parr, studied with her stepdaughters, princesses Mary and Elizabeth, took the scholar Jane Grey into her household and created a study centre for reformed religion in her rooms, translating the gospels from Latin and co-writing the *Book of Common Prayer* with Archbishop Cranmer. Parr taught herself Latin and Greek, and published translations and an original work. Jane Grey taught herself Greek and Hebrew.

All the Tudor princesses and many of their ladies were highly educated; some of them were exceptional scholars and poets. Margaret Roper, daughter of the saint, scholar and writer Thomas More, was a translator and writer of philosophical texts. Mary Sidney, Countess of Pembroke, sister to Philip Sidney, ran a literary salon at Wilton House and rewrote her brother's poem *Arcadia*. Anne Cooke, the wife of Sir Nicholas Bacon, published a translation from the Latin of John Jewel's *Apology of the Church of England*. Her sister, Mildred Cecil, was manager of huge lands and an extensive fortune in the frequent absence of her husband Sir William Cecil at court. She studied Protestant theology and published translations of Greek into Latin. A third sister, Elizabeth Lady Russell, published theology translated from French, and the youngest sister Katherine translated works from Hebrew as well as Latin and Greek.[198] The court poet Aemilia Lanyer was tutor to Lady Anne Clifford. In

1580, a commentator, Richard Mulcaster, addressing the intelligence of girls, noted that they learned faster than boys, but quickly reassured his readers: 'For all that seeming it is not so … their natural weakness, which cannot hold long, delivers very soon.'[199]

Education for women fell out of fashion with the arrival of James I, whose daughter Elizabeth Stuart studied only 'female arts'.[200] When a female scholar, Bathsua Makin (1600–75), known as 'England's most learned lady', presented the king with a book of poems in six languages, *Musa Virginea*, he is said to have asked: 'But can she spin?'[201]

Hilarious.

Bathsua Makin survived the stupidity of King James and was invited by his son Charles I to teach his daughter six languages and mathematics. When the princess Elizabeth Stuart was arrested by the Parliamentarians, Bathsua Makin stayed with her as a servant, rather than abandon her to her father's enemies. In 1673, Makin established a school for girls in Tottenham, London, where she practised her theories of women's education outlined in her book *An Essay to Revive the Ancient Education of Gentlewomen* (1673). She did not demand equality for women, but recognition. This was not lack of conviction but doubt of success: 'Let not Your Ladyships be offended that I do not (as some have wittily done) plead for female Pre-Eminence. To ask too much is the way to be denied all.'

Many noblewomen not only studied languages and theology but published under their own names, as revealed by a 2012 exhibition, Shakespeare's Sisters, featuring 50 women writers from these years, some of them hardly known, even now.[202]

The nobility created a network of training and education for their daughters. Katherine Dudley, Countess of Huntingdon, wife of Henry Hastings, kept a 'kind of finishing school for the children of the nobility' at the end of the sixteenth century.[203] Margaret Dakins (later Margaret Hoby, the diarist) lived with the childless countess, as did Dorothy Devereux, Dionys Fitzherbert and Penelope Devereux, who was fluent in French, Italian and Spanish. Other elite households employed educated gentlewomen as tutors and teachers for their children. Margaret Hexstall signed an indenture to care for the Duke of Buckingham's children at Bletchingley during the indefinite absence of the parents. She worked with five staff – two other gentlewomen and a laundress – to look after four children.[204]

Being an elite companion was not always an agreeable experience. Joan Thynne wrote to her fiancé:

'My lady keeps her accustomed courtesy towards me which I may count a hell to heavenly joys or such lady's love that will force me to leave this country, which I would be loath since your pleasure is to the contrary, but I hope you will not have me stay where I shall be so vilely abused as now. I am, more meeter for some servant than for one of my estate.'[205]

Some of the nunnery schools for girls of middling class survived the dissolution: St Mary's Winchester had 26 pupils, boys and girls, in 1535. There were also village schools or even private tutors: Mrs Evans, a brewer's wife, took in a wealthy orphan girl and taught her lessons. Rivington Grammar School, founded in 1560, accepted girl pupils – Alice Shaw attended in 1615. Girls attended the free school in the old parish church of Wigston in Leicestershire, and at Norwich even the poorest girls were educated, though they might leave school to go to work at the age of six, while their brothers continued their studies. The wife of Richard Dawes had her own school in Essex in 1590 for boys and girls.[206]

Some schools were founded between the 1590s and the 1630s for lower-class pupils. Bunbury School in Cheshire, a school in Essex and one in West Chilcompton in Sussex admitted girls but specified that they could only attend up to the age of nine or ten and were only to be taught to read English – not to write. Some schools specified that they would only teach boys: the 1590 rules at Harrow explicitly excluded girls, as did St Olave's in Southwark, Felsted in Essex and Tiverton in Devon.[207]

In the Tudor years, upper-class women left on the country estates, relied on writing to stay in touch with their husbands and kin. Lady Margaret Hoby's spiritual journal from 1599 to 1600 recorded her thoughts and prayers.[208] During the civil wars women joined the written political debate and – divided from their families – wrote personal letters. Even working women wrote and read: Susan Rodway, a common soldier's wife, wrote to her husband who was serving Parliament in the London Trained Bands, besieging Basing House. Sir Simon Harcourt reminded his wife to write: 'My dear, let me hear often from thee.'[209]

For the first time in English history there were women wanting to write about themselves and read about each other. A domestic servant, Isabella Whitney, taught herself to read and write and in 1566–67 published *The Copy of a Letter, lately written by a gentlewoman in metre to her unconstant lover*, the first volume of verse published by a lower-class Englishwoman, followed by a second book in 1573. Dorcas Martin, a townswoman, married to the Lord Mayor of London, published an essay in the two-volume anthology of religious and devotional writing *The Monument of Matrons* of 1582. Two years later, Anne Wheathill composed and published a book of prayers, *A Handfull of Wholesome (though Homely) Herbs*, linking women's speciality – herbalism – with religious expression. Anne Dowriche composed a historical poem; Elizabeth Melville published *A Godly Dream* in 1603. Aemilia Lanyer – the mistress of Elizabeth I's cousin Henry Carey, Lord Hunsdon – published her book of verse in 1611. The daughter of an Italian Jew, she compared the original sin of Eve with the far worse sin of all men – that of executing Jesus Christ:

> Her sinne was small, to what you doe commit;
> This sinne of yours, surmounts them all as farre
> As doth the Sunne, another little starre.
> Then let us have our Libertie againe,
> And challendge to your selves no Sov'raigntie;
> You came not in the world without our paine,
> Make that a barre against your crueltie;
> Your fault beeing greater, why should you disdaine
> Our being your equals, free from tyranny?
> If one weake woman simply did offend,
> This sinne of yours, both no excuse, nor end.[210]

The first childcare manuals by women written in English were published before the civil wars: Dorothy Leigh's *The Mother's Blessing* in 1616 and Elizabeth Jocelyne's *A Mother's Legacy to her Unborn Child* in 1624. Hannah Woolley wrote on cookery and also published a successful herbal and domestic advice book. The Protestant scholar and writer Anne Locke pioneered the spiritual journey style that was to become fashionable after the civil wars.[211] Katherine Jones, Viscountess Ranelagh (1615–91), was an Anglo-Irish scientist, philosopher and political thinker, a member both of the 'Hartlib Circle' (a protestant spy network that spread from Europe to America), the Great Tew Circle of humanist philosophers, and the so-called 'Invisible College' around Robert Boyle.

Not everyone was a fan: 'When any of our Sex doth Write they Write some Devotions or Romances or Receipts of Medicines for Cookery or confectioners or Complemental Letters or a Copy or two of Verses ... which express our Brief Wit in our Short Works.'[212] This harsh critic was Margaret Cavendish, Duchess of Newcastle, who also aspired to the philosophical circles and spent a fortune on publishing her own books, which ranged from natural science to philosophy. She wrote a play and a science fiction romance. Original and eccentric, she was a determinedly innovative thinker, corresponding with philosophers and scientists of the day, respected mainly for the wealth of her husband's fortune and her social position.

Mary Evelyn (1636–1709) – a writer herself – argued that women should not study: 'All time borrowed from family duties is misspent; the care of children's education, observing a husband's commands, assisting the sick, relieving the poor, and being serviceable to our friends, are of sufficient weight to employ the most improved capacities amongst us.'[213]

Medicine

Medicine, chemistry, herbalism and surgery were widely practised by elite women on their households, estate workers, tenants and – during warfare – injured soldiers.

Margaret Colfe, wife of Abraham Colfe, rector of Lewisham, was described at her funeral, 'for Yeares a willing Nurse, Midwife, Surgeon, and in part Physitian to all, both rich and poore; without expecting reward'.[214]

All gynaecology and obstetric examinations and treatments were exclusively performed by women, some of them highly skilled practitioners. Some of the surgeons at the newly formed St Thomas's Hospital in London were women.[215] Elizabeth Hall was on call at St Bartholomew's Hospital in the capital in the 1550s. Elizabeth Fysher cured Thomas Bedforde of Coventry of a very 'great swelling', buying spices from apothecaries to make her own medicines. Elizabeth Eston nursed her employer Thomas Gawen for 12 years, on the promise of a rental property on his death, a promise he died without honouring. Catherine Studley of Aldgate Street, London, received Henry VIII's ward Thomas Philpot in her house when he was near to death. She nursed him back to health over eight months and charged the king, his guardian, 18s a week for his care, an extraordinarily high fee which reflected her skills. Most board and lodging was between 1s and 2s a week.[216]

Mother Edwin worked as a surgeon at Christ's Hospital, London, in 1563; Mrs Cock was the surgeon-apothecary there in 1576, as was Alice Gordon in 1598. Cecily Baldrye got her surgery licence from the Bishop of Norwich in 1568. Only one woman in Exeter was licensed to be a surgeon in the whole of the reign of Elizabeth: Mary Cornellys of Bodmin.[217] Isabel Warwike was allowed to practise as a surgeon in York in 1572 because of her good reputation. Two named women physicians emerge from the Kent probate records: Mrs Wright, who provided physic and advice and was fetched from her home in Canterbury to a dying patient in 1635, and Mrs Jacob of Canterbury, who was one of a family of physicians in 1613. She was probably still working, with her son, in 1649 when she was named in the probate records of her patient.[218] A midwife in Southampton was so skilled that she was rewarded with the freedom of the city in 1601. The honour was given to her husband because she had been 'for many years the chief midwife in the town and hath taken great pains and honest care in her function'.[219]

Women nurses, rockers and governesses who bonded with their young noble charges often became permanent members of the household or were paid a lifetime salary or pension. Alice Davy, a wet nurse in Henry VII's royal nursery to Princess Margaret Tudor, went on to serve the new baby Princess Elizabeth Tudor in 1492.[220] In 1553, 25 nurses were employed at Christ's Hospital, in the capital, to look after orphan children.[221]

Nursing opportunities for low-paid women expanded as the Elizabethan parishes were obliged by law to provide poor houses and hospitals for the poor. As it was disagreeable, dangerous and badly paid, male professionals did not compete for the work. Elderly poor women were employed by Norwich in 1570 to nurse patients in almshouses. By the end of the century, women were working in most parishes to inspect dead bodies for cause of death, to prevent the spread of plague.[222]

A law regulating physicians and surgeons passed in 1512, apparently to prevent 'sorcery' and 'witchcraft' among medical practitioners, signalled the start of a campaign to drive folk-healers and cunning women out of business.[223] The College of Physicians, formed six years later, claimed that any practitioner outside the college was not to be

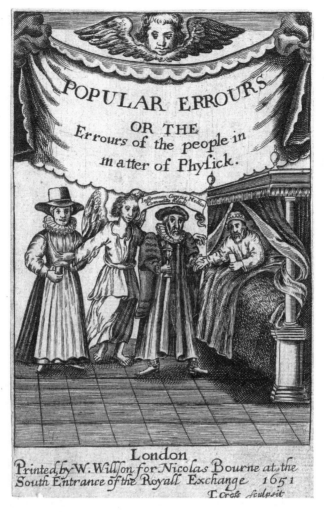

A dangerously incompetent woman doctor is held back from killing a patient, by an angel: frontispiece, *Popular Errors or the Errors of the People in Matter of Physick*, 1651

trusted – and, of course, women could not join the college or attend men-only universities. Wealthy patients were persuaded: moving from female healers to members of the college in the sixteenth century. The College of Physicians undertook 29 prosecutions of women between 1550 and 1600, and issued unknown numbers of formal warnings and exclusions to prevent anyone from practising surgery and doctoring without one of its licences.[224] In Norwich in 1561, the male barber-surgeons drew up new rules to ban all women from practising medicine and surgery in the town.[225]

James Primrose published *Popular Errors or the Errors of People in Physicians* in 1651, with a frontispiece that shows a female doctor being held back from the bedside of a sick patient by an angel so that a male doctor can save a life.

The only patients left to women practitioners were poor people and those in remote areas who could not afford to send for an expensive male doctor. Gynaecology and obstetrics remained women's specialities – unpopular among medical men because of the intimacy with women in labour, the long hours and the fear of failure.[226]

The campaign against female physicians created a prejudice against all traditional healers that played into the rising persecution of wise women and cunning women from the Tudor laws to the witch-hunts of the 1600s.[227]

Witchcraft

The declining respect for women healers may have been caused by the failure of remedies to prevent the plague, and by men moving out of 'cunning work' and folk medicine, for which payment was also falling, and into 'medical' work as apothecaries, physicians and different grades of surgeons. The Physicians' and Surgeons' guilds tried to professionalise medical work by rejecting experience as a qualification and requiring a university degree to enter the profession (which women could not attain), by publishing medical books in Latin (which no one but highly educated women could read) and by informally banning entry to women healers. They improved their own status by speaking derogatively of women practitioners. As the status of folk medicine and herbalism fell, as the pay for healing fell, men moved out of the craft of healing and tried to enter the professions of medicine and surgery, leaving folk-healing and cunning work to women.

The increasingly negative definitions of the 'nature' of women found in the women-hater pamphlets matched the supposed 'nature' of witches: emotional, angry, credulous, easily tempted, indecisive and uncontrollably oversexed.[228] Most of those accused of witchcraft were women – and two-thirds of them were poor single women.[229] The

Malleus Maleficarum – the paranoid 1486 handbook for finding witches – focused almost exclusively on women, especially old, poor and marginal women, depicting their easily tempted natures, hunger and greed, and describing them as viciously resentful of their wealthier neighbours, the new middling classes.

The medieval world remained a highly superstitious society. When anyone was struck by bad luck – illness or death or accident – they sought an explanation from the spirit world. Yorkshire landowner Lady Margaret Hoby believed that God had sent her illness as a 'gentle correction' in 1599:

> After priuat prairs I went about the house and read of the Bible and wrought tell dinner time: and after dinner it pleased for a Just punishment to correct my sinnes, to send me febelnis of stomak and paine of my head, that kept me up on my bed tell 5:a clock: at which time I arose haveing release of my sickness, according to the wonted kindnes of the Lord, who, after he had Let me see how I had offended, that so I might take better heed to my body and soule hereafter, with a gentle corriction let me feele he was reconsiled To Me.[230]

Protestant theology suggested that God Himself sent trials, that the devil and his agents walked the world making mischief, and disaster could be called down on a prosperous house by an envious neighbour or someone with a grievance, landless because their shared fields had been enclosed, envious of the rise of the 'middling' people; some were squeezed out of profitable work and named as quacks and witches; and some were genuinely cursing their 'betters' and wishing them ill – regretting the loss of 'good lordship' when they could have expected help from the kitchen door of the grand house. The idea of a fatal 'Beggar's Curse' originated in the folklore of the past and would hold sway for centuries.

A new law brought in by Henry VIII in 1542 to make witchcraft a hanging offence was expanded by Elizabeth I in 1563 to make a new crime of the summoning of spirits and causing death by witchcraft, punishable by death.[231] A witch who killed a farm animal would serve a year in prison. The first woman to be prosecuted under the new law was Agnes Waterhouse – her trial was reported in a pamphlet widely sold at the time.

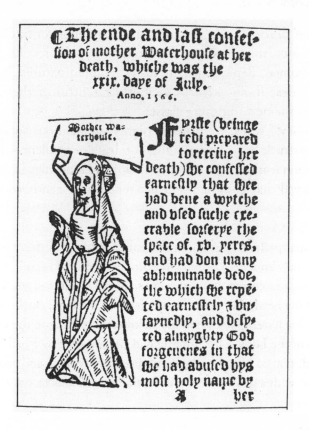

'The examination and confession of certaine wytches at Chensforde', 1566, by John Phillips, detailing the trial of Elizabeth Fraunces, Agnes Waterhouse and her daughter Joan

Agnes, her sister Elizabeth Fraunces and her 18-year-old daughter Joan, from Hatfield Peverel, were accused at the Chelmsford Assize court of killing a neighbour, William Fynee, by witchcraft. Agnes admitted the crime – and more. She also confessed that she had murdered her husband because they lived 'somewhat unquietly' together. Her sister Elizabeth had given her a cat called Sathan – and it was Sathan who had performed the murders.

Agnes' daughter Joan was also accused of tormenting a neighbour, 12-year-old Agnes Brown, with a black dog that came to their dairy holding a key, damaged the butter and offered the young girl a knife to kill herself, telling her that it was his 'sweet dame's knife'. The girl told the court that the dog had indicated that he came from the Waterhouse cottage: 'he wagged his head to your house, mother Waterhouse'.

'Sathan': first described as a white cat, a toad and then a black dog with an ape-like face and horns

Agnes Waterhouse confessed to the murder of two men; but denied the satanic dog, and the knife. She might have been guilty of the murders, or she may have been exhausted and delusional after witch tests and sleep deprivation and made a false confession, or she may have pleaded guilty to the murders in order to make a more convincing 'not guilty' plea to the joint accusation with her daughter Joan – and save her. If that was the plan, she succeeded. Agnes Waterhouse was executed for witchcraft, but she saved her daughter: Joan was declared innocent.[232]

Within a year of the arrival of James I in England in 1603, he enlarged the law to make almost all forms of witchcraft punishable by death and inspired a boom in witch hunting. The new Witchcraft Act required prosecutors to show that witches had worshipped the devil or associated with evil spirits. This extra requirement caused a decrease in convictions, from 41 per cent of those charged (1598–1608) to only 17 per cent (1608–17), but the stage was set for the witch-hunting craze of the 1640s.[233]

Interrogations changed: sleep deprivation and bullying began to be widely used, and JPs and specialist witch-hunters learned from the witch-hunting handbooks, and the new law, how to prompt accused women with leading questions. English women started to confess to a relationship with the devil in person, and even to having sex with him.[234] This emerged as rather a disappointment – the women reported that Satan had a tremendously cold penis and a short span of attention; the Prince of Darkness sounded remarkably like an inconsiderate lover who failed to produce a good dinner or sexual pleasure. Worst of all, the women divulged that Satan sometimes charged them pennies for the experience.

All the written reports from the 1500s of covens, flying on broomsticks, naked dancing, use of familiars (pet or wild animals) and sacrifice of babies emerged after the genre of witch-fantasy confessions had been established, and they were written by magistrates who had learned what they should be looking for, what questions to ask and what trials a witch should endure. The sometimes gruesome, sometimes pornographic 'confessions' read like male sexual fears and fantasies, at a time when men felt increasingly anxious about female sexual appetite. Some humane and sensible JPs never elicited a witchcraft confession and remained unconvinced by the witchcraft scares.

One of the largest groups of people to be charged and executed for witchcraft – the Pendle witches – were an unpopular local family. In 1612, in rural Lancashire, a young woman, Alizon Device, asked a pedlar for some pins. He refused to sell, and then suffered a fall and a fit. Alizon was accused by the pedlar's son of using witchcraft. When she was interrogated, she confessed that she had been initiated into witchcraft by her maternal grandmother, an 80-year-old blind widow Elizabeth Sowthernes known as 'Old Demdike'.[235] Alizon also named another local elderly woman as a witch: Anne Whittle, known as 'Old Chattox'. Both old women confessed to witchcraft and Whittle also confessed to killing two men with magic. Elizabeth Sowthernes'[236] daughter, Elizabeth Device, was examined and a 'witch's mark'[237] – a birthmark or mole – was found. Sowthernes accused her other daughter, Anne Redfearn. The five women were imprisoned in Lancaster Castle. Another Device girl, nine-year-old Jennet, accused her mother Elizabeth of witchcraft and murder, and said that at a meeting at the Demdike family home they had agreed to blow up the castle, release the prisoners and kill the jailer. A further ten people were arrested.[238]

At the trial of 19 witches, more than half were found guilty and hanged, including Elizabeth Device, her sister Anne Redfearn, her daugher Alizon and son James, and the old lady, Anne Whittle.[239] Eighty-year old Elizabeth Sowthernes died in prison before her trial. Twenty years later, in 1633, a Pendle boy named Edmund Robinson reported being kidnapped by witches and identified 17 alleged witches, including the now adult Jennet Device. She was found to have two witches' marks and was convicted of killing a woman by witchcraft, but she was not executed. Robinson's story was eventually discredited but Jennet remained in prison for several years.[240]

Witch-hunting peaked in England in 1644–47, during the unrest and anxiety of the first civil war at a time when witch-hunting swept other European countries and was exported to colonial America. The English experience was led by one man: the self-styled 'Witchfinder General', Matthew Hopkins, who was responsible for 250 trials. At least 80 per cent of the witches he accused were women, and perhaps as many as 200 of them were executed.[241] The high conviction rate (55 per cent) came down to Hopkins' interrogation techniques. He used 'tests' of witchcraft such as stripping a woman naked to look for witches' marks, pricking to see if she bled, and 'swimming her' – roping her and throwing her into deep water to see if she would float. But he denied that women were 'extraordinarily walked till their feet were blistered and so forced through that cruelty to confess'.[242]

His first conviction was against Elizabeth Clark, who was accused of bewitching the wife of John Rivet in Manningtree, Essex, in February 1645. Hopkins said that he found marks on her, and his assistant John Stearne claimed to have witnessed her assistants from the devil – imps. Elizabeth confessed and implicated other women, who were investigated by Hopkins and Stearne. Within three weeks, six Manningtree witches had been imprisoned awaiting trial – Elizabeth Clarke, Rebecca West, her daughter Anne West, Elizabeth Gooding, Anne Leech and her daughter Helen Clarke.[243] By the end of July, 36 witches had been tried at Chelmsford and 19 of them hanged.[244] Hopkins and his associates travelled through the counties of Essex, Suffolk, Norfolk and Huntingdon, charging a fee to frightened communities to rid them of witches. Another spate of hangings took place at Bury St Edmunds in August, when 16 women and two men were executed for witchcraft. John Stearne wrote that there were 120 more accused witches imprisoned awaiting trial, of which 103 were women. Mass executions of up to 70 witches were conducted at Bury St Edmunds.[245]

One of the women, Susanna Stegold, confessed to killing her abusive husband through malicious thought. She told her investigators in 1645 that she first realised her magical powers when a pig died after she wished it would stop eating. Anna Moats was also found guilty at Bury St Edmunds in August after she confessed within two hours of her arrest that the devil had appeared to her 'when she was a lone in her howse and after she had been curseinge of her husband and her childeringe'.[246]

In early September that year, a woman named Mother Lakeland was accused of killing her husband with witchcraft and was found guilty of petty treason – a worse crime than witchcraft – and condemned to death by burning.[247]

Matthew Hopkins died aged only 27 or 28 – he may have been hanged by angry villagers from the Manningtree area in retaliation for the deaths of their relatives and neighbours. The story that he himself was accused of witchcraft and drowned while being 'swum' is (sadly) unlikely. Hopkins' death did not put an end to the witch-hunting craze in the east of England, and in Bury St Edmunds in 1662, two elderly widows – Rose Cullender and Amy Denny – were accused of bewitching local children and causing one death. They were found guilty of 13 charges of using malevolent witchcraft and hanged.[248]

Concern that witches were being forced into false confessions, and that the witch-hunting books were coaching inquisitors, caused an increase in scepticism in the 1660s. The Restoration brought in a more sophisticated culture and doubts about witchcraft. Trials for the practice collapsed, conviction rates fell and reprieves and pardons became frequent. On at least one occasion, in 1664–5, the Privy Council stepped in to prevent a major witch hunt, when a Somerset justice of the peace had gathered evidence and the confessions of 25 suspected witches.[249]

Faiths

Women retained their roles as religious leaders and defenders of their faiths. When the civil wars broke out, Dorothy Kelly – who had founded her own separatist church – packed sandbags and defended Bristol's Frome gate against the attack led by Prince Rupert, and when the Royalist army took the city, the little church went into hiding, with a woman brewer, Mrs Nethway, in Lewin's Mead. They emerged, with Dorothy Kelly at their head, as a successful church that lasted through the Cromwell years.

The poet Lady Eleanor Davies acted as a prophetess advisor to Oliver Cromwell himself, after correctly predicting the death of the Duke of

Buckingham. Elizabeth Poole bore witness to her visions before the Army Council.

In 1647, George Fox and Margaret Fell founded the Society of Friends – known as Quakers. Their first convert, Elizabeth Hooton, became a preacher, frequently arrested and imprisoned for her faith. Fell was the mother of seven daughters, three of whom became preachers too. Quaker women had equal status in the movement, and it was two women – Isabel Buttery and her female companion – who established the first meeting of Friends in London, bringing a sermon written by Quaker founder George Fox to the capital in 1654. They stayed with two converts in Watling Street and Moorgate.[250] Quaker women took responsibility especially for domestic morals in families, and grew increasingly radical.[251]

Margaret Fell spoke for tolerance, both for herself and for others, when she argued in favour of the readmission of Jewish men and women to England. Oliver Cromwell had proposed this to the council without gaining official consent; but from 1655 small numbers of Jewish men and women returned to England. And, in 1659, in a petition composed by Mary Forster, more than 7,000 Quakers lobbied against paying tithes to the Church of England, and Margaret Fell would go on to petition Charles II for the release of 700 Quakers, including the founder George Fox after he had been imprisoned.[252]

Women at Play

A celebration of sport and games for men and women was started by Robert Dover in 1632 in Chipping Campden. The collection *Annalia Dubrensia* described the Cotswold 'Olimpick Games', with women shown dancing jigs on the frontispiece to the book. A song recorded by diarist Nicholas Blundell described how the girls 'daunced till thire bones did ake … and did swett themselves into a Jelly'.[253]

In 1638, Sir Dudley Digges of Kent left money in his will for prizes for annual footraces, for bachelors and for maids, to commemorate his birthday, 19 May. The prize money of £10 was the same for each category, making it the most valuable running prize in the whole of England till the nineteenth century. There were so many entrants that there had to be qualifying races to choose the contenders to race at Old Wives Lees.

Frontispiece, *Annalia Dubrensia*, 1636, showing Robert Dover's Olimpick Games – see women competing in dancing in the top-left corner

Not all sport was sponsored and encouraged by the elite. Football was banned on more than 30 occasions between 1314 and 1667 because so many matches – rival teams chasing cross-country after a ball – ended in violence and disruption. Women played, sometimes as teams of married women against single women.[254]

The Invention of 'Women's Work'

Elizabethan regulations kept workers in their villages at low pay and enforced lower wages for women, so the guilds and even the hiring fairs tried to exclude women workers to keep up wages and favour male workers.[255] An understanding that women's work was underpaid, less skilled and without prospects took root. The idea of 'women's work' was invented to identify work so disagreeable or badly paid that men did not want it.

By the end of the 1400s young men were more and more favoured for apprenticeships.[256] Even London – the city of female opportunity – had become oversupplied with labour, and women were being squeezed out of business and property owning. Men rather than women were making, inheriting and consolidating fortunes.[257] In Bristol in 1461, and in Norwich in 1511, male weavers protested against women workers entering the trade.[258] The 1550 Ordinance of the Weavers' Company ruled that no weaver could reveal trade secrets to 'any maiden, damsel, or other woman'.[259] A study of women in the Oxford guilds shows husbands and wives entering their names as equal members until 1540. After then, the name of the wife tended to be omitted.

A London draper was refused by the guild officers to register his female apprentice in 1570, despite 'much murmuring, since many in the company suspected that the woman did indeed have the right to be enrolled'.[260]

Only 73 girls are known to have enrolled as apprentices in the first half of sixteenth-century London, and they worked, often for a woman master, in trades regarded as 'suitable' for women. From 1580 to 1640, there are no girls' names recorded as entering craft guilds in London.[261]

Exeter women were only allowed to apply to be freemen of the city if they were widows who had worked alongside their deceased husband and were continuing their trade after his death.[262] Every town admitted fewer women into the 'freedom', and male workers competed strongly with women for work in all the skilled trades and profitable work.[263] Bristol had used the convention of femme sole to enable women to enter trade in the city, and as late as the 1530s about five girls a year were being signed as apprentices and training as 'sempstresses and tailors'. Later in the century, the apprenticeship system for girls steered them into domestic work. Bristol girl apprentices were to be found in food production, while some trained as 'housewives and sempstresses' – in effect, domestic servants. Since they were said to be 'apprenticed', they could be unpaid or work only for their keep. Helen ap Richard moved to Bristol from Tintern in Gloucestershire in October 1542 and signed up for a seven-year apprenticeship – to serve in a shop and sew. Her master was a grocer, Roger Jones, and his wife was a seamstress.[264]

Apprenticeship contracts started to name housework and spinning as a 'skill' that would be 'taught', allowing employers to take on girls for seven years of unpaid work.[265] In Coventry in 1595, there were 12 female apprentices working for female spinners. William Copeland took on a female apprentice at his inn at Romford in 1594: she served as his cook.[266] Elizabeth Deacon was bound as an apprentice in Salisbury in 1612 to study 'the mystery and sciences of housewifery and flaxdressing': housework and spinning, ordinary domestic work with no training or promotion.[267]

In the 1600s, the number of girls taking up apprenticeships doubled but the girls were not getting a training that would lead to them being 'masters' of their trades; they were doing domestic chores and sewing, spinning or keeping the shop – the so-called 'apprenticeships' were hidden servitude.[268] The young women signed up for as many as seven years, working unpaid, receiving only food and lodging. Being apprenticed to a guild had been a specialist traineeship, leading to a skilled job and full membership of a guild. For boys it still was.

In the later sixteenth century, skilled women traders and even full guild members found themselves squeezed out of work by local licensing arrangements. Control and discipline of women increased and many women owning or managing ale houses came under suspicion. Ale houses were profitable; and the local authorities helped men into the ale business. In 1540, the town of Chester ruled that no woman aged between 14 and 40 years could keep an ale house or serve as a tapster, imposing the staggering fine of 40 shillings. In 1566, 16 women were prosecuted for trying to work in their traditional trade.[269] York, where almost all the brewers had been women, including some single women, changed the licensing system in 1562, specifying that licences should go only to 'honest citizens'. The city fathers found 139 honest citizens to licence – 125 of them happened to be men; only 14 women were deemed suitable for a licence.[270]

More women disappeared from the inn and brewing business in the seventeenth century as tastes changed from ale, which could be brewed on a small scale domestically from malt, to beer – which was brewed in greater amounts, in specialist brew houses from hops. Brewers of beer had to have capital or credit to set up breweries with vats, pipes, fuel, kegs and a transport and distribution system. They had to be able to buy large supplies of hops for large-scale brewing. Beer kept for longer than ale and could be transported to distant customers, or even exported overseas. Traditional ale wives could not compete with the male brewers of beer. The widow who had raked her malt in her little malt house, advertised that she had fresh-brewed ale by putting out a branch of a tree over her door and served till the keg was dry, could not enter such a capital-intensive business. The drink trade, which had been almost all-female, became capitalised, extended, mechanised – and passed into the hands of men to make their fortunes.

From 1600, women hucksters had to have licences to sell their wares in the streets and markets, and these became more and more difficult for a single woman to obtain, and would be withdrawn if there were any complaints against her.[271] When times were hard, poor men applied for huckster licences and moved into the work. Even a woman working with her husband as a pedlar could come under scrutiny. Isabel Wyld was arrested with her husband Thomas under the Vagrancy Laws in 1582, although she was a pedlar, covering 260 miles in a fortnight, over 18 miles per day, through six counties, selling the goods she carried in her pack.[272]

The fortunes of upper-class women declined as well. By the 1600s, only a few wealthy women were able to enter the new booming money market. Lending developed into formal mortgages, secured against land, so women found themselves unable to compete with men, as they could not hold the title deeds or pursue defaulters in the courts unless they were registered as a femme sole. Women were almost entirely excluded from the growing credit economy and could not borrow capital to set up businesses in the expanding manufacturing industries, nor international trade.[273] They continued as moneylenders and credit agents only at a small level, between trusted partners. A woman's 'credit' rested on her reputation and her good name, personal attributes, not on the quantity of her business.

Shops and shopping became 'women's work'. In the early Elizabethan years, women owned shops, inherited them or entered into partnership with their husbands to buy or rent them.[274] Women shopworkers were preferred to serve customers in the fashionable retail shops such as those in the Royal Exchange in London. But after an early flourish of elegance, the Exchange became a magnet for assignations and prostitution; and male customers joked that female shopkeepers were themselves for sale.[275] In other later shopping 'exchanges', women retailers bought or rented nearly half the shop spaces in their own names. The majority of shop-workers were poorly paid women.

Buying goods in the towns and in London had been the work of gentlemen – who visited urban areas for business and networking more frequently than the wives they left at home. Two generations of women from the Thynne family, running Caus Castle and Longleat while their husbands were in London, sent detailed lists. Joan Thynne wrote to her husband John on 15 November 1600:

> Good Mr Thynne, since the writing of my letter unto you I have called to remembrance that the barrel of salad oil last bought is all spent. Wherefore I pray you may it please you to, in respect you are there, to make a choice yourself to buy a jar of oil of like quantity as the last which was bought. Also, if it so please you, to buy a keg of sturgeon which will be very serviceable for your table and will be kept until you pleased to have the same spent, both which are very necessary … I heartily thank you for the wires you sent me and do request you to speak to mistress Lincoln to make for each of your children to her wires and two robes.[276]

The increasing wealth of gentry households meant more money for the consumption of luxuries and more leisure time. Upper-class women started to visit London and the growing towns to make their own luxury purchases, and merchants and traders designed new shops to attract them with 'Ladies Markets'.[277] In 1609, the New Exchange opened for elite women shoppers, targeting lady customers with luxury items.[278] Attractive shops and window displays turned retail shopping into a new leisure activity for wealthy women served by poor women.[279]

As soon as shopping was identified as 'women's work', it was criticised by male commentators who associated it with extravagance, vanity and time wasting. Commentators complained that women were going out of their homes into the streets for their shopping, unprotected, unsupervised and undisciplined and 'wasting' money. The concerns about women being at liberty to shop, tapped into traditional fears about female vanity, female sexuality, female profligacy and Eve's weakness to temptation. The high fashion excesses repelled Puritan thinkers. There were class anxieties too: commentators worried that the middling-class women were dressing above their working-class roots, breaking the sumptuary laws that were supposed to limit them to dark colours and serviceable fabrics.

Even the all-women rituals around childbirth, absolutely exclusive to women, became regulated, under the growing concern that women might be vain or extravagant, and should be not allowed to do their work as they wanted. The byelaws of Chester were amended to control the hidden traditions and rituals of childbed and churching. The male lawgivers claimed that 'gret excesse and superfluose costes and charges' should not be undertaken by the poorer people, who were getting into debt by copying their betters. Only the mother, sisters and sisters-in-law, and a midwife might attend the labouring mother in the town, and they were not allowed to overdress for the occasion.[280]

In the 100 years from 1550 to 1650 casual work – preferred by working wives – had been better paid than work agreed by the year or half-year.[281] Women's casual, seasonal and temporary rates of pay were equal to those of men.[282] But from about 1650 the cash pay for full-time workers living 'out' increased, compared with those who took some of their wages as bed and board (like women servants) or those who were paid by the day (often women again). Even if the wage rate was the same, the workers paid in cash who benefited from free bed and board at home became better off. Wage-setting by rings of employers held all wages down. Slowly, after years of legally enforced inequality, it was thought that women's wages were somehow 'naturally' less than men's wages – even less than half the man's wage.[283] In fifteenth-century Norwich, where a subsistence wage was 8d to 1s a week, a master weaver could earn 3s a week, while the average unskilled female worker could barely survive on her wage of 8d a week.[284]

A pay gap between men and women in both casual and contracted regular work opened up. Male workers were paid an average wage of 10d a day, while women received less than half that – only 4d for a woman in regular work and 3d (the old rate for both men and women) for casual labour.[285] In the late 1600s, Norfolk sheep shearers were paid 6d a day if they were women but between 7d and 14d if they were men.[286]

By 1620, most women worked inside the family business – for their father or husband-employer, unable to seek work from the competition, forced to accept the rate of pay that he could afford from his own wage or profit, or went unpaid.[287] It benefited the family business if a wife took as small a wage as possible, produced as much food and goods as she could at home, and took no pay for raising the children and maintaining the home. The 'double shift' was her gift to the business and family.

The so-called 'golden age for women' was certainly over by the 1600s. Increasingly bound to their houses, women workers could not organise with others, or exchange information about the market or opportunities. They could not leave to find better wage rates, nor travel and take up better work. 'Women's work' was paid at about half the male rate and in many places the differential was enforced by law. 'Women's work' was work that men did not want to do, fitted around the 'women's work' of producing for the family and maintaining a home unpaid. There is no promotion in 'women's work', no career structure, no retirement age and no pension. Actually, there is no end – only death released a working woman from her work.

Protest

In the sixteenth century, the ownership of land became increasingly defined and contested. Industry, building and shipping all needed wood and fuel from the forests and ore from mines. Moorlands and waste lands which had been left empty and used by the nearby villages became valuable. The monarchs – trying to 'live off their own' – exploited the massive royal landholdings, selling them off, renting them or exploiting them.

The destruction of the religious houses at the Reformation released land to new landlords who had no tradition of benevolent local lordship. As the 1500s progressed, they demanded more grazing land for sheep for the all-important wool trade – soon there were twice as many sheep as people. They enclosed the shared fields and common woodlands to bring more land into sheep farming. They ploughed up the communal arable strips and enclosed woodlands and moorlands for hunting. Up and down the country, landowners closed whole villages, driving the tenants away. In some counties, one in six villages were destroyed by their landlords from the mid-1400s to the mid-1500s.[288]

This did not take place without struggle, rarely recorded by the published writers of the landlords' class. They concealed the landowners' actions and glossed over the protests, calling the food rioters a mindless mob and the breaking of new fences criminal trespass. As lawmakers and the enforcers, landlords ruled in their own favour against their tenants and workers. It is not surprising that the very few accounts describe ignorant peasants fighting inevitable change, stupidly at war with their own 'true' interests.[289]

Women were at the forefront defending their gathering, gleaning, hunting and fishing rights on common and waste land and in the forests. Thorpe Moor in Yorkshire was kept free from enclosures by the 'wyves of Kirkby Malzeard' who took on their landlord, the Earl of Derby in 1549. Less than fifty years later, the new earl was also defeated by his tenants and then a new landlord, Sir Stephen Proctor, bought into the valley of Nidderdale in Yorkshire and attempted to enclose Thorpe Moor. He faced rebellions in 1597, 1600 and 1601, and assassination attempts – one by a local sorcerer hired by his gentry neighbours.[290] His neighbours contrasted his Protestant, profit-seeking style with their own tradition of 'good lordship' – violent and personal control of their tenants. Lady Jolyan Yorke, his neighbour, said 'Sr Steven had undone all th[e] country.'

Poor people and dependant tenants and workers were recruited on both sides. Poor cottagers who had built little shacks for homes on Thorpe Moor were attacked: one woman said she and her children were beaten and pushed out of their home in a night-time attack; another poor pregnant woman nearly died from a premature birth after an attack by a crowd of masked men, intent on protecting the Moor from incomers. Villagers and tenants drew on folk memories and on a deep knowledge of the law to preserve the common land against incursions by Proctor or his workers. They appealed to him directly – the women of Kirkby Malzeard 'made humble suite' for their commons to Proctor, 'the most p[ar]te of them kneelinge upon their knee', and a yeoman's wife, Dorothy Dawson, acclaimed as Captain Dorothy, assisted by Alice Bayne led a band of 37 women into a pitched battle against hired miners in 1604. Seventeen women were prosecuted.[291] A woman marching with them told the Star Chamber – the highest court on landowning – that the women had broken down fences to maintain 'their rights of common'.[292] The commoners of Kirkbyshire agreed to give up a third of the common land if the Countess of Derby would buy out the hated Proctor. When she did, the tenants reneged on their agreement and refused to give up their common. On May Day 1615, the Kirkbyshire tenants and commoners joined together with a secret password, broke down fences and said they would be ruled by 'club law' – the agreement of the community.[293]

James I and then his son Charles I were driven to exploit the royal forests by their need for money. To avoid going to Parliament for taxes, they sold land and tenancies in the royal forests and expanded the forest boundaries. Local people were banned from thousands of acres: at first 3,000 acres in the Forest of Dean and then 22,000 acres in 1639, 4,000 acres in Braydon Forest, 460 acres in Feckenham Forest, 1,589 acres in Leicester and a third of Malvern Chase – about 3,000 acres.[294] The people who survived by gathering harvesting and gleaning in the forests rose up against the new enclosing landlords in a series of actions named the 'Western Rising'. The first riots took place in Gillingham Forest, Dorset, in 1626 led by 14 men and 12 women who were arrested and fined. It was not a question of finance for them but a sense of belonging. They told the sheriff: 'Here were we born and here we will die.'[295]

Two years later, royal soldiers joined the people in destroying some of the new enclosures, killing deer and burning crops. Arrested rioters were rescued by the crowd, royal messengers were assaulted and the crowd defeated the sheriff of Dorset with an arrest warrant for 100 so-called rioters.

In the Forest of Dean in March 1631, the anti-enclosure rioters came in force. Five hundred people – led by men dressed as women[296] – with drummers and a fife and flags were said to have assembled 'armed with gunnes, pokes, halberds and other weapons' to break fences and in-fill mining pits. A shot was fired at one land agent and an effigy of another was buried in his own ore pits. The next month even more people turned out: 3,000 marched with banners and drums and tore down the fences and attacked houses. Action continued over the next two years, people taking down fences as soon as they were repaired. In April 1631, 3,000 rioters with banners and drums removed most of the remaining enclosures in the forest. By the end of the month, all of the earlier enclosures had been removed. Over the next two years, the rioters attempted to destroy enclosures as they were put back in place.

One thousand rioters, wearing women's clothing, assembled at Braydon over the summer of 1631 to break down fences and threaten the landlord. A servant who reported the rioters to the authorities had his home vandalised, and the sheriff and a court official representing the king were driven away with shots being fired.

The riots at Feckenham were not named as part of the Western Rising, but they followed the same pattern: people threw down the new fences in March 1631 after their appeal for foresters' rights failed in court. The next year, 300 people rioting against enclosure had a pitched battle with forty armed men, the sheriff, a deputy lieutenant and a justice of the peace, who recorded that the foresters 'in a most daring and presumptuous manner presented themselves unto us with warlike weapons (vizt) pikes, forrest bills, pitchforks, swords and the like'.

In Leicester, the local authorities supported the people in the anti-enclosure riots of 1627 and 1628. The Corporation of Leicester and residents appealed to the Privy Council against a new, enclosing landlord. The landlord was supported by the Privy Council and the House of Lords; but arrests and prosecutions of the rioters were quietly dropped.

Both the Forest of Dean and the Braydon/Chippenham riots were mustered by a call from 'Lady Skimmington' – an alias for several leaders, and invoking a woman's leadership of a riot. Only a very few of the male rioters dressed as women – perhaps no more than seven – and they may have done this as a disguise and to invoke the traditional play of the skimmington ride – a community reproof. When the leaders were arrested, women's clothing was used as a mark of shame: the male leaders of the Braydon Forest riots were set in the pillory – the public stocks – dressed in women's clothes.

Many of the rioters were women defending what was seen as a particular women's cause: their way of life on the land. Certainly, a woman's productivity could only feed her family and support the economy if she had access to common lands. Common lands were sometimes described as the farmer's spouse – his supporter and helper, and hedges were derided as girdles, as if the encloser was trying to tie a girdle around a fertile woman and keep her for himself. Many women hoped they would have immunity from arrest because of their inferior legal status. The Star Chamber confirmed in 1605 that husbands were responsible for the actions of their wives: 'If a woman offend in trespass, riot or otherwise and an action is brought against her and her husband, the husband is answerable, notwithstanding the action was without his privity.'[297]

Women were more than supporters in food riots – they were almost always the leaders. Far from being mindless outbreaks, the riots were choreographed events, in which ordinary women insisted that food be sold at the usual price in the market so that they could feed their families. Sometimes they captured wagons taking food away from the market; they broke into grain stores and weighed out the grain themselves, often paying what they thought was a fair price; they challenged the town millers or bakers for underweight measures. Typically, there would be plenty of threat but little or no physical violence, as the profiteers bowed to the numbers of furious women, reduced prices or gave up exporting food and sold it locally. Ideally, the riot would be ended by a local authority, usually the justice of the peace, coming into the marketplace, weighing the food and agreeing a fair price – endorsing the women's action.

In 1629, a slump in the cloth industry led to hardship across England. Corn merchants bought up grain stocks of wheat and rye in the local markets to ship to towns, and even abroad. Local magistrates in Maldon, Essex, reported that rioters were trying to hire muskets and had threatened to 'kill farmors, or anye other factors yt wear imployed to buye or sell any Corne'.[298]

Poor women labourers and wives of labourers or craftsmen marched with their children to the quayside, where several grain ships were being loaded. They boarded the ships and filled their bonnets and aprons with rye to take away to mill into flour for bread.[299] Just like the women rioting against enclosure, the women believed they were not under the law. They said: 'Women were lawless and not subject to the lawes of the realme as men are but might ... offend without drede or punishment of the law.'[300]

They were right – seventeenth-century advice for magistrates read: 'If a number of women (or children under the age of discretion) do flocke together for their own cause, this is none assembly punishable by these statutes, unlesse a man of discretion moved them to assemble for the doing of some unlawful act,' meaning that a crowd of women assembling spontaneously is not a crime.[301] It is only a crime if they are led by a man of importance. An all-woman uprising cannot be prosecuted.

One of the rioting women was Ann Carter, who had been the wife of a prosperous butcher, mistress of her own house, employing two servants only the previous year. Her husband lost his business and the family home, and Ann was thrown into poverty. Another was Elizabeth Sturgeon, a labourer's wife who said she was 'in pouertie and wanting victuall for her children'.[302]

Ann Spearman, a day labourer, said she went to steal rye from the ships 'because she cold not have Corne in the m[ar]kett and [because] certaine fflemishe shipps ... [lay] at Burrow Hills ... there to receiue in Corne to carry beyond sea'. Margaret Williams told magistrates that she went to the ships 'amongst others of her owne accord ... Corne being deare and ... being carried awaie ... and she being a poore woeman'. One woman was asked who had incited her to riot and she answered, 'The Crie of the Country and hir owne want.'[303]

Only a few of the rioters were arrested and they were not accused or convicted of any crime but were 'bound over' to keep the peace. Ann Carter denied leading the riot, and she too was bound over. The local magistrates searched the grain ships for other food that was needed locally, such as bacon, cheese or butter. The leading townsmen – bailiffs, aldermen and head burgesses – agreed to buy the corn at their own expense and sell it at an agreed price, to the poor: 'the Corne [p]rovided by Mr Jacobs the marchant now lyeing within the Burrow shall be bought at Convenient price if yt maybe had for our poore and so to make stay of yt from transportinge'.

The riot was a completely successful performance by both common people and the elite who recognised their appeal. The initial threat of violence was followed by non-violent direct action by women. The magistrates supported their action and the townsmen set a fair price for the food. They even won a national concession: the Privy Council announced that grain should not be taken from any hungry areas and sold elsewhere. It must be offered first in the local market.

But only three months later, there were more ships loading grain at Maldon. This time Ann Carter openly led the rioters, and as merchants continued to ship corn out of hungry areas she travelled around the clothing townships, to drum up support, and sent out letters, which she signed as 'Captain':[304] 'Come, my brave lads of Maldon, I will be your leader for we will not starve.'[305]

As many as 300 men and women, unemployed cloth workers, marched with Ann Carter, boarded a ship, assaulted the crew, stole the cargo and forced the vessel to sail away empty. Another group of rioters broke open a warehouse and carried off more grain. They assaulted the leading merchant, Mr Gamble, and made him give them £20. He called the magistrates and the crowd melted away as the JPs arrived.

The Privy Council set up a special court to try the rioters for a crime that they described as 'being of so high a nature and of so dangerous consequence that it amounteth to little less than a rebellion'.[306]

Ann Carter, the shop owner who had fallen into poverty, who had called herself 'Captain', was hanged. So were four rioters charged with taking away 15 quarters of rye grain; but the riot that Carter had summoned forced regulation of the market. Essex magistrates imported and sold grain to the poor at less than the market price, and special care was taken to see that Maldon and the clothing towns were well supplied.[307]

Women took to the streets for many causes – almost always defending their traditional rights. Women rioted against Fenland drainage schemes, which changed the way of life in the marsh areas: there were rioting women at the Isle of Axholme in the late 1620s and 1630s, and they rioted there again at the end of the century. On one occasion they were led by a gentlewoman, Catherine Popplewell, who recruited a crowd of men, women and children at Belton to destroy fences and crops on the newly drained fields.[308]

As Charles I attempted to raise funds with new and illegal taxes, women were in the forefront of resistance. In Litchborough, Northamptonshire, in 1637, tax collectors came for 'ship money' – a tax traditionally levied only on port and coastal towns. Male householders melted away as the women barricaded themselves into their houses refusing to pay, and were supported by a crowd of women and children who drove the collectors away. Sarah Walter, a yeoman's wife in Newcastle, refused to pay hearth tax in 1663 and said she would raise an army against anyone who demanded it of her.[309]

Through the 1600s, women continued to participate and sometimes lead so-called 'riots' in defence of traditional rights, and they policed prices and practices of local markets, especially food markets. Southampton women boarded a grain ship before it could sail for London and demanded the stores that it carried in 1608; Dorchester women rioted in 1630 and the following year over food supplies. A Newcastle woman hoped that she would see Charles I 'hanged at a horse tail and the dogs run through his puddings'.[310]

A radical London woman supported the execution of the king and predicted that the restoration of his son in 1660 would last no more than a year.[311]

Wives defended their husbands. In Newcastle, in 1653, the 'mighty clamour' of 50 wives forced Bartholomew Yates to discharge the newly recruited crew from his ship. He had probably press-ganged them into a long dangerous contract to serve the Navy, but the women rescued them. Women joined with male rioters in the London weavers' riots of 1675, when women called for the new engine looms to be broken.[312]

Almost 2,000 wives of enslaved seamen, held by the Turks in Salé, Morocco, demanded that the Lord Admiral, the Duke of Buckingham, help their husbands. They complained that an earlier petition to the king had been ignored. Here, as in other protests, women seem to have felt that direct action was allowable as a last resort if the rulers and landowners had failed to respond to earlier milder protest. When Charles I visited York in May 1642, 100 women complained to him about local issues; when he arrived in Leicester in July, he faced a deputation of ladies complaining about the sheriff. Women also invoked the traditional image of a queen's mercy when in 1634 they appealed to the queen, Henrietta Maria, for the release of husbands who had been arrested after a protest about wages and conditions in the lead mines of Derbyshire.[313]

Women defended local churches, especially during times of religious change. In 1538, Exeter women armed with staves and pikes broke into St Nicholas Priory to stop workmen demolishing the rood loft – the gallery that runs along a rood screen, dividing the body of the church from the altar, typical of Roman Catholic churches. The commissioners for Henry VIII's dissolution of the monasteries had ordered the rood screen to be taken down, so that parishioners could see the altar, but the women were having none of it. They chased the workmen up the tower, where they had to jump out to escape. An alderman, sent to explain the changes to the women, was assaulted and ran away, and finally the women barricaded themselves into the church for a short siege.[314]

Bishop Grindal was twice lobbied by 60 London women churchgoers demanding the return of a Puritan lecturer in 1566. During the northern rebellion in favour of Roman Catholicism in 1569, a churchwarden's daughter, Barbara Collyng, organised the women of Long Newton, County Durham, to reinstate the old stone altar in the eastern end of the parish church, restoring it as a Roman Catholic place of worship.[315]

Another gentlewoman, Mary Villars, and nine parishioners in Oadby, Leicester, called for the removal of their 'drunken and idle' minister in 1581; Margaret Frith signed a petition in January 1641 to complain of the gross negligence of the minister at St Mary Cray, Kent. In August 1577, the chapel at Brentwood in Essex was defended from closure by 30 women armed with agricultural and kitchen implements – and a kettle filled with boiling water. They were led by a woman: Thomasina Tyler. When the sheriff arrived to make arrests, half of them escaped and the remainder were released because no one was certain if they could be made to answer for themselves.[316]

Some demonstrations sent clear signals that women were hoping not to be held criminally accountable for the action. In 1642, women in Yorkshire organised a protest to look like a traditional feast day, bringing a bagpiper and cakes and ale to their demonstration, probably in the hope of getting a sympathetic hearing from traditional-minded magistrates. Some public actions were genuinely more of a feast-day event than a riot of protest – like a 'rag', a playful show which might have a serious point. Some demonstrations were quiet and peaceful: Leicester council was urged to allow a turner the freedom of the town by ten women stockingmakers who took it upon themselves to tell the city fathers in 1658 that the town needed a good turner.[316]

Women also came together to maintain standards in their own community. Three women in Kent beat up a husband who was abusing his wife in 1612.[317] But it was transgressive women who bore the brunt of most community punishments, like 'rough music' when neighbours clattered pots and pans and played instruments, or the skimmington ride – an elaborate pantomime of disapproval, with players seated on a horse sometimes costumed, sometimes wearing cuckold horns.[318] Agnes Mills, wife of a cutler, complained to the authorities that three or four hundred men came armed, and banging drums, beat her, threw her into a wet hole and planned to duck her on a ducking stool in Calne, Wiltshire, in 1618. She was probably believed to be violent, adulterous or a scold: most demonstrations against women were directed at those who challenged male authority. Community punishments against rebellious individual women were intended as a warning to all women. One of the men at a 'riding' in Suffolk in 1604 said that the pantomime was not only that 'the woman which had offended might be shamed for her misdemeanour towards her husband [in beating him] but other women also by her shame might be admonished [not] to offend in like sort'.[319]

Community actions against women maintained standards and were supported by women community leaders against women transgressors. In Maidwell in Northamptonshire, in 1672, Lady Haslewood – the wife of the squire – called for a 'riding' against a woman who beat Anthony Cable, her drunken husband, a smallholder in the parish. Lady Haslewood's husband, Sir William, banned the riding as Anthony was a favourite of his.[320]

Women's complaints against 'scolding' women equalled the number of complaints to the courts made by men. In the panic after the civil wars, it was local women who were prominent accusers and witnesses, maintaining the reputation of the community and enforcing conventions about 'good' female behaviour.[321]

But in Bristol in 1667, an elite man, William Bullocke, said to be a 'gentleman wife-beater', had to hire a constable to protect him from the fury of the people, led by women. In 1616, five London women demonstrated before the magistrates to complain of a sailor who beat his pregnant wife until she miscarried. A Holborn parish official who tried to ship a pregnant woman to another parish while she was in labour was prosecuted by eight women when the baby died.[322]

Women defended women against injustice in their community: 25 women bore witness in support of Goodwife Taylor of Saffron Walden when she was accused of failing to attend communion in 1631. Women used coded behaviour to discipline the community – a village wedding at Ratcliffe in Leicestershire in 1610 was interrupted by young spinsters dancing with a willow garland 'In a very profane manner'.[323]

Some women staunchly refused to recognise the authority of the civil powers. A Stratford woman accused of brawling by the Elizabethan court shouted at the magistrates: 'God's wounds! A Plague of God on you all, a fart of one's arse for you!'[324]

Women continued to use the loopholes in the law which only referred to men to escape punishment: Margaret Ridhall's husband told the London church in 1588 that he held himself to blame and he 'submitteth himself to take double punishment if he failed to prevent her committing such an offence in future'. In the highest court in the land, the Star Chamber, in 1603, an argumentative female plaintiff was named as 'clamorous' and was whipped, and her husband was fined £20 for failing to govern her properly.[325]

In the increasing radicalism of the seventeenth century, women began to expand their repertoire of protest from wordless direct action to written petition, from food riots to political protest. The 1600s would be called 'the century of riotous Englishwomen'.[326]

During the civil wars, women led women marchers in protests calling for peace and, after the Parliamentary victory, women protested against the Cromwell government and called for the restoration of the monarchy. As poor and working women formed the political leadership of their communities through the chaos of the war years, women's involvement in political life reached a 'high tide' that would not return for centuries.[327]

Petitions

Petitions to Parliament offered a well-established route for men to raise grievances, but in 1642, for the first time, women wrote and published as a collective, composing a written claim and signing their names to it. Three big petitions said to be written by women appeared around this time, demanding help for trade, protection from Roman Catholics, religious reform and peace.[328] Two of the appeals were copied from previous male petitions, and may even have been written by men, but one – presented by Mrs Anne Stagg, wife of Giles Stagg, a poor member of the Brewers' Guild, almost certainly a brewer herself – was probably written by women for women. Claiming to be by 'Gentlewomen and Tradesman's Wives In and About the City of London', Anne Stagg's petition in February 1642 demanded the expulsion of the bishops and Roman Catholic peers from the House of Lords, that the Roman Catholic mass be banned and that the army support Protestants, believed to be in danger from Roman Catholic rebels in Ireland: 'The thought of which sad and barbarous events maketh our tender hearts to melt within us'.[329]

The citing of feelings, and the dramatic expression of fear of violence from Roman Catholics, are unique to this petition and suggest that it was composed by a female author. The tone is deferential: 'We doe (this) not out of any selfe-conceit or pride of heart, as seeking to equall ourselves with Men either in Authority or wisdom. But according to our places to discharge that duty we owe to God, and the cause of the Church, as farre as lyeth in us, following herein in the example of the Men, which have gone in this duty before us.'[330]

Mrs Stagg and her women colleagues were met at the door of the Houses of Parliament by John Pym, the Parliamentary leader. They were not invited in. He told them: 'Repair to your Houses and turne your Petition which you have delivered here into Prayers at home for us; for we have bin are and shall be (to our utmost power) ready to relieve you, your Husbands and Children, and to perform the trust committed onto us.'[331]

Anne Stagg, a deferential woman petitioner, was thanked and sent home, and told to pray at home while the government helped her and her fellow signatories.

In August 1643, another group of several hundred women were met outside Parliament as they called for peace in the English civil wars. The next day they returned in their thousands, demanding to see John Pym and present their plea, 'The Petition of Many Civilly Disposed Women'. One newspaper account estimated they numbered 5,000–6,000 poor women, wearing white ribbons in their bonnets for peace. One report claimed they were 'whores, bawds, oyster-women, kitchen-stuff women, beggar women and the very scum of the suburbs, besides a number of Irish women'.[332]

It is more likely that these were working women experiencing hardship because of the disruption of trade during the civil wars and the absence of their husbands away at war. They brought the traditional choreography of women's protest to Parliament and blockaded the entrance. The MPs did not respond as traditional community leaders would – hearing the protest and making changes. Instead, Sir William Waller's horse regiment was called out to clear the streets and, according to one witness, Thomas Knyvet, 'There was much mischief done by the horse and foot soldiers.'[333]

The women rioters stoned the troops and shots were fired – one of the women was armed with a rusty old sword. Reports called her a 'virago'. A young woman and two men were killed and many of the rioters were injured. A newspaper report said, 'Tumults are dangerous, swords in the hands of women do desperate things.'[334]

Later women petitioners also demanded that they be heard and specifically refused to stay at home. In 1649, Elizabeth Lilburne, wife of John Lilburne, the radical leader, took over his 'Leveller' campaign when he was arrested and imprisoned. She and other Leveller women demanded the release of their husbands using mass petitions, pressure groups and demonstrations.[335] She presented a famously 'acerbic' women Leveller petition:[336] 'And are we Christians and yet must we sit still and keep at home? … and shall we shew no sense of our sufferings? … Let it be accounted folly, presumption, madness or whatever in us, whilst we have life and breath we will never leave them.'[337]

These women were not met at the door of the house with agreement. The Sergeant at Arms incautiously told them, 'The House gave an answer to your husbands and therefore that you are desired to goe home, and looke after your owne businesse, and meddle with your huswifery.'[338]

The women did not go home, but held another demonstration the very next week and continued to petition Parliament. In 1653, another Leveller woman, Katherine Chidley, led a group of women to Parliament with a 6,000-name petition attacking the luxurious lifestyle of the members and claiming the right to be heard – she said that since God heard women, Parliament could do no less.

A small private petition from one woman and her son, Johanna and Ebenezer Cartwright, lobbied the government for a return of the Jews to England. This was a welcome suggestion to Oliver Cromwell, who wanted the financial stimulus and international contacts of successful Jewish citizens. In 1655, Parliament agreed that no actual law forbade readmission, paving the way for Jews to return to England.[339]

One appeal from Royalist women would not even address the victorious Parliament, but was published instead of petitioning. In 1660, they wrote a public 'declaration' of women against their government: 'The Royale Virgin; Or, The Declaration of Several Maydens in and about the once Honourable City of London'.[340]

This publication, like other petitions by women, with the exception of Anne Stagg's, was met with exaggerated denial, refusal and even outrage. Claims that women wanted a 'parliament of women' were rolled out by opponents to any female contribution after 1647.[341] But this was a male fantasy. No women petitioners called for the right to sit in Parliament, or even to vote. Women only wanted to state their case to the House; they did not demand to stay as legislators. They were there to make a point about specific issues – they did not claim a right to represent their communities as spokeswomen or members.

Despite the king's trial and execution in January 1649, there was no suggestion that now that men had been freed from the rule of a male monarch, women also were free. Apparently, the overthrowing of the king was not the overthrow of male power. Philosophical debate made it clear that although the figurehead of the king had gone, all the other instruments of male rule – law, religion, marriage and misogynistic traditions – remained. Oliver Cromwell led a rebellion against kingly tyranny, not against domestic tyrannising over wives and children, and certainly not against legal oppression of women. Most Parliamentarians would have thought that Queen Henrietta Maria had not been oppressed nearly enough.

The huge disruption of a long civil war against the Stuarts and then a Puritan government created a climate of uncertainty and anxiety, not radicalism – and certainly not feminism. There was no sense of unity for women across the classes, there was no sisterhood. Literate women asked only for greater respect – not for rights. They redefined the role of Eve in the Creation story, they searched the Bible for examples of 'good' women; but they went no further. They tried to improve the image of women but no one called for increased opportunities for women, education for women, votes, or for equality before the law. But even so, there was a panic about the rise of women and a belief in their determination to overturn the rule of men.[342] The men who had taken power from the king became more anxious and defensive about keeping it from women.

It was a 'world turn'd upside down' in the powerful old phrase – but not turned upside down for women.[343] Gerrard Winstanley, who wrote poetically and urgently about transforming the countryside so that every man might have his own plot of land, did not raise the rights of women landholders; he barely mentioned the backbone of the agricultural work-force – women.

The small extreme religious sects remained the only places where women were seen as equal with men before God. Only they argued in favour of more freedoms for women or granted women rights within their groups. None of the major radical groups of the 1650s argued for the equality of women, and women writers limited their claims to moral equality, not equality before the law or in politics.[344] As a 1632 pamphlet on 'Women's Rights' explained: 'All of them are understood either married or to be married and their desires are subject to their husband.'[345]

Marriage

Early marriage arranged by parents was still common for upper-class women. Heiresses, especially, were placed into their future husband's families while they were still children. Margaret Plumpton was sent away from her home to live with her future husband's family when she was four years old in 1464.[346] Katherine Willoughby's guardian, Charles Brandon, 35 years her senior, ordered her marriage at the age of 14 – to himself. She wrote: 'I cannot tell what more unkindness one of us might work more wickedly, than to bring our children into so miserable a state, not to choose by their own liking, such as they must profess so strait a bond and so great a love to forever.'[347]

Consent of the bride was meaningless when she was a little girl under the command of her parents. Mary Boyle's father Richard, the Earl of Cork, married all his daughters to his financial advantage before they were old enough to refuse. But Mary (1625–78) defied her father when she was only 14: 'I still continued to have an aversion to maridge, liveing so much at my ease that I was unwilling to Change my Condition, and neaver could bring my selfe to close with any ofred match but still begd my Father to reafuse all the most advantageous profer, though I was by him much prest to settell my selfe.'[348] She went on to marry for love and became Mary Rich, Countess of Warwick.

Mary Rich was an exception. Most young brides could not refuse; it was the task of the minister to observe that the child-bride consented, as her father handed her to her husband. That was enough.

Some young couples chose each other and married, even against their parents' wishes. Sixteen-year-old Maria Audley met Thomas Thynne at a family party under the supervision of her mother Lucy, Lady Audley, and they were married the same evening, and were put to bed together, fully clothed, so that the marriage should be considered as consummated. It was a year before Thomas's parents, Joan and John Thynne, found out that their son was married and they tried to declare the union invalid, even taking the case to court.[349] The story of the wedding and the feud may have been the inspiration for *Romeo and Juliet*.

Some pregnant lower-class brides were induced to marry to provide a father to their child; some may have seen the church wedding as the confirmation of a marriage already agreed, under folk traditions: 25 per cent of Tudor brides were pregnant on their wedding day.[350] In Norwich in the 1600s, fathers 'sold' the bride in a traditional 'wife sale' to an agreed bridegroom.[351]

The law was unclear as to how violent a husband might be when disciplining, punishing or abusing his wife. Hate-filled advice books recommended violence: a 1671 pamphlet recommended that a husband should 'Teach her manners with a crabtree cudgel'.[352] A popular saying of 1591 'Women and Hens are Lost by Gadding' changed in thirty years to be:

The honest Maid (is) better at home with a bone broken, than
   a-gadding,
The woman and the Hen are lost with straggling.[353]

A sixteenth-century London bye-law ruled that men might not beat their
wives after 9 p.m. to avoid disturbing the neighbours.[354] The execution
of the king in 1649 made all male heads of households more nervous:
rhetoric against rebellious women – despite their small numbers –
increased, and advice books focused on containment and control of
women.

The emerging middling classes did not – in theory – approve of physical violence, especially in marriage, and 'conduct books' that offered tips
on how to lead a respectable life advised against it.[355] But the restraint did
not filter up to the aristocracy, nor down to the labouring people, and
when violent men were brought to a court, juries took a tolerant view.[356]
It was generally agreed that husbands should stop short of murder: no
marital beating should cause injuries so serious that the wife died; but
those few husbands who were charged with wife murder could easily turn
such a charge into a confession of an accidental death after 'reasonable'
violence. Juries were reluctant to bring a guilty verdict in for a wife
murderer when the punishment was hanging and disembowelling. The
all-male juries preferred to find men guilty of accidentally killing their
wives. Men were the principal domestic murderers: an average of
three-quarters of marital killings were husbands killing their wives.[357]

The crime of a woman killing her husband, though rarer, was seen as
far more serious, since she was attacking the head of the family: the
God-appointed master.[358] Husband-killing was called 'petty treason', as
the murder of a king was high treason. The punishment was death by
being burned alive but this happened rarely until the 1400s, when
Parliament introduced burning alive as a standard punishment for heretics.[359] Margery Mills was burned to death for poisoning her husband at
Charlwood in Surrey in September 1599.[360]

Some women may have reacted to the increasing oppression by men.
One woman, wife of a Yorkshire yeoman, refused to give him access to
the property she brought to the marriage, which was his – by law and
custom. On 1 January 1648, he recorded in his journal: 'This morn, I
used some words of persuasion to my wife to forbear to tell me of what
is past, and promised her to become a good husband to her for the time

to come, and she promised me likewise she would do what I wished her in anything, save in setting her hand to papers; and I promised her never to wish her there unto.'[361]

Before the Reformation, there was no divorce – only annulment of marriage on very limited grounds by the pope himself. Once Henry VIII had granted his own divorces, his subjects could apply at great cost for a specific Act of Parliament to end their marriage on very limited grounds. Adultery by a wife could be cited as grounds for a divorce, but a husband's adultery was legally allowed. A study of the wills of aristocratic men of 1450–1550 showed that of 763 noblemen, 51 left bequests to mistresses or illegitimate children. If the wives did not know about these infidelities before, they knew on their husbands' death, when the widow – as executor in most cases – had to pay an inheritance to mistresses and bastards.[362] It must have taken the edge off deep grief.

Most marriages were ended more simply by separation or desertion, and many of the households headed by single women were caused by husbands running away. A husband deserting a wealthy wife could take their children and all her family money. A separating wife had to leave her children in her husband's care; she could not remarry and had no right to any payment from the family fortune.[363] Lower-class marriages could still be ended by agreement in folk rituals such as 'wife sale', often to her lover, to signify the end of their union and the start of a new one.

A new Adultery Act was passed in 1650, under the moralistic Cromwell Parliament. The short-lived law 'for suppressing the detestable sins of Incest, Adultery and Fornication' punished acts of incest and adultery, but only by wives and their lovers, male seducers and 'bawds' – as well as women soliciting for sex and sexually active women. Three women were hanged for adultery before the act was repealed on the return of the notoriously promiscuous Charles II.

Parliament made another change to the wording of the marriage service. The promise of sexual willingness and warmth by a wife was now omitted. The public endorsement of sexual arousal of a wife with her husband disappeared. So too went the promise of female happiness: 'Bonoure and buxom in bed and at borde'. The new *Directory for the Public Worship of God* of 1645 ruled for very short and simple marriage vows in church. Now the husband had to promise 'to be a loving and faithful Husband unto thee until God shall separate us by Death'. And the bride promised the same love and fidelity – but also obedience: 'To be a loving faithful and obedient Wife unto thee until God shall separate us by Death'.[364]

These promises were fulfilled in some marriages. Journals kept by literate women (only upper-class women, and not many of them) showed that of 21 marriages, happy marriages outnumbered unhappy ones by 15 to 6.[365] Tombstones, memorials, poems and letters for husbands and wives refer to companionable and loving marriages till death. Lady Anne Harcourt makes it clear what a lucky find a good husband was for a seventeenth-century wife: 'I had much mercy in my marriage with him, he being th' answer to my prayer, he being a religious, prudent and loving husband.'[366]

Widows

The treatment of widows deteriorated in the seventeenth century from their prominence as heads of 10 per cent of early medieval English households,[367] surviving their husbands in 69 per cent of aristocratic and gentry marriages,[368] and position in the London property market. Widows had been widely trusted by their first husbands in the 1500s: 89 per cent of widows in Abingdon were named as executors of their husband's will and their inheritance was not conditional on them remaining single.[369] But from the 1600s widows were impoverished by their husbands' wills, which started to rule that a widow would lose her inheritance on remarriage. Husbands developed a new idea: creating an 'entail' on property, to make the disinheritance of all women compulsory. An entail turned 'patrimony' from the Norman tradition to a legal obligation on a family forever,[370] bequeathing the estate away from the widow or female descendants to a male heir – however distant. Entail became increasingly popular in the 1600s, reducing the inheritance of widows and daughters, and making their work for the family to the benefit only of the oldest male heir. Male heirs were well aware of the advantage of inheriting property with a built-in experienced manager. A friend of the heir to Caus Castle told him to work with his mother in her project of lead mining in the Mendip Hills: 'during her own life she can benefit therein, but you and yours may receive a commodity thereof forever; you should be contented to allow her the better share (two thirds), one third to you [if] you contribute one third of the charge when finished.'[371] Entail impoverished women for centuries – Jane Austen's novels (200 years later, in the early nineteenth century) show fictional women's anxiety about the future hardship for widows and their daughters from entail.

A study of women in Abingdon, Berkshire, between 1540 and 1720 suggests that from the early 1600s, widows increasingly chose not to remarry. The only widows who did marry for the second time were those with young children. This change to the traditional ways in Abingdon was probably reflected in the rest of the country. It seems that for much of the sixteenth century an Abingdon widow was a true heir – the person to inherit her husband's fortune. But after about 1570, the wills provided for her only if she did not remarry. In the 1600s, the concern became that sons should inherit, but their mother, the widow, was apparently not trusted to guard their inheritance. After 1660, trust in widows as executors of their husbands' wills declined: only 74 per cent of widows were named as executors.[372]

Some Abingdon widows were left fortunes and some demonstrated entrepreneurial skills by improving on their late husbands' work. Isabel Pophley inherited her second husband's brewery and went on to buy and run a number of inns. She died a wealthy woman, owning several properties, diamond jewellery and investments.[373]

Single Women

The loss of the nunneries, convents and abbeys meant the loss of a career path with high social status for single women after 1536. There was no work outside the family home or business for aristocratic single women, except that of serving as companions for wealthy relatives or patrons, or – for very few – at court.

As anxiety about single women increased in the late 1500s, few escaped suspicion and surveillance by the authorities.[374] Only the single women whose means were established and who owned their own houses, older women who might be trusted not to corrupt anyone's morals or have a bastard child at the cost of the parish and those who had been living with a parent who had recently died, avoided censure. All single women were regarded with less tolerance than that afforded widows, who could inherit houses and sometimes workshops and membership of guilds or townsman status. A single woman, Ann Faulkner, and her widowed sister Mary

Stokes jointly inherited their mother's trading business, but were recorded in the Southampton city records as one trader – the widow. As a single woman, Ann was assumed to be dependent on her sister Mary – the widow – although they had inherited equally.[375]

In the seventeenth century, the single women population peaked at about 30 per cent of the country – an unusually high proportion.[376] Single labouring women supported themselves by their own earnings or joined households as servants for their bed and board and wages, or lived with their families contributing to the household with their work or earnings.

Women Loving Women

Anxiety about sexual practices in same-sex relationships was prevalent throughout Europe, but only male sexual intimacy with men was both banned by the church and illegal.[377] The laws explicitly described acts that were banned for men, but since there were no criminal laws against women's sexual practices with women, there were no official descriptions of women's sexual practices with women. Women lovers could believe that their affection and actions were both without sin and outside the law.

Women had routinely lived intimately together: sleeping in the same bed at night, spending all day in each other's company – sometimes choosing to live together rather than with their families or with a husband – but it was rarely recorded that they found sexual pleasure with each other. There are two records of bishop visitations to convents before the Reformation where women were discovered sleeping together. In Littlemore – a priory reported as having several financial and discipline problems – the prioress was accused of sleeping at night with one of the nuns in her bed. No mention was made of any sexual relationship, but the inspecting Bishop Alnwick ruled that the women must sleep apart. In Flamstead Priory in 1530, one of the nuns, Johanna Mason, said that she slept with another nun so that they could wake each other up for matins. The inspecting bishop – John Longland – said that this must stop.[378]

Some women's love for another woman was till death: Kateryn Parr, last queen of Henry VIII, was deeply loved by a number of her ladies who risked their safety to stay with her. Her friend and fellow church reformer Anne Askew chose torture and death by burning rather than incriminate her. It is hard to imagine a greater love than this.

Part 5

1660–1764
Locked Out and Locked In

Land Grab

Therefore be content with lowly degree
And (God) will provide for thy children and thee.[1]

So advised the *Poor Man's Counsel* (*or, The Marryed Man's Guide*) – not a ballad written by the people rooted in their experience, but a nastier thing by far: a ballad written by a wealthy aristocratic writer to persuade the poor that they were lucky to be where they were and to be content with their lot, and never – ever! – to rebel again.

Not that the revolution had served the poor. Although radicals in the civil wars demanded that the land enclosures be returned and the poor restored to the land, the Commonwealth government failed to live up to its promises or its name. Nor did the return of the monarchy with Charles II, in 1660, mark a return to 'good lordship'. The pace of enclosures increased, driving women from the land, as the pleasure-loving leisured court preached a work ethic for labourers.

In just 40 years, about a quarter of the entire area of England was taken into private ownership: wasteland, forest, upland and floodlands were declared as private property, enclosed with walls and hedges or brought under the plough, in as many as 1,700 separate Acts by the land-owners' parliament.[2] The beautiful landscapes that are the setting for the great eighteenth-century country houses were rolled out over emptied villages and ruined lives. The tracks made by people who had lived on the land for generations were blocked; the common lands where they collected fuel and grazed their animals were hedged and gated. No more could people turn out animals to graze, set out their beehives, gather berries, mushrooms and nuts, collect firewood and freely hunt game. No longer could a country family live off the land. It was an extraordinary theft by the elite – especially from a people who had already lost so much common land to enclosures. Villages that used to work collectively suddenly found that the richest few families had engrossed all the land, and villagers became employees of their former neighbours; more efficient farming methods and increased production followed. The impact upon the poor working country people was severe, and regretted even by some of the elite: Thomas More's *Utopia* (1516) and Oliver Goldsmith's poem *The Deserted Village* (1770) more than two centuries later both lamented the ruin of country life. The working people wrote their own ballads – not of nostalgia but of anger:

> The law locks up the man or woman
> Who steals the goose off the common
> But leaves the greater villain loose
> Who steals the common from the goose.

> The law demands that we atone
> When we take things we do not own
> But leaves the lords and ladies fine
> Who takes things that are yours and mine.
> The poor and wretched don't escape
> If they conspire the law to break;
> This must be so; but they endure
> Those who conspire to make the law.

> The law locks up the man or woman
> Who steals the goose from off the common
> And geese will still a common lack
> Till they go and steal it back.[3]

Even those communities that managed to keep common land lost their traditional rights. Game – venison from deer, hare, rabbits, pheasants, partridge, grouse – all now belonged to the landlord, and shooting for sport developed into a craze for the wealthy. In 1671, new laws declared it illegal for a tenant to take game, even on her own land.[4] Once fox-hunting became a sport – almost an obsession – for the elite, working people might not kill foxes preying on their hens. Even the fish in the river and ponds were off-limits under the newly invented fishing 'rights'. In 1723, the notorious 'Black Act' created more than 200 new offences, which were expanded over the subsequent years, each punishable by hanging – all of them aimed at country people trying to live off their former lands. Anyone poaching game, stealing crops, burning hayricks or breaking down the hated fences could be sentenced to death.

Women suffered the most. It was no longer possible for a woman to make a good living from her shared village fields – they were gone. She could not graze her animals on the common land – that was enclosed. She was excluded from woodlands where she used to gather firewood or graze pigs. She could not fish in the stream or river or take rabbits or pigeons for food. Now, paid at a lesser rate for the casual work at which they had excelled, women could not make a living in cash work either.

Women were driven off the common lands to work for others, to earn money to buy goods that they had previously produced themselves. In turn, this created a surplus of workers, which caused wages to halve. Country people who could not work for their neighbours had to go on the road for seasonal work, or migrate to the cities.[5] The Elizabethan-Stuart laws that had ordered that women must stay at home suddenly dissolved.[6] All of a sudden it was socially and morally acceptable for a single woman to leave home seeking work; indeed, it became illegal for her *not* to have work. Bristol more than doubled its population from 21,000 in 1700 to about 50,000 in 1750. Manchester went from a population of about 18,000 in 1750 to 89,000 in 1801.[7] A quarter of the population would be living in towns by 1800, often in terrible urban slums.[8]

Single women and widows could no longer support themselves in their cottages. They went as domestic servants and into the workshops in the growing towns to live in with employers. But a woman tied by her dependants at home in the country could neither earn money without access to the common lands, nor go to the towns for work, she was trapped in the country, producing food from the little garden that remained her own, giving birth, breast-feeding – actually producing the milk for the baby – maintaining the health of the children, supporting the elderly and the sick, making textiles and clothing, making food and drink, providing wood for the fire and sometimes wax for the candles. If the families were to survive, all the wives' labour, all their productivity, had to be given to the households for free to release the man of the household to work all hours for cash wages. The value of wives' unpaid work was obscured.[9] The tradition that women work for their families without payment, and that men dedicate themselves to wage earning, became established by the enclosures of common land in the seventeenth century – long before the rhetoric of a 'breadwinner wage' was invented.

The gulf between wages for men and those for women had been set locally by magistrates since Elizabethan times. But now landlord-JPs changed the way they set wages: no longer did they specify a minimum wage that employers must pay; instead they set a maximum limit that local employers might not exceed. Quite deliberately the magistrates held down wages and held down women's pay. The pay gap between men and women workers remained. A man making hay in 1684 could not be paid more than 10d a day, while a woman working alongside him, doing the same work, could not be paid more than 6d or even less. In the booming servant business a live-in male cook earned £4 a year, a woman cook £2.5s.[10]

England was a poor country in the late 1600s – nobody was measuring, but there was no surplus balance of payments, there were frequent epidemics and when the harvest failed people starved. More than a third of all children died in childhood, and the population declined from 5.23 million in 1660 to 4.93 million in 1680. Daniel Defoe identified different classes: the rich, the middle sort and 'the working trades who labour hard but feel no want; The country people, farmers etcetera, who fare indifferently; The poor, who fare hard; and the miserable, who really pinch and suffer want'.[11]

Protest

The great land grab did not take place without a fight. The people challenged almost every field, taking legal action – appeals to landlords, pleas to the church, petitions – and illegal – riots, breaking fences, sabotaging machines, poaching and arson. Protest followed the draining of wetlands like the Fens, the ploughing up of old meadows and other changes of use. There were protests around the cost of food, the sale of food and the export of food away from the local market. Sometimes these could be violent and riotous. Major uprisings occurred all around England during years of hunger in every decade from 1740.[12] In one year alone – 1766 – there were more than 130 riots up and down England, as poor people tried to force farmers and corn merchants to keep grain for bread in the country where they had harvested it. The landlords and the wealthy described the uprisings as 'riots' and the people as a 'mob'. But many of them were continuing the well-understood tradition of tenants and labourers' protest and landowners making concessions.

Women led the complaints. They were the greatest presence in the markets, putting pressure on food retailers, food producers, middlemen and farmers to keep prices down and to keep foodstuffs local. Working-class women led direct action which was so well understood by the elite that one historian called it the 'moral economy of the crowd'.[13]

A group of women rioted at Lyme in 1678, protesting the import of linen and canvas. Many of the rioting women were from families who would later join the Duke of Monmouth's rebellion against the tyranny and Roman Catholicism of James II – part of a tradition of public protest and political radicalism in the prosperous Dorset town.[14] A bad harvest in 1693 caused Northamptonshire women to carry knives to market and force grain retailers to sell locally at fair prices. In Oxford market, millers and bakers and corn factors were stoned by a mob of women.[15]

In Nottingham market, a riot lasting several days broke out to prevent Lincolnshire merchants from taking hundreds of pounds of cheeses out of the county. One warehouse owner mustered his own mounted troop to find the stolen cheeses at Castle Donington, 14 miles away. But here the traditional-minded elite sided with the traditional-minded poor against the new money men. The Castle Donington JP refused to sign search warrants to allow the private troop to search local houses. In response, the troop arrested suspect rioters and besieged the magistrate's house, demanding that he hear the case against the rioters. This in turn triggered an uprising by local women and children who defended the magistrate and rescued the rioters. The women and children drove the troop out of town.[16]

Even a woman acting alone might summon a sympathetic response. According to the scandal sheet the *Newgate Calendar*, a woman, Ann Flynn, was arrested in 1750 and imprisoned for five weeks before appearing in court, charged with stealing a shoulder of mutton. She told a tale of woe that penetrated every heart. She acknowledged the robbery; but solemnly declared she was urged to it by the most afflicting distress. Her husband had been ill and unable to earn a shilling for twelve weeks, and she was driven to the last extremity, with two infant children. In that deplorable situation, continued the unfortunate woman, while the tears ran down her wan cheeks, she desperately snatched the shoulder of mutton – for which she had already been confined five weeks.

According to the scandal sheet, the jury faltered as they found her guilty and the recording judge said, 'Gentlemen, I understand you.' The elite men responded to the plea of a poor woman. The recorder ordered that Ann Flynn be released after paying a shilling fine – and the jury paid it for her.[17]

Many crimes of hunger were ignored; many country riots burned out without being recorded; many ended early when magistrates made on-the-spot rulings about prices, and even distributed food to the poor. But attitudes seem to have hardened throughout the 1700s and magistrates came to side more and more with the profiteers. Radical thinking – which would go on to inspire violent revolution in France and then in America – originated in England, where anger about greed became widespread and the greedy elite increasingly anxious. London was the most tumultuous city in the Western world before 1789.[18] In England, as in the French Revolution, women were foremost in radical thinking and violent action.

Women also protested against the new machines and new practices that threatened wages or put skilled artisans out of work. In 1675, women rioters destroyed engine looms in Spitalfields, defending craft practices against machines. In 1697, as many as 5,000 women lobbied Parliament against foreign competition in the silk weaving industry.[19] The women brought their children and organised the protest: 'They pooled their half-pennies and paid the bell woman to "go about to raise the weavers and so go to Westminster and petition parliament".'[20]

William Blackstone thought it necessary to note in *Commentaries on the Laws of England* (1771) that women had no legal right to riot and should not be allowed to hide behind the claim of having no legal identity. The fear of riots became so strong that the Riot Act of 1714 was created. It defined a 'crowd' as more than 12 people. A magistrate or civil authority was to read the act to any gathering of more than a dozen people, and one hour after the reading, soldiers or militia were allowed to shoot to kill. It was an extraordinary, aggressive act from an elite against their own people. It may have had more impact on women than men. It has been suggested that women feared the act and cleared the streets promptly, thus disappearing from the records.[21]

Power Grab

The restoration of Charles II in 1660 was the visible return of patriarchy. The men who had invited monarchy to return – for lack of any other idea – made conditions. Charles had to give up his traditional royal rights and accept the end of all remaining feudal fees, fines and dues.[22] From now on, English men would have no masters. It was the final and complete end of feudalism for such men. It was a power grab. English men became legal beings with rights under the law; the royal family became great landowners and kings. But English women – who had argued and preached and fought for English freedom – gained nothing from the overthrow of the Parliament and the return of the king. Women entered the pre-modern world just as they had the medieval world: as serfs, owned by their husbands without a legal presence.

Shaken by the civil wars, English thinkers were comforted by the European-wide revolution of thought (now called the Age of Enlightenment) that argued that progress was upward and humanity would improve and become more civilised, cultured and logical. New sciences developed, based on observation of the real world rather than speculation; rational thought was valued over inspiration, and logic over magic. All the natural world was closely observed and recorded by self-styled scientists who thought that the rich diversity in nature would be understood by being defined and categorised. The diversity of human beings, the one human body that could have both male and female qualities, and change from female to male, did not fit this new hunger for precise and limited labelling. The new philosophers decided that there were only two sexes: fixed and unchanging, completely opposite, male and female, normal and other.[23] They saw this simple binary model because they favoured it; they found it because they looked for it, because it fitted their ideas of male and female status. When they saw behaviours or nature that did not support a rigid binary model, they explained them away. The changing sex of the developing fetus, the presence of all the sex organs in early development was ignored.[24] Two sexes, completely opposite, were never a genuine observation supported by all the other evidence, but an intellectual fashion in all modernising European thought; invented to explain and justify sexual inequality.[25]

New theories about women's bodies were based on the dissection of corpses and use of the newly invented microscope. The word 'vagina' was invented in the seventeenth century to define a 'female' organ that previously had been named as an internal or reversed 'yard' – a penis.[26] Women's nature was now deduced from their bodies: the dangerous rage and madness created by the wandering womb, greensickness caused by sexual frustration, moodiness caused by menstruation, the deterioration of menopause. The new 'Enlightenment' thinkers agreed that women were the opposite of 'normal' men: female irrational minds were compared with stern male logic, emotional feelings with controlled thinkers and frail bodies compared with male strength.

These ideas gained ground as elite male philosophers observed the increasingly leisured women of their own class. John Locke – one of the great thinkers of the Enlightenment – advised women that lifting heavy objects 'belongs not to their sex' and 'endangered their health', blind to the world around him filled with labouring women working alongside men.[27] The only thing made lighter for women to lift was their pay packet.

The Royal Society, an association of scientists and philosophers founded in 1660, excluded women for 285 years, demonstrating – by its membership list alone – the superiority of the male mind. Since women were believed to be creatures of feeling and men were creatures of thinking, women could have no place in a society devoted to rational logic. As founder Joseph Glanvill said, 'Truth has no chance of being declared, when the affections wear the breeches, and the female rules.'[28]

Men were intellectual, but women were sensual, driven by their emotions and uncontrollable physical passions. The womb was 'an animal inside an animal'.[29] The bawdy comic writers of the Enlightenment still maintained that women were sexually voracious. Rabelais observed women 'insanely chasing the codpiece'.[30]

Even women's ability to bear children was derided as an animal-like function, unlike the brilliant ideas gestated in the rational male mind. As the commonplace book said, 'None but fools were fit to bear children.'[31]

There were good reasons for elite philosophers and so-called scientists to argue that women's nature was unreliable and women were unfit for authority. Protesting, radical lower-class women had been leaders in the chaos of the civil wars, fighting alongside men in defence of towns and houses, preaching and prophesying in the small religious sects, entering politics, arguing and petitioning, and always at the forefront in direct action against enclosures, food shortages and disruption to the market. Aristocratic women held besieged houses against impossible odds, and maintained the wealth, status and unity of the family in the absence of men. With all these women in control, the country had gone to hell. Commentator Richard Allestree observed: 'Everything seems inverted, even sexes. Whilst Men fall to the Effeminacy and Niceness of Women, and Women take up the Confidence and boldness of men.'[32]

Now that the king was restored, it was hoped that assertive women would retire to domestic peace. The she-soldiers who had marched out and fought, and the lady generals who had held the siege of their houses, were sent back into their onerous domestic and civilian work. Historians noted: 'No one wanted a heroine in everyday life. On the contrary, women were expected to relinquish extraordinary roles as their contribution to what everyone presumably desired, a return to normality.'[33]

Enlightenment thinkers agreed that good women were naturally modest, and if they were not, they must be taught. As Rousseau said, 'If the timidity, chasteness and modesty which are proper to [women] are social inventions, it is in society's interest that women acquire these qualities; they must be cultivated in women.'[34]

Disappointingly, it seemed that women had to be coached into their modest and timid nature. A major work to do just that, hugely popular in the seventeenth century, was *The Ladies Calling*, written by Richard Allestree in 1673, reprinted nine times by 1727. Such books became known as 'conduct books' as they taught the readers how to conduct themselves: how to behave. It was a turning point in the creation of modern English femininity.[35]

Allestree had been a Royalist soldier during the civil wars restored to his vocation as a Church of England minister by the return of Charles II. From this eminence of royalism, spiritual authority and worldly experience, he explained the true nature of women, to women: 'Let it be admitted that in respect of the intellect they are below men; yet sure in the sublimest part of humanity they are their equals: they have souls.'[36]

Allestree's comment was a huge concession to women, contradicting the widespread earlier belief that women did not have souls but, like animals, were bodies only. As possessors of souls, women could spiritually lead in private, while being safely governed by men with superior minds in the wider world.

The Ladies Calling warns women, in truly gruesome detail, of how they appear when they lack modesty and meekness, and how by practising these virtues, a woman will be more attractive to God and to society (and attract a husband) than those who are immodest. Affability and compassion are not just significant virtues in themselves – they are how a woman succeeds in society (and attracts a husband). Devotion to God is important too, because it helps a woman become a valued member of society (and attract a husband). Written for literate women – the middling classes and those above them – the book plays on crass snobbery to discourage bad behaviour, and repeats over and over that demanding, verbal, assertive behaviour belongs to the lower classes and would not be practised by a lady. 'A scold ... being a creature to be look'd for only in Stalls and Markets not among persons of quality.'[37]

A 'lady' is a being recognisably different from a working woman. The 'nature of women' now comes to mean this refined creature who has the time and the need to perfect this limited behaviour. Female sexual self-control – indeed, sexual frigidity – is the prime ladylike quality. The myths of courtly love and the entertainments based on the courtly love stories returned with the monarchy, and the lady of the castle blended seamlessly with Allestree's bourgeois heroine. Both of them were sexually chaste, perhaps frigid. Both of them had to protect themselves and their reputation against male aggression and their own betraying desire: 'She that listens to any wanton discourse has violated her ears. She that speaks any: her tongue. Every immodest glance vitiates her eye, and the lightest act of dalliance leaves something of stain and soilage behind it.'[38]

If marriage cannot be achieved by a woman, Allestree promises there are pleasures in spinsterhood – only he describes them so briefly, it is clear there are none. Even if marriage is a prison for a woman, Allestree says it is 'better to be a Prisoner to one's home, than a Stranger'.[39]

Political Protest

The restored monarchy was openly antagonistic to protests from the lower classes, especially those of women. New laws against petitioning, mass demonstration and press freedom were passed in 1661 and 1662.[40] Some women refused to be silenced; they argued for women's education, preached in women-only sects and worked in the underground press, like the heroine Elizabeth Calvert who was a printer and bookseller alongside her husband Giles at the Black Spread Eagle, in St Paul's Churchyard, and the Black Spread Eagle, Barbican. After the Restoration, Elizabeth led in publishing radical pamphlets, even when her husband was imprisoned. She worked with other female publishers, Hannah Allen, Joan Dover (later Darby) and Ann(a) Brewster, on anti-monarchy texts, and was arrested twice. Widowed in 1663, Elizabeth continued to print seditious material and was arrested with her maid Elizabeth Evans, her apprentice Mathias Stephenson and her son Nathaniel. She was imprisoned in 1664, and her son died before she could win her release to nurse him. Although her print shop was destroyed in the Great Fire of 1666, Elizabeth Calvert continued to print radical texts and send them all over England.

Her secret press outside the City limits was found and broken in 1668 but she returned to St Paul's Churchyard a year later to open another press and was arrested and tried for publishing another banned book. She absconded from her trial in 1671 and charges against her were dropped, but she was arrested again three years later for another offence. Undeterred, she signed on another apprentice, before making her will in favour of her only surviving son Giles, a rebel to her death in 1675.[41]

Other women wrote books against the restored king, published pamphlets and spoke out against him: 11 per cent of the cases of seditious speech against Charles II prosecuted in court were spoken by anti-monarchy women.[42] Women defied the new laws banning petitions. Working women, silk weavers and glass-makers intimidated their MPs and forced the Houses of Parliament to hear their concerns about their trades.[43]

Women flocked to join the rebellions against the restored monarchy. London sugar-baker Ann Smith hid Archibald Campbell, the Earl of

Argyll, during his first uprising against James II, the brother and heir to Charles II. Smith and her husband fled abroad with Argyll, and financed his second uprising against James in Scotland in 1685. Despite this extraordinary act of treason, she was given a pardon in 1686. Deborah Hawkins promised that she would 'put on breeches myself to fight for the Duke of Monmouth' rather than see the Roman Catholic James inherit the throne.[44] The bastard son of Charles II, Monmouth also attracted the 'Maids of Taunton', 20 schoolgirls who embroidered a banner for him and hailed him as king under the leadership of their schoolmistress, Mrs Musgrave. They were all arrested for treason and sentenced to transportation as indentured servants to the Sugar Islands. Mrs Musgrave died in prison but the girls' families were allowed to buy pardons from James II's second wife, Queen Mary of Modena, their 'owner'.[45]

Elizabeth Gaunt, a London shopkeeper, hid one of the conspirators of the Monmouth uprising but was betrayed by him. As a woman, with no direct connection to the conspiracy, she expected to face a minor charge, but instead she was accused of treason and sentenced to death by burning, without the mercy of being strangled first. However, the public execution ordered by James II backfired. Elizabeth Gaunt's courage won support for her cause. Hers was an entirely unapologetic scaffold speech, written in her own hand for publication, and she proclaimed it in her own voice, before her terrible death by burning:

> I leave it to him, who is the avenger of all such wrong who will tread
> upon Princes as upon mortar, & be terrible to the Kings of the earth;
> & know this also, that tho' you are seemingly fixed, & because of the
> power in your hands, are weighing out your violence, & dealing with
> a despiteful mind, because of the old & new hatred, by
> impoverishing & every way destressing those you have got under
> you, yet unless you can secure Jesus Christ & all his holy Angells, you
> shall never do your business, nor your hand accomplish your
> enterprizes; for he will be upon you ere you are aware; and therefore
> that you would be wise, instructed, & learn, is the desire of her that
> finds no mercy from you.[46]

Another woman, 68-year-old Alice Lisle (1617–85), was accused of treason for harbouring two rebels on the run. She argued that she had not known they were rebels and she thought that one of them was merely a radical preacher. As the widow of a regicide who had agreed the execution of Charles I, she faced a trial that was prejudiced against her from the start. Her husband John Lisle had fled the country at the restoration of the monarchy and been assassinated by a Royalist spy in exile at Lausanne in 1664. Twenty years after his death, 36 years after his regicide, his act counted against his widow. Judge Jeffreys ruled that Alice Lisle could not speak in her own defence, because Charles I had not been allowed to speak in his defence; and the jury reluctantly found her guilty of treason. James II delayed for a week after her sentence, finally commuting the penalty as she was an aristocratic woman from burning alive to the more merciful beheading. She was decapitated in Winchester market – the last woman to be legally executed in this way in England.[47]

One young woman killed a Royalist officer with his own sword while he was raping her mother after Monmouth's defeat at Westonzoyland in Somerset. Mary Bridge, aged only 12, seized the rapist's sword and stabbed him through the heart. She was the only Monmouth supporter ever released by the notorious Judge Jeffreys, who gave her the sword as a souvenir. It was passed down through her family and can be seen today, at the Museum of Somerset in Taunton.

Protest flared up against Judge Jeffreys who hanged hundreds of Protestant and Puritan rebels fighting for the Duke of Monmouth in 1685. The widows and daughters of the hanged and transported men wrote a specifically female petition denouncing Jeffreys and invited him to return to visit them in the West Country: 'Where we, the good women in the west, will be glad to see him, and give him another manner of welcome than he had three years since.'[48]

Fears of Roman Catholic James II and his wife Mary of Modena peaked with the surprising birth of a son – almost immediately denounced as a changeling by Protestant rabble-rousers. The fear of a Roman Catholic Prince of Wales inspired a second uprising against James II, this time encouraged by his two Protestant daughters, princesses Mary and Anne, and led by a group of lords, who offered James's throne to his Protestant daughter Mary and her husband William of Orange. The couple took up a joint monarchy by invitation, and their royal powers were limited yet further by a Bill of Rights in 1688.

The new monarchs were not universally welcomed. Some women still supporting the exiled Stuart king James II, after he had run away, threatened to scratch out the eyes of the mayor who backed William and Mary at Kingston upon Thames in 1716.[49]

Once again, England had a regnant queen in Mary, daughter of James II, and the Parliament and the queen herself tried to establish her common-born husband's supremacy over his royal wife. Queen Mary's biographers suggest that she was bullied into complete submission by her emotionally cold husband. Even before they were offered the throne, she had promised to make him king for life and obey him, putting her marriage vows of obedience before her royal status as a queen. Although Mary was heir to the throne, William insisted that he also be crowned, to rule jointly. The lords who invited the couple needed Mary's line to the throne to give the appearance of legitimacy to an invasion by her husband's army. Of course, they had no interest in the rights of women monarchs and readily agreed that the couple, one a royal Stuart, the other an elected ruler, be crowned as equal king and queen.

The Bill of Rights, presented to the ruling queen and king, often hailed as one of the heroic steps towards democracy, does not even mention women. It was designed only to protect the rights of men in Parliament, Protestant men and male juries. It was inspired by the work of thinkers around John Locke, including women – Mary Astell and Damaris Cudworth – who argued that there was no 'natural state' of monarchy – the power of kings was only established by agreement with the people. But although there was no natural monarchy, there was such a state as natural patriarchy: a tyranny of men over women – given by God and maintained by man's superior physical strength: 'But the husband and wife, though they have but one common concern, yet having different understandings, will unavoidably sometimes have different wills too; it therefore being necessary that the last determination – i.e., the rule – should be placed somewhere, it naturally falls to the man's share, as the abler and stronger.'[50]

It was a brilliant side-step to preserve patriarchy after the decapitation of the monarchy, to hold up the authority of men while diminishing kings. Not even Locke's opponents, pro-Royalist women philosophers, could speak up for women. As Royalists, they were bound to argue for male authority in throne room and home. As Royalists they named the king as the father of the nation and the head of the household. They

could not develop rebellious ideas against male authority, while supporting the ultimate male authority: the king.[51]

Two successive queens made no improvement in the status of women
– neither Mary, nor her sister Anne who eventually succeeded her,
encouraged women into positions of authority, nor paved the way for the
rise of powerful royal princesses, and both died without female heirs – or
any direct heirs at all. Mary's submissiveness to her husband meant that
even when she acted as regent during William's frequent absences,
nobody had the sense of a woman taking over.

Queen Anne, though she emphasised her lack of education and struggled with ill health caused by 17 pregnancies and no surviving child,
attended more council meetings than any previous monarch and took a
keen interest in the politics of her time. But as politicians grouped into
the two opposing rivalrous parties – Whigs and Tories – and as she was
powerfully influenced by women favourites, Anne won the reputation of
being overemotional, changeable and easily influenced. And her hard
work was forgotten.

Work

Most women were still supporting themselves, in a countryside that was
less and less open, in an economy deliberately closed against them.
Women living at home tried to fit cash-earning work around their
production for the household. Jane Milward, the wife of a miner in the
late 1700s, fed her husband Richard and their six children, as a report
described:

> The management of the ground is in good measure left to his wife
> Jane, although her husband always assists in digging after his hours of
> ordinary labour (in the pit). In 13 years their scrap of ground yielded
> good crops of potatoes peas and cabbages, which she sold in
> Shrewsbury. She kept a pig and used its droppings for manure along
> with what she and the children could scrape off the roads. Without
> Jane's efforts, a family of six children would have been reduced to
> pauperdom.[52]

When times were hard, women and men had to take any work to keep themselves and their family alive. Mrs Jones of Ruthin in Wales in the late eighteenth century forged an agreement with her husband that he should take over traditional female work to set her free to knit the wool from the family sheep. Although they owned a small farm, they could not survive on their own produce: the farmer had to take on his wife's work to set her free to make the cash produce – butter and knitting. Her son remembered what she said:

> 'I'll make a bargain with thee; I'll see to food for us and both the children all winter if thou, in addition to looking after the horse, the cattle, and pigs, wilt do the churning, wash-up, make the beds, and clean the house. I'll make the butter myself.'
> 'How wilt thou manage?' asked my father.
> 'I will knit,' said she. 'We have wool, if thou wilt card it, I'll spin.'
> The bargain was struck, my father did the housework in addition to the work on the farm, and my mother knitted, and so it was she kept us alive until the next harvest.[53]

Single women headed households as independent widows, deserted wives, single mothers and spinsters, earning their own livings, often on the breadline in rural communities, but sometimes very successful in towns: especially in luxury goods and retail businesses, lending small amounts of money to familiar faces – trusted creditors. Law court records show that most wives were self-sufficient: 60 per cent of them attending court said they kept themselves by their own labour.[54] Of London women, 77 per cent of single women and 71 per cent of widows earned their own living in paid work,[55] and about 40 per cent of London shops and businesses were owned by women.[56]

Some businesswomen were hugely successful. Elinor Mosley, a single woman, gained the freedom to trade in London by joining the Clockmakers' Guild, though she herself was a milliner, and employed four female apprentices as well as women servants in her home and workshop at Gracechurch Street. She married at the age of 47, but kept the business and her membership of the guild in her single name. The business was probably taken over by her sister.[57] Single women traders ran or owned 36 shops or trades in Southampton by 1750, and one of them, Jane Martin, a milliner, carried so much stock that she used carts with metal wheels for deliveries – and was fined under city regulations for damaging the paved ways.[58]

Records from other towns suggest that a woman had to show income or status before she could open a business on her own and earn. Women who opened shops in Oxford had to have capital or family connections. In London, they had to be heiresses from merchants or tradesmen, backed by family money, or able to buy into a guild with liberal regulations.[59]

Even very small-scale women traders might make a fortune. Alice Dant was a pedlar, selling little items of clothing: ribbons and stockings, from a backpack. She left a fortune of £9,000 to the poor. Samuel Pepys, the diarist, was surprised by the competence of a woman merchant, Mrs Bland: 'It seem she doth understand it and perform a great deal.'[60]

One woman was so hugely successful as a silk designer that her signed design books were preserved. Anna Maria Garthwaite (1688–1763) was the daughter of a provincial clergyman in Grantham. Her extraordinary talent for design and colour prompted her to train as an apprentice to a London master weaver – probably a woman master – who entered her into the Weavers' Company. Garthwaite joined an artistic and scientific circle of apothecaries and botanists who specialised in botanical drawings.[61] She may have known a successful botanical artist, Elizabeth Blackwell, whose book *A Curious Herbal Containing Five Hundred Cuts of the Most Useful Plants, Which Are Now Used in the Practice of Physick, to Which Is Added a Short Description of ye Plants and Their Common Uses in Physick* went through many editions in 1737.

Garthwaite rose to the position of a master weaver and, inspired by flower and plant drawings, designed and made gorgeous silks that were used for gowns, upholstery and decoration, and exported. She took her sister and her ward to live with her in her grand master weaver's house in Spitalfields – the centre for high-quality silk weaving. Her neighbours were successful women weavers too: Sarah Gabell, who 'was paid thirty pounds to train Henrietta Griffith', and in 1742, Elizabeth Forward, a spinster, who accepted £60 to train the daughter of a vicar as her apprentice.[62]

A widow of a weaver, Margaret Hey, took up her husband's position in the Weavers' Company and trained several male apprentices. Another female weaver was Mary Willis, who worked alongside her husband and was a member in her own right in the company, remaining in business and in the Weavers' after his death.[63] Phoebe Wright (d. 1778) was another silk designer whose creations for the loom also included embroidery. Under the patronage of Queen Charlotte, wife of George III, Wright established the Royal School for Embroidering Females, with her niece, Nancy Pawsey, and wove and embroidered the throne canopy in the king's audience room. Wright used the flower paintings of Mary Moser (1744–1819) as the basis of her designs. Moser was one of the two women members of the Royal Academy of Arts in the 1700s.[64]

Women dominated other textile industries too. Doncaster was famous for the women stockingmakers who knitted in home-based workshops and were notorious for bursting, uninvited, into inn bedrooms to ambush travellers and sell their wares.[65]

Women continued to dominate the food business, both as producers and retailers. Street markets all around the country were dependent on women bringing fresh and produced foods.[66] In 1662, Eleanor Davies, of The Maypole, Strand, was licensed 'to kill and sell all manner of fresh meat except beef during the ensuing Lent'.[67] Women street vendors had their own agreed rounds; they sold from baskets carried on their arms or sometimes balanced on their heads with seasonal fruits and vegetables such as strawberries, asparagus and cherries. Women preparing food and selling retail goods became even more important in the growing towns as many urban households bought in meals from the bakehouse, such as pies and cooked meats, as well as breads and puddings. Londoners, whose houses were too small to have a bread oven, bought their bread from the bakers, and brewing at home stopped, as the cycle of using yeast from brewing in home-baking was broken.[68]

The new 'exchanges' were purpose-built buildings with retail shops inside, rather like a modern mall. Shop women were hired to serve in the new units.[69] The 'exchanges' became centres of shopping as a leisure and social activity, dominated by women shopkeepers in the 1600s. By 1690, nearly half of the shops inside the exchanges were owned by women (47 per cent), and 46 per cent of them were kept by women shopkeepers. Daniel Defoe described: 'The two great centres for women merchants; I mean the Exchange shops, particularly at the Royal Exchange and the New Exchange in the Strand.'[70]

Women in the Royal Exchange owned businesses in light, decorative and textile trades: haberdashers, girdlers, drapers, mercers, embroiderers, milliners, grocers and clothworkers. But there were also women's businesses offering paint-staining (portrait painters), leather sellers and merchant tailors. Women were vintners, goldsmiths, barbers, barber-surgeons, and doctors of physic, scriveners, notaries, upholders, smiths, booksellers, iron mongers, pewterers, armourers, saddlers, joiners and salters.[71] Some women retailers were so well established that they issued their own coins – trade tokens to use as small change during the constant shortage of official coinage. Six trade tokens struck by women dating from 1660–70 have survived.

A woman's currency: a halfpenny token minted by Mary Long at the sign of the Rose in Russell Street, Covent Garden, 1669

The restoration of the monarchy allowed the reopening of theatres, fairs and entertainments, and women returned to their work as entertainers, dancers, acrobats and musicians. At the 1698 Bartholomew Fair, in London's Smithfield, female tightrope walkers and aerialists were much admired.[72] In the 1720s in the capital, a young woman was known as the European Championess for her prizefighting – boxing – which was probably contested with few rules and bare knuckles.[73] Women appeared for the first time on stage in women's parts, and there was an outpouring of women's creativity. Women writers produced plays, poems and books; women artists produced popular paintings – Mrs Mary Beale charged £10 for a full-length portrait in 1671.[74] Mary Beale was part of a small band of female professional artists working in London. She became the main financial provider for her family – a career she maintained from 1670/71 to the 1690s. Explorer Celia Fiennes (1662–1741) took advantage of the new freedoms to travel thousands of miles on horseback and on foot in England as a single woman, accompanied only by servants. She wrote a private journal of her travels but did not publish.

The only work open for a lady without loss of genteel status was governess to elite children in a private house, or companion to an upper-class lady. These gruelling and humiliating posts of 'companions' were created by the requirement of the ladies of the family to show delicacy and fragility: they now had to be attended, chaperoned, guarded or served. Poor middling- and upper-class single women or widows, trying to retain their status, might find themselves at the whim of an employer, producing nothing of value, virtually unpaid. Some posts were literally without pay, as sought in the *Daily Advertiser* on 7 July 1772:

> A Widow lady about 40, of Family, Character and Education, would like to superintend a single Gentleman's family that is but small and who is a Man of Good Morals and not under the same Age. The lady expects to be treated as a Friend and Companion as no Salary is required unless the Gentleman has children and should like the Lady to act in the capacity of a Governess, being properly qualified to undertake the Care of Young Ladies; has no objection to Town or Country.[75]

Women had positions of authority and were leaders of their communities, in local institutions, in public health and on their private estates. Anna Maria Garthwaite, the silk weaver, acted as executor of her father's estate when she was 27 years old.[76] Respectable lower-class women reported illicit sex, illegitimate children and infanticide, making up 'juries of matrons' at the request of the court to rule on pregnancies and impotence. Women juries and 'watchers' aided the detection and prosecution of witches. Women taught in free schools and supervised pauper apprenticeships, served as keepers and matrons for the poor. During plague years, they searched the dead and dying for signs of the disease and kept the lists of the dead of the parish.[77]

Between 1688 and 1755, a quarter of British jails had a widow as a keeper.[78] Often a widow would inherit the post from her dead husband. Eliza Prince, widow of John at a Berkshire house of correction, remarked rather pointedly to the authorities that she could continue in the family tradition of keeping the jail or she could fall on the parish which would then have to support her and her eight children, as well as pay the wages of a new jailer.

That your petitioner's husband and his father and grandfather have been keepers of the house of correction at Abingdon for a great many years, and your petitioner has a brother and a brother in law very well qualified and willing to assist her in the future management of that prison, and she can find sufficient security, if required, for her faithful discharge of the office of Bridewell keeper. Your petitioner therefore humbly prays to be continued in the office of keeper of the house of correction, that she may be thereby able to provide bread for her family, which must otherwise be unavoidably thrown on the parish for maintenance.[79]

Sextons – employed by parish churches to keep the graveyard and ring the bells – were often women, especially in London.[80] A woman appointed to a London church as sexton in 1739 took her case to the King's Bench when parishioners tried to replace her with a man. The court stated that there were 'many' women sextons in London. A ruling later in the century decreed that a woman could undertake the post since it was 'a private office of trust',[81] reflecting a growing feeling that women could do 'caring' work. At the Quaker burial ground near Bunhill Fields, Deborah Morris inherited the post of sexton and gravedigger from her father for twelve years from 1745 to 1757, and then handed it on to her husband.[82]

Women served as overseers of the poor – an important and demanding task that affected public order and dispensed local charity. The continuing uncertainty about women under the law in the eighteenth century was exploited by Mary Jacques of Derbyshire who successfully wriggled out of her civic duty by explaining 'She, as a woman, was not capable of the office nor by law compellable to serve it.'[83]

The female governor of the Chelmsford workhouse was confirmed in her role despite legal challenge. But the court noted that although women were freeholders and contributed to the public charges, they could not vote for members of Parliament or coroners, and they could not hold public office.[84]

The late seventeenth century saw the deliberate exclusion of women from civic posts.[85] Increasingly, women had to choose a deputy – a man – to publicly do the work. Only if no man was available could a woman take up the responsibility that had previously been an automatic part of her elite social position. Legal opinion volunteered that it was 'inappropriate' for women to take office.[86]

The squeezing out of women voters from the electorate started in 1640 and was mostly completed by 1690 when it was generally accepted that women did not vote.[87] In a 1739 King's Bench case, the judges agreed that women could legally vote, but advised that they should not do so: since women 'lack judgement' on public issues.[88]

Education

Women were hired as teachers – but mainly teaching girls. Elite young women received their education from governesses – whose low status and pay were the subject of hand-wringing sermons and poignant novels; but no improvement. Some home schooling for girls could be of a high standard. Anthony Cook's daughters were highly educated in a deliberate experiment to test female abilities; Lucy Hutchinson (b. 1620) was bilingual in French and English and could read at the age of four. In 1698, Viscount Hatton's daughters were said to be 'good Latin scholars'.[89]

Girls of the middling sort were increasingly sent to school, creating a community of educated women in the residential schools, a helpful development for single women of the middling classes who did not want to marry or work as a housekeeper or companion. Mary Ward's Roman Catholic convent at Mickelgate Bar, York, expanded into a boarding and day school, surviving constant harassment from no-popery mobs. The mother superior was imprisoned in 1694, the house attacked in 1696, and the convent was only saved by a spectral St Michael riding a horse through the mob – according to legend.

Women who preferred the company of other women were attracted to the new schools that opened in London and the bigger towns. The new girls' schools were all single sex, and the curricula varied from the highly scholarly – Henry Purcell wrote *Dido and Aeneas* for the famous pupil choir at Josiah Priest's Girls' School to perform in 1688[90] – to little more than preparation for married life: decorative hobbies, amateur music, light reading and above everything else, etiquette.

From 1670, academies for non-Church of England Christians called 'Dissenting Academies' were allowed to offer a university-standard education for religious radicals who would not take the oaths required at Oxford and Cambridge universities. Some Dissenting colleges allowed women to attend – but no woman could graduate.[91]

After 1660, a small group of women including Bathsua Makin, Elizabeth Elstob and Mary Astell publicly criticised the English education system, linking the poor education of women with women's lack of status. The times were against them and their comments were mostly ignored. As Richard Brathwaite pronounced, in a tract of 1642, 'a proper gentlewoman desired not the esteem of any she-clerks; she had rather be approved by her living than learning.'[92]

Exclusion

From the 1700s, women were excluded from more and more areas of life: voting, community leadership, work, entrepreneurship and even as inventors: no more women registered their patents after 1660.[93] Women were squeezed out of paid, high-status or professional work, or any work that required a formal education or high-level skills. This was justified by the new 'science' about women's bodies and women's nature. No longer would philosophers argue that men should speak for women and rule over them because they had authority from God in the Bible and men could represent women: they were the same sort of beings. Now, men should speak for women because they were completely the opposite of women: capable where women were incapacitated.[94]

Even upper-class women were excluded from public life, and from profitable work. The sisterhood of women's sex was subdivided by class and working-class women were demonstrably inferior to everyone. The idea that ladies should lead very different lives from other, lower-class women was vigorously promoted from 1760.[95] Dr John Gregory wrote A Father's Advice to his Daughters, an immediate bestseller, capturing and describing the mood of the times that defined 'a lady' as emphatically non-productive. Even a lady's hobbies must be valueless. Dr Gregory recommended needlework, netting, knitting, art and handicrafts. Activities were designed to fill up hours spent at home. Even going out was discouraged.[96]

By 1730, 42 per cent of London wives claimed they had no paid employment and were almost all kept by their husbands.[97] The work of running the home – maintaining the outward appearance and the smooth functioning of the household, networking with clients or customers, supervising servants, ordering and controlling food and services to the household, producing children, educating and raising them, managing and maintaining the family social life and its presentation to the world – all this, and much more, was done by middling and upper-class women, but was defined as leisure, done as part of her daily life by the lady of the house; unpaid in families who wanted to appear so genteel that the women of the family were idle.

The all-male professionals waxed loudly critical of experienced but unqualified women. Women doctors, nurses and surgeons now found themselves excluded from the professional guilds, which demanded a university degree when no woman could attend a university.[98] Patients, who had been persuaded that prescribing medicine and surgery had to be learned at university and licensed by a guild, came to choose male doctors, and women healers were pushed into poorer patients or nursing. In 1650, only about 65 per cent of health practitioners claimed to be professionally qualified and registered; ten years later, this had risen to 75 per cent.[99]

Elizabeth Cellier (?1640–after 1688), an experienced midwife, described the dangers for women in childbed when they were attended by a highly qualified but inexperienced male doctor, 'especially such as confess they never delivered Women in their lives, and being asked "what would they do in such a case" Reply "they have not yet studied it but will when occasion serves".'[100]

Cellier argued that there should be a college of midwives, so that women could increase their traditional skills, obtain certification and form a working guild. She published *A scheme for the foundation of a royal hospital ... and for the maintenance of a corporation of skilled Midwives.*[101] No corporation was founded, and midwives were employed by poor patients while qualified but inexperienced men attended and billed the middling and upper classes.

Records of medical spending in Kent show wealthy patients transferring their spending from nursing care (mostly women) to physicians (mostly men).[102] Those women physicians who hung on to their practice moved to the care of women patients and children. Of 43 payments to women for assistance during illness in the Kent records, 2 were for serving as messengers, 7 were for tending children and 13 were for dealing with minor ailments. Only 21 payments were made to women for performing surgery or prescribing for patients; compared with 1,756 payments to male physicians and surgeons.[103]

In this period, banking and international money-dealing grew very quickly and women, who already dominated small-scale credit and moneylending businesses, should have been well positioned to join the massive global expansion. But they were unable to expand because of their lack of legal status. No woman's loan or mortgage could be enforced by a court. Women were limited to small loans that they could personally cover and collect, and to a clientele that they knew could be trusted. Women were not able to expand their credit and pawn businesses to work with strangers, let alone international finance.

Jewish women proved the exception, specialising in international trade and moneylending, as their word was uniquely reliable. Oliver Cromwell's encouragement of the return of Jewish people to England for the benefit of international trade meant that by 1660 there were 35 Jewish families in London alone. The original settlers from Spain and Portugal were followed by Jewish families, mostly from Amsterdam and the Low Countries. The Ashkenazi Jews formed their own congregation in 1690 and acquired a synagogue in Duke's Place. The Spanish and Portuguese Jews may have had two synagogues: one in Creechurch Lane and another at St Helens.[104] By 1690, there were around 400 Jews in London and the 1695 census list showed 48 of 110 parishes in the capital with Jewish inhabitants; most of the population were in All Hallows, London Wall; St Andrew, Undershaft; St Helen, Bishopsgate; St James, Duke's Place; St Katharine Cree, Aldgate; and St Katherine, Coleman.[105] The safety of the Jewish community had been guaranteed by the returned king himself, desperately short of money, needing moneylenders.[106] Their success prompted one commentator, William Erbery, to ask if Muslim people should not also emigrate to England: 'This Christian Common-wealth, appearing so favourable to the Jews, why not to the Turks?'[107]

The Bank of England was established in 1694, while Child's, Coutts and the partnership that would become Barclays Bank started to hold large reserves of cash and lend internationally. Banker Edward Blackwell had 1,000 clients and held £500,000 on deposit.[108] Interest rates averaged 5 per cent in the middle of the seventeenth century.[109] The expansion of trade to the Far East – and, above all, the global trade in slaves – meant that banking in all its forms took off in the seventeenth and eighteenth centuries; but women – without legally enforceable contracts to their name – could not join it.

The trade of printing was widely hit by the restoration of Charles II. Religious and instructive tracts had seen a boom in the civil wars and Cromwell years: there were 132 women printers in the century before the return of the monarchy,[110] but the market for Puritan sermons plummeted under the new pleasure-loving king. To reduce the number of printers, the Stationers' Company in London refused licences to the poorest printing houses, all of which were run by widows – the survivors of husband-and-wife printing teams. Only the most substantial widow printers survived.[111]

Guilds and professional associations of all sorts continued to close their doors to women members and women apprentices, to exclude them from the most profitable work, leaving them the least rewarding parts of the business. While widows and wives of tradesmen might still be admitted as a gesture of respect to the more important man, still important even though deceased, single women entrepreneurs found themselves banned. They were literally on their own: Jane Zains had to pay a fee up to 30 times more than that of a male trader or a widow, when she opened her linen drapery business in Southampton in 1680.[112]

From 1731, English men and women of African ancestry were excluded from training in London by a proclamation from the lord mayor: 'No Negroes or other Blacks be suffered to be bound apprentices, at any of the Companies of this City to any freeman thereof'.[113] When laws against 'gypsies' were repealed by Queen Anne in the early eighteenth century, it disrupted the campaign of Northumberland magistrates against bands of men and women who they did not name as 'gypsies' but as 'Baleys Shaws Falls or ffawes have of late to come into this country and keep themselves together ... threatening to burn houses and are suspected of burglaries theft and other evil practices and ride armed to the great terror of her Majesty subjects.'

A 'large number' were arrested but most of the men broke out of prison, leaving the women and children behind. The women were whipped and the children kept in the poor house until apprenticed. In later years, some of them would be recaptured and transported as indentured servants – servitude – to Virginia.[114]

Even the little business of selling fresh foods in the street became more hostile towards women at the end of the eighteenth century. Women traders walking the streets and in the outdoor markets came under increasing pressure, blamed for disorder, false measures, selling stolen goods and blocking the highways. In London especially, local bye-laws were passed to limit and control women vendors. Street trading had been the marketplace for those who could not afford to buy and rent stalls or shops, but now even the streets closed to women.

Craftsmen and women who made their products at home – such as tailors or cobblers – opened their front windows to the streets and traded with passers-by, and in the mid-1700s all sorts of retailers opened in the front-facing rooms of domestic houses. As domestic premises, they were officially owned by the male householders; a woman might be the only shopkeeper, she might own all the stock, she might have made everything herself, but officially it was not her shop: only 6 per cent of shops were recorded as being kept by women, and only 4.5 per cent as owned by women.

Even spinning – the constant occupation of all working women – was threatened by a new invention. According to the origin legend, James Hargreaves, a hand-loom weaver, saw his wife's spinning wheel fallen on the floor with the wheel still turning and the spindle still winding thread in their home at Oswaldtwistle, Lancashire. He realised that a wheel mounted sideways could feed many threads to many spindles – and the spinning jenny with multiple spindles was invented. The machine broke the home-based trade that had been the economic foundation of almost all women. The first machines were set up (sometimes hired) in homes and in workshops and operated by women at low pay; but when they became bigger and heavier, from 1720 onwards, they were moved into factories powered by water. Spinning became mechanised and industrialised: hundreds of new machines were housed in the new buildings known as mills – after the earlier corn mills – and women were transformed from individual craft workers into factory 'hands', working in shifts at the speed that suited the machines, forced out of a craft that had been known as 'women's work' for thousands of years. In the early years of high pay in the industry, women were even squeezed off the machines as male spinners tried to have them excluded from well-paid work.

The trade of silk weaving, threatened by cheap foreign imports, became increasingly unfriendly to women. Most male silk weavers in the 1600s had owned the family looms and employed family members: children to watch the threads, a wife to set the threads and weave beside him or spin the thread. Apprentices were brought into the family home for training, and worked and lived with the family, setting up their own family workshops when they qualified as master weavers themselves.[115] By the 1700s, the guild was discouraging the family business, preferring men to qualify as weavers, join the guild and then train a limited number of male apprentices. The master weavers now aimed at keeping trained apprentices in the business, holding wages down and maximising profits. A gulf developed between workers and the masters, and they both tried to exclude women. The Weavers' Company, which had accepted the extraordinary talent of Anna Maria Garthwaite, was now urged by its members to exclude women from the trade. A ballad of the 1720s complained bitterly against the company admitting women:

But now we find the Masters another way has ta'en,
For to admit the Women for to increase their gain,
For since they hear from home, so many Men are gone,
They think it fit, for to admit the Women in their room,
… You Widows, Wives, and Maidens, that hath a mind to be,
Admitted as free Weavers into our Company,
Three Pounds it is the Price, then take my kind advice,
Your Money tender they'll a Member make you in a trice,
And so to assure you they take it not amiss,
The Masters will discharge you with a kind loving kiss,
For now you have a call, from the Masters of the Hall,
For to admit, if you think fit, your Boys and Girls and all.[116]

In 1769, six men broke into the house of a pattern drawer, Daniel Clarke, demanding 'where the B——h his wife was, saying they would murder her directly, and they would cut his ears off, if he did not come up and show them where the work was'.

Clarke agreed that his wife had drawn the patterns for the silk that was on his loom, but 'they might depend upon it, she should make no more of it'. The men went upstairs to where the loom was kept in the Clarke family home and cut the half-finished silk from it, a two-coloured flowered satin, or 'Leopard spot'. As Elizabeth Clarke said later, 'I did it, they were offended because it was a work too good for a woman to have a hand in.' Daniel Clarke was later suspected of giving evidence against rioting silk weavers and was lynched by a mob of 3,000 people and drowned in a pond.[117]

As foreign imports introduced new fabrics like calico and cottons from India, hardship in the silk trade spread. Women consumers were blamed for preferring foreign cloths, and women workers were blamed for entering the trade.

For seamstresses, the arrival of the 'mantua', a new form of dress, offered an opportunity to move into tailoring. A loose-fitting gown that came into fashion in the 1680s, originally as an overgown, without any internal boning or corsetry, the mantua could be made by someone without a lengthy professional training as an apprentice under a master and without a large workshop or lots of different materials. Women petticoatmakers easily transferred to mantua-making, exploiting the opportunity. As soon as the Tailors' Guild realised that mantua gowns were a profitable, and booming market, they started to campaign for laws to prevent 'Manto-makers' from working. The guild pursued relentless prosecutions against seamstresses, often poor single women working alone, arguing that they were trespassing on tailoring work.[118] The Mercers' Company, which included tailors, haberdashers, milliners, grocers and ironmongers, also prosecuted single women traders. The seamstresses were trapped in a no-win situation – not allowed to work without guild membership but not allowed to apply for membership of the men-only institution. Ann, an Oxford Milliner, published this letter in *Jackson's Oxford Journal* in September 1771:

> The Mercer's (but more properly the Merciless Company)
> threatening me with an immediate Distress, if I do not leave off my
> Business or purchase a Freedom of the Company which would cost
> about £20; a Sum almost equal to the whole I possess.[119]

Women banned from the guilds were forced into working for themselves, without any protection of a trade association. If the work could be done with small capital outlay, or in a small workspace, or fitted into domestic work at home, they worked alone. If they could find a guild member prepared to bend guild rules for the profit of exploiting unregulated workers, they might work for a master in his workshop, without training, without regulation and without guild membership. When economic conditions worsened in the 1700s, the women workers were without protection, and their poverty forced them to accept poor wages. This confirmed the guilds' suspicion: that women workers would bring down the wage rate for everyone.[120] Matters became so dire for the mantua-makers that the job title 'mantua-maker' was understood to signify prostitute; most woman mantua-makers had to perform sex acts to earn money or food to survive.[121]

Prostitution

The mantua-workers were one trade of many where women workers moved into sex work to supplement their earnings, and moved out again as soon as they could. In London and in provincial cities, there was a wide range of prostitution – from women street walkers and beggars to high-class brothels and privately 'kept' mistresses. Some brothels could be elegant and expensive, copying the style of gentlemen's clubs, and were visible and tolerated for the years from 1660 to the early 1800s. Some were specialist: seven young women established a house in London's Covent Garden during the Commonwealth and served as 'confessors', offering absolution as Roman Catholic priests, alongside sexual services[122] – both roles equally troubling to the Puritan mentality.

One of the first guides to prostitutes in London was published in 1691: *A Catalogue of Jilts, Cracks & Prostitutes, Nightwalkers, Whores, She-friends, Kind Women and other of the Linnen-lifting Tribe* lists the women available at Bartholomew Fair. Among the 21 women listed, it noted Mary Holland – 'tall, graceful and comely, shy of her favours' – who was said to be available for £20, and her sister Elizabeth, who was said to be 'indifferent to Money but a Supper and Two Guineas will tempt her'.

Prostitution, especially in London, was widespread and there were post-Restoration calls for sex work to be legalised in specific areas, but these were opposed by another wave of Puritanism, which came in with the Protestant House of Orange (William and Mary) in 1688. From then, prostitutes could be publicly whipped in the streets, and societies to persecute brothel-keepers and prostitutes were formed in London and many provincial towns. It was the new moral associations – not the traditional JPs – which brought most of the prosecutions against prostitutes: in London, there were more than 1,000 a year.[123]

Men, as clients, were never prosecuted for prostitution. A rare man appeared in court in 1721. Thomas Brass admitted soliciting a woman in the street, using her for sex and paying her, but was accused of nothing. He appeared as a witness for her prosecution as a prostitute. His evidence persuaded the magistrates to send her (her name not listed) to the Middlesex House of Correction for 'picking him up in the streets and carrying him into a tavern and agreeing to let him lie with her for 4s 6d'.[124]

It was widely believed that it was best for everyone if elite men restrained their sexual appetite in the elite domestic home and used poor women for sex. Enlightenment beliefs about the healthy balance of humours dictated that men should avoid sexual frustration.[125] Pornography was widely available for literate men after the end of the Licensing Act in 1695,[126] and mostly described male lust and female passivity,[127] for use by men to masturbate – which was not considered unhealthy or a social evil until the nineteenth century.[128]

Poor women could also be used as an outlet for homosexuals. Lady Saville was said to have converted her son, Sir George, from homosexuality in 1750 by taking him away from a male lover, a waiter at Mount's coffee house, into the country to have sex with servant girls and agricultural workers. Henry Harris reported the cure: 'Lady Saville has taken her younger twig of Sodom into the country, and by way of weaning him from that unnatural vice, takes great pains to cocker him with every Abigail in her house and all the milk maid cunts in the neighbourhood.'[129]

Slaves and Slave Owners

Wealthy English women were involved in the growing trade in slaves as owners. Queen Catherine of Braganza bought shares in her husband Charles II's company, the Royal Adventurers Trading into Africa, founded in 1660 to kidnap and ship enslaved people from the continent. Charles's mistress Louise de Kérouaille had a portrait painted of herself with her arm around an apparently adoring page.

The women of the slave-trading Morice family took the compliment of having slaver ships named after them: *Anne*, *Katherine*, *Sarah* and *Judith*. Other slave merchant and sugar plantation daughters consolidated slaving fortunes with advantageous marriages.[130]

The royal court contained African-born slaves, including one man bought for £50. James II continued investing in the slave trade and his daughter Queen Anne signed a contract worth £7.5 million for Britain to supply slaves to the Spanish West Indies, taking 20 per cent for herself.[131]

Slaves were not only traded across the Atlantic to the plantations in the New World, but imported into Europe. In England they were mostly used for domestic service and it became fashionable to have African-born page boys and girl companions. An eight-year-old Black girl was publicly auctioned in Liverpool in 1765: 'To be sold by auction at George's coffee house betwixt the hours of 6 and 8 o'clock a very fine Negro girl about eight years of age, very healthy, and hath been sometime from the coast. Any person willing to purchase the same, may apply to Captain Robert Syers, at Mr Bartley Hodgett's, Mercer and Draper, near the Exchange where she may be seen till the time of sale.'[132]

An enslaved six-year-old girl with white skin, brought from Jamaica, was exhibited as a novelty at Charing Cross in 1756. Spectators paid a shilling each to see her. The offensive language of the time said she had 'all the features of an Ethiopian with the flaxen woolly head, a skin and complexion as fair as alabaster'.[133]

Slaves were brought to England with their returning colonial owners, who continued to exploit them as slaves in England, though there were doubts about the legality of slavery in England. An enslaved woman – Katherine Auker – won partial freedom in the Middlesex court in 1690. She told the court that she had been brought to England by her master Robert Rich, a planter in Barbados, six years earlier. She had managed to get religious instruction and baptism at St Katherine's Church, near the Tower of London. Some people thought that baptised people were automatically freed, but the Rich family did not free Katherine Auker. They physically abused her – her statement says she was 'tortured and turned out of doors' but they did not officially discharge her from slavery. When the family returned to Barbados, they kidnapped her and threatened to cut off her nose and ears, but she managed to get away. Nobody would employ a woman enslaved to another owner, so she was destitute. It was probably her poverty which might be a charge on the parish that earned her a sympathetic hearing at the court, which ruled: 'Order for Kath' Auker a Black to be at liberty to go to service until her master shall return from Barbados and provide for her.' She was not freed from slavery, but she was allowed to work as a servant until her slave owner returned, when she would return to slavery and become his responsibility. Probably, she was able to disappear into work in London and take her own freedom.[134]

Eighteenth-century newspapers often included advertisements for the return of runaway slaves – many threatening sympathisers not to hide or protect them:

> Run away from her Master at Black-Heath, A Negro Woman, aged about 25 Years, pretty fat, (went by the Name of Cælia) and is indented by the Name of Cælia Edlyne, and has several Years to serve. She has a Cross, the Mark of her Country, on one Cheek, just under her Eye, and walks lame, being a little inclinable to the Dropsy: She Washes, Irons, Clear-starches, and remarkably Darns well. Whoever secures her, and gives Notice at the Bar of the Jamaica Coffee-House, so that she be brought to Justice, shall have Two Guineas Reward; but whosoever entertains her, shall be prosecuted with the utmost Rigour.[135]

Clearly, runaway slaves found a welcome and a refuge in white working-class communities. Christmas Bennett ran away to Whitechapel – a working-class area of London:

> RUN away last Thursday Morning from Mr. Gifford's, in Brunswick-Row, Queen-Square, Great Ormond-Street, an indentur'd Negro Woman Servant, of a yellowish Cast, nam'd Christmas Bennett; she had on a dark-grey Poplin, lin'd with a grey water'd Silk, mark'd under each Ear with having an Issue, and a Seeton behind her Neck, and suppos'd to be conceal'd somewhere about Whitechapel. Whoever harbours her after this Publication shall be severely prosecuted; and a Reward of a Guinea will be given to any Person who will give Information of her, so that she may be had again.[136]

Historian Peter Fryer said there was an awareness in both white and Black communities that they should unite: 'They saw black people as fellow victims of their enemies, fellow fighters against a system that degraded poor whites and poor blacks alike. With their help, London had by the 1760s, become a centre of black resistance.'[137]

Black men and women developed their own communities in England: a London newspaper reported a party at which people 'Supped, drank, and entertained themselves with dancing and music, consisting of violins,

French horns, and other instruments, at a public house in Fleet Street, till four in the morning. No Whites were allowed to be present for all the performers were Blacks.'[138]

In remote areas of England, ex-slaves were both more isolated and visible; but there were friendships and marriages between white and Black people. The apparent 'disappearance' of thousands of African and Caribbean people brought into England as slaves and runaways was caused by intermarriages for love between the immigrant population and the indigenous people.

Literary Work

There was an extraordinary growth of women writers and an explosion of book production in the seventeenth century: between 1616 and 1620, only eight new books written by women had appeared but in the later years of the century women would be producing hundreds: 653 new titles by 231 named authors, some of them writing multiple books.[139] This boom in publishing was powered by women authors writing to keep their families together after the civil wars, recording their extraordinary times, and gaining confidence to publish their practical, spiritual and political insights. This is the time that women publish themselves.

Quaker women, whose theology taught that women could bear witness, were especially prominent, contributing 20 per cent of the women's publications for the century, and women prophets from other religions also wrote and published their visions. Widow Joan Whitrowe published her advice to Queen Mary in 1690,[140] telling King William: 'Take this Counsel, though from a woman. The Lord is no respector of persons.'[141]

The philosopher Lady Anne Conway developed a theory of religion, reading the Kabbalah, the Quran and Quaker texts.[142] But few prophetesses enjoyed the accuracy of Lady Eleanor Davies, who predicted that her husband would die within three years of an argument in which he burned her manuscript. He died in the same week that he destroyed her manuscript.[143] (Rightly so.)

Practical advice books by women for women became popular from 1640, with women publishing medical books and books of recipes. The numbers of women authors may have been underestimated because male editors, male publishers and male readers did not always acknowledge women's authorship of science and medical works. *Opuscula Philosophica* by Anne Conway was not credited to her, but to the man who translated her Latin text into English. Anonymous books were attributed to men if they were not thought suitable subjects for a woman author. Readers of non-fiction preferred their books to be authored by men, but women authored medical researches and recipes for medicine, including: the Countess of Arundel, Althea Talbot; Viscountess Ranelagh, Katherine James; the Countess of Kent, Elizabeth Grey; Hannah Woolley; and the Countess of Cumberland, Margaret Clifford, and her daughter the Countess of Pembroke, Anne Clifford.[144]

Ladies like Mary Sidney and Anne Conway wrote philosophical and natural science treatises. Best known of the polymath ladies, singled out by contemporaries and then historians for her eccentricities, was the Duchess of Newcastle, Margaret Cavendish.[145] The uncompromising duchess, writer of plays, an autobiography and a biography of her husband, studied and wrote about science. Known as 'Mad Meg', she believed female ignorance came from lack of experience:

> We are kept like birds in our houses not suffered to fly abroad to see
> the several changes of Fortune and the various humours ordained and
> created by nature, and wanting the experience of nature, we must
> needs want the understanding and knowledge, and so consequently
> prudence and invention of men.[146]

These years also see the rise of diaries written by elite women. They are not a reliable picture of normal women's lives: there is no recorded diary or journal written by a poor woman before 1660 (which is not to say that none were written – just not valued enough to be kept).[147] Some were edited by friends and family. Some were spiritual exercises, with sins and omissions exaggerated for effect. They all report that the only way to complete their spiritual exercises and stay on top of their long, arduous working days is to rise very early and go to bed late. Mary Rich, the Countess of Warwick, was responsible for the running of her home at a manor house in Essex; she personally supervised the dairy and the henhouse, as well as the management of the entire estate, and raised her husband's three nieces. She kept the account books of household and estate, working as the lady of the house and the estate manager. Her neighbour Elizabeth Walker, who also kept a diary, did very similar work, as well as physically labouring on her land.[148]

The diaries show some elite women enjoying the seclusion and protection of a marriage in which the husband represented the family in the wider world of business, law and politics, and his wife undertook the burdens of running estate and house. But some women, such as Lady Anne Clifford, wanted more: 'All this time my Lord was in London where he had all and infinite great resort coming to him … I stayed in the country having many times a sorrowful and heavy heart … so as I may truly say I am like an owl in the desert.'[149]

Since the diaries were often written as a spiritual exercise, they emphasise spiritual life and sometimes an intense emotional – even sensual – relationship with God. The Countess of Warwick wrote of 'warmth' and 'fire' in times of spiritual emotional intensity. Some wives explicitly recorded that their marriages were unhappy, and some wrote of deep relief at the death of the husband.[150]

Katherine Philips (1632–64) was a poet, translator and dramatist who refused to publish but circulated her poems among friends and family. The poems were published without her permission to her distress: 'Tis only I … that cannot so much as think in private, that must have my imaginations rifled and exposed to play the Mountebanks, and dance upon the Ropes to entertain all the rabble.'[151]

Despite her aversion to publication, Philips became known as the 'Matchless Orinda' as she used classical names for her friends. Passionate female friendship was her principal theme, and she was regarded as one of the great poets of her day. Her friend Sir Charles Cotterell intended a compliment in his backhanded praise in 1667: 'Some of [her works] would be no disgrace to the name of any Man that amongst us is most esteemed for his excellency in this kind, and there are none that may not pass with favour, when it is remembered that they fell hastily from the pen but of a woman.'[152]

Almost every topic was open to the female author of the early 1700s, including criticism of the condition of women and speculation about the alternatives to marriage. The only subject that women authors avoided completely, until the end of the century, was contraception, it being 'obvious' that the first duty of a wife was to produce children.[153]

Hannah Woolley (1622–75), daughter of a woman physician, founded her own girls' school in Hackney, teaching genteel craft skills, and wrote *A Gentlewoman's Companion*, arguing that a lady should know all the practical tasks of the household including physic and medicine. She burst out: 'Man is apt to think that we were merely intended for the world's propagation and to keep its humane inhabitants sweet and cleane; but by their leaves, had we the same Literature he would find our brains as fruitful as our bodies.'[154]

Fifteenth- and sixteenth-century authors were defensive about women: their titles spoke of 'sanctuaries' and 'protections' for women. But by the seventeenth and eighteenth centuries, authors had become bolder, speaking of 'female advocates' and 'ladies' defences'.[155] Increasingly, women authors argued that if women received an equal education to men they would be their equals, even superiors.[156]

The first periodical specifically aimed at women was launched in 1693 with *The Ladies' Mercury*, and was followed by many others, mostly edited by professional women writers, some of them successful novelists, providing an opportunity for freelance women writers and inspiration to women readers. They tended to be short-lived, squeezed out by the more established, and more prestigious, men's publications, especially the *Gentleman's Magazine*.[157]

The first woman to make a living from writing was the notorious playwright, novelist and sometime royalist spy Aphra Behn, who published 16 plays in 19 years from 1670. Her 1682 novel *Love-Letters between a Nobleman and His Sister* ran to 16 editions. She wrote bawdy, witty plays for the women actors who now took to the stage, including the new king's mistress Nell Gwynn. Behn, who claimed that arranged marriages were little better than prostitution, would be widely condemned for the sexual freedom of her writing; but she was hugely successful.[158]

With rare exceptions, early women authors found it hard to make a living from writing. Those who had no family support turned their hands to all sorts of authorship: journalism, pamphleteering, research and factual writing, other forms of fiction and publishing serials. Writers such as these, trying to earn a living from 'hack' work – named for the London parish of Hackney where they lived – found themselves forced to take writing commissions from any publisher that would pay them. Such female authors lost status by being women for hire, unlike genteel authors who could pass off their writing as an elegant hobby. Jane Barker

(1652–?), one of the first women to make a living from her writing, supplemented it with the sale of her own patent medicine, and gave herself a doctor's title: *Dr Barker's Famous Gout Plaister*. Eliza Haywood (1693–1756) salvaged her reputation as a runaway wife, playwright and novelist of bawdy love stories by turning to novels about female suffering and female sexual restraint.

The new form of fiction – the novel – developed through many early literary experiments in form and genre from about 1720, until it became the dominant voice of Romanticism. Readers were said to prefer female authors for novels, many of which were published anonymously – by 'A Lady'. Some of them may even have been ladies. A survey of titles between 1750 and 1769 shows more women than men authors in 11 of the 19 years; but few women were as well paid as men.[159]

Women writers could face criticism for speaking out, since the convention that they should be silent and above all 'modest' remained strong, and was growing. Some women tried to avoid censure by claiming to write only for their own sex, or chose a subject that was appropriate for women, such as domestic skills or devotion to God. Some developed a habit of apologising for publishing and blamed an inadequate education for any flaws in their work, in the hope of making male critics more generous in their criticism. A study of prefaces to poetry between 1667 and 1750 revealed that half apologised for the author being a woman, reassuring the reader that she was not a professional poetess and had not intended to publish.[160]

But by writing and publishing under their own names, women challenged the belief that they were naturally unintelligent, incapable, incoherent, overly emotional. The seventeenth-century women writers – by their very presence – contradicted the conventional assumptions and increasingly loud assertions about women's lack of abilities, lack of intelligence and their restricted opportunities. The 1660s see the first consciously feminist thinking, with women authors declaring that there was no justification for restrictions on women or their lack of opportunities: not in the Bible, nor in the nature of women. An author calling herself 'Esther Sowerman' turned the Creation story around to prove the superiority of the woman, claiming 'that women were superior to men as they were created from Adam's rib and not from dust'.[161]

Mary Astell (1666–1731) argued that there could be no logical reason for male dominance, that men were not born free and women were not born slaves.[162] Her book *A Serious Proposal to the Ladies* (1694) proposed residential centres for single women as places of education and refuge – like Protestant nunneries – where women could live apart from men. She took inspiration from Queen Anne, her patron, and her friends included Lady Mary Wortley Montagu, Judith Drake, Elizabeth Elstob and many others. They were the forerunners of the eighteenth-century 'bluestocking salons' – women-organised gatherings of intellectuals in London, whose leading lights would be Hester Thrale, Hester Chapone, Elizabeth Montagu and Elizabeth Carter: all writers who supported other women writers.[163] Other women corresponded with male philosophers and scientists.

Mary Astell's book on marriage, *Some Reflections on Marriage* (1700), suggested that a union could become a relationship of tyranny and slavery.[164] A wife had chosen a 'monarch for life', with nothing to do but 'please and obey'.[165] She urged readers that there was nothing terrifying about the name 'Old Maid' and that they could be 'absolute Monarchs in their own Bosums'.[166]

Astell challenged the idea of the superiority of men by citing the paradox of the 'Queen's footman', an example of how inequality based on sex (the footman was superior to the queen) conflicted with inequality based on class (the queen was superior to the footman): 'If every Man is by Nature superior of every Woman, it would be a sin in Woman to have Dominion over any Man, and the greatest Queen ought not to command but to obey her footman.'[167]

Sport

After twenty years' of Parliamentary suppression of sports, the Restoration heralded a return to public exhibitions of women footracing, pitching the bar, playing football, cricket and fighting in public competitions for wagers, challenges or prize money. Samuel Pepys watched girls running for wagers at the Bowling Green, London, in 1667. In Manchester 1681, three women raced naked for the prize of a Holland shift – a typical prize of a petticoat or an overgown of good quality 'Holland' material. In Lancashire in 1696, at a horse race meet, girls ran a race for a smock and a guinea. In Berkshire a year later, at another race meeting, women raced each other for a smock.[168]

By the middle of the eighteenth century, several women's annual foot-races had been organised across the country, with winners from one race excluded from the others, the first example of a set of interrelated women's races. Many were so-called 'smock or shift' races with dresses or petticoats for the prize. Women raced barefoot, wearing white waistcoats and drawers, and sometimes naked. Women runners dominated the sport, running the same distances as men, and often further. Fast runners became famous, challenging each other: in 1712, 'The Flying Milk Woman of Ormond-Street' ran against 'The Mad Bess of Southwark' for 5 guineas a side on Hounslow Heath.[169]

Record crowds gathered in the windows and balconies of the houses on Pall Mall for a race in 1732 that was won by Hannah Williams, who scooped the prize of a fine Holland smock. Hannah's husband made her sell her prize and buy two of 'coarse thread' in its place.[170]

Women were renowned for their skills as boxers and prizefighters. Elizabeth Wilkinson Stokes was called a championess, even though the most able male boxer James Figg was not called a champion.[171] She published a challenge in the *London Journal* in June 1722: 'I, Elizabeth Wilkinson, of Clerkenwell, having had some words with Hannah Highfield and requiring satisfaction, do invite her to meet me on the stage and box with me for three guineas, each woman holding half a crown in each hand, and the first women that drops her money to lose the battle.'[172]

Hannah replied: 'I, Hannah Highfield of Newgate Market hearing of the resoluteness of Elizabeth Wilkinson will not fail, God willing, to give her more blows than words, desiring home blows, and of her no favour. She may expect a good thrumping.'[173]

Elizabeth Wilkinson introduced rules and a dress code to women's matches, with fighters expected to wear 'cloth jackets, short petticoats coming just below the knee, Holland drawers, white stockings and pumps'. Although famous for her fist-fights, she also fought with swords, knives and quarterstaff. A spectator at a fight in 1728 described:

a small Englishwoman, full of fire and very agile … she wore red ribbons. They began to fight with 'a sort of two-handed sword, three or three and a half feet in length; the guard was covered, and the blade was about three inches wide and not sharp only about half a foot of it was, but then that part cut like a razor.' After some sparring, the Irishwoman was cut across her forehead and the fight was stopped for the wound to be sewn up by a surgeon, and a plaster applied to it. She then took 'a big glass of spirits to revive her courage' and the fight resumed, this time with each fighter 'holding a dagger in her left hand to ward off the blows.' The Irishwoman was wounded again, and again the fight was stopped for her to be sewn up. When it was recommenced, the women held wicker shields for defense, but the Irishwoman received 'a long and deep wound all across her neck and throat,' which again was sewn up but she was too badly hurt to continue. With 'the combatants ... dripping with perspiration, and the Irishwoman also with blood,' the fight came to an end, and coins were thrown to the fighters.[174]

Elizabeth Wilkinson was known as the prime English fighter until her name fell from the record in the last years of the nineteenth century, when boxing became known as a male sport and she was forgotten.[175]

'The greatest cricket match that was played in this part of England,' according to the *Reading Mercury* of 1745, was between the Bramley maids in blue ribbons and the Hambledon maids with red ribbons on their heads: 'The Bramley girls got 119 notches and the Hambledon girls 127. There was of bothe sexes the greatest number that ever was seen on such an occasion. The girls bowled, batted, ran and catches as well as most men could do in that game.'[176]

The earliest report of a game of football with modern-style rules is of a women's match. In 1726, women were reported playing a 'friendly' match of six-a-side football at the Bowling Green, Bath, on a weekday, but playing professionally for money on Sundays on a pitch before paying spectators.[177]

Romanticism

From about 1740, the Enlightenment insistence on the superiority of thought (male) over feelings (female) started to be challenged by a new insistence on the merit of strong feelings and the revelation of deep truth in deep emotion. This was 'sensibility'.[178] Only the upper classes possessed sensibility. Adam Smith, father of the Enlightenment, declared that it was 'much beyond what is possessed by the rude vulgar of mankind'.[179]

A whole new gulf was opened up between women, separating those who were stoical and unresponsive from those who were highly strung. Ladies were supposed to be born with a refined sensibility that prompted them to virtue, while working-class women were the 'rude vulgar of mankind'. People came to believe that women of the aristocracy, gentry and rising middle classes were so different from women of the labouring classes as to have almost nothing in common, almost another species. Even their biology – physical strength, sexual response, pain threshold – was said to be different.[180]

Of course, this confirmed courtly love ideas about the delicacy and frigidity of elite women, and was supported by the conduct books which had taught for more than a century that ladies should be non-productive, sexually cold and inactive. These hard-taught traits were now observed in genteel ladies as if they had occurred naturally – and were described as the 'natural' difference between ladies and lower-class women. Observers noticed a complete difference between virtuous upper-class women and the untutored bawdy women of the lower classes.[181]

The research in women's sex organs was used to confirm women's difference from men, their inferiority to men, and their general unfitness for life. By the end of the 1600s, the belief that upper- and middling-class women's nature was maternal, tender, emotional and illogical, and that they were physically frail or at least inactive, implied that ladies were obviously unfit for public office or responsibility outside the home.[182] Working-class women were excluded from authority on the grounds that they were ignorant and ill-judging through lack of education, and 'naturally' inconsistent and unreliable because female.

Novels replaced conduct books as the most popular way of teaching literate women the qualities they needed to demonstrate gentility. Passionate feelings about Nature or Art could shake a lady and move her to tears or even faintness; but sexuality was completely repressed. Heroines in the eighteenth-century novel were highly emotional but never sexually voracious. They felt passionately; but they did not lust. In life, and in literature, almost all the interest in female behaviour focused upon how a woman repressed sexual appetite; and a woman's 'virtue' came to mean nothing more than her sexual inactivity.[183]

The stories initially followed the literary tradition of 'histories' – fictionalised biographies. As the many anonymous and named women authors made the form their own, they developed it to suit their own particular tastes and based it on their experience. No longer would the heroine be a woman of classical times, or a royal mistress in France; the elite English women authors set the fictions in the place they knew best: the imaginary English home and the imaginary English countryside. This was far from the real English upper-class home, which was arduously supported by the underpaid work of an army of domestic servants, financed by the underpaid labourers in a distant factory and slaves in a distant land. This was not the real English countryside: increasingly a place of struggle for women being driven from the land to earn a living. It was a fantasy England from an imaginary golden age of good lordship, happy peasantry and ladies in a big house or castle.

The typical heroine of the new novels is courted by a totally suitable young man, of superior status and wealth, and then separated from him by circumstances. As the novels became more 'gothic' – darker, exotic and unlikely – the heroine found herself kidnapped and abused by enemies. Those stories that remained English and domestic usually involved mistaken identity or the interference of false friends to separate the well-suited couple. The adventure of the story was the heroine learning to understand herself, experiencing emotion, repressing emotions, finding virtue and finally seeing the suitability of her suitor – who usually came into a substantial fortune during their separation and his own emotional journey. Then they married with the consent of parents and guardians, which had often been withheld earlier.

The new novels taught readers – the literate elite – that to be a successful lady was to be a highly tuned string, thrilled by moral feelings and higher emotions. In *Pamela* by Samuel Richardson, and then in his *Clarissa*, the adventure for the heroine was to control her own sexual desire (identified as 'liking' or 'love' but never 'lust') and guide a predatory man to respectable marriage. 'Virtue' in the eighteenth-century novel deteriorated to mean sexual repression. Of the 150 most popular novels in the commercial circulating libraries between 1739 and 1801, only two heroines had sexual intercourse outside marriage, and one of those was raped. Both died.[184] Julie in *Julie or the New Heloise* died of an illness, brought on by remorse for having enjoyed adulterous sex; Clarissa blamed herself for her own rape by her fiancé. It was not the rape that made her suicidal, but that she had allowed herself to be attracted to her suitor. These two were the first fictional self-harming victims of the double sexual standard – women who held themselves to a higher standard than men and punished themselves for failure.

Love and Marriage in Novels and Life

Love as a good reason for marriage – preferable to arranged marriages – emerged first in the novels and then in life in mid-1700s England. Before then, elite marriage had been a business matter for the family fortunes: Frances Langdale (1710–73) met her future husband for the first time when he was three weeks into the negotiations of their marriage. He met with her father and her grandmother weeks before she set eyes on him, and by then the deal was done.[185]

Arranged marriages became a plot device in the novels to create conflict, distress to the heroine and an obstacle to her marriage to the man of her choice. This fictional development had an impact on the real world: the English middle and even upper classes began to consider the preferences of the bride or bridegroom and allow them the right of a veto, though European parents were slower to change.[186] The advice book *The Ladies Calling* had ruled in 1673 that the choice of husband should be made by parents, and young ladies allowed only a veto.

But fortunes must be made and estates merged; socially ambitious entrepreneurs bought themselves status by endowing a daughter to marry upwards. Marriageable people could not be allowed to roam freely and find a partner at random. Marriageable young men and women were introduced to each other inside the narrow circle of wealthy friends and families. In every English town, especially London, where the 'season' (April–November) featured parties and even ticketed assemblies for elite youth, communities organised meeting places and events to introduce the wealthy young people to each other. The cost, the etiquette and the private entrance requirements meant that only those with aristocratic patrons or wealth could enter, meet and choose from a rigorously pre-selected field.

Even then, it was not free choice for women. A woman could consent, but she could not propose. The tradition was that the man sought permission from a woman's family and proposed to her; she consulted her family and friends, and accepted or refused him. The tradition of a woman proposing to a man she liked did not expand from the working classes. This put all young ladies in the social difficulty of encouraging a suitor, without overstepping the razor-thin line of modesty. Thousands of words of advice were written or whispered to young ladies about how to stand out but not push in; how to lead up but not lead on.

Even worse for ladies, the system of male choice ranged women as competitors against each other. In previous generations, when elite marriages were arranged between strangers, a woman's friendship with another woman was often the most significant relationship in her life. But in the new system of women competing for a bridegroom, every woman was a rival.

The trend towards love as a motive for marriage caused great concern to the fathers of heiresses. Fear of secret and informal weddings between wealthy women and opportunistic men rose again in the middle of the 1700s as the novels praised marriages for love and fictional heroines defied their fictional families. In 1753, a new law ruled that all weddings must be performed in church, by an ordained minister, before registered witnesses either with a special licence or after the calling of banns. Under the new restrictions, runaway brides had to go north, across the border into Scotland, where 'handfasting' informal weddings were still possible. The first village over the border was Gretna Green, where one blacksmith alone estimated that he performed the marriage ceremony over the traditional anvil for more than 100 runaway couples a year.[187]

It was hard for an individual woman to find a man she liked and attract him, defeat her rivals, and persuade her parents to offer the best economic package, in the narrow window of time when she was at peak beauty and could afford a 'season'. John Gregory advised his daughter in 1761: 'Without an unusual share of natural sensibility and very peculiar good fortune, a woman in this country has very little probability of marrying for love.'[188]

A wife who had been chosen for her craft skills, the wealth she would bring and the children she would bear might be reasonably hopeful of a satisfactory marriage. But a bride chosen for love had to deliver all these benefits, as well as making her husband happy – a very ill-defined goal. The marriage for love did not create an equal marriage: the work of emotional intelligence fell mostly on the wife. Richard Steele, eighteenth-century social commentator and founder of the *Spectator*, made it clear: 'With love the wife owes her husband or friendliness and kindness of conversation. She is to endeavour, to bring him as much assistance and

Comfort of life as is possible, so that she may answer that special end of the woman's creation: the being of help to her husband.'[189]

Some husbands tried to be loving and considerate. The smaller sizes of elite and middle-class families in the eighteenth century may indicate that considerate husbands were trying to avoid dangerously frequent births by withdrawal before ejaculation, or even by avoiding full intercourse.[190] One seventeenth-century woman complained: 'Her husband did not deal with her as befitted a married man and what seed should be sown in right fine ground, he spent about the outward part of her body, and with that, threatened that if she were with child, he would slit the gut out of her body.'[191]

Not much marital tenderness there.

The idealised wife in the Romantic novel of sensibility might choose her husband for love but always happened upon a fortune. The story of the hugely successful novel *Pamela*, supposedly a tale of true love overwhelming a heartless man, is really that of successful social mountaineering. All the advice about 'happily ever after' was completely silent about the source of the money that pays for the happy home. No fictional women earned their own money or worked or ran a business after marriage. Heroines, like wives, do no-work and are not-paid.

The other great absence from the novels was female sexuality. Although love provided the only valid reason to marry, it was an ethereal love. Female arousal, when described at all, sounded like illness: faintings, nosebleeds and palpitations. Author Henry Fielding argued in 1746 that upper-class female sexual desire and activity must be repressed. Ladies must 'Preserve their Natural Innocence and Purity'.[192]

In the real world of the upper classes, virginity in brides – always a requirement by men, wanting to be sure that the heir was their own son – was now compulsory, and demonstrated by coolness, even frigidity, by young women before marriage. Any intimacy was banned even during long engagements, and chaperones and strict visiting times guaranteed that there was no opportunity. Even after marriage, genteel wives were warned that any sexual eagerness would lose their husbands' respect. Bernard Mandeville reported of the successful repression of passions in women in 1742: 'To counterbalance this violent natural desire, all young women have strong notions of honour carefully inculcated into them from their infancy.'[193]

After 1750, the conduct books no longer needed to advise about the importance of repressing female sexual desire – it no longer existed – not even as a problem. By the end of the century, in the eponymous novel by Fanny Burney (1796), the heroine Camilla is deeply in love but completely free of lust. Her father assures her: 'You have no passions, my innocent girl, at which you need blush.'[194]

Upper- and middle-class women were neutered by a potent combination of medical theories about female bodies and the novels' descriptions of women's nature. The fashionable and expensive male doctors – who only observed upper-class women patients – recorded that women were incapable of orgasm, and some were repelled by sexual intimacy. The doctors claimed that sexual appetite in a lady was abnormal and should be eliminated by a starvation diet, drugs, prayers and sometimes physical restraint. Just as fear of competition from women was eliminated in the guilds and the professions by excluding women from craft work, the old fear of voracious female sexuality was eliminated by excluding women from sex.[195]

The homes of the middling- and upper-class families became the ladies' quarantine bubble. Dirt, sin and real-world problems must stop at the front door. The virtuous wife made a sanctuary for herself and her family. The ancient Greek theory from Aristotle that home and business were distinct and different places was adapted to suggest that ladies were different from men and in need of a different space. The phrase 'separate spheres' – a sort of sexual apartheid – dominated ideas about where women ought to be, and how they should behave.

The unit of the family as a godly unit – husband, wife and children – was reflected even in the use of pews in church. Upper-class families, who had previously stood nearest the altar, with ladies behind gentlemen and servants behind them, now paid a fee for the parents and children to occupy pews at the very front, and sat together. These formed family pews, occupied by the nuclear family headed by the father, not for the wider household of visitors, apprentices, servants, retainers and hangers-on.[196] Pews became high-walled units with doors, sometimes locked, as if the 'bubble' of the separate sphere had come to church.

Despite the enthusiasm for marriage in the novel, women who had experienced a real-life marriage as opposed to reading about it seemed reluctant to undertake a second one. A substantial number of widows – up to a quarter in one seventeenth-century parish – did not remarry. In contrast, men tended to remarry after the death of a wife: there were about 90,000 widowers to 275,000 widows in 1688.[197] The cheerfully selfish explanation of an eighteenth-century Essex farmer revealed why a man might want to marry again … and why a widow might not: 'Having experienced much comfort in the marriage state and my children requiring some careful female to manage and bring them up I soon determined to look out again.'[198]

Whether married for love or married by arrangement, it was almost impossible for a wife to get a marriage dissolved. The Adultery Act – which had made infidelity a criminal offence, punishable by death – was repealed in 1660 as part of the return of the sexually liberal royal court. Thirty years later, under the more repressive William and Mary, another attempt to criminalise adultery and punish it with death or transportation failed in 1698.[199]

Divorce was still only allowed by an individual decree of Parliament, which cost hundreds of pounds to obtain and favoured the husband, who could divorce his wife for her adultery alone – wives needed to show a more serious offence than male infidelity. Most separating wives complained of violence; but domestic abuse was not grounds for divorce.[200] A divorcing wife had to prove her marriage had been bigamous – her husband was already married to someone else – or that it had been forced on her by rape, or that her husband sodomised her: anal sex, or vaginal penetration with equipment. Few women had the means or the witnesses to prove such complaints; but even a wife successfully leaving a bigamist, rapist or sodomist would lose her children and any fortune she had brought to the marriage, or made during the marriage. All her wealth and children were the property of her husband.[201]

Unsurprisingly, there were only two successful divorce petitions from injured wives to the House of Lords in the 200 years from 1650 until the law was changed in 1857.[202] Whether marriage was for 'love' or by arrangement, women were still legally bound paupers in their husbands' keeping.

One highly unusual woman used her own personal wealth and extraordinary boldness to give her a unique escape route from the law covering wives. Mary Edwards (1705?–43) was the only child of wealthy parents; her father owned property in the home counties and London. Her mother came from a wealthy Dutch family and made no claim on the Edwards' estate but passed it all to 23-year-old Mary, who was said to be the wealthiest woman in England. Within two years, Mary Edwards was in love and claimed to be secretly married to a young aristocratic ensign in the Guards, Lord Anne Hamilton, younger son of the 4th Duke of Hamilton. The announcement of the marriage appeared in the *Gentleman's Magazine* in July 1731: 'Lord Anne Hamilton, to Miss Edwards, of very great fortune'.[203] The marriage was said to have taken place in the Fleet Prison, where clergymen were available to marry couples in a hurry and those wanting secret weddings.

In March 1733, Mary Edwards gave birth to a son and defied scandal declaring herself a single woman on his baptism certificate, naming him 'Gerard Anne Edwards, 'Son of Mrs Mary Edwards, Singlewom.', without naming his father. But in the same year, she extended the use of her coat of arms to Lord Anne who took Edwards as his middle name in 1733.

The family lived together and commissioned Hogarth to paint a portrait of the three of them on the terrace of their home in Kensington. Shortly after this scene of virtuous domesticity, Mary Edwards discovered that her husband had stolen £17,000 worth of her shares in the Bank of England and the India Company. She instructed her lawyers and demanded the return of her funds, describing herself as 'Mary Edwards, spinster'. In effect, she denied any marriage and thus blocked his rights as a husband to her fortune, declared her son a bastard and herself a woman whose reputation was ruined. It was a move of extraordinary daring. The lawyers forced Lord Anne Hamilton to return the money and he left her and his son.

Social ruin did not follow. Mary Edwards' wealth and courage saved her from exclusion from polite society and she continued to live with her son in the country village of Kensington and the grand town house of St James' Street, a well-known patron of the arts. In 1742 she sat for her portrait by Hogarth, draped in jewels, surrounded by symbols of independence – and resistance to tyranny: a bust of Alfred the Great who resisted the Vikings, and Elizabeth I who resisted the Spanish. A globe indicates her freedom in the world and a scroll reads:

Remember Englishmen the Laws the Rights ...
So dearly bought
the Price of so much Contest
Transmit it careful to Posterity ...

An adoring spaniel (not a lady's lapdog) sits under her extended hand. And look at that smile!

In the same year that Mary Edwards commissioned the portrait celebrating her single state, Lord Anne Hamilton (33) married a 16-year-old heiress, Anna Powell. The law and her guardians apparently accepted that there had been no previous marriage.[204]

Poor and working-class people who wanted to end their marriages simply separated. Ten per cent of marriages in Colyton, Devon, ended in separation in 1725–65. Mostly it was husbands leaving wives: 33 men left their wives compared with 6 women leaving their husbands. Some separations were public and formalised by folk rituals like jumping backwards over a broom or the public performance of 'wife sales'.[205]

Women's Love for Women

The Restoration court of Charles II and the culture of London that copied it were sexually permissive; both homosexual and lesbian flirtations and courtships were openly enjoyed. Two of the king's mistresses were said to have gone through a marriage ceremony – perhaps an erotic game for Charles's entertainment, perhaps an expression of their genuine desire.[206] There was well-circulated gossip that Barbara, Lady Castlemaine, and Frances Stewart slept in Castlemaine's bed, but as mistresses of Charles II, this may have been a play for royal attention.

Women at court and in everyday life were friends and lovers. Women proclaimed intense friendships that were allowed, even encouraged by society.[207] Those who described their relationships seem to be passionate even erotic – but not mimicking heterosexual intercourse. Many of them praised their loves as more spiritual than the carnal love of men.

'I am just like one that has lost the sunshine that makes everything cheerful,' wrote the philosopher-philanthropist Elizabeth Burnet (1661–1709) when her friend Sarah Churchill left after a visit. Author and heiress Lady Rachel Russell (1636–1723) spoke of her 'delicious friend'. Letter-writer Anne Dormer (1648–95) wrote to her sister: 'You know so well that I love you dearer than my own life that it is needless for me to tell you so.'[208]

Some women authors were sexually attracted to women but only described their feelings in the most ethereal terms. The poet Katherine Philips published this love letter to another woman:

My excellent Lucasia, on our Friendship:
I did not live until this time
Crown'd my felicity
When I could say, without a crime
I am not thine, but Thee[209]

There were many interlinked passionate friendships at the Stuart court: Anne Killgrew, a maid of honour at the court, wrote a series of passionate poems to 'Eudora' that were explicitly love poems but so respectable as to be published after her death by her father. A contemporary, Countess of Winchilsea Anne Finch, who wrote as 'Ardelia', composed an erotic love poem to Anne Tufton, Countess of Salisbury, claiming to be a white mouse that might be caressed, creep into her 'brown tresses' and be admitted to her bosom.[210] Anne Finch was friend to Elizabeth Singer Rowe, who was in turn the passionate friend of poet Frances Thynne, Countess of Hertford. All these elite women poets wrote sensual love poetry to women.

In the court of the first Duchess of York, Anne Hyde, wife to the future James II, there were scandalous reports of flirtations between ladies-in-waiting. Her daughters, both royal princesses and heirs to James, had openly passionate relationships with women friends. Princess Mary, wife of William of Orange, who would become Queen Mary II, was intimate with Frances, Lady Bathurst, for 20 years, the two writing to each other under pet names and referring to each other as husband and wife. In 1678, Mary described her pregnancy with her husband as if she had betrayed their love: 'Though I have played the whore a little, I love you of all things in the world.'[211]

Mary's sister and successor, Queen Anne, was openly in thrall to Sarah, Duchess of Marlborough, who was only supplanted by a new favourite, Abigail Masham. Shocking reports that the queen was spending her nights with women were carefully framed to avoid a legal challenge.[212] But the press spoke of 'the disagreeable expression of the dark deeds of the night'. The rejected Duchess of Marlborough claimed that Queen Anne had 'Noe inclination for any but of one's own sex'.[213]

Sarah, Duchess of Marlborough, seems to have been confident that accusing the queen of a same-sex attraction to a lady-in-waiting would not raise questions over their own previous relationship. She may have thought that she was protected from gossip about her intimacy with the queen by her own love-marriage and she was also protected from scandal by her political allies and her aristocratic status – far higher than that of her poor-relation successor.

A working-class woman poet wrote passionate poetry about female friendship. Elizabeth Hands, who worked as a domestic servant, described 'Maria's friendship, more to me than love'.[214]

Jane Barker, attached to the court of James II, made it clear that female friendship was not only a purifier of feelings, but of a higher order than other earthly relationships. The fictional heroine of *Patchwork Screen for Ladies* (1723) lived as a single woman, supported herself and enjoyed women-only friendships. She wrote in praise of female friendship:

> Friendship is that mysterious thing alone
> Which can Unite and make two Hearts but one;
> It purifies our love and makes it flow,
> In the clearest stream that's found in Love below.
> It sublimates the Soul and makes it move
> Towards Perfection and Celestial love.[215]

The sentimental friendships were described by the women as 'love'. Constantia Fowler wrote of her sister-in-law in 1630: 'For never creature was more fortunate than I in gaining affection from her. For I believe I am blest with the most perfectest and constant lover as ever woman was blest with.'[216]

In a poem by Anna Seward, one friend feels complete despair when her best friend is engaged to marry and she foresees their cold future encounters:

> When thou shalt pass me with averted eyes,
> Feigning thou seest me not, to sting and grieve,
> And sicken my sad heart, I could not bear
> Such dire eclipse of thy soul-cheering rays
> I could not learn my struggling heart to tear
> From thy loved form, that thro my memory strays;
> Nor in the pale horizon of despair,
> Endure the wintry and the darken'd days.[217]

Marriage to a man became known as the 'funeral or grave of friendship' by the 1700s.[218] But some married women continued intense relationships with women after marriage. The early feminist Mary Wollstonecraft, who would go on to have two scandalous love affairs with men, fell in love with her friend Fanny Blood at their first meeting. Wollstonecraft encouraged her sister Eliza to desert her husband to live with her, and urged Fanny to join them in a male-free household, teaching at a school. When Fanny left the household, to marry, Wollstonecraft declared, 'The world is a desert to me.' She followed her friend Fanny to Portugal to attend her in childbed, and was there at her death.[219]

Mary Astell, the pioneer educator, proposed an all-women's academy for women and girls living together. It never opened, because of the hostility to a 'convent' structure. Mary Astell promised that scholars and staff would enjoy 'Noble, Vertuous, and Disinteresst'd friendship', but confessed that she had a 'weakness for loving women'.[220] She surrounded herself with women friends throughout her life, sometimes troubled by the intensity of her feelings, which were not always reciprocated. Some biographers suggest that she turned to the love of women after a proposal of marriage collapsed. This is a traditional belief that suggests that women seek the company and love of women when they cannot get a man. It is more likely that Mary Astell saw the failure of the betrothal as a lucky escape. In later life, she was openly critical of marriage – she called it a 'tyranny' and a 'slavery' – and made a satisfying attachment with a woman friend, Lady Catherine Jones (1672–1740), who lived with her till her death.[221]

Lady Catherine Jones went on to live with Mary Kendall (1677–1710) – a relationship so highly regarded that it was celebrated by the church authorities and Kendall's cousin, who installed a marble statue of her in the chapel of St John the Baptist in Westminster. The inscription celebrates: 'That close Union and Friendship, In which she lived, with the Lady Catharine Jones; And in testimony of which she desir'd That even their Ashes, after Death, Might not be divided.'[222]

Anna Maria Garthwaite, the silk designer, moved in with her married sister Mary when their father died. Mary called her 'my loving sister' and at her husband's death left her house in York to join Garthwaite in her London house and workshop, where they lived together in an all-female household, with two female servants and their ward.[223]

Mary Kendall (1677–1710) monument, St John the Baptist Chapel, Westminster Abbey. Her ashes were later mingled with those of Lady Catherine Jones

The playwright Catherine Cockburn, née Trotter, a philosopher and moral theologian, was deeply involved with women and maintained a passionate relationship with her patron Lady Sarah Piers. Cockburn wrote the play *Agnes de Castro* for the London stage in 1795. The hugely successful drama tells of a woman who has an equal love for her husband and her woman friend. The story ends tragically, but not before the wife has specifically said that the love of her woman friend is equally precious as her husband's love. There were other plays celebrating aristocratic sentimental women friendships.[224]

The author of *Clarissa*, Samuel Richardson, collected a circle of women friends who praised the passionate female friendships in his novels and engaged in intense sentimental friendships with each other.

Elizabeth Carter, the classical scholar and translator of the Greek poet Epictetus, called Catherine Talbot 'my passion, I think of her all the day, dream of her all the night and one way or another introduce her into every subject I talk of.'[225]

Although elite women's loving friendships were sometimes hailed as a higher love, free of lust and typical of their refined nature, scandalous and amused references to women having sex with women started to appear in scandal sheets, plays and pornography. Coded accusations were printed in the scandal sheets, usually referring to corrupt aristocrats or foreign royalty. A so-called 'history' by the Seigneur de Brantome, *Lives of Gallant Ladies*, uses the word 'lesbienne' and describes 'fricarelle' (rubbing) as the sexual activity of women lovers, who are only driven to each other by the absence of men and who 'loathe' the practice, once they are able to get a man.

A mock-epic poem *The Toast* by William King first used the phrase 'lesbian loves' meaning sexual intimacy between two women, in 1732; and later the words 'tribadism' and 'sapphic passion' were used to describe sexual intimacy between women. But a 'tribade' could also mean a hermaphrodite – now diagnosed as a medical condition – and it could mean a man or woman who had lovers of both sexes. The practice of same-sex love for women was sufficiently well known for it to enter into slang; it was called 'A game of Flats' and lesbians were called 'tommies', perhaps matching the slang word for homosexuals, 'mollies', or perhaps short for 'tom-boys'.[226]

Under increased scrutiny and more critical commentary on single women and their friendships from the early 1700s, women's passionate expressions of friendships became more subdued, women more discreet in courting other women. In 1724, an anonymous pamphleteer describes English ladies '*Kissing* and *Slopping* each other in a lascivious manner and frequently repeating it'. By the end of the century, women who lived flamboyantly and openly together, especially the less respectable actresses, singers and artists, came under serious scrutiny.[227] All female friendships had to be firmly defined as asexual, and named 'sentimental friendships'.

The belief that all lower-class women were sexually active meant that working class women friends were suspected of sexual activity, and from 1700 single women friendships came under scrutiny and suspicion. Working-class women living and working together could be separated by the labour laws, which allowed magistrates to rule how and where women worked. Four women at South Milton, Devon, who had been self-suffi-cient in a spinning house together, were ordered to go into domestic service, where they would almost certainly be separated. Quaker women who lived communally faced prosecution, such as Jane and Anne Wright, who were separated and taken from their home even though they were sisters.[228]

A medical tract described the differences between a healthy sexual working-class girl and a delicate young lady. Another, from 1725, *Supplement to Onania*, a warning against masturbation, explains that 'EN', an upper-class girl, was taught to masturbate by a servant: 'EN, of a tender make and naturally inclin'd to be weakly, developed a number of disorders as a result.' On the other hand, the female servant who had initiated the young lady 'ails nothing, is a strong wench of twenty seven'.[229]

Those medical texts that mentioned upper-class female sexuality at all described it as an aberration. All discussion was intended to discourage female sexuality, not to diagnose. Women who touched genitals with other women were said to be likely to die from diseases of the womb. M. Tissot's book, translated by A. Hume, *Onanism: Or, A Treatise upon the Disorders produced by Masturbation; Or the Dangerous Effects of Secret and Excessive Venery*, has only one generalised chapter on women: 'Women have been known to love girls with as much fondness as ever did the most passionate of men, and conceive the most poignant jealousy when they were addressed by the male sex upon the score of love.'[230]

Novelist Henry Fielding concludes his account of a 'female husband' with a plea against same-sex love, which though it is 'Viciously and Equally detestable in both Sexes', it is worse in women: 'Nay, if Modesty be the Peculiar Characteristic of the Fair Sex it is in them most Shocking and Odious to Prostitute and Debase it.'[231]

By the end of the 1700s, both the enthusiasm for women's passionate friendships and the later panic about women's sexual intimacy were over. Fewer texts appeared complaining of women's excessive love for women. The repression of upper-class female sexuality meant that women's friendships, also appeared to be non-sexual. The earlier alarm over the general fashion for friendships between women became avid curiosity about the exceptional few and comment on them became harsher.

Female Husbands

Popular ballads and plays about women marrying women usually showed the women motivated by greed and ending in despair. The ballad 'She-Wedding or a Mad Marriage at Deptford' (1684) tells of a fraud played on a family by a pregnant maidservant. Another, 'The Scornful Damsel's Overthrow' (1685), depicts a woman rejecting male suitors who get their revenge when she is seduced by a cross-dressing woman. The bride kills herself when she discovers her husband is a woman.[232]

In 1680, Amy Poulter, the wife of Arthur Poulter, dressed herself as a man and named herself James Howard, to woo 18-year-old Arabella Hunt, a famously beautiful professional singer and musician at the court of Queen Mary. Their summer-long courtship was approved by Arabella's mother and James married Arabella before witnesses, at St Marylebone parish church on 12 September that year. The young couple lived together in Arabella's mother's house in the capital's Haymarket for six months.[233] A witness to the wedding, Sara Cunningham, aged 24, told the London consistory court that James 'went most in womanish apparel and especially when she went into the City pretending there were very great reasons and circumstances for her going so'.[234]

Six months after the wedding, Arabella applied for an annulment to the marriage at the consistory court, claiming that her husband James was 'one of a double gender, an hermaphrodite'.[235]

Amy Poulter was widowed by the death of her husband Arthur in January 1681, four months into her marriage to Arabella. She told the court that she had been 'Seduced by some evil company and counsel', and that she had courted Arabella dressed both as a man and as a woman – 'not seriously but rashly and unduly and in a frolic jocular and facetious manner ... made suit to Arabella Hunt in a way of marriage'.

Amy said that as soon as Arabella understood she was a woman, 'they did forthwith forsake ... the company of each other ... and they have ever since lived, and do now live apart from each other, as they ought to do, this respondent well knowing ... that she was in error, and that she then was, and still is a woman and a perfect woman ... and no man, and no hermaphrodite or person of double gender'.[236]

The court called a jury of five midwives, who examined Amy Poulter and announced that she was a woman – 'perfect ... in all her parts'.

This was an advantage to Amy Poulter. If she had been declared a hermaphrodite by the court, or even declared as a man, she might have lost her annual widow's dower from her Poulter marriage, and been publicly shamed.[237]

The court ruled the marriage null and void not because it was undertaken by two women – there was no specific law against same-sex unions[238] – but because Amy Poulter had already been married at the time of the wedding. The court annulled the bigamous union, reported the midwives' account that Amy was a 'perfect' woman, and noted that both women were free to marry in future. There was no other charge to answer.

Arabella continued her career as a highly regarded court musician, and died single in 1705; but only five weeks after the court annulled her marriage as a 'female husband', Amy Poulter died and was buried at Cottered in Hertfordshire.

Theirs was not the only female marriage recorded in this period. In 1694, a young woman (unnamed) was accused of marrying a young maid for her marriage portion and planning a second marriage with another woman. Her love letters were read aloud to the amusement of the criminal court. She was ordered to be whipped and kept at Bridewell until the court should decide her punishment.

In 1719, Catherine Jones appeared before the criminal court of the Old Bailey in London charged with bigamy for making a second marriage when her husband of six years, John Rowland, was abroad. Her defence was that her marriage to Constantine Boone was no real marriage as Boone was a hermaphrodite.

According to the less-than-reliable record of the *Newgate Calendar*, a witness told the court that Constantine Boone had been raised as a girl and taught needlework until she ran away to sea as a 12-year-old boy. Catherine Jones said in her defence that Constantine Boone had been exhibited as a hermaphrodite at Bartholomew Fair and other places. Constantine Boone confirmed that this was true, and other witnesses said that Constantine Boone tended to be more female than male. The jury accepted the defence – that there was no marriage since Constantine Boone was a hermaphrodite, and released Catherine Jones from the charge of bigamy.[239]

In 1720, Sarah Kerson, calling herself John, tried to marry Anne Hutchinson – the court assumed the motive was to defraud Anne of her money. Like most same-sex marriages for women, the case reached court only when there was a criminal complaint attached to the wedding. Marriage between women was not a criminal offence of itself, and there may have been many female husbands and wives who never attracted the attention of the authorities. One female marriage was recorded without comment, by the clerk to the church in Taxal, Cheshire, in 1707: 'Hannah Wright and Ann Gaskall, Parish of Prestbury, 4th September 1707'. And a year later, in Prestbury church: 'Ane Norton and Alice Pickford, Parish of Prestbury, 3rd June, 1708'.[240]

A few decades later, in 1734 in London's Soho, the clergyman would not issue a marriage certificate to John Mountford (tailor) and Mary Cooper, a spinster, making a note that he 'Suspected two women no Certif'.[241] Which suggests that he did not marry them – but only because they had no licence for their marriage.

A clergyman in 1737 officiated at the wedding of John Smith and Elizabeth Huthall, and later recorded his doubts: 'By Ye opinion after matrimony my Clark judged they were both women. If ye person by name John Smith be a man, he's a little short fair thin man not above 5 foot.'[242] But apparently the wedding went ahead, and the authorities were not alerted.

In 1747, a newly married couple – John Ferren and Deborah Nolan – were discovered to both be women after the wedding, but the marriage was not challenged: 'The supposed John Ferren was discovered after ye ceremony were over, to be in person a woman.'[243]

The Marriage Act of 1753, which required the calling of banns in local parishes or the issuing of special marriage licences, and the recording of all weddings, was intended only to prevent entrapping weddings by fortune-hunting grooms. The act was not against same-sex weddings for women, which continued throughout the eighteenth century. Indeed, female marriages may have quietly grown in popularity through this period. Certainly, the numbers of individual reports increase and the phrase 'female husband' is used without explanation as an everyday event.[244]

One woman who had lived as a man, a husband and a soldier was only discovered during a visit to hospital in Edinburgh in 1759. Another wife loved her female husband so dearly that when they were exposed by an old acquaintance, she travelled to York 'in great affliction begging that they might not be parted'. In the same year, a female husband, Samuel

Bundy born Sarah Paul, was arrested for fraud upon her wife, Mary Parlour, who reported them to the authorities. When the case came to court, the wife Mary refused to appear against her female husband and the case was dropped.[245] In 1764, a female husband, John Chivy, died after living as a farmer and a husband for more than 20 years.

Another woman who tried to live as a man and married not one, but three women, was fictionalised by Henry Fielding, the magistrate-novelist. He claimed his account was drawn from court papers, but it was published as a novel titled *The Female Husband* in 1746.

Nothing sentimental about this novel! The voice is from the Age of Enlightenment, not the Romantic movement: the novelist adopts a hard-hearted, cynical approach and takes a forensic interest in the heroine and her downfall. Fielding claims that Mary Hamilton was born on the Isle of Man in 1721 to a well-off widow and a retired army sergeant and was seduced by an older woman who had herself been corrupted by Methodists. Mary Hamilton fell passionately in love with her seducer and was heartbroken when she was rejected as the other woman chose to marry a man. Fielding makes the traditional claim of the superiority of heterosexual intercourse over female intimacy, with Mary's former woman lover urging her: 'Follow my example now, as you before did my temptation and enter as soon as you can into that Holy state into which I was yesterday called. In which, tho' I am yet but a fellow Novice, believe me, there are delights infinitely surpassing the faint endearments we experienced.'[246]

Instead, Mary Hamilton took ship to Dublin, claimed to be a Methodist minister, and courted and married a wealthy older widow, who discovered that Mary was a woman on the wedding night. Mary fled to the West Country and courted and married two other women, each time discovered as a woman and running away. Her final marriage lasted three months and the bride was deeply attached to Mary, who now claimed to be a doctor of medicine named George Hamilton and lived with the bride in her family home. A chance encounter with someone who had met George during a previous marriage led to gossip, and a magistrate issued a warrant for arrest – not for same-sex marriage, not even for bigamy, but for a criminal vice that was not described. A search of Mary/George's possessions revealed 'Something too Vile, Wicked and Scandalous in Nature'.

This is all that Fielding says about the discovery that was perhaps some sort of fake penis with which to mislead the final two brides, who were said to be virgins on their wedding night. If a dildo was used to penetrate the brides, it would have been a criminal offence of sodomy. But Hamilton was not accused of sodomy. She was committed to Bridewell and charged under the Vagrancy Act for 'having by false and Deceitful practices endeavoured to impose on some of His Majesty's subjects'.

The judges handed down a verdict on Hamilton without ruling on whether they were male or female: 'That the he or she, prisoner at the bar is an uncommon, notorious cheat, and we, the Court, do sentence her, or him, whichever he or she may be, to be imprisoned six months, and during that time to be whipped in the towns of Taunton, Glastonbury, Wells and Shepton Mallet, and to find security for good behaviour as long as they, the learned justices aforesaid, shall or may, in their wisdom and judgment, require.'[247]

Hamilton was publicly whipped in four market towns and imprisoned for months. Fielding alleges that on the night of the worst beating, she tried to bribe the jailer to bring a young woman into the prison for sex – a development almost certainly fictional, designed to show the moral corruption of a female husband. Until then, even Fielding's own account describes Hamilton as neither predatory nor promiscuous, but only persistently trying to create a marital home with a specific beloved woman, for profit, love and sex. In fact – just like a male husband.

Cross-dressing Women

There was no law against women dressing as men, but the biblical injunction remained, and cross-dressed women could be prosecuted for being disorderly. Even when women dressed as men for their own safety, like on long journeys, they felt the frisson of social anxiety about a woman not conforming to her social place.

The theatre, back in business after the shutdown of the Cromwell years, not only allowed women on stage, but created 'breeches' parts in which the actresses wore men's breeches and showed silk-stockinged legs and garters for the enjoyment of the mixed audience. Cross-dressing women proved popular with all audiences, and would be specifically requested on 'ladies nights' by the all-women audiences. They remained hugely popular with audiences until the 1700s rise of unease about ladylike behaviour and anxiety about same-sex female eroticism. Some historians suggest that breeches plays were discouraged when it became clear they were favoured by women audiences; breeches parts signalled female independence, female sexuality and female preference for other women – and were phased out.[248]

A woman who played herself on stage, dressed as a man, and occasionally passed as a man in real life, was the so-called German Princess, Mary Carleton (1634–73). Born Mary Moders, the daughter of a Canterbury musician, she first married a local shoemaker before running away to Barbados. She then married a surgeon, Thomas Day – leading to an unsuccessful trial for bigamy.[249] On her release she went to Cologne, where she was 'mistaken' for another woman, and adopted the identity of Maria de Wolway, returning to London as a German countess. She was tricked by a lawyer's clerk into marriage, and when he discovered she had no fortune, his father sued her for bigamy.

She claimed to have trained as a male lawyer at the Inns of Court and conducted her own successful defence, released by a jury to public acclaim. She wrote her own account of her life, which was dramatised as *A Witty Combat, or, The Female Victor*, and played herself on the London stage; the diarist Samuel Pepys attended a performance. Carleton continued with criminal deceits until she was arrested in 1671 for stealing a silver tankard. The death sentence was commuted to exile to Jamaica, but she returned early, to continue with more deceits and a theft, and was once again arrested. She dressed very fashionably at her trial and on her last journey to the gallows. She was hanged at Tyburn on 22 January 1673.[250]

An actress who wore breeches on stage and in real life, Charlotte Charke (1713–60) published a fictionalised version of her life story in 1755, and described being raised as a tomboy, being unhappily married and forced by poverty onto the stage, where she played both women and breeches parts. When travelling she dressed as a man, calling herself Mr Brown and flirting with women, declaring that she was incapable of conventional female skills and behaviours. She lived for much of her life with her woman friend and manager, and they travelled as husband and wife. Charlotte's cross-dressing led her into a courtship with an heiress and the possibility of a profitable marriage to a wealthy woman – but she withdrew from the relationship as she said she did not feel she could be a 'female husband'.[251]

A woman of African descent who refused to be confined to conventional female behaviour in conventional female clothes disguised herself as a man, calling herself John Brown and volunteering as a soldier in the Royal Africa Company – the slaving company. Perhaps she was trying to get to Africa – it is possible that she had been slaved from the Guinea coast and was trying to get home. If anybody asked her what she intended, they did not record the answer. But she succeeded in making the voyage. The captain of *The Hannibal* of London, Thomas Philips, explained in his ship's log in November 1693 how she was discovered:

> This morning we found out that one of the Royal African
> Company's soldiers, for their castles in Guiney, was a woman, who
> had enter'd herself into their service under the name of John Brown,
> without the least suspicion, and had been three months on board
> without any mistrust, lying always among the other passengers, and
> being as handy and ready to do any work as any of them: and I
> believe she had continu'd undiscover'd till our arrival in Africa, had
> not she fallen very sick, which occasion'd our surgeon to visit her,
> and ordered her a glister: which when his mate went to administer,
> he was surpriz'd to find more sally-ports than he expected, which
> occasion'd him to make a farther inquiry, which, as well as her
> confession, manifesting the truth of her sex, he came to acquaint me
> of it, whereupon, in charity, as well as in respect to her sex, I ordered
> her a private lodging apart from the men, and gave the taylor some
> ordinary stuffs to make her woman's cloaths; in recompence for
> which she prov'd very useful in washing my linen, and doing what
> else she could, till we deliver'd her with the rest at Cape-Coast castle.
> She was about twenty years old, and a likely black girl.[252]

An entire genre of popular writing described women passing themselves off as soldiers. In 1692, the *Gentlemen's Journal* told the story of a beautiful English woman who passed as a male soldier for two years with the French army, promoted to 'the Governor of Pignerol's Gentlemen of the Horse until she was discovered as a woman playing with another of her sex'.[253]

An Irish woman, Christian Cavanagh (1667–1739), ran a Dublin inn with the help of her husband Richard Welsh who disappeared, probably pressed, into the British army. Aged 26, 'Kit' Cavanagh dressed as a man and enlisted as an infantryman to find her husband in 1693. She was captured by the French at the Battle of Landen and released – still undiscovered – to Captain Tichborne's company in a prisoner exchange. A quarrel with a company sergeant over a woman led to a duel, when Kit Cavanagh killed the sergeant and was discharged from the army.

She enlisted again with the Scots Greys and fought with them until the Peace of Ryswick, re-enlisting with the Greys in 1701 for the War of the Spanish Succession. She continued fighting even when wounded at the Battle of Blenheim. In the aftermath she found her long-lost husband, who was with another woman. Kit Cavanagh agreed that she and her husband should pass as brothers and continued in the army until the Battle of Ramillies, when she fractured her skull and was discovered as a woman.

From *The Girl's Own Annual*, 1904, Kit Cavanagh (Christian Davies, 1667–1739), who served with the British Army and was buried with full military honours

The Scots Greys brigadier Lord John Hay ordered that she should continue to draw her pay until she was formally discharged as a trooper and taken on as a cook. Her unfaithful husband was killed at the Battle of Malplaquet in 1709 and she searched for his body and buried him. She married another dragoon Hugh Jones, and then lived with Captain Ross of the Scots Greys, taking the name Mother Ross.

When the Greys were demobbed in 1712, Kit Cavanagh was presented at court to Queen Anne, who granted her £50 and a pension of a shilling a day for her extraordinary military service. She married for the third time and finally retired to the Royal Hospital Chelsea as a pensioner, where she was interviewed by writer Daniel Defoe, who published her story. She died aged 72 and was buried with full military honours at the hospital.

Several women were known to have passed as men to serve in the army and navy, according to the *Gentleman's Journal*: 'We have had but two years ago a young lady on board the Fleet in man's apparel, who show'd all the signs of the most undaunted valour. Several others are still living, and some of them in this town, who have served whole campaigns, and fought stroke by stroke by the most manly soldiers.'[254]

Another woman recruit to the British army was not celebrated for her courage, but arrested, whipped and put to hard labour in 1704. Elizabeth Morris had dressed as a man and enlisted as a soldier in Lt General Steward's regiment.[255] Perhaps she drew such condemnation because she was not following a husband, but pursuing her own wishes.

Two notorious cross-dressing women became female pirates: Mary Reid and Anne Bonny, whose story was published as *A General History of the Pirates* in 1724. Born around 1700 in Ireland, Anne Bonny was dressed as a boy and named 'Andy' in the hope he would become a lawyer's clerk. The family emigrated to Carolina, where Anne married a pirate named James Bonny against her father's wishes. After the couple moved to the Bahamas, Anne became the lover of pirate Jack Rackham, ran away with him on his ship and disguised herself as a male member of his crew, which already included Mark/Mary Read (or Reid), who had dressed as a boy from early youth to win an inheritance and later to join the British army. Mark/Mary had married as a woman and moved to the West Indies with her husband, but when he died she joined Rackham's crew, as a man – Mark. Rackham was jealous at first of the friendship between Anne Bonny and Mark Reid – until Mark/Mary

Anne Bonny (*c.*1697–?1721) in *A General History of the Robberies and Murders of the Most Notorious Pyrates*, 1724, by Captain Charles Johnson, possibly a pen name for Daniel Defoe

revealed herself as a woman, when he allowed them to be loving woman friends.[256]

Anne Bonny married Jack Rackham at sea and he, Anne and Mark/Mary stole the ship *William*, recruited a new crew and worked as pirates until October 1720, when they were attacked by a sloop commissioned by the governor of Jamaica. The crew were said to be too drunk to fight and were taken to Jamaica, where they were hanged. Anne Bonny's last words to her husband were: 'Had you fought like a man; you need not have been hanged like a dog.'[257]

Mark/Mary and Anne both pleaded their bellies, and execution was delayed. Mark/Mary died in prison and Anne disappeared from the record.

An illustration of pirate Mary Read (1695–1721) in 'The Adventures and Heroism of Mary Read', *The Pirates Own Book*, 1837

Nottinghamshire has a well-told story (probably a fiction) of a highwaywoman: Joan Phillips, the daughter of a wealthy farmer who was persuaded by her lover to dress as a man and hold up a stagecoach on Loughborough Road. She was said to have been tried at the Lenten Assizes in Nottingham and hanged in April 1685 on a gallows erected at Wilford Lane, close to where she had been captured.[258]

Hannah Snell (1723–92) took her brother-in-law's name, James Gray, and dressed in his suit of clothes, to search for her deserting husband. Discovering he had been executed for murder, she decided to continue in a male identity and joined John Guise's 6th Regiment of Foot when they marched against the Young Pretender, Charles Edward Stuart, in 1745. However, she deserted after a brutal whipping from her sergeant, and joined the Marines instead, sailing for India.

She was wounded in the legs and groin – but had the bullet taken out by a local woman so that the regimental surgeon should not discover her sex. On return to England in 1750, she revealed that she was a woman and appealed for a pension. She published her story as a book, *The Female Soldier*, and created a theatrical act: showing military drill and

Hannah Snell (1723–92) in full military uniform, painting by Richard Phelps, engraved by John Young, engraver to His Royal Highness the Prince of Wales

singing songs in uniform. She was honourably discharged and granted her pension.

On retirement, she married twice and had two children from each husband, and at her death was buried at the Chelsea Hospital, a gesture of respect to her military service.

A popular genre of ballads celebrated women who went to war in the army or navy dressed as men. Mostly, the ballads celebrated the women's adventure, and their return to civilian life and womanhood – but the possibility of a successful life as a man was publicised and popularised.[259]

Some women dressed as men to be freed from the conventions of ladylike behaviour. Sally Salisbury did it to go out with rowdy male friends. There is a record of an affray in a pub in Gateshead, where one of the drinkers was found to be a woman dressed as a man. Catherine Meadwell, an estranged wife, wore men's clothes and used the name of

Captain Clark to meet her lover. Perhaps the most surprising story of all is that of a coachman, in service for 16 years to the aristocratic Harvey family, who was only discovered to be a woman when she gave birth.[260]

The seventeenth-century accounts of cross-dressing women's lives were mostly a narration of a woman's adventure, not a condemnation. Literature advising on appearance focused on dressing appropriately for social status, as if class mattered more than sex. But at the end of the century, writers began to urge women to dress as women and identified cross-dressing as a social problem, a moral failing, or even a symptom of madness.[261] The new unease developed, as women cross-dressed in public, taking a stage costume into everyday life.[262] Assuming men's clothing, not as a joke or a performance, was seen as a threat by women who might want to assume men's authority too.

Although commentators increasingly insisted there were two sexes, and only two sexes, there was a continued awareness of people known as 'hermaphrodites'. A 1718 pamphlet on hermaphrodites mostly discussed women changing into men, since it was still thought – as the Greek philosophers – that a physical body would change to improve, that a woman would become a man. What was the benefit of going in the opposite direction? Anyone of indeterminate sexuality was most likely to be a women turning into a man.[263]

The 'mollie' culture of homosexual males included men passing as women, even identifying as women. There were mock-weddings in the 'mollie' houses, and even 'mock births' when a 'mollie' would retire into a room and simulate labour.[264]

Around 1770, young noblemen who shared a love of Italian culture called themselves 'macaronis' and dressed elaborately, wearing high heels, high powdered wigs, white-powdered faces and face patches. Although their appearance was feminised, their intention was not to pass as women, but to be very glamorous men. However, the *Oxford Magazine* described them as a new gender: 'a new kind of animal, neither male nor female, a thing of the neuter gender, lately started up amongst us … it talks without meaning, it smiles without pleasantry, it eats without appetite, it rides without exercise, it wenches without passion'.[265]

The magazine might express distaste, but there was no moral panic, as there had been for women wearing male clothes. Men were not endangered by feminine men, as they were threatened by manly women.

Single Women

In the 1500s, a 'spinster' meant someone who spun wool for a living; 100 years later, the word 'spinster' came to denote a single woman, even in court and official records.[266] Fifty years after that – in 1650 – it had become an insulting term for a woman who had failed to find a husband. It had lost its connotation of productive trade; it meant only a woman who had failed in her only work – that of marriage. There were more single men than single women in the population, but bachelors were thought to live worthwhile, enjoyable lives, while single women were forever disappointed.[267] Young bachelors were regarded indulgently for delaying marriage, as men could wed at any time – they were not preferred as fresh-faced virgins. Men had other career options than marriage – it was neither duty nor destiny for men at all but more like a hobby. Given the freedoms, and the higher wages, being a bachelor must have been a more enjoyable state than being a single woman. Phrases such as 'sowing wild oats' from 1576,[268] and 'boys will be boys', which originated in 1569 as 'children will be children', indicated the acceptability of male misbehaviour and even crime for young single men.

The attitude to single women became more and more contemptuous. England (far more than in any other country in Europe) saw increased abuse of single women in the eighteenth century. In 1713, an anonymous poem, 'Satyr upon Old maids', celebrated the abuse of single women and described them as 'nasty rank rammy filthy sluts', who ought to marry lepers and lechers, rather than be 'piss'd on with contempt'.[269]

Although writers mostly urged single women to marry in order to increase the population and to ensure women came under the control of husbands,[270] a quarter of all women chose not to marry in the 1660s.[271] Since 20–30 per cent of all brides were pregnant at their weddings, it may be that some had been forced to marry by the pressure on sexually active single women, and single mothers.[272]

Some single women made successful personal and financial lives, creating homes with women and leaving bequests to other single women and family members. At least 50 pairs of unmarried sisters lived together in 1745 Southampton, many of whom worked together, and they often left their savings to other single women relations.[273]

By the middle of the eighteenth century, it was widely understood that a woman's destiny was to marry: only one popular novel offers a different destiny for women. *Millenium Hall* (1763) was written by Sarah Scott after her husband had committed suicide and left her with enough money to live as a widow. She chose not to remarry but seized the opportunity to develop a women's commune with her sister Lady Barbara Montagu, Sarah Fielding, Jane Collier, Elizabeth Cutts and Margaret Riggs who lived with Margaret Mary Ravaud. Scott and Montagu shared a house at Batheaston – a village outside Bath – and taught 12 working-class boys and 12 working-class girls in the commune, employing them to sew necessities for the neighbouring poor.[274]

Scott described a fictional women's commune in her novel, which became a bestseller, one of the few dissenting voices in the rising tide of conduct books and stories claiming that women lacked reason, were driven by their feelings and were safe only at home in the care of a father or husband. But Scott's praise of a single life in a virtuous commune was restricted to genteel ladies. Working-class girls at her fictional school were taught domestic skills and prepared for a life of service and marriage.

Some of the negativity towards single women occurred as population growth stalled in England while continental populations were rising. Economists believed a large workforce to be essential for wealth, and imperialists wanted a surplus population to send overseas. Fertile women who refused to marry were viewed as failing to contribute to the nation's well-being; women preferring women, or even preferring spinsterhood, were unpatriotic, as well as personally selfish.[275]

Crime and Punishment

The majority of female murderers were charged under the Infanticide Act of 1624, which assumed that any single woman with a dead baby had deliberately killed it. There was no assumption of innocence, and no accusation of the father. It fell to the accused woman to prove that she had *not* killed her dead child. A woman who could not prove her baby was stillborn would hang because her baby was dead.[276] In London, in the hundred years from 1660, 46 women were found guilty and executed for infanticide, 28 for murder and 10 for petty treason: killing their husbands or employer.[277]

Despite evidence to the contrary, women were believed to be naturally murderous. The explosion in publishing after the civil wars exploited moralising stories about husband-killers far more than stories of more common murders: men killing men in street violence, and their wives at home. But husband-killers became a literary fashion: hugely popular as entertainment, as reason for suspecting women and as propaganda against disobedient women.

The scandal sheet the *Newgate Calendar*, the unreliable recorder of court hearings at Newgate Prison, loved nothing more than a story of a murderous wife. Catherine Hayes was reported as killing her husband in 1726 by getting him drunk and beheading him. The *Calendar* gleefully recounted that when she was shown the severed head of her murdered husband, she caressed it and asked for a lock of hair as a keepsake. She was sentenced to be hanged and her body burned alive for the 'petty treason' crime of husband-killing, and the *Calendar* reported the gruesome details when the hanging failed and the live woman pushed away the burning faggots, taking three hours to be burned.[278]

But stories of husband-murderers proved to be complicated. Any attempt to explain the murderous wife's point of view led into the difficulties and even injustice of her position. Mary Channel, a young woman of only 18 from Dorchester, was forced to marry a wealthy old neighbour, a grocer in the town. Mary hated her older husband and fed him rat poison. Easily convicted for murder, she was ordered to die by burning. But there was no gloating over the pain for this young woman:

> she was guarded by proper officers to the place of execution, with her hood veiled over her face. After she had uttered some private ejaculations she pulled off her gown and white silk hood and delivered them to her maid – who accompanied her to the stake – and then suffered death, according to the sentence before pronounced against her, declaring her faith in Christ; and to the last continued to exclaim against her parents' constraints, which had been the sole cause of her torturing death. Thus, at a small distance from the town of Dorchester, she yielded her breath, in or about the month of April, Anno Domini 1703.[279]

Many stories revealed that murderous wives had been cruelly treated; one described a midwife who turned on her husband after a lifetime of beating and sexual assault so extreme that she had once raised a hue and cry against him for her rape. But describing any justification undermined the accusation of petty treason, for which there could be no defence. To describe a murderous wife as a woman defending herself, was to see her not as a stereotype of wickedness but as a mistreated woman, a person with her own opinions and her own dangerous power.

Such accounts of murderous wives contradicted the church teaching that husband and wife were of one flesh and challenged male supremacy. Little wonder that a male writer at the time said that an undutiful wife was a 'home-rebel, a house-traitor',[280] linking the domestic with the political, calling for domestic crimes to be severely punished, in a society that was becoming more and more afraid of rebellion.[281]

The law that ruled that a wife and a husband were one person in law, and that an accomplice might be punished for murder, bore down very hard on Deborah Churchill, who stepped between her armed husband and his armed friend during their quarrel. The friend was killed, the husband escaped and Deborah Churchill was charged at the Old Bailey, June 1708, for being an accomplice to the stabbing. She was convicted and pleaded for mercy as she was pregnant. A jury of matrons, called to confirm the pregnancy and save her life, avowed that they could not say whether or not she was pregnant. On 17 December that year, after six months with no sign of a baby, she was hanged at Tyburn, guilty of nothing more than being the bystander wife of a murderer.[282]

Most women criminals were thieves and fraudsters, outnumbering male thieves in the London prisons between 1670 and 1720. Women thieves specialised in stealing from shops, from their domestic employers, pickpocketing, and receiving and selling stolen goods. They preferred the women's speciality of clothing and household linens, with women in towns more likely to turn to crime than country women, probably because they were on their own, trying to survive on poor wages.[283]

Alice Gray was hanged in 1708 for assisting in the rape of a 10-year-old girl, who was co-sleeping with Alice when Alice brought a man John or Thomas Smith to their bedroom. He gave the child a venereal disease and Alice Gray said nothing in court but swore to the court clergyman that she was innocent.[284]

Some women criminals operated on a grand scale. Nan Hereford, a swindler, employed an older, respectable-looking woman to befriend a local apothecary in King Street, London. The older woman told the wealthy medical man that her niece was an heiress looking for a husband. The apothecary paid her £100 for the introduction and gave his new wife £250 on their wedding day for her expenses before she could draw down her inheritance. After they consummated the marriage, the apothecary went to the house of his bride's wealthy uncle to collect the inheritance. There he found he had been swindled. The householder produced his own nieces – and knew nothing of the apothecary's wife. He raised a hue and cry against her, but Nan Hereford was long gone with her £350.

She shoplifted with great profit for six years, impersonating a great lady, often using a sedan chair as a getaway vehicle, until she was caught by a linen draper who refused a bribe of 100 guineas not to prosecute. Hereford was arrested and taken to Newgate where, in a dramatic escape attempt, she set fire to her cell. After the incident, she was kept in hand-cuffs and fetters until her hanging in December 1690.[285]

Mary Young fell into a life of crime after she could not make a living as a seamstress in the capital. She joined 'a number of men and women, assembled in a kind of club, near St Giles's. These people gained their living by cutting off women's pockets and stealing watches, etc., from men in the avenues of the theatres, and at other places of public resort.'[286]

Mary served an apprenticeship in the art of pickpocketing and rose to become a senior member of the gang, christened with the name of 'Jenny Diver', specialising in stealing watches off their chains and even a ring from a gentleman's finger when he held her hand to help her into church. As gang leader, she choreographed mass thefts by the entire gang work-ing together. On two occasions she pretended to fall ill in the street and picked the pockets of the people who helped her to her feet, while her pretend servants picked the pockets of those nearby and the rest of the gang moved through the crowd. She led the gang on an expedition to Bristol to steal and defraud at the fair. Back in London, she executed a fraud and a theft on a young man who had seen her at the theatre. He thought he was meeting her at her home for a clandestine love affair. Jenny Diver got into bed with him before a gang member, pretending to be a housemaid, knocked on the door saying that the master, her husband, had come home. Diver took her frightened lover's clothes, the contents of his pockets, his jewellery and his silver-topped cane and

The lusciously imagined death of Lady Jane Grey by Paul Delaroche in 1833, complete with a red-legged executioner with a most suggestive dagger. Jane Grey was very far from a blindfolded victim in virginal white, fumbling for the block. Aged 16, she walked to her scaffold on Tower Green, and told the waiting crowd: 'Good people, I am come hither to die.' She read from her prayer book, before asking the executioner to 'despatch her quickly.'

Overleaf: The inspiration for the jacket of this book, and for all women trapped in marriage with a dishonest husband! This is William Hogarth's portrait of Mary Edwards (1705–43), who discovered her husband was stealing her fortune. Divorced, she would have lost her fortune and their son – instead, she denied they had ever been married, declared herself a spinster and her son a bastard, and risked her reputation to be free of him.

Arabella Hunt (1662–1705), a famously beautiful professional singer and musician at the court of Queen Mary, who had her marriage to James Howard dissolved when she discovered he was a woman named Amy Poulter who was already married. Arabella never remarried, and Amy died five weeks after the marriage was ended.

The Chevalier d'Éon (1728–1810) was raised in France as the male heir to the de Beaumont family. The decorated soldier dressed as a man to serve as a captain of Dragoons, and as a woman named Lia de Beaumont to spy for France on Russia and England. A master fencer, the Chevalier is shown here on the right in a celebrated match against Chevalier de St Georges. This was painted by Alexandre-Auguste Robineau c.1787.

This painting of Dido Elizabeth Belle (1761–1804), daughter of a slave, with her cousin Lady Elizabeth, by David Martin in 1778, is typical of slave portraits. Dido is shown in exotic costume carrying a tray of fruits – plantation produce. She stands behind Elizabeth, who carries a book, and rather awkwardly holds her at arm's length.

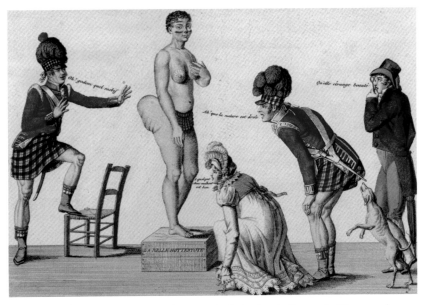

This print of Saartjie Baartman (1789–1815), by Louis François Charon, shows shameless exhibition spectators: a young woman trying to peep under the loin cloth, while others – Highlanders in kilts – expose their own legs and buttocks. The enslaved woman looks directly out from the print, as if hoping for release. She died the year that this print was made, aged 26.

locked him naked in the bedroom to keep him safe from the imaginary jealous husband, while the gang cleared out of the rented house.

Jenny Diver arranged insurance for her criminal gang: if any were unable to join a thieving trip because of illness the others should allow them 10 per cent of the profit until they were well again. She continued with a career of deception and theft, was caught twice and transported twice, returning early both times, but was apprehended pickpocketing and executed in 1740.

Highwaywoman Ann Holland worked alongside her second husband James Wilson, who was said to find her most helpful in his trade. After his execution she remarried and became a fraudster and an extortionist with her third husband until her capture and execution in 1705.[287]

Harsh punishments for petty crimes fell hard on the petty criminals: women and children. Women and girls found guilty of stealing goods less than 10d in value would be whipped at Bridewell, or through the streets. If the goods were worth more than 12d (a shilling), they could be hanged or transported overseas as an indentured servant for up to ten years to the English colonies.[288] In 1667, a woman who had already been branded for a previous offence was found guilty of stealing two shirts and four smocks, valued at 8d. As it was a repeat offence, she faced the death penalty, but an application for pardon was made to the king, as she and her husband 'are very desirous for her to be transported to the plantations'.[289] In 1659, Margaret Griffiths begged to be sentenced to transportation to Virginia where she could serve under her brother.[290]

The cruelty of the law was often softened by juries, who could under-value stolen goods and so allow the accused to avoid a death sentence. Sometimes a woman managed to escape execution by 'pleading her belly' and getting her sentence deferred until the birth of the baby – time for a pardon, or a reduction of sentence, or even an escape. Women tried to get pregnant while awaiting trial or before examination by having sex with jailers or other prisoners. Sometimes women helped women offenders. The jury of matrons who examined a woman due for execution reported pregnancies with surprising frequency – in 1685, 27 per cent and in 1686, a staggering 43 per cent of women sentenced to hanging at the Old Bailey were found to be pregnant and had their executions delayed or cancelled.[291]

Women remained at a disadvantage because of their lack of legal status. Elizabeth Gaunt, accused of harbouring a rebel after the defeat of the Duke of Monmouth's forces, was named by a man already outlawed for treason – and yet his word was taken over hers. As she said in her speech before being burned for treason: 'My blood will also be found at the door of the unrighteous Jury, who found me guilty upon the single oath of an out-lawd man.'[292]

A large prisoner population of innocent people was created when the new poor laws took children from destitute parents and imprisoned unemployed adults. The first workhouse – a forced labour camp – was set up by the London Corporation of the Poor in 1662, and the first privately owned workhouse imprisoned paupers three years later. Married couples were separated, and men and women housed, fed and forced to work under strict supervision in their own sections, and only released if they could find work outside. By 1712, 14 towns in England had opened their own workhouse,[293] imprisoning people guilty of nothing but being poor.

New institutions – houses of correction, halfway between a jail and a workhouse – began to be developed around the country on the model of the first house for women at Bridewell in London and were often named 'bridewells'. These were for men and women convicted or named for trivial offences against public order, like vagrancy, begging and stealing food. Work was punitively hard, on starvation rations. The punishment fell hardest on women, who made up two-thirds of the national Bridewells' prisoners. Some poor women were pitied and some were blamed. Pauper widows – favoured by the parish overseers as 'deserving' – might be allowed to stay in their own homes and given between 6d and 12d a week – hardly enough to buy food. But young women in the parish, especially independent single women, were expected to find work and pay for their own keep, and could be arrested if they were found without work or refused to take a job. If a woman went on the road looking for work, she could be stripped and whipped by the overseer of any parish she entered and then driven out, for fear of her conceiving a bastard and putting the cost of the child on the parish. Women vagrants were moved out of the parish bounds whenever possible – sometimes with brutal force – or imprisoned in a house of correction and then driven on.[294]

Middling- and upper-class women rarely appeared in the courts since they were not driven by poverty into petty crime. From 1693, educated women could escape an accusation, when literate women as well as men were allowed to plead the so-called 'benefit of clergy', proving that they could read, and so be punished less harshly.

As the idea of female frailty took hold, magistrates tended to believe that husbands forced wives into crime and that women were innocent. When compelling evidence of female crime existed, women were judged more harshly – they had offended against the social code of female 'goodness' as well as the criminal law.[295]

Witchcraft

The persecution of unpopular working-class women under the pretext or belief that they were witches did not continue far beyond the Restoration. Women were still accused of witchcraft, but the days of widespread witch-scares or mass trials prompted by witch-hunters were over.

One of the last fatal trials came in 1682 and resulted in the deaths of three elderly women. Temperance Lloyd was accused by her neighbours in Heavitree, Exeter, of using image magic (symbols) to cause illness and death, and of consorting with the devil, She was questioned and confessed to being in league with 'a black man' – a devil. Mary Trembles, a beggar, was accused of causing illness and an epileptic fit by witchcraft. She said she had been initiated into witchcraft by another old woman beggar – Susanna Edwards – and she in turn blamed Temperance Lloyd. All three women were found guilty and executed on 25 August at Heavitree.[296] The last woman to be legally executed for witchcraft would die at the same spot two years later. Alice Molland was hanged there for bewitching three women in 1684.[297]

The last person to be legally convicted of witchcraft appeared in Hertfordshire in 1712. Jane Wenham was a widow with a local reputation for 'witchcraft, swearing, cursing, idleness, thievery and whoredom'.[298] She quarrelled with a neighbouring farmer and was accused of causing fits and delusions in his servant, Ann Thorn. Jane Wenham asked to be swum to prove her innocence, but the local justice Sir Henry Chauncy refused the swim test and instead imposed a test of reciting the Lord's Prayer. After she stumbled in the prayer, Jane was imprisoned and tried for witchcraft. At the trial, the jury found her guilty, but she was reprieved from hanging by the judge, Sir John Powell, who doubted the evidence and obtained a royal pardon for her. Wenham had to leave her village for her own safety, but she was lucky enough to be housed by a wealthy patron.[299]

In 1735, the new law on witchcraft followed the increasing scepticism of the lawmakers: now the offence was not witchcraft, it was pretending to perform witchcraft. But suspected women were attacked until the end of the eighteenth century. Alice Green, the wife of a labourer, was swum in December 1748 after 'malicious and evil people having raised an ill report of her being a witch'. Ruth Osborne, more than 70 years old, was publicly swum with her husband John in a pond near Tring in 1751. A crowd of 1,000 people gathered to watch, some of them paying for the spectacle. Ruth died during the ordeal and her husband died soon after. The local justices found Thomas Colley guilty of her murder, and sentenced him to death when it was proved that he had repeatedly used a stick to push Ruth Osborne underwater and collected the fees from the spectators.[300]

Violence

In 1674, a court ruled that violence to a wife was illegal in England: husbands might only scold and imprison wives. Legal expert William Blackstone disagreed and in 1764 restated that husbands could beat their wives within 'reasonable bounds':

> The husband also, by the old law, might give his wife moderate correction. For, as he is to answer for her misbehaviour, the law thought it reasonable to intrust him with this power of restraining her, by domestic chastisement, in the same moderation that a man is allowed to correct his apprentices or children; for whom the master or parent is also liable in some cases to answer. But this power of correction was confined within reasonable bounds, and the husband was prohibited from using any violence to his wife.[301]

The definition of 'reasonable' was key. A beating once or twice was reasonable, in private was reasonable, a beating that stopped short of attempted murder was reasonable. English common law allowed a wife to 'pray the peace' against a violent husband, before a magistrate who could order the husband not to assault his wife again. This was done only rarely and granted only after repeated severe and public assaults.[302]

In 1669, a neighbour was recorded telling a husband that he was 'A very ill man to beat his wife at such a rate'.[303]

Public violence to wives and wife-beating became unacceptable in the middling classes as polite behaviour and etiquette were adopted; and in the working classes, community disapproval turned on violent husbands. Public demonstrations, mockery and abuse that had rained down on husbands who failed to control scolding or adulterous wives were now directed at husbands who did not control their own anger. Women led a demonstration against a known wife-beater in 1747 at Billingshurst, Sussex, and a year later in Islington, near London, but violent abuse of wives continued among the lower orders.[304] Domestic violence, especially among poor and labouring people, may have been intensified by the arrival in England of strong, cheap spirits – in particular gin introduced from Holland by the Hanoverian monarchy.

Men were the violent sex: accused of 91 per cent of all murders in eighteenth-century Surrey.[305] On average, there were two murderous husbands to every murderous wife.[306]

Rape now defined as a personal assault was still used as a technique of kidnap. 'Sibble' Morris, a 16- or 17-year-old heiress, was kidnapped by John Wheeler who – helped by two women, Mary Hendon and Margaret Pendergrass – forced a false marriage on the young woman. Richard Russel raped her, infecting her with a venereal disease. The three were accused of 'forcibly and unlawfully marrying and defiling Sibble Morris; against her Will' in 1728. Richard Russel was not arrested, and John Wheeler was a servant of Margaret Pendergrass so only the two women accomplices were found guilty and hanged.[307]

By the seventeenth century, rape was defined as a personal assault, and the woman herself – not her guardian, husband or father – might be compensated and the rapist punished as a criminal. Even a pregnant rape victim might be believed when she said she had neither consented nor orgasmed, as understanding about conception improved. But a woman's word remained 'naturally' unreliable. Many men brought to trial simply denied the act, winning an innocent verdict by giving their word.[308] As a seventeenth-century Lord Chief Justice remarked, 'In a rape case it is the victim, not the defendant, who is on trial.'[309]

Although legal opinions reflected a 'general horror of rape',[310] judges rarely found it. In the 150 years or so from 1558 to 1700, only 48 convictions for rape were recorded in Sussex, and 21 in Hertfordshire.[311] Juries were far readier to convict murderers than rapists. In Surrey between 1660 and 1800, there were more than twice as many convictions for murder than for rape (2.5 times more). Eighty-five per cent of accused murderers were found guilty, but only 55 per cent of accused rapists. Convictions for attempted rape were higher: 64 per cent of the men accused of attempting rape were found guilty.[312] The death penalty may have discouraged magistrates from accusing men of rape and jurors from delivering a guilty verdict, preferring an accusation of attempted rape with a physical punishment and fines, and some rapes may have been attempted and interrupted by people who then became witnesses in court to the lesser crime.

Forced, violent or unwanted sex in marriage was not a crime because a wife's consent was understood to be given once and for all on her wedding day and could never be withdrawn. But children under the age of 12 were not able to consent – any sexual intercourse with a child was rape. In the 1751 Account of the Proceedings of the Governors of the Lock Hospital for Venereal Disease, it was noted that more than 50 children aged between 2 and 12 had been treated in the four years since the hospital's opening, having contracted the disease because of sexual attack. The governors believed this to be the result of rapists attempting to cure themselves of venereal disease by having sex with a virgin, and campaigned against the myth.[313]

Health

Epidemics, including the great plague of 1665, continued to sweep the country. In London, probably about 20 per cent of the city's population died of the plague, with especial impact on women, since working city women were particularly poor and underfed, and they often worked in dirty and cramped quarters in nursing, health and the sex trade. 'Searchers' employed by the parish to identify plague victims and close up their houses were mostly women, so women experienced a small peak in employment in these ill-paid (4d a day for searchers), highly dangerous and unpleasant jobs.[314]

The greatest danger to women's life came from childbirth. In an age when marital rape was not a crime, without efficient contraception and with no understanding of how infections were transmitted, childbirth was a constant threat to wives.

The arrival of male physicians to replace traditional female midwives did not make childbirth any safer, despite the claims of the all-male guilds and colleges. While Dr Peter Chamberlen invented forceps, a mechanism to grip a baby stuck in the birth canal and pull it out, he kept his life-saving invention a strict secret: three generations of his family – Chamberlen, his three sons and a grandson – made their fortunes from the suffering of women and babies.[315] The Chamberlen doctors would only produce the forceps in the birthing room after they had blindfolded the labouring woman so that she could not see their instrument and – if she survived – describe it to rivals.

Without forceps, the only way to deliver a baby stuck in the birth canal was to wait for the mother to die and then perform a Caesarean section on her dead body. It says much for the attention to women and babies that the Royal Society of Physicians allowed the Chamberlen men to profit from the exclusive use of his invention while physicians and midwives without the life-saving equipment continued to supervise dying mothers and babies.[316] The average death rate for women in childbirth in the eighteenth century was about one in 40 women.[317]

Conception, pregnancy and birth remained a mystery and not even the greatest women in the land trying to give birth to a royal heir could be sure of a safe outcome. Queen Anne endured 17 pregnancies and died without producing a Stuart male heir. She had seven miscarriages, five stillbirths and two babies died as newborns. Two toddlers died of smallpox, and her only surviving child died aged eleven.[318]

Condoms were used to protect the man from infection, not to prevent pregnancy; and herbs causing miscarriage, and surgical abortions, were the most readily available contraception. In 1732, abortionist Eleanor Beare, a herbalist (and alleged poisoner), was sentenced to the pillory by a court in her home town of Derby. She was pelted with vegetables and eggs and then stoned by an outraged crowd who were said to have been ready to kill her if the parish officers had not protected her. She was one of several abortionists reported in the *Newgate Calendar*.[319]

Renaissance thinking, which had identified men as reasonable and self-controlled and women as unreasonable and highly emotional, made allowances for occasional irrationalism in men. 'Love-sickness' was a male disorder, when a man might lose his usual reason in the grip of desire – the character of Romeo provided a recognisable male sufferer in *Romeo and Juliet*, written in the 1590s. Love-sickness could be described by the more bawdy commentators as exaggerated lust: 'cunt-struck'.

But by the middle of the eighteenth century, influenced by the Romantic movement, high emotion came into fashion for both sexes, and symptoms of mental illness were suitable for everyone. Men of heightened sensibility, like the heroes of the sentimental novels, could act-out their emotions with tears, despair, running away, anger, sleeplessness, fasting and even suicide – as in Johann Goethe's hugely popular novel *The Sorrows of Young Werther* (1774). Men of sensibility expressed despair at the cruelty of the world.

In the case of women, emotion was expressed more modestly. They did not have the option of travel or escape, and they did not violently commit suicide with guns; women in the novels modelled self-harming in more passive ways, like fasting, neurotic behaviours, starving themselves or declining into exhausted or even catatonic states.

A cluster of symptoms shown by young women were named 'greensickness', said to be caused by sexual frustration and cured by penile penetration.[320] But as young ladies were expected to be increasingly sexually cool, 'greensickness' could not be caused by a young lady pining for sex. Instead the symptoms of 'greensickness' were normalised and considered to be part of female maturing. Menstruation, or delayed and irregular menstruation, eating disorders, fainting, tearfulness, exhaustion, depression, fragility and malaise became increasingly seen as normal elite female behaviour.

The growing belief in female asexuality, and uninterest in sex, meant that doctors finally observed that female orgasm was not necessary for conception. They went further – there was no female contribution to conception at all! Experts believed that the whole embryo was contained in the sperm, and the ovum in the woman was merely a passive receptacle for the baby to grow[321] – it was a nest, not an egg. A woman was indeed an empty vessel. As Lady Peregrina Chaytor complained of her pregnancy in 1701, in a letter to her husband, 'I must wish you had not given it me at this time, when I would think of better things.'[322]

There were still no anaesthetics, and medical opinion in the eighteenth century stuck firmly to the view that pain in childbirth was ordained by God as part of the punishment of Eve. So to offer pain relief went against the will of God and was therefore a sin, 'to contravene the operations of those natural and physiological forces that the Divinity has ordained us to enjoy or to suffer'.[323]

Not even the determination to strengthen the health of aristocratic heirs, so that a vigorous nobility might be restored alongside the returning king in 1660, had any impact on childrearing practices and failed to persuade elite families to let mothers breast-feed their babies. The belief that breast-feeding prevented conception meant that for those men determined to get more heirs, it was more efficient to send a baby to a wet nurse and conceive another child than to keep the first baby with the mother. The working-class woman who became a wet nurse had to send her own child away, or feed it after the client baby, displacing her own newborn baby and endangering its health. Wet nursing used the working-class mother as a milk-producer, like a cow. It was a cruel and expensive elite practice; ironically, it caused a higher death rate among aristocratic babies than among those of the poor. One in five elite babies died in infancy, but one in seven lower-class babies. The increasing emphasis on female frailty as a sign of being a 'lady', and the sense that genteel women disliked physical functions, meant that the use of wet nurses expanded down the classes. Social climbers did not breast-feed any more than aristocrats. Jane Austen herself – that expert on bourgeois ladylike behaviour – was sent away from home as a newborn at the end of the eighteenth century to a wet nurse.[324]

Part 6

1765–1857
Making a Lady

Slavery

In 1761, an African girl, aged only seven years old, was sold in Liverpool, nearly 4,000 miles away from her family in The Gambia. She had survived kidnap, separation from her parents and a six-week voyage from Africa to the Sugar Islands imprisoned below decks. At the Sugar Islands, most of the slaves had been dragged up into the sunlight, washed and cleaned for sale, as the homebound load of sugar, rum and molasses was loaded into the stinking hold; but she was kept on board, probably part of the 'Captain's perks', an allowance of slaves given to slave-trading captains for their private use or sale. She was bought by Henry Hervey Aston and his wife Catherine, a Liverpool business family, to be a playmate-slave for their two daughters. They named her Chloe Gambia for her lost homeland, and she served as a domestic slave and then their housekeeper. She died at the age of 68, and – as a baptised Christian – was buried with a headstone in St Peter's churchyard, in Aston, Cheshire.[1]

Chloe was one of many millions of men and women kidnapped in Africa and one of the thousands shipped to England, to work as slaves and domestic servants, or even (in the case of little children) as companions in white English households. Slaves were a sign of high status among the elite from the mid-seventeenth century until the abolition of slavery in England in 1833 and though boys and men were preferred as footmen and page boys, enslaved girls and women were also brought into the country. According to Lord Chief Justice Mansfield, there were at least 14,000 African-born slaves in England in 1772.[2]

Although the work was lighter than the fatal labour of the American and West Indies plantations, the treatment of men and women slaves in England was often intensely cruel, sometimes ending in death. Black women as well as men were branded and whipped, as proved by the scars on runaways described in advertisements for their return: 'Run away from Mr. Shute, Merchant in Pudding Lane, near the Monument, a Young Negro Woman, Yellowish Complexion, Middle-Stature, and Slender, with two Fl[e]sh Marks one above the Shoulder, the other above her Breast below her Collar-bone.'[3]

It was widely believed that the state of slavery in England had been abolished with feudalism, but in practice slaves brought into England from the colonies – where slavery was a legal state – were not automatically freed on arrival. Most slaves freed themselves by running away, but those who managed to escape found it hard to survive in a society where there was little help and support for the native poor, let alone newcomers. Newly free women had no home parish, no right of residency anywhere and nowhere to claim charity. Many had no education and little training in English domestic work. 'Charlotte' was brought to England by her owner Captain Howe who died. 'Charlotte' was refused poor relief by the parish overseers of Thames Ditton, and the case went to court, appearing before Lord Chief Justice Mansfield in 1785. Mansfield supported the parish and not the destitute woman, ruling that since she had not been hired for a wage, she was not entitled to charity.[4]

One woman escaped from slavery on the death of her owner and became, for a time, a hugely successful prostitute and brothel-owner. Her life was described in a guide to the sex workers at a London brothel at King's Place. The pamphlet, *Nocturnal Revels*, describes an African girl, born in Guinea, West Africa, who was kidnapped very young, sold into slavery, survived the Atlantic crossing to Jamaica and was sold to a planter. He gave her a schoolmaster to teach her to read and write and made her the supervisor of the house slaves. He raped her repeatedly, and she gave birth to two of his children; after three years in Jamaica, he brought her to England as his slave – some accounts say he married her and that she was known as his wife.

NOCTURNAL REVELS:
OR, THE
HISTORY
OF
KING's-PLACE,
AND OTHER
MODERN NUNNERIES.
CONTAINING THEIR
MYSTERIES, DEVOTIONS, and SACRIFICES.
Comprising also, The
ANCIENT and PRESENT STATE of PROMISCUOUS
GALLANTRY:
WITH THE
PORTRAITS of the most CELEBRATED
DEMIREPS and COURTEZANS of this PERIOD:
AS WELL AS
Sketches of their Professional and Occasional Admirers.

By a MONK of the ORDER of St. FRANCIS.

IN TWO VOLUMES.
VOL. I.

THE SECOND EDITION, CORRECTED AND IMPROVED,
WITH A VARIETY OF ADDITIONS.

Il vero est, quod ego mihi puto palmarium,
Me reperisse, quo modo adolescentulus
Meretricum ingenia & mores possit noscere:
Mature ut cum cognorit, perpetuo oderit.
TER. EUN. Act 5, Sc. 4.

LONDON:
Printed for M. GOADBY, Pater-noster-Row.
1779.

The guide to London's prostitutes was written under a fictitious name. The 'Order of St Francis' probably refers to Francis Dashwood's high-society gentlemen's clubs

The *Nocturnal Revels* described her life in England with her owner, in the offensive terms of the time:

Notwithstanding the beauties of this Island often attracted his attention, and he frequently gave loose to his natural appetites with his own country women, still she remained unrivalled as a constant flame; nor was it in some respect extraordinary, although her complexion might not be so engaging as that of the fair daughters of Albion, she had many attractions that are not often met with in the female world who yield to prostitution. She was faithful to his bed, careful of his domestic concerns, exact in her accounts, and would not suffer any of the servants to impose upon their master, and in this respect, she saved him some hundreds a year. Her person (to follow her) was very alluring: she was tall well-made and genteel, and since her arrival in England, she had given her mind to reading, and at her master's recommendation, had perused several useful and entertaining books, calculated for women, whereby she had considerably improved her understanding, and had attained a degree of politeness scarce to be paralleled in an African female.[5]

Despite her loyal service, when Harriot's master died of smallpox, he left her with nothing but her clothes, some trinkets and £5 in cash, and she joined a brothel and became the favourite of 'a score of peers and 50 commoners who never presented her with anything less than a soft paper commonly called a bank note'.

She earned enough from prostitution to buy her own house in King's Place, London, and hired her own girls to work as prostitutes. The *Nocturnal Revels* reports that she fell in love with a guards' officer, paid his debts and refused to have sex with other men. A visit to Brighton left her London servants unsupervised and they stole her goods and ran up debts that she could not meet. At the time of the writing of the *Nocturnal Revels*, Harriot was in the King's Bench for debt, and there is no apparent record of her release or life after imprisonment.

Other African women worked as prostitutes in London; another guide mentions: 'The curvaceous Miss Lowes of Upper Charlotte Street, Soho, and Miss Wilson of Lichfield Street, Soho, who was of very pleasing features and intelligence and frequently to be found at the theatre in the evening.'[6]

Some women managed to free themselves from slavery and make successful lives in England. One of these was Mary Prince, who was born into slavery in Brackish Pond, Bermuda, in 1788, the daughter of a sawyer and a house slave. When the plantation owner died, Mary's mother and her six brothers and sisters were sold to a new owner as house slaves. Mary was the companion slave of the new owner's granddaughter, but when she was 12 years old she was hired out to another owner and had to leave her mother and siblings: 'I cried bitterly at parting with my dear mistress and Miss Betsy, and when I kissed my mother and brothers and sisters I thought my young heart would break it pained me so; but there was no help I was forced to go.'[7]

Mary was beaten by her new owner and his wife, and sold into hard physical labour in the Salt Ponds, in the Turks and Caicos islands, where she worked waist-deep in water shovelling salt to dry. After ten years she was taken to Bermuda by her master on his retirement and from there to Antigua. She had painful rheumatism and was regularly beaten, but she attended a Moravian church, where she met her husband, a carpenter who had bought his freedom. Mary saved money from extra work and tried to buy her freedom, but her owners – the Woods family – refused to sell. They whipped her for marrying without their permission and separated her from her husband, taking her on a visit to England without him, growing more impatient as her poor health worsened. Finally, after several quarrels, they threw her out:

> I did not know well what to do. I knew that I was free in England; but I did not know where to go, or how to get my living; and therefore, I did not like to leave the house. But Mr Wood said he would send for a constable to thrust me out; and at last I took course and resolved that I would not be longer thus treated, but would go and trust to Providence. This was the fourth time they had threatened to turn me out, and go where I might, I was determined now to take them at their word; though I thought it very hard, after I had lived with them for thirteen years, and worked for them like a horse, to be driven out in this way like a beggar.[8]

Mary found her way to the abolitionist Thomas Pringle and became a servant to him and other abolitionists. Her legal position was uncertain. She had been born into slavery – a legal state in Bermuda – and although she had been thrown out by her owners in England, she had not been officially freed by them, and they would not allow her to buy herself out of slavery. After a year's stay in England, her owners prepared to return to Antigua. Mary was trapped in England – if she returned to her husband Daniel in Antigua, she would return to a state of legal slavery and would belong to the Woods family again. A petition to Parliament failed, and when the family sailed for Antigua, Mary was left behind, a free woman only in England, but separated from her husband in Antigua. She dictated the story of her life to a sympathetic white woman – Susanna Moodie, sister of the historian Agnes Strickland – and it became the first female slave narrative to be published. After publication, she disappears from the record. All slaves were freed in Bermuda and Antigua in 1834 by the legal abolition of slavery, so she could have returned as a free woman to her husband then.

Dido Elizabeth Belle (1761–1804) is perhaps the best-known English slave, thanks to the fame of her owner, and books and a film about her. She was born to a slave mother Maria Belle in the West Indies, the daughter of Sir John Lindsay, a naval officer who took the four-year-old girl with him when he returned home to England. Rose-tinted accounts of his relationship with her mother suggest that he may have rescued her from slavery while on an anti-slavery patrol and cared for their baby at her death,[9] but as an enslaved woman she had no consent to give. Whether rapist or rescuer, Lindsay took the child to his uncle at Kenwood House, London. William Murray and his wife Elizabeth, a childless couple, were raising their legitimate white niece Lady Elizabeth Murray, and the little girl Dido was raised with her to serve as her companion.

William Murray was 1st Earl of Mansfield and Lord Chief Justice, sitting on several important cases testing the legality of slavery in England. His prolonged and thoughtful deliberations were intentionally ambiguous. Though often hailed as the English judge who freed slaves in England, he only ever made individual arguments for the freedom of individual slaves and speaking generally he said: 'I don't know what the consequences may be if the masters were to lose their property by accidentally bringing their slaves to England. I hope it never will be finally discussed; for I would have all masters think them free, and all negroes think they were not, because then they would both behave better.'[10]

Dido Belle lived with Lord Mansfield's family as a poor relation – present at family occasions but not at large dinner parties, a companion and a family member but not a social equal, paid a smaller allowance than her white, legitimate cousin. She lived the life typical of a poor genteel relation to an elite family as companion, personal assistant, even secretary to William Murray. But the difference between the white heiress Elizabeth and her illegitimate cousin Dido was noted at the time. The portrait of Elizabeth Murray (see plate section) shows Dido Elizabeth Belle in an exotic costume with a turban headdress, placed behind her kinswoman, carrying pine cones. The young white woman holds a book in one hand with the other hand resting rather awkwardly on Dido's arm – as if holding her back.

The portrait is not a sentimental depiction of a tender relationship. It is a quite typical example of slave paintings, in which Black slaves or servants are contrasted with their white owners, demonstrating the owner's wealth, and emphasising the physical beauty of both slave and owner – with the spotlight on the white person, who commissioned the painter and owned the slave. Other portraits of slaves and owners also feature the slave carrying exotic fruit or flowers: a picturesque emblem of the slavery work of production.

Despite Lord Mansfield ruling on the freedom of individual slaves in England, he was so doubtful of Dido Belle's safety that he 'confirmed' her freedom in his will – to make it clear that whatever she had been during his life – she was freed by his death. He left her a small inheritance that enabled her to marry a white upper-household servant and set up house with him in middle-class Pimlico: a typical marriage and home for a poor relation of an elite family.

Saartjie Baartman was the daughter of a cattle drover of the Khoikhoi people of Southern Africa. She was brought to England in 1810 with her master, Hendrik Cesars, a freed slave, by Alexander Dunlop, a surgeon in the Cape Slave Lodge, who had a sideline in showing exotic animals in Europe. Dunlop showed her, as the 'Hottentot Venus', for 2s per person in London, one of several Khoikhoi children exhibited as curiosities.

The African Association took Saartjie Baartman's case to the King's Court and argued that she was enslaved and had been described by Dunlop as 'property'. The inquiry accepted the claim that Baartman was free, was working as she chose and would be paid half of the profits of her exhibition. Cesar and Dunlop took Saartjie to country fairs for exhibition and in 1811 she was baptised a Christian in the name of Sarah Bartman, and married a man of African descent.[11]

Despite the promises of her freedom, she was sold to a French owner, exhibited in Paris for 11 hours a day, and after her death in 1815 her body was dissected and her remains kept in a museum, only returned to South Africa for burial in 2002.

Matilda Foster was born a slave in 1818 on the Elim Estate in St Elizabeth parish, Barbados, and conceived a child to a white man and gave birth to a daughter, Fanny, a year after the legal abolition of slavery, so the baby was born free.

Matilda and her daughter got to England and were recorded in the 1851 census living in St Pancras: Matilda working as a laundress and

Fanny as a domestic servant. Fanny married or lived with James Eaton, a porter, and had ten children with him. As well as domestic work, Fanny Eaton worked as an artist's model at the Royal Academy of Arts, often posing as a non-white heroine for a sketching club that included some of the pre-Raphaelite painters. She also modelled for artists Rebecca Solomon and Joanna Wells, but her modelling fees were not enough to free her from domestic service. She ended her days living with one of her married daughters, and died at the age of 88.[12]

Theories of racial inferiority developed after the first African kidnaps, as an attempt to justify and excuse the massively profitable growing transatlantic slave trade. When slaves had been kidnapped from Ireland in the seventeenth century, a myth of Irish inferiority had arisen as justification; earlier racism had been directed towards other exploited groups: Jewish people and so-called 'gypsies'. The fanciful notion that African people were suited for slavery, and even that slavery was beneficial for them, was put forward by the people who profited from slavery. Racism became a hugely popular concept – but only in countries that had profited from slavery and longed to believe that enslaving someone proved the superiority of the slaver. It is no coincidence that the modern expression that 'might is right' was coined by an abolitionist in 1846: '"Might makes right," and hoary folly totters on in her mad career, escorted by armies and navies.'[13]

English imperialists on their mad career escorted by armies and navies had already persuaded themselves that they were innately superior to all women, Jewish peoples, Irish people, some Asian peoples and people of the first nations in the Americas, and in Australia. Racism and sexism justified the rule of elite white men over half their own country and potentially all the rest of the world. Citing God (and finding racism and sexism in the Bible), citing the classics (and finding misogyny and slavery in ancient Greece), citing the new sciences which conveniently found whatever anyone wanted, English imperial men used religion and science to justify kidnap, slavery and excluding people from their own lands, opportunities, education and freedom.

Racism was a transparent attempt to justify slavery and the British Empire; it did not cause it. Belief in female inferiority was trumpeted after the oppression of women – it did not cause it. In the eighteenth century, some women saw the connection and protested both, and some women saw the benefits they gained as slave owners and elite women and made no protest. Elite women directly owned slaves, and when compensation was paid to slave owners for their losses at abolition, 41 per cent of the payments would be made to identifiable women.[14]

Mary Seacole (1805–81), now hailed as a heroine of nursing, was rejected as a nurse by the British government and the official charities because of prejudice against her colour. She was the free descendant of slaves, the daughter of a lodging house keeper and a British army lieutenant, raised, married and widowed in Jamaica who had worked on the island and in Panama as a health practitioner. She arrived in London to volunteer as a nurse for the British army in the Crimean War but was rejected both by the government and by the official charity, the Crimean Fund. She thought it was racial prejudice: 'Did these ladies shrink from accepting my aid because my blood flowed beneath a somewhat duskier skin than theirs?'[15]

Thought to be one of only two original photographs of Mary Seacole (1805–81), found in Winchester College archives where Mary is the only non-combatant in the collection

Florence Nightingale (1820–1910) claimed she only sat for one photograph – at the request of Queen Victoria. Here's another, by Regent Street portraitist William Edward Kilburn

Mary Seacole applied directly to Florence Nightingale's assistant: 'Once again I tried, and had an interview this time with one of Miss Nightingale's companions. She gave me the same reply, and I read in her face the fact, that had there been a vacancy, I should not have been chosen to fill it.'

Seacole took passage on a ship to Crimea, where she built her own boarding house from the wreckage of other houses destroyed by shelling in the ruins of a town only a mile from the British headquarters. She nursed wounded soldiers and supported them as they returned from the fighting to be shipped home, providing food and drink for paying officers and for wounded soldiers for free. It was said that you could buy anything from an anchor to a sewing needle from 'Mother Seacole'. She had a cool meeting with Florence Nightingale (1820–1910) in Crimea. Nightingale wrote: 'I had the greatest difficulty in repelling Mrs Seacole's advances, and in preventing association between her and my nurses (absolutely out of the question!) … Anyone who employs Mrs Seacole will introduce much kindness – also much drunkenness and improper conduct.'[16]

Mary Seacole won a bet that she would be the first English woman into Sebastopol, entering the town with the triumphant British army in September 1855 and serving the soldiers until the end of the war, at a financial loss. She was awarded the Crimea Medal, and several fundraising events were held to celebrate her service and pay her debts.

She published her autobiography, *Wonderful Adventures of Mrs. Seacole in Many Lands*, in July 1857, before returning to Jamaica for a visit, eventually making a comfortable home in London, where she died in 1881, leaving £2,500 in her estate. She was proud of her mixed race and her history:

> I am a Creole, and have good Scots blood coursing through my veins. My father was a soldier of an old Scottish family … I have a few shades of deeper brown upon my skin which shows me related – and I am proud of the relationship – to those poor mortals whom you once held enslaved, and whose bodies America still owns.[17]

Servitude

To be an apprentice in eighteenth-century England, especially one of the increasing number of children legally kidnapped from their parents by the poor laws, was to be in a state of short-term slavery: servitude, bound for seven years to a master, unpaid and exposed to criminal cruelty. Sarah Metyard and her daughter owned a millinery workshop at Bruton St, in the capital, with five pauper apprentice girls from parish workhouses. The two women tortured one girl, Anne Naylor, tying her up, beating her and starving her to death, but were only arrested four years later when parts of the girl's body were found. Metyard and her daughter were executed for murder at Tyburn in July 1762.[18] The scandal-loving *Newgate Calendar* reported Elizabeth Brownrigg, a midwife, living with her husband, a plumber, at Flower-de-Luce Court, Fleet Street, who tortured and starved three young girls who had been put in her care from the poor house. When one girl escaped and reported her injuries, the local authorities released her from her apprenticeship, but failed to pursue the Brownrigg family. Neighbours reported the torture of another girl who died after her release, and Elizabeth Brownrigg was finally arrested and executed at Tyburn in September 1767, while her husband and son were sentenced to six months imprisonment.[19]

There was no room in the Foundling Hospital for a two-year-old toddler, found on a doorstep at Castle Street, Holborn, in 1809, and the child was sent to the parish workhouse and 'dropped' – left to die of exposure – by Thomas and Elizabeth Pugh, who claimed that the deserting father had promised them £300 for his child's death. They were imprisoned for six months each.[20] In 1829, Frances Colpitt, a ten-year-old girl was apprenticed by the parish to Mrs Esther Hibner, to learn tambour work. All apprentices at the workshop were cruelly treated, starved and beaten, and Frances died. During the trial it was discovered that another child apprentice had died too. Hibner was executed; her daughter and their assistant Anne Robinson were found guilty of assault and imprisoned in the house of correction.[21]

Slaves Protest Against Slavery

The most effective protest from enslaved women and men in England was to simply run away. A majority of the people of African descent in England in the eighteenth and nineteenth centuries courageously took their own freedom, some repeatedly escaping until they found a hiding place – often with white working-class families. A very few slaves were freed on arrival, as their owners believed that no legal state of slavery existed in England and employed them as servants, paying a wage. But when these owners wanted to return to their colonial homes, they often tried to take servants back with them – returning to legal slavery and enslaving them all over again. Many slaves fled to avoid return, and many accounts describe runaways and rescues from ships returning to the West Indies or the Americas. Some ex-slaves helped others to get away. The *Daily Advertiser* of 17 June 1743 recorded:

A Black Negro Woman, about nineteen Years old, with two Letters on her Breast and Shoulder, made her Escape out of the Ship Hannah, Capt. Fowler, for Jamaica, the 6th inst. goes by the Name of Sabinah, is suppos'd to be deluded away by some other Black

about Whitechapel, Rag-Fair, or Rotherhith. Whoever brings her to
the late Mr. Neale's, on Lawrence-Pountney-Hill, shall have three
Guineas Reward; or if put on board the Ship again any time between
this and next Tuesday, Ten Shillings more.[22]

In the *Gazetteer and New Daily Advertiser* on 25 March 1765:

RUN away from her Master last Friday evening, a Negroe Woman,
named Joan, about 18 Years old, speaks nothing but English; had on
when she went away, a brown Stuff Gown, red Cloak and black
Leather Shoes; has very thick Lips, about five Feet five Inches high.
Whoever will give Notice where she may be found, or bring her to
Capt. John Grant, at Mr. Stewart's, Finch Lane, shall receive Two
Guineas Reward, and no greater will be given, as proper persons are
employed to find her.

N.B. Any Person who conceals her, will be prosecuted.[23]

Ellen Craft was born into slavery, the illegitimate daughter of a woman
slave and her white owner in Clinton, Georgia, in America. At 11 years
old she was given as a gift to her owner's daughter – her white half-sister
– and taken with the household to Macon, Georgia. Ellen married a
skilled carpenter, William Craft, who had been born into slavery, and the
two of them planned an extraordinary escape. Ellen disguised herself as
an elderly slave owner, and her husband pretended to be her slave, to
make a perilous journey by train and boat of more than 800 miles to
freedom in Philadelphia.[24] They lived in Boston as free people, but were
hunted by slave-takers so fled to England, where Ellen said she would
'much rather starve ... a free woman, than be a slave for the best man
that ever breathed upon the American continent'.[25]

On arrival, they were helped by men and women abolitionists and
Ellen Craft took work as a lodging house proprietor, while her husband
William worked as a cabinet-maker. They campaigned for the end of
slavery, telling their own life histories to anti-slavery audiences and working for the London Emancipation Committee.[26]

Born free in West Africa and slaved to Boston, New England, as a
little girl of eight years old, Phillis Wheatley (1753–84) would be highly
influential for Black and white Englishwomen. John Wheatley bought

her as a domestic servant for his wife, Susannah: 'A slender, frail female child … for a trifle'.[27] They guessed she was about seven years old as she was losing her milk teeth. Taught by their daughter Mary, by the age of 14 the little girl was reading Greek and Latin and had published a poem on the death of a minister. At 20 years old, in search of a publisher, she was brought to London by the Wheatleys' son Nathaniel, and in 1773, under the patronage of Selina Hastings, the evangelical Christian Countess of Huntingdon, published her collection of poems, the first such book written by an American Black woman. Her owners granted her her freedom.

Phillis Wheatley followed other English writers and composed in the classical tradition – but her biographer suggests that she specialised in the elegy due to her roots in West African culture, where young women traditionally sang the praises of the dead. Returning to America, a free woman, Phillis married a free African-American entrepreneur and self-styled 'lawyer' John Peters, in Boston. They had three children who died in infancy. The family fell into poverty, and John Peters was arrested for debt. Phillis worked as a scrubwoman in a boarding house while continuing to write poetry. She died in poverty in December 1784, with 143 poems unpublished.[28]

Phillis Wheatley condemned slavery, but celebrated that it had taken her from what she described as her pagan culture in Africa. Her language is of its time:

On Being Brought from Africa to America
By Phillis Wheatley

'Twas mercy brought me from my Pagan land,
Taught my benighted soul to understand
That there's a God, that there's a Saviour too:
Once I redemption neither sought nor knew.
Some view our sable race with scornful eye,
'Their colour is a diabolic die.'
Remember, Christians, Negros, black as Cain,
May be refin'd, and join th' angelic train.[29]

In 1787, 40 women of African origin and 70 white women took the extraordinarily courageous decision to travel to Sierra Leone to create a

Phillis Wheatley (1753–84), portrait from the frontispiece of her book
Poems on Various Subjects, Religious and Moral

settlement of free people. Funded by the Committee of Black Poor, organised by white volunteers and famous Africans Ignatius Sancho and Olaudah Equiano, 280 African men, along with the African women and white wives and girlfriends, took a ship to West Africa. The settlement – neglected by government – failed within two years and all but 60 of the pioneers died.

Some people of African descent lived free in England. As well as the runaways and freed people, some African children had been sent by their parents for their education, using contacts (made through the slave trade) to enter English schools with the hope of joining English society and taking up business opportunities. By the end of the eighteenth century, several schools in the slaving ports of Liverpool and Bristol would be teaching free African children, sent from Africa by families who wanted a child raised in English culture.[30]

A freed slave, as a property owner, was able to vote in an English election before free white women won the vote. Ignatius Sancho, the writer, musician and entrepreneur, opened a grocery shop in Charles Street, Westminster, and, as a property-owning man, cast his vote in 1780.[31]

Elite White Women Protest Against Slavery

The founder and leader of the anti-slavery movement, William Wilberforce, specifically ruled women out of the campaign: 'For ladies to meet, to publish, to go from house to house stirring up petitions – these appear to me, proceedings unsuited to the female character as delineated in Scripture.'[32]

Many ladies agreed. Eliza Conder insisted that women belonged in their homes: 'If we are thus to start out of our spheres, who is to take our place? Who, as "keepers at home" are to "guide the house", and train up children? Are the gentlemen kindly to officiate for us?'[33]

Despite not being wanted – told that scripture was against them – upper- and middling-class women engaged in the campaign for the abolition of slavery from 1772, when the first English slave was freed in England by a court case, through to 1807, when slave trading was made illegal, to 1833 when the state of slavery was made illegal in the English overseas territories. By 1820, women's names filled the petitions: leading women writers against slavery included Ann Yearsley, Hannah Moore and Anna Barbauld,[34] and the first call for immediate total abolition was published in 1824 by a woman – the radical Quaker Elizabeth Heyrick. Her belief in instant abolition eventually became the national policy of the campaign, after six years of resistance from the more moderate men's executive who wanted gradual change.

In 1825, ladies founded the first women's anti-slavery organisation, in Birmingham, boycotting sugar and raising money through bazaars selling ladies' home-made productions.[35] Within six years, 70 ladies' anti-slavery associations had been set up.[36] By 1850, women's anti-slavery associations outnumbered men's, a national female network with international links, sending petitions to Parliament, and highly effective canvassers and pamphleteers.[37]

The ladies met in parallel with the men's societies, in ladies-only groups, unable to sit on policy committees and not invited to speak, but offering advice to the men's committee, support and fundraising. Only in the second half of the nineteenth century would some lady abolitionists work alongside men as equals. In 1853, the first co-ed anti-slavery society was founded in Leeds, and the next year the Manchester society sent the first two women delegates to the men-only British and Foreign Anti-Slavery Society meeting. In 1859, two African-American women, Sarah Parker Redmond and Ellen Craft, joined the London Emancipation Committee, which was open to everyone regardless of colour or sex, and Sarah Parker Redmond spoke in public on lecture tours in England.

Upper- and middle-class women believed that they could comfortably support the abolition of slavery, as their campaigns expressed 'Pity for suffering and the desire to relieve misery which are the natural and allowed feelings of women'.[38]

The elite white English women's view of slavery was that while no woman should be enslaved to a master, women could and should be protected and controlled by a husband or father. The ambition of these white abolitionist ladies was that enslaved women should exchange their legal status as chattel to a master to that of chattel to a husband or father. They believed their own lives provided an example of all the freedom that an enslaved women would want and should have: freedom under the rule of a husband or father. An enslaved woman should not be freed to behave like a man; she should be freed to take up her domestic place as a woman: secondary to a man, free to 'occupy her proper station as daughter, wife and mother'.[39]

The benign combination of the slavery of marriage and abolition was explicitly celebrated at the wedding of the abolitionist Priscilla Buxton, which took place on 'emancipation day', 1 August 1833, when the law to free English slaves was officially passed. The bride's fellow abolitionists raised their glasses in a toast, wishing that the bride 'might long rejoice in the fetters put on that day, as well as over those which she had assisted to break'.[40]

Priscilla Buxton – and most elite women – believed that women should be limited by, almost confined inside, family life. They felt justified in interfering in the issue of slavery because charitable, evangelical and even political work formed part of their duty to maintain family life – that of other families as well as their own.

Sarah Ellis argued in her book *The Wives of England* (1843) that ladies should step out of their domestic roles to confront issues like the 'extinction of slavery, the abolition of war in general, cruelty to animals, the punishment of death, temperance, and many more, on which, neither to know, nor to feel, is almost equally disgraceful. In short, women's politics must be the politics of morality.'[41]

Most elite women did not think they should go beyond trying to reproduce the ideal upper-class home among enslaved and poor women. Few ladies thought they should campaign on anything other than domestic issues until the middle of the nineteenth century. Courageous campaigning women could be against women having a vote. Sarah Dymond, of the Taunton Ladies' Anti-Slavery Society, wrote: 'I will engage to get up a public meeting, which I think I can do without stepping out of my proper sphere; I am decidedly opposed to the woman question.'[42]

Working-class White Women Protest Against Slavery

Few working-class women had either the time, the money or the invitation to attend an elite anti-slavery meeting. Their own drudgery, poverty and exposure to abuse meant that working-class women in England were all too familiar with some of the conditions of slavery, and revelations of the abuse of enslaved women did not shock them. They demanded that all working people – enslaved, in servitude and free – should have better treatment.[43] They used slavery as an illustration of their own oppression. Working-class abolitionists believed that slavery was wrong, but questioned why African slaves should be freed while white workers were left in servitude. Such women saw the abolitionists adopt a patronising concern for the oppression of distant foreign women and a blindness to the oppression of women at home.

Nineteenth-century campaigners for better conditions for women workers, such as Robert Sherard, a writer and philanthropist, used the phrase 'white slavery' to emphasise the hardship suffered by white working-class women in England, in a mixed message that evoked Black slavery as a terrible wrong; but actually directed attention away from abolition, by comparing it to the legal exploitation of sweated workers and describing his own elite white male distress: 'The pale procession of the White Slaves of England, I could see nothing but sorrow and hunger and grime, rags, foul food, open sores and movements incessant, instinctive yet laborious – an anvil and a hammer ever descending – all vague, and in a mist as yet untinged with red, a spectacle so hideous that I gladly shut it out, wondering for my part, what in these things is right.'[44]

Despite the hardship of their own lives, many working-class women called for the abolition of slavery, signing the petitions in their thousands and boycotting slavery goods. Women famously led the rejection of produce such as sugar, tea, coffee and chocolate, although very poor women could not afford such luxuries for their families. Lydia Hardy wrote to her husband Thomas – the founder of the London Corresponding Society, the first working-class political association – from Chesham in 1792: 'The people are here as much against that as enny ware and there is more people I think hear that drinks tea without suger than there is drinks with.'[45]

Mass meetings to protest against slavery were held in industrial towns, even in the slaving ports. Many of the working-class abolitionists went on to campaign for workers' rights – further separating the working-class abolitionist movement from the elite abolitionists. In 1788 alone, there were 100 petitions demanding abolition from working-class radical organisations.[46]

Working-class communities welcomed, supported and hid runaway slaves, seeing slavery as a problem of class exploitation: elite employers oppressing both free and enslaved workers. Even abolitionists could be the enemy – cruel employers of poor people, both Black and white. Slavers and elite white people complained that runaways and freed men and women were helping new immigrants to their freedom. Edward Long claimed: 'Upon arriving in London, these servants soon grow acquainted with a knot of blacks, who having eloped from their respective owners at different times, repose themselves here in ease and indolence, and endeavour to strengthen their party, by seducing as many of these strangers into the association, as they can work to their purpose.'[47]

Free men and women of African descent organised escape routes into sympathetic white working-class communities. London magistrate John Fielding said in 1768: 'Blacks, intoxicated with liberty, enter into societies, and make it their business to corrupt and dissatisfy the mind of every fresh black servant that comes to England ... They have the mob on their side.'[48]

William Cobbett, an observer of the English labouring classes, believed that the English, uniquely, lacked white racism and that runaway and freed slaves could easily find white women who were glad to marry them. His language is too offensive to repeat, but he concluded that English white working-class women were not racist: 'He will, if he be so disposed, always find a woman not merely to yield to his ... embraces ... but to accompany him to the altar to become his wife ... this beastly propensity is I assert, with sorrow and with shame, peculiar to the English.'[49]

'Breadwinner Wage'

Persuasive – but mostly nutty – theories about economics, religion, class and gender drove poor and working women from the country and into the sweatshops of the early factories in the middle of the eighteenth century. The new so-called 'science' of political economy argued that everyone should sell their labour at the price they could get, and employers pay as little as possible, trusting the market to find the right price just above starvation wages. Puritans and Protestants preached that God rewarded true believers with wealth, so poor people had only themselves to blame. Doctors identified the especial sensibility of upper-class women, who should be protected from disagreeable realities; but the insensitive nature of working-class women suited them to arduous, disagreeable and dangerous labour.

From around equality in the thirteenth and fourteenth centuries, the gulf between the average pay of men and women had fluctuated dramatically before falling to a steady rate of half-pay for women, now with support from most political economists; with the honourable exception of John Stuart Mill. Elite, mostly male, thinkers remained convinced that men should be paid more than women, and the government passed the 1834 new Poor Law on that assumption:[50]

> It is clearly a waste of strength, a superfluous extravagance, (an economic blunder) to employ a powerful and costly machine to do work which can be as well done by a feebler and a cheaper one. Women and girls are less costly operatives than men … what they can do with equal efficiency it is therefore wasteful and foolish, economically considered, to set a man to do. By employing the cheaper labour, the article is supplied to the public at a smaller cost and therefore the demand for the article is increased.[51]

From 1850 it was widely accepted that a woman would and should be paid about half a man's wage, if she worked at all, and the living wage – only earned by men – became known as the 'breadwinner wage'. The 'Law of Unequal Exchange', invented in 1808 by French political economist Jean Baptiste Say, argued that since a woman's economic needs were met by her husband, she was not disadvantaged if her wage was less.[52] He could earn the wage that fed the family, he could win the 'bread'. From 1821, the phrase 'breadwinner' came into use, almost always meaning the man earning enough for his family.[53]

A parliamentary committee set up to explore the wage gap in 1840 heard from a handloom weaver from Stockport:

> Joseph Sherwin … usually earned 6s 6d a week, and his wife 3s by winding bobbins for two other looms. However, he failed to subtract from his wage, and add to hers, the value of her winding services for his loom. Mrs Sherwin received for winding 3d out of every 1s earned by each of the two weavers who hired her services; each of these weavers, then, earned only 9d for every 1s worth of cloth. Since she could wind for three looms (her husband's plus two others), Mrs Sherwin could earn the same amount as these two weavers (9d = 3 x 3d). Joseph Sherwin admitted 'I must pay three-pence out of every shilling, if I had no wife.'
>
> His true wage, then, was only 4s 10d, and his wife's true wage was 4s 7½d. What by his statement appeared to be a wage ratio of 0.46 (3s / 6s 6d) turns out to be, in truth, almost equal wages. If the wage

data that we have overstate male earnings and understate female earnings, then there may be no wage gap to explain.[54]

Indeed – the committee were on to something! It was not that women were somehow naturally earning a lesser rate – it was that they were not getting paid at all! When Mrs Sherwin worked as a winder for weavers, she was paid, but when she worked for her husband, she was not paid at all. If women were paid money for all the work they did – for husbands as well as employers – there would be hardly any wage gap between men and women. The gap had been created by the tradition that women's work inside their home is done for free. Even when she was producing sellable goods, Mrs Sherwin earned no money – just as she did when she was producing goods consumed in the home: growing food, cooking, cleaning, home maintenance. Alas! This blinding revelation to the committee made no difference at all in real life – women continued to work for their husbands for free and hours of their labour went unpaid – reducing their earnings and their rate.

The making of pins and needles provided an example of how well-paid craft work that could have been done by well-paid artisan men or women was divided into low-paid piecework, mechanised and – once it was sufficiently low paid and de-skilled – allocated to unskilled women labourers. In 1728, *Chambers's Encyclopaedia* described a craftsman's workshop: 'The artisan is at the heart of the production process ... the tempo of production is fixed, and each task requires considerable skill.'[55]

A century later, in 1835, observer Andrew Ure saw the drive for machines to take skilled work away from artisan workers: 'Whenever a process requires particular dexterity and steadiness of hand, it is withdrawn as soon as possible from the cunning workman ... and it is placed in charge of a peculiar mechanism, so self-regulating, that a child may superintend it.'[56]

Karl Marx described the outcome in 1867: 'In the automated factory ... one woman or one girl superintends four ... machines, and so produces nearly 600,000 needles in a day.'[57]

Wherever possible, a skilled artisan, making one object from start to finish, was replaced by a team of workers making parts of the object, and then by a machine, making multiples, supervised by a badly paid woman, and often maintained and cleaned by child workers. The woman and children were not to be paid a breadwinner wage since they were supposed to be supported by the father of their family. They needed no training, and they served no apprenticeship to a guild that could set wages. Working in a deafening factory or even in a sweatshop attached to their own homes or set up in their living area, they could not organise for better conditions or wages, and if they complained, they could be easily replaced by other poor untrained women.

The breadwinner wage was explained to working people by political economists who now believed the prosperity of the country depended on low population – as few passengers as possible – and high productivity – a strong engine – which would be achieved by responsible breadwinner men. It was taught by middle-class reformers who believed that a full-time woman homemaker offered the solution to poverty, disease and immorality. It was preached from the pulpits as the way for women to become spiritual leaders in their homes. It was willingly paid to skilled men by the booming industries as the piecework process pushed more and more work towards badly paid women and children. It was agreed by male guilds and unions to protect men's wages and men's jobs against women workers. It suited the professions that had already excluded women. It was glamourised in the conduct books and novels that imagined that a true woman could only fulfil her nature in the separate sphere of her home, far from work, unsoiled by cash. It even won over some working-class wives who exchanged poorer wages for themselves for better pay for their husbands. The Female Political Union of Newcastle noted in 1840: 'Is it not true that the interests of our fathers, husbands, and brothers, ought to be ours? If they are oppressed and impoverished, do we not share those evils with them?'[58]

The call for a breadwinner wage became a cycle reinforcing inequality for women, as low rates of pay and exclusion from both training and skilled work forced them to depend on men who then had to earn a wage for at least two people,[59] demanding a breadwinner wage for skilled male work which employers could afford by paying minimum wages to unskilled women. The many women who could not marry a good earner had no prospect but poorly paid work. Women became 'industrial lepers',[60] in unskilled jobs that men left vacant because they were so ill paid.

Women's Work

By the 1850s, women of all classes found themselves deliberately excluded from profitable work, from education, from training, from the guilds and trades, and from the professions and from authority. Even women of property and high status started to nominate a male deputy to perform civic tasks.[61]

Education and guild membership became exclusively male. Journeymen book binders excluded women from their union in 1779 and tailors from London tried to ban women even from working at home.[62] Trades that had been dominated by women were now 'manned', and women supported and assisted the spinner, weaver, baker, miller and brewer trades that had been their own. Women could not raise the capital to buy licences and rent equipment and property for big commercial businesses. The booming luxury goods businesses like bookshops, jewellery stores and pharmacies were closed to women, both by the guilds and by the demand for start-up capital. Women could not enter international trade without a bank account and insurance in their own name.[63] They were even discouraged from the sport of boxing, where they had earlier been sporting stars. The tone of newspaper reports turned critical, describing women prizefighters as domineering and unwomanly.[64]

'Women's work' came to mean hard, nasty, low-paid work. As historian Dorothy George commented: 'It can almost be said that there is no work too heavy or disagreeable to be done by women provided it is also ill paid.'[65]

Only a shortage of labour – as happened in early nineteenth-century Coventry, Yorkshire and the West Country – saw women work alongside men and get paid the same rate.[66]

When Samuel Crompton's long-handed or double spinning mule came into cotton factories from 1820, men captured the new machine. They claimed it was too heavy for women and defined the task as 'skilled' work, demanding – and getting – a skilled wage. When the technology changed again, with the invention of the much lighter self-acting mule, which was brought into factories from 1840 and could be worked by women, male spinners refused to allow women on the new machines, forcing them into unskilled tasks as 'piecers, carders, and tenters' on lower wages – usually half those of a mule spinner.[67]

By 1830, women workers outnumbered men in the factories of the cotton industry: 65,000 women to 60,000 men.[68] A factory commissioner reported in 1844 that women were doing harder shifts than men: 'Their labour is cheaper, and they are more easily induced to undergo severe bodily fatigue than men.'[69]

The introduction of mechanised weaving told the opposite story. Handloom weavers had been the well-paid elite of labourers, mostly working in their own homes, with their wives and children assisting. It was such well-paid work that men tried to exclude women from weaving in the mid-eighteenth century, breaking their looms and threatening women weavers. When power looms were brought in to factories around the end of the century, the weavers opposed them in violent machine-smashing riots. But employers stood firm, employing women and children until extreme poverty, even starvation, forced the traditional weavers into the hated factories on the machines. But they had left it too late to make factory weaving an exclusively male trade. They found women weavers trained up to work on the power looms, organised and paid as skilled workers. In north-east Lancashire in particular, men and women weavers recognised their shared interests and organised together to get equal pay and conditions.[70]

Not all trade organisations were anti-women. The Grand National Consolidated Trades Union of 1833 recruited women into women-only sections. Lodges included lacemakers, straw bonnet-makers, shoebinders, laundresses, milliners and even ladies' maids. A lodge for women working in their own homes was proposed; but associations of unskilled poorly paid shift workers could not organise effectively; only when women dominated an industry might they be successful. In Stockport in 1840, the majority of the power loom workers were women (58 per cent) and they undertook industrial action with men. Women stood alongside male workers in strikes and demonstrations from 1808 in Manchester, and in the general strike of cotton workers in 1842. Women organised their own strikes: Loughborough lace runners walked out in 1811 and Kensington washerwomen went on strike in 1842.[71]

The breaking down of production into small, less skilled tasks meant they could be done by poor women in their homes. The 'putting out' or 'piecework' system broke the craft of, for instance, tailoring a garment, into many less-skilled repetitive tasks. Women would be supplied by the middlemen with parts of tailoring, lacemaking, shoemaking, buttonmaking and small metalwork – and repeatedly do one part of the process. Sometimes they had to pay a deposit for the raw materials, which could be so expensive that they had to offer their labour for free till the debt was paid off. The materials themselves could be hazardous. Women handled and stored toxic or dangerous products in their homes and could fall sick or be sacked without financial support. Isolated in their dwellings, with wages set as low as possible by the middlemen, the women had little opportunity to compare rates or organise together for better terms. Even after tasks had been mechanised and moved to the factories, women and children were still employed for preparing and finishing factory-made articles in their homes.

Women workers, especially those in their homes, constituted a 'reserve' work force. When the government needed uniforms and clothing for the 12 years of the Napoleonic wars (1803–15), the work was mostly done by women at home under the 'putting out' system, in defiance of the tailor's guilds trying to protect rates for their male members. Work that could be done more cheaply in a woman worker's home was called 'slop work' and was known to be 'sweated' – overworked and underpaid to tight deadlines. The early profits of most industries came not from mechanisation and factories, but from the sweated labour of home-based women workers.[72]

The widespread use of such women for slop work, even as late as 1906, was highlighted in a report from the *Women's Trade Union Review*:

cigarette-making, the beading of ladies' shoes, the stitching of gloves, chainmaking and the manufacture of hosiery, jewelcases, tennis-balls, belts, ties, furniture, brushes, and saddlery were all homework trades, in which a twelve to sixteen hour day brought in, on average, earnings of 5s (25p) to 7s (35p) a week … a dress could have been made by a reasonably paid seamstress in an airy workroom, while the buttons and trimmings were produced by a sweated worker … wedding cakes manufactured in hygienic conditions were likely to be packed in attractive boxes glued together in a disease-ridden tenement.[73]

Not until the nineteenth century would anyone have any concerns that women and children were risking their safety and health in terrible conditions:

The Royal Commission of 1842 included graphic illustrations of women and children working in coal mines

Women commonly worked underground in coal mines, primarily as part of family teams. While men worked the coal face, women carried or dragged the coal in sledges or tubs through the tunnels to the lifts, or on occasion even up to the surface ... At lime kilns, women were employed carrying baskets of coal and chalk, while men broke the chalk loose, screened it, lifted the baskets onto the women's heads, and threw the chalk into the kiln. Both sexes helped hack the coal and chalk into small pieces and fill the baskets ... Women were employed in the loading of slate onto boats in Devon (after it was quarried by men), where the work was described as 'immoderately hard' (by Richard Ayton, an observer in 1814), yet women 'accomplish as much in a given time as the men do.'[74]

The terrible work and conditions for women and children working underground came to public notice after an accident at Huskar Colliery near Barnsley in 1838, when 26 children (11 girls) were drowned while working. An inquiry reporting on the conditions made the point that women stripped naked to the waist to work in the heat of the mines and wore trousers for the heavy work. This was as shocking to the elite as the danger of the job.

It was well known that hard-working women could be as productive as men. The journalist Henry Mayhew watched a male dust collector in the East End of London in 1840 who was:

shovelling the sifted soil from one of the lesser heaps, and, by a great effort of strength and activity, pitching each shovel-full to the top of a lofty mound, somewhat resembling a pyramid. Opposite to him stood a little woman, stoutly made, and with her arms bare above the elbow; she was his partner in the work, and was pitching shovel-full for shovel-full with him to the summit of the heap. She wore an old soiled cotton gown, open in the front, and tucked up behind in the fashion of the last century. She had clouts of old rags tied around her ankles to prevent the dust from getting into her shoes, a sort of coarse towel fastened in front for an apron, and a red handkerchief bound tightly round her head. In this trim she worked away, and not only kept pace with the man, but often threw two shovels for his one, although he was a tall, powerful fellow.[75]

Most gravediggers were women. Sarah Arnold worked as the gravedigger for the Southwark burial ground at Long Lane, Bermondsey, for eight years from 1786, taking over from her husband John at his death. Mary Davis dug the graves for a year at Whitechapel in 1785 and Mary Harper was Wandsworth's gravedigger in 1786.[76] Women sextons (or sexton-esses) were common across London, responsible for organising the digging of graves and supervising the parish churchyards.[77]

The emergence of fixed shops in prime locations created roles for shop assistants. Women had been squeezed out of retail work by the belief that it was improper for a young woman to serve at a shop coun-ter, but as the work was de-skilled and devalued, shop work became instantly recognisable as 'women's work' – unskilled and underpaid.[78] Most positions were live-in and notorious for extremely long hours and low wages. In 1842, there was an unsuccessful attempt to regulate the working hours, and in the 1860s an effort to frighten women out of the bad habit of evening shopping by alerting them to 'endangering the health of their own sex, and especially that of the mothers of the future generation'.[79] Aristocratic ladies – four duchesses, two marchionesses and six countesses – set an example by agreeing not to shop after 2 p.m. on Saturdays.

No working-class woman, labouring as hard as a man in equally dangerous and unhealthy work, was encouraged to think of herself as morally superior and physically frail. No one thought working-class women were naturally unsuited for the world of work and should be protected in the home. Indeed, the men who brought in the new industries drove working-class women to work harder than ever. The wealthy men protected their wives and daughters, encouraging them into light spiritual work at home as suiting their fragile nature, while brutally exploiting working women in fields, mills, mines and on the streets.

Only when cheap male labourers became widely available did employers and male workers claim the work was too hard or unsuitable for women. There was no official concern about women doing hard labour until 1808 when the Poor Law commissioners worried that women farm labourers were inadequate homemakers because they had no proper domestic training: 'Agricultural work, if habitual, accustoms the whole frame to action upon too broad a scale for domestic life; the eye becomes regardless of precision and cleanliness, the habits undomestic and unfavourable to personal subordination. It seems agreed on all hands that much field-work in early life is a bad exercise for a woman's future duties.'

Women labouring hard alongside men were said to be 'coarse, licentious wretches, scorning all kinds of restraint, and yielding themselves up, with shameless audacity to the most detestable sensuality'.[80]

'Chivalrous' campaigns to keep women out of hard or dangerous work only appeared after working men realised that if conditions were improved for women and children, they would improve for everyone. Women and children found themselves increasingly banned from factory and industrial work in the later years of the nineteenth century, but they continued to struggle for a living in unregulated trades. Henry Mayhew, who observed the poor of London, gave this account of flowersellers in 1851:

Sunday is the best day for flowerselling ... in the height and pride of the summer four hundred children were selling flowers on Sundays in the streets. The trade is almost entirely in the hands of children, the girls outnumbering the boys by more than eight to one. The ages of the girls vary from six to twenty, few of the boys are older than twelve, and most of them are under ten.

Of flowergirls there are two classes. Some girls, and they are certainly the smaller class of the two, avail themselves of the sale of flowers in the streets for immoral purposes, or rather, they seek to eke out the small gains of their trade by such practices. Their ages are from fourteen to nineteen or twenty, and sometimes they remain out offering their flowers until late at night.

The other class of flowergirls is composed of girls who, wholly or partially, depend upon the sale of flowers for their own support or as an assistance for their parents. They are generally very persevering, more especially the younger children, who will run along barefooted, with their, 'Please, gentleman, do buy my flowers. Poor little girl!' or 'Please kind lady, buy my violets. O, do! please! Poor little girl! Do buy a bunch, please, kind lady!'[81]

Poor girls who could get neither education nor training grew into poor women. Mayhew saw women who were so-called 'mudlarks', searching the riverbank and tidal ponds for washed-up goods to sell:

Among the mud-larks may be seen many old women, and it is indeed pitiable to behold them, especially during the winter, bent nearly double with age and infirmity, paddling and groping among the wet mud for small pieces of coal, chips of wood, or any sort of refuse washed up by the tide. These women always have with them an old basket or an old tin kettle, in which they put whatever they chance to find. It usually takes them a whole tide to fill this receptacle, but when it is filled, it is as much as the feeble old creatures are able to carry home.[82]

Flower girls, prostitutes, criminals and housewives would be among the 6.5 million women listed as 'unoccupied' in the 1851 census. The 'unemployed' women and 3 million unemployed men included the elite, who would declare themselves to be at leisure – though perhaps supervising land, investing in shares, renting property and profiteering from assets. Most women who described themselves as 'in work' were working in manufacture, from piecework at home to shifts in factories: 1 million women and 1.7 million men. More than in agriculture and fishing: 700,000 women and 1.6 million men.[83]

Women could not make a good living in the country after they were driven from the common fields and forests by land enclosures. Women smallholders and food producers were squeezed out of the local markets. By the end of the eighteenth century in Billericay, Essex, women of middling fortune were no longer running the stalls in the weekly markets – men had them and the women traded from carts. In Oxfordshire at the same time, women had given up the expensive trades: horses, livestock and grain were all being sold by men, while women were selling fruit and vegetables.[84]

The mechanisation of farming brought men into women's jobs. Cheese and butter-making had been a traditional skill of milk maids and dairy maids, who maintained and milked the dairy herd, skimmed the cream, churned the butter and pressed the cheeses by hand.[85] The bond between women and their herds was famous, as was the need for cool hands and a light touch with dairy products. But when the dairies were mechanised, men entered the work and demanded a man's wage to match.

A few women in agriculture became landowners and prosperous tenants working in profitable agri-businesses. Women landowners had traditionally managed their lands during the regular absences of their husbands in earlier centuries, but from the mid-eighteenth century farming and landholding became a fashionable occupation for men. Increasing profits after the enclosures attracted male investors into land, and the snob appeal of the country estates encouraged middle-class tradesmen to buy land. The arrival of capital, machines and scientific theories into traditional agriculture put women landowners at a disadvantage with no access to a science, engineering or financial education. Nor could women farmers easily raise capital to buy new agricultural machines. The growing belief from the Romantic movement, that men had scientific and rational brains whereas women were emotional and responsive to wild Nature, provided further discouragement for women trying to make a living from farming. As one embittered woman farmer said in Gloucestershire in the early 1800s: 'A woman undertaking to farm is generally a subject of ridicule.'[86]

One women entrepreneur managed to transform her bankrupt inheritance into a hugely successful industry. Eleanor Coade (1733–1821) conducted her successful London linen business with a stock of cloth worth £200 in the mid-1760s. Despite the bankruptcy and death of her father, she increased her stock to a value of £4,750 in 1767, before leaving the business and going into partnership with Daniel Pincourt, a maker of so-called 'artificial stone'. When Pincourt claimed he was the sole proprietor of the venture, Coade sacked him and took the company under her own control. She developed her own formula for the stone, called Lithodipyra or Coade stone, a ceramic stoneware that could be poured into moulds and come out looking like carved stone. It was made of clay from the West Country (her family home was at Lyme Regis) mixed with flint, sand and glass, and fired twice at high temperatures.

Eleanor lived on the factory premises at Narrow Wall in Lambeth and made a huge success of her products, designing classical statuary and dressing for buildings. She exhibited her work at the Society of Artists. In 1774, she showed five pieces:

> A chimney piece, in artificial stone, for a nobleman's hall. From a
>   design of Mr. Johnson's.
> A vestal and pedestal; in artificial stone.
> A sybyl in artificial stone.
> A statue and pedestal for a candelabrum.
> A tripod.[87]

Though manufactured and not carved, the statues and ornaments were still expensive: a 9-foot-tall garden statue cost 100 guineas, while a Corinthian capital was £14.[88] Coade stone dominated the market. She

A modern photograph of the South Bank Lion shows the lasting qualities of Coade stone. He was cast in 1837 in Eleanor Coade's workshop

produced stoneware for the gothic screen at St Georges Chapel, Windsor, stone for the Royal Pavilion, Brighton, Carlton House, London, and the Royal Naval College at Greenwich. Shortly after her death, her company produced a large quantity of stoneware used to refurbish Buckingham Palace. Belmont House, the Coade family home in Lyme Regis, is decorated with Coade stone motifs and the handsome South Bank lion on Westminster Bridge in London is made of Coade stone.

Eleanor Coade never married, but took the courtesy title of 'Mrs' Coade. She sold her factory to her manager in 1813 for £4,000 – he had hoped to inherit it for free. At her death in Camberwell in 1821, she left her fortune to charity schools, clergymen and different members of her family. She specified that her bequests to married women friends were not to be controlled by their husbands.

Domestic work employed 466,000 women and 150,000 men.[89] By the middle of the nineteenth century, over three-quarters of servants were women. Domestic service formed the biggest single occupation for women and it was the fastest growing – but despite elite advisors' enthusiasm for working-class women going into service, the work was widely hated by the women themselves. Wherever other work could be found locally, women preferred it. In York in 1851, 60 per cent of the working women toiled in domestic service, but in Stockport and Preston, where the textile mills provided alternative arduous work in terrible conditions, only 3 per cent of women chose domestic service.[90]

Men servants were better paid and conferred more status on the elite home. In 1798, a footman in a big house was paid £50 a year and could expect to be given a livery to wear, his keep and tips.[91] The upper women servants earned less than half that: up to £20 a year. A female cook received between £7 and £15, housemaids between £4 and £10, and the lowly kitchen scrubs £2 a year. Servants in middle-class houses earned half the wages of elite servants, and a cleaner in public buildings or a barmaid or waitress would make less than £2 a year and was unlikely to 'live in' or receive meals.[92] This would not be enough to support herself – she would have to take another job, depend on someone else, steal or sell sex.

Many of the working-class women said to be 'unemployed' in the 1851 census should have been named as 'unpaid'. They were productive in their homes, maintaining the family at their own expense – working for the family but 'not paid', labouring, assisting or even a full partner with their husband – but drawing no pay and receiving none of the profits. Children, too, worked unpaid in the family business. A witness to a parliamentary committee in 1840 described a handloom weaver at work: '1. The man was in the loom weaving, 2. A boy of 10 years of age was winding bobbins, 3. The wife was at her husband's elbow, picking the work. 4. His daughter was at the back of the loom, taking up the broken threads of the warp, for it was not a good warp ... the piece was ... the work of the family.'[93]

Money also flowed towards men in the elite. Although a fifth of all British companies were owned and run by women entrepreneurs in the nineteenth century, a rich bride endowed her husband with everything on her wedding day, unless special provision had been made for her. Women investing in the family business were not recognised as investors, shareholders or proprietors, and were not paid a dividend.[94] Women's names disappeared from the lists of directors, and company names boasted the 'Father and Sons' style – even with daughters working in the business. The exclusion of women as significant entrepreneurs in a family business was confirmed by the Company Acts of 1856–62, which created full limited liability and freed a business from family ownership and kinship control.[95] When both husband and wife had their own business, her earnings would be expected to pay family expenses or support the husband's business but his did not contribute to hers.[96]

Women continued to work successfully in the theatre, where they might attract upper-class men who could afford to keep them as mistresses. One who nearly made the transition to wife was a Jewish woman: Hannah Norsa.

The first Jewish woman to star on the English stage, as Polly Peachum in *The Beggar's Opera* at Drury Lane in 1732, Hannah Norsa was the daughter of a tavern keeper, Isaac Norsa, and his wife, Esther de Aharon de Chaus. Hannah caught the eye of Robert Walpole, Earl of Orford, and lived with him as his wife at Houghton Hall in Norfolk, welcoming guests and moving in the first circles of society. A local lady reported: 'She is a very agreeable Woman, & Nobody ever behav'd better in her Station, She have every body's good word, and bear great Sway at Houghton, She is every thing but Lady, She came here in a Landau & Six horses & one Mr Paxton a young Clergyman with her.'

Walpole planned to marry Hannah Norsa when his wife died, but the countess did not oblige, and he died before her, in debt. Hannah's theat-

MISS NORSA.

Hannah Norsa (1712–84), actress and singer, lived with Robert Walpole, Earl of Orford, at Houghton Hall after he separated from his wife, until his death in 1751

rical friends gave a benefit performance for her, and she lived as a single woman, dying in 1784, leaving a considerable fortune.[97]

Elite women's work was to advertise the class and wealth of the family, by showcasing expensive clothes and jewellery, now freed from the old controls over what each class might wear. The landed elite enclosed parkland and used agricultural land for sport, and the urban elite founded more and more invitation-only exclusive venues. Even if an aspirational family failed to rise very high, they could at least deploy elite etiquette to distinguish themselves from their working-class origins. Middle-class people studied newspapers, scandal sheets, conduct books and copied upper-class manners and domestic arrangements in an attempt to demonstrate that they had risen above their working-class origins. The greatest indicator of a family's arrival in the middle classes proved to be the leisure of women.[98]

Even the phrase 'pin money' – which had previously meant a significant annual allowance paid by a husband to his wife for her household expenses – now came to mean trivial earnings that a wife might keep for petty cash. But even this, like housekeeping money given to a wife, remained, in law, the property of her husband and he could demand its return.[99] If she made savings, they were legally his, and he could demand they be given to him. The husband of a wealthy woman reported on her income, paid the tax due from her money, but could even claim her tax rebate for himself. The 1824 Tax Act defined wives among a group of people whose tax must be paid by a trustee, guardian, tutor or curator. The others were 'infant, lunatic, idiot, or insane':

'And be it enacted, that the trustee, guardian, tutor, curator, or committee of any person being an infant or married woman, lunatic, idiot, or insane, and having the direction, control, or management of the property of such infant, married woman, lunatic, idiot, or insane person … shall be chargeable to the said duties.'[100]

Women had been excluded from almost all medical work by the end of the 1800s. Patients who could afford to pay almost all consulted a member of a physician's or surgeon's organisation – exclusively male. Even the work of midwifery became dominated by male practitioners, probably because women midwives could not get access to the new techniques and technologies – such as forceps for difficult births. Elite families preferred fashionable male midwives – the 'accoucheur', whose French name indicated his high status. The very poor might still resort to cheap women practitioners but by the 1851 census only about 2,000 midwives reported that they were in work, and they were all part-time.[101]

Women continued to work unpaid for the Church of England, even though they held no recognised position in the church. But they were able to organise and even preach in the growing dissenting churches.

John Wesley (1703–91) allowed women to teach Bible classes in his new Methodist Church, and one – Mary Bosanquet – argued that a woman should preach if she experienced a 'special calling'. Wesley agreed. When the number of pupils in their class exceeded its capacity, Bosanquet and teacher Sarah Crosby preached to crowds of hundreds. Crosby left her husband to live with Bosanquet and two other prominent women preachers, Sarah Ryan and Mary Clark. United in a joint spiritual mission, inspiring each other, facing difficulties and sometimes danger, Methodist women experienced intense loving relationships living and working together, separated from men.[102]

After Wesley's death, the Methodist Church banned women from preaching and the inspirational Methodist women speakers retreated from public occasions to become teachers for children at Sunday schools and organisers of social events. Methodist magazines had published thumbnail sketches of single women preachers in the eighteenth century, but by the early nineteenth century they disappeared in favour of ministers' wives.[103]

So-called Primitive Methodists, a splinter group, began their mission in 1805 and allowed women preachers to go into working people's homes and communities to speak, often entering the new urban areas and slums, which were not served by a parish church and never saw a Church of England minister. Typically, women preachers were young, around 20 years old, and came into the ministry after a spiritual experience in adolescence. Women such as Elizabeth White, Harriet Randborn and Harriet Maslin were inspired during their teens and took up preaching as very young women. Elizabeth Gorse Gaunt and Hannah Howe preached in remote areas of Derbyshire. Mary Thorne and Johanna Brooks, both older women, preached for the Bible Christian denomination in Devon and Cornwall, accompanying younger travelling preachers such as Em Cottle and Elizabeth Dart.

The Primitive preacher Ann Carr (1783–1841), a poor and uneducated woman raised by her aunt and uncle, turned to evangelical preaching after her fiancé died young. She became a travelling preacher, joining the Primitive Methodists and bearing witness in mill yards, streets and camp meetings, travelling with Hannah Woodhouse and Sarah Eland. When the Primitive Methodist leaders tried to bring these charismatic preachers under control, she created a new denomination of women-only preachers – the Female Revivalist Society – speaking in cottages and factory yards, especially to women workers. As part of the group, Elizabeth Tomlinson and Sarah Kirkland travelled with Ann Carr around the textile industry villages of Nottingham and Derby, before moving on to Leeds, the centre of the West Riding woollen industry.

The Female Revivalist movement peaked in the 1830s with a savings club, an adult education programme and a Sunday school, but collapsed on the death of Ann Carr in 1841.[104] Her friend and colleague Martha Williams wrote her biography. The death of Carr and the closing of the Female Revivalist Society marked the end of women preachers in England until a new wave in the 1860s, which excluded working-class women, and specialised in 'lady preachers' who prided themselves on preaching only when formally invited by a church, never impromptu or out of doors, and only with the permission of their husbands or fathers.[105]

Quaker women, who had been famous prophetesses and preachers, were also discouraged from public witness by the elders of their faith. They were encouraged instead to hold separate women-only meetings and to specialise in charity to the poor and moral discipline.[106]

Joanna Southcott (1750–1815) formed a society around her prophecies that survives to this day. She predicted the end of the world (it's OK, it was 2004). Born to a Devon farming family and going into service and shop work in Honiton, Southcott joined the Wesleyan Methodists and then went to London to sell 'seals of the Lord' – tickets to heaven for people elected to eternity. She could be extremely persuasive, claiming 10,000 followers in London alone. Southcott promised that she was about to give birth to the new Messiah, but she died without a baby shortly after the due date.

The hugely influential evangelical revival of the national church from 1780 fuelled and enhanced claims of the spirituality of women, encouraging devout women to practice spirituality at home and support works in the churches; but evangelical Church of England women never became preachers. Evangelists emphasised the importance of good works rather than ritual, and upper- and middle-class women were encouraged to meet together to perform charitable and reformist work and to go into poor homes on a mission to improve the poor – teaching women refined behaviour, good housewifery and church attendance. The women's social work – sometimes very patronising – led a few to see the intolerable conditions that poor women endured, and encouraged some ladies into more informed political work for social change.

There was great benefit to men – especially incompetent men of all classes – in excluding women from profitable and interesting work. If women were regarded as irrational, they could be banned from universities and space left for men of less ability. If women were forbidden from the professions and from profitable work, there was less competition for men practitioners and more profit for them. If women were encouraged to spend and consume, they drove a market for the new goods of industrialisation. If wealthy women handed over their fortune to their husbands on marriage, the booming profits of enclosure, slavery and the industrial revolution could be banked by men. Whenever women are banned from the starting blocks, a man is bound to come first and if anger is banned from the ladylike behaviour, nobody is going to raise her voice in protest.

Education

Girls from poor homes were offered an education, though it was not the equal to that for boys. Every village school provided lessons in reading and writing for girls, and in towns and cities some schools catered exclusively for girls. Their studies were designed to give working-class girls minimum literacy: enough to follow instruction and to prepare them for a life of low-skilled work.

Education for girls of the middle classes mostly avoided academic subjects, unlike that of their brothers, who were expected to go to university or law college as part of their development to male maturity. Elite and middling girls were taught reading, writing and arithmetic, perhaps a foreign language, and music, art, sewing, crafts and deportment to a level suitable for the drawing room. A small market town like Chester had about a dozen girls' schools,[107] some of them providing an academic education, others the most superficial of lessons. The growing publicity about the fragility of female bodies advised that scholarship and study might be too great a burden for elite girls.

Some exceptional women managed to get a scholarly education, and some of them managed to publish and be recognised for their contribution to science. Margaret Bryan, an eighteenth-century schoolmistress, published *A Compendious System of Astronomy* in 1797. Lady Hester Stanhope identified an ancient Palestinian site from a medieval manuscript and excavated it herself. Palaeontologist Mary Anning discovered the first complete Plesiosaurus dinosaur at Lyme Regis, and in 1836 Etheldred Bennett was appointed a member of the Imperial Natural History Society in Moscow, a male-only institution so impressed by her collection of thousands of fossils and confused by her first name that they mistook her for a man and gave her a diploma. Two women – Mary Somerville and Caroline Herschel – were elected to the Royal Astronomical Society in 1835. Ada Lovelace invented an algorithm for a yet-to-be-built computer in 1843. Anna Thynne built the first self-sustaining aquarium, and Mary Anne Whitby – a Western pioneer in the cultivation of silkworms – worked with Charles Darwin on caterpillar genes. Mary Horner Lyell's work as a geologist and expert on land snails in the Canary Islands is partly concealed by her more famous husband Charles Lyell, who is credited with work that may be hers.

Health

Despite the vaunted male expertise, the infant mortality rate and the deaths of women in childbed remained high: 7.5 per 1,000 births in 1750 and 5 per 1,000 births in 1850.[108] As England expanded its empire overseas, soldiers and seamen, pioneers and administrators were needed for the growing empire, and there was increased concern at the infant death rate. Commentators blamed the easy target – the failure of working-class women as homemakers and mothers: 'Whatever sanatory or architectural improvements may be made in artisans' dwellings, it will still be found, while wives remain as they are, that ... one will be a veritable little palace in point of comfort, while another will be a domestic Slough of despond.'[109]

If only women would stay home all day, their presence alone would cure rising damp, filthy water, mouldy walls, infectious diseases, hunger and illiteracy!

In fact, the high death rate from post-birth bacterial infections was mostly caused by busy male doctors going from one patient to another without sterilising their equipment, changing a gown or apron, or even washing. Epidemics occurred at lying-in hospitals; in 1770, at the 63-bed Westminster lying-in hospital, 19 women contracted puerperal fever, and only six survived.[110] A breakthrough came in 1795, when a naval surgeon, Alexander Gordon, noted the pattern of infections during an epidemic in the Poor Hospital and came to the conclusion that midwives and surgeons were infecting their patients: 'It is a disagreeable fact that I, myself, was the means of carrying the infection to a great number of women.'[111]

The suggestion that an elite man might be responsible for infecting working-class women was so offensive to the elite doctors that Gordon was hounded from practice. Instead, people continued in their beliefs that 'Doctors are gentlemen, and gentlemen's hands are clean.'[112]

The work of Louis Pasteur (1822–95) and Joseph Lister (1827–1912) finally proved the existence of bacteria and from the late 1800s practitioners started to use antiseptics, which reduced infection. Responsibility for public health was now understood to be a task for government, not just for working-class women who – until then – had been the only ones concerned with the cleanliness of slum houses, the only ones asking for clean water and working drains.

Kitty Wilkinson (1786–1860) saved thousands of lives during the 1832 cholera
epidemic by opening her Liverpool laundry to her neighbours

One such working-class woman was Kitty Wilkinson, an Irish migrant
in Liverpool who had been a cotton mill worker and a domestic servant.
She opened up her laundry business to her poor neighbours for a penny
a week, allowing them to use her boiler and bleach to disinfect their
clothes during the 1832 cholera epidemic. She became known as the
'saint of the slums' and campaigned for public bathhouses for the poor.
In 1842, she was appointed superintendent of the baths, her public
service recognised with the gift of a silver teapot from Queen Victoria.[113]

Separate Spheres

The idea that women and men inhabited different worlds – 'separate spheres' developed from ancient Greek philosophers, glamourised by courtly love, restated during the Enlightenment and popularised by the Romantic movement – received a huge boost from the acceptance from the seventeenth century that there were only two sexes: men and women, and they were opposites. Different lives and activities were suited to the two different sexes. The male sphere comprised the active outer world: military conquest, commercial success, executive power and action suited to his logical, decisive brain and powerful body. The ladies' sphere encompassed domestic, spiritual, emotional, maternal and wifely work in the home, suited to her emotional, sensitive nature, unreliable body and fragile health.[114]

Sensitive beings, without logic, sexually frigid, bodies without power, domestic rather than worldly, easily persuaded even when temptation was fatal: of course, such a fragile being must be protected by someone stronger and kept somewhere safe. In time, men modified the world to make it suit them even more, creating men-only institutions: centres of learning and of sport, leisure activities and games for men, the clubs that only 'gentlemen' could join – on streets that were already declared unsuitable for ladies. Women took what power they could in their own sphere of the home: creating etiquette and morality rules and limiting entry. In time, women believed that they could take this elite home-making out into the world – that they were responsible for all homes: slavery homes, labouring class homes, poor homes – and it was the moral duty of ladies to teach poor women how to behave. A remarkable number of elite women transformed the separate spheres home from a fortress to protect and isolate women into a springboard to action in the world.

Sex

Chastity no longer had to be enforced by men policing women's behaviour; every genteel woman was expected to police herself and reassure men with her complete self-control. The philosopher David Hume pronounced: 'A female has so many opportunities of secretly indulging ... that nothing can give us security but her absolute modesty and reserve.'[115]

From the eighteenth century, ladies were said to be completely unlike their bawdy, earthy medieval foremothers. By the early nineteenth century, more and more experts were advising that gentry women were naturally frigid.[116] 'Woman seldom desires any sexual gratification for herself. She submits to her husband's embraces, but principally to gratify him.'[117] Doctors agreed that ladies never undertook heterosexual intercourse for pleasure but only as their duty to their husband and to conceive children.

Maternal love predominated in ladies, and husbands were advised not to risk trying to arouse their wives.[118] In 1850, the *Westminster Review* wrote: 'With the exception of "fallen women", nature had made sexual desire in women dormant "till excited by undue familiarities".'[119]

Upper-class women who felt sexual desire probably denied the feeling or concealed it. Anne Lister (1791–1840), an elite woman in Yorkshire, thought that she was a rarity. Her uneasy sense of uniqueness existed not only because she desired women, but that she felt any arousal at all. Lister described her feelings of desire as 'manly', as if she had no words for female desire.[120]

Ladies who admitted they felt sexual desire and girls and ladies who were caught masturbating were diagnosed with 'hysteria' and 'nervous excitation' and treated with cold baths, rest and a restricted diet. But chaste virginity brought its own problems. According to one expert, R.J. Culverwell, in 1844, older celibate women were prone to nervous disorders: 'as is truly attested by the miseries of hysteria and other nervous derangements, that pervade the junior and elderly maiden branches of every family, and constitute so formidable an enemy to domestic felicity.'[121]

Hysteria was a disease unique to elite women, diagnosed by the doctors who specialised in elite women, in a self-fulfilling circle. Hysteria proved to be mysterious: it had no apparent physical cause, it was changeable, different in every patient, perhaps caused by the erratic movement of the womb, by female sensibility, even by inherited madness or masturbation. There were so many symptoms that it was easy for nineteenth-century doctors to diagnose more and more women as suffering from hysteria and, with this publicity, it became more widespread and more extreme.

Patients could sink into passivity, even into something like a coma, or they could become hyperactive, with fits, faintings and sometimes violence.[122]

As men and women were defined as complete opposites, the new belief that elite women were naturally frigid meant that their opposites – men – must be naturally lustful and driven to seek sexual satisfaction. The myth of the tyrannical male sexual drive – glamourised in the stories of courtly love – was revived to help shore up the contrasting natures of the two sexes. Women were frigid and men were lustful. But there was a problem. Male doctors felt certain that sexual frustration was hugely damaging to male health. Nobody had worried very much about this before but now there was a panic. Sexual restraint weakened male will and body and could lead to fatal disabilities and disease. But so too did masturbation. How to satisfy men whose health depends on them never hearing 'no'?

The solution was the exploitation of poor women to service elite male sexuality just as they did all the other disagreeable, tiring, low-skilled, poorly paid work. Nobody suggested that labouring women were so refined as to have lost sexual desire. Nobody suggested that they were so fragile that they should be protected from male lust. The double standard of sexual morality – where men are sexually active and women are not – allowed elite virgins to become frigid upper-class wives shielded from marital demands for sex, as elite husbands satisfied themselves on poor women that they could imagine as robust and sexually willing. One conduct book for servants warned that, while male servants would not be pursued by their mistresses, it was 'very likely that maids would be attacked by their masters or fellow servants.'[123]

Once it was understood that conception was not caused by female orgasm, and agreed that ladies did not orgasm, men were released from any expectation that they would give sexual pleasure to their partners – wives or anyone else. Female sexual arousal was no longer a male ambition. Now, sexual intercourse was defined as penile penetration of the vagina, best performed in the position recommended by the church: face to face, man on top. This put pace, pressure and duration under his control and the conclusion was his ejaculation. This upper- and middling-class definition of sexual intercourse was taught to the labouring classes and changed courtship traditions already under pressure from urban life.

In pre-industrial villages and small country communities, the courtship rituals had involved the whole community, the young, the newly married and the older people who gathered for seasonal work or celebration and casually supervised the games and dancing. Young people paired up and changed pairings, and courtship took place in semi-public with other couples nearby. A young woman might enjoy light-hearted encounters with several partners before settling on one – or not settling at all. Hand-holding, kissing, mock-fighting and physical play were all part of a light-hearted approach to intimacy that took place in the safety of the community. Courtship traditions like 'bundling' – sexual touching without penetration 'bundled' up together – and courtship games where couples paired off and hid together, or kissing games where couples might seek each other out, were a light-hearted and easy approach to sexual desire and pleasure. Social condemnation, the church or the law would only be invoked if something went wrong – a pregnancy with a deserting father, an adulterous relationship or scandalous promiscuity. Sexual activity in many forms was permitted, even encouraged, inside community control. The phrase 'to make love' did not mean sex; it meant to court, to flirt, to engage and charm.[124]

But communal courtship rituals of village life with lifelong friends, under the tolerant scrutiny of the entire community, could not be transferred to urban settings with strangers, and town life and industrial hours did not provide approved events or spaces for courtship. Novels publicised the idea of 'falling in love' as a rapid, even instant event, and described encounters that took place in the privacy of the upper-class home, in the presence of one other person – a chaperone – to prevent any sexual intimacy. A couple chose each other and were exclusive to each other, from the very start of the story. They progressed through shared experiences and conversation to marriage and from then – unspoken but understood – to elite sex: penile penetration, dominant male, male orgasm. The middle-class ideas about sex were preached from the pulpit, taught in the conduct books and retold in novels and scandal sheets. The sexual playfulness of the working classes gave way to the genteel taboo on intimacy before marriage; sexual touching became only a stage on the way to penetration, sexual intercourse meant only penile penetration, and female arousal and satisfaction became irrelevant.[125]

Pornography drawings that had previously shown kisses and caresses in imaginative positions and combinations now depicted penetrative sex with men on top. Pornographic novels that had told stories of lustful women's enjoyable progress through many experiences to a late repentance now told stories of female passivity and even victims. Any fictional women who engaged willingly in sex were either hypersexual or morally lost, or both.

The trend to penetrative intercourse instead of 'bundling' and courting rituals is shown in the rise of pre-marital pregnancies. By the start of the nineteenth century, the proportion of pregnant brides and bastard children had both doubled. Women pregnant on their wedding day accounted for 33 per cent of all brides, and 5 per cent of live births were to unmarried mothers.[126]

Not all men bought into the opportunities for sexual satisfaction on unenthusiastic partners. The Romantic movement promoted the ideal man with heightened feelings and awareness, and this combined with the evangelical enthusiasm to suggest male sexual self-denial before and even during marriage. Some couples promised highly spiritual unions with sex only for the conception of children. Some husbands – of all classes – practised restraint to avoid frequent pregnancies. At a time of unreliable contraception, when male accoucheurs did not provide abortifacients, like the earlier women midwives, middle- and upper-class couples could only prevent pregnancies by sexual restraint.

Women Divided

One of the least explored effects of separate spheres was the division of women from women: it created a massive gulf between the 'lady' of the elite and the 'woman' of the classes below her. Elite women were thought to be culturally and even biologically different from working women and were required to lead very different lives.[127] A rift opened between the women who were encouraged to be weak in the drawing room and frigid in the bedroom and those who would only survive the fields, sweatshops, factories and streets if they were extraordinarily strong and resilient.

Behind high factory walls without windows, deafened by the noise of the machines, exposed to danger and to assault, injured, ill and underfed, the mill girls were invisible to the ladies who bought the linen in the elegant draper's shop. Warm bright fires in middle-class drawing rooms burned the coal that a woman collier had dragged, harnessed like a pit pony, through the mine, that the maid had laid in the fireplace where a child had swept the chimney. Ladies could nibble on delicacies because underpaid women grew the food, brought it to market, shopped for it, prepared it and served it, and cleaned up afterwards. A sweet-smelling lady of leisure, beautifully dressed, was supported by an invisible army of working women, carrying the hot water for her bath up the narrow back stairs, making the soap, washing her linen, even physically dressing her with the complicated fastenings on gowns that were changed several times a day for different events, braiding her hair into the elaborate styles that needed a hairdresser every evening.

Despite enthusiasm for Nature by Romantic writers and readers, the elite women avoided seeing the destruction of the lives of poor women in the countryside just as they avoided seeing the exploitation of poor women in the industries and in the towns. The enclosure of common land and the changing use of the countryside, the exploitation of rural workers and the particular cruelty to women are never mentioned in the novels, though authors and readers were of the landowning classes. There is plenty of maypole dancing, but no enclosures.

Even women radicals from the upper classes could not bridge the class divide. The daughter of Elizabeth Fry, the great Quaker reformer, was attending an anti-slavery meeting in Norwich in 1840 when it was disrupted by Chartist women calling for the vote for all men. She described the working-class women reformers in nightmarish terms: 'I also saw some women who excited the men, and whose shrill voices out screamed the roar of the men. I heard they were three well known Socialist sisters, the vilest of the vile.' Another woman radical, Elizabeth Pease, risked her status by supporting Chartism and said it was an 'almost outrageous stance for a lady'.[128]

Class hostility went both ways. Working women publicly abused ladies wearing foreign silks and the new Indian calicoes that were spoiling the business of English textile workers at the end of the eighteenth century. In 1804, Worcester women glovemakers attacked ladies wearing silk gloves for choosing the new fashion over locally made leather.[129]

Another terrible divide opened up between women: that of race. English elite women abolitionists excluded ex-slaves from their committees. The only women of African descent to share a platform with English elite abolitionists were from America: the ex-slave and abolitionist Ellen Craft and the free woman and abolitionist Sarah Parker Redmond.

The famous anti-slavery token made by the Wedgewood pottery in 1787 entitled 'Am I not a Man and a Brother?' was popular among abolitionists in England. But it would be 1838 before a coin was struck for enslaved women's rights – 'Am I not a Woman and a Sister?' – and then it was made for the American Anti-Slavery Society and popular in America.

English elite women did not feel a sisterhood with women of a lower class or another race.[130] Elite women called for political rights for their own class, not for anyone else. They even used the example of slavery to support their campaign – comparing their inequality to slavery. Mary Wollstonecraft, the philosopher and writer, wrote: 'I called women "slaves" I mean in a political and civil sense.'[131] Wollstonecraft defined

'AM I NOT A WOMAN AND A SISTER' – the 1838 American copper medallion shows a freed woman slave. There was no UK equivalent

white middle- and upper-class women as slaves to their husbands and fathers, and compared them to slaves in the sugar plantations, to emphasise her call for the freedom of elite women: 'Is half of the human species, like the poor African slaves, to be subject to prejudices that brutalise them … only to sweeten the cup of man?'[132]

The tin-eared comparison of the life-threatening, violent enslavement of African women to the oppression of elite white women was a tragic failure of sisterhood in a woman who is rightly famous for her campaigns for women. Wollstonecraft wrote *A Vindication of the Rights of Man* to argue against monarchy and aristocracy, followed by her finest work, *A Vindication of the Rights of Women*. Though passionate for women's education and keenly aware that girls were groomed as companions for their future, more important husbands, Wollstonecraft never advocated equal rights for all women. She supported class – different and better lives for upper- and middle-class women to those of working-class women. She was in favour of education for poor girls, but only up to the age of nine, when they should be entered into a trade or unskilled work. 'Rights for women' meant for Wollstonecraft, rights for ladies – and this was true for almost all the active political radical women of the eighteenth century and early nineteenth century. The equality Wollstonecraft imagined was equality for elite women with elite men. She did not demand equal rights for working-class women, or enslaved women.

The expanding British trade and then the British Empire created a need for a racist narrative to justify oppressing indigenous people, destroying their lives and taking their lands. The racist theories caused a gulf between women, as white women supported the imperial adventure. Women missionaries and wives and daughters of missionaries committed themselves to converting people of Africa, India and Asia. Donations from women's groups funded 70 per cent of English missionary work.[133] Women medical practitioners formed a crucial part of imperial expansion, since only women could attend Indian women in seclusion, and women missionaries enter Indian homes. Middle- and upper-class women seeking husbands also travelled throughout the empire, especially to India. Once married, they reproduced as far as possible the 'separate sphere' home: classist, racist, permissive for men and exploitative of enslaved or servant women. Indian women lovers of English officers found themselves excluded from the elite white women's social circle; even Indian wives were frowned on.

In 1857, the First War of Indian Independence broke out. It was known in England as the 'Indian Mutiny' – projecting an image of a ship with a crew sworn to obedience, rather than a land invaded by outsiders who imposed military rule. After the war it was impossible to maintain the fiction that the English had been welcomed or invited into the Indian kingdoms and the few social contacts between Indian and English women fell apart. Women knew that a fissure of class and race ran through the sisterhood of sex. As Sarah Ellis said in 1845, 'What should we think of a community of slaves who betrayed each other's interests or a little band of shipwrecked Mariners upon a friendless shore who were false to each other?'[134]

Elite Women Protests

The doctrine of separate spheres persuaded elite women that their proper place was inside their home and their best companions were other women. Excluded from politics and higher education, discouraged from money-making and steered into the home, forced together with nothing important to do, upper- and middling-class women met each other in the endless round of social events, and soon found causes to unite them.[135] Energetic women could not be persuaded to live inside a domestic bubble for ever. Harriet Martineau wrote in 1832: 'I want to be doing something with the pen since no other means of action in politics are in a woman's power.'[136]

An early and exceptional woman politician was Georgiana, Duchess of Devonshire. As an extremely wealthy aristocrat in an unhappy marriage, she took up a life of political campaigning, holding salons in support of Whig policies and Whig politicians, against tyranny and monarchism. She even campaigned in public hustings for the Whig party in 1784 and 1788 – facing slander, condemnation and mockery for speaking out in the streets. Her private life was hailed as a contemporary scandal. She supported the limitation of royal power and the Whig agenda, calling for better governance: but not for democracy – and certainly not for votes for working men. She was not in favour of women of any class having a vote – she wanted influence, not a vote for women. She saw herself and all upper-class women as advisors and supporters to the male voters and politicians.

The defence of marriage proved a natural cause for women, the subject of the greatest women's petition since the English civil wars, when in 1820 the king, George IV, tried to divorce his estranged wife Queen Caroline. At least 17 women-only petitions were sent to support the queen. One from London elite women alone bore nearly 18,000 signatures and was signed by 'Married ladies of the metropolis'.[137] The upper- and middle-class wives supported a fellow wife, whose arranged marriage had so spectacularly failed. Caroline of Brunswick had been married to George, Prince of Wales, in 1795, although he was widely known to be already secretly married. The royal couple separated shortly after the birth of their daughter, and he falsely accused her of adultery and immorality. Caroline was banned from seeing her child and moved abroad. In 1817, after learning of the death of her daughter in childbirth, Caroline returned to England to claim her position as queen. George IV's attempts to divorce her publicly failed and, in 1821, he barred her from his coronation. There was an extraordinary scene when she hammered on the locked doors of Westminster Abbey for admittance. Luckily for him, she died shortly afterwards, leaving as her legacy the disturbing question as to how separate spheres benefited women if husbands took advantage of their freedom, and abandoned their dependent wives? If they chose to do so, there was no home for a woman to make into a separate sphere. There was no home for her at all.

High-status women still had some political rights. They could promote their preferred candidate for Parliament, and they might publicly campaign for him, especially if he was a relation, as a respectable part of their duty to their families. The 10 per cent of women who were land-owners with tenants had the power to nominate a candidate for election and took it upon themselves to order their tenants to vote for him – that was their responsibility as landowners. But even though they could nominate the MP and order their tenants to vote, such women had no direct vote of their own in national politics. When the Chartist petitions demanded the widening of the vote to working men, the contradictions became more glaring. It seemed absurd to elite women that a poor uned-ucated man should demand the right to vote when his female social superior could not: it was the contradiction of the queen's footman all over again. Of course a man was superior to a woman; but not when he was a footman and she was a queen? The anomaly prompted some women to argue that elite women must have the vote – and others that the vote could not be given to working-class men.

Elite women who had joined together, and even spoken in public for the abolition of slavery, pressuring some MPs and encouraging others, naturally started to wonder why they should not directly choose their MPs. If women could influence MPs, why should they not be MPs themselves? Some of the ladies-only anti-slavery committees developed into suffrage societies calling for votes for elite women and a place for elite women in public life. Suffrage societies in London, Manchester, Bristol and Edinburgh all sprang out of the anti-slavery movement.[138]

It was an elite single woman who first raised the issue that as a property owner she had a vote, but as a woman she did not. In 1832, Mary Smith, from Yorkshire, argued that since she paid the same taxes and rates as a male elector she should have a vote as he did. She persuaded her MP, Henry Hunt, to raise the matter in Parliament – but he was laughed down,[139] and the Representation of the People Act of 1832 was passed to explicitly ban women from voting for Parliament. The language of the law was changed from 'persons and people' – implying women as well as men – to 'men' – clearly excluding women. The Act referred specifically to male voters and votes for men, removing ambiguity and solidifying the tradition of the male-only vote into law.[140] Ironically, the bill that excluded women is known to history as the Great Reform Act as it abolished the small, often corrupt rural constituencies and redrew the boundaries so that the new growing towns had their own MPs. It widened the franchise to include more men of the middling classes like businessmen, shopkeepers, wealthy farmers and small landowners. This makes it a 'Great Reform' to parliamentary history – but not to women's history since women were explicitly excluded, whatever their wealth or status, from voting in national parliamentary elections.

But in 1850, apparently reversing the ban on women voters, the Interpretation Act ruled that laws citing 'men' and 'male' should be understood as meaning 'people', so including women. Not so! Not so! The attorney general himself announced that was 'really a most unaccountable supposition'![141] In response to this new law, thousands of elite women registered to vote. In 1867, a court case ruled that judges would look at the usual custom and practice of each individual area to follow local tradition; and were not obliged to allow women voters.[142]

Some philanthropic women who had worked together on the abolition of slavery campaigns tried to create social change directly. Secure
that they were safely inside their 'sphere' if they concerned themselves
with domestic life, they ventured into working-class homes. There they
discovered the sexual abuse and violence endured by women. Their
concern about this added to a national anxiety about marital violence,
publicised by Caroline Norton, who could not obtain a divorce from her
husband on grounds of his cruelty even though he had thrown books and
an inkstand at her, scalded her with a tea kettle and may have caused her
to miscarry.[143] An imperial nation with a queen on the throne, priding
itself on chivalry, was shocked by the reports of abuse, and the ensuing
moral panic about domestic violence resulted in the passing of a bill
against assault in 1853. MP Henry Fitzroy told the House of Commons:
'No one could read the public journals without being constantly struck
with horror and amazement at the numerous reports of cases of cruel and
brutal assaults perpetrated upon the weaker sex by men who one blushed
to think were Englishmen, and yet were capable of such atrocious acts.'[144]

Most of the nineteenth-century commentators felt that the appalling
conditions of working-class homes were the failure of working-class wives
and mothers to reproduce the virtues of middle-class family life. Advice
books like William Cobbett's *Cottage Economy* taught that a successful
working-class home could only be created and maintained if a woman
was full-time at home, not out at work making money.[145] It proved a
persuasive combination of the concept of separate spheres and the breadwinner wage. Wives should not compete for work and drive down wages
but stay at home, in their separate sphere, while the husbands earned a
breadwinner wage enough to support a family.

As the desire to improve the lives of the poor grew more urgent, more
and more 'improving' and charitable committees and associations with
separate female branches appeared and, by 1840, thousands of women
volunteers.[146] Urban elite women gathered together and divided up
working-class areas for uninvited visits, dispensing advice and sometimes
resources; while ladies in the rural areas continued the elite tradition of
visiting and supervising tenants and rural poor, as landlords had always
done.[147]

Visiting the poor, always part of aristocratic patronage and control of
their poor neighbours, tenants and employees, now became a feature of
middle-class life too, and visiting committees organised themselves into

wards and locations, and inspected prisons, hospitals, orphanages and asylums. Men sat on the boards of charities and took the business and administration decisions; ladies raised the funds for the charities, especially with sales of the endless bits of tat of domestic arts and craft products. 'Bazaars' for charities gave elite women a chance to meet and organise, without political content or unladylike public appearance. All the philanthropic work was aimed at raising working-class women and their families to elite standards of cleanliness, health, safety – and discipline. Elite women wanted working-class women to create homes to a so-called respectable standard ... and stay in them.[148]

Genteel women wanted to help but not be tainted by association. Donations to the Lock Hospital for Venereal Disease were made anonymously – sexually transmitted disease was taboo.[149] But gradually, elite women became bolder in their public work, putting their names to causes, specialising in temperance, rescuing and reforming prostitutes, and improving the conditions of factory workers, especially women and children. In the course of their charitable work, ladies entered working-class homes intending to improve them and then realised that hardship and poverty were caused by inequality – the elite home and lifestyle rested on the exploitation of poor people, especially women. For some of the ladies – who would go on to campaign for public health, or for safety in mines and factories – it was a revolutionary insight.

Working Women Protests

Working women persisted in defending their families against hunger, the loss of their lands, the attack on their traditional lives, the undermining of local prices in local markets, and deteriorating wages and work conditions. In 1769, Benjamin Franklin wrote: 'I have seen within a year, riots in the country about corn; riots about elections; riots about workhouses; riots of colliers; riots of weavers; riots of coalheavers; riots of sawyers; riots of Wilkesites; riots of government chairman; riots of smugglers, in which custom-house officers and exciseman have been murdered, the Kings armed vessels and troops fired at.'[150]

All of these disturbances were riots led or supported by women, working-class women. Gentry observers continued to describe working-class protest as dangerous riots; denying that they were a well-understood theatrical act by working people performed by women to appeal – over the heads of the merchants, profiteers and traders – to a traditional authority figure, the local justice of the peace. If he did not arrive, or if he did not judge in favour of the crowd – as he weighed the loaves, examined adulterated flour or set the price of grain – the protest continued to escalate, to violence against property or people.[151]

In 1766 Exeter, local men and women caught a cart leaving the town with a load of dry peas and brought the carter before the magistrate to insist that the peas be sold locally. When the magistrate refused to play his traditional part in price-setting, the situation grew more threatening. Other groups broke open stores around the town, taking the food they needed and preventing other food carts from leaving.[152]

War with France in 1793 blocked imports from Europe, and a bad harvest in 1794 caused a new and widespread outbreak of popular protest, with people out on the streets and soldiers in the markets. In 1815, the parliament – mostly wheat-growing MPs – ordered that no foreign wheat could be imported until the local price for English producers had hit a peak – set at £4 a quarter. Wartime prices of the previous decade and a half had fluctuated from £2.8s a quarter to an unaffordable £13.3d.[153] This law – the Corn Law – was believed by many to ban cheap foreign wheat from the poor people of England, so that landlords could profiteer.[154]

Working women, as always, were prominent in riots, especially those trying to keep food in the neighbourhood, and prices down. In Gloucestershire, after a poor harvest and a cold winter, five women were accused of 'having riotously and tumultuously assembled, with divers other persons, on the 24th of June instant, within the parish of Tewkesbury aforesaid, to the terror of his Majesty's subjects, and in breach of the peace'.[155]

It was a typical food riot, led by women to stop wheat flour going out of their town to a more profitable market. The judge at their trial, Sir Alexander Thomson, reported to the home secretary that a crowd of people demanded that the local corn factor Richard Jenkins tell them what he was doing with a barge, loaded with flour, moored in the middle of the river, out of their reach. Jenkins told them to disperse and spoke to the woman leader, 21-year-old Helen Macmaster. He said, 'She was hollering.'

Local JPs arrived and called on the crowd – now about 200 people – to disperse. The Riot Act was read but had no effect. By four o'clock, the crowd got hold of the barge and were helping themselves to flour. Helen Macmaster and Anne Mayall, two young wives with hungry children, spoke to the corn factor. They 'dammed him, and said he was as great a rogue as the next'.

Sarah Kinson and Mary Aldridge, both aged 16, 'were not mere spectators, but taking an active part in the disturbance'. Another young woman, Haptia (Happy) Fielder said 'she wished she could leap over the bridge into the barge, and she would throw the flour into the water'.

One witness caught Helen Macmaster carrying flour away, held in her apron, and warned her of the consequences. She replied, 'Never mind that, will you give me a dobbin?' He gave her one and a halfpence to go home but she said 'she would have her bit of flour …'.

The five young women were arrested and sent to the borough jail – away from the town of Tewkesbury, where there might have been a rescue attempt. They were found guilty of rioting and sentenced to six months' imprisonment, which they served in the Bridewell division of the Gloucester jail – isolated from other women, who were mostly confined for debt.[156]

Women led by Margaret Boulker attacked a steam-powered corn mill at Snow Hill, Birmingham, after a woman customer complained her loaf was illegally undersize. They stoned the mill and got into the counting house. The Yorkshire Yeomanry were called out and working men joined the riot. Two men were shot dead,[157] and Margaret Boulker was hanged at Warwick.[158]

In 1795, a 'little MOB OF WOMEN' was said to have held up a miller's cart at Bexley, Sussex, and in Brighton that year a crowd of 200 women and girls paraded with a loaf of bread on a stick – symbolising the threat of bread or violence. The local authorities usually understood this pantomime of unrest. One magistrate was prosecuted for helping a women's riot at Somerton, Somerset, in 1795, when he supported the women preventing a load of corn from leaving the town.[159]

In the town of Seaford, Sussex, members of the Oxford Militia looted a mill, shops and inns, commandeered a ship laden with flour, and sold bread and food to local families at a 'fair price'. Soldiers Edward Cooke and Samuel Parrish told the tribunal that they had stopped the food being sent out of the county when their families were starving. They were shot for mutiny and others were sentenced to execution, transportation and lashings.[160] In 1799, another bad harvest and a downturn in the economy led to more rioting by poor and hungry people. Again, women were in the lead of the rioters. In Bath an old woman overturned a large basket of overpriced potatoes, which were quickly collected by women and children. In the riot that developed all the sacks at the market were raided and the potatoes stolen. The crowd then marched to nearby Walcot and found potatoes hidden by a farmer; they assaulted him and stole the potatoes.[161] In Nottingham, women attacked the baker's shop, sampled the bread and showed that he had been mixing chalk and alum with the flour. A mob in King's Lynn – 'chiefly women' – only gave up an attack on the miller's house when the Riot Act was read.

The government attempted to resolve the high price of wheat by persuading the poor to eat other grains. The Brown Bread Act, commonly known by sceptical housewives as 'the Poison Act', banned millers from making anything but wholemeal flour in 1800.[162] In Horsham, Sussex, a women's riot went to the windmill:

A number of women proceeded to Gosden wind-mill where, abusing the Miller for having served them with brown flour they seized on the cloth with which he was then dressing meal, according to the directions of the Bread Act, and cut it into a thousand pieces; threatening at the same time to serve all similar utensils he might in future attempt to use in the same manner. The Amazonian leader of this petticoated cavalcade afterwards regaled her associates with a Guinea's worth of liquor at the Crab Tree public house.[163]

Bad harvests and shortages triggered riots until 1801, and in many cases the authorities – whether gentry in little market towns or the government itself – responded to the demands of hungry people by distributing food, setting up relief for the poor and ordering profiteers not to export food from local markets or increase the price.[164] The Bread Act would be repealed two months after the protest at Gosden windmill.[165]

A letter to the *Gentleman's Magazine* in 1795 made it clear that some of the elite understood that their own survival depended on not leaving the poor to starve: 'Many plans are laid, and schemes proposed to keep our poor from perishing for want of bread; but alas! … I doubt whether it be any charity, except to ourselves – to prevent their rising and knocking us on the head.'[166]

Already frightened by rising radicalism at home and in France, the government tried to reduce the price of food, especially wheat. The use of grain for distilling was banned, as were exports of wheat, while imports were allowed and a new system of poor relief was introduced in some areas, forcing the parish overseers to pay a supplement to a father's wages if the price of bread rose above an agreed level. Punishments increased: people could be arrested without charge or trial; 'treason' was redefined as bringing the government into contempt; and crowds were banned – any gathering of more than 50 people had to be licensed by a magistrate.[167]

It did not stop women joining and leading food riots, nor demonstrations to protest enclosure: grazing animals or gathering food or kindling on land that had been held in common. One woman, denied her right to glean in a farmer's field in Easthorpe in 1799, obeyed the farmer and left the grain that had fallen on the ground after the harvest, but returned the following night with 30 other women.[168]

Women were specifically summoned in Wakefield, Yorkshire, in 1795:

To Give Notice
To all Women and inhabitants of Wakefield they are desired to meet at the New Church ... on Friday next at 9 o'clock ... to state the price of corn.
By desire of the inhabitants of Halifax
Who will meet them there.[169]

A wagon with sacks of wheat and flour was intercepted at Handborough, Oxfordshire, in 1795. Women climbed aboard and threw the sacks on the roadside, setting the price at 40 shillings a sack for flour, '... and they would have it at that, and would not give more, and if that would not do, they would have it by force. The owner (a yeoman) at length agreed: "If that must be the price, it must be the price."'[170]

Working-class women led other riots too: against turnpikes which charged travellers on the road, against local taxes and against the new machines in the cloth trade – rightly predicting that the machines would put them out of work.

In Shepton Mallet in 1776, women spinsters and male weavers attacked the town workhouse, where a spinning jenny had been set up to demonstrate the benefits of the new machine.[171] Later machinery-breaking of 1811–12 and the 'Plug Riots' – the destruction of factory boilers by pulling out the plugs in 1842 – was mostly carried out by small associations of men, supported by crowds of rioters including women. In the 1830 attacks on threshing machines, in the country around London women were charged with arson and sending threatening letters.[172]

Some rioting men dressed as women, probably as a form of disguise that was less likely to draw a punishment than going masked, and echoing the costumes of skimmington rides. West Country rioters against the new charges for use of the road frequently dressed in skirts and women's high crowned hats. Further west, in Wales in the 1830s, the cross-dressed attacks on tollgates and turnpikes were known as 'Rebecca Riots', a reference to sisterhood – from the blessing given to Rebecca in Genesis: 'Thou art our sister, mayst thou increase to thousands of thousands, and may thy seed possess the gates of their enemies.'[173]

In London riots, women were estimated to represent about 39 per cent of the crowd.[174] Robert Southey complained in 1807: 'Women are far more likely to be mutinous, they stand less in fear of law, partly from ignorance, partly because they presume upon the privilege of the sex, and therefore in all public tumults they are foremost in violence and ferocity.'[175]

The 'privilege of the sex' was probably more visible to an upper-class man like Robert Southey than to the poor women rioting for food. Hannah Smith of Manchester led raids by men, women and children on potato carts and shops in 1812 and boasted that she could 'raise a crowd in a minute'. She was captured in a food riot but charged with highway robbery, which carried a death sentence. Hannah Smith was hanged. Not much privilege of sex there. The working-class women were said to be 'the backbone of protests, as they were the backbone of their communities, patching up the wounded and covering up for those sought by the authorities ... They were also the ones who had to carry on maintaining the family when male breadwinners went to jail.'[176]

In 1780, women were involved in London's anti-popery protests known as 'the Gordon Riots', after Lord George Gordon who headed the Protestant Association to oppose the Papists Act of 1778, which had proposed more toleration for Roman Catholics. Calling 60,000 people together for a rally, claiming that Roman Catholics would undermine the British army and other British institutions, Gordon was supported by the 'respectable' working classes: tradesmen, clerks, apprentices of London. However, orderly protests turned into the most destructive riots in the capital's history, including attacks on Newgate Prison and the Bank of England, only suppressed by sending in the army with brutal consequences: 300–700 people were killed. Of the 110 rioters prosecuted, 20 were women, some of them of African descent.[177] Charlotte Gardner, an African woman, was hanged on Tower Hill for helping to tear down a publican's house during the riots.[178]

Miss Sarah Burney, daughter of the composer Charles Burney, watched the attack on the house of a magistrate, Sir William Hyde, who had previously read the Riot Act and called out the army against the rioters. Despite her horror at the people she called a 'Mob' and 'so many Furies', she described a demonstration that followed community rules. Even in the heat of violence, the rioters brought a fire engine to hose down neighbouring buildings and prevent damaging the adjoining houses:

St Martins Lane, London, 8 June, 1780.
When Hyde's house was emptied of all its furniture, the Mob tore away the windows & window Frames, & began to pull up the Floors, & the pannels of the Rooms, till some of the Neighbours, (Who had however hung blue Ribbons from their Windows the whole time to prove their Religion, & many of whom perhaps had particular reasons to rejoice in the Justice's Disaster,) entreated them not to keep up so strong a fire before their Houses, as they had the greatest reason to fear they would soon catch, & that the whole street wd, be in a blaze notwithstanding the Engine – Upon this the Ringleaders gave the word, & away they all ran past our windows to the bottom of Leicester Fields, with lighted firebrands in their hands, like so many furies – Each carried something from the fires in our street, that nothing might escape – they made in Leicester Fields one Great Bonefire of them – the Women like the Furies were more active & busy in the business than the Men – & they continued pulling down Pannels, Doors, &c till between two & 3 in the Morning to keep up the Bonefire & totally destroy the Poor House.[179]

When the soldiers arrived, called out to quell the riots, they seem to have been in sympathy with the rioters:

> Early in the Eveg. about 30 foot Guards wth. an Ensign at their
> Head marched into the street – but the daring Populace appeared not
> the least alarmed, on the contrary they welcomed them with loud
> shouts & huzza's – The Ensign made some speach to them – but as I
> suppose he dared not oppose so many hundred People as were here
> assembled after a very short discourse wth. them, he turn'd round, &
> march'd out of the street as he came into it, the Mob shouting &
> clapping the soldiers as they pass'd on their back as they passed &
> one of these even joined in the huzza. This was more alarming than
> any thing – for if the Military power would not act, & was not fear'd
> by the Populace, what chance did there seem to be of an End to the
> outrages they might be disposed to commit.[180]

The ritual of the riot is clear, even in this London anti-Catholic riot of urban workers. The working-class people – mostly respectable tradesmen and their wives[181] – enacted a protest; elite families, watching from their elegant drawing room windows, made no attempt or gesture to prevent or stop the riot, and actually performed their own theatre of support, displaying ribbons and shouting approving slogans:

> While Mr. B: My sister & I stood at the Window, the Crowd being
> then greatly diminished, as Nos. had flown to attack other places – I
> saw about 10 men & women in a Groupe looking up at our
> Windows – 'No Popery,' cried they – & repeated this 2 or 3 times –
> but as Men, Women, & Children had been crying No Popery a
> thousand times during the Evening, & indeed all the day long, we
> had no idea that we were ourselves addressed at this time, till one of
> the Men sd. to the rest pointing to us, 'They are all 3 papists.' – 'for
> God sake, cried poor Etty, Mr. Burney call out no Popery or
> anything' – Mr. B- accordingly got his Hat & Huzza'd from the
> window – It went against me to hear him, tho' it seem'd no joke in
> the present situation of things to be mark' d out by such wretches, as
> Papists – God bless your Honour,' they then cried, & went away very
> well satisfied.[182]

As Miss Burney's account shows, a very small gesture from the elite satisfied these rioters. Like the weighing of loaves by the JP in the market, it was the assurance to the working class that the elite understood their demonstration, and agreed with them.

Women did not only protest through riot – as the eighteenth century went on they created formal associations, sometimes in writing. They set up friendly societies, for mutual support, insurance and as a place where members could share information about working conditions or the rate of pay. The increasing poverty of working families inspired workers to form new organisations, like early trade unions, called 'combinations'. Some were co-ed but when women workers were excluded from men-only associations, they formed their own. Women spinners in Leicester formed the 'Sisterhood of Leicester' in 1780.[183]

Riots in the north of England centred around the textile mills when the new machines replaced handlooms. Handloom weavers had been the wealthiest of the craftsmen with their loom set up in their cottage, the family spinning to provide thread, and the weaver collecting raw wool or cotton and returning cloth on a regular schedule for good wages – a lifestyle that was ended by the invention of the power loom, which mill owners installed in huge buildings beside the rivers (for water power) in north-west England from 1780. As the Napoleonic wars and poor harvests brought starvation, and the power looms undercut craftsmen's wages, violent mass protests broke out. Most of the machine-breaking riots were started by men, led by an imaginary mythical figure, 'Ned Ludd', and the rioters were named after him as 'Luddites'. Some women rioted alongside the men, calling themselves 'Ludd's wives', and in April 1812 some men wore women's costumes and took the name 'Ludd's wives' in an attack on a Stockport mill. A woman calling herself 'Lady Ludd' led a women's food riot in Leeds that year.

On 20 April, four women – Alice Partington, Anne Dean, Ann Butterworth and Millicent Stoddard – were arrested for riot, tumult and breaking windows at Burton's power loom mill, Manchester, and sentenced to six months in prison. Four days later, two young women led rioters into the steam-powered Westhoughton cotton mill at Bolton in Lancashire: 'About fifty assembled near the mill … They smashed through the gates and started to break windows … led by two young women, Mary Molyneux, 19, and her sister Lydia, 15, who were seen … with Muck Hooks and coal Picks in their hands breaking the windows of the building ... shouting "Now Lads" to encourage the men on.'[184]

The men set fire to the building, destroying all the machinery, the raw cotton and the woven cambrics. The women were arrested for 'wilfully and maliciously & unlawfully setting Fire to and burning the Weaving Mill, Warehouses and Loop Shop of Messrs Rowe and Duncough at Westhoughton with intent to injure the said Messrs Rowe & Duncough'.[185]

As trade unions evolved in the nineteenth century, they based themselves around the old skilled male workers' associations – mostly men-only and excluding women workers, who they blamed for bringing down wages. The London Corresponding Society, formulating policy for working men, had a men-only membership in 1792.

All radical voices were suppressed by the frightened government during the French Revolution but the recovery from 1815 proved more open to women. At an open-air public meeting in 1818, the radical weaver Samuel Bamford argued that women should be allowed to vote at such gatherings. He wrote: 'This was a new idea and the women who attended numerously on that bleak ridge were mightily pleased with it – and the men being nothing dissentient when the resolution was put, the women held up their hands, amid much laughter; and ever from that time women voted at radical meetings.'[186]

Workers in Manchester and the surrounding areas had been meeting in small committees and then in larger public meetings since the early years of the nineteenth century, calling for an end to government corruption, free trade to lower the price of food especially bread, better pay and conditions, and votes for men. In July 1818, there was a strike of cotton spinners, in September a strike of weavers, and a march of 1,222 men and 355 women that won an increase in wages.[187]

A radical newspaper described the women calling for reform: 'Their arguments are very forcible. They say that since the men abandoned the cause of freedom, they will support it. They say freedom was a woman and therefore every woman ought to be free. Man, they say, has shamefully deserted his post – and has no right to control woman; – since he has lost the power of defending himself ... that woman can expect no protection from the cowards that cannot protect themselves! And they demand Universal Suffrage in its fullest extent.'[188]

A January meeting in 1819 Manchester was attended by 8,000 working people, despite some employers locking men and women in their factories to prevent them from taking part. The radical MP Henry Hunt called for votes for 'individuals': 'That every individual, of mature age, and not incapacitated by crime or insanity, has a right to a vote for the election of a Representative in Parliament.'[189]

The women of Blackburn organised a Female Reform Society, and – wearing a green favour for liberty in bonnets and caps – proceeded towards the stage for an outdoor meeting in June 1818. Alice Kitchen gave a short speech in which she said the women linked the poverty of their homes and their hunger with the corruption of government. She ended:

> We the Female Reformers of Blackburn, therefore earnestly entreat you and every man in England, in the most solemn manner, to come forward and join the general union, that by a determined and constitutional resistance to our oppressors, the people may obtain annual parliaments, universal suffrage and election by ballot, which alone can save us from lingering misery and premature death. We look forward with horror to an approaching winter, when the necessity of food, clothing, and every requisite will increase double-fold.[190]

A woman from Ashton wrote to the Blackburn women's committee calling for revolution: 'We are on the precipice from which there is no retreat … let us boldly take the plunge for there is no other way left but either slavery or exertion. Let us prove we are true-born English women and that we are determined to bear this illegal oppression no longer.'[191]

Female Reform Society members were harshly criticised in elite newspapers for failing to keep to their homes and perform their domestic duties. The idea of separate spheres was invoked to identify them as women who had wrongly stepped into men's business. But the Manchester Female Reform Society reached over the class divide and wrote an open letter to upper-class women, calling on them as sisters and describing the poverty of their lives that was the result of elite men profiteering in industry and corrupting government.[192] They did not receive a reply – but they were voicing an idea of sisterhood more important than class. Theirs was one of the few voices to challenge the division of women.

In August 1819, the largest public demonstration in favour of universal suffrage, government reform and free trade summoned a crowd of about 60,000 people to St Peter's Fields in Manchester. Societies from all around the area marched with bands and singing, the women often in all-white dresses with flags, bonnets of liberty and green sashes or ribbons. Radical Samuel Bamford described the march of the Middleton Reform Society to St Peter's Fields:

> Our whole column, with the Rochdale people, would probably consist of six thousand men. At our head were a hundred or two of women, mostly young wives, and mine own was amongst them. A hundred or two of our handsomest girls – sweethearts to the lads who were with us – danced to the music, or sung snatches of popular songs: a score or two of children were sent back, though some went forward; whilst, on each side of our line walked some thousands of stragglers. And this, accompanied by our friends, and our nearest and most tender connections, we went slowly towards Manchester.[193]

The Female Reform Society was calling for cheaper food, and for votes for men: 'as wives, mothers, daughters, in their social, domestic, moral capacities, they come forward in support of the sacred cause of liberty'.[194]

The crowd gathered to hear MP Henry Hunt on the platform, surrounded by the Female Reform Society holding banners, when the Manchester and Salford Yeomanry were called out by the local magistrates to arrest him.[195] The Yeomanry charged into the crowd, knocking down a woman and killing a child, and arrested the MP. The Cheshire magistrates ordered the 15th Hussars to disperse the crowd and the soldiers charged with sabres drawn and killed as many as 17 people, including four women: Margaret Downes, Manchester – sabred in the breast; Mary Heys, Chorlton Row – trampled by cavalry and died of her injuries four months later after giving birth prematurely; Sarah Jones, Silk Street Manchester – truncheoned on the head by a special constable; and Martha Partington, Barton – crushed to death in a cellar. Elizabeth Gaunt miscarried after the attack and her baby died. Between 400 and 700 people were injured. A radical supporter recorded what he saw:

> The Yeomanry made their charge with the most infuriate frenzy: they cut down men, women and children indiscriminately, and appeared to have commenced a premeditated attack with most insatiable thirst for blood and destruction … The women appear to have been the

particular objects of the Cavalry Assassins. One woman, who was near the spot where I stood, and who held an infant in her arms, was sabred over the head and her tender offspring DRENCHED IN HER MOTHER'S BLOOD. Another was actually stabbed in the neck with the point of a sabre which must have been a deliberate attempt on the part of the military assassin. Some were sabred in the breast: so inhuman, indiscriminate, and fiend-like, was the conduct of the Manchester Yeomanry Cavalry.[196]

The 'massacre' targeted women, who numbered only one in eight of the crowd, but a quarter of the injured (100 of the 400 wounded).[197] They were not – as one report claimed – crushed trying to escape but struck by truncheons or cut by sabres.[198]

Some of the crowd fought back, one among them 'a young married woman of our party, with her face all bloody, her hair streaming about her, her bonnet hanging by the string, and her apron weighted with stones, kept her assailant at bay until she fell backwards and was near being taken; but she got away covered with severe bruises. It was near this place and about this time that one of the yeomanry was dangerously wounded, and unhorsed, by a blow from the fragment of a brick; and it was supposed to have been flung by this woman.'[199]

Women survivors gave evidence at an incomplete inquest on one of the protesters. Elizabeth Farren, of Lombard Street, Manchester, said: 'I was with this child ... I was frightened for its safety, and to protect it, held it close to my side with head downwards, to avoid the blow. I desired them to spare my child, and I was directly cut on my forehead.'

Ann Jones of Windmill Street said, 'I saw a great many people wounded, and very bloody indeed ... a great many people in my house, and all was in great confusion, and some of the special constables came up in great triumph before my door, calling out, "This is Waterloo for you! This is Waterloo."'[200]

A magistrate observed that working-class women were revolutionary, the enemies of his class: 'It was very general and undisguised cry amongst them that the gentry had had the upper hand long enough and that their turn has now come.'[201]

It was true that working-class women saw that the only way that Parliament would serve working-class interests was if working-class men had the vote. The Manchester Female Reformers were clear why they were supporting votes for men: 'We can no longer bear to see our husbands and our little ones clothed in rags.'[202] They did not demand votes for women – that was thought to be too radical, and might risk the whole campaign. The Blackburn Female Reform Society's founding statement in 1819 declared its purpose 'To assist the male population of this country to obtain their rights and liberties'.[203]

The nationwide petition for votes for men became the predominant campaign of the nineteenth century, with the 'People's Charter' attracting 50,000 women's signatures in the first week.[204] But the Chartists were careful not to call for votes for women. Many Chartists, like many working-class people, were persuaded by the theory of separate spheres. They wanted votes for men only – so that a parliament of working men could enforce a minimum wage high enough for a male breadwinner to keep his wife and family at home.[205]

The doctrine of separate spheres made sense to working class women too, who justified forming women's-only associations to win votes for men because government policies endangered their homes. The 1839 Stockport Women's Association said: 'We regret that we should be driven by dire necessity to depart from the limits usually prescribed for female duties; but when ... even with the most rigid economy we are unable to provide for the actual necessities of subsistence ... we can feel justified in declaring our conviction that nothing less than the adoption of the principles of the People's Charter can effectively remove the existing distress.'[206]

But in the same year, the Female Political Union of Newcastle disagreed – they thought that women should not be confined to domestic concerns: 'We have been told that the province of women is her home, and that the field of politics should be left to men; this we deny. It is not true that the interests of our fathers, husbands, and brothers, ought to be ours? If they are oppressed and impoverished, do we not share those evils with them? If so, ought we not to resent the infliction of those wrongs upon them? We have read the records of the past, and our hearts have responded to the historian's praise of those women, who struggled against tyranny and urged their countrymen to be free or die.'[207]

Three giant petitions, the last accompanied by a huge demonstration in 1848, called for the vote for working men, but in the face of government refusal and a troubled leadership the Chartists could not maintain momentum.

Other associations of women almost always justified themselves by being in defence of the home. Occasionally – as during the protests against the new Poor Law of 1834 – they were joined by elite women. In Elland, Mrs Susan Fierly spoke of the 'Dignity and equality of the sex', in a rare example of an upper-class woman identifying with poor women. Outside the lecture, the working-class women protested in the old way: stealing a cartload of bread intended for the workhouse, throwing stones at the Poor Law guardians, disrupting a meeting of the Poor Law commissioners and even going so far as to roll the gentlemen commissioners in the snow.[208]

Sisterhood across the classes remained rare. Working-class women increasingly understood that their safety and the survival of their families was a class issue – a living wage would only be won by entering the Houses of Parliament and voting against the landlords and employers, and stopping the laws from destroying the lives of the poor with enclosures, wage controls and punitive charity. Naturally, they did not look for help towards the landlords and employers and their wives and daughters.

Crime and Punishment

Prosecutions of women for witchcraft declined with the reduction of superstition, especially among the middle and upper classes; but there were still flare-ups in villages and working-class communities, where suspicion of neighbours or eccentric women might sour into a ritualised lynching. In 1785, Sarah Bradshaw was accused by her neighbours and chose the traditional test of 'swimming' a witch to see if the devil helped her to float. Bradshaw sank beneath the water and was dragged out and proclaimed innocent.[209] In 1792, an old lady of Stanningfield, Suffolk, let herself be swum before the community in a final attempt to clear her name of longstanding accusations of witchcraft. She also sank and although she was dragged out, she was 'almost lifeless'.[210]

One woman, called 'the Yorkshire witch', claimed to cure curses.[211] According to the *Newgate Calendar*, Mary Bateman – a deserted wife and small-time thief – set up as fortune teller and charmer at Marsh Lane, near Timble Bridge in Leeds. She had the good luck to be sent for by a terminally ill woman, Mrs Pirgo. Mary Bateman offered hope, saying that she could lift the curse. Mrs Pirgo gave Mary Bateman money: coins and notes, which she tied into silken purses to be sewed into the sick bed. Mrs Pirgo also paid for household goods and food for Mary, who cooked up puddings for her patient and gave her honey laced with mercury. This diet proved fatal for Mrs Pirgo, but her husband William continued to follow Bateman's prescriptions and only called in the authorities when he found that the silk purses that had been sewn into his bed, which should have contained notes and guineas, held only cabbage leaves and coppers. The jury found Mary Bateman guilty of murder. She pleaded her belly, which would require examination by a committee of matrons or midwives. Her claim 'created a general consternation among the ladies, who hastened to quit the court, to prevent the execution of so painful an office being imposed upon them. His lordship, in consequence, ordered the doors to be closed, and in about half-an-hour, twelve married women being empanelled, they were sworn in court, and charged to inquire "whether the prisoner was with quick child?" The jury of matrons then retired with the prisoner, and on their return into court delivered their verdict, which was that Mary Bateman 'is not with quick child'. Mary Bateman was executed in 1809.[212]

From the mid-1700s the increasing belief that women had a nature – quite unlike men's – that was 'pure' and 'selfless' and that they were weak and fragile made the judiciary more likely to blame a woman's crimes on a bad husband. Between 1600 and 1800, women were charged with only 13 per cent of property offences in Sussex and 24 per cent in Surrey.[213] Many women thieves and even murderers found themselves released because their husbands were regarded as the main criminal, according to the *Newgate Calendar*.

Charlotte Walker was repeatedly released by sympathetic juries because her youthful slight appearance made them doubt that she had robbed or assaulted grown men. She was only four foot eleven inches and 23 years old when she first appeared in court charged with assault in 1777. She would be arrested for stealing on 27 occasions, and released 15 times. She defended herself, cross-questioning the men who said she had robbed them, painting a picture of them as immoral drunkards and picking on their inconsistencies. Her demolition of Joseph Bowman, robbed by her in French Horn Yard, was irresistible: 'He said ... I held him together by both his arms, and so robbed his Worship: I said I must have three hands to rob him when I had hold of both his arms.'

In 1800, Walker faced trial for theft and was found guilty and sentenced to death, commuted to transportation to New South Wales, where she set up house with a time-served shoemaker 14 years her junior and lived with him till her death in 1806.[214]

Some women were ambitious and imaginative criminals. One fraudster, Elizabeth Harriet Greeve, passed as an aristocratic woman. She appeared in the *Newgate Calendar* for her convincing pretence to come from an aristocratic family, offering the patronage of her friends for a price: 'With one of the dupes of her artifice she was first cousin to Lord North; with another, second cousin to the Duke of Grafton; to a third, nearly related to Lady Fitzroy: on some occasions she affected great intimacy with Lord Guilford; and had the young Premier then ruled the State she would, without much doubt, have boasted the patronage of Mr Pitt.'

She was arrested in November 1773 for promising a coach-carver that she could get him the place of a clerk to the stores in the Victualling Office. She took his life savings of £36. She promised William Kent of Streatly in Berkshire the place of a coast-waiter, and took £62 from the husband of another woman: 'Elizabeth Cooper next appeared before the magistrates and charged the prisoner with defrauding her late husband of sixty-two pounds on a similar pretence to the last case, the loss of which, and his disappointment, the poor afflicted widow said, broke his heart.'

Elizabeth Harriet Greeve was recognised as a fraudster who had already been transported and had returned before serving her full sentence. She was transported again.[215]

Chloroform had first been used to make a patient unconscious in 1847 and only three years later, in 1850, an innovative criminal, Elizabeth Smith, known as 'Fat Beth', accosted a young solicitor named Frederic Jewitt in London. The young gentleman presumably paused at the offer of sex and as he considered the price, she pressed a handkerchief soaked with chloroform over his mouth, causing him to fall unconscious. He woke up in a lodging house in Thrall Street, Spitalfields, stripped naked and without his watch, ring or money. Miss Smith – 'Fat Beth' in the court documents – tried to escape the hue and cry by hiding in a notorious brothel in George Street, not far away, but was arrested and sentenced for theft, the first recorded criminal to use chloroform.[216]

Women fighters, pugilists, became increasingly criminalised. But in 1795, Mary Ann Fielding fought an unnamed woman – 'a noted Jewess of Wentworth Road' – with the well-known male boxing champions

'Gentleman' Jackson and Daniel Mendoza as their seconds; and in 1789, an unnamed 'Colonel' advertised in *The Times* newspaper for a rematch against a woman boxer who had beaten him.[217]

A new offence was created in 1803 to criminalise abortionists. Performing an abortion after the 'quickening', when fetal movements were felt by the mother, now carried the death penalty. But a successful prosecution depended upon the woman who had sought the abortion telling the court that she had felt the movement of the baby before the procedure. Rather than rely on such an unlikely betrayal, the male doctors called for a redefinition in 1837 to make abortion a crime at any stage of the pregnancy – and the mother's opinion as to 'quickening' irrelevant.[218]

The crime of 'petty treason' – the specific murder of a wife killing a husband or a servant killing a master – was abolished as a distinct offence from murder in the Offences against the Person Act 1828. In 1868, public hanging was ended, and the last woman to be hanged in public was 25-year-old Frances Kidder for the murder of her stepdaughter.[219]

There was a boom in prostitution in the eighteenth century, mostly women selling sex when other work could not be had or was paid so poorly that a single woman worker could not survive. Prostitutes were so widely used that philosopher Bernard Mandeville wrote *A Modest Defence of Public Stews* in 1724, arguing that there should be state-run brothels to allow men to satisfy themselves, safe from criminals and venereal disease. In London alone the police estimated there to be 7,261 prostitutes in 1851.[220] By the 1900s, this had risen to 50,000,[221] and to 80,000 by the middle of the century.[222] The *Westminster Review* of 1850 reported even higher numbers – it claimed up to 360,000 prostitutes were working in the capital – a quarter of all the working women in the city.[223] The Vagrancy Acts of 1822, 1834 and 1844 included a clause that forbade 'soliciting' for sex and living off 'immoral earnings'; but while there was a belief in the imperative needs of men, there was little real determination to reduce the numbers of available women. The law against soliciting was largely used against homosexual men, and the 'immoral earnings' clause mostly directed against male pimps. Prostitution by women on the streets, in ale houses, bawdy houses and high-class brothels was tacitly allowed. Women apprehended on the streets were rarely arrested for soliciting – only if they were indiscreet, when they would usually be charged with being disorderly, drunk or vagrants: 'Of the several hundred prostitutes who appear in the charge books of Saint James' in London between 1733 and 1739 many give false names, the favourite being Miss Nobody.'[224]

Such women must have felt like 'nobodies'. Social reformer and journalist Henry Mayhew called a meeting of needleworkers in London in 1849, and an anonymous older woman told him:

> The most I can earn is about 3s 6d a week. I get my lodging only
> from the person that employs me. I'm sometimes obliged to work till
> twelve at night for my 3s 6d; and now in these short days I can
> scarcely earn anything. I've been obliged often to go to prostitution.
> These twelve years I haven't been altogether on the streets, but have
> been almost as bad. I can scarcely earn, sir, what I eat. I think the
> small number of us present arises from the shame of the women to
> come … But I'm not ashamed to tell the troubles I've had through
> distress. Bad payment for the work obliges us to do wrong. It's
> against our will to do such a thing. And now, for a woman of my
> years, it's getting almost more than I can bear, sir.[225]

A guide to London prostitutes, published annually, was priced at 2s 6d a copy and sold around 8,000 copies a year for 18 years from 1757 until it fell out of fashion. It described up to 200 women working as prostitutes in such detail that the booklet may have been bought and used for masturbation – but the descriptions were often based on real women, and may have been accurate in the language of the time:

> Sally Robinson Maiden Lane
> The origin of this lady is a little obscure, but she sold sausages about
> the streets till above 15 years old, when the celebrated Mrs Cole had
> a casual sight of her maidenhead for thirty guineas, out of which she
> generously made Sal a present of five shillings, to cure her of the clap,
> which she got from her deflowerer. She is a tall fat girl, but not
> ungenteel, nor her face disagreeable but she is as mercenary as the
> devil, which lessens all her other good qualities.[226]

The list includes young women:

Miss – 44 Newman-street, Oxford St
This petite belle has not yet attained her sixteenth year, and to make amends for her deficiency of height, she is elegantly formed, nor does she lack beauty … Two guineas will bring you better acquainted with this charmer nor will you have cause for disagreeable reflections from her acquaintance.[227]

The list also includes a rare mention of a Jewish woman. I quote the misogyny and antisemitism for the benefit of accuracy:

Miss Lawr-e, No 6, Church- St. Annes Soho
The religion of the Jews will not permit them to eat pork, or feast with Christians; how strictly this lady may adhere to particulars in her articles of faith we cannot positively tell; but this we can say for truth, that she has not the least objection to Christian concupiscence, and will open her synagogue of love, even on the Sabbath, either to Jew, Turk or Infidel, if they think proper to call on her as above. This young Israelite renounced her Levitical friends for the sake of a Christian, who gave her inward proofs of a new faith, which were so convincing to her, that she has continued a thorough orthodox convert ever since. She is of a sprightly disposition, has good teeth, dark hair, black eyes, a Roman nose, a fresh colour, of a middle size, and is very wanton in her looks.[228]

A *List of Covent Garden Ladies* describing prostitutes and their prices was published by 'Mr Harris' for 30 years from 1760 as a guide for two generations of elite male customers. By the 1830s, there were too many houses to describe: 900 brothels and 850 houses of 'ill fame'.[229]

A few full-time professional prostitutes made a good living from sex but most of the women on the streets were selling sex for food, or a bed for the night, alcohol or gifts. Their numbers boomed as the breadwinner wage for men forced down women's wages. A child thief, Ellen Reese, stated that 'she did not become a regular prostitute till shoplifting failed – was miserable both ways, but going on the street was more profitable'.[230]

Ann Illiard and her daughter, fined and imprisoned for keeping a brothel, were probably arrested and convicted in April 1809 – not for managing a brothel but because of the 'vast number of disorderly women' and the 'indecencies' – 'within fifty yards of a charity-school for females, in Cavendish court, Houndsditch'.[231] The parish officers applied to Mrs Illiard, a widow, to close her house but she refused, telling them she had 'no other means to obtain a livelihood'. They arrested her and her daughter. The court found the women guilty and fined the mother, aged 60, £150, and the daughter, who was about 30, £50: 'The daughter then begged to say a word or two to the Court, in which she declared her innocence; said she had only been to see her mother, whose line of life she lamented; and that she was unable to pay even 50s. She added that the names they went by were not their real names, and that the premises belonged to others, who let them to her mother at a weekly rent, and who had now abandoned her. She then retired, apparently overpowered by her feelings.'[232]

The problem of sick and poor prostitutes inspired some elite philanthropists to open the first 'Magdalen Hospital' in London in 1758. Named for Mary Magdalen, the penitent prostitute forgiven by Jesus, they were not designed to help prostitutes as much as prevent women from entering prostitution. Young women who had been seduced or raped once were preferred: regular prostitutes were thought to be too difficult to reform. Anyone pregnant or with a sexually transmitted disease was directed to the lying-in hospitals for pauper women or the Lock hospitals – jails for the diseased. The poverty of working-class women meant that there were always far more applicants than places available. They applied once a week, queuing up for interviews, which were intended to discover 'whether they had a heart to reform or just a desire for relief from poverty'.[233]

The London Magdalen admitted nearly 4,000 young women in fifty years from 1758. Most were taught domestic skills and left to go into service or returned to their birth families, while about 15 per cent were expelled for 'improper behaviour'. A further fifth of the women left early or died.[234] The Magdalen was run by male governors; but upper- and middle-class women were patrons. Its chapel, with the Magdalen Choir, became a fashionable church to attend, and the girls at work could be viewed by appointment; but they could refuse to be exhibited to previous employers or acquaintances. By 1800, about 300 Magdalen houses had been created across England, increasingly specialising in laundry work. Some evolved into homes where unmarried mothers were set to work and their illegitimate babies taken from them for adoption.

For elite women in England, the abuse of working-class women for sex could no longer be a secret prop for the sex-free marriages of the elite. The crisis of confidence in English superiority caused by the 1857 First War of Indian Independence spread widely. The moral superiority of the elite English home financially supported by a breadwinner husband and ornamented with a wife in her separate sphere no longer seemed successful at home and compelling abroad. Prostitutes challenged the picture of white male moral superiority as much as rioting Indians, and the women represented a visible flaw in the master race, a vector for disease, a sign that men were not as they claimed: morally and socially superior. How could England claim to be a master race, moving outwards to conquer the world, if it could not demonstrate moral superiority at home?

Rape

The widespread belief that elite men could use working-class women for sex probably caused a rise in middle- and upper-class men raping and a reluctance to report. Only one elite man was accused of child rape in London. Sir John Murry was found not guilty in 1719.[235] A man publicly known as the 'Rape-Master General of Great Britain', Francis Charteris, was convicted of raping his servant Anne Bond, but pardoned by the king in April 1730.[236] Of 45 rape cases heard at the Old Bailey from 1770 to 1799, nine (20 per cent of the recorded rapes) were committed by an employer or his kinsman on a servant. Most London rape cases seemed to be lower middling-class rapists and lower middling-class women acquaintances, or fellow workers; in only 27 per cent (12) of these cases was the assailant a stranger – perhaps because it was thought too difficult to find a man who had not been identified by the woman.[237]

In Surrey between 1660 and 1800, a rape case was brought to the assize court once every year and a half. In the Sussex courts over the same period, this happened even less frequently, on average one case every four years.[238] In Surrey, twice as many women brought charges of attempted rape to the courts between 1660 and 1802 than for rape itself – 86 to 42[239] – which probably reflected the jury's willingness to convict on a lesser charge. At the Old Bailey in London between 1770 and 1800, 43 rape cases involving women and girls over the age of 12 were tried, 7 per cent (3 men) were found guilty, while in 15 cases in the North-East

Assize Circuit over the same period, 13 per cent (2 men) were convicted.[240]

If the victim of rape was under the age of nine, it was considered rape regardless of any argument brought by the accused.[241] The death penalty for adult rape or for sex with a child under the age of ten was abolished in 1841; it had been in effect since 1540.

Local women had authority in rape and incest cases. Juries of matrons might inspect a victim for virginity or disease or pregnancy, report on her reputation and even recommend a verdict.[242] A woman's prior reputation was a deciding factor, and other women would attest to it. But in 1836, all defendants accused of all crimes were given the right to have a defence lawyer to speak for them, to interrogate witnesses and to challenge evidence against them.

Rape cases became a theatre in which qualified and highly educated men rehearsed explanations and excuses for an accused rapist. Upper-class lawyers questioned a poor woman complaining of rape about her character, history and reliability. The village women who knew her no longer made their contribution. This was devastating for women reporting a rape, who now found themselves facing a hostile interrogation as the prime witness of a crime done against them.[243]

Sport

In London in 1768, the greatest tennis player in England, Mr Tomkins, was beaten 2–1 by a 40-year-old French woman, Mme Bunel, who wore 'a short skirt and an easy jacket, which placed no restraint upon the activity with which she flew from side to side of the Court'.

Furious gamblers who had backed Mr Tomkins called for a rematch. Mme Bunel accepted the challenge and played the champion again, for a considerable purse. It was an important political and social occasion, attended by the French ambassador and the nobility. Mme Bunel beat him again, this time 4–2.[244]

A woman horse rider, Alicia Meynel, challenged her brother-in-law, Captain Flint, to a race over four miles in 1804, and she led for most of the race on her mare, *Vinagrillo*, before she had to pull her horse up, lame. A reported 10,000 spectators watched the race, some carrying signs that read 'PETTICOATS FOREVER'. A huge purse of £3,000 was offered in a return challenge, which was taken up by Mr Bromford, who withdrew during the race. The following year Alicia Meynel challenged the most successful jockey in England, Francis Buckle, three-time winner of the Derby, with a string of classic winners behind him. Before a crowd reported to be 30,000 strong, the two raced to an extremely close finale, with Alicia Meynel beating the champion by half-a-neck in a storming finish – and she was riding side-saddle.[245]

English rower Ann Glanville achieved national fame in 1842, becoming known as the champion female rower of the world, beating the ten best male crews in France. She raced pilot gigs with an all-female crew. Ann married John Glanville, who worked as a waterman on the River Tamar, raised 14 children and took on the job of waterman when her husband was ill.[246]

Defining Girls and Training Ladies

The Romantic movement opposed swaddling a baby on a board, preferring a freer, more tactile relationship. More babies were breast-fed as parents were warned that a baby might be morally corrupted or infected by a wet nurse. Attachment to the mother became fashionable even among the upper classes and endorsed the belief that women were not sexual but highly maternal.

From the 1700s, the availability of washable textiles – cotton, linen and muslin – meant that even working-class parents could afford to dress babies in white gowns until they started to crawl, when the gowns were hemmed up to make 'short coats', with no distinction between boys and girls. But the increasingly strident teaching that there were only two rigidly defined sexes with no variation meant that it became vital to identify the sex of a baby at birth and raise a child to suit his or her future. The state registration of births in 1837 required the father to decide the sex of his child at birth and register him or her (there were no other options) with the authorities. Behaviour appropriate to the defined sex was taught to children from an early age. Sarah Stickney Ellis wrote in 1843: 'Boys were accustomed to a mode of treatment as much calculated to make them determined, frank and bold, as that of girls to induce the opposite extremes of weakness, artifice, and timid helplessness.'[247]

It was a struggle to teach healthy girls to restrain and repress themselves; but the elite clothes, with tight bodices and long skirts, crushed

This 1883 advertisement from *Harper's Magazine* promotes matching 'perfect health corsets' for mother and child

lungs and stomach and limited mobility. Women's fashions disabled growing girls: 'As women's bodies were deformed from the age of two by metal stays that contracted their upper torsos (and rendered their health attractively delicate), so their minds were deformed by the injunctions to remain silent and silly.'[248]

The evangelical movement – a renewal of enthusiasm inside the Church of England – defined the middle-class home as the centre of moral virtue and women's religiosity: 'What can be found in the whole circle of fashionable pleasures that can produce such exquisite feelings of delight as the affectionate husband enjoys, when he returns home from the business and fatigue of the day, and finds his wife engaged in domestic cares?'[249]

The home was the best place for a lady; soon it was the only place for her. In the eighteenth century, the London streets that housed 'gentlemen's clubs' became closed to elite women, who would not be seen in them, and by the nineteenth century only those streets designated as shopping streets were visited by ladies. Newspaper reports of rape cases in the early 1800s increased fear about the wider world, and soon it was widely believed that it was not safe for women on the streets.[250]

As women were idealised, impossible behaviour began to be demanded of them. Art critic and philosopher John Ruskin, disappointed first in his mother and then in his wife, fixed the blame fast: 'There is not a war in the world, no, nor an injustice; but you women are answerable for it. Not in that you have provoked; but in that you have not hindered. There is no suffering, no injustice, no misery in the earth; but the guilt of it lies with you.'[251]

The semi-enclosed lady of the house was the hallmark of the upper- and middle-class home. She became a model for aspirational middle-class families, who made their wives and daughters idle in order to qualify for entry to the upper classes. Even working-class families tried to demonstrate their prosperity and respectability by making wives and daughters unpaid. In 1849, Henry Mayhew, the great observer of the working people of London, said that: 'The more respectable portion of the carpenters and joiners will not allow their wives to do any other work than attend to their domestic and family duties.'[252]

Young Victoria

The crowning of a young woman of 19 years old as queen of England in 1838 triggered an enthusiasm for the monarchy and offered a live model for the idealised elite woman. The doctrine of separate spheres designed to produce modest, delicate, semi-educated, non-productive girls had a prime example in the new queen. She had been raised in near-seclusion, protected by her strict mother from the loose-living royal court of her disreputable uncles. The emphasis upon her sheltered upbringing, her maidenly modesty and her dependence on her first prime minister, William Lamb, Lord Melbourne, emphasised the subservience of all women – even a queen – as suggested by the theory of separate spheres.

Poet Elizabeth Barrett Browning imagined the young queen shedding tears on her coronation – because of her modesty as a girl, her innocence as a virgin and the overwhelming power of her emotions as a woman. Known as the 'rose of England', Victoria was contrasted with her unpopular predecessors – the Hanoverian kings: 'England was sick of the coarse masculine vices of the Kings who went before her, of their greed for public money, of their gross bodies and grosser minds, their absurdities and want of decorum ... The nation delighted to associate the ladylike manner, youthful freshness, and purity with the scepter and robes of state.'[253]

On her marriage to Prince Albert in 1840, Victoria signalled her obedience to her husband as master of the household, her deference to him as an advisor and her role as a domestic woman: a wife and mother, supporting the idea that a happy marriage was created and nourished by

Queen Victoria with a laurel wreath of roses, thistles and leaves, *c*.1841–50

female submission, however important the wife might be. After marriage, Victoria deliberately changed her image from that of a beautiful young woman to dowdy and matronly.[254]

Marriage

The Marriage Act introduced by Lord Hardwicke in 1753 banned all marriages except those conducted in the local church of either the bride or groom, by a Church of England clergyman, after the calling of the banns, except with a special licence. Quakers and Jews might use their own places of worship but no one was allowed to merely promise before witnesses any more. This was designed to prevent kidnap of heiresses, elopement weddings over the Scottish borders, marriages of minors without parental consent and secret marriages in locations like the Fleet Prison.

Such an attack was made on Miss Ellen Turner, a 15-year-old heiress, daughter of the high sheriff of Cheshire, when she was lured from Mrs Daulby's boarding school at Liverpool in February 1827 by barrister Edward Gibbon Wakefield, his brother William and Mrs Frances Wakefield. The fraudsters took her in a chaise and assured her that her father was going to be made bankrupt by the failure of a bank, but that a marriage with William Wakefield would introduce capital and save him from disgrace. Persuaded by this story, Miss Turner went to Gretna Green in Scotland and was married to Wakefield by the blacksmith at his forge – a legal wedding in Scotland. The three tricked Miss Turner onwards to France, now pursued by her uncle and a Bow Street Runner, who caught them at Calais. William Wakefield reassured him: 'You may dispose of your niece as you think proper, but you receive her at my hands as a pure and spotless virgin.'

The brother kidnappers were imprisoned for three years each, but the heiress's father did not proceed against Mrs Frances Wakefield, since he thought her a woman who had been misled by her husband. Miss Turner was released from her marriage vows by a motion of annulment in the House of Lords.[255]

The stricter regulation of weddings protected elite wealthy heiresses; but its wider effect was to further divide working people's lives from elite lives, as working people could not afford an official church marriage and many lived in urban slums without a parish church or any religious ministry. Many working women continued to co-habit, 'marry' and part using folk rituals like the 'wife sale', moving from a previous partner to a new one by staging a public 'sale' to a new man of their choice. Some local Poor Law commissioners even forced husbands to sell their wives, to avoid maintaining the family in workhouses. At least one early nineteenth-century magistrate said he did not believe he had the right to prevent wife sales. The English custom of wife selling spread to Wales, Scotland, Australia and the Americas, before finally dying out in the early years of the twentieth century.

Embarrassed elite observers condemned folk marriages and folk divorces – sales, plighting of troths, and jumping backwards over the broom – as pagan, anarchic and degrading. Some sales may have been the open transfer of a wife as a chattel from one 'owner' to another. Some working women disrupted wife sales in the 1820s and 1830s, suggesting that they felt it to be no longer a 'folk marriage' but a way of men avoiding their domestic responsibility to women that they lived with as husbands and fathers.[256]

Working-class marriages did not mean a wife became dependent on and submissive to her husband, until the nineteenth century when low wages for women made it almost impossible for a woman to survive alone. Popular ballads like 'I'll Be No Submissive Wife' invoked the arguments against slavery and applied them to tyrannical husbands.[257] Violence in working-class marriages was a regular topic, with some songs celebrating wife-beating and others condemning it. No widely popular songs hymned companionate and egalitarian marriages, but the radical Samuel Bamford wrote tender love poems to his wife and children.

> How happy may we be, my love!
> How happy may we be,
> If we our humble means improve,
> My wife, my child, and me.
> Our home shall be a turtle's nest,
> Where duty, peace, and love,
> Shall make its inmates truly blest,
> And sorrow far remove.

And if the world upon us frown,
Still peace serene is ours;
It cannot bear the free mind down,
With all its tyrant powers:
For if they bear me far away,
And bind me with a chain,
Our nestling will beside thee stay –
Then do not, love, complain.[258]

As an active Chartist, handloom weaver and protester at the Peterloo demonstration, Bamford made it clear that the happy marriage depended upon the couple improving their 'humble means' and braving tyranny.

Love became the dominant motive for marriage in the nineteenth century, for both elite and working-class people, and stories about love found, lost and regained offered the main adventure for the popular novels mass-produced for the growing female readership. Middle- and upper-class women learned to conform to the etiquette around virginity: a woman should not even verbally express her feelings until the man had told her that he loved her and proposed marriage. The engagement – the gift of a ring and the announcement of their intention to marry – was now supposed to take less than a year, as longer engagements brought the danger of temptation to pre-marital sex. Working-class women apparently succumbed: a large proportion conceived before their wedding day. Between 20 and 40 per cent of brides were pregnant at the altar of English country parishes in 1800–48.[259]

As work opportunities diminished for elite women, marriage became the only acceptable ambition, and the fiction of union for love sweetened the hard commercial deal. Courtship became an essential skill, the wedding an increasingly significant social ritual, virginity a pre-requisite and de-flowering a debutante moment.[260]

A gown of white – the chosen colour for debutantes at the queen's drawing rooms making their entry into social life – was now the preference for brides making their entry into married life. Queen Victoria wore one, marrying in a court dress of white lace. The hugely popular engraving of her and Prince Albert on their wedding day in 1840 shows him gazing straight at the viewer while directing his bride and her gaze out of the frame. She is half a step behind him, her hand resting in his. He points their direction with an index finger, her lips are slightly parted. Clearly, they are going where he leads; and she is thrilled.

The increasing rituals around the marriage vows – the bride leaving her house, handed over by her father, the change of her name, the wearing of a special dress and the permanent wearing of a ring on a particular finger to signify the ownership of her husband – are exact mirrors of slavery rituals: 'The ritual of enslavement incorporated ... first, the symbolic rejection by the slave of his past and former kinsmen; second, a change of name; third, the imposition of some visible mark of servitude; and last, the assumption of a new status in the household or economic organization of the master.'[261]

Victorian wives entered into a state of legal coercion and control in an elite home that was acknowledged as a protective prison for wives in the court case of Cecilia Anne Cochrane, who had lived apart from her husband for some years but was kidnapped by him in 1840. The judge, Mr Justice Coleridge, would not release Cecilia Anne Cochrane, not even to her own mother, who demanded her daughter under the old habeas corpus law that prevented imprisonment without evidence of wrongdoing. The court supported the husband's right to imprison a wife:

> A husband has custody of his wife and may confine her if he sees fit.
> However, when a wife absents herself from her husband on account
> of no misconduct on his part, and he afterwards, by stratagem
> obtains possession of her person, and she declared her intention of
> leaving him again, whenever she can, he has a right to restrain her of
> her liberty until she is willing to return to a performance of her
> conjugal duty.[262]

A husband had a right to imprison a runaway wife until she agreed to have sex with him and stay with him. The judge went on: 'For the happiness and honour of both parties (the law) places the wife under the guardianship of her husband, and entitles him, for the sake of both, to protect her from the danger of unrestrained intercourse with the world, by enforcing cohabitation and common residence.'[263]

Mr Justice Coleridge ended his ruling with the statement that Cecilia Anne Cochrane's personal happiness was less important than the stability of marriage, proclaiming: 'Let her be restored to Mr Cochrane!'[264]

Even those marriages that were not a nightmare of legal coercion could be tyrannies. A contributor to the *Spectator* pointed out the pleasures of being a husband: 'Nothing is more gratifying to the Mind of Man than Power or Dominion, and this I think my self amply possessed of, as I am the Father of a Family.'[265]

Domestic work was now described to middle- and upper-class brides as an opportunity for self-expression. The Romantic movement that had gilded the inequalities between men and women combined with the enthusiasm of 1800s evangelism to promote domestic work as a chance for a woman to shine as a wife, a mother and a spiritual guide: 'A true wife in her husband's house is his servant; it is in his heart that she is queen.'[266]

The increasing demand for more healthy children to labour in the industries and to support British imperial expansion saw women encouraged to become wives and mothers. The empire needed officers and cannon-fodder, and assaults on marriage came to be seen as both 'unfeminine and unpatriotic'.[267]

Women writers learned to keep any criticism they might have of the state of marriage to their private papers. In 1819, Hester Thrale wrote sarcastically of the pleasures of her marriage – 'Holding my head over a bason six months of the year' – but she did not publish.[268]

Although elite women were supposed to be immune to sexual desire, their sexual activity was recorded and publicised as never before when newspapers and pamphlets started reporting on trials for compensation brought by cuckolded spouses seeking divorce under the 1670 law, designed to replace violent reprisals for a husband's honour by setting a monetary compensation to be paid to him for the damage to his property – his wife.[269] Upper-class adultery compensation cases turned into a bestselling feature, salaciously describing sexual activity and naming the participants in an easily read code of 'Lady M' and 'Sir –', in stories that became known as 'crim cons' from the hearings of 'criminal conversations', meaning adulterous sexual intercourse. The accusations of adultery and the evidence of servants, friends or spies made riveting reading, and the settlements could be astounding: the Duke of Cumberland was ordered to pay Lord Grosvenor £10,000 in 1769. In 1807, Lord Cloncurry brought an action against his former friend Sir John Piers and was awarded damages of £20,000, for adultery.[270] The guilty couple were supposed to have been so absorbed in love-making that they failed to

'Crim. Con. A Sketch taken from Life by Seignoir Gabrielli. Valued by 12 Connoisseurs at Twenty Thousand Pounds!' – the huge damages awarded to Lord Cloncurry on his divorce

notice an Italian artist, Gaspare Gabrielli, up a ladder, painting a fresco on a wall in the same room.

Inevitably, description of the adulteries revealed that aristocratic women were sexually active – seeking and enjoying sex with men and with other women. In an attempt to maintain the purity of the separate sphere home, and the double standard of sexual repression of wives, all divorcees were immediately ostracised, with upper-class social occasions and clubs closed to any woman named in a divorce, or to any woman separated from her husband for almost any reason. Any woman tainted by scandal would be frozen out of elite events and barred from elite establishments. Any upper- or middle-class woman unlucky enough to be caught in any sexual act was shunned or exiled abroad, while adulterous husbands might remain respected members of society, enriched by a deserted wife's fortune, raising their children.

Single Women

When the 1851 census revealed that of the population of 20 million people, 2.5 million women were single, and that women outnumbered men by half a million, it triggered misogynistic outrage.[271] It was the first time single women had been counted, as it was the first time that marital status had been reported, and many commentators were horrified. Single women – many already banned from profitable work and meaningful lives by the need to protect them from the danger of 'unrestrained intercourse with the world', as Mr Justice Coleridge would say[272] – were thought to be unproductive and parasitical. They were increasingly called 'surplus women'.

Victorian political economist W.R. Greg wrote a stand-out pompous essay on the 'surplus woman' problem, proposing that if only ladies were more charming and wives less demanding of husbands, women would find that bachelors were willing to marry them: 'As wives become less expensive and less exigeant, more men will learn to prefer them to mistresses.'[273] Remaining single women should be shipped out to the colonies, where there were proportionately more bachelors, and they were ready to marry anyone.

'We have a million and a half adult unmarried women in Great Britain. Of these half a million are wanted in the colonies, half a million more are usefully, happily, and indispensably occupied in domestic service. The evil thus viewed assumes manageable dimensions, and only a residual half million remain to be practically dealt with.'[274]

Language about single women deteriorated. 'Surplus' women implied that any unmarried woman was valueless, and 'spinster' and 'old maid' became insults. But the increasingly hostile climate and the outburst of commentary on surplus women did not persuade them to take the 10,000 ships that Greg thought were needed to export single women to the colonies; instead it created the first awareness among single women of their numbers, and of themselves as a community.

Sapphism

'Whenever two ladies live too much together ... has a Greek name now, and it's called sapphism.'[275]

So said writer Hester Thrale in one of her fake shock moments about the changing attitudes to sex. Everyone agreed that all bodies were now either male or female, with no gradations, and so women who loved women could not be excused by being almost-men, hermaphrodites, and driven by manly lust. Instead they were fully women and only women, and so were wrong to experience desire, horribly wrong to enact it, and doubly wrong acting with the wrong sex.[276] The self-styled experts agreed that women were wilfully perverse in choosing to love women.[277]

Sexual intimacy between women was not widely known outside sophisticated circles. Hester Thrale, also a patron of the arts, revered sentimental female friendship and was horrified to think that women living together might be sexually active: 'Tis my Scourge to think better both of the World & of all the Individuals in it than they deserve; that House of Miss Rathbone's is now supposed to have been but a Cage of Unclean Birds living in a sinful Celibat. Mercy on us!'[278]

One woman who knew herself to be sexually attracted and sexually active with women thought that she might be all but alone in the world. Wealthy landowner Anne Lister (1791–1840), nicknamed in her home in Yorkshire as 'Gentleman Jack', used her wealth and status to shield and permit her sexual seduction of many women. She recorded her experiences of multiple partners and many sexual incidents in secret, coded diaries. One of her dearest loves was a neighbour, Marianna Belcombe. Lister described a night of lovemaking with Marianna in which they both experienced multiple orgasms. Marianna Belcombe was obliged by her family, and her own desire to conform to conventions, to marry a wealthy man. After her marriage she could meet Anne only under the pretence of friendly visits, when they co-slept as apparently non-sexual friends. They both contracted a sexually transmitted disease – probably from Marianna's husband.

Anne travelled Europe, exploring her love of women, often assertively even aggressively sexual with more than one hesitant lover, before abandoning them and moving on. She had read of women lovers in classical literature and was curious to hear of a woman in her neighbourhood who was said to be sexually attracted to other women: 'She was the character I had long wished to meet with to clear up my doubts whether such a one really existed nowadays ... are there more Miss Pickfords in the world than I have ever before thought of?'[279]

Anne Lister also visited a famous female couple, the 'Ladies of Llangollen', and described her experience in a letter to Marianna Belcombe, who asked if the Ladies of Llangollen were sexually active: 'Tell me if you think their regard has always been platonic & if you ever believed pure friendship could be so exalted ... I cannot help thinking that surely it was not platonic. Heaven forgive me, but I look within myself & doubt. I feel the infirmity of our nature & hesitate to pronounce such attachments uncemented by something more tender still than friendship.'[280]

In later life, Anne Lister fell in love with a wealthy heiress, Anne Walker. The two went through a private ceremony in church when they took communion together, which they regarded as a binding marriage ceremony, and lived together until Anne Lister's death.

Sexual activity between women, which had previously been ignored, glossed over or referred to only in discreet private letters, started to be discussed more widely, and gossip and accusations published. Women lovers of women were called 'tommies' in slang, but the classically educated spoke of 'sapphists' – from the Greek poet Sappho who wrote of her love for women.[281]

One elite woman publicly reviled as a sapphist was Anne Seymour Damer (1749–1828), an English artist and novelist with connections to the aristocracy of England and Europe. Widowed by the suicide of her husband, and heiress to Horace Walpole, Anne Damer combined financial independence with artistic genius working as a sculptor. She wore male-style jackets and shirts with skirts and was lampooned in a published poem, which named her as a sapphist and first published the word 'tommy' as slang for a female lover of women. The mock epitaph in 1780 said she was 'liable to foibles which rigid virtue censures'.[282]

She was again publicly accused of lesbianism in a pamphlet, *The Whig Club*, in 1794, blamed for seducing actress Elizabeth Farren: 'Superior to the influence of MEN she is supposed to feel more exquisite delight from the touch of the cheek of Mrs D ... r than from the fancy of any novelties which the wedding night can promise.'[283]

As a wealthy widow, Damer could afford to work at her sculpture, book collecting, acting and writing. She moved in the elite circles of

Europe and was close friends with Georgiana, Duchess of Devonshire, and Georgiana's friend and her husband's mistress, Lady Elizabeth Foster. Damer knew Sarah Siddons, and her name was linked with the actress Elizabeth Ashe, the writer Mary Berry and Emma Hamilton, the well-known mistress of Admiral Nelson. The English disapproval of Mrs Damer's conduct came at a time when lesbianism was identified with foreign influences and with bohemian and artistic behaviour. Marie Antoinette, Queen of France, was named for 'sapphic orgies',[284] the slur combining – in one inclusive accusation – anti-Gallicism, anti-women and anti-monarchy.

The storm of negative publicity that followed Anne Damer and those other women suspected of 'sapphism' meant that by the end of the eighteenth century even the most sheltered elite women were aware of the potential physical and erotic component to passionate female friendships. But they could choose to ignore it.[285]

Since sexual intercourse was firmly defined as penile penetration of even the most unenthusiastic woman, the sensual intimacy of women alone together was not sexual intercourse. Without a man with a penis, sexual intercourse could not exist. This was of enormous advantage to women lovers who escaped observation, their mutual desire hidden by the belief that women had no sexual desire and that whatever they did together, it could not be 'sexual intercourse'. This mystification hid women lovers for centuries and kept lesbianism from being criminalised in the law books, as some lawmakers thought it was simply not possible, while others preferred to be ignorant.

Female friends and lovers could move in the highest social circles without slander as long as they defined their friendship as sentimental, highly emotional and even passionate, and concealed any sexual intimacy. Some women couples lived together for years in the tradition of 'sentimental friendship' and indeed many may never have been sexual. Edith Simcox, the writer and reform leader, expressed a passionate life-long adoration of Mary Ann Evans (George Eliot, the author), which was reciprocated only with friendship. Geraldine Jewsbury wrote as a lover to the wife of Thomas Carlyle, Jane Welsh Carlyle: 'Oh Carissimia, you are never out of either my head or my heart. After you left on Tuesday, I felt so horribly wretched, too miserable even to cry – and what could be done?'[286] The women were loving friends until Jane's death in 1866.

The 'Ladies of Llangollen' was the name given to Eleanor Butler (*c.*1738–1829) and Sarah Ponsonby (*c.*1755–1831). The women met when Eleanor was 29 and Sarah only 13, becoming inseparable friends. At the age of 23, Sarah escaped a proposal of marriage and ran away with the 39-year-old Eleanor to live in a house in Llangollen, Wales, and pursue a life of retired friendship, culture and gardening. They became known as the 'Ladies of Llangollen' – an eccentric couple who dressed in masculine jackets over long skirted riding habits. They considered suing a newspaper for libel after it implied that Eleanor took a masculine role and Sarah was more feminine, but their friend, philosopher Edmund Burke, recommended that they ignore the slander: 'Your consolation must be that you suffer only by the baseness of the age you live in, that you suffer from the violence of calumny for the virtues that entitle you to the esteem of all who know how to esteem honour, friendship, principle, and dignity of thinking, and that you suffer along with everything that is excellent in the world.'[287]

Burke reminded the ladies that their elite status alone should defend them from accusations by the vulgar. They could choose to define their relationship as 'sentimental' and no one could contradict them. But if they sued the journalist for libel, they would have to give evidence in court to prove that his implication – that one was taking the male part and the other the female – was untrue. By ignoring the slander, they avoided a court appearance and continued to claim the high ground of a 'pure' example of sentimental friendship. Sarah Ponsonby's tombstone in Llangollen churchyard describes Lady Eleanor Butler as her 'beloved companion'.

They were not the only women accused of having sex with women to publicly deny the accusation and cite elite status as proof that sexual intimacy did not take place. Eliza Frances Robertson, a schoolteacher in Greenwich in 1795, was accused of fraud, cross-dressing, posing as a man and having sexual relations with her friend and colleague at the school. Robertson's defence, written and published from Huntingdon jail, deliberately used high-flown and religious language – she wrote as a middle-class woman who might be expected to be sexually frigid: 'The Cavillers at the motives of attachment between my friend Miss Sharp and self, seem to enter very little into feelings described in holy writ such as the friendship of Naomi and Ruth ... Our Saviour not only approved of an attachment between persons of the same sex, but has himself consecrated friendship by divine example.'[288]

Another pair of school teachers, Marianne Woods (1781–1870) and Jane Pirie (1779–1833), were ruined after making the mistake avoided by the Ladies of Llangollen. They brought a libel trial against a pupil's guardian, who had accused them of being lovers. While the Ladies of Llangollen, with independent means, could afford to ignore comments, the middle-class schoolteachers could only earn a living if their reputation was without the stain of sexuality. Lady Helen Cumming Gordon told other parents and guardians that the two 20-year-old schoolteachers called each other 'darling', shared a bedroom and a bed in the boarding school they owned in Edinburgh, and had been heard kissing, caressing and panting. The two young women sued for libel and won their case at appeal in the House of Lords, on the basis that since sexual intercourse meant only penile penetration of a vagina, and since only penile penetration of the vagina could cause female orgasm, whatever they were doing was not sex. Their lawyer told the court: 'Their private parts were not so framed as to penetrate each other, and without penetration the venereal orgasm could not possibly follow.'[289]

However, most of their £10,000 award went on legal fees and they parted: Marianne to return to her previous employer in London and Jane Pirie to stay in Edinburgh, probably excluded from educational work and deeply depressed.

Georgiana, Duchess of Devonshire, endured a triangular relationship with her disagreeable husband, William Cavendish, 5th Duke of Devonshire, and his mistress, her friend Lady Elizabeth 'Bess' Foster, for years. Her sexual adulteries with men were widely publicised and the two women also had a deep attachment and perhaps a sexual connection: 'My dear Bess,' Georgiana wrote, 'Do you hear the voice of my heart crying to you? Do you feel what it is for me to be separated from you?'[290]

Women Representing Themselves as Men

Increasing emphasis on ladylike modesty – even on the stage – turned the fashion against cross-dressing actresses and the 'breeches' parts. Benjamin Victor, a commentator on London theatre, expressed the turning of the tide in the middle of the nineteenth century: 'And now, ye fair ones of the Stage, it will not be foreign to the Subject to consider whether it is proper for you … to perform the characters of men. I will venture in the

Name of all sober, discreet, sensible spectators to answer *No!* there is something required so much beyond the Delicacy of your sex to arrive at the Point of Perfection, that if you hit it, you may be condemned as a Woman, and if you do not, you are injured as an Actress.'[291]

Some women dressed as men for safety in a misogynist world. Some dressed as men to accompany their husbands – sometimes into military service. Christian Davies, Mary Knowles and Mary Talbot became popular heroines in the eighteenth century, like Hannah Snell, disguising as men to follow their husbands.

'Le Petit Matelot' – the little sailor boy – provided the code name for an English woman spy acting as a courier for the British government in a spy ring in Paris in 1795. The widow of a British soldier, Arabella Williams disguised herself as a cabin boy to carry money and messages for two years or more until May 1801, when the French authorities arrested her.[292]

The *Newgate Calendar* called Sarah Penelope Stanley 'The Female Trooper' when she was accused of petty larceny in 1796. She had been born the daughter of a land steward and apprenticed to a milliner at Lichfield. After deserting her husband, a poor shoemaker, to go to London, she dressed as a man, taking work as a clerk, and was eventually recruited to the Ayrshire Fencible Cavalry, a regiment of light horse. Stanley served for a year before being promoted to corporal, and ultimately revealed to be a woman. The commander of her troop arranged for her honourable discharge and befriended her, as did other officers and some of the people of Carlisle. Returning to London, she fell on hard times and stole a cloak – she told the court it was her first offence and she intended to repay and dress as a woman in future. The court clearly sympathised with her: two under-sheriffs and the keeper gave her money on her release.[293]

Anne Jane Thornton, a 15-year-old girl, dressed as a cabin boy on a transatlantic voyage to find the man she loved, who had gone to America in 1832. On arrival, she found he had died so she took posts on other ships, calling herself Jim Thornton. On her return crossing to London on *The Sarah*, a crew member noticed that she was a woman and she was taken to the ship's captain, who kept her on as a crewman.

He said, 'She would run up the top gallant-sail in any sort of weather and we had a severe passage. Poor girl, she had a hard time of it, she suffered greatly from the wet but she bore it all excellently and was a

Sailor Anne Thornton's (1817–77) identity was discovered after she refused to have sex with a crewman who had glimpsed her naked

capital seaman.'[294] Anne Thornton wrote her own biography, *The Interesting Life and Wonderful Adventures of that Extraordinary Woman Anne Jane Thornton, the Female Sailor*, and received a grant from the king, a donation from the citizens of London and the tenancy of a farm in Ireland. Though greeted by an admiring crowd, she would later be assaulted by her male neighbours, who demanded that she marry. She wedded the male friend who rescued her from them in 1836.

Women prizefighters continued to train and fight for substantial 'purses' in public, but criticism of them in newspapers and journals derided either femininity – that made them poor boxers – or lack of it, when they stripped to the waist to box. One witness at a court case against disorderly women fighters said – disparagingly – it was not possible to tell if they were men or women.[295]

Other women found themselves prosecuted for dressing as men: Mary Jones was arrested for wearing men's clothes and making a disturbance in Tummil Street, London, while Ann Lewis was detained for dressing as a sailor – both of these women may have been charged with rowdy public behaviour, a worse offence than discreetly cross-dressing.[296]

While visiting Newgate jail to set up a school for the children of women prisoners, the Quaker Elizabeth Fry witnessed scenes 'too bad to be described', including 'begging, swearing, gaming, fighting, singing, dancing, dressing up in men's clothes'.[297]

Some women's fashion earned condemnation for nothing more than a nod to male style. The arrival of the 'masculine' jacket on women's riding habits upset commentators John Gay and Joseph Addison, who said it was blending the sexes, which should be kept completely separate.[298]

Female Husbands

A woman who passed as a man to live with another woman, or even with a succession of women, found herself called a 'female husband', which became a popular and widespread term. Some female husbands were part of a sexually intimate pair of women finding acceptance in society with one partner passing as a man; some were women who had adopted a temporary male identity to seduce a woman; some may have felt they should not have been born as women; and some were going in disguise. In the magazines and newspapers of the eighteenth century, reports of female husbands proliferated.

In June 1773, a young woman was reported to have dressed as a man and married a wealthy older woman: 'The design was to get possession of the money and then to make off, but the old lady proved too knowing.'[299] In July 1777, the *Gentlemen's Magazine* reported on 'a woman sentenced to six months in gaol for going in Man's clothes and being married to three different women by a fictitious name and for defrauding them of money and effects. Jane Marrow was sentenced to sit in pillory. The rubbish thrown at her during her time in the stocks, left her blind.'[300]

Elite women continued to use the privilege of class and the assumption of frigidity to live together, and even describe themselves as married, without suspicion. Elizabeth Barrett Browning recorded this exchange with Mrs Cochrane, about Matilda Hays (my great-great-great-great aunt!) and Charlotte Cushman, an actress who had, according to Browning, an 'unimpeachable' character:

I understand that she and Miss Hayes have made vows of celibacy and of eternal attachment to each other – they live together, dress alike … it is a female marriage. I happened to say: well I never heard of such a thing before! Haven't you? said Mrs Cockrane. Oh, it is by no means uncommon.

They are on their way to Rome so I dare say we shall see a good deal of them. Though an actress Miss Cushman has an unimpeachable character.[301]

Elizabeth Hughes Steele, a so-called 'masculine'-looking woman, was friend and manager to the hugely successful actress Sophia Snow Baddeley (1745–86), who was appearing in Shakespeare roles at Drury Lane Theatres in the mid-eighteenth century. Baddeley financed a famously extravagant lifestyle with wealthy lovers, which Elizabeth Hughes Steele managed when at home in London, dressing as a man and passing as a husband when they were travelling. On one occasion she challenged a man who had insulted Sophia Baddeley to a duel, and took his pistol off him. She was said to be 'fitter to be a man than a woman'.[302]

In 1766, the *Gentleman's Magazine* reported that Mary East (*c.*1739–80), who had been 'disappointed in love' at 16 years old, had chosen to live with her best friend, also 'disappointed in love', as husband and wife.[303] East called herself James How, and together the couple ran a number of public houses, finally settling in the White Horse, in Poplar, London. Although generally accepted as husband and wife, the couple were blackmailed by a man who had known Mary East before she became James How. They paid for his silence until the death of Mrs How in 1765, when James How refused to make another payment and was attacked by the blackmailer. How took the extortionist to court and assumed his previous identity as Mary East to win the case, seeing the crook pilloried and sentenced to four years' imprisonment. Mary retired from work and from her male identity but stayed in Poplar as a respected member of the community until her death in 1780, when she was buried at St Matthias Old Church.

The writer born as Mary Diana Dods (1790–1830) took the pen name David Lyndsay while living with her widowed sister. Later, in a partnership with a woman, Isabella Robinson, Mary Diana Dods adopted a male identity and the name of Walter Sholto Douglas. The two passed as husband and wife and Walter Douglas claimed to be Isabella's legal husband and the father of her daughter. The author Mary Shelley helped the couple to obtain passports as husband and wife, and they left England to live together in France.[304]

Everything we know of Sarah Geals (1824–?) was recorded at her trial for accidentally shooting her employer, James Giles, a shoemaker. Giles told the court that Sarah Geals had changed her sex and become William Smith after 'a disappointment', living with a lover, Caroline, as husband and wife for 17 or 18 years in a small house and working for Giles as a clicker or leather-cutter.

Giles said in evidence: 'I paid her regular wages, the same as the men working in the same capacity – I had no idea that she was not a man – I believe she held herself out as a married man, but I do not know that I pointedly put the question.'[305]

Giles employed William Smith's wife Caroline to care for his sick wife, and when his wife died Caroline continued work as his house-keeper. Some months later, she told him that her husband William was, in fact, a woman named Sarah, and the shoemaker invited her to leave their home and marry him. They persuaded William Smith to accept this separation and take on women's clothing – becoming Sarah and accept-ing a rented shop at Bow by way of compensation. When the shop failed to make a profit, the newly married Giles couple rented an apartment for Sarah. But they had a quarrel – Sarah objected to how James Giles treated Caroline, the wife he had taken from her, and decided to leave England altogether. She wrote to James:

38, Grafton-street, June 12,-65. –
Sir, – I have been thinking of our quarrel, but you were the cause, and not Caroline. I know she would come and see me often, but you keep her away, and she is very submissive, and you do not care how hard she slaves, like some poor drudge of a servant. If you loved her you would not allow it, in her declining state of health. Since you have had her you have broke her spirit. If the dinner is not ready to a minute, look at the agitated state she is in, frightened almost to death. As I told you last Sunday, I am the woman for spirit, and you held my arms till they were black and blue the other day. Sir, I am still inclined to come to terms, to save any more bother or further trouble, as you know what I mean – the affair between you and me

that has taken place at Bow. The best thing you can do is to supply me with a few pounds, and I will go to New Zealand, and then you will be rid of those you have acted so wrong to. I must have an answer to this. Tell Caroline to bring or send me a few shillings. I will pay her again. This is not her fault, but yours, sir. Remember. P. S. – Sir, I want the answer."[306]

When James Giles did not reply, Sarah Geals took a loaded pistol to the workshop. There was an accident and it misfired, and she gave herself up for arrest. Sarah Geals was not prosecuted for passing as a man nor for being a female husband, and there was no inquiry as to the female husband and wife sexual activity. She was accused only of attempting to murder James Giles, and the misfiring of the pistol meant that her sentence was five years' penal servitude.[307]

Lia de Beaumont, Mademoiselle d'Éon, a French-born aristocrat, became the subject of a huge wager in London in 1776, printed in the *Westminster Gazette*:

This gentleman declares the d'Eon (alias the Chevalier d'Eon) a WOMAN in the clearest sense of the word; this declaration he supports with a bet of any such sum of money from one to five thousand guineas, or he proposes to any one, who will deposit five thousand guineas in the hand of his banker, to pay £10,000 if d'Eon proves herself either a MAN and HERMAPHRODITE or any other animal other than a WOMAN.[308]

Charles Geneviève Louis Auguste André Timothée d'Éon de Beaumont (1728–1810) had been declared a boy at birth in order to inherit the male-line title. Raised as a boy, he became a French lawyer and intellectual, disguised himself as a woman to spy on Russia, but then reverted to male appearance to serve as a French diplomat, a captain of Dragoons and the leader of the French peace delegation to London. He was awarded with a royal and military order and the title 'Chevalier', and ordered by the French to spy on England and prepare for a French invasion.

The Chevalier d'Éon dressed as a woman for the spying mission, and moved in London society as Lia de Beaumont. After doubts were raised about her sex, a betting pool started on the London Stock Exchange, offering odds of 3:2 that the Chevalier was a woman.[309] Lia may have planted the rumours herself, to prompt her return to France as a patriotic heroine, or she may have been getting a commission on the bets.[310]

The death of Louis XV closed the spy network and the new king, Louis XVI, paid for secret papers and a trousseau of women's clothes for Lia de Beaumont to wear on her return to France. She entered elite French society dressed as a woman. A contemporary described her in the terms of the time: 'He was made to resume the costume of that sex to which in France everything is pardoned. The desire to see his native land once more determined him to submit to the condition, but he revenged himself by combining the long train of his gown and the three deep ruffles on his sleeves with the attitude and conversation of a grenadier, which made him very disagreeable company.'[311]

In August 1777, Lia de Beaumont chose a male identity and wore a grenadier's uniform to volunteer for military service in the American War of Independence, but was prevented from joining the conflict, refused permission to return to London and ordered to continue to wear women's clothes. She went back to London eventually, but after the execution of some of the d'Éon family during the French Revolution, the family income dried up. She paired up with an actress, Mrs Bateman, to give fencing displays and the two performed a fencing duel at the Haymarket Theatre in 1793.[312] She petitioned the French National Assembly to lead a division of female soldiers against the Habsburgs.

Lia de Beaumont died at her home in London aged 81 and a medical examination revealed 'male genitals in every respect perfectly formed, breasts remarkably full, and unusual roundness in the formation of limbs'.

Part 7

1857–1928
Separate Spheres

Protest

In 1854, a young single woman, aged 27, with no legal training or previous publications to her name, wrote and published a pamphlet on English laws that applied to all women – not just the rich and well-born. Barbara Leigh Smith (1827–91) was not thinking only of her own rights. One of the progressive feminist thinkers who were called the 'Ladies of Langham Place' – an informal think tank on women's rights[1] – she set up the *English Women's Journal*, to look at the conditions of all women of all classes. She campaigned against slavery, for women's suffrage and contributed to the founding of Girton College, Cambridge, in 1869.

Barbara Leigh Smith, unlike other thinkers of her time, considered women as a group – as a sex, not divided by class, wealth, status, colour or religion. This was a historic moment – a turning point in the history of women who had previously seen themselves through their relationship to a man, or in their class position – whether a 'lady' or not. Now a few individuals considered women as an identifiable group with shared needs. This new attitude inspired some of the campaigns at the turn of the nineteenth century and its absence explained the failure of others.

Unity was hard to achieve for women. Some working-class women did not welcome elite women advising or campaigning for them. Some elite women regarded the poor as almost a different species; racism divided women, and marital status divided wives, widows and spinsters.

Barbara Leigh Smith's own class position was ambiguous. She was the illegitimate child of a radical elite man, Ben Leigh Smith, and a milliner, Anne Longden. According to his beliefs, all the children had been educated at the local school alongside working-class children. The parents lived together openly, but never married. Barbara Leigh Smith's pamphlet *A Brief Summary in Plain Language of the Most Important Laws Concerning Women Together with a Few Observations Thereon* demanded a change in the law for all women. She wrote: 'A man and wife are one person in law; the wife loses all her rights as a single woman and her existence is, as if entirely absorbed in that of her husband. He is civilly responsible for her wrongful acts ... and she lives under his protection and cover.'[2]

Her summary was deliberately provocative: 'A woman's body belongs to her husband she is in his custody: and he can enforce his right by a writ of habeas corpus.'[3]

Barbara Leigh Smith (1827–91): feminist law reformer

Palaeontologist Mary Anning (1799–1847) was known around the world for her Jurassic discoveries in the fossil beds at Lyme Regis. Her findings changed scientific thinking about prehistoric life yet she was not eligible to join the Geological Society of London. In her lifetime, her extraordinary finds were rarely published or credited to her, and she was paid little money for them. This portrait of Mary and her dog Tray, by Benjamin Donne, a neighbour, is a copy of an 1842 painting.

This portrait of the Ladies of Llangollen goes some way to repeat the slander against them: that they were an 'odd' couple, dressed in masculine clothing and mimicked husband and wife. James Henry Lynch copied Mary Parker's secret drawing of the faces of these inseparable friends, Eleanor Butler (c.1738–1829) and Sarah Ponsonby (c.1755–1831), without permission and added the manly jackets, men's top hats and their well-known garden scene, and mass-produced the image.

Augusta Ada King, Countess Lovelace (1815–52), a skilled mathematician, was the daughter of Lord Byron and a friend and colleague of Charles Babbage: 'the father of computers'. In 1843, she published a translation from Italian of a 'sketch' of Babbage's analytical engine with her own notes. It suggested the 'engine' could do more than calculation; she described an operations sequence, the first computer program.

Fanny Eaton (1835–1924) was the daughter of a slave, born just after the abolition of slavery and brought to England by her mother. Fanny had two children and worked as a domestic servant and as an artist's model at the Royal Academy of Arts. Simeon Solomon featured Eaton in his painting, The Mother of Moses, and she was a favourite subject for the Pre-Raphaelite artists. This chalk drawing is by Walter Fryer Stocks c.1859.

Dame Millicent Fawcett (1847–1929) is portrayed in this intimate painting by Ford Madox Brown (*c.*1872), dedicating her life to her blind, much older husband, Henry Fawcett. She was also a leading light of women's causes: uniting 17 suffrage societies to found the National Union of Women's Suffrage Societies, helping found Newnham College Cambridge for women, supporting the abolition of the slave trade and supporting women and children endangered during the Boer War in South Africa. She lived long enough to see all women get the vote.

'Can you cook dinner?' shouted a heckler. 'Yes! Can you drive a coach and four?' replied Constance Markievicz (1868–1927) on her campaign for women's votes driving her carriage with four matched grey horses. The daughter of an Arctic explorer in an Anglo-Irish family, she fought against the British occupation of Ireland and was sentenced to death, though released in 1917 under a general amnesty. Arrested again the following year for protesting conscription in the First World War, she stood for Sinn Féin and took 66 per cent of the vote from prison, and refused to take her seat – though she was in any case, still imprisoned.

Maud Allan (1873–1956), an internationally acclaimed musician, actor and dancer known for her seductive performances, lost one of the most sensational libel trials of the 20th century against a right-wing MP who accused her of being a lesbian and a spy. The judge remarked that the costume Maud wore for her performance, was 'in fact …worse than nothing'.

Leigh Smith did not exaggerate. Not even habeas corpus – the law enshrined in English life from the twelfth century to prevent anyone being imprisoned unlawfully – could rescue women confined by their husbands.[4] As M.S. of Bedford Street, London, wrote to the *Daily Telegraph* on 21 August 1888: 'Married when only a girl, after a few years, I am practically a widow, having been obliged, from my husband's brutality, to seek a separation. This was not until, through his brutality, I lost an eye, principally owing to the very merciful law which compelled me to live with a man until I was maimed for life.'[5]

Another powerful voice for a change in the laws on marriage was that of Caroline Norton, an aristocratic author who left her drunken and unfaithful husband George in 1836 intending to live on her earnings as a writer. George successfully claimed her earnings, kidnapped their sons and accused Caroline of an adulterous affair with her friend Lord Melbourne, the prime minister. Melbourne successfully defended himself against a charge of adultery and won his case; but Caroline Norton's reputation was destroyed. George refused to divorce her and kept their three sons from her. He summoned her (too late) to their younger son's deathbed, after his fatal accident. She wrote to Parliament supporting a change in the law: 'What I suffered respecting those children, God knows … under the evil law which suffered any man, for vengeance or for interest, to take baby children from the mother.'[6]

A wife, whether divorcing an adulterous and abusive husband, or deserted by him, automatically lost her children, whatever the reasons for the break-up. All husbands took custody of all children of any age, and a divorcee might never see her children again.[7]

All divorces had to go first before the ecclesiastical court and then through a civil court to compensate a husband for the loss of his adulterous wife, and finally through a private act of Parliament in the House of Lords. This cost an astronomical fee – from £200 to £5,000[8] – at a time when a labourer's weekly wage was 9s 3d.[9] It put divorce beyond the reach of anyone but the very wealthy. In reality, only wealthy men could divorce. In two centuries the House of Lords granted 321 divorces to men, and four to women, and two of those were annulments of bigamous marriages. The only two divorces for women were for those whose husbands were adulterous with their own sisters.[10]

The Matrimonial Causes Act of 1857 improved the lives of wives, allowing them to keep their earnings from a deserting husband and to apply for maintenance for the children of the dissolved marriage. In addition – as long as they were not the offending partner – they might be allowed to keep their children, and wives might regain the money they brought to the marriage. In 1870, the Married Women's Property Act allowed all married women, as well as estranged wives, to keep their own income or inheritance. Anna Grenville, first Duchess of Buckingham and Chandos, wrote plaintively to her husband, who had wasted his own fortune and was hoping to work through hers: 'If I had not brought you one penny being your Wife I should have had a right to your confidence but … surely I have an additional & powerful right to be consulted, so large a portion of the property being mine.'[11]

Parliamentary opponents feared the acts would 'create a factitious, an artificial and an unnatural equality between man and woman'. They were completely right. Now that women did not lose everything – children, home, wealth – on divorce, there was more equality in marriage.

The new court for divorce received a flood of petitions: 253 in the first year, 580 in 1911, and demand grew so rapidly that appeals for maintenance from abused or deserted wives had to be transferred to local magistrates – to the tune of 11,000 a year.[12] The changes in the law for married women saved Emily Hall, who had married Edmund Jackson in 1887 but left him a few days after the ceremony. He won a court order that she should return to him (and have sex with him) but she defied him and the court. Edmund kidnapped Emily in 1891 and held her against her will. Her sisters sued for a writ of habeas corpus and the case went before three senior judges.[13] Court ushers brought in chairs for the three wives of the judges, who took their seats to observe their husbands hand down the judgment on whether it was legal for a runaway wife to be kidnapped and held by a violently abusive husband.[14] The judges, under the steely gaze of their wives, decided that it was not, and Emily Hall was released to her family.

The judgment proved unpopular, with crowds demonstrating outside her home, singing 'For he's a jolly good fellow' in praise of a man who had kidnapped his wife from her family in broad daylight. Although Emily was not forced to live with her husband, he would not release her from her marriage and she died as his wife – he even tried, unsuccessfully, to attend her deathbed.[15]

No longer did women authors avoid criticism of marriage. Mona Caird wrote in the *Westminster Review* of 1888 that the institution itself was a failure, forcing women to become the property of their husbands, repressing their minds and spirituality. She called for education for girls so that they might be morally and financially independent of husbands, and for greater liberalisation of divorce so that unhappy wives could lead independent lives.[16]

Victorian wives replied to her in 27,000 letters, such as this one from a merchant's wife in Worthing: 'I myself am a deserted wife and my husband has treated me with exceptional contempt and unkindness, but I am proud to say that so great is my reverence for the sanctity of the marriage vow, that if my husband sent for me to return to him tomorrow; I would go, and with a hearty will and friendly affection, strive to do my duty to him.'[17]

Women had absorbed the lessons of teachers, preachers and conduct books that they were born inferior to men and that a woman's true happiness must lie in the home, in a subservient role. Once established, this belief would prove long-lasting.

But some women rebelled.

Edith 'Biddy' Lanchester (1871–1966), the daughter of a Hove architect, studied higher maths at London Polytechnic and Botany and Zoology at Birkbeck Library and Scientific Institute. She became a schoolteacher and worked as a secretary for Eleanor Marx, daughter of Karl, and spoke at meetings and rallies.

In 1895, at the age of 24, she fell in love with a factory worker, James Sullivan, and since she was opposed to the bridal vow of obedience, they decided to live together without marriage. The night before they moved into their home, her father, brothers and a so-called expert, Dr George Fielding Blandford, interviewed Edith Lanchester and agreed that she was insane. The doctor explained his diagnosis: 'If she had said that she contemplated suicide a certificate might have been signed without question ... I was equally justified in signing one when she expressed her determination to commit this social suicide.'[18]

The doctor issued the certificate giving the cause of her mental illness as 'over-education'. She was handcuffed by her father, and taken, protesting, to an asylum where she was bullied, coerced and assaulted. Her case caused a scandal. Fellow members of the Socialist Democratic Federation sang the revolutionary anthem 'The Red Flag' under her barred hospital window, and after four days she was released, when the commissioners diagnosed her as 'sane; but foolish'.[19] Edith Lanchester went on to have two children with James Sullivan and supported radical causes all her life.

Biddy Lanchester, a soldier of liberty. She had 'not been a mere dummy in the hands of the Power; a satellite borrowing light entirely … she has shone'

The Matrimonial Causes Act of 1923 ended the double sexual stand-ard in the law whereby a wife's adultery was cause for divorce but the husband's was not. From that year, adultery by either partner in a marriage was grounds for the marriage to be ended. The proportion of petitions filed by wives rose from 41 per cent in 1921 to 62 per cent.[20]

Ironically, by making it possible for wives to divorce husbands guilty only of adultery, the many abused and raped wives no longer reported the violence against them in order to obtain a divorce. Marital violence slipped from the records.[21]

Some educated women, such as Barbara Leigh Smith, prompted reforms that benefited all women and saw themselves as 'feminists' – interested in the progress of all women of every class. But many middle- and upper-class women campaigned for poor women as a form of benevolent patronage. As the Women's Co-operative Guild explained,

'Many organisations at this time were run by middle class women doing things "to" working women.' In contrast, the Women's Co-operative Guild, founded in 1883, encouraged working-class women into co-operatives to work together on the issues that mattered to them.[22]

Protest against the poverty and ill health of working people spread when doctors discovered 'germ theory' and understood that infections generated in the slums were being transmitted to upper- and middle-class homes. The government passed the first public health laws in the 1840s. An epidemic of cholera in 1854 – which would kill more than 10,000 people throughout the country – was blamed in Soho, London, on the quality of the drinking water. Dr John Snow showed that the water – contaminated with cholera germs from pollution, overflowing cesspits and open drains – was piped to free street pumps and into the houses of the rich. Disease had no respect for class. In 1858, the 'great stink' of the River Thames made all of London unbearable for everyone, from the slums to the Houses of Parliament. Michael Faraday, the scientist, wrote to *The Times*: 'The smell was very bad, and common to the whole of the water; it was the same as that which now comes up from the gully-holes in the streets; the whole river was for the time a real sewer.'[23]

Fear of the epidemic diseases of the nineteenth century – smallpox, typhus, cholera, yellow fever, scarlet fever and TB, or 'consumption' – increased, thanks to a lack of certainty as to how diseases were transmitted, and by the lack of a cure. Campaigns to prevent disease were directed against poor housing, poor hygiene and poor people, something all women could support and that would benefit all women. Health campaigns took on a moralising overtone and to the Methodist founder John Wesley, there was little distinction to be made between 'dirt' and 'sin':[24] 'Together with the more important lessons, which you endeavour to teach all the poor whom you visit, it would be a deed of charity to teach them two things more, which they are generally little acquainted with: Industry and Cleanliness.'[25]

The middle classes took the lesson to heart and believed the cleanliness and order of their houses, and the elegant leisure of their women, distinguished them from their poorer neighbours. Spirituality became respectability and the spiritual passion of the Romantic revolution ended in an outward show in the service of snobbery. Historian Barbara Ehrenreich calls this 'An organized political offensive against poor and working people ... – not as sisters, but *uplifters*.'[26]

The campaigning ladies continued to organise themselves into teams to visit entire wards and enter every working-class home. The visitor met either a wife whose husband earned enough money to keep her at home, a woman working at home in sweatshop conditions, or a woman disabled because of pregnancy, injury, incapacity, disease, mental illness or alcoholism. It was a shocking experience for women who had been shielded from reality.

The visitors offered advice on housekeeping, encouraged churchgoing, and Sunday schools for children, promoted healthy living – and especially abstinence from alcohol: all the churches offered temperance clubs.[27] The hope of the visitors was that their presence alone would transform working-class homes. The National Society for the Prevention of Cruelty to Children said in its report for 1902 that the example of elite women was all that was needed: the ladies' 'example of refinement and delicacy of manner, speech and habits unconsciously set before them a higher ideal of living than they have been accustomed to'.[28]

A few middle-class women who had approached the poor as patrons gained such expertise through their voluntary work that they were offered official posts as government inspectors, visitors and wardens. As the work had grown from separate sphere philanthropy, they felt able to take professional posts without loss of gentility. By 1900, an estimated half a million women were working as unpaid volunteer campaigners or as professional and semi-professional philanthropists.[29] A few were appointed to the Boards of Trade from 1909, to advise on a minimum wage in industries that were known to be 'sweated': chainmaking, ready made tailoring, paper box making, machine lacemaking and finishing trades – work typically done by women. One of them was Beatrice Webb (1858–1943), who wrote a minority government report against linking pay to a person's sex: the pay should be for the job and not for the sex of the worker; but majority advice was that a fair breadwinner wage should be twice the pay needed by a single woman.[30]

The problem of sexually transmitted disease inspired the breakthrough campaign that brought ladies out of the separate sphere of their protected homes into partnership with the poorest of working-class women – prostitutes. It became clear that the home could not be isolated from the world, and that freedom for male sexuality came at a cost to both his wife and his prostitute. In the early nineteenth century, it had been assumed that chaste and monogamous women were safe from disease, inside the separate sphere of their exclusive home. Syphilis, the worst of the sexual diseases, was thought to generate spontaneously inside the bodies of promiscuous women and was then given to men. Doctor William Acton (1813–75) said a prostitute was 'a mere instrument of impurity ... a social pest, carrying contamination and foulness to every quarter to which she has access'.[31]

The Contagious Diseases Act passed in 1864 forced prostitutes in naval ports and garrison towns to report to police stations for regular inspection for diseases. Any woman could be arrested on suspicion of prostitution and forcibly physically examined by a (male) army surgeon. One woman described the experience of being examined by a speculum: 'Often they use several. They seem to tear the passage open first with their hands, and examine us, and then they thrust in instruments, and they pull them out and push them in, and they turn and twist them about.'[32]

Arrest, examination and treatment were made deliberately painful and humiliating as a deterrent to the women. Campaigner Josephine Butler called it 'surgical rape'. As a Kent woman accused of prostitution said: 'It is men, only men, from the first to the last that we have to do with! To please a man I did wrong at first, then I was flung about from man to man. Men police lay hands on us. By men we are examined, handled, doctored. In the hospital it is a man again who makes prayer and reads the Bible for us. We are had up before magistrates who are men, and we never get out of the hands of men till we die.'[33]

If a woman was found to be infected, she was imprisoned either in a Lock hospital or in the workhouse, and sentenced to three months of treatment – later extended to a year. There was no known cure for the diseases but mercury, a poison that could cause kidney failure, was widely used as an ointment, inhaled, ingested and inoculated.

Only women suspected of selling sex found themselves arrested and treated. The man's sexual act and his payment were not illegal. No men were forcibly treated, none were even challenged by the police and they were never named in court. But despite the harsh treatment of women it was clear, in 1875, that the diseases were not confined to prostitutes – they were spreading even beyond male clients to their wives and unborn children.[34]

Two women were admitted to the Central London Sick Asylum in Fitzrovia, in February that year, one a 19-year-old prostitute with ulcers developing across her body. The doctors named the patient 'AG' when they wrote up her notes and observed the spread of the disease for which there was no cure: syphilis. The other patient, who they named 'AP' in the anonymised notes, was a married lady from the middle classes, 30 years old, well educated, who had endured seven years of miscarriages, a large sore on her tongue and a constant headache. The doctors noted that she spoke as if she were 'deranged' and admitted her for observation. She too had contracted syphilis; but as a virgin bride and a celibate wife, she could not possibly have generated it by her sexual promiscuity.[35]

The only explanation – however disagreeable to elite doctors and their genteel patients – was that sexually promiscuous women were not generating syphilis in themselves. Mrs AP's infection must have come from *Mr AP*. He – like thousands of other men – used poor women for sex and carried syphilis into their own homes. The disease was widespread: 30 per cent of soldiers and sailors reporting sick were found to be suffering from venereal diseases,[36] and in 1916 a royal commission report estimated that more than 10 per cent of people in towns had syphilis and even more had gonorrhoea.[37]

The prostitute AG died a week after being admitted to the hospital. No family demanded her body for a respectable burial so the doctors were able to do a post-mortem, which found that the membrane around her brain had turned to jelly.[38] The other patient, AP, admitted at the same time, lost the ability to speak and died a few weeks later.

Sheltered ladies stepped out of the protection of their homes and spoke in defence of prostitutes. Campaigner Josephine Butler said: 'It is unjust to punish the sex who are the victims of a vice, and leave unpunished the sex who are the main cause, both of the vice and its dreaded consequences.'[39] The pioneer of competent nursing, Florence Nightingale, a single gentry woman, had the courage to publish an essay opposing the police regulation of prostitutes, demonstrating with data that arrests of women had little effect in controlling disease. Nightingale's reputation as the heroine of the Crimean War earned her a respectful hearing, but the infamous Contagious Diseases Act was extended in 1868 – from all naval ports to 138 towns and later to a 10-mile radius around each town.

Elite women were banned from the first campaign against the Contagious Diseases Act as the men-only committee felt such a taboo topic to be unsuitable for ladies. Florence Nightingale, Elizabeth

Wolstenholme and Josephine Butler established their own association: the Ladies National Association for the Repeal of the Contagious Diseases Acts, an active campaigning committee that identified the assault on working-class women as an assault upon all women. They did not recommend that prostitutes reform but that the Contagious Diseases Act was at fault, since it was not a genuine provision for public health, but a veiled attempt to provide men with women who were free of disease. All women taking part in the campaign – both rich philanthropists and poor women – were radicalised and educated by the protest, and many of them made a connection between the abuse of women and their lack of legal rights.[40]

The committee listed the great names of nineteenth-century feminism. Josephine Butler toured Britain speaking of the 'sistership' of women. She held 99 meetings in 1870. For many it was shocking to hear a lady speaking publicly about sex and prostitution, and she was attacked by men who used prostitutes, by pimps and by brothel owners. In Pontefract in 1872, her lecture room was set on fire, as the police watched and did nothing.

A huge petition of 2.5 million signatures was presented to the Houses of Parliament and the acts were suspended and repealed in 1886 – but only in England.[41] They still applied in the empire, where the laws were used to segregate Indian sex workers from their families and their communities. Indian women servicing English troops were forced to live in special housing, next to military cantonments, and have sex with white men only.[42] Josephine Butler argued for sisterhood despite race as well as despite class: 'Our poor Indian sisters claim our sympathy, even more than our own countrywomen, who were subjected to the C.D. Acts, for not only are they women oppressed by men, but they are the women of a conquered race oppressed by their conquerors. Their hope of deliverance must seem to them so very far off.'[43]

Butler went on to campaign against child prostitution in England and the trafficking of enslaved women and children to Europe. In 1880, she identified a child sex abuse ring involving the head of the Belgian Police's vice squad and her evidence led to the trial, conviction and imprisonment of the head of the squad, his deputy and 12 brothel owners. With Florence Soper Booth, Butler persuaded the editor of the *Pall Mall Gazette* to demonstrate the abuse of children by buying a 13-year-old girl from her mother for £5. After a long campaign, Parliament raised the age at which a child might consent to have sex from 12 to 13, and finally, in 1885, to 16 years old.[44]

Another member of the Contagious Diseases Act committee, Elizabeth Wolstenholme, established the forerunner of the Women's Social and Political Union (WSPU) with Richard and Emmeline Pankhurst in 1889. She would live long enough to see women get the vote, dying aged 84 in March 1918. Her colleague Millicent Fawcett, another Contagious Diseases campaigner, organised the National Union of Women's Suffrage Societies (NUWSS), founded Newnham College, Cambridge, and other women's campaigns.

As Christabel Pankhurst said: 'The cause of sexual disease is the subjection of women. Therefore to destroy the one we must destroy the other.'[45] Pankhurst linked the liberation of women gaining the right to vote to freeing women from male sexual demands with her slogan: 'Votes for Women! Chastity for Men!'[46]

(Amazingly, it didn't catch on.)

Women Against the Vote

Not all women made the connection that in order to change the laws on women, they must become lawmakers themselves: MPs and voters. Caroline Norton, the bereaved mother whose children were taken by their father and who almost single-handedly won changes to the law with the Custody of Infants Act of 1839, never supported women's suffrage: 'The natural position of a woman is inferiority to man. Amen! That is a thing of God's appointing, not of man's devising. I believe it sincerely, as part of my religion. I never pretended to the wild and ridiculous doctrine of equality.'[47]

Many other women wanted to be part of public life but stay out of political life. Campaigners like Etta Lemon, whose extraordinary crusade won conservation controls on the trade in wild bird pelts and feathers, also founded the Women's National Anti-Suffrage League – a campaign *against* women having a vote in national elections. An 1896 pamphlet linked the two causes: 'If women are so empty-headed and stupid that they cannot be made to understand the cruelty of which they are guilty in that matter, they certainly prove themselves to be unfit to be voters.'

The National Anti-Suffrage League began in 1908 with a roster of great women, including Lady Jersey, Mrs Humphrey Ward the novelist, Gertrude Bell the explorer, social reformers Sophia Lonsdale and Violet Markham, and Beatrice Chamberlain the educationalist daughter of Joseph Chamberlain. It was hugely successful at first, presenting a petition of 337,018 signatures and recruiting a fee-paying membership of 9,000 in 1909 – far greater than any pro-suffrage campaign. By 1913, it boasted 270 branches with more than 33,000 members, when the suffragettes' Women's Social and Political Union had 2,000.[48]

The Anti-Suffragists argued that women were not competent to run a large and complex empire. Women were 'debarred by nature and circumstance from the average political knowledge and experience open to men'. The league argued that since reforms for women had been successfully brought by women from outside Parliament, it proved that women had influence beyond partisan politics. They believed that women should be consulted by the government on women's questions, and proposed a Women's National Council or Advisory Committee to advise and influence the all-male Parliament.[49] They were happy that women vote in local elections, and even serve in local government offices, as parish and county was an extension of a woman's 'home', where she ought to have moral authority. But national commerce, finance, war and diplomacy remained the business of men, and it should be men who elected male MPs. To allow women a vote in national, parliamentary elections would put the great powers of the state in the hands of an inexperienced and ignorant electorate: bad for the empire, and bad for women.

Eliza Lynn Linton compared suffragists to prostitutes: 'The fast young lady and the strong-minded woman are twins, born on the same day and nourished with the same food; but one chose scarlet and the other hodden grey, one took to woman's right to be dissipated and vulgar, the other to her right to be unwomanly and emancipated.'[50]

The real, unstated fear was that if everyone, men and women, had the vote at 21, there would be a female majority. Women, including all those surplus spinsters, would outnumber men. This was the greatest obstacle to giving women the vote … and it was barely mentioned.

Inevitably, an association founded to prevent women from attaining political power attracted women recruits who demonstrated incompetence. 'It was our fate, as Antis, to attract all the ultra-feminine, and the ladylike incompetents,' said one anti-suffrage woman organiser – sadly lacking any sense of sisterhood.[51]

Evelyn Baring, Earl of Cromer, held the presidency of the Men's League for Opposing Women's Suffrage in 1908. When the men merged with the ladies' association, he naturally assumed control of the new co-ed National Anti-Suffrage League, making it clear why women should not have the vote: 'Extreme sentimentality … vague and undisciplined sympathies, hasty generalisations based on inexperience, and inaccurate information: qualities which are, broadly speaking, characteristic of the majority of the female sex.'[52]

The lady members agreed they were incapable. As Caroline Norton wrote to William Gladstone in 1850, 'I have not ventured upon proposing improvements in the law. I am too sensible of the ridicule my attempting to adjust a framework of legal possibilities even if I believed myself capable of a task, which is utterly beyond woman's province.'[53]

The gentlemen supporters intended to dominate the merged association. They wanted women members to help them, but not to make policy: 'I am physically incapable of doing eternal battle to all these rampaging women,' wrote one. 'With her ideas of the way to treat the male sex, Miss Lewis ought really to be a Suffragist; it is a mere accident that she has drifted into our camp.'[54]

Queen Victoria, one of the most powerful people in the world as the Empress of India, remained passionately opposed to women getting the vote. In an 1870 letter, Theodore Martin, trusted friend of the queen, wrote: 'The queen is most anxious to enlist everyone who can speak or write to join in checking this mad, wicked folly of "Women's Rights," with all its attendant horrors, on which her poor feeble sex is bent, forgetting every sense of womanly feeling and propriety … Woman would become the most hateful, heartless, and disgusting of beings were she allowed to unsex herself.'[55]

Women for the Vote

The voting system in England was hopelessly corrupt, and a wealthy woman could select the MP for her area by simply bribing the electorate. Open voting, without a secret ballot, meant that any elite woman with tenants or employees could simply order them to vote for the man of her choice. Mrs E.H. Bruton wrote to all her tenants before the 1868 election: 'SIR – I request you will vote for my father, J.W.S. Erle-Drax, Esq., on receipt of this.'[56]

Even when the vote was expanded to middle-class men in 1884, the word 'men' in this instance meant only 'men'. Women were still excluded. Helen Taylor, the daughter of suffragist Harriet Taylor and the stepdaughter of John Stuart Mill the philosopher, stood for election as an Independent Radical Democrat in Camberwell in 1885, while the Women's Suffrage Bill was actually going through the Houses of Parliament.[57] Some people feared her candidacy would threaten the progress of the bill, while her opponents called her 'an unsexed woman agitator'.[58]

On nomination day, the presiding officer at Camberwell refused to accept her papers and she stepped down. The *Standard* mocked her, writing that she had 'shown a lack of knowledge of the elementary rule of grammar in the differentiation between masculine and feminine genders'.[59] The Women's Suffrage Bill failed and other women who had also registered to vote were refused in a series of court cases.

In 1894, the Local Government Act expanded the right to vote in local elections to all women who owned property in their own name. This was a compromise – it avoided swamping the male vote with women, kept the vote among the property-owning classes, and divided women by class: property-owning women got the vote, poor women and married women whose houses were in their husbands' names did not. At a stroke the 'votes for women' became 'votes for single ladies', no longer a feminist campaign for the benefit of all women.

Some working-class women campaigned for themselves. In Lancashire, where women held the majority in the textile mills, the so-called 'mill girls' retained a keen political awareness. They understood that only a Parliament that responded to women voters, and staffed with women MPs, would end the exploitation of working women. The Lancashire women actively campaigned for votes for working-class women,[60] and in 1902 women textile workers from all over northern England presented a petition to Parliament with 37,000 signatures demanding votes for women.[61]

They were the exception to the general rule of snobbery. Other suffrage campaigns, run by elite women, called only for the vote in all elections to be extended to propertied women: they were upper- and middle-class women campaigning for themselves. Millicent Fawcett (pictured in the plate section), the daughter of a liberal middle-class family, united 17 suffrage societies to found the National Union of Women's Suffrage Societies, campaigning for votes for middle-class, property-owning women using peaceful protest. Campaigning peacefully, holding meetings and proposing reform through Parliament, the NUWSS was the biggest organisation to campaign for votes for women: more than 3,000 women marched in support in February 1907 – on 'the mud march'! They were far more numerous and influential than Emmeline Pankhurst's Women's Social and Political Union founded in 1903. But the Pankhurst group would take the headlines and dominate the historical record because of their campaign of civil disobedience, terror attacks and suffering. Even the WSPU demanded the vote only for wealthy women.

From 1905, the WSPU campaign became more violent: breaking windows, arson, planting bombs and handcuffing themselves to railings, campaigning under the motto 'Deeds Not Words'. In June 1908, over 250,000 people attended the 'Women's Sunday' demonstration organised by the WSPU at Hyde Park – the largest political rally of the century in London. When Prime Minister Herbert Henry Asquith refused to meet them, the suffragettes smashed windows in Downing Street and tied themselves to railings. The WSPU newspaper had a circulation figure of 20,000 subscribers in 1909.[62] In 1910, after a parliamentary bill for votes for propertied women ran out of time, 300 women marched on the Houses of Parliament and were met by policemen, who were said to have been deliberately drafted in from working-class areas and instructed to beat and abuse genteel women. The government denied this. A journalist reported the reaction of one of the demonstrators, Miss H: 'One policeman ... put his arm round me and seized my left breast, nipping it and wringing it very painfully, saying as he did so, "You have been wanting this for a long time, haven't you?"'[63]

In 1913, Emily Wilding Davison ran in front of the king's horse at Epsom race course, perhaps trying to pin suffragette colours to the reins, and was trampled and died. The increasingly violent tactics of the WSPU, particularly its 1912–14 bombing and arson campaign, alienated it from the public and from some of its members. Five people were killed during the bombing campaign (including one suffragette) and at least 24 were injured (including two suffragettes). The WSPU invented the letter bomb, and twice bombed the home of the chancellor, David Lloyd George, in 1913. Emmeline Pankhurst herself was sentenced to three years in prison for her role in the attack.

Many suffragettes imprisoned for violence undertook hunger strikes and were force-fed. Mary Richardson described the torture she experienced in 1914:

> They fed me five weeks by the nose and at the end of that … it would not pass into the throat even though they bent it and twisted it into all kinds of shapes. Instead, it went up to the top of my nose and seemed to pierce my eyes … Then they forced my mouth open by inserting their fingers and cutting my gums … and the lining of my cheeks … when I was blind and mad with pain, they drove in two large gags. Then the tubes followed and they pressed my tongue down with their fingers and pinched my nose to weaken the natural, and also the purposeful, resistance of my throat.[64]

In an attempt to prevent women dying in prison, Parliament introduced the Prisoners (Temporary Discharge for Ill-Health) Act, or, as it was known, the 'Cat and Mouse' Act. Hunger-striking women were released until they recovered from their ordeal and then re-imprisoned.

Offering violence and experiencing violence from police and bystanders, members began to leave the WSPU and by 1914 it was said to have only 5,000 members, compared to the peaceful NUWSS, which reported 50,000.[65] Both groups halted campaigning during the First World War and encouraged women to join the war effort.[66] Emmeline Pankhurst and her favoured daughter Christabel organised demonstrations to encourage women to take up war work and were part of the 'white feather' campaign by women, presenting the feathers – an accusation of cowardice – to men in civilian clothes.

The post-war Representation of the People Act of 1918 was intended to resolve a number of interconnected problems. Working men without savings or property, who had been conscripted and forced to risk their lives in the high-fatality world war, had to be given the vote at the age of 21, as a reward for their service. But if all the women over 21 were given the vote they would outnumber men. Nobody – not even the pro-vote campaigners – wanted the female population majority to be reflected in the democracy. When the male vote was extended to all men over 21 years, the women's vote was limited to women over 30 years who owned their own houses. It was votes for older rich ladies – not votes for women. Lord Cecil admitted the compromise in Parliament: 'The age limit of thirty was introduced, in order to avoid extending the franchise to a very large number of women, for fear they might be in a majority in the electorate of this country. It was for that reason only, and it had nothing to do with their qualifications at all. No one would seriously suggest that a woman of twenty-five is less capable of giving a vote than a woman of thirty-five.'[67]

The arithmetic suited men who wanted to keep power for men: 8.4 million women joined the register. Women were less than half – 40 per cent – of the electorate, even though they outnumbered men in the country. The compromise satisfied the genteel ladies campaigning for the vote, but it betrayed the working-class women who were still disenfranchised. It solved the conundrum of the 'queen's footman'. She was his social superior and although he now had a vote, she had one too.

The first woman to be elected to Parliament by the electorate of carefully restricted women voters was Constance Markievicz (1868–1927), the daughter of an Arctic explorer, in an Anglo-Irish family. She entered political life campaigning for votes for women, driving her own carriage with four matched grey horses. When a man shouted, 'Can you cook dinner?', she replied, 'Yes. Can you drive a coach and four?'

She was jailed for protesting against the visit of King George V to Ireland, and joined the Irish Citizen Army to fight with 70 other women in the Easter Rising against British occupation. She wounded a British army sniper, she may have shot a policeman and she held out for six days in a siege at St Stephen's Green, Dublin.

She pleaded not guilty to rebellion but was sentenced to death – the sentence commuted to imprisonment for life. She is reported as saying: 'I do wish your lot had the decency to shoot me.'[68]

Released from prison under a general amnesty in 1917, Markievicz was back inside in 1918 for protesting the conscription of men for the war. She stood for Sinn Féin from prison and was elected as MP for the Dublin St Patrick's constituency – then part of the United Kingdom. She took 66 per cent of the vote, which made her the first woman elected to the House of Commons, but she supported the Sinn Féin boycott of the imperial Parliament and refused to take her seat.

This was something of a technicality as she was still imprisoned in Holloway.

In the absence of Constance Markievicz, the first elected woman MP took her seat at Westminster in 1918. Hurrah. But actually, it had been her husband's seat. Waldorf Astor, MP for a safe Conservative seat at Plymouth, inherited his father's peerage and moved to the House of Lords, recommending his parliamentary seat adopt his wealthy American social-ite wife as their MP in his place. Nancy Astor, who had shown absolutely no previous interest in women's suffrage, was elected. Suffragists and suffragettes celebrated the arrival of an upper-class wealthy Conservative woman to Parliament. Nancy Astor later explained that it was helpful that the first woman MP was a wealthy woman, as it enabled her to hire the best people to support her.[69] A third of the women elected between the wars (ten of them) would move into their husbands' parliamentary seats. Finally, in July 1928, the Representation of the People Act was passed, giving a vote to everyone – men and women – over the age of 21.

At this point it became clear that there was no such thing as women's politics or women's issues that united all women. The great terror of the 'Parliament of women', a gynocracy which would ruin the nation, feared from the sixteenth century, did not come into being with women MPs. Women voters were divided over almost all issues – even those directly affecting the rights and freedoms of women. Race, class and other inequalities divided sisterhood. There was no such thing as a united women's vote.

Working-class Protest

Some women's organisations were egalitarian, like the Women's Protective and Provident League, founded in 1874 by headmaster's daughter Emma Paterson, modelled on women's unions in America. The league worked with female associations of bookbinders, sewing machin-ists, upholsteresses, spinners at Leeds and the woollen weavers of Dewsbury and Batley. It set up a mutual credit association, the Women's Halfpenny Bank, in 1879, and became the National Federation of Women Workers in 1906. Lucy Re-Bartlett of the WSPU's campaign for women's votes said that there was a new conscience arising in women at home and abroad.[70]

The crest of the Dewsbury, Batley and surrounding District Heavy Woollen Weavers Association, founded by Ann Ellis. Their slogan: Unity is Strength

In 1875, women workers led their first organised strike in West Yorkshire. In February, a rumour had started that the masters were going to cut wages for the 'shoddy' workers – those working on reclaimed wool. A young married weaver – Ann Ellis of Skelsey Mill – was appointed by men and women weavers to organise a protest. She formed the Dewsbury and Batley Weavers' Committee of 13 women to represent 25,000 workers, and on 16 February addressed her first meeting of 9,000 striking weavers in a field near Spinkwell Mills, Dewsbury. According to the *Dewsbury News*, 'She had never stood on a platform as she did at present until this strike … She would bundle up and go, rather than give in to the masters … the women had begun the battle and would have to get on with it.'

The men were clear that this was a unique act of leadership by the women: 'Coming to the front and taking on labour – and there wasn't another place in England where they had done that,' reported the *Huddersfield Examiner*.

The all-women committee of the striking weavers rejected help offered by the Women's Protective and Provident League, and by the National Union of Women Workers: they did not want external middle-class women organisers – they wanted to organise their own strike and set their own terms. The male strikers refused to join the men-only Operative Union and got behind the women to lead the strike. One man told the *Examiner*: 'The men should be faithful and true to the women … a man who won't back a woman is no man at all.' Another man said that the women 'would need cheek'.[71]

Despite the masters threatening the committee members individually, telling them that their husbands would be sacked, the women refused to negotiate a pay cut, demanding the full rate of pay and nothing less. Ellis said that workers would not be able to live on anything less than full pay – it would not cover their rent, heating and food bills. Workers from surrounding industries and the nearby mines gave money for a strike fund enabling the women workers to stay out on strike for six weeks. Finally, the masters capitulated, reversing the proposed cut in wages and paying the agreed rate, in all but two of the mills.

Elsewhere, male unionists were reluctant to welcome women into the campaigns. One male union member wrote to headquarters in 1889 that women as well as men should be organised locally: 'Please send an organiser to this town as we have decided that if the women here cannot be organised they must be exterminated.'[72]

One of the greatest joint actions by women workers, organising themselves, came from the women chainmakers of the West Midlands. These women made light chains in forges attached to their cottages, more than 2,000 of them in Cradley Heath alone. A middleman or middlewoman called a 'fogger' would deliver three-metre-long rods of iron to each chainmaker, who would cut the rods into links, and heat and hammer the hot iron into 5,000 links of a chain, working in the forge for up to

A Cradley Heath chainmaker in 1910

12 hours a day. The fogger then collected the finished chains, delivering more rods. After deducting about 25 per cent for providing the service, the fogger paid the employer's preferred rate for the work. Women usually earned between 4s and 5s a week. The rate was set by Boards of Trade but the employers, who sat on the board for their particular craft, defined the maximum that they would offer, usually fixing women's wages at about half the male rate.[73] Social commentator Robert Sherard described a chainmaker's forge:

> One may come across sheds with five or six women, each working at her anvil; that are all talking above the din of their hammers and the clanking of their chains, or they may be singing a discordant chorus; and at first, the sight of this sociability makes one overlook the misery which, however, is only too visible, be it in the foul rags and preposterous boots that the women wear, or in their haggard faces and the faces of the frightened infants hanging to their mothers' breasts, as these ply the hammer, or sprawling in the mire on the floor, amidst the showers of fiery sparks.[74]

In March 1910, the Board of Trade set new wages for women chainmakers, at a minimum rate of two and a half pence an hour, in place of the old payment by weight. It was as high as the employers would go and should have doubled the women's pay for a 55-hour week. With no intention of paying the new rate, the chainmaker employers began stockpiling old chains and refused to supply rods to chainmakers unless they agreed to work for the old rate. Employers sent out contracts at a low rate of pay and tried to persuade the women chainmakers – most of whom could neither read nor write – to sign them. Three representatives from the National Federation of Women Workers – Julia Varley, who had started work as a 13-year-old mill girl; Mary Macarthur, a draper's daughter; and Charles Stitch, who had started chainmaking at the age of eight – visited the chainmakers: 'We went into the forges, talking to the women as they hammered away, awakening their consciousness to their responsibilities, appealing to their pride and their motherhood,' said Varley.[75]

When the women chainmakers demanded the new pay rate – as agreed – the masters started a 'lockout', not buying new chains, but selling their stockpiles. The standoff lasted for seven months until the weight of public sympathy, and international interest in the treatment of the chain-makers, forced employers to agree to pay the new rate and eliminate foggers from the system. It was a victory for sweated women workers, and for the National Federation of Women Workers.

It became clear that the breadwinner wage – a male supplement – was working not only against the interests of single women but even against those of men, as wherever possible, employers de-skilled jobs and passed them to low-paid women and children. Increased mechanisation and inventions made more and more jobs lighter and low skilled.

It was a woman who explained this rather obvious fact in 1888, when Clementina Black told the Women's Trades Union Council that when women were 'employed merely because they were cheaper, all work gradually fell into their hands ... and that this resulted in lower (wages) to the general injury of men and women alike'.[76]

In 1888, another women's strike seized international interest and became a model for the general dock strike the following year. Most British matches in the nineteenth century were made using poisonous white phosphorus, and most of the workers in the industry were women: 1,276 of them and 245 men in 1897.[77] The giant match factory of Bryant and May in London's East End employed more women than anywhere else locally, yet most of the work was done not in the factory but in 'sweatshop' conditions in workers' homes, in order to avoid safety requirements.

The work could be fatal. The poisonous phosphorus in the match-heads, which workers were accidentally eating and inhaling in the crowded factory and sweatshops, caused their jaws to crumble – a condition called 'Phossy jaw'. Their pay was reduced by fines for minor offences: the company claimed it paid 10s–12s a week to 'steady workers' but in 1888 women workers reported they got only 4s a week. They had no union representation at all, and as part-time and casual workers found it hard to organise.

After five women workers – Mary Driscoll, Alice Francis, Eliza Martin, Kate Slater and Jane Wakeling – were suspected of having told radical journalist Annie Besant about the conditions at the factory, three of them were dismissed.[78] As a result, 1,400 women workers walked out in protest and a few days later the factory stopped production. Bryant and May management suggested that working-class women would only have taken action if they had been influenced by outside agitators. The chairman

'Pass the poisoning': Annie Besant's scathing article told shareholders of the toxic conditions at the Bryant and May factory

told shareholders: 'You are all pretty well aware what this strike has arisen from. For a considerable time, an agitation has been at work in the East-end of London tending to ... upset the minds of the workers.'[79]

The delusion of 'outside agitators' was designed to comfort shareholders, writhing from an excoriating article by Annie Besant in the newspaper *The Link*, on Saturday 14 July 1888. She wrote:

Do you know that the women and girls whose labour made the 22½% dividend paid in February last are living, or dying, in Old Ford, Bromley, Tiger Bay, and other districts of East London, on wages varying from 4s to about 13s a week? That sometimes the wage goes even below 4s, and that a girl of sixteen years of age, a fortnight ago, was discharged with 2s 8d to represent the results of a week's toil? Do you know that it appears even from the miserable shuffles of your secretary, Mr Carkeet, that the 'average wage' of the 'adult female workers' in your employ is only 11s 2d per week? And consider, the fact that there is an 'average wage' of 11s 2d does not help women, who, like the twenty-nine-years-old wife of a dock labourer, the mother of five children, took home 5s 6d last Saturday week ... How would you like, wife of a clerical shareholder in Bryant and May's, to keep house for a week on 11s 2d? How would you like to start for your work at half-past five a.m., and reach home again at seven p.m., having been on your feet nearly all the time, and after doing this for five days, with an additional half day on the Saturday, to take home 11s 2d as a reward? And if you did reach the average, but only got the 5s 6d, and had been at the work for fifteen years, might you not say, like my poor friend said to me the other day, 'I'm most tired of it'?[80]

It was the working-class women of Bow who called the strike and held it, winning the reinstatement of the women organisers, proper lunch breaks in rooms away from the poisonous phosphorus, clean washrooms, an end to fines and a proper rate of pay. They founded one of the country's biggest trade unions, the Union of Women Matchmakers, to protect their working conditions in the future.[81] The first women factory inspectors were appointed to enforce safety, especially in businesses that employed many women, and white phosphorus would finally be banned from matches in England four years after the 1906 Berne Convention.

Throughout, the striking women were known as 'girls', and the protest is still widely referred to as the 'Matchgirls' Strike'. But despite the patronising language, the walkout had a profound effect, inspiring the great dock strike the following year. When the leader of the dockers John Burns called on a meeting of thousands of dock workers, he said: 'Stand shoulder to shoulder. Remember the match women who won their fight and formed a union.'[82]

The years between 1907 and 1911 were years of the 'great unrest' when women's union membership increased and women undertook industrial action. In London alone, unionist Mary Macarthur organised 20 simultaneous strikes involving 200 women. Women understood that they had to have equal pay, or they would be used to undercut men's wages. As Eleanor Rathbone said: 'If the wages of men and women are really based on fundamentally different conditions and if these conditions cannot be changed then it would seem that women are the eternal blacklegs, doomed, despite themselves, to injure the prospects of men whenever they are brought into competition with them.'[83]

Women were determined not to be 'eternal blacklegs' bringing wages down and breaking strikes. In the bad jobs usually delegated to them, they went on strike to raise pay and improve conditions. Jam- and pickle-makers, ragpickers, bottle-washers, laundry women, envelope-, biscuit-, cocoa- and tin box-makers, and distillery and confectionery workers – all low-skilled, low-paid light work, some of it in sweatshop conditions – went on strike from 1910–14. Women's actions emerged as the old food riots used to emerge: when an incident triggered a widespread sense of outrage. In 1911, a herring fish-wife put a red rag on a broom and carried it before her like a flag, going around the yards to call out workers on strike.[84] She had no union assistance and no outside agitators: it was women standing up for women.

In the housing estates and slums of the new industrial towns, women's protest took a new form: the rent strike. In the first years of the First World War, with many men away, many women could not pay their rents, especially when landlords imposed a 25 per cent increase, as they did in Glasgow's Govan area in 1915. The unrest spread to other Scots' towns and to the English towns of Leeds, Bradford, Edmonton, Barrow, Workington, Coventry and Birmingham, until it was so widespread that the government created the Rent Restriction Act of 1915, and in 1919 ordered towns to provide new good-quality social housing for working people.[85]

In Bradford, working-class women used this new tactic of a rent strike to control an abusing man. They forced a private landlord to exclude a man and his mistress from the family home by withholding their rent until he had been evicted. Wood, a dyer's labourer, made no financial contribution to the family home but lived off his wife – a daily domestic cleaner who sold goods door to door. The couple had four children, one of them a girl named Maud. When Maud was four, the heavy-drinking Wood brought his mistress to live in the family home. When Maud was ten years old, her father sexually assaulted her, and gave her an infection which prompted her to tell her mother. The quarrel between husband and wife was heard by the neighbours. Later, as an adult Maud said: 'The happiest day of me life is when I came home from the mill, and he'd gone. Me mother says "he's been thrown out". The neighbours signed a petition saying they would withhold the rent if me father weren't thrown out. Well, the woman next door lived wall-to-wall, and they could hear it carry on, they could hear it, and they thought my mother had had enough. So she got the petition up, and he had to go, and take his fancy woman with him.'[86]

A spontaneous strike by women bus drivers and workers brought wartime transport in London and other cities' to a halt in 1918, when a group of women, without union support, met at Willesden Bus Garage and demanded that the 3,500 women employed by the London General Omnibus Company should get equal pay to men for the same work and be paid a 5s male bonus. Both male trade unions and male employers were committed to a breadwinner wage favouring men. The Willesden women went on strike the next day and were joined by women from Acton, Archway, Hackney and Holloway bus depots and garages. Other women working on the London Underground came out too, bringing the Tube to a halt, and women strikers walked out of garages at Bath, Birmingham, Bristol, Hastings and Southend. About half of all the women employed in transport – 18,000 women – stopped work for a few days before they were offered the 5s bonus (but still not equal pay to men) and returned to work.[87]

The post-war recession prompted women workers to drop the campaign for equal pay, calling instead for job creation and better pay for everyone. Groups of unemployed women joined together informally for mutual support, and the Women's Group in the 1922 Trades Union Congress demanded unemployment insurance for domestic servants, cleaners and home-workers.[88]

In 1926, private coal mine owners attempted to reduce miners' wages and the Trades Union Congress called a General Strike. The unions were so afraid of sparking political unrest that they limited the strike to heavy industries: 1.7 million workers went on strike, and some more radical women workers, such as the sweetmakers at Rowntree's in York, walked out to support the striking miners. Government reaction was immediate and hostile. The strike was broken in nine days, largely by gentry and white-collar volunteers called out by the government. Union member-ship collapsed under the pressure of anti-trade union legislation and the gruelling experience of defeat in the strike itself. The miners themselves held out for a further six months until forced by absolute poverty to go back to work at lower rates.

The General Strike proved a deeply divisive experience for English women. Working-class women in mining areas experienced terrible poverty, causing one Labour campaigner to describe the affected neighbourhoods as 'famine areas'. Women stormed the dole office in Merthyr when benefits were cut, and Rhondda women broke through three police cordons to take their complaints to the Prince of Wales.

A miner's wife wrote for help: 'I am pregnant. The children have no boots or clothes, and to make things worse we have not a bite of food in the house and the children are crying for bread ... If you visit us you will find things worse than what this letter says we are, but I have no more writing paper to say more – Please believe me.'

Many women from the wealthy and working classes sympathised deeply with the miners and the terrible poverty their families suffered without pay for six months. Marion Phillips, the chief woman officer of the Labour Party, set up the Women's Committee for the Relief of Miners' Wives and Children. The all-women committee organised appeals, flag days, sales of goods, concerts and a 'boot day' to raise money to buy shoes for miners' children. People donated clothes, food and money, and a scheme for miners' children to stay with temporary foster families saw women opening their homes to poor children: 'The hostesses came from every class of society, from those who owned motor cars to working people living in small flats, but the children seemed to fit in very readily with all. Often when they came, "aunts" were very troubled about their food. They had become so accustomed to having little, and probably in addition, arrived so tired with the journey, that at first they would eat nothing but bread and jam, to the bitter disappointment of the hostess who had been looking forward seeing them enjoy their first solid meal in weeks.'[89]

Not all women responded with sympathy. The Women's Guild of Empire led by Mrs Flora Drummond – who had worked on a campaign by the Pankhursts against wartime strike action – urged wives to discourage their husbands from striking: 'It is up to us to do all we can to save these women from themselves.'[90]

Apparently, miners' wives did not want to be saved from themselves. A meeting of the Women's Guild for Empire needed a heavy police presence to protect the speakers from a crowd of 500–600 people, 'mostly women', who protested and threatened a 'riot'. Mass rallies of women supporting their husbands' strike action were held in May 1926, with

10,000 women attending. In June, there was a near-riot in Blaenavon, where 2,000 people (mostly women) locked the 'relieving officer' in his office after he refused relief payments to husbands unless they signed receipts. Some so-called 'riots' seem to have had echoes of early community protests. Miners' wives in Wales attacked 'blackleg' or strike-breaking men in processions very like medieval skimmington rides. In Bryneath Colliery, some wives got hold of a strike-breaking miner, William Gregory, on his way to the pit. They dressed him in a white shirt and took him to his home in Coity in a wheelbarrow while playing a concertina. Six women were charged with unlawful assembly and intimidation; all but one went to trial and were bound over to keep the peace for 12 months.[91]

For many elite women the General Strike gave them an opportunity to play at working-class jobs, sometimes even dressing up in faux uniforms. Few volunteered to replace striking men and do hard or dirty work. Volunteers chose jobs that they thought they would enjoy: male students took on the roles of driving buses and trains and volunteered their private cars as taxis, while upper- and middle-class women volunteers did household chores to support them – cooking hot food, serving in canteens and cleaning up afterwards. Gentry women undertook work usually done by their servants: laundering clothes and making up beds in the temporary camps set up in parks in London and at railway stations.[92] One upper-class volunteer said: 'I can remember enjoying the General Strike very much, with never a thought for the miners. We were quite sorry when it came to an end. My contemporaries and I had no particular feelings about the rights or wrongs of the strike, we simply had no feelings either of sympathy or antipathy towards the miners; but felt that it was our job to help the country as a whole to be as little affected as possible.'[93]

Lady Lindsay (formerly the Duchess of Westminster) saw the strike as an interlude in the social season: 'In a way, we all had great fun you see. As I said, we weren't at all seriously interested in the problems of the day. I really didn't know whether the miners had enough or not. It sounds bad; but I mean that is the truth of it! We were *so young!* I don't remember anybody sort-of discussing the rights and wrongs. You did what your parents said … It was … rather a joke. When the strike was over, we just went back the way we were, shook out our party dresses and went to the next ball.'[94]

The party atmosphere was very far from the experiences of working-class women. The newspaper *Labour Woman* wrote: 'The women of the governing classes of to-day have enjoyed the brilliancy of the season. Let them go. After all, they are of the past, lingering on the scene too long. The women of the future, the women who will help to make our country great, not with "seasons" but with all-the-year-round happiness, are to be found in other places. Above all amongst the women in the coalfields.'[95]

The Nature of Women

'Have you any notion how many books are written about women in the course of one year? ... Are you aware that you are perhaps the most discussed animal in the universe?' wrote Virginia Woolf in 1929.[96] The greatest men of the century explored the new sciences and found they proved – just like the old ones! – that men were indeed superior. This from Charles Darwin himself: 'The chief distinction in the intellectual powers of the two sexes is [shown] by man attaining to a higher eminence, in whatever he takes up, than woman can attain – whether requiring deep thought, reason or imagination, or merely the use of the senses and hands ... Thus man has ultimately become superior to woman.'[97]

Darwin – one of the greatest observers of the natural world – concluded not only were women naturally inferior to men, but they would evolve to become more inferior. While men evolved greater superiority in all their diverse talents, women would only become more fertile and successful as child-bearers.[98]

Darwin's idea was confirmed by other thinkers like Karl Vogt, who believed that evolution made the sexes more and more specialist – making men stronger and women frailer: 'The inequality of the sexes increases with the progress of civilization.'[99]

An 1859 conduct book writer understood that science confirmed the God-given superiority of men. A husband should 'consider himself the divinely appointed priest of his own household'.[100]

Obviously, women should be encouraged to specialise in the only thing they could do well: conceiving and giving birth. Motherhood was elevated to religious heights by philosophers as if to console women that it was the only thing they could do. One male self-styled expert recommended: 'A new philosophy of sex which places the wife and mother at the heart of a new world and makes her the object of a new religion and almost of a new worship that will give her reverent exemption from sex competition and reconsecrate her to the higher responsibilities of the human race.'[101]

Motherhood, performed on the most elevated plane, would save the world, according to psychologist G. Stanley Hall: 'Women in parliament and in journalism, their representation in the local and general government, in peace congress, in workingmen's meetings, in science and literature: – all this will produce small results until women realise that the transformation of society begins with the unborn child ... This transformation requires an entirely new conception of the vocation of mother, a tremendous effort of will, of continuous inspiration.'[102]

In this thinking, women's demand for equal pay and opportunities could only be a doomed conflict against women's physique, nature and evolutionary destiny, as W.R. Greg knew:

> Those wild schemers ... who would throw open the professions to women and teach them to become lawyers and physicians and professors, know little of life, and less of Physiology. The brain and the frame of woman are formed with admirable suitability to their appropriate work, for which subtlety and sensitiveness, not strength and tenacity of fibre are required. The cerebral organisation of the female is far more delicate than that of the man. The continuity and severity of application needed to acquire real mastery in any profession, or over any science, are denied to women, and can never with impunity be attempted by them: mind and health would almost invariably break down under the task.[103]

Once women had been defined as completely different from men, indeed the 'opposite', it became more and more important to identify a baby's sex: that parents and adults might respond appropriately to either a boy or his infant opposite, a girl; that the child might be taught from the first moment how to behave appropriately for his or her sex, and to firmly fix from the moment of birth, one of two possible sexual identities.

By the middle of the nineteenth century, babies wore gowns only in the early months of infancy and were then put into short coats called 'rompers' or 'Russian skirts'. They were the same style for boys and girls, but coded by colour so that total strangers should know at first sight whether the baby was a 'strong little fellow' or a 'pretty little love'. A little boy would be dressed in pink, as it was a 'strong' colour, while for a girl it would be pale blue or pale yellow.[104] As Jo Paoletti recorded: 'The cherubic white dresses of infancy, once worn well into the third year, shifted in less than a generation from being exactly right for babies to not only wrong but harmful for boys. A boy was not a girl and should never be mistaken for a girl. Banishing white dresses was just the beginning; lace, ruffles, gathers, flowers, kittens, and a sizable portion of the color spectrum were all eliminated from little boys' clothing over the course of several decades.'[105]

Little boys had to be taught early that they must be manly, but little girls could be infantilised. *Harper's Magazine* wrote in December 1876: 'The girl wears forever the infant petticoat, with all its power and privileges.'[106]

By this time, the petticoat with 'all its powers and privileges' had become a disabling burden for elite women. The gown was supported by a wired crinoline, composed of many layers, tiers and flounces, with pantalette worn underneath and a huge bell-shaped skirt on top, a bodice and jacket often on top of that, a shawl on top of all that, and hair styled elaborately in braids and always worn pinned up. It was clothing that inhibited movement, prohibited action and deterred deep breathing and even digestion. It was an appearance that could only be achieved with a background of servants to make, launder and repair, and a maid to help the lady dress. The clothing not only made elite women dependent on others for dressing and undressing, it disabled them, making walking an arduous exercise, running and any form of sport impossible. The fashionable look for elite women became more and more doll-like, pale, fragile, with a tiny waist. Elite women took poison, including arsenic, to lose weight and bleach their skin; they swallowed tapeworm eggs with the intention of growing a parasite worm in their stomachs to eat their food until, when the ideal weight had been achieved, ingesting a dose of antiseptic or mild poison to kill the worm.[107] It was hoped the worm would die and be passed, but some grew very large and strong.

Elite women wore whalebone corsets that were tightly laced, pulled in by an assistant dresser to achieve a 22-inch waist (10 inches smaller than today's average female waist).[108] The ribs were deformed and the spine permanently curved.

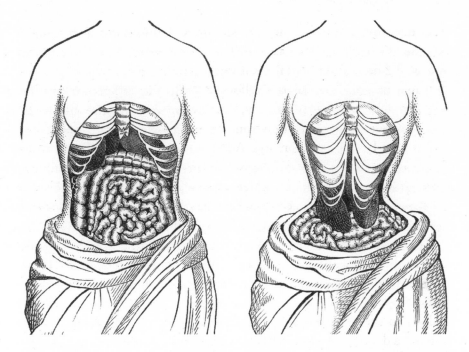

Physiology for Young People, 1884, showed the deformed position of the liver and the stomach, from tight lacing in corsetry

Ladies reported shortness of breath as their lungs were compressed, constipation and painful indigestion. Over time, the corsets could cause more serious injury: 'bent or fractured ribs, displacement of the liver, and uterine prolapse (in some cases the uterus would be gradually forced, by the pressure of the corset, out through the vagina)'.[109]

So-called doctors, physicians and scientists had viewed elite women as 'naturally' more frail than men for more than a century. But in the nineteenth century new diseases and new diagnoses suggested that elite women were not only fragile, they were unfit for life.

The genuine frailty of elite women, created by avoiding healthy food in sufficient amounts, little or no exercise, no sexual pleasure, extreme repression and painfully low mental stimulus, could now be observed in their daughters who had fasted and rested all their lives, under tremendous psychological stress from repression and social anxiety. From about 1900, research into menstruation showed that it was unique to women – and therefore a sign of weakness. Doctor and sexologist Havelock Ellis wrote, 'Even in the healthiest woman a worm however harmless and unperceived, gnaws periodically at the roots of life.'[110] It was evident to male doctors and scientists that women's bodies were 'naturally' prone to failure. Women's normal state was to be sick.[111]

It was true that elite women's lives made them sick. Not only did they starve themselves and take no exercise, they were exposed to diseases by close contact in unventilated rooms. Women were thought to be especially vulnerable to tuberculosis, which was generated by poor housing and hygiene in the crowded slums and spread easily from servants and sweatshop workers to their employers and clients. In nineteenth-century London, a quarter of all deaths were caused by tuberculosis and in the last half of the century millions of people died from consumption in England.

It became identified as a 'tragic' disease. Patients tended to behave with frantic energy or with melancholy exhaustion – rather like the heroines of the Romantic novels, now a behaviour associated with ladies of

The 'tragic' disease: consumption

sensibility. The progress of the disease could be slow, giving patients time for deathbed farewells – which were often recorded in prose, poetry, fiction and paintings. It was nicknamed the 'Romantic Malady' and the typical patient's appearance – pale skin and flushed lips – became so fashionable that even healthy women reproduced the feverish flush with white powder and rouge. The belief that consumption was linked to masturbation in women gave the disease an extra taboo allure.[112] The novel *The Lady of the Camellias*, by Alexandre Dumas, tells the story of a beautiful high-class courtesan who (spoiler alert) dies tragically of consumption and was adapted into a successful stage play and then the opera *La Traviata* by Verdi, confirming the link between female sexuality, illness and death, in high art.

Women's mental health was said to be further weakened by menarche, menstruation, the menopause, the spontaneous wandering around of the womb inside the body and sexual arousal. There was no discreet silence about sex, usually attributed to the Victorians – they had a constant heated discussion about pornography, masturbation, sexual release as essential for men and dangerous for women. Male commentators endlessly remarked on the dangerous sexuality of the working classes, the dangers of corruption to the young and that sexual ignorance was not a state of unknowing but the greatest virtue.[113]

Advisors to upper- and middle-class women continued to insist that they did not orgasm but now believed they experienced no pleasure at all. A 1918 advice book, *Conjugal Happiness*, states: 'Sensible and fine feeling women, who are devoted to their husbands ... would willingly submit to their spouses' demands, even though sexual intercourse may give them little or no pleasure.'[114]

As late as 1928, a question in a private medical questionnaire about the sexual feelings of wives was considered shocking and inappropriate, because sexual feelings were generally understood to be abnormal in married women.[115] Even so, wives were expected to volunteer for regular sexual intercourse to conceive children and satisfy husbands, who otherwise would be driven to rape, turn to adulterous sex with more obedient women, or be forced into unhealthy masturbation.[116]

Elite women's gynaecological health continued to be an area of mystery and great interest to male doctors, partly because of the tremendous fees that could be earned by persuading women that they were both physically sick and mentally disturbed. Removal of the clitoris as a cure for masturbation, sexual appetite, or almost any behaviour that fell outside the doctor-defined limits of elite female behaviour, was probably widely recommended by family doctors and discreetly performed by surgeons. Isaac Baker Brown was criticised not for performing female genital mutilation on his patients but for publishing *On the Curability of Certain Forms of Insanity, Epilepsy, Catalepsy, and Hysteria in Females* in 1886. He recommended removal of the clitoris in patients whose husbands or families reported that they were interested in sex, or who had been caught masturbating, or who were regarded as over-emotional in any way at all.[117] Removal of both ovaries was tried from 1870 and was regarded as an instant success in curing what was known as 'failures of femininity': not just physical but nervous disorders – and any symptoms for which doctors had no ready diagnosis.[118]

Believing gynaecology to be directly linked to female mental health, doctors continued to experiment on disturbed, unhappy or rebellious patients. Dr Bennet, a famous English gynaecologist, advocated placing leeches on the vulva or inside the vagina on the neck of the uterus, although he warned any doctor doing this to count the leeches as they dropped off when satiated and might be lost inside the vagina. He remarked that he had known adventurous leeches to advance into the cervical cavity of the uterus itself, saying: 'I think I have scarcely ever seen more acute pain than that experienced by several of my patients under the circumstances.'[119] (This is a reputable gynaecologist who lost leeches in the vaginas of 'several' patients – who exactly was crazy here?)

A modern review of the mental health of nineteenth-century elite women suggests that many suffered from depression, caused by 'sexual harassment, subservient domestic roles that required self-sacrifice and internalization, feelings of helplessness due to lack of social power, diffused sense of purpose following the Industrial Revolution altering the role of wives and mothers, gender-biased psychological treatments that were harmful, and perpetual pregnancies, which often involved complication.'[120]

The mental health of elite women deteriorated so badly during the years of expansion and prosperity for England that historians describe an 'epidemic of hysteria'.[121] One highly regarded authority, Dr Henry Maudsley (1835–1918), the leading British psychiatrist of his day, was clear that young women could not study, their 'nerve centres being in a state of greater instability, by reason of the development of their repro-ductive functions, will be the more easily and the more seriously deranged'.[122] American doctor Silas Weir Mitchell diagnosed hysteria in men and women in the 1850s and prescribed male patients to take regular and frequent outdoor exercise. But for women exercise was not the answer – they must have the 'rest cure':[123] 'For approximately six weeks the patient was to lie on her back in a dimly lit room. If her case was particularly severe, she was not even permitted to get up to urinate. She was to be fed soft, bland foods to gain weight daily and have a daily massage on the entire body, increasing in vigour as the cure went on.'[124] Anything the woman enjoyed must be kept from her. Virginia Woolf was not allowed to write and during the course of her 'rest cure' gained three stone in weight. Her husband, Leonard, consulted five of the best British doctors of mental health and said they knew 'practically nothing'.[125]

By the middle of the nineteenth century, the condition of hysteria proved the diagnosis when almost any character change was observed in women, especially sadness, boredom or fatigue. It was only when the intolerable terror of modern warfare in the Great War produced symptoms among officers and men similar to those that had been called 'hysteria' that doctors had to reconsider the condition and the name. Enlisted men showing symptoms of post-traumatic stress disorder after the horror of trench warfare were diagnosed with the female condition of 'hysteria'. But officers from the upper classes could not be labelled with a condition that was typical of distressed women. By 1916, elite men showing symptoms of mental illness were diagnosed as suffering from 'neurasthenia', a different name for the same disease of their inferiors.[126]

It was evident to doctors that ladies of the upper and middle classes were too weak and delicate for anything but the gentlest exercise, sexually frigid and incapable of concentration on any task, but working-class women were robust, sexually active, fertile and fit for hard labour with no psychological weakness.[127] The opposite was true. In reality, working-class women – with poor diets and housing – died earlier and were more often ill. They were underfed even in breadwinner households because of the tradition that men and boys ate first. Working-class women could not rest before or after childbirth, and infant mortality and low birth rates were caused by the disease of rickets – triggered by a lack of vitamins which made bones twist even in the pelvis, obstructing labour and sometimes causing the deaths of mother and child.[128]

Some working-class women escaped puerperal fever because they could not afford an expensive doctor or to go into the fee-paying hospitals. Only 15 per cent of women went into hospitals for birth in 1927. The safest births were those in rural areas with a midwife or practitioner who stayed with the mother throughout labour, did not attend other infectious patients and avoided intervention.[129] In 1914, free school meals began to be made available for children, and poor families started to receive greater health and welfare support. By 1920, infant mortality rates had fallen.[130]

Upper- and middle-class families suffered from disproportionately high infant mortality and death in childbed because their wealth and high status exposed them to the infections that were carried by fashionable and expensive medical practitioners from one patient to another. The maternal mortality rate in middle-class areas of Leeds was nearly double that of poor neighbourhoods – as middle-class women were attended by doctors with poor practices of hygiene; but the poor continued to give birth at home, sometimes without any professional attendance.[131] Dora Russell coined the phrase 'it's four times as dangerous to bear a child as to work in a mine', comparing the maternal death rate in 1920 of 4 per 1,000 births with the deaths in mining accidents of 1 in 1,000 miners.[132] Safety in childbirth would not improve until the 1930s when practitioners – including the expert obstetricians – understood that they were spreading infections.

Working-class women, afraid of dying in childbed or feeling that they could not raise a child, continued the folk tradition of 'bringing on' bleeding – causing abortion. Drugs said to bring on bleeding were advertised in newspapers and sold openly. Methods of abortion included scalding hot baths, gunpowder mixed with margarine, slippery elm and penny royal herbs. In 1905, doctors reported seeing blue lips in patients who had tried to bring on a miscarriage by poisoning themselves with lead.[133] Secret abortions, and the many women and babies who died when they went wrong, were not recorded.[134]

Rubber condoms were cheaply available from the 1900s, replacing animal skins. Contraception was associated with men who wanted sex for pleasure without conception or disease, and the women they used for sex, not with wives who were not thought to take pleasure in sex, and who only endured it to conceive children. Many wives associated condoms with prostitution: an applicant for a divorce in 1872 – Louisa Birch – included the complaint that her husband insisted on using a condom with her.[135] Feminists opposed them because it meant that men could have sexual intercourse safe in the knowledge that they would neither get an infection nor conceive a child. Husbands who had planned their families by abstaining from sex could use condoms and demand sex every day of the month, even from frail, invalid and disabled wives.

Vaginal pessaries were available from pharmacists (and also home-made) from about 1880. But after the First World War, theories about eugenics – in particular the low birth rate of the officer class and the increase of their social inferiors' – led sociologists to recommend controlling the population of the poor. The heroic work of Marie Stopes in bringing reliable contraception to working married women was partly inspired by the desire to prevent 'unfit' people from breeding.[136]

Paleobotanist Marie Stopes (1880–1958) published an advice manual, *Married Love*, in 1918 after the failure of her first marriage. Inspired by female sexual pleasure, which she described in idealistic and spiritual terms, Stopes fervently believed that pregnancies should be spaced in a family and people that she called the 'worst end of the community' should be discouraged from growing faster than her own class. She founded the Society for Constructive Birth Control and Racial Progress in 1920, supported by former suffragettes, and opened free clinics to married women, offering the cervical cap, which had the massive advantage of being re-usable and under the control of a woman. Stopes opposed abortion, favouring sterilisation of people that she thought unfit to breed.[137] She opened the first clinic for married women in Holloway, London, in 1921.

Middle- and upper-class families were using contraception from the 1920s to control the size of their families but fear of working-class women's sexuality meant that it would not be until 1930 that the Ministry of Health allowed publicly funded nurses and doctors to give contraceptive advice to poor married women and then only on medical grounds.[138]

One of the heroines of the history of contraception and sex education for women was Annie Besant. Born in 1847 to an evangelical middle-class family, she married a clergyman and bore two children in three years. She described her youth in her autobiography: 'I feel a profound pity for the girl standing at that critical point of life, so utterly, hopelessly ignorant of all that marriage meant, so filled with impossible dreams, so unfitted for the role of wife.'

After the marriage broke down, Annie moved to London, taking only her daughter, Mabel. She worked as a governess, wrote short stories and delivered a lecture on the political status of women. Put on trial for

Prolific writer, speaker and activist Annie Besant (1847–1933) campaigned for exploited workers, education on birth control, and Irish and Indian home rule

obscenity for republishing a contraceptive pamphlet with her friend and comrade Charles Bradlaugh, she defended herself and walked free from court but with her reputation in tatters. Her husband took her daughter from her because of her poor moral character. In 1888, she worked with the women matchmakers of the Bryant and May strike, saying: 'Better remain silent, better not even think, if you are not prepared to act.'

Besant converted to the philosophy of theosophy, travelling as a missionary for the religion to India, where she campaigned for education and Indian independence, becoming the first leader of the Congress Party, adopting an Indian boy who she believed to be the messiah.[139]

Single Women

The deaths of 700,000 British men in the First World War increased the proportion of single women in the population, especially among the officer classes where mortality was high. As educated and literate social commentators, women were quick to observe: there were more middle- and upper-class single women than there were men to marry them – most of them would never be wives.[140] By the time of the 1921 census, there were 1,158,000 unmarried women and 919,000 unmarried men between the ages of 25 and 34.[141]

Many women were shipped out by their hopeful families to the imperial lands in Africa and India, with the ambition of marrying an officer of empire, surviving the posting and retiring wealthy to England. Known as the 'fishing fleet', the women entered a deeply hierarchical racist clique and most of them did nothing to improve it.

Single women who remained in England were blamed for their failure to marry:[142] the lifelong 'spinster' was suspected of man-hating,[143] and some feminists confirmed their disdain. Christabel Pankhurst said: 'There can be no mating between the spiritually developed women of this new day and men who in thought and conduct with regard to sex matters are their inferiors.'[144]

The idea that a single woman might think of herself as the equal to a man was derided by the late nineteenth-century radical thinker and poet Edward Carpenter, who said in 1897 that spinster feminists were 'out of line ... Such women do not altogether represent their sex; some are rather mannish in temperament; some are "homogenic", that is inclined to attachments to their own sex rather than the opposite sex; such women are ultra-rationalising and brain-cultured; to many, children are more or less a bore; to others, man's sex-passion is a mere impertinence, which they do not understand, and whose place they consequently misjudge.'[145]

Despite condemnation by the radical left, the misogyny of the sexologists, and condemnation by the conservative right, many unmarried women created interesting and worthwhile lives for themselves as single women choosing to marry late or not at all. Women took pride in the friendships of other women as their main source of emotional life. The Victorian emphasis on women's lack of sexuality elevated women's friendship as more ennobling and more pure even than marriage.[146] The lack of financial profit between equal elite friends further raised the status of the relationship in a society that was uneasily obsessed with profit. The friendship of ladies who had nothing material to gain from each other and were idle together was the doctrine of the separate spheres in action: domestic, profitless, workless, detached from reality, spiritual, emotional, effortless.

Some single women used the absence of a husband as the key to leave the separate sphere, to live alone in their own lodgings, pursuing careers that were slowly opening on the fringes of the professions, or working in family businesses, or to live together in the women-only educational schools and colleges, or as companions and friends or lovers. Many took their freedoms and had adventurous lives identifying themselves as 'new women' by more practical clothing.

More than half of the women in feminist organisations were unmarried, or married late in life, inspired by the example of other happy single women, and drawn to feminist organisations by a wish to live and work with women.[147] Those that worked on causes around male violence, the double sexual standard, the breadwinner wage and the campaign for the vote, mostly without support from men, inevitably radicalised to become 'anti-man' – as they were accused. More moderate single women looked at the disadvantages of marriage even after the 1850s reforms, and decided against or deferred it till later in life. One of the Langham Place activists, Bessie Rayner Parkes (1829–1925), who ran the Victoria Press and edited *The English Woman's Journal*, married at 38 years old, but refused an earlier suitor. She wrote in her diary of 1859: 'To live with him and give up in *some* measure my beloved Emmie and Barbara, to be dependent on that quiet … face for my intellectual nutriment … To give up as I then must very much; my dear cousin Sam and my dear brother Frank; oh never never. A single woman is so free, so powerful.'[148]

Women Loving Women

Elite women who made lifetime loving attachments to female partners continued to be well regarded in society and could socialise as a recognised couple without scandal about their sexuality. They kept silent about their private intimacy and generally escaped comment since they were ladies who were expected to lack sexual desire.

Hostile or satirical comment about women loving women actually diminished in the middle of the nineteenth century as it became widely believed that women lacked erotic desires for anyone – especially for each other. From 1830, discussion about sexual intimacy between women was either medicalised or 'pornified' – the only descriptions were from doctors or pornographers.[149] Some doctors' descriptions of female sexual activity managed to be both a doom-laden warning and titillation.

In the agreed silence about women's sexuality with women, many relationships thrived in the 1860s and 1870s, socially accepted as lifetime friendships and were even described as 'marriages'. Matilda Hays, who was introduced to Elizabeth Barrett Browning as the married partner of the 'unimpeachable' actress Charlotte Cushman, went on to make a long-term live-in relationship with Theodosia Dowager Lady Monson. Frances Power Cobbe (1822–1904), a single woman, lived most of her life with sculptor Mary Lloyd whom she addressed as 'husband', 'wife' and 'beloved friend'. Both women described their friendship as 'marriage' and were part of a high-status, highly respectable friendship group that included John Stuart Mill, William Gladstone and Charles Darwin, who wrote to the two women as a couple and invited them as a couple to social events.[150]

Sophia Jex-Blake had a deeply loving relationship with Octavia Hill, the philanthropist, describing her as 'my dear loving strong child', and in retirement lived with Dr Margaret Todd, a fellow pioneer doctor and novelist. Jex-Blake saw herself as invulnerable to male attraction, saying of herself: 'I believe I love women too much ever to love a man.'[151]

These public relationships were not necessarily privately or secretly sexual. Sophia Jex-Blake's intense and loving letters to Margaret Todd contain no sexual references. As a doctor, Jex-Blake would have been taught that sexual feelings and practices in women led to mental and physical disease; but she expressed no anxieties about her feelings, nor did she compare herself, or the women she loved, to patients said to be sick with sexuality. She described feelings of intense love but none of sexual arousal, and she showed no doubt or embarrassment about them.[152]

Edward Carpenter, the poet and 'sexologist', rejected the idea of different sorts of love in 1912: 'No hard and fast line can at any point be drawn effectively separating the different kinds of attachment ... friendships so romantic in sentiment that they verge into love ... loves so intellectual and spiritual that they hardly dwell in the sphere of passion.'[153]

Some relationships were profound experiences. Pioneer sportswoman and commentator Marjorie Pollard killed herself rather than live without her companion May Morton. Marie Correlli, the novelist, had a lifetime partner and biographer in Bertha Vyer. They were a recognised couple. One diarist saw them together at an evening party: 'They did not dance but spent most of the evening with their arms around each other looking on at the rest.'[154]

Catherine Bradley and Edith Cooper were childhood friends. When they began to write together, they combined their nicknames into a pseudonym: Michael Field. Publication of joint volumes of poetry and drama proved successful, until it was discovered that Michael Field was two women, then their work fell out of fashion. They wrote: 'My love and I took hands, and swore against the world, to be poets and lovers evermore.'[155]

Some women reproduced the old belief that a female husband was the last resort of the woman who could not catch a male one. Maria Richmond wrote to her friend: 'I sincerely hope, dear Margie, that should you continue single … you will, however old you may be, come out and marry me, helping to farm my little estate, and lecture my nephews and nieces.'[156]

Women, deeply attached to each other, might introduce a friend into their marital home without scandal. No less a wife than that of the Archbishop of Canterbury, Minnie Benson, had a close woman friend to live with her and her husband and their children, but felt deep guilt.[157] She prayed for a spiritual union with her friend and the death of 'carnal affections': 'Once more, and with shame oh Lord, grant that all carnal affections may die in me, and that all things belonging to the spirit may live and grow in me. Lord, look down on Lucy and me and bring to pass the union we have both so blindly each in our own region of mistake continually desired.'[158]

The husbands and wives who lived openly with an intimate woman friend on the assumption that the friendship was not sexual were deeply disturbed by the 'Codrington divorce', when in 1863 Helen Jane Smith Codrington was accused by her divorcing husband of adultery with a fellow officer and others. Her friend, Emily Faithfull (1835–95), a well-known philanthropist who founded the Society for Promoting the Employment of Women, with Bessie Rayner, lived with the unhappily married couple and – as was announced in court – the two women slept in the same bed, when Helen Codrington refused to sleep with her husband. The implication, that the women were sexually intimate, and that Helen Codrington was bisexual and promiscuous, persuaded the jury, who gave her husband a divorce. It was a disastrous and shaming process for all three. Helen Codrington never saw her children again and disappeared in disgrace from elite society and from the historical record. Emily Faithfull, publicly humiliated by the suggestion made in court that she was sexually active with her woman friend, was dropped by the Langham Place feminist group, but courageously continued to campaign for women's rights. Later, she lived with her friend Charlotte Robinson, to whom she willed her property, thanking her for the 'happiest years' of her life.[159]

Some families, alerted by the Codrington divorce, aware of the numbers of women who would not or could not marry, became increasingly wary of daughters who did not conform to the female ideal, sought education or independence, or appeared – as the families said – to be 'manly'.[160] Such girls might attend the new women's schools, colleges and even universities, where middle- and upper-class like-minded young women could meet each other without interruption from men. Political campaigns for women provided the same opportunities for female friendships that were 'intense, passionate and committed'.[161] Religious organisations that promoted same-sex missions also provided a place where women could meet and unite passionately in service of a cause. Girls born in the 1850s came of age and into independence in a society that allowed more independence and education for women, and some found partners and lovers.[162]

Kissing, embraces and touching were rarely described, and may have been rare in life, as in letters. Frances Wilder, a young woman, wrote a searingly honest letter to Edward Carpenter for his advice on her sexual desire for women, describing a relationship with another woman that 'never went further than a handshake': 'I was 28 when I again fell in love with a girl about my own age. I made it my business to cultivate her, but soon found that tho' she was quite friendly and admirable, she cared less for me than I did for her. Often when alone with her, I had a strong desire to caress & fondle her; but I am naturally reserved & restrained and we never advanced further than the formal handshake. I had no sexual desire in connexion with her & I couldn't quite understand my feelings towards her ... but my attachment for this girl was quite emotional. I loved to be with her, to hear her talk, even though I seldom agreed with her.'[163]

Letters, accounts and fiction based on these lives emphasised a passionate, sentimental, not genital love between girls and women, which generated its own slang in words like 'crush' and 'pash': a shame-free enthusiasm and expression of single-sex love. The genre of fiction termed 'school novels' celebrated the passionate attachment of a young woman to an older mentor in a single-sex environment.[164] These bonds between women could be described by authors and biographers without shame or self-consciousness. The books are clear that deep and passionate attachments between women were normal and healthy – and non-sexual. There was no shame, and no concealment – the fictional women were confident that they were better women for loving each other.[165]

These women were reacting against the separate spheres doctrine that had left women without education or opportunity. They saw themselves gaining an adequate education in order to become financially independent women, free from the limitations of their family homes and free from the dominance of men.[166]

As the new century began, the idea of sexual intimacies between women appeared in the pages of feminist journals like the gloriously named *Shafts* (1892–6) (no! referencing arrows) and *Freewoman* (1911–12).[167] By this time a greater openness about women's sexual desires in bohemian, progressive and cosmopolitan circles had created a breach among feminists: some wanted to openly acknowledge sexual interest and desire for men, some felt they had to keep their sexual desires secret as they were only directed to other women, and some continued to feel no desire for men or women.

The term 'lesbian' was not used until the twentieth century. Sexologist Havelock Ellis (1859–1939) called both homosexuality and lesbianism sexual 'inversion', a definition that – although it limited the imagination to only two genders – may have helped some women understand and name their desire for other women, as 'normal' womanhood 'inverted'. But they would have had to be brave women to seek his diagnosis: Ellis believed that a 'true invert' came from a family with mental illness. He described one woman, Alice Mitchell, who had cut her lover's throat, as 'typical'. 'Homosexual relationships are also a cause of suicide in women,' he wrote.[168] Ellis himself had an open marriage with writer Edith Lees, who was sexually active with women during their relationship, without murdering anyone.

The word 'inversion' or 'deviant' started to be widely used among progressive thinkers and theories also spread that there was an 'intermediate sex' in which one could be both male and female. Frances Wilder, writing to Edward Carpenter, said: 'I concluded that I had … a dash of the masculine. (I have been told more than once that I have a masculine mind.)'[169]

Wilder's letter may be typical of how a young woman who always preferred women to men as friends and companions came to understand her feelings as sexual – once she was able to attach a name, even an invented name, to her feelings. Carpenter wrote of same-sex desire as 'Urania' from ancient Greek writings and named those people who loved others of the same sex as 'urnings'. Wilder wrote to him in the hope of meeting a woman who felt like her. Her letter, among his papers without a note as to whether he replied, is a rare example of the solitary voice of a single woman struggling with her feelings for other women:

I voiced my need in a little pacifist & socialist paper asking if any lonely woman rebel would care to correspond with another.

I had about 16 answers. The first was from a girl or woman – with whom I am at the present time in love – she is rather younger than myself & has all the characteristics which I most admire in women. She is delightfully self-reliant, capable & humorous. It was she who introduced me to your book, and somehow made me realise that I was more closely related to the intermediate sex, than I had hitherto imagined & she also I think (though I haven't questioned her on the subject) is certainly not a normal female – she is much too nice! When I think of her, I have physical desire, and should love above all things to be able to live with her & be as intimate as it is possible to be & I don't feel that this desire is at all immoral or degrading. It is not merely or chiefly physical desire – I cannot bear the idea of losing her friendship, even if the physical desire is never gratified & I don't for a moment expect it will be. I should be intensely grateful if I could just hold her hand and tell her how much I love her. This may look awfully stupid on paper, but it is very real to me. I feel there is nothing I wouldn't do for her that I could do.

... I long more than I can say to love a woman completely and absolutely and to have it returned. The world would say that a physical relationship between two of the same sex is an unspeakable crime.

But after a few weeks consideration I have come to the conclusion that this relationship can never be as degrading as the normal sex relationship can be and usually is. I know it is a big thing to say that the normal sex relationship of men and women is more degrading than the other but it will be true *wherever & so long as women are in economic slavery to men* & I think you will agree.[170]

At the beginning of the twentieth century, the greater visibility of women who expressed themselves in masculine ways, in either dress or behaviour, and the numbers of women who openly desired other women increased abuse about female love and open criticism of 'tommies', though there was no outright persecution of women who loved women.[171] In 1919, a libel trial pursued by Maud Allan, a dancer, brought the question of female sexuality with women to the newspapers and public notice.

Maud Allan (1873–1956), a musician and designer, gained international fame for her dancing and acting, especially her *Vision of Salome* based on Oscar Wilde's play, which included the 'Dance of the Seven Veils'. An English independent MP published an article entitled 'The Cult of the Clitoris', in his own magazine, claiming that Allan was not only a lesbian but also (indeed therefore) a German spy – he alleged that there were 47,000 homosexual men and lesbian women vulnerable to blackmail by German agents. He suggested that the former prime minister's wife Margot Asquith was Maud Allan's lover – since Margot Asquith indeed paid for Allan's London apartment. The dancer sued him for libel, and his defence argued that since she knew the meaning of the word 'clitoris', she must be a lesbian. The jury agreed: Allan lost her case; the accusation that she was a lesbian was held to be true.[172] The slur that Margot Asquith was friends with a lesbian dancer shadowed her reputation, but there were no subsequent trials. Maud Allan taught dance and lived with her lover Verna Aldrich, moving to Los Angeles and working as a draughtswoman for Macdonald Aviation.

In 1921, a law to criminalise lesbian sexual activity was proposed in the House of Commons. Lesbianism had not been banned before, and the majority of legislators thought it safer not to draw the attention of chaste women to such possibilities. Conservative MP John Moore-Brabazon instructed ignoring lesbians: 'Leave them entirely alone, not notice them, not advertise them. That is the method that has been adopted in England for many hundred years.' MPs agreed that sex between women was too dreadful to describe and there was total official silence on women loving women even when other sexual acts were openly discussed.[173]

Female Husbands

Lillias Barker (1895–1960) was born into a middle-class family and volunteered for the Voluntary Aid Detachment of nurses and the Women's Royal Air Force during the First World War. She married her husband at the end of the war but left him after only six weeks of marriage. She lived with a male lover in Paris, giving birth to two children before the family moved back to an English farm, where she met Elfreda Haward in 1922 and persuaded her that she was a man, injured in the war, only dressing as a woman to oblige her family. The two women moved into the Grand Hotel, Brighton, under the name of Sir Victor Barker and, pressured by Elfreda's parents, they married – Sir Victor declaring himself a bachelor on the marriage certificate.

Victor acted with Brighton Repertory Company and joined the cricket club as 'Captain Barker', but he left Elfreda in 1926. He joined the National Fascisti movement, and lived at its headquarters in London, training recruits and boasting of his past: street-fighting with 'reds'. He named himself as 'Colonel' in 1928, opening a café with his new partner, an actress. When the café went bankrupt he was prosecuted for fraud and this led to his discovery as a woman in Brixton Prison. He was convicted of perjury – false information on the marriage certificate – and sentenced to nine months in the women's prison at Holloway.[174] After his release, he lived as a manservant and was later prosecuted for theft.

Some men lived as 'male wives' in single sex couples. From the 1800s, men were recorded identifying as women, forming partnerships, engaging in marriage ceremonies and pregnancy rituals, with one of the couple taking the role of the wife and mother.[175]

Colonel Victor Barker, one of their many aliases, who was charged with fraud, perjury and later theft

After the First World War the phrase 'sex change' began increasingly to be used to describe people who dressed and lived as the opposite sex from their birth sex. Better understanding of psychology and increased medical intervention made it possible for people to transition – most of them from female to male. Almost all of the stories reported in the press were those of people who believed themselves to have been assigned the wrong sex at birth. London's Charing Cross Hospital became known as an international centre specialising in medical and even surgical help, and patients would usually be allowed to freely choose their sex.[176]

Marriage

Sex in upper-class marriages continued to puzzle doctors, who were divided between the 'sexologists' who said that all women could and should feel sexual desire and those who idolised 'ladies' as being above such feelings. Romantic love as a motive for marriage grew, love inside marriage became a goal, and moral husbands hoped to get sexual satisfaction from their wives and not from prostitutes.

Some sexologists rebelled against the widespread belief that women were sexually frigid and argued that women were in an almost constant state of arousal about conception, carrying a child and giving birth, and mothering. According to Iwan Bloch: 'Procreation is their proper element, and when they are engaged in it they remain at home in their own sphere; we for this purpose must go elsewhere, out of ourselves. In the matter of time also, our part in procreation is concentrated. We may devote to the matter barely ten minutes; women give as many months. Properly speaking, they procreate unceasingly, they stand continually at the witches' cauldron, boiling and brewing; while we lend a hand merely in passing, and do no more than throw one or two fragments into the vessel.'[177]

Husbands were assured that wives could be aroused by male persuasion, according to Havelock Ellis, and that women were attracted to strong, decisive and even violent men, and enjoyed forcible seduction. Because of this desire in women, actual rape – sexual intercourse without a woman's consent – rarely occurred, according to Ellis.

An 1890 textbook stated: 'A fully matured woman in full possession of her faculties, cannot be raped, contrary to her desire, by a single man.' This myth was repeated by Gurney Williams, author of the *International Clinics* paper 'Rape in Children and Young Girls', first published in 1913: 'The mere crossing of the knees absolutely prevents penetration.'[178]

Forced sexual intercourse in marriage was still not defined as rape. In one case, *R v Clarence* in 1888, a husband was charged with malicious infliction of bodily harm and grievous bodily harm after he gave his wife a venereal disease while raping her. The rape was not illegal – but knowingly infecting her was a crime.[179]

The doctors' discussion about the damage of rape moved from the danger to the happiness of the marriage and from there – as if by magic

– to the danger to the happiness of husbands. In 1869, a so-called scientist, John Cowan, wrote that husbands who raped their wives made themselves ill with a 'weakness of the nervous system', a 'weakening of the joints' and a 'want of strength'.[180] Wife rape was physically damaging for the rapist-husband and should be avoided for that reason.

As the middle-class home was idealised as a place of culture, health and affection where male leaders could experience rest, and enjoy the spiritual high standards and elegance of their wives, marital rape and domestic abuse became more and more unacceptable. There is no reason to think that domestic violence and marital rape stopped. But no longer would neighbours witness, complain or interrupt the abuse of middle-class wives. The aspirational home locked its doors and kept matters private.[181]

Victoria, Wife and Empress

Queen Victoria, succeeding the often unpopular, sometimes dissolute Hanoverian kings, consciously decided to bring the morality and style of the upper- and middle-class home to her reign. Partly, this was her own personal style – deeply attached in youth to a middle-class governess, living in a separate sphere from the royal court, her own religious background and her passion for her strict and respectable husband who she regarded as her superior. Victoria created a family both bourgeois and royal to rule the greatest empire in the world, linking the dominance of the English with extraordinary prosperity, inequality, racism and sexism.[182]

The massive increase in the wealth of the nation – from the profits of slavery, enclosure and agriculture, industrialisation and empire – powered the prosperity of everyone but the poor and excluded and grew the middle classes. Working people rose from poverty into better-paid work, farmers grew wealthy with improved agriculture and industrialists made profits. The 'elite' class became less exclusive as the middle classes continued the rise they had been making for centuries, merging with the upper gentry who were marrying into the aristocracy, all investing or active in the empire, trade, church, administration, industry and landowning. Minute social distinctions identified old families' money from new, old titles from new, the established from the arrivistes.

But the newly conscious middle classes did not form a bridge to the poor. They viewed poverty as a disgraced state from which they or their parents had triumphantly escaped. They adopted elite practices: employing poor people at low rates, charging high rents for inadequate housing, supporting either the church which stuck to the old established parishes and ignored the slums, or the evangelical wing that entered the slums bringing God, hygiene, snobbery, sexism and racism. The people they categorised as 'deserving poor' became the target of advice and charity, and the rest – paupers, beggars, addicts, the insane, criminals, the hopeless, social offenders, protesters, prostitutes, people of other races and religions – were viewed from a distance, with increasing alarm, regulated and punished. About a quarter of the population could be called middle class by 1850 – their numbers doubled in the next 20 years.[183]

Although Queen Victoria was an active and domineering monarch – arguing with prime ministers, quarrelling with her husband, ruling for 40 years without him as a widow, and placing her children on most of the thrones of Europe to ensure Great Britain's continuing position of power – she portrayed herself as a deferential and adoring wife. She might be a reigning queen and then an emperor, but she was determined to show that her husband was the patriarchal head of a model family, promoting Prince Albert as father of the family and of the empire, and herself as a subservient wife and, later, grief-stricken widow.

'Let women be what God intended, a helpmate for man, but with totally different duties and vocations,' she wrote.[184]

She employed governesses and tutors to educate her daughters: Vicky, Alice, Helena, Louise and Beatrice received educations that included physical exercise and practical skills fit for their future careers as wives to monarchs, steering their countries towards a British-type constitution and middle-class way of life. Both parents and first-born Vicky regretted that she had not been born a boy, as she showed more promise than her brother, Prince Edward. Vicky always took the boy parts in family theatricals, dressing as a boy for the stage, with the encouragement of her parents.[185] Their ambition for her led them to allow her to choose her own royal husband and her engagement at the age of 15 to a man nine years older than her, in the hope that the young couple would create a British-type constitution in his home country of Prussia. Like all middle-class mothers, Victoria believed in exporting the standards and style of her home, even to families (or entire nations) that did not want it.

All of the princesses supported programmes for women's education and nursing training. The girls followed their royal mother's example in attempts to improve the behaviour of women rather than change their circumstances.[186] Princess Louise, the second youngest, was a talented artist. The queen allowed her to attend the National Art Training School, and she specialised in sculpture. Louise supported the education of girls, but her husband thought his wife should not speak before an audience. Obediently, the princess educationalist sat in silence, while he took to the stage to read her feminist speech.[187]

Queen Victoria struck one outstanding blow for the freedom of women from pain when she accepted chloroform for the birth of her last two children, Leopold (1853–84) and Beatrice (1857–1944), against the advice of churchmen, ending centuries of a tradition of female suffering based on the Christian belief that pain in labour was a God-given curse on women for Eve's sin, as written in Genesis: 'Unto the woman he said, I will greatly multiply thy sorrow and thy conception; in sorrow thou shalt bring forth children; and thy desire shall be to thy husband, and he shall rule over thee.'[188]

Queen Victoria avoided the pain that was one of Eve's punishments for her sin. The other punishment handed down to women was desire for a husband, and the rule of husbands over wives. If the three curses are understood as one, Victoria's defeat of pain in childbirth suggests that a woman might avoid the other curses: chastity for wives and the rule of men. This was revolutionary – understandably, nobody remarked on it.

Although she gave birth to nine children in 17 years of marriage, Victoria was – like many aristocratic women – remote from her children, refusing to breast-feed, and handing them over to nannies and governesses. She may have suffered from undiagnosed post-partum depression, speaking of 'lowness and a tendency to cry … it is what every lady suffers with more or less and what I, during my first confinements, suffered dreadfully with'.[189]

She was closest to her youngest daughter, Princess Beatrice, and expected her to remain single and live all her life as a companion and secretary. But Beatrice got engaged in secret and her mother did not speak to her for six months, recovering enough to insist that the young married couple live with her, so that she could see Beatrice every day. The princess obeyed and stayed with her mother through her married life, and after – during her own widowhood. Like a typical middle-class daughter, Beatrice was expected to work as a companion and assistant in the family business, without recognition or pay.

Victoria's opposition to the campaign for women's rights was known, but not publicly stated. Her frequently quoted critiques of the 'mad folly' of women's rights were made in private. Yet her position as ruling queen inevitably raised the paradox of one woman whose signature was on the laws, while her married female subjects were excluded from them. Caroline Norton, no friend to women's suffrage, whose own divorce led to agonising separation from her children, said it was a 'grotesque anomaly' that married women were legally non-existent in a country governed by a female sovereign: 'The signatures of married women are legally worthless; where they cannot lay claim to the simplest article of personal property – cannot make a will – or sign a lease – and are held to be non-existent in law.'[190]

As a woman who concealed her hard work and was not visibly paid, Victoria provided a model for the middle-class wife who also was not paid for all the work she concealed. In that sense, Victoria was like so many women – an unintentional feminist, determinedly modelling womanly subservience but constantly demonstrating ability.

Sport

Most doctors advised against women taking up sport. Physiologist Alexander Walker made a long study of women in 1892 and concluded: 'Happily, the athletic temperament does not occur in women.'[191]

Doctors agreed that the best exercise for women was walking in fresh air. Others warned women against competing with men. But in 1890, Margaret Villiers, Countess of Jersey, a woman who believed that women's role was to be a 'helpmeet' to her husband and to the world, defended the possibility of a woman doing something because she enjoyed it: 'Is it quite just … as is very commonly taken for granted, when a woman attempts anything which is more ordinarily done by men she therefore desires to emulate or rival man? Is it not conceivable that she may sometimes like the work or sport for its own sake, without any thought of competition with the other sex?'[192]

Upper-class women needed sports and crafts and arts to fill the long hours of leisure prescribed for ladies. According to *Harper's Monthly* in

1866, there was an epidemic of croquet, a game suitable for upper- and middle-class ladies, putting them under little strain and requiring little energy. It was exclusive – needing specialised equipment and a well-prepared lawn. Quickly, women found themselves accused of cheating, scuffling the ball into place with their long skirts. An 1865 manual warned women: 'Don't cheat. We are aware that young ladies are proverbially fond of cheating at this game; but as they only do it because "it is such fun" and also because they think that men like it ... The practice spoils the game so much that, if it is allowed, the rules may as well be done away with at once.'[193]

When interest in croquet waned, lawn tennis took over, even more exclusive, requiring more specialist equipment and a specially prepared and equipped lawn. The first club opened in 1874 and ladies' events were introduced at a handful of English clubs from 1881. Maud Watson's first competition came at Edgbaston that year. She won the singles title and the doubles, in partnership with her sister Lilian, at the age of just 16. In 1884, Wimbledon added a singles Ladies Championship, which Maud also won after beating Lilian. Entrants were allowed to the Wimbledon event only two weeks in advance, but 13 players entered, including Blanche Bingley, who would go on to be a future champion. Maud Watson won 54 matches consecutively, losing only 12 sets, until in 1886 she was defeated at Bath by Lottie Dod, who would become not only the youngest ever singles champion at the All England Club in 1887, but also Ladies Golf Champion in 1904 and an Olympic silver medallist archer in 1908.

In 1900, Charlotte Cooper from Ealing added two Olympic golds to her list of victories, winning the ladies singles and the mixed doubles, making her the first Olympic tennis champion and the first individual female Olympic champion. Cooper, deaf since the age of 26, is still Wimbledon's oldest ladies champion and her record of eight consecutive singles finals stood until 1990 (when Martina Navratilova achieved nine).[194] In 1908, Dorothea Douglass, also from Ealing, won another Olympic tennis gold for GB, beating Dora Boothby who took silver. Dorothea published *Tennis for Ladies* in 1910.

Alice Legh has been called the greatest woman British archer of all time, winning the British national championship 23 times between 1881 and 1922. (Her mother also won it four times.) She was the first female archer to describe her technique and philosophy in detail.[195] Legh did not go to the 1908 Olympic Games in order to prepare for the World Championship, which she won, beating the Olympic champion by a substantial margin.

The All England Women's Hockey Association was founded in 1895, excluding daughters of tradesmen not because they should not be admitted to an exclusive club, but to spare them from extra exertion, according to *Hockey Field* in 1910:

> Is not hockey too violent an exercise and too prolonged a strain for those who often spend much of their time in heavy manual work? ... Very often these girls, in addition to close application to wage-earning work ... have the heavy part of the household work in their

Alice Legh (1855–1948) said, 'Even quite old ladies can shoot, and shoot well too.' She retired as national champion aged sixty-seven

own homes to perform ... and get a liberal allowance of exercise in washing clothes or scrubbing floors – which last is a fine exercise, but somewhat 'self-sufficing' from an athletic point of view ... For girls who do this kind of thing daily ... are not violent games unnecessary, and likely to take them 'beyond the health limit of fatigue'.[196]

The ladies were not welcome in the all-male Hockey Association, and in reply they refused to allow men to serve on the Women's Hockey Association committee.[197] They agreed to exclude working-class people and scheduled friendly matches during working hours, midweek. Both the women's and men's associations were based in the south and did not welcome a northern Ladies' Hockey League, formed in 1910, barring its clubs.

Northamptonshire's Marjorie Pollard played hockey for England nearly every year from 1921 to 1937. As well as editing and writing the *Hockey Field* and *Women's Cricket*, she was also a sports journalist for national newspapers and in 1935 she became the first woman to commentate on sport for the BBC, during a men's cricket match.

The 1870s saw a resurgence of cricket for all, and with girls not admitted to men's clubs a group of women hockey players, including Marjorie Pollard, travelled to Colwall to play cricket in 1926 and founded the Women's Cricket Association. Pollard remembered: 'After play was over, we sat in the Park Hotel at Colwall ... and discussed how cricket could become real for us – no longer to be an elusive thing, that one played half afraid of ridicule. We pondered, mused, talked.'[198]

Golf was considered an acceptable sport for women, as long as it was not too energetic. Doctors in 1899 advised women only to putt, and if they insisted on driving, to take only a half or three-quarter swing.[199] A purpose-built 18-hole ladies' course opened in 1868 in Devon (a year after St Andrews in Scotland) and English women played a tournament, accompanied by gentlemen caddies resplendent in scarlet uniforms. The ladies' club supported itself, with lady members responsible for building work and repairs to their own clubhouse (which served cold food only), plus heating and the maid's wages. They also had responsibility for the maintenance of their course, the mowing machine and the greenkeepers' wages.[200] At Berwick, a 'ladies' course was laid out in 1867. Its ladies' club was formed 20 years later and the women managed the lease of the course and employed their own greenkeeping staff.[201] By 1893, the number of ladies clubs had grown to 63, and they called a meeting to form the Ladies Golf Union. Around this time, leading woman golfer Issette Pearson invented the handicapping system, which would eventually be adopted by the men's game.

Only Barnehurst Golf Club in London offered men and women equal membership, equal use of the links and similar access to the clubhouse, although certain rooms were reserved for each sex. Women mostly either opened their own clubs or joined ladies' sections of men's clubs. Some clubs created shorter, simpler greens for women – and allowed competitive female golfers with low handicaps specified time on the men's greens, but women had to give way to men on the greens. Women were rarely welcome in all the parts of the clubhouse. At Beverley and East Riding, the women could rent a room in the clubhouse and receive refreshments through a hatch. At Littlestone, one of the very few clubs where women and men shared unrestricted use of the course, women only entered the clubhouse by special invitation at Christmas, and never by the front door. When a group of visiting women found doors locked, they had to eat outside in the rain.[202]

Despite the difficulty of getting on to long courses, women golfers learned to compete. Issette Pearson was defeated by Lady Margaret Scott in the first British Ladies Championship, in a field of 38 players. Margaret's father, Lord Eldon, delivered her acceptance speech for her, and although she won two more championships, she retired on her marriage in 1897.[203] Dorothy Campbell won both the British and American Open Championships in 1909. Charlotte Cecil Leitch won the English and French Championships before the war, and the British in 1920 and 1921. In 1921, she beat the legendary Joyce Wethered in the British and French Opens, to become the only person ever to have beaten Miss Wethered twice. Their great rivalry continued until 1929 when Joyce married Lord Heathcoat-Amory and retired from competitive golf.

Horse riding became a sport for wealthy women, with the rise of fox-hunting in the nineteenth century. Catherine 'Skittles' Walters[204] was a highly skilled horsewoman and renowned beauty, an elite prostitute in London in the 1860s, where spectators admired her riding in 'Rotten Row', Hyde Park, on the finest mounts in the tight habits made specially for women.[205] 'The real objection to the hunting field for ladies and parsons was in the manners and language of some foxhunters of old,'

The last Victorian courtesan, Catherine 'Skittles' Walters' (1839–1920) first love was horses

wrote the *Ladies Field* magazine. 'Now the manners of the hunting-field and the drawing-room are the same.'[206]

The manual *Riding for Ladies, With Hints on the Stable* reversed earlier advice and said that women riders did not need to be guided through a day's hunting by a man leading the way. Women need not move out of the separate sphere of domestic life to be a good horsewoman. Training horses and arranging their transport fell within 'natural feminine qualities of compassion and affection', according to Mrs Power O'Donoghue.

Women who had been riding side-saddle, wearing breeches underneath the newly designed safely skirt, took to riding astride from 1910, wearing knee-length coats for modesty, adopting the same position as girls on bicycles.[207] Diarist Arthur Munby watched French women cyclists from the Paris Hippodrome in 1869 and judged there to be 'nothing indecent in their performance, or in the girls' behavior, if once you grant that a woman may, like a man, wear breeches and sit astride in public'.[208]

The popularity of the bicycle in the 1890s created a dilemma for doctors: it could improve the health and physique of women, strengthen the abdominal muscles, invigorate the respiratory system and stabilise the nerves. But they feared that women would overstrain the heart and suffer spinal deformities. Excessive pedalling would lead to uterine displacement and spinal shock and might lead to masturbation. One American doctor warned of 'bicycle-face', a facial disfigurement in which all of the features moved to the centre of the face.[209] In 1893, at the age of 16, Tessie Reynolds set a record for cycling from Brighton to London and back in just 8 hours 30 minutes.[210]

In 1895, Nettie Honeyball assumed her false name and advertised for players for a British Ladies' Football Club, supported by Lady Florence Dixie, the explorer, war correspondent, feminist and aristocrat.

Together they founded the British Ladies' Football Club with mainly middle- and upper-class women who had the time and means to play

Nettie Honeyball (dates and real name unknown) founded the British Ladies Football Club in 1895 – their first match in 1895 was watched by a crowd of 12,000 spectators

daytime matches and travel to away matches all around England. A game played in 1895 against the Ladies Reading team drew a bigger crowd than the men's team.

Women like the Carlisle Munitionettes played football during their lunch breaks and after their war work shifts. The manager at Dick, Kerr and Co., an ammunitions factory, suggested to one of the players, Grace Sibbert, she should establish a factory team. Dick, Kerr Ladies became famous for the quality of their play and the size of the crowds they drew – far bigger than for the men's game, even when men came back from the war. They played more matches in 1920 than any men's team and their Boxing Day match at Goodison Park in 1920 sold out the 53,000-capacity stadium. A French team played exhibition matches against the Dick, Kerr Ladies on a tour of England and in the return tour of France, the English women remained unbeaten.

The following year the English Football Association announced the game was 'not fitted for females', accused women players of corruption and banned women's teams from FA grounds. Alice Barlow of Dick, Kerr Ladies said: 'We could only put it down to jealousy. We were more popular than the men and our bigger gates were for charity.' Without grounds, banned by the national association, women's football disap-

The most successful football team in England: Dick, Kerr & Co factory team in 1921 – the year they were banned from Football Association grounds

peared.[211] While a handful of teams, such as Dick, Kerr's, found alternative venues, the FA's decision saw most women's teams disband and reduced spectator numbers for the few who remained.

Some women were paid for swimming and coaching. 'Natationists' were commercial swimmers, diving, holding their breath, performing synchronised swimming, racing and lifesaving in venues like Westminster Aquarium, where women received £2 a week in 1897 and Anne Luker, the high diver, was paid substantially more. Nellie Easton, a swimming mistress at nine metropolitan baths, staged aquatic displays with women pupils, advertising that she never wore corsets in the water. She died in 1919, leaving a fortune of £2,723 10s 9d.[212]

Pools segregated men and women swimmers and often offered inferior pools for women. As a woman Belle White, the first British diver to win an Olympic medal in 1912, could only get access to the high diving board at Highgate Ponds one day a week. White was also a proficient swimmer and competed at three further Games, winning gold at the Europeans in 1927 when she was 33. In 1924, Lucy Morton became the only non-American woman to win a swimming medal at the Olympics, unexpectedly taking gold in the 200 metres. Lucy trained at her local pool, where she had been given permission to swim before and after work, when the pool was usually closed.[213]

The ice skating world championships were considered unofficially to be men-only but when Madge Syers entered the competition in 1902, organisers could find no rule banning women and the judges had to allow her entry. She took second place and went on to beat her husband at the Nationals. She also won two of the new Women's World Championships, and gold at the London Olympics in 1908. Syers began the trend of calf-length skating costumes to show her footwork.[214]

The first recorded ladies' gymnastic event took place in 1904, at a club competition won by Lozells Athletic Club. Twenty years later, a British championships for women were held in Swindon, and in 1928 the British women's team took bronze at the 1928 Olympics.

In 1921, on their return to England after winning the first leg of the Olympiade athletics series in Monte Carlo, the victorious women's team decided to form the London Olympiades Athletic Club.[215] The Men's Amateur Athletics Association did not welcome women members and the Women's Amateur Athletic Association held its first championship in 1923, at which Mary Lines won 4 of the 10 titles. By the time of the

Amsterdam Olympics in 1928, the International Olympic Committee had introduced five women's events: 100 metres, 800 metres, 4 x 100 metres relay, high jump and discus. But it was believed that the strain of running the 800 metres caused women athletes to collapse, and women would be banned from the race until 1960.[216]

Work

The 1851 census had defined housework as 'work',[217] but in 1881, the census-takers decided that if housework was done by 'ladies', it could not be work.[218] So domestic duties undertaken at home by women who were not paid was 'not work'. This resulted in a dramatic fall in the number of women who were counted as employed – from 98 per cent in the 1871 census to 42 per cent ten years later, an apparent disappearance of 56 per cent of the female workforce.[219]

Ten years on, the civil servants planning the 1891 census had another change of mind. Observing the household duties of elite ladies – dusting the delicate china, maintaining social relationships, commissioning gowns, writing letters, planning parties, keeping accounts, planning menus and supervising and disciplining servants, making appointments for husbands and sometimes doing the family business accounts, investing in their business and maintaining their clients, birthing, feeding and raising children – these officials decided that the activities done by women at home were, after all, work: 'The nature of daily occupations of such persons being thus evident, they would be properly reckoned in Domestic Service.'[220]

Good Lord: no! Of course, the daughters, sisters and wives of gentlemen could not be listed like maidservants in 'Domestic Service'. A change had to be made to maintain the illusion that such women were leisured. So in 1901 the census office announced, 'We came to the conclusion that on the whole it would be better to revert.'[221] Women's work remained, but the figures changed. By 1911, only 10 per cent of wives were recorded as working, compared to 70 per cent of single women.[222]

Domestic occupations may have been renamed as leisure to satisfy genteel families who wanted to claim that the ladies of the household did not work, but the re-definition affected everyone. Domestic work in their own home by women had now been defined as an economic zero – 'not paid' and 'not earning', and now not reported. This hid the huge cost of producing babies and children, housing, clothing, feeding and nursing the family so that children could enter education, training and work, and husbands could attend wage-earning work. The census definition of unpaid work also ignored all food or goods produced by the women of the household and consumed by the family, and anything that might earn money but which was not known as 'work' – like craft, art and writing, and all the unpaid clerical, administrative and other work that wives did automatically for husbands. Women of all classes were expected to help their husbands, and this invisible work was so widely understood that many posts were given to men in the knowledge that their wives would work for them, unpaid: 'Most schoolmaster posts went to married men on the understanding that his wife would act as a matron or house-mistress at a boarding school or teacher's assistant at a day school.'[223]

This gave employers and husbands a licence to exploit their wives. Both elite and working-class women, engaged in the endless round of labours inside the home, were, officially, at leisure. As it was not work, it needed no pay. Women's activities in the home had no measurable value. Their time was valueless. Officially: women were doing nothing for no measurable reward.

Ironically, most paid labouring women were working in homes as domestic servants. In 1901, service in private houses formed the biggest single occupation of women, at 31 per cent of women workers.[224] It was badly paid work with long hours, open to girls as they left school at the age of 12. A woman worker wrote in 1906: 'When I was about fourteen years of age I went to service for about eighteen months and I did not like it at all because you was on from morning to night and you never did know when you was done and you never did get your meals in peace for you are up and down all the time, you only get half a day a week and you never get very large wages in service. You never know when you are going to get a good place.'[225]

Many servants hated their work. Middle-class Frances Wilder explained how she entered domestic work after the death of her father, a senior civil servant: 'Though he was one of the best of men in a general way he did not think it necessary that his daughters should have more than a very secondary education, and ... I was quite unfitted to earn my living which I had to do. I took up domestic work – the condition and spirit of which I loathe ... I have not felt in my element with employers who (as so many still do) possess the feudal spirit towards those who serve them.'[226]

Domestic work was physically arduous, with long hours, a female speciality – unsurprisingly, it was badly paid. The value added by workers in the factory was evident; the value added in the home was invisible. Servants too were expected to be invisible, cleaning and lighting fires in empty rooms, silently preparing the house in the morning and closing it down at night. Architectural changes, like servants' quarters, back stairs, basement kitchens and tradesmen's entrances further hid servants and their service from their employers 'upstairs'. Domestic servants lost status as the family rose through the levels of the middle classes, and they were not considered part of the family.

Better education for girls of the middle and upper classes continued, and the 1870 Education Act required all girls to attend school from the age of five to 13, with the 1880 Act making attendance compulsory. In 1873, the government required girls to receive some sort of physical exercise, adopting the Swedish system of gymnastics while boys did military drills. By the 1890s, such was the concern about the health of children that physical education was made compulsory. Boys were encouraged into competitive team games like football, hockey and cricket, and girls were offered netball and rounders. The poorest schools had to make do with drill and Swedish gymnastics, but working-class girls, expected to help at home, had no time to practise after class. Girls' sports usually ended when they left school.[227]

More girls stayed on later, working as pupil-teachers in their school, which would be enough to qualify them as governesses or teachers. The pay and conditions were extraordinarily poor. But one commentator, W.R. Greg, explained it was women's own fault: 'It was ill paid and ill esteemed because it was ill done. Governesses were a depressed and despised class (where they were so) for the same reason that needle women were a distressed class: because, as every woman could read and write and use a needle, as every woman could teach a little, and sew a little, every uneducated woman who was destitute became a sempstress, and every educated or half-educated woman became a governess.'[228]

By 1900, Church of England day centres had begun to train teachers and university colleges opened. Amazingly, the low pay for women teachers continued even when they were better trained. Women accepted low pay because the work was respectable in clean conditions and might even take them – as governesses – into elite homes. By 1901, three-quarters of all teachers were women.[229]

Elite women who could afford the time and the fees could attend lectures; first at Cambridge and then London and Oxford universities, and from the 1870s they were allowed to take the final exams.[230] But at Oxford they were not allowed to graduate or be awarded a degree until 1920, and not until after the Second World War at Cambridge (1948), where male graduates were so appalled that female graduation had even been proposed to the Senate in 1946 – and defeated – that a mob of hundreds of men marched on the women's college of Newnham, broke windows and battered the college gates with a handcart, trying to break in.[231] Sarojini Naidu, poet and campaigner for Indian independence, was the first Asian student to study at King's College London, and Girton College, Cambridge, in 1895–8, and Amy Ida Louisa King was the first woman of African descent to graduate from Girton in 1903.[232] But women who had fought hard to get to university and study found professions closed to them: 80 per cent of female Oxbridge graduates became teachers – earning about three-quarters of their male colleagues' wages.[233] When Gwyneth Bebb and two other women challenged the Law Society for admittance after they graduated with law degrees, their case went to the High Court, where the judges ruled that women's ban from the law was part of 'long, uniform, and uninterrupted usage; which we ought to be very loath to depart from'.[234]

The idea of religious work for both Roman Catholic and Anglican women started to become popular from 1850. Convents opened for religious professionals, providing an easy solution to the so-called problem of 'surplus women', and 3,000 Roman Catholic nuns joined 235 convents in England in 1837; by 1900, they numbered around 10,000 women in 600 convents. Anglican sisterhoods had also developed and by this time 90 Anglican convents had been established.[235] Women, who were already thought to be more spiritual than men, could now live in a completely separate sphere enclosed in a convent, emerging only to perform charitable and spiritual missions. Ironically the high quality of convent schools caused alarm that girls might be getting a superior education to boys.[236]

By 1870, women preachers were mainly to be found in the newly established Salvation Army, a radical, joyful, exuberant evangelical organisation aimed at the working-class poor. Founder Catherine Booth and her daughters, known as 'Hallelujah Lasses', deliberately created a carnival atmosphere for their message. Booth worked alongside her husband William, declaring that no woman was 'subject to man in any sense in which one man is not subject to another; both the law of God and man recognize her as an independent being'.[237]

Women became leaders in other religions. Fatima Cates was a founding treasurer of the Liverpool Muslim Institute, which established an orphanage, a school and a mosque – the first in England, where Sadika Hanoum (birth name Teresa Griffin Viele) worked as a journalist. The first purpose-built mosque in Woking was funded by Begum Shah Jahan of Bhopal.[238]

The Church of England and evangelical sects saw a new wave of preachers known as 'lady preachers' emerge from the 1840s. The women presented themselves as conventional respectable women, trying to bring a complementary spirituality to the men's ministry.[239] In the parishes, from 1862, women could take up the post of 'deaconess', which required no educational or professional qualifications and was not residential. The unordained women were allowed to assist parish priests but not administer any of the sacraments. The church discussed the possibility of women being spiritually equal in the ministry in the 1920 Lambeth Synod – and decided against it. Opponents argued that women were not designed by God for leadership but should be subordinated to male authority.'[240] The synod was proud to be exceptionally resistant to women: the Church of England would argue for the 'disability of sex' long after other professions had allowed women equal entry.[241]

Opponents of female ministry cited St Paul: 'As in all the congregations of the saints, women should remain silent in the churches. They are not allowed to speak, but must be in submission, as the Law says. If they want to inquire about something, they should ask their own husbands at home; for it is disgraceful for a woman to speak in the church.'[242]

Others felt that women wanting to be priests were ambitious: and this was a bad thing. Bishop of Exeter Gascoyne Cecil hinted at other feelings: 'The religious instinct and the sexual instinct were too close to be allowed to be brought into close contact.' The dean of Canterbury, Henry Wace, added the extraordinary claim of spiritual gender: 'There were differences not only in the physical but in the psychical constitution of women which rendered the office of regular public preaching unsuitable.'[243]

England was the last major country in the world to train women doctors.[244] English women had to go abroad to get medical training and qualify in European and American medical schools and universities. The first school for women physicians opened in London in 1874 to a handful of students. The first English woman doctor was Elizabeth Blackwell, who had to practise in the US, followed by Elizabeth Garrett Anderson, who received her licence from the Society of Apothecaries in 1865. The Medical Act passed in the same year tried to prevent women doctors training abroad by forcing all doctors to register with the government. One of the heroines of the women's campaign for medical training was Sophia Jex-Blake. Refused admission to study medicine at the University of Edinburgh, on the grounds that they could not make provision for a single lady, Jex-Blake advertised for other women to join her and six other women studied with her for a medical degree despite verbal and physical abuse from male students. Arriving to sit an exam, they were blocked from the exam room by a mob of 200 men; when they passed their finals, the university refused to let the women graduate. Jex-Blake qualified abroad and put up her brass plate as a doctor at No. 4 Manor Place, Edinburgh, and created Scotland's first hospital for women.

Women doctors, who struggled so hard for qualification and recognition, would be essential to the success of empire when the British state expanded into countries where women were in purdah. Previously abused and excluded, female doctors became an extraordinary asset, helping prise open occupied countries.[245] But progress would be slow. There were only 553 women doctors in Britain in 1912.[246]

Clerking had been an exclusively male job. Younger sons and potential managers entered as clerks to learn the business and work their way up to senior roles. The specific skills of shorthand and typing were originally seen as part of a clerk's repertoire from 1890 and men learned both skills, until they correctly identified that shorthand and typing did not lead to promotion up the managerial ladder: 'Shorthand and typing soon came to be seen as dead-end tasks, men eschewed them, while female clerks were hired exclusively to fulfil them.'[247] When women came into offices from the 1900s, they were restricted to shorthand and typing. Clerking skills did not lead to management posts for women. A woman typist remained as a woman typist until she married – when she automatically left work and was not allowed to return.

Almost all posts in industries, government and educational institutions included a marriage bar, requiring women to leave work after their wedding. No married women could apply for the better-paid office jobs, and a single woman had to leave when she married. Some senior professions did not admit women at all: the upper levels of the civil service, law and accounting remained closed to all women, single and married.[248] This was not seen as a loss to the country of half of the potential labour force. On the contrary it was regarded as beneficial that elite women should be protected from complex work. A 'double-shift' of raising children in an adequate home *and* competing with men at work was thought to damage elite women. It was too much for single women too. It was widely believed that if a woman had to work hard and think, she would become infertile. Neurologist Paul Möbius wrote: 'If we wish woman to fulfil the task of motherhood fully, she cannot possess a masculine brain. If the feminine abilities were developed to the same degree as those of the male, her material organs would suffer, and we should have before us a repulsive and useless hybrid.'[249]

Rigorous demands for appropriate ladylike behaviour filtered down the classes and restricted women in all trades – even women prizefighters. Though fighting professionally as a woman was not in itself a crime, 96 of 166 known female prizefighters were arrested for disorderly behaviour in the second half of the nineteenth century. Eight of them were good enough boxers to beat up the arresting officers and get away.[250]

While women working at home were officially defined as idle, there was a contradictory emphasis on the skills and ability needed to produce a high-quality home. No longer could the wife demonstrate her husband's wealth by her appearance and leisure alone; now she was required to demonstrate his high standards, morality and taste by a beautiful, efficiently functioning, well-run, godly home. Elite women were expected to interfere in the lives of their tenants, while evangelist homes expected ladies to perform church, charity and missionary work in working-class homes.

The first magazine to focus on home management was *The Englishwoman's Domestic Magazine*, published in 1852 by Samuel Beeton.[251] His wife Isabella Beeton wrote *Mrs Beeton's Book of Household Management* in 1861, with 900 pages of recipes and 300 pages of domestic advice, ranging from fashion to servant management, poisons and 'mothercraft'.

Naming 'housework' as a craft or later even claiming for it the status of a science made it worth the effort by an intelligent and educated wife to perform herself, for free. It was not 'charring' or 'skivvying' – unskilled domestic service, to be done by servants – it was a newly named craft. The idea of mothering, cleaning, cooking and maintenance being a worthwhile full-time occupation was not forced on women, it was 'sold' to them, by magazines, journals, books and even lessons in schools. Creative, energetic and entrepreneurial women, confined at home by the doctrine of separate spheres, craved to make something meaningful out of their domestic lives. Mrs Beeton recommended 'an educated approach to household chores ... fill the domestic void and thus preserve the home'.[252]

Domestic work was made more complicated by newly invented equipment. The New Suburbia Gas Cooker in 1929 made cooking more technical but promised more leisure when the adverts invited wives to 'Come out of the kitchen. It does all the cooking while you shop or play.'[253] Despite the promises, mechanisation in the home did not create leisure for women. Closed stoves made cooking more complex and the multiple functions meant that different dishes were expected at the table at the same time. Domestic washing machines enabled laundry to be done at home and done more often; the new vacuum cleaners (available domestically from 1915) forced a solitary woman, working alone, to clean the rugs more frequently in the home – the chore had once been a family effort of hauling them into the garden and beating them.[254]

The new equipment in a mechanised kitchen became the mark of an elite household but required many new skills, and these fell on wives to learn, to operate, clean and maintain, and produce superior results. On average, women spent as many hours reaching higher standards with labour-saving gadgets as they had done before without them.[255]

As middling- and upper-class wives found themselves held to higher and higher standards, training themselves to work harder, while agreeing that this wasn't work, the working women – married or single, ill or fit – were enduring the agonising experience of long factory hours, hard labour in heavy industries (including mining and quarrying) or the arduous work of service in an elite household – and then going home to do their own domestic work in housing that could not be thoroughly cleaned, ventilated or heated, without access to clean water or good food.

The Great War transformed the lives of every woman, even without universal conscription for women. It saw the campaign for votes for women halted and both of the national groups calling for women to have the vote – the NUWSS and the WSPU – split internally over the war, between pacifists who were against and pro-war campaigners. The

National Union of Women's Suffrage Societies set up a register of work vacancies for women volunteers to fill, and the leader of the Women's Social and Political Union, Emmeline Pankhurst, demanded that its women members should serve their country and so earn the right to vote. A grateful government granted her a wartime passport to travel to America to campaign for US support for the Allies. In contrast, some left-wing campaigners for the vote – such as Emmeline's Parkhurst's daughter Sylvia – disagreed with the war, claiming that women were innately opposed to militarism. Sylvia demanded better pay and conditions for working-class women.

One member of the WSPU proved a determined pacifist. Alice Wealden made a poor living from second-hand clothes dealing in Buxton, Derbyshire. On the outbreak of war, she and her daughter Betty joined the 'No Conscription Fellowship' and helped in the underground network set up to hide conscientious objectors from the draft. In 1916, she was approached by a government spy to ask her son-in-law – who was a dispensing chemist – for poison. At her trial – orchestrated by government spies – she was accused of planning to assassinate the prime minister, David Lloyd George, with a poison dart while he was playing golf with King George.

The gothic implausibility of the plot did not deter the jury, who found Alice Wealden and both her daughters guilty. They had been told that the three women were not only politically deviant but abnormal women who had 'transgressed the moral boundaries of gender'. Alice was jailed for conspiracy in 1917 and – like her former WSPU comrades – went on hunger strike. She would be freed in a post-war amnesty but her health had been damaged by her treatment in prison and she died in 1919.[256]

The war also divided the anti-suffrage movement between supporters and pacifists, but as women moved into men's jobs and even into auxiliary military service during the war years, anti-suffrage leaders could no longer argue that women did not participate in the man's world but should stay in a separate sphere of women's influence.[257] The conflict shattered the argument of the separate spheres as a justification for keeping women from power – but the division between so-called 'ladies' and working-class women endured.

Many women supported the war and entered war work on patriotic and feminist grounds. Vera Brittain's courage in stepping out of a comfortable safe elite life led her to volunteer as a Voluntary Aid Detachment nurse, drafted to France. She was prompted to action by her feminism: 'I do not agree that my place is at home doing nothing,' she said.[258]

The welcome women received to wartime work was mixed. Professional medics and the military doubted the commitment of enthusiastic volunteers. Some voluntary associations started life as openly elitist – like the First Aid Nursing Yeomanry (founded 1907), which was open only to young ladies who owned their own horse! When war broke out, the English government declined the help of the FANYs, and the corps – only six women – volunteered to the allies, travelling to Belgium to

Heiress, tennis player, fencer, May 'Toupie' Lowther (1874–1944) mustered an all-woman ambulance unit in the First World War and was awarded the Croix de Guerre

nurse French and Belgian wounded soldiers. They would only be invited to drive British ambulances in 1916.[259]

The extraordinary sportswoman, motorist, fencer, weightlifter, jiu jitsu champion and international tennis player, May 'Toupie' Lowther (1874–1944), organised her own team of women ambulance drivers – the Hackett-Lowther Ambulance Unit – and took 20 cars and 30 women to France. The British army did not use the all-women ambulances, who attached instead to the French Third Army for nearly three years of wartime service. Lowther was awarded the French military medal, the Croix de Guerre, for her service.

Many women's service units grew out of voluntary associations led by elite philanthropic women that were invited to become part of the official services when it became clear how demanding the war would be on manpower. Units like the Women's Land Army, the Women's Army Auxiliary Corps, the Women's Royal Naval Service (WRNS) and the Women's Royal Air Force (WRAF) became official organisations. For many upper- and middle-class women, working alongside other women in wartime was the first time they had met working-class women as equals and learned of the obstacles they faced. But for others, wartime experience perpetuated the class divide: FANY ambulance drivers could wear their fur coats over their uniforms,[260] and it was widely understood that Wrens and FANYs were drawn from elite families, and neither welcomed working-class women.

The history of women in espionage for England has been obscured by the desire to imagine women spies as glamorous double-dealing sexually predatory amateurs. But Gertrude Bell reported to the government on her travels in the Middle East from 1900, and in 1916 she was hired with T.E. Lawrence (Lawrence of Arabia) to work for the so-called 'Arab Bureau'. She was then appointed as an army political officer in the Indian Expeditionary Force. She pretended to have no idea of the value of her work: 'I believe I am to have pay, but fortunately I need not wear uniform! I ought to have white tabs [sign of rank], for I am under the Political Department. It's rather comic isn't it?'[261]

Between 1909, when the British Secret Service Bureau was formed, and demobilisation in 1919, 6,000 women would be recruited. The Field Intelligence Department had 132 officers and thousands of employees of English and African descent. The intelligence establishment paid badly and was unreliably organised, depending heavily on strong-minded,

Flora Sandes (1876–1956), the only known female soldier in the First World War, served as a sergeant-major in the Royal Serbian Army on the front line

discreet women who worked for patriotism and the sense of achievement.[262]

Flora Sandes (1876–1956) was the only English woman to fight as a soldier in the First World War. She joined the FANY with her horse, but left to join Mabel St Clair Stobart's Women's Sick and Wounded Convoy Corps, transporting wounded soldiers in the First Balkan War in 1912. From there, she joined the Serbian Red Cross and supported the wounded during the 'Great Retreat' through Albania, when – as all the other medical staff were killed or ran away – she was enrolled in the Serbian army and advanced on Bitola (Monastir), where she was wounded in hand-to-hand fighting. Promoted to sergeant major and decorated, she spent the rest of the war running a hospital and was later commissioned as the first female officer of the Serbian army.[263]

The English government banned women combatants but actively recruited women into war work factories, trebling the numbers of women in government-controlled workplaces as essential military and munitions industries needed workers when men were conscripted into military service.[264] By the end of the war, 46.7 per cent of the workforce would be female.[265]

Even women at home were required to contribute. The National Food Economy League, the National Union of Women's Suffrage Societies Patriotic Housekeeping Exhibition, and the Food Reform Association all demanded that women at home contribute to the war effort. As one government poster read, 'The British fighting line shifts and extends and now *you* are in it. The struggle is not only on land and sea; it is in *your* larder, *your* kitchen and *your* dining room. Every meal you serve is now literally a battle.'[266]

Women married to men of other nationalities could find themselves under suspicion, or even interned. After the 1914 Nationalism Act, English women lost their nationality on marriage to a foreigner, but an English man marrying someone of any nationality remained English. The 1914 Aliens Restriction Act meant that a foreign-born wife, or an Englishwoman married to a foreign man, could not own a wireless or signalling equipment; some had to register where they lived; some were imprisoned. Later in the war people were forbidden from anglicising a foreign-sounding name – as the royal family did, changing from Saxe-Coburg to Windsor in 1917. Some aliens – people born abroad – who had taken British citizenship found that it was revoked.[267]

One English woman, Martha Earle, was arrested and imprisoned for a year in the women's prison at Holloway for writing to her sister in Germany using what she said were family code words. 'I have never been in such a situation as I have been today and I am nearly mad,' she wrote in May 1918. 'I never thought my letter to my sister would be taken as a crime.'[268]

The moral panic was directed at non-English people, especially women. German-born Frieda Lawrence and her husband, novelist D.H. Lawrence, had to leave their cottage in Cornwall as it was feared that she could see vessels in the shipping lanes and would report to Germany. Margot Asquith, already suspect for her glamour, her friendship with Salome-dancer Maud Allan and for visiting a prisoner-of-war camp, was accused of espionage in a letter sent to the Criminal Investigation Department.[269]

Wartime commentators called for the rooting out of 'disease' in society, meaning anyone who seemed 'different'. Edinburgh University fired all its German members of staff in September 1914, and the internment of all 'aliens' was triggered by public outrage at the sinking of a civilian English ship, the *Lusitania*, with the loss of 1,198 passengers and crew in 1915. Public violence erupted against businesses with German names and against people thought to be German. Englishwomen married to non-English husbands faced deportation and by 1915 nearly 7,000 women – foreign born or foreign-married – had been repatriated, and more were threatened with deportation if they did not leave voluntarily. Because of the shortage of space in internment camps, some women had to be kept in prisons with criminals. Women accused of spying or offences under the Defence of the Realm Act were held with female convicts in the Aylesbury Inebriate Reformatory.[270]

Antisemitic pogroms in Russia before the war had driven 120,000 Russian Jews to the UK, but as the fighting began all Jewish people – about 300,000 – found themselves coming under increasing suspicion in England. Milly Witkop (born Vitkopski), a Jewish anarchist born in Ukraine who had worked in a garment sweatshop in London before the war, lived with a German radical, Rudolf Rocker. Witkop was arrested in 1916 and held without trial under the Defence of the Realm Act. Her partner and older son were interned in a male camp, leaving her eight-year-old boy without his family. She represented herself to the board considering her case in 1917: 'You have kept me in prison for fifteen months without trial. Why do you treat me differently from my comrades Shapiro, Linder, and Lenoble? Why shouldn't we all be allowed to go to Russia? You know that I was arrested because of my political views. Yet I was put in prison with criminals, with prostitutes, with women suffering from disease, with whom I have to share toilet, bath, and crockery.'[271] Milly Witkop demanded deportation from England to the Soviet Union but refused to leave without her partner and son. She remained interned until 1918, when she joined them in the Netherlands.

In 1916, the government introduced conscription for single men aged 18–41, later raising the age to 50 and including married men. Their civilian jobs had to be filled: in essential production, where 2,479,000 women were working in 1916,[272] and on the farms producing food, where 260,000 women in the Women's Land Army started work.[273] Women were persuaded into war work as their form of 'service' to the nation to compare with the military service of the men, and many of them, working-class and elite, rose to the challenge.

Labour boards recruited women workers, moving them to essential work like munitions and housing them in hostels. Married women tended to volunteer in local heavy industry and in outdoor work like farming and hard labour, because those employers provided help with childcare or food shopping to attract workers.[274] Some workplaces received subsidies to offer women special privileges to keep them and their children safe and healthy.

Single women, who could travel, found themselves allocated to the munitions factories, where they loaded explosives into shells, in constant danger of accidents and explosions, and risking TNT poisoning. The factories employed doctors to monitor the workforce for toxic jaundice and the many other illnesses that followed handling, inhaling or ingesting TNT; but they were instructed to prioritise production of the shells and only then to treat patients. Doctors were there to manage the workforce, removing workers who were so heavily jaundiced that they were likely to die, then to obscure the cause of death on certificates and avoid paying compensation where possible.[275]

The cheerful nickname given to jaundiced women of 'Canaries', for their yellowing skin, denied the seriousness of the poisoning. The women, most of them young and single, away from their homes, observed that their skin went yellow and their hair fell out from working with TNT but only later learned that this was a symptom of toxic jaundice. As the war progressed, protective equipment would be issued to munitions workers, and they would be given free milk and subsidised meals to counteract the poison, with shifts reorganised to move women around to give them breaks from the most dangerous areas.

The media churned out charming propaganda about the munitions workers, as journalists and later historians enjoyed the idea that women of all classes had come together in essential war work:

> They have come from the office and the shop, from domestic service
> and the dressmaker's room, from the High Schools and the Colleges,
> and from the quietude of the stately homes of the leisured rich ...
> Even in the early days of the advent of women in the munitions
> shops, I have seen working together, side by side, the daughter of an
> earl, a shop keeper's widow, a graduate from Girton, a domestic
> servant, and a young woman from a lonely farm in Rhodesia, whose
> husband had joined the colours. Social status, so stiff a barrier in this

country in pre-war days, was forgotten in the factory, as in the trenches, and they were all working together as the members of a united family.[276]

Sisterhood in wartime work, like unity in the wartime nation, was a dream of propaganda. The majority of the 200,000 women who worked in munitions were working-class women, mostly escaping domestic service. Very few wealthy and privileged women took on dirty or dangerous work, and many used the excuse that they had to keep households running for returning officers – whose comforts were more important than returning soldiers. It was difficult to match the very limited skills of elite women volunteers with the needs of wartime industry. They were accustomed to giving orders, but unused to hard labour, so they were

1916 recruiting poster for women munitions workers. The infantryman behind waves goodbye as the woman pulls on her overalls to work with toxic chemicals

rarely useful even as managers or supervisors. Often they were allocated to food preparation in the factory canteens. Sometimes they brought their maids to do the work.[277]

The relatively few upper- and middle-class women who volunteered for patriotic reasons found themselves unpopular on the factory floor when they did not support workers' demands for better conditions or pay. Going home to comfortable houses after work, they did not particularly need better conditions at work – according to the memoirs of one middle-class munitions worker, Joan Williams, 'There was much more romance about "war work" when you weren't made too comfortable.'[278]

Philanthropic and charity work suited ladies far better than hard war work in factories. The Duchess of Westminster and Sutherland set up hospitals abroad, and Lady Hamilton (wife of the Commander-in-Chief in the Mediterranean) co-ordinated specific funds and relief efforts in support of her husband's troops.[279]

Women who replaced men were supposed to receive the full male rate of pay in a transparent plan between the all-male government and the all-male trade unions to use women for war work during wartime but prevent them from becoming cheap competition to returning soldiers after the war. Despite the agreement, women were still often paid less than the male rate. Even at the Woolwich Arsenal, the biggest of the munitions factories, where the government was desperate to attract and keep workers, only women crane drivers, inspectors and wages clerks were paid the same as men – and that took two strikes to achieve.[280]

A secret report by the Ministry of Munitions explained that the working men believed they would only get their jobs back after the war if women workers were paid at male rates. The policy of equal pay for war work was in place only to enable women's redundancy, their expulsion 'from the industrial regions into which they have penetrated during the war. Curiously enough the women do not seem to see this.'[281]

Actually, women workers were fully aware that they had to move out of well-paid work to make room for returning soldiers. Many thought it their duty to do so. The government's smug assumption that women did not observe that they were being used in wartime in jobs that would not last, missed the patriotism that drove women into war work – responding to the 1915 government call: 'Do Your Bit; Replace a Man for the Front.'[282]

Most women left their jobs to make work available for returning men without complaint. Fewer women declared themselves in work in the 1921 census than in 1911 – some of them permanently retiring from workplaces that did not want them. There was a rhetoric – widespread and reassuring for men – that the returning men were better at work than the women who had been urged to replace them and then urged to go away again. Women's trade unionist Mary Macarthur described the exclusion of women from work: 'Now the woman is being turned out of her war employment and it is explained that she was never really as satisfactory as she might have been.'[283]

During the war, the WSPU had changed its slogan from 'A woman's right to work' to the more deferential 'A woman's right to serve', and after the war nobody – least of all the suffragette ladies – demanded that a woman had a right to work. One letter writer to the *Daily Herald* said: 'No decent man would allow his wife to work, no decent woman would do it if she knew the harm she was doing to the widows and single girls who are looking for work … send them home to clean their houses and look after the man they married and give a mother's care to their children.'[284]

The larger National Union of Women's Suffrage Societies changed its name to the National Union of Societies for Equal Citizenship in 1919, and pursued a policy of 'new feminism' under leader Eleanor Rathbone, which was focused on women's work as wives and mothers: 'The majority of women workers, are only birds of passage in their trades. Marriage and the bearing and rearing of children are their permanent occupations.' Her views split the membership but played into the return of women into the home after the First World War.[285]

But women had been changed by the experience of a world war. Some had been paid a fair rate for the job for the first time in their lives. Some had been protected by a union, with shopfloor representatives for workers. Some had seen worker representatives reduce unsafe work practices or bargain for better conditions. Some had experienced good conditions like clean washrooms and canteens, and some had enjoyed benefits such as subsidised food or health care. Women working and sometimes living together found it easy to take collective action. Working-class women who had travelled far from their homes and worked for different employers gained confidence and skills. Women who had been provided with food for their families as part of a wage deal to attract them into dangerous or hard labouring work demanded a peacetime welfare payment for each child, and better education, and better-quality food. Women sacked from redundant factories and squeezed out of men's jobs demanded equal unemployment benefit to men.[286]

In many cases, with fathers and brothers away from home at war, the patriarchal discipline in the home broke down and women lost their deference to male authority. Young women in some industries earning equal pay with male workers won admiration for their determination or even heroism; some took the new freedom and enjoyed it, buying the new silk stockings and cosmetics. Some commentators saw moral breakdown and the Defence of the Realm Act was invoked to put curfews on port towns and ban women from pubs and bars. Women's Patrols were formed in many towns with military camps to protect women from soldiers. Advertisements for volunteers were published in the *Suffragette*, the newspaper of the Women's Social and Political Union. Once active they ended up patrolling the streets and arresting women for doing nothing more than meeting soldiers.[287] Far from controlling predatory men, they were keeping surveillance on the so-called 'dangerous' behaviours of women.[288] As a letter from 'a general' confirmed: 'The services of the two ladies in question have proved of great value. They have removed the sources of trouble to the troops in a manner that military police could not attempt. I have no doubt whatever the work of these two ladies is a great safeguard to the moral welfare of young girls in the town.'[289] Not everyone agreed that civilian women should be 'removed' from being sources of trouble. 'Three Respectable Maids' complained of the 'League of Decency and Honour', set up by the National Union of Women Workers: 'It is a poor do if we men and women cannot look after ourselves ... these so-called ladies ... ought to mind their own business, and instead of joining the League of Honour ought to join the League of Hard Work, and then they would not have so much time to bother about other people's affairs. We think it is one of the most wicked insults to us girls and also to the soldiers.'

This was an ideal moment for advisors and commentators to suddenly recall the importance of home-making and the essential presence of the wife and mother at home. These two strands of thought – getting women out of competing for paid work and glamourising unpaid work at home – prompted the TUC to call for a 'mother's pension' in 1919, and for a government committee to remind women that they had a purpose far more important than wage work: 'The primary function of women in the state must be regarded ... she must be safeguarded as homemaker for the nation.'[290]

Asian and African women and their descendants particularly suffered from the shrinking of the labour market as wartime work was cut back and returning soldiers demanded their previous civilian jobs. When sailors and soldiers from imperial countries were demobbed, there was a drive to make the men return to their former homes abroad. White working-class men led race riots against demobbed men of colour. Black seamen were attacked and abused in the streets of port towns like Liverpool and Bristol in 1919, during days of riots and pitched battles in the streets. In one night alone in Liverpool, 700 men, women and children of colour had to hide in a 'Bridewell' and in other prisons from a race mob.[291] A riot developed in Newport after it was said that a Black man had made a remark or embraced a white woman, and in Cardiff racists attacked a coach party of Black men with their white wives.[292] The white rhetoric around the riots – all caused by white lynch mobs motivated by racial hatred and economic grievances – demanded the soldiers of colour return to their colonial homes and an end to association between them and white women. The irony of a colonial race insisting that people stay in the land of their birth was invoked by Felix Hercules, of the national liberation movement in the British West Indies, in *The Times* of June 1919:

> I do not believe that any excuse can be made for white men who take the law into their own hands because they say they believe that the association between the men of my race and white women is degrading.
>
> If ... the problem can be solved by sending every black or coloured unit forthwith back to his own country, then we should be compelled to see that every white man is sent back to England from Africa and from the West India islands in order that the honour of our sisters and daughters there may be kept intact.[293]

White women were used as an excuse for racist complaints and as a justification for riot. Their own safety or feelings were never considered. White women were accused of immorality if they befriended, loved or married men of African or Asian descent. A panic was created around future children, and racism was fuelled by the government's slowness and indecision in sending colonial troops home when they were demobbed and even failing to recognise or reward their service.[294]

The most noticeable change in work patterns after the war was the flight from domestic service. Nearly a third of working women had been servants before the war, but in the first post-war census (1921), only 19 per cent of women remained in service. Many had transferred into offices and shops: 7 per cent of the female workforce had been working in retail in 1901, but by 1921 the figure was 10 per cent. Most had gone to offices, as the increase in clerks and typists showed: 1901, 2 per cent; 1921, 10 per cent.[295] The decline in the numbers of women in the textile trade was caused by further mechanisation and a general slump in the business.

Some wartime professional women complained of being excluded from work by the marriage bars imposed in teaching, nursing and the civil service, and in many commercial companies.[296] The need for these skilled workers gave rise to the 1919 Sex Disqualification (Removal) Act, which ruled that: 'A person shall not be disqualified by sex or marriage from the exercise of any public function, or from being appointed to or holding any civil or judicial post, or from entering or assuming or carrying on any civil profession or vocation.'[297]

Many women professionals took the passing of the act as a starting pistol and were off the blocks and into law, veterinary surgeries, JP and graduate roles. But an unofficial bar stayed firm in many places. A large number of civil service posts remained men-only, and the sensitivity about protecting women's innocence led judges to exclude them from juries,[298] and even ask qualified women lawyers to leave their clients without representation in the courtroom if the evidence was thought to be 'unsuitable' for a lady to hear.[299] The law would be one of the last professions in the UK to admit women; preferring male juniors in cliquey lawyers' chambers and refusing applications to the Law Society.[300] The shortage of lawyers during the 1914–18 war and after, thanks to death and injury, finally forced the Law Society to open its doors to women lawyers.[301]

In some companies, women were segregated in women-only departments with their own entrance and hours. A Bank of England report in 1921 admitted that women were kept apart – not to protect their respectability, but to prevent the women on the 'ladies' floor' from seeing the more interesting work that was being done by men elsewhere in the building.[302]

Women expanded their role in education post-war at all levels: by 1930, 14 per cent of university teachers were women – though some Oxford colleges remained men-only.[303]

The first women's police volunteers split over the decision to curfew women around military camps, and two organisations were formed which expanded to police women workers in the munitions factories during wartime, safety legislation in factories, women and children on the streets and even traffic. By 1917, there were 500 women police officers, but with the end of the war they were demobbed and the service became the Women's Auxiliary Service. The Metropolitan Police for London recruited 100 women constables for a women's patrol from 1919.[304] A woman doctor, Letitia Fairfield, reassured an anxious parliamentary committee that a woman could, without grave damage to her health, be on her feet for eight hours a day. (Good news, eh?)

Elite women became professional nurses, progressing naturally from part-time voluntary work. A separate training programme for 'lady' probationers began in 1860, requiring an elite woman to complete her training in one year, rather than the two or three years for working-class recruits, and housed lady probationers in their own exclusive halls of residence.[305] The Royal College of Nursing (for training nurses) was founded during the war, in 1916.

After centuries of criticism, midwives received official training in 1902, and in 1910 those who were not certified were banned from practising.[306] This represented a further attack on experienced but unqualified women healers and had the effect of medicalising birth and driving pregnant women from their homes and into hospitals to give birth. But midwives who could afford the training and gain the qualification won professional status and membership of a professional association.

But women doctors were excluded from training and work after the war, in order to accommodate men who wanted to return to medicine or train as doctors. St George's Hospital, London, stopped admitting women as clinical students in 1919, fearful that new male doctors would have to work under a better-qualified woman: an 'intolerable' position for 'an ex-Service man who has, perhaps, as his House Surgeon over him, a girl of twenty-two', according to medical students complaining of the competition. The London Hospital promoted a woman doctor to a residency in 1922 and her male colleagues threatened to resign. Hospitals all around the country refused to train women, explaining that women would marry and give up their practice, and that the course covered topics inappropriate for them.[307]

Part 8

1928–1945
Into the World

Women Get the Vote

For the first time in England, in May 1929, all women over the age of 21 had the right to vote in the general election. Nicknamed the 'flapper election' by the popular press, denigrating the seriousness of the young female vote, the three parties – Conservative, Liberal and Labour – specifically campaigned to young women. Labour and Liberal emphasised equality for women in their posters, while Conservatives offered welfare for mothers and families and dedicated an entire poster campaign to cheaper tea.

The 1929 Conservative Party poster campaign calling women to show their gratitude for the suspension of tax on tea

Some women who had spent their lives campaigning for the vote believed they had won it for their war service; others thought they had only been given it so that no working-class men would have a vote when elite women did not – a bitter victory. Votes from the newly enfranchised men and women were spread across the three parties, and the Labour Party formed a minority government, with 14 women MPs – only 2.3 per cent of the whole. One was Ellen Wilkinson, who called herself a 'flaming socialist'.

She believed that class not sex caused working women's suffering: 'The woman who earns her living, whether as a wife or a wage earner ... is suffering mainly from the wrongs that afflict all her class,' she wrote. Wilkinson, and many post-campaign women, wanted an improvement for all working and poor people.[1]

Women found it hard to identify and campaign for women's causes – there was rarely a united female response to any single question. Class remained deeply divisive: upper-class ladies had little in common with working-class women; middle-class women measured their social rise by leaving their working-class roots behind.[2] Women employers, landowners and business people had a vested interest in keeping wages down and rents up. Even when feminists demanded equal wages for equal work, they favoured single women as the surviving marriage bars in some professions put wives out of work. Ironically, when feminists called for a benefit to be paid to mothers, it only rewarded married women who stayed at home.[3]

The Great Depression stalled discussion about working women's rights, causing devastating unemployment, which fell hard on women workers. Britain's world trade halved, and in 1932, 3.5 million people (of a population of 18 million) found themselves out of work. Heavy industries, mostly sited in northern England, were hit the worst, with unemployment reaching 70 per cent in some regions. People went hungry and childhood malnutrition became common. The counties around London avoided the worst poverty, thanks to the development of new light industries of electrical goods and cars, and a boom in house-building.

Poor women grew poorer as wealthy women maintained their high standards of living. The defeat of the trade unions in the General Strike meant they were too weakened to defend the poor and unemployed against economic collapse and new laws. Jean Edmonds, daughter of a Liverpool docker, remembered: 'Poverty was all around us and it was only later that I was to discover the reason for my own father's irregular and low paid work. In 1926 during the General Strike in support of the locked-out miners, my father had been involved in active strike action and as such, had been a marked man ever since … It was that huge defeat and betrayal of the 1926 General Strike that made it so hard for us to fight against the most horrible mass unemployment, hunger and poverty in the 1930s.'[4]

Marjorie Broad, a schoolgirl in Yorkshire, remembered the miners' children: 'Our village school also took pupils from the nearby mining village of Moorends; they often came to school shoeless, even in winter … I recall there was a "Poor Law" official who, if you applied for help, would come to the house and assess your request. But you'd have had to sell your furniture to raise funds first, only being allowed to retain the beds.'[5]

The Labour Party was anxious not to appear radical. A woman minister of labour and former trade union leader, Margaret Bondfield, passed the Anomalies Act of 1931, disqualifying 180,000 wives from a benefits scheme even though they had paid contributions. Welfare payments were set below the minimum amount required to buy food and maintain health, according to the British Medical Association in 1933.[6]

The Means Test of 1931 gave inspectors the right to examine the finances of the whole household before granting any benefits to wives, mothers or children. Jean Edmonds in Liverpool remembered 'the neighbouring family being visited by a means test inspector on the eve of their baby son's funeral and told that they would have to pawn the table under the coffin, before they could qualify for unemployment relief'.[7]

In October 1936, Ellen Wilkinson led 200 unemployed men on a march from the town of Jarrow in Tyneside, north-east England. Eighty per cent of the workforce in the steel and shipyard town were unemployed; child mortality was double the national average.[8] The unemployed men marched nearly 300 miles to the House of Commons, with a 12,000-name petition, begging for help. Official trade unions refused to support the march, and Prime Minister Stanley Baldwin would not meet them. After the marchers had delivered the petition, it was promptly lost – the matter was not debated in the Houses of Parliament, and the government offered no assistance.[9] It was a dramatic demonstration of the indifference of the wealthy men and women in government to the want and despair of the working classes.

Nora Boswell, a girl of the middle classes, said: 'Aged 24, my mother went to see the Jarrow marchers at Covent Garden. When she saw

'Jarrow's plight, is not a local problem. It is the symptom of a national evil.'
Ellen Wilkinson (1891–1947), Labour MP on the hunger march of 1936

students throwing cabbages at them, she laughed. Years later, she told me she had never ceased to feel guilty for that laugh. It was, I think, a moment that began a change in her view of others.'[10]

The Great Depression divided politicians proposing political and economic solutions from the left and right wings. Women also joined both political extremes, as shown in women's response to the Spanish Civil War when they volunteered on both sides. Edith Pye from the Society of Friends, the Quakers, brought 4,000 refugees from Bilbao into England.[11] The Communist Party of Great Britain recruited women into leadership roles but had no specific policies on women's rights or sexism.

The British Fascisti, Britain's first fascist organisation, was formed by former Scout and ex-servicewoman Miss Rotha Lintorn-Orman (1895–1935) in 1923,[12] but her movement lost members to the British Union of Fascists (BUF) under Sir Oswald Mosley. Lady Maud Mosley (Sir Oswald's mother) launched a women's section, with some confusion over fascist policy on women, some of whom expected equality in the front line of the struggle, while other women recruits rather hoped that they would be paid to stay at home.[13] Lady Mosley handed over leadership to activist Mary Richardson, who had slashed a famous painting, the Rokeby Venus, in a suffragette protest in 1914. She wrote in *The Blackshirt*, the movement's magazine: 'I was first attracted to the Blackshirts because I saw in them the courage, the action, the loyalty, the gift of service, and the ability to serve which I had known in the suffragette movement.'[14]

Fascist women supported male political campaigners and acted directly, stewarding meetings, where they targeted women demonstrators, campaigning on the streets and standing for Parliament: 10 per cent of BUF candidates were women, a proportion that would not be achieved by other parties until the 1980s.[15] The BUF produced feminist policies: Anne Brock-Giggs explained that housewives would have proper representation, there would be equal pay and higher wages, and the bar on married women working would be abolished in order to free women to work for the nation. Women would be helped with families too – financial and medical assistance would improve the health of the nation's poor, and contraception would be available in the hope of reducing the family sizes among those considered inferior.[16] Fascists believed that women should 'fulfil their nature': Oswald Mosley wrote, 'We want men who are men, and women who are women.'[17] So that's clear.

Antisemitism was introduced into the BUF's rhetoric from German Nazis and the fascists started to attack Jewish people. In Stepney, London, there were frequent attacks on the streets,[18] and a mob stoned the windows of a laundry to prevent Jewish girls attending a laundry class.[19] The BUF planned a huge march through London's East End, but the display of militaristic power, which they hoped would overawe people, actually united the poor, working class, immigrants and Jewish people of the area into determined opposition to the march. Local people acting in spontaneous self-defence, blocked the proposed route and fought hand-to-hand with the police who attempted to clear the way for the fascist parade. Later named the Battle of Cable Street, it proved a turning point for British fascism, which found working people, Jewish and Irish people united against it.[20]

Women joined in the battle: of 79 anti-fascist protesters arrested at Cable Street, 8 were women. Local communist activist Phil Piratin recalled: 'It was along Cable Street that from the roofs and the upper floors, people, ordinary housewives, and elderly women too, were throwing down milk bottles and other weapons and all kinds of refuse that they didn't any longer want in the house onto the police.'[21] Women were on the street as well. Sarah Wesker, a Jewish trade union organiser, led protests, and Jewish 12-year-old Joyce Rosenthal said: 'The police … were just hitting everyone. There were women going down under the horses hooves.'[22]

Rosenthal saw a 16-year-old boy climb a lamppost and shout to the crowd: 'Don't be yellow bellies, forward, we are winning!' Four years later they met, and she asked him if '"he was the nutcase up the lamp post?" … he was just her type'.[23]

Another eyewitness at the police station said he saw 'a huge policeman drag in a young woman, rip off her blouse and hold his truncheon as if to strike her in the face. She stared straight at him and, with defiance in her voice, said: "I am not afraid of you." As the room went quiet, the policeman called her a Jewish bitch and put her in a cell.'[24]

The people who protested at their neighbourhood being cleared so that a militaristic parade could be marched through their streets found themselves accused by the pro-fascist newspapers of leaderless riot. *Time* magazine wrote: 'Ignoring orders from the Labour Party and prominent British Labour leaders, half a million British proletarians liberally sprinkled with Jews went on an anti-fascist rampage last week which turned out to be London's biggest riot in years.'[25] It was the traditional complaint that a spontaneous uprising of poor people was a 'riot'.

As tensions grew in Europe, preparation for another war stimulated the economy with increased demand for munitions, and sidelined the debate over feminism and women's rights. Women divided into those who were for and against the coming war. Even women pacifists were not united, as some called for peace despite the defeat of the Spanish government and the rise of Nazi Germany, and some supported rearmament to enforce peace from a strong negotiating position.[26]

Work

The Great Depression drove more women out of work and contributed to a sense that they should not be employed. Nostalgia – for the time before the First World War – rekindled the separate spheres dream of a breadwinning father successful in the wider world and a wife and mother providing a nurturing, spiritual home. No longer were men idolised as adventurers, explorers and soldiers; doubts about empire and the horror of the war inspired an appreciation of peaceful domestic lives, 'family' men, good husbands, fathers and fair-playing sportsmen.[27] The separate spheres ideal evolved into an imaginary partnership where an ideal husband was still the chief breadwinner but now he participated in family life. The wife and mother was still the creator of the home, managing ethics and appearances, but this ought not to be self-sacrifice – now the stay-at-home wife was supposed to find her home a source of emotional satisfaction and pride.

The falling birth rate meant smaller families and higher expectations of mothering. Children – now banned from work – should be at home and school, being improved rather than exploited. Mothering – defined as natural to all women – was heavily promoted as a 'noble calling'. Although childcare was supposed to come naturally to women, and all women instinctively know how to care for a baby and child, there was a rapid expansion of expert advisors and child psychologists who taught that babies and children needed firm discipline, clear boundaries and a regular timetable. Mothers were expected to know by their nature what they should do, but natural informal spontaneous behaviour was wrong. Childcare required a strict timetable, just like industrial work. Children should be prepared for the working world.

The war raised questions about the quality of men available to serve as soldiers. Many conscripted men were rejected by the army for disabilities and poor health, and this was believed to be the fault of inadequate mothering. It was widely agreed that women must leave the jobs that should only ever have been temporary, get back into the house and make good homes for working men and healthy children.[28]

Housework too must be made more efficient and scientific. Specialists in housework, now rebranded as 'Domestic Science', advised women in magazines, and girls at school, that it was a serious profession, suitable for an educated woman.[29] But the equipment for housework and cooking, built in factories and serviced and maintained by specialists, did not empower housewives – it turned them into workers who operated machines, without knowing how they worked, or even what was the value of their work.

Whatever they were called, housewives were not 'home-makers', 'domestic scientists' or 'home technicians' – they were consumers, working unpaid, buying kit to do simple tasks, using chemicals as instructed on the packets. Traditional skills of baking and brewing, cleaning and textile work were lost from women and passed from the kitchen to the factory. New gadgets may have been 'labour-saving' – doing work faster or more efficiently – but the time saved was not taken by women for leisure. The gadgets raised standards and so created more work, and longer hours for women.[30]

The expansion of light industry and the invention of the assembly line suited women workers and the new factories paid better wages to attract all women without a marriage bar. In the aftermath of the Great Depression, some families were wholly dependent on the woman's wage. But unions tried to preserve jobs for men and maintain unequal wages to advantage men: 'Most of our present ills are traceable to the policy of employing less men and more women,' wrote the general secretary of the Post Office Workers' Union in 1931.[31]

Women managed to get a 'Domestic Servant Charter' and a 'Nurse Charter' on the trade union demands, but they were opposing a mood – supported by fascist propaganda, plus the new fashion for domesticity, plus the old breadwinner wage argument, plus the separate spheres ideology, plus the new science of mothering – that women should be at home. It was a perfect storm that blew women back into unpaid domestic work in their homes.

The Married Women's Property Acts of the nineteenth century had created, by accident, a situation in which wives might control their own wealth but husbands were still liable for their wives' debts. 'In this case we ought to consider the rights of husbands,' said Lord Chancellor Viscount Cave in 1925. Husbands – who had enjoyed the wealth of their wives for more than 800 years – rushed to resolve injustice when it went against them, and got the anomaly fixed in a record 50 years.[32]

The Married Women's Property Acts left some women's fortune in trusts controlled by male trustees. Edwina Mountbatten (1901–60), one of the richest women in Britain, heiress to the financier Sir Ernest Cassel, ran up tens of thousands of pounds in debt as Vicereine of India (wife to Earl Mountbatten of Burma), and brought a private bill to Parliament to allow her to break the restraint on her inheritance. The government introduced its own bill and the Law Reform Act of 1935 abolished trusts to serve as restraints on heiresses and ended the liability of husbands for their wives' debts.[33]

Health

More women were dying in childbirth in 1921 than they had been a decade earlier, but health visitors were not allowed to advise on contraception – even to married women. One mother of eight children living in two rooms in Battersea told an inquiry: 'I had a bed in the back for the two girls, a bed for the boy which I take down every day and put up at night to make more room. We have our food in this room, I do all my cooking here. In the other room is my bed, a bed I make up for the other little boy on the settee, and the pram the baby sleeps in.'[34]

Stopes clinics for working women were few and far between, but patent medicines to 'bring on' bleeding were widely advertised and sometimes effective. Most of the customers for the widely advertised pills to 'restore health' were married women of all classes who preferred to induce a miscarriage than to birth or raise another child. When a woman could not afford the pills, or found them ineffective, she resorted to all sorts of interventions, some effective and some dangerous. One reported: 'In the thirties, my aunt died self-aborting. She had three children and couldn't feed a fourth … So she used a knitting needle. She died of septicaemia leaving her children motherless.'[35]

At least 15 per cent of women who were registered as dying in childbirth – about 300 women a year in the decade from 1923 – died from abortions, and that number was almost certainly an underestimate because doctors would conceal a fatal illegal abortion on the death certificate to spare the feelings of the family.[36]

Women were frequently prosecuted for abortion, and there were generally up to 50 women abortionists imprisoned in Holloway Prison at any given time, serving sentences of as much as 14 years. The women were unqualified but not incompetent, and not all of them worked solely for the money. One said: 'I knew it was against the law but I didn't think it was wrong. Women have to help each other.'[37]

Abortions were legal if two doctors agreed that the mother's life was endangered by the pregnancy or she would die in childbirth. In 1938, this inadequate abortion law was challenged by a London obstetrician, Dr Aleck Bourne, who treated a 14-year-old girl with cognitive disability. She had been raped by five off-duty guards officers, who had invited her

Beecham's Pills to cause abortions were advertised to 'assist Nature in her wondrous functions'

to the Royal Horse Guards Barracks, promising her a horse with a 'green tail'. When her mother took the girl to St Thomas's Hospital, the consultant refused to abort, saying that since the five rapists were officers, 'she might be carrying a future prime minister'.[38]

The highly regarded Dr Bourne agreed that although there was no immediate danger to life to the girl – as required by the law for an abortion – there were such risks to her physical and mental health that 'If one waited for danger to life, the woman would be past assistance.'[39]

He carried out an abortion and was taken to court, accused of performing illegal surgery. The judge ruled that doctors might perform surgical abortion (before 28 weeks) to protect a woman's mental and physical health. She did not have to be at risk of death from the pregnancy or birth to justify an abortion.

The Women's Co-operative Guild congress of 1934 – continuing its remarkable campaign for the rights of working-class women – called on the government to legalise abortion like any other surgical procedure.[40] The Abortion Law Reform Association was formed in 1936 by Stella Browne, Dora Russell, Frida Laski and Joan Malleson, and in three years had nearly 400 members – mostly working-class women. Browne, courageously, spoke of her own abortion when she gave evidence to the 1937 Inter-Departmental Committee on Abortion: 'If abortion were necessarily fatal or injurious, I should not now be here before you,' she said.[41]

Stella Browne (1880–1955) believed that women should be able to have sexual experiences outside marriage and control of their fertility.[42] She linked the ban on abortion to the many ways that women were controlled: 'What is this ban on abortion? It is a sexual taboo, it is the terror that women should experiment and enjoy freely, without punishment. It is the survival of the veiled face, of the barred window and the locked door, of burning, branding, mutilation and stoning; of all the pain and fear inflicted ever since the grip of ownership and superstition came down on women, thousands of years ago.'[43]

Childbirth itself was a dangerous procedure, especially for poor women. Giving birth could be fatal for women suffering from malnutrition and 'rickets'. Country women and poor women attended by a midwife who did not go from patient to patient still had more healthy births than those in towns attended by professional men with multiple patients.[44] Sepsis and puerperal fever continued to cause many deaths until the male medical profession finally agreed to basic hygiene practices, such as wearing masks, gloves and aprons, and antiseptic procedures.

Women Loving Women

The new professional sociologists (all men) discussed love between women but – as sexologists – they were mostly interested in women's love if it was sexual. Women's love for women came to be defined as a sexual experience using genital touching to stimulate orgasm, and everything else was defined as platonic love, meaning non-sexual, or friendship. Female lovers were assumed to be attempting to reproduce heterosexual intercourse as best they could without the necessary equipment. Women's desire for other women was said to be an 'inversion' of their true nature, which was assumed to be heterosexual. The same belief when applied to homosexual lovers led some sexologists to suggest that both lesbians and homosexuals were 'inverting' their natural desires, and they created and named a new third sex called 'inverts'.

For men, the definition of homosexuality as a hereditary disability could be helpful as it provided a defence against the severe laws that banned homosexual acts. For women, it defined what had been a normal and widespread loving relationship as an act of genital sexuality, a sin, and a disability or illness. Passionate female devotion was both sexualised and pathologised.[45]

Some women found the new label helpful as yet another definition of female nature – but one that widened the parameters of expected behaviour. Some acknowledged their sexuality and deliberately created an androgynous or manly appearance. Some were glad to break the 'asexual' model of romantic female friendship and claim their own erotic nature.[46] But some women continued to insist that a deep love for women could be untouched by sexuality. The notes on one of Havelock Ellis's own patients, who he described as a 'true invert', read more like a woman whose love was not sexual but highly spiritual. 'Miss M' told him: 'I love few people … But in those instances when I have permitted my heart to go out to a friend, I have always experienced most exalted feelings, and have been made better by them morally, mentally, and spiritually. Love is with me a religion. The very nature of my affections for my friends precludes the possibility of any element entering into it which is not absolutely sacred.'

Vera Brittain's biography of her friend Winifred Holtby specifically described a lasting love between two women without erotic overtones. She was clear that women's shared love was ennobling and would lead to other spiritual loves: 'Loyalty and affection between women is a noble relationship which far from impoverishing actually enhances the love of a girl for her lover, of a wife for her husband, of a mother for her children.'[47]

Women at War

All single women between 19 and 40 years of age were conscripted into National Service in December 1941. Wives, mothers and those single women who headed a household with servants – so upper- and middle-class single women – were exempt.[48] Conscripted women had to choose a wartime occupation, such as mechanic, engineer, munitions worker, air raid warden, bus and fire engine driver. Within two years, almost 90 per cent of single women and 80 per cent of married women were employed in essential work in heavy industries like engineering, metals, chemicals, vehicles, transport, energy and shipbuilding.[49]

Women could choose to join one of the auxiliary services – the Auxiliary Territorial Service (ATS), the Women's Auxiliary Air Force (WAAF) or the Women's Royal Naval Service (WRNS) – but they could not be combatants.[50] Class snobbery persisted in the services: the ATS, the Women's Army Auxiliary Corps and the Women's Voluntary Service were all headed by elite women, indicating the suitability of these services for middle- and upper-class conscripts. Many ladies volunteered for patriotism, and some hurried into snob services before they were allocated to lesser-status company.[51]

A total of 640,000 women enlisted in women's divisions of the armed forces.[52] The ATS first recruited women as cooks, clerks, orderlies, store women or drivers in 1938, but they went on to serve in anti-aircraft command, on searchlights – the 93rd Searchlight Regiment were all female. They also worked in mixed batteries on anti-aircraft guns, despite officially not being allowed to fire them.[53] Their marching to the tune of 'Anchors Away' suggests different:

> We are the ATS marching along
> We are the Ack Ack girls
> and this is just our marching song
> We joined the Royal Artillery
> to fight for yours and mine
> And when we see a jerry plane
> we shoot the blighter
> Shoot the blighter down[54]

Women aged 18–50 and living near naval ports could apply for shore-based jobs in the WRNS to release men for service at sea. Wrens played a major part in the planning and organisation of naval operations, serving at Bletchley Park and its out-stations, operating machines used in code-breaking.[55]

Wren Gwyneth Verdon-Roe wrote home in 1944: 'I am so glad I am a plotter – it is the most exciting job because we are in on everything that is happening. The night of 4th-5th June I was on all night. We worked flat out till dawn and then the whole thing was called off because of bad weather. The disappointment was terrible, the anti-climax after all the stress. We were tearful and tired and had never felt so low in all our lives.'[56]

There were far more women code-breakers than men at the now famous Bletchley headquarters – 8,000 of them to 2,000 men. One was Joan Clarke, recruited to break the Enigma Code. She worked alongside Alan Turing and they were briefly engaged to marry. Even as a lead code-breaker she was paid less than the men.

ATS plotters at Coastal Artillery Headquarters in Dover, December 1942

Founded in 1939, the Women's Auxiliary Air Force compiled weather reports, maintained aircraft, served on airfields and worked in intelligence.[57] Women also worked in the Royal Observer Corps, maintaining and flying barrage balloons.[58] The Air Transport Auxiliary (ATA) were known as the 'Attagirls', delivering planes to airfields all around Britain, often in bad weather and in unfamiliar planes.

'You didn't know what type of plane you were going to fly that day,' said Joy Lofthouse. 'You'd get out of a Tiger Moth after delivery and then into a Wellington bomber. After that, you could be flying a Spitfire.'

Instead of flying the plane using the instruments, the women were told to stay within sight of the ground and navigate using maps, a compass and a watch. It was extremely dangerous in bad weather or poor visibility. One woman, Mary Wilkins, was known as 'Fog Flyer' for her bad-weather navigation.[59] Jackie Moggridge joined ATA at the age of 18 and ferried 1,438 planes to waiting RAF pilots, flying 82 different types of aircraft. She later became the first female commercial airline captain.[60]

Jackie Moggridge (1922–2004) flew as a pilot with the ATA during the Second World War, and later with the RAF Voluntary Reserves. Pictured here after the war with her daughter Candy Atkins

The iconic fighter plane the Spitfire was designed by a woman draughtswoman. Stella Rutter finalised and corrected the drawings that were prepared by three male draughtsmen working under her, and checked them again before they were printed as manufacturing guides for the Vickers-Supermarine factory in Southampton. She was paid the same as the men: £3 a week. Her security clearance was so high that when the Allied Command was looking for a 'lady' to host the leaders before D-Day at a top-security dinner, Rutter was invited to attend:

> That was a huge responsibility for a woman of my age. There was great trust being put in me, one which I never betrayed. I was requested to help all of these commanding officers to eat, drink, dance, sit down and meet other officers who would be on their right and left on the battlefield, and meet them and know them by sight. I think approximately sixty-two other officers were in attendance and Major General Omar Bradley turned up as well, and as a hostess I was, of course, introduced to and worked with them all.[61]

Not even on the eve of the decisive battle of the Second World War should a man have to pour his own drink.

Women also volunteered for the First Aid Nursing Yeomanry (FANY), Women's Voluntary Service (WVS) or served in Civil Defence, the National Fire Service or in military nursing.[62] Thousands of FANYs were recruited for the Special Operations Executive and about 60 were trained as spies, parachuting into occupied countries to organise resistance fighters preparing the way for the Allied invasion. Among the heroines were French-born Vera Leigh, captured and murdered,[63] and Odette Sansom, captured while serving with the French resistance and tortured by the Gestapo.[64] Violette Bushell, a shop girl inspired to serve by the death of her husband Étienne Szabo of the French Foreign Legion, was dropped into France twice, before being captured, tortured, sent to Ravensbrück concentration camp and executed, aged 23, in 1945. Pearl Witherington was said to be the best shot of the SOE and served in the French resistance with a million-franc bounty on her head. She survived the war and explained that she had wanted to defend France: 'I just thought, This is impossible. Imagine that someone comes into your home – someone you don't like – he settles down, gives orders: "Here we are, we're at home now; you must obey." To me that was unbearable.'[65]

British resistance agent Noor Inayat Khan (1914–44) was posthumously awarded the George Cross for her courage as an SOE radio operator in occupied Paris and a prisoner at Dachau

Noor Inayat Khan was the daughter of an Indian Muslim family of musicians and poets, a descendant of the ruler of Mysore, Tipu Sultan. She overcame her Buddhist belief in not taking life because of her opposition to Nazism and her hope of making common cause between Indian and English people. 'I wish some Indians would win high military distinction in this war,' she said. 'If one or two could do something in the Allied service which was very brave and which everybody admired, it would help to make a bridge between the English people and the Indians.'[66]

She was the first woman radio operator ever dropped into France, and she chose to stay on in Paris as the only English radio operator, even when her circle was broken up and she was offered evacuation. Life expectancy for a radio operator, who had to reveal their location with every transmission, averaged six weeks. Arrested by the Gestapo, she escaped, only to be recaptured and spend ten months, shackled hands and feet, in solitary confinement. Transferred to Dachau concentration camp, she was shot in 1944.

The Women's Auxiliary Service (Burma), or WAS(B), consisted of a band of 250 British women, also known as the Chinthe Women, who worked alongside troops during the Burma campaign. One soldier remembered a 'Chinthe Woman':

> The Burma Road was being washed away as my Platoon was marching towards Pegu. In the distance we saw a lone lady standing by a table in the rain, and as we got nearer we saw she had lots of mugs of hot tea on the table. She gave us all tea and a packet of cigs and a wad. She was a lovely Scots lady who must have been 50 years old. I spoke to her and told her she was too near the guns, and she should go to a safer place, after all the Japs were only 4 miles up the road. She would not leave and said, 'There will be other soldiers behind you who will want tea. I am just a WAS(B).'[67]

The women who worked on British farms came to be known as 'Land Girls' of the Women's Land Army, paid directly by the farmers who employed them.[68] The average wage for male agricultural workers had been 38s per week, but the women who replaced them were paid 28s per week, with 14s deducted for board and lodging, and a basic working week of 48 hours in winter and 50 in summer, and no holidays. Conditions improved after 1943 with the introduction of the 'Land Girls Charter', giving them a week's holiday a year and raising the minimum wage.[69] One woman – Amelia King from Stepney, of African descent – was rejected by Essex County Council, which said that farmers would not want her labour and local people would not provide housing. The racist rejection was raised in the House of Commons, which could think of no solution but that Amelia King apply to another service.[70]

The Women's Timber Corps, known as 'Lumber Jills', were recruited to fell trees and manage forests for essential wood supplies.[71] Annice Gibbs, who worked for the corps, said: 'We soon got used to heavy work, such as lifting pit-props and cutting them into various lengths for the coal mines. There were no mechanical devices used then and every pit-prop was cut by hand ... [at the dinner break] we sat under a tree eating beetroot sandwiches.'[72]

Victory depended on the women at work, and the government provided inducements, opening 1,341 new nurseries for the duration and recommending equal pay. Some employers agreed to pay male rates – if the women were doing a man's job, 'without assistance or supervision'; but most women's pay remained around half that of the men workers they had replaced. Semi-skilled and unskilled jobs were newly defined as 'women's work' and exempt from equal pay negotiations. Women injured during enemy bombing raids or while serving in Civil Defence received a third of the compensation paid to men – 7s a week for a disabling injury compared with 21s a week for men. Equal rates would only be introduced after campaigns by women in Parliament and trade unions in April 1943.[73]

Married women remained barred from the professions, but in 1944 they were admitted as teachers in schools to act as role models for schoolgirls, who were now staying on until they were 15 years old. Parliamentary secretary Chuter Ede explained that it was unhealthy for schools to be staffed by 'too many' spinsters: 'thwarted, sex starved and repressed'.[74]

The war on civilians shattered the idea of the home as a separate sphere where the wife's task was to create a superior domestic world. When bombs were falling through the roof, what was the point in women being advised to stop the worries of the outer world at the doorstep? Most households were headed by women as men were drafted into service. Women undertook voluntary war work as well as their day jobs. In 1944, Olive Owens, aged only 17, was working as an air raid warden in Croydon, Surrey: 'One day when I was on duty, a V2 rocket dropped on the corner of Park Road and King's Road ... It was complete devastation. We dug and dug until our fingers bled. My most vivid memory is of an arm raised, to call for silence, when someone heard tapping among the ruins.'[75]

Diarist Nella Last, an 'ordinary housewife' who joined the Mass Observation Archive in 1937 and spent thirty years recording the daily observations of British life, said in her entry on Sunday 12 April 1942, 'I feel this conscription of women will be a backward step, for it is taking the best, most formative years from a girl's life and giving her a taste of freedom that many crave for. Will they settle later to homes and children?'[76]

Shopping during wartime became a time-consuming, anxious task, with long queues forming at shops, as people waited for hours to buy rationed goods, which often ran out. Women conscripted into war work had to use their breaks to queue, and some mothers had to take their children out of schools to stand in line for the family's food. Women were urged to return to the tradition of self-sustaining households by growing their own food, and many took on the task of food production as well as their household work.[77]

The order for the first wave of evacuations from England's towns came two days before the declaration of war in September 1939. In only three days, 1.5 million children, pregnant women, women with infants and chronic invalids left towns and cities to go to the country to stay with unknown hosts. The Women's Volunteer Service assisted with the journeys, billeting children with local families. Trains ran out of London stations every nine minutes for nine hours.[78] Many institutions, universities, businesses and families organised their own evacuations from endangered towns to safer areas of the country. Altogether about 3.5 million people moved for some, or all, of the war.[79] When no attacks came in the early days of the war, some children returned home, but another evacuation started after the intense bombings began in 1940.

The numbers of illegitimate babies doubled during the war. In 1945, they accounted for 9.1 per cent of births, but the boom was caused by a fall in weddings. Wartime marriage rates fell from 22 per 1,000 in 1940 to 14 per 1,000 in 1943–44, and some of those missing their weddings were pregnant brides.[80] A third of pre-war brides had conceived before marriage, but 70 per cent of them got married before the birth. About the same proportion of women – 37 per cent in 1945 – found themselves pregnant but were unable to marry the father of their baby in wartime.

No national records were kept of illegitimate births, but in Birmingham in 1944–45, a third of all illegitimate children were born to married women, half of them servicemen's wives. When the husband returned home, it was his decision whether to raise another man's child in his home. He might decide that the child be put up for adoption, or he might choose to divorce his wife for adultery. As the husband, it was his decision – his wife, and the father of their baby, had no legal rights in the matter.[81]

At least 22,000 children were fathered by American servicemen, stationed in the UK, about 1,700 of whom were of African-American descent. Official concern about fraternisation between white women and African-American troops caused the troops to be banned from some hotels and bars. Despite efforts to segregate them, many English women enjoyed the company of American soldiers, and there were genuine love affairs. Dawn Yardy was engaged to marry Stewart Kroger, an American army corporal of the Choctaw people who lost his life in the Normandy invasion.[82]

Street fights between African-American GIs and white Englishmen sometimes broke out, like the one in 1944 in a Manchester station after an African-American sailor and a white English woman exchanged a kiss. Some hotels banned all non-white people, including pre-war immigrants from the Caribbean. Women protested outside one GI camp, singing 'Don't Fence Me In' when the men were confined before being sent home. Avoiding the English police protection, the soldiers broke out of the camp to meet with the women and the American military police had to be called to separate them.[83]

African-American GIs could not marry without permission from their commander, and even in the case of men who had fathered children, this would almost always be refused. African-American GI Ormus Davenport wrote in the language of the time that the US army unofficially had a 'gentleman's agreement' which in practice became official policy. The agreement said 'No negro soldier or sailor will be given permission to marry any British white girl!' 'Not one GI bride going back to the US under the US government scheme is the wife of a Negro,' he wrote.[84]

Up to half of the white English mothers of African-American GI babies were already married and about half of the babies would be given up for adoption. White American soldiers could get permission to marry their partners. By June 1950, 37,879 British women had emigrated to the United States with their white husbands as 'war brides', with 472 'war children'.[85]

Some white women protested the official advice not to fraternise with men of African ancestry – both men from the Caribbean and African-American troops. The advice was given in order not to offend racist segregationist American allies, stationed in England, who expected their home colour bar to be applied in England. Four WAAF members were posted away from their base for refusing to obey the order not to fraternise with Black troops.[86]

Women Loving Women at War

The demand for wartime recruits to all the Women's Services meant that women loving women were officially mostly ignored.[87] Letitia Fairfield, a senior medical officer in the ATS, was asked to compose a memo on lesbianism for senior officers. She suggested that women with an 'excessive attachment' should first be 'diverted by other interests' and only separated by posting if the excessive attachment continued. Only the most serious cases of 'perverted practices', or corrupting 'other women by talk or example', were to be considered for discharge.[88] In an echo of the earlier belief that female intimacy did not necessarily mean sexual intimacy, Fairfield wrote that co-sleeping for women should be allowed, as it was not an indication of sexual practices. She reassured her fellow elite officers that bed sharing was normal for working-class women and nothing for them to worry about. Some units expelled women who were caught together in the same bed, but it was generally understood in both the WAAF and the ATS that only relationships that disrupted discipline need be investigated.[89]

Violette Trefusis-Forbes explained how to approach an airwoman or officer: 'We should point out to her that her behaviour is that of a schoolgirl and that these sentimental attachments are not what we expect from airwomen who must necessarily always set a good example to others. That unless she can behave herself as a sensible adult, we consider that she will have a detrimental effect on discipline generally [and] we would have to dispense with her services.'[90]

A pair of lovers at RAF Upwood were accused of being lesbians after their letters were read by their commanding officer in 1941. The officer reported: 'In view of the fact that the writers of both letters are obviously in a highly temperamental and peculiar state of mind and are miserable if parted for a few hours at a time leads me to suppose that their work is unlikely to be as efficient as it would otherwise be. Since these two airwomen appear to be unable to behave like grown-up people who belong to a fine service and that their childish conduct cannot be overlooked any longer, they must be separated.'[91]

Women Dressing as Men … and Becoming Men

The need for practical clothing that could be recycled during clothing rationing caused a change in attitude towards women's clothes. 'Make Do and Mend' and 'Sew and Save' schemes advised women how to re-fashion and recycle clothes. Leading designers worked on the 'Utility' scheme, using materials to produce functional clothing. Trousers became acceptable for women, and cropped hair styles were safer around machines; they were no longer a visual code about sexuality. Unisex clothes – like the siren suit – were worn by men and women.[92]

Mark Weston (1905–78) was defined as a girl at birth and named Mary Weston. She became a highly successful field athlete and competed in the shot put at the 1928 Olympic Games in Amsterdam, coming sixth. After the games, Weston said she could no longer continue to live

Mark Weston (1905–78) was defined as a girl at birth and became a highly successful world field athlete, before surgeries and choosing to live as a man

as a woman and consulted specialists at Charing Cross Hospital, undergoing surgery in 1936. After the successful operation, Mark Weston registered his new identity, married Alberta Bray and they had three children together.[93]

Laura Maud Dillon (1915–62), daughter of a baronet, attended St Anne's College, Oxford, and competed in the Women's Boat Race in 1935 and 1936, preferring to wear men's clothing and live as a man. She took a course of hormones and was accepted as a man, working as a driver and a fire watcher during the Second World War, undergoing breast removal and changing her birth certificate in 1944 to Laurence Michael Dillon – now the male heir to a baronetcy. His transition would be discovered by the entry in Debrett's Peerage in 1958, which was altered to show a new heir to the baronetcy. Dillon enrolled in a school of medicine at the end of the war and undertook at least 13 sex-reassignment surgeries. He wrote: 'Where the mind cannot be made to fit the body, the body should be made to fit, approximately at any rate, to the mind.'[94]

Protest

Union membership increased, as women worked long, arduous hours in factories, from 5 per cent of the workforce at the start of the war to 23 per cent in 1943. Women demanded factory nurseries, wheeling prams decorated with the slogans 'We Want War Work. We Want Nurseries.'[95]

No provision was made for women to register their opposition to the war and refuse to join the war effort. Conscientious objectors were defined as men refusing to fight, who were deployed into non-combatant war work. But some women decided not to support the war, even refusing to be conscripted into work they had done voluntarily: 272 women were arrested and 214 of them served prison time. But unlike men, there was no mechanism for a woman's pacifist beliefs to be registered and women were not counted as British conscientious objectors until December 1941, when the government ordered all single women aged 20–30 to serve in either the Civil Defence or the armed forces.[96] More than 1,000 women protested. The first woman to be imprisoned as a conscientious objector was Connie Bolam, a domestic servant in Newcastle upon Tyne. Bolam was ordered into non-military work, but she objected to the order as coercion, spending a month in prison before being persuaded to go into the work allocated to her. While most tribunal chairs gave male conscientious objectors a scrupulously fair hearing, the leader of the Northumberland and Durham Tribunal told Connie Bolam: 'We on the tribunal have some commonsense; and you have none. It is no good talking rubbish to us like that.'[97]

Conscientious objector status would finally be granted to 911 women by tribunals, and most of them accepted non-military roles such as fire-watching, land or ambulance work.[98]

Protest was widespread against rationing, food shortages and the hours that had to be spent queuing for food by the women who already had the burden of war work, raising children and running a home, often as the sole head of the household with a husband away fighting. Women complained bitterly when essential food stuffs were rationed and argued against government rationing. The protest would intensify when the war ended but rationing did not.

In 1940, the revived Women's Freedom League – an old suffrage organisation – started to ask some awkward questions about women's role in society. Margery Corbett Ashby claimed that voluntary work by elite women was keeping women out of official paid positions and increasing unemployment for professional women. Dorothy Evans queried the allowance for foster mothers – and demanded proper payment. It proved the first of many so-called 'Women's Parliaments' that raised women's issues throughout the war years, demanding equal pay and equal compensation for wartime damage and injuries. Issues that had been viewed as 'women's issues' – the health of children, safety at work, access to laundries and childcare – now came to be seen as things a wartime government had to take seriously to ensure the health and safety of the civilian population.[99]

Demobilisation

When peace was declared, most women were expected to leave work, as wartime nurseries closed, or they were laid off, but some organisations kept going.[100] The Women's Land Army continued in work, producing food until 1950, and both women's auxiliary forces and the Women's Voluntary Society became permanent, with the WVS receiving royal patronage.[101]

Trudy Murray, who served in the Women's Auxiliary Air Force, remembers mixed feelings at the end of the war: 'Demob was a big disappointment to a lot of us. It was an awful and wonderful war. I wouldn't have missed it for anything; some of the friends we made were forever.'[102]

As had happened at the end of the First World War, women were demobilised from so-called 'men's work' to make way for the returning servicemen, but this time the war was followed by a period of rebuilding and economic growth. Some industries without unions to protect men's jobs and rates kept women workers on as a cheaper workforce, and labour shortages in the late 1940s pushed the government to launch campaigns to encourage women into work and invite workers from British colonies.[103] The ship the *Empire Windrush* brought 1,027 Caribbean migrants to England in 1948, 292 of them women, of whom 178 were travelling alone to make their lives in England.[104] The post-war boom would be powered by a new underclass of English women: immigrant women, who would face racial prejudice as well as misogyny and exploitation.

The Last Witch

The last witch to be sentenced under English law, Helen Duncan, was a fraudulent psychic, pretending to give people messages from the dead and producing 'ectoplasm' – mostly cheesecloth. She picked up gossip of the sinking of HMS *Barham* with a loss of 861 lives in 1941 and told a public seance that the spirit of a drowned sailor had come to her. She was charged with seven counts under the Witchcraft Act of 1735, alongside the owners of the Portsmouth Psychic Centre and her agent. She served nine months in prison and on release continued to hold seances. Her trial, which Winston Churchill called 'absolute tomfoolery', was the last witchcraft trial in England, and in 1944 the witchcraft law would be repealed.[105]

Part 9

1945–1994
A Woman Today

Women Endangered

The death penalty for 'petty treason' – killing a husband or social superior – remained in law since 1351, even when capital punishment for all other murders was abolished in 1965. It stayed on the statute book until 1998, when it was abolished, along with piracy with violence, high treason and arson in dockyards!

Mary Elizabeth Wilson (1889–1962), 'The Merry Widow of Windy Nook, was convicted of killing two husbands and suspected of killing two more. She was sentenced to death but died while imprisoned in Holloway

Mary Elizabeth Wilson (1889–1962) married her first husband John Knowles in 1914 and they lived together at Windy Nook in Gateshead. The couple were joined by Mary's lover John Russell, and after her husband died in 1955, Mary married Russell. A year later, he too died. The two men had left her a total of £42. A year on, she married a retired estate agent, Oliver Leonard, who died only 12 days after the wedding, leaving his widow £50. At her fourth wedding, to Ernest Wilson, Mary was said to have joked that the wedding cake should be saved for the funeral, and indeed, Ernest died a year after their marriage, bequeathing her £100, a bungalow and his life insurance. She did not attend his funeral but the police later claimed that she had asked for a trade discount from the undertaker. After exhuming the bodies of Ernest Wilson and Oliver Leonard, the police found high levels of phosphorus. Mary Wilson was convicted of murdering two husbands with insecticide, and her previous two husbands were also thought to have been poisoned. She was sentenced to death, but the sentence was commuted to life imprisonment and she died in prison.[1]

The last woman to be hanged in England was Ruth Ellis (1926–55), a British nightclub hostess and mother of two, who repeatedly shot her lover David Blakely with a borrowed gun in 1955, after years of abuse in which she had attended hospital with bruises and miscarried a baby after he punched her in the stomach. The public expected that the death sentence would be commuted to imprisonment and the Home Office received 600 letters asking for mercy. One woman wrote: 'Only a woman understands, that has been in the same position like myself, and millions of others, beaten by our husbands.'[2]

But the violence Ruth Ellis suffered was not considered a mitigating circumstance, especially as she was seeing and receiving money from another man, and married to neither. Her beauty and her work as a nightclub hostess also probably counted against her. But ten years after she was hanged, the death penalty was abolished in 1965.

Most murdered women are killed by their husbands or partners: 58 per cent in 1967–74, usually in their own homes.[3] The reports read like a list of war dead. This slightly edited list – excluding road traffic accidents and terrorist attacks – is drawn from the original, compiled by Karen Ingala Smith on her website Counting Dead Women for the year 2019:

1 January 2019: Charlotte Huggins, 33, was stabbed in the early hours of New Year's Day in London by her ex-partner.

1 January 2019: Jay Edmunds, 27, was killed in a house fire in Kirton, Lincolnshire, started by her ex-partner who also died.

4 January 2019: Simbiso Aretha Moula, 39, was found dead with her husband in Rainham, Essex. Police believe he strangled her and hanged himself.

5 January 2019: Sarah Ashraf, 35, was found dead at home in London. Her brother was found guilty of manslaughter on the grounds of diminished responsibility.

11 January 2019: Asma Begum, 31, was stabbed more than 50 times, in her head and neck by her husband in their home in east London.

13 January 2019: Luz Margory Isaza Villegas, 50, was murdered by her husband. He burned and buried her body in a suitcase in a shallow grave in Hertfordshire.

13 January 2019: Christy Walshe, 40, was shot in the face by her partner in Southend, Essex.

14 January 2019: Leanne Unsworth, 40, died of head injuries inflicted by an acquaintance in Lancashire.

16 January 2019: Alison Hunt, 42, was stabbed 18 times on the doorstep of her home in Swinton by her ex-partner.

22 January 2019: Mary Annie Sowerby, 69, known as Annie, was stabbed repeatedly in her chest and neck by her son in her home in Cumbria.

23 January 2019: Julie Webb, 44, was found with serious head injuries in a house in Birmingham and died in hospital the next day. Her partner was found guilty of her murder.

26 January 2019: Margaret Smyth, 29, known as Maggie, was missing for six days before police found parts of her body under rubble at a former pub in Bolton where her ex-partner had been working. He was found guilty of her murder.

29 January 2019: Susan Waring, 45, from Darwen, Lancashire, was last seen alive in January 2019. Two years later, her partner was convicted of her murder and of offences against four other women, including causing grievous bodily harm and making threats to kill.

31 January 2019: Mary Page, 68, was kicked and punched by her son, before he killed her by hitting her over the head with a bedside table at her home in Wolverhampton. He was found guilty of manslaughter due to diminished responsibility.

1 February 2019: Libby Squire, 21, disappeared after a night out in Hull, her body was found in the Humber estuary 7 weeks later. A man was convicted of her rape and murder in February 2021.

1–2 February 2019: Antoinette Donnegan, 52, was found strangled in a flat in London, strangled by clothing. Her lodger was convicted of manslaughter.

5 February 2019: A 73-year-old woman died 11 days after being mugged in Birmingham. A 15-year-old boy was found guilty of manslaughter.

7 February 2019: Rosie Darbyshire, 27, was found dead in the street in Preston, Lancashire, with serious head injuries. Her boyfriend was convicted of her murder.

8 February 2019: Aliny Mendes, 39, died of multiple stabbings in the street by her ex-husband as she collected her children from school in Surrey.

11 February 2019: Sarah Henshaw, 40, was attacked with a hammer and then strangled with a vacuum cord whilst in bed in her home in Leeds, by her ex-partner.

14 February 2019: Dorothy Bowyer, 77, was stabbed to death by her grandson in Derbyshire. He was found guilty of manslaughter on the grounds of diminished responsibility.

15 February 2019: Leah Croucher, 19, was killed by a man who killed himself afterwards.

19 February 2019: Susan Howells, 51, was killed by her partner who was found guilty of her murder and of preventing her burial.

25 February 2019: Jodi Miller, 21, was kicked and stabbed by a man who had repeatedly accosted her and tried to pay her for sex which she refused, in Leeds.

1 March 2019: Jodie Chesney, 17, was stabbed in the back whilst walking through a park with friends in east London. Two men, aged 19 and 17, were convicted of her murder.

2 March 2019: Elize Stevens, 50, was stabbed 86 times in London, by her partner, who claimed that he feared she would leave him.

6 March 2019: Laureline Garcia-Bertaux, 34, was found naked, wrapped in bin-bags in a shallow grave in her garden in west London. She had been strangled by her ex-boyfriend.

7 March 2019: Allison Marimon-Herrera, 15, and her 37-year-old mother, Giselle, were found dead. Giselle's partner was thought to have killed them before hanging himself.

9 March 2019: Lalal Kamara, 26, was found dead in a flat in Denton, Greater Manchester. She was murdered by her boyfriend's brother.

10 March 2019: Alice Morrow, 53, was found dead following an assault in Belfast. Her partner admitted her murder.

17 March 2019: Rachel Evans, 46, was stabbed or slashed more than 100 times by her ex-partner after ending her relationship with him.

20 March 2019: Alison McKenzie, 55, was stabbed to death by her son in Middlesborough. He was found guilty of manslaughter on the grounds of diminished responsibility.

22 March 2019: Janette Dunbavand, 81, and her husband were found dead in their home. He shot her before shooting himself.

27 March 2019: Barbara Heywood, 80, was stabbed to death at her home in Manchester. Her 88-year-old husband was arrested and detained under the Mental Health Act.

2 April 2019: Paula Meadows, 83, was found dead at home. Her 84-year-old husband is believed to have killed her before killing himself.

17 April 2019: Sarah Fuller, 35, was strangled to death by her partner in Exeter.

20 April 2019: Megan Newton, 18, was found dead at Stoke-on-Trent. A former schoolfriend, 18, was convicted of her rape and murder.

21 April 2019: Leah Fray, 27, was found dead in a burning flat in Leicester. A man, 18, was convicted of murder, rape and arson.

23 April 2019: Siama Riaz, 33, was found dead after police were called to attend to a stabbing in Rochdale. Her husband was convicted of murder.

23 April 2019: Sammy-Lee Lodwig, 22, was found stabbed with cuts to her throat, forehead and chest in Swansea. Her 'boyfriend' had tied her up on the bed before killing her.

26 April 2019: Amy Parsons, 35, was bludgeoned to death with a metal bar whilst in the shower by her partner.

29 April 2019: Emma Faulds, 39, from Kilmarnock, was killed by a friend, 40.

30 April 2019: Lauren Griffiths, 21, was found dead in her flat in Cardiff. Her partner, 22, was jailed for murder.

3 May 2019: Ellie Gould, 17, was stabbed to death by a school friend in Wiltshire, after refusing to be his girlfriend.

6 May 2019: Joanne Hamer, 48, was found dead at home in Lincolnshire after police were called. Her husband was found guilty of murder.

10 May 2019: Mavis Long, 77, died in hospital after her husband, 80, strangled her. He was convicted of manslaughter.

12 May 2019: Julia Rawson, 42, was identified by her dental records in Tipton, Yorkshire. Two men, 28 and 23, were found guilty of her murder.

20 May 2019: Tatiana Koudriavtsev, 68 and 69-year-old husband were stabbed to death by their son in London.

24 May 2019: Jayde Hall, 26, was stabbed to death in Stoke-on-Trent, after ending her relationship with her boyfriend.

27 May 2019: Elizabeth McShane, 39, was found dead with her partner, 33, in a flat in Glasgow. Police were treating their deaths as murder-suicide.

29 May 2019: Linda Treeby, 64, died of serious head injuries after emergency services were called to a caravan site on the coast of Lincolnshire. Her partner, 50, was jailed for murder.

5 June 2019: Regan Tierney, 27, was found stabbed to death in Salford probably by her ex-partner, 31, who died in hospital.

7 June 2019: Paige Gibson, 23, was stabbed to death in Halifax, W. Yorkshire by a 16-year-old male who was jailed for 16 years.

9 June, 2019, Neomi Smith, 23, was stabbed to death in Aberdeen by her boyfriend.

15 June 2019: Valerie Richardson, 49, was killed in her home in Fife by a friend, 39, who killed himself.

17 June 2019: Safie Xheta, 35, was killed by knife wounds to the neck. Her husband was treated for injuries and later jailed for her murder in Oxford.

24 June 2019: Lucy Rushton, 30, died of multiple injuries in Andover. Her estranged husband was convicted of her murder.

29 June 2019: Kelly Fauvrelle, 26, was stabbed at home in an attack that also killed her unborn baby. Her ex-partner, 25, was jailed for their deaths.

29 June 2019: Julia Flynn, 74, died in a fire at her house set by Tyler Flanagan, 17, who pleaded guilty to manslaughter.

1 July 2019: Joanna Thompson, 50, died from neck injuries at her home. A teenage male was arrested and later detained under the Mental Health Act.

2 July 2019: Ligita Kostiajeviene, 42, died of severe head injuries following an armed siege at a house in Peterborough. Another woman and a child were injured in the attack. Her husband was jailed for murder, attempted murder and assault on an emergency worker.

11 July 2019: Carol Milne, 59, was found dead in her home in Aberdeen. Her son admitted culpable homicide due to diminished responsibility.

12 July 2019: Layla Arezo, 74, and her husband Akbar Arezo, 64, were stabbed to death in their home in south-west London. Their son was sentenced for manslaughter at the Old Bailey.

15 July 2019: Doreen Virgo, 89, was found dead in a care home in Norfolk; she had been strangled. Her husband, 81, was ruled to be responsible for the act but unfit to stand trial.

18 July 2019: Diane Dyer, 61, died of blunt force injury to the neck and face in south-west London. Her boyfriend, 54, was jailed for life.

21 July 2019: Kayleigh Hanks, 29, was strangled to death in her home in East Sussex by her on-off partner, 36.

25 July 2019: Christine Ford, 71, died of multiple injuries after an attack by her landlord Brian Coote, 65, in Flamstead.

28 July 2019: Dr Leela (Premm) Monti, 51, and her partner Robert Tully, 71, were found dead in their home in Lincolnshire. Her son, 22, was found guilty of murder.

30 July 2019: Kelly-Anne Case, 27, was found dead after a fire at her home. A man, 28, was jailed for murder.

30 July 2019: Tracey Walker, 40, died from stab wounds in Lerwick. Two friends, Dawn Smith, 29, and Ross MacDougal, 32, were found guilty of murder.

3 August 2019: Dorothy Woolmer, 89, was raped and murdered in London. She died of multiple blunt force injuries. A man, 22, was jailed for murder and sexual assault.

5 August 2019: Kathleen (Gwen) Gold, 78, was killed by her husband who then killed himself.

12 August 2019: Lindsay Birbeck, 47, was found strangled in a graveyard in Lancashire on 22 August. A 16-year-old male was jailed for murder.

17 August 2019: Belinda Rose, 63, a care worker was stabbed to death in Birmingham in a property she supervised. A businessman, 52, admitted manslaughter on the grounds of diminished responsibility.

17 August 2019: Pamela Mellor, 55, was found dead in a house in Handforth, Cheshire. A man, 43, was found to have unlawfully killed her and was detained indefinitely under the Mental Health Act.

19 August 2019: Linda Vilika, 41, was stabbed to death in Essex by her husband, 42.

25 August 2019: Michelle Pearson, 36, died of injuries in an arson attack at her home in Salford in December 2017 which killed four of her children. Two men were sentenced to life imprisonment in May 2018.

26 August 2019: Rebecca Simpson, 30, died in hospital after being found with serious head injuries in Castleford, Yorkshire. Her boyfriend, 32, pleaded guilty to her manslaughter.

28 August 2019: Jacqueline (Jackie) Kirk, 62, was killed by her ex-partner.

29 August 2019: Alice Farquharson, 56, was found dead at her home in Aberdeen. Her husband, 60, was jailed for murder.

29 August 2019: Laura Rakstelyte, 31, was stabbed to death in Ilford, London, by her ex-boyfriend, 43, who fatally stabbed himself.

31 August 2019: Sandra Samuels, 44, was found dead in Hackney, London. A man, 40, was jailed for her murder.

1 September 2019: Janet Lewis, 77, was stabbed and clubbed as she slept at her home in Essex. Her husband of 60 years was convicted of her murder.

6 September 2019: Marlene McCabe, 71, had suffered serious head and face injuries before dying in her home in Blackpool. Her grandson, 25, pleaded guilty to manslaughter by reason of diminished responsibility.

11 September 2019: Lana Nemceva, 33, was found dead with her husband in the home in Burton, Staffordshire. Police believed her death was murder and his suicide.

12 September 2019: Bethany Fields, 21, was stabbed multiple times in the street in Huddersfield. Her ex-boyfriend was sent to a secure hospital for his role in her death.

18 September 2019: Serafima Mashaka, 58, was killed in Ealing, west London. A man, 41, was jailed for her murder.

19 September 2019: Vera Hudson, 57, was murdered by a neighbour, 25.

19 September 2019: Keely Bunker, 20, was found dead in woodland in Tamworth, Staffordshire. A man, 19, was found guilty of her rape and murder.

21 September 2019: Cristina Ortiz-Lozano, 28, suffered multiple stab wounds and died at her home in Southampton. A man, 29, was jailed for murder.

24 September 2019: Emily Goodman, 42, was found stabbed to death by police investigating the death of a man, 37, who fell from the 14th floor of a block of flats in Oxford.

24 September 2019: Katrina Fletcher, 64, was killed by her partner, 62. He had a history of convictions for violence against her and was convicted of manslaughter.

27 September 2019: Margaret Robertson, 54, also known as Meg, was found dead at home in Aberdeen. A man, 40, was jailed for her murder.

2 October 2019: Arlene Williams, 46, was found stabbed to death at her home in Enfield, London. Her son, 28, admitted manslaughter by diminished responsibility.

6 October 2019: Sarah Hassall, 38, was found dead in her house in Pontypridd, Wales. Brian Manship, who had raped and stabbed her multiple times, was found guilty of murder.

8 October 2019: Suvekshya Burathoki, 32, known as Fatima, was found stabbed to death at her home in Leicester. Her former partner, 29, was jailed for her murder.

9 October 2019: Natalie Harker, 30, was stalked, abducted and murdered by her ex-partner who was found guilty of her murder at Catterick.

10 October 2019: Niyat Berhane Teklemariam, 21, was found dead with a neck wound. Her probable killer, 38, committed suicide in a central London Tube station.

10 October 2019: Lesley Spearing, 55, was stabbed at her home in Rainham, east London. Her son, 27, was held in relation to her death.

21 October 2019: Zoe Orton, 46, was found dead at her home in London. Police believe she was strangled.

22 October 2019: Thi Tra My Pham, 26, Thi Van Nguyen, 35, Thi Nhung (Anna) Bui, 19, Thi Thanh Tran, 41, Thi Tho Tran, 21, Thi Nhgoc Oanh Pham, 28, Thi Mai Nhung Tran, 18, Thi Ngoc Tran, 19, were refugee women of 39 refugees suffocated in a container lorry organised by people smugglers.

25 October 2019: Annie Temple, 97, was found dead in her bed. The son of her late GP was found guilty of defrauding her and of her murder.

26 October 2019: Beatrice Yankson, 59, died of burns and inhalation of smoke in a fire at her home in London. Her son, 35, was detained indefinitely.

28 October 2019: Evie Adams, 23, was poisoned by her ex-partner, who faked her suicide note. He had been earlier suspected of murdering his two children. He was found guilty of all three murders.

3 November 2019: Levi Ogden, 26, was attacked and fatally injured in a street in Halifax, W. Yorkshire. Her boyfriend, 26, pleaded guilty to manslaughter.

9 November 2019: Tsegereda Gebremariam, 29, was stabbed to death probably by her former partner, 28, who also killed himself.

13 November 2019: Nicola Stevenson, 39, was found dead in a wheelie bin in Lewes, E. Sussex. She had suffered blunt force injury to her head.

13 November 2019: Mandeep Singh, 39, was found dead in a house in Nottingham alongside her husband, 57.

21 November 2019: Alison McBlaine, was killed by a car deliberately driven into her. Four males were found guilty of her murder and a fifth was convicted of manslaughter.

27 November 2019: Katy Sprague, 51, was found strangled in Cambridgeshire. Her neighbour, 36, was jailed for her murder.

15 December 2019: Marion Price, 63, was found dead in her car, she had been shot. Her estranged husband, 69, and his accomplice, 60, were found guilty of murder.

16 December 2019: Jolanta Jacubowska, 50, was stabbed to death in Watford. A 17-year-old male was charged in relation to her death.

17 December 2019: Kayleigh Dunning, 32, was found dead in Portsmouth. Her partner, 48, was convicted of her murder.

18 December 2019: Nelly Myers, 58, was found dead in Sussex. Her lover, 35, was jailed for her murder.

19 December 2019: Angela Tarver, 86, died after being almost decapitated. Her son was jailed for her murder.

22 December 2019: Amy Appleton, 32, was beaten to death in the street in Sussex by her husband, who also killed a passer-by, Sandra Seagrove, 76, when she tried to intervene.

23 December 2019: Frances Murray, 37, was found dead in Belfast with her partner Joseph Dutton, 47. A man admitted unlawfully killing them.

25 December 2019: Vivienne Bryan, 74, was found dead in a house in Fairbourne, N. Wales. Her 75-year-old husband was convicted of her manslaughter.

31 December 2019, Stacey Cooper, 34, was found dead in her home in Redcar. A man, 27, was charged with her murder.

In addition

March 2019: A woman whose body was found in a stream in the Yorkshire Dales in 2004 was identified as Lamduan Seekanya/ Armitage. She lived in the UK between 1991 and 2004.

26 April 2019: Mihrican Mustafa, 38, and Henriett Szuchs were two women whose bodies were found in a freezer in east London. A man, 35, of Newham, east London, was jailed for life.

12 July 2019: The remains of Brenda Venables who died in 1982, when she was 48 years old, were found in a sceptic tank. An 86-year-old man was held on suspicion of murder.

Waiting for further information regarding the deaths of other
possible victims Alem Shimeni, Annabelle Lancaster, Marie Gilmore,
Debbie Twist, Amanda Gretton, Melanie Jane Spence, Donna
Boden and Sarah Hopkins.[4]

It took a surprisingly long time before women realised that they were
being singled out for murder, and the murderers were usually their
husbands or partners. The phrase 'domestic violence' – suggesting a sort
of home-made, amateur cruelty – came into use in the mid-1970s in
England after the launch of the first organisation to defend women
assaulted and abused by their male partners.[5] Erin Pizzey set up the
Chiswick Women's Family Aid, and in the same year the National
Women's Aid Federation began to support, educate and re-house abused
women and children.

In the UK at the time of writing, one woman is killed every three
days.[6] In the year 2022, there were 107 murders of women.[7] The slight
drop in 2022 deaths from the numbers recorded by Ingala Smith for
2019 may be a result of lockdown rules during the pandemic forcing
women to stay with men who would have murdered them if they tried to
leave. Latest details (from 2020) show that most women – 68 per cent
– are killed inside their homes, 61 per cent by a male partner, 41 per cent
of them murdered by their partners after deciding to separate.[8]

The 1976 Domestic Violence and Matrimonial Proceedings Act
created protection orders to ban violent partners from approaching their
wives and girlfriends. Victims of violent husbands have described the
orders as 'worse than useless'.[9]

Prosecutions for men breaking the orders fell from more than 10,000
in 2017 to less than 7,000 in 2021, of which only 5,500 received
sentences. Although protection orders for women victims of violence
increased by nearly half (48 per cent) in the two years from 2018, about
a quarter of them were violated. One man repeatedly breached the
order over seven years, threatening his ex-wife and two daughters. She
said: 'He made threats to kill me … I was just constantly looking over
my shoulder all the time … We were just petrified, fearing for our lives.
We didn't feel safe whatsoever. We were just waiting for something to
happen.'[10]

Research into men who assault their wives and partners suggests that
domestic violence is a 'gateway' crime to other crimes of violence. More

than half of the men who killed women in 2018 had been previously violent to their partners or to other women. Three men had killed women before. Some men who are violent against women go on to other victims; some progress to terrorism. A third of men linked to terrorism had been involved in domestic violence in 2019.[11]

Men who attack their wives and partners can be excused by the woman's 'provocation' – that her behaviour was so maddening that a husband could not stop himself lashing out and killing her by accident, his responsibility diminished by rage. In 2001, Mr Justice Rougier, at Winchester Crown Court accepted that Jean Betambeau, 62, was guilty only of manslaughter on the grounds of diminished responsibility, after he stabbed his wife ten times with a carving knife, fell with her to the kitchen floor and tied a plastic bag over her head. The judge said: 'I accept that your wife was a difficult woman to live with, and offered you a fair degree of provocation … Also you are a relatively elderly man and prison would be very hard for you. I accept this was a single incident and the risk of you re-offending is minimal to zero.'[12]

It is probably true that Mr Betambeau was unlikely to re-offend, given that the wife who had irritated him has now been permanently silenced. It is to be hoped that he does not remarry, or that the second Mrs Betambeau is not prone to argument. Mr Justice Rougier might have considered that other men, also irritated by their wives, might be encouraged by the legal defence that a nagging wife is responsible for her own murder. Lady Rougier might have had thoughts about this too.

But women who kill their husbands find it hard to persuade the court that they too had a 'fair degree of provocation'. Even the understanding of Battered Woman Syndrome – where a woman cannot defend herself, but may act, years after the first abuse, has found little traction in the courts. A sudden flare into murderous violence is understood by the courts; a woman's painfully slow arrival to murderous despair is not. The law on the provocation to murder describes, understands and excuses the sudden blow-up of murderous male rage. But attacks on abusive men by their wives, long after the initial provocation, are excluded from the defence.[13]

Mrs Sara Thornton was physically and emotionally abused by her alcoholic husband for the eighteen months of their marriage – a neighbour gave evidence that she had been taken to hospital unconscious, 'black and blue'. Sara Thornton asked for help from her doctor, from her local church, from social services, from Alcoholics Anonymous, from the Marriage Guidance Council and from the police – who were called five times and charged Malcolm Thornton with assaulting his wife. When he threatened her, and her ten-year-old daughter, Sara Thornton stabbed him once with a knife, as he lay asleep on the sofa. She was found guilty of murder in 1989, the judge ruling that there was no excuse for the murder as it did not take place during a 'sudden and temporary loss of control'. He said she could have 'walked out or gone upstairs'.[14]

Thornton served six years of her prison sentence until the charge was changed to that of 'manslaughter', after psychologists argued that she had been mentally disturbed by long-term abuse and that this was as valid a defence against the charge of murder as a sudden loss of temper from 'provocation'.[15]

Kiranjit Ahluwalia was found guilty of murder in 1989 when she set fire to her husband's bedding while he slept, after he had told her their marriage was over, demanded £200 and threatened to beat her and burn her face with an iron. She was sentenced to life imprisonment (for a minimum of 12 years), but on appeal in 1992, the court accepted a plea of manslaughter on the grounds of diminished responsibility owing to her prolonged and deep depression after years of abuse. The defence of only a 'sudden and temporary loss of control' was wrong, the judges ruled, and declared that a delayed response was possible ... but their honours warned that the longer the delay between the assault and the defensive attack, the less likely that such a plea would be accepted.[16]

It became clear that in order to win a claim of self-defence, a woman had to show a set of acceptable behaviours, even while being beaten into despair and obedience. A wife in the dock had to prove that she was sexually faithful, devoted to her family and had previously allowed her husband's violence. She had to demonstrate that she was a loving, passive person: a 'normal' woman.[17]

Most serial killers are men – most of their victims are women. Serial attacks on ten women from 1969, and the murder of at least 13 but possibly more, in the north of England between 1975 and 1980 by Peter Sutcliffe, nicknamed 'the Yorkshire Ripper', revealed the vulnerability of prostitutes to assault and murder.[18] Police incompetence, which left Sutcliffe free after nine police interviews in five years, was partly caused by lack of concern for prostitutes. A senior West Yorkshire detective said in 1979 that the then unknown murderer had 'made it clear that he hates prostitutes. Many people do. We, as a police force, will continue to arrest prostitutes. But the Ripper is now killing innocent girls. That indicates your mental state and that you are in urgent need of medical attention. You have made your point. Give yourself up before another innocent woman dies.'

Rape

The increasing freedom for women, out of the home and into the wider world of work and community, was blamed for exposing women to sexual attack. After a recorded decline in rape in the mid-nineteenth century, numbers of reported rapes rose steadily until the mid-1960s, when they soared in a trajectory that still continues upwards. It was easier to blame women for being 'in the wrong place' or 'at the wrong time', or dressed in the 'wrong clothes' than to inquire, arrest and try a man for doing 'the wrong thing'. The 1960s successful, single, white, educated women were accused of competing with men, rivalling them, disempowering them and so turning them to sexual violence.[19]

The increase in rape after the 1960s was caused by a boom in reporting of so-called 'date rapes' – where the rapist and the woman were known to each other before the assault. In the UK in 1973, 14 per cent of the rape convictions were those of 'date rapists'. Twenty years later almost all rapes reported were 'date rapes' – 45 per cent of rapes were committed by acquaintances and 43 per cent were 'domestic rapes' by partners or family members. Strangers were responsible for only 12 per cent of the reported rapes.[20] It may be that courtship and date etiquette became more sexual and violent towards the end of the twentieth century; or that women were resisting male assumptions that a date meant consent to sex, or a greater readiness to report threatening and violent men.

Rapists could still expect a sympathetic hearing, if summoned to court. In 1977, a Northern Irish guardsman named Thomas Holdsworth had his three-year sentence for rape reduced to six months by the appeal judges, who said: 'We have a man of previous good character whose army career would be completely destroyed if this sentence were to stand.'[21]

This good-character guardsman had sexually assaulted a 17-year-old girl, ripping out her earrings, fracturing her ribs and causing serious vaginal injury. One appeal judge, Mr Justice Slynn, remarked that

Holdsworth had 'lost his self control or allowed his enthusiasm for sex to get the better of him'.[22] Another, Mr Justice Wild, observed that the young woman would have been 'less severely injured if in fact she had submitted to rape'.[23]

But this guidance from the bench – to submit to rape to avoid injury – was contradicted by the honourable judge himself, in a later trial. Then, Mr Justice Wild explained that only determined resistance proved that a woman was refusing sex: 'Women who say "no" do not always mean "no". It is not just a question of saying "no", it is a question of how she says it, how she shows and makes it clear. If she doesn't want it, she only has to keep her legs shut and she would not get it without force and there will be marks of force being used.'[24]

Law lords ruling on another appeal decided that three men were *not* rapists after they dragged a sleeping woman, Daphne Morgan, out of her bed and each had sex with her, holding her mouth and nose when she screamed to her children to call the police, because they sincerely believed her husband, who had told them that her refusal and resistance was part of a sex game. The case prompted a change in the law to say that a man's belief in consent must be 'reasonable'.[25]

Poor women, students or unemployed women are more likely to be raped or sexually assaulted than well-off women.[26] Women of colour are less likely to be believed than white women, when they complain of a rape.[27] One survey of women attending rape crisis centres suggested that 23 per cent of them were Black and mixed race.[28] Women with Asian ancestry were less likely to be raped, according to government statistics.[29]

Of course, many rapists claimed that their partners or friends were willing. He could claim that he was being 'rough' or 'playful' and that the misunderstanding was all hers. But if the 1960s had really ushered in a new world, where many women enjoyed being surprised with rough sex, the era should not have seen a rise in female fears. Women expressed greater anxiety about their safety and especially fear of sexual assault increased.[30]

In police interviews and in court, the rapist's definition of what was and what was not sexual abuse gained equal status to the woman's definition of what was and what was not 'rape'. The cliché of 'he said/she said' showed that denial was granted the same authority as the accusation – a dream situation for a guilty man. He could define the act as 'bad sex' that failed to please her, or that she regretted, or that she tricked him into sex in order to accuse him of rape for blackmail or the chance to shame him. The inquiry turns on the woman and her motive, and can inquire into all the surrounding circumstances. As a witness to the act she does not make much of a contribution – all she has to offer is that she did not consent. Her evidence is explored only to discover if she is dishonest. Women reporting rape find that it is their own life that comes under scrutiny. Their mobile phones are almost always confiscated and police officers search for evidence of previous sexual relationships, diseases, previous complaints of rape or mental illness. If a raped woman refuses to give up her phone, the investigation into her rape is almost always halted. A report by the Crown Prosecution Service found its own demands to download phones to be 'irrational and over-intrusive' in 60 per cent of the cases.[31]

A rape case rarely gets to court within a year, and then the woman is expected to relive the assault in front of a public court and in view of her rapist. Her behaviour is key to his conviction. While his criminal history is confidential, and his privacy defended by a qualified lawyer, her life is scrutinised and she has no support or representation in court. One of the leading historians of rape writes: 'Her clothes, hairstyle, posture, accent and tone of voice, all take on immense significance. The woman is reduced to her body: what she was wearing, how she walked, and her sexual attractiveness. Consent is inferred through the female victim's body, rather than the male perpetrator's actions. In this reduction of the woman to her body, she has diminished as not a full person under the law, and indeed within society … Few women are able to bear the burden of performance.'[32]

A new so-called science of 'victimology' was developed after 1940. Some rapes were said to be a 'victim-precipitated crime' that occurred because of the sexual provocation of the woman, her inability to defend herself because of physical weakness, drunkenness or fear and the absence of guardians such as parents, friends or police.[33]

Despite the fact that most rapes and assaults on women took place in the home, by known assailants, the emphasis on stranger rape was revived in the 1990s with true-crime and dramatised crime on television. Repeated, painful and complicated domestic assaults by drunk and angry men were not material to draw audiences; but stranger rape suited the entertainment industry, and it suited the rapists themselves. The murderous rapist psychopath became a staple of entertainment and entered the understanding of rapists. According to Joanna Bourke: 'Rapists who were diagnosed as psychopaths found the emphasis on pathology congenial. It did, after all, separate them from common criminals, and landed them in hospitals (where 15 per cent were able to escape).'[34]

The glamourisation of rape into a crime of unstoppable sexual desire sometimes accompanied by psychopathic violence does not reflect the regularity and frequency of sexual assault for normal women in England. A study in 2002 of 1,882 men on a university campus found that 120 men (6.4 per cent of the sample of male students) said that they had undertaken 483 sexual acts that the researchers defined as rape or attempted rape.[35] Of them: 44 said they had only raped or attempted rape once, and 76 were repeat rapists. Of the 76 who said they had raped or attempted rape more than once, 34 reported 2 rapes, seven reported 3 rapes, nine reported 4 rapes, four reported 5 rapes, five reported 6 rapes, three reported 7 rapes, three reported 8 rapes, and an astounding eleven reported between 9 and 50 rapes.

Since the survey respondents were students at a university, it might be thought that the 44 who raped once were just getting started on a career of multiple rapes in adult life.

The UK is one of the least successful countries at convicting suspect rapists, unlike Germany, where the majority of prosecutions end in a guilty verdict. In Britain in 1977, one in three reported rapes were prosecuted and the rapist found to be guilty – that fell to one in four by 1985, one in ten in 1986. In that year police chose not to prosecute 25 per cent of the rapes reported to them in England. Fewer than a third of those questioned were charged; only 25 per cent of them went on to court, and 5 per cent of those cases were dropped by the prosecution. Of those few arriving at court, only 6 per cent were convicted. By 2007, this miserable conviction rate had dropped to one conviction for every 20 reported rapes.[36]

In an attempt to improve this, the Crown Prosecution Service took the extraordinary decision to prosecute only those rape cases it thought certain to win. The first year of this experiment saw 1,000 potential prosecutions dropped for being too difficult, and the next year 2,000. By December 2021, 67,125 rape offences were reported but only 2,409 of them taken to court and only 1,409 ended with a conviction: a success rate of 2 per cent. Victims' Commissioner Dame Vera Baird estimated that because of this there could be 'almost 1,500 rapists per year who are still on the streets who could have been convicted if this decision had not been taken'. In her words, 'We were witnessing the effective decriminalisation of rape.'[37]

Rapists walked free in the distant past as now, because neither medieval magistrates nor modern police believed women who complain of rape. The belief in the 1960s that working-class women and children were likely to be making false claims against their 'betters' – for malice and fraud – grew into a suspicion of the so-called 'liberated' single women said to be aggressively feminist, and anti-men.[38] In the 1970s, police believed one in every five rape reports to be false.[39] In 2005, a review suggested that about 3 in 100 accusations of rape were untrue,[40] but a 17-month-long experiment in 2011–12, in which all suspect women were prosecuted for lying, resulted in only 35 cases of false allegations being brought to court – compared with 5,651 rapists. Thirty-five women had been lying about having been raped – less than 1 per cent (0.61 per cent) of all complaints.[41] A genuine rape victim, taking her complaint to the police, is far more likely to be suspected of making a false allegation (20 per cent) than her rapist is to be convicted (2 per cent).

Since many rapes are not reported to the police at all, this conviction rate is probably worse than 2 per cent. In the year 2000, the British Crime Survey estimated that 61,000 women aged between 16 and 59 had been raped in England and Wales, but only 20 per cent of these were reported and recorded by police (12,200).[42] The charity and campaign group Rape Crisis agreed with that estimate, suggesting that in 2021–22 over 350,000 rapes may actually have taken place – making the likelihood of a rapist being convicted in fact less than 1 per cent.

In 1992, the English Law Commission reported that rape by a husband was equally as distressing for a woman as rape by a stranger. The old church law that ruled that a wife gave consent once on her wedding day, for the duration of her marriage, meant that marital rape was legal until 1994, when the law was changed to make a husband raping his wife a criminal act – probably the most frequently occurring rape.[43] For the first time in English law since 1066, a husband did not have feudal rights over his wife's body.

This attack on traditional marriage sparked an outcry of protest at the assault on marriage, but the expected 'epidemic of prosecutions' did not occur. Although surveys suggested that between 8 per cent and 14 per cent of wives said they had been raped by their husbands, accusations to the police were few, and charges were often dropped. Of the 450 marital rapes reported in 1996, only 22 sustained an accusation against their husbands – only 5 per cent felt able to pursue the complaint, and a horrifying 95 per cent of women who went to the police to tell them that they had been raped by their husbands went home to the man they had accused without pursuing charges. Women who complain of rape at home are the most likely to withdraw the complaint. In 2000, 42 per cent of women who withdrew accusations of rape after going to the police had named their current or former partner.[44] As the evidence of wife murders makes clear, it was probably the safest thing to do. Unless she has a refuge, and reliable police protection, it is safer for wives to stay at home with a violent man or rapist than to accuse him and leave.

There is a significant proportion of women rapists. Most surveys suggest that between 6 per cent and 24 per cent of all rapists are female, abusing other women or men. A small survey of men in a London clinic found that 18 per cent of them had been forced to have sexual activity by a woman. Female rapists have been ignored partly because men who have been raped are reluctant to report, because of the continuing belief in female lack of sexual appetite, and the belief that rape is performed by a penis: until 2003, UK law defined rape as penile penetration. Experts have suggested that those few women who do rape or sexually assault unconsciously wish to be men, or are 'nymphomaniacs' and/or insane.[45] Current thinking about rapists of any gender suggests that the crime is one of anger and an expression of power, not of sexual desire.[46]

There has been little research into violent and sexual assault in women's prisons. The first studies, conducted in the 1990s, suggested that violent sexual assault among women occurred less often than in men's prisons, but there was more coercion. Assault by male and female prison staff on inmates takes place routinely, as 'strip and search' and disciplinary procedures.

Recent research has only been undertaken because of expressed anxiety about transgender women in women's prisons. While some of the assailants in women's prisons have identified as transgender women, there are too few reports to show a clear pattern. Of the 97 sexual assaults recorded on women prisoners in England and Wales in the 3 years from 2016, 7 were committed by transgender women prisoners.[47] In March 2022, there were 43 trans women prisoners being held in England and Wales and 187 trans men: a total of 230 trans prisoners. From 2023, trans women with male genitalia, or trans women with a record of violence, were held in male prisons unless granted individual permission to move.[48]

Greater care in the management of trans women prisoners in women's prisons from 2019 has meant that no assaults by trans women have been recorded on women prisoners since then. Despite this progress, in 2022, the government responded to huge anxiety about prisoner safety by ruling that trans women with intact male genitalia should be housed in men's prisons, exposing them to greater risk. There is more violence in men's prisons; in 2019–20, 3.42 per cent of victims of assault were transgender.[49]

The question of where transgender criminals should be kept has become a highly publicised debate, with media and public apparently deeply concerned about the dangers of assault in prisons by trans people; not so much about assaults on trans people.

Especially bad for women is the tendency of the courts to imprison women for 'consumer offences' like shoplifting (21 per cent of prosecutions) and failing to have a TV licence (18 per cent of prosecutions). Once imprisoned, they are not kept safe. Thirty-five per cent of women prisoners harmed themselves in 2021, despite asking for help with mental health problems, money worries, housing difficulties and drug and alcohol addictions.[50] Incidents of self-harm are a far more frequent occurrence than any relating to transgender people in prisons and are a far greater danger to women. But it is of less interest to people who like a moral panic about women.

Equally cruel, and also racist, is the UK tendency to lock up disproportionate numbers of women of African or Asian ancestry. In 2017, Black women were 25 per cent more likely than white women to be sentenced to prison, and 18 per cent of the women's prison population were Black, Asian and minority ethnic women, from an overall population of women of 11.9 per cent.[51]

Work

In 1946, the Royal Commission on Equal Pay decided that women workers were less efficient and might be paid less than men. The commission quoted women's inferior physical strength to that of male workers, and said that women were less able to deal with 'surprise situations'.[52]

Despite this lack of alertness, women were not at all surprised to find their wages fell from 53 per cent of the male rate to 45 per cent.[53]

Although officially inferior, women were not obliged to give up work and return to their homes after the Second World War. Even wives should stay at work, according to the *Spectator* in 1946, though it was hardly a resounding accolade for women: 'To dismiss women automatically on marriage is to waste education and training and ... the female staff of the Civil Service will lack broad-mindedness if it is entirely composed of spinsters.'[54]

Women might keep their jobs, but many people thought the nation's success depended on underpaying women at all levels in all industries. The 1946 Royal Commission on Equal Pay believed 'the British economy would collapse if women obtained pay parity with men'.[55] Scientist Rosalind Franklin complained vociferously about being paid less than men doing the same job.[56] Her contribution to understanding the double-helix structure of DNA not only earned her less money, but it went uncredited. Her male colleagues used her crucial X-ray data without acknowledgement and the discovery secured them the Nobel Prize four years after Franklin's death in 1958.

Equal pay for women was granted by London County Council in 1952, to women civil servants in 1955, and to teachers in 1956, followed by workers in the National Health Service and nationalised industries.[57] In the 1960s, a series of strikes by women workers challenged the value that was put on their work compared with that of male workers in similar tasks. The strike of women workers at the Ford factory in Dagenham was followed by that of women at the Lucas factory at Acton, and women bus conductors – put out of work by the introduction of the one-man bus – demanded that their union, the Transport and General Workers' Union, allow them to retrain as drivers.[58] In 1963, the Post Office allowed married women to retain their jobs after their weddings.[59] Women rose into senior positions, mostly in retail, hotels, catering and local government. One of those was Diane Abbott, fast-tracked through the civil service and elected to Westminster City Council in 1982; by 1987 she had secured a seat in the House of Commons for Labour, becoming the first Black woman to become an MP.[60] In 1988, 15 per cent of managers were women, but only 6 per cent of company directors.[61] In the library profession, women pulled ahead by 1930 and accounted for 80 per cent of librarians by 1960.[62] Women entered the

Foreign Office in 1951 as equal diplomats – but they had to resign when they married, until the rules changed in 1973. In 1976, the first female ambassador, Anne Warburton, moved into the UK embassy in Denmark.[63] It was not until the mid-1980s that the Metropolitan Police Force admitted that its unofficial policy of keeping the proportion of women at about 10 per cent of the rest of the force was discriminatory, and even now women make up less than a third of the UK's police forces (29 per cent).[64] It turns out that favouring men recruits to the police may not have been helpful – in 2023, the London Metropolitan Police were found by Baroness Louise Casey to show 'widespread bullying, discrimination, institutional homophobia, misogyny and racism, and other unacceptable behaviours which are a far cry from the high ethical standards the public rightly expects of its police officers'.[65]

When the Labour Party came to power in 1974, the government passed laws against sexual discrimination, including equal pay, pensions for women working for their families, maternity rights, and establishing the Equal Opportunities Commission. The numbers of women working steadily increased, and women's pay rose to a dizzy 75 per cent of the male rate. But in 1978, it started to decline.[66] Employers avoided the new legislation. Part-time workers were not given rights, and pro-women campaigns tended to focus upon social benefits to poor families instead of equality for all women.

The financial crisis of the mid-1970s prompted the Labour government to give up on equal pay. Instead, it cut benefits and created a hostile atmosphere towards the poor, the unemployed and people with disabilities. Unemployment rose, and women of colour were especially affected by abuse from employers. An Asian woman forced out of Uganda to live and work in England said: 'There was no question of whether you wanted to or not – you had to work, so you did. And wherever you found work, you had to take it. It wasn't that you were educated, so you only wanted certain kind of jobs – we had to work in factories and that's how we brought up our children … We used to have people working for us, and now we had to work for others. That's life … Of course I felt sad.'[67]

The rise of unemployment in England hit women workers nearly twice as hard as men: while male unemployment rose 146 per cent, women's went up by 276 per cent in the early 1980s.[68] Work began to be outsourced from poor women in England to even poorer women in the developing world and many English factories closed. The slump in manufacturing hit women of colour in low-paid non-union jobs very hard as their work was outsourced to women working in their homes at even poorer rates. Christina, a Greek-Cypriot clothing worker for 20 years, said: 'Chinese, Turkish or Indian ladies are working at home now, so all the work from the factory is going to these people.'[69]

The 'putting out' system of employers delivering parts of work to women for them to assemble or complete in their homes was assumed to have ended with industrialisation, but in fact home-working (slop work, piecework) increased through the 1970s, and women who worked part-time or in their homes, unprotected by unions or even factory inspectors, found their rates falling, bringing women's rates of pay down against the male rate overall.[70] A list of occupations undertaken by homeworkers in north London in 1972 found women making 'hats, belts, ties and buttonholes … packing crackers, stuffing toys, pasting jewellery, knitting, crocheting, making hooks and eyes, carding buttons and thread, wiring batteries, or making and mending netting. Equally a home worker might do skilled administrative work like copy-typing, addressing or stuffing envelopes.'[71]

The minimum wage was introduced in 1999 and set at £3.60 an hour.[72] In 1995, women were packing tights in their homes for 36 pence an hour.[73] Women of Asian descent reported that when men could not get jobs, women were forced into work at home, as they had to have a wage but their families did not want them working outside the home. Most of the homeworkers used their earnings for food and children's clothing, and large families could barely make ends meet.[74]

When women did return to employment in the boom period of the 1990s, it was often to low-paid service jobs and part-time work – less and less protected by either unions or wages councils. At the same time as driving down wages, the Margaret Thatcher Conservative government privatised many public services such as care homes and the provision of school dinners, as well as services like cleaners. In these places, the new private employers made workers part-time wherever possible, without sick pay or pensions. Some posts paid by the hour and hired when needed.

Concern for poor working women translated into nostalgia for a fantasy past that never existed, where stay-at-home wives were fully catered for by reliable husbands. Some surprising people kept the happy dream alive: the chair of the Equal Opportunities Commission in 1978,

Elspeth Howe, commented: 'The traditional single role family where the wife stayed at home and the husband went to work is disappearing. As a society, we are right to worry about what is happening to women, as they struggle to carry the double burden of their traditional duties and their role as workers.'[75]

We are indeed 'right to worry about women carrying the double burden', but we could have worried about this any time in the last 900 years. Working-class women have carried the double burden of wage work and production for the family ever since wages were paid for work and they had to go outside the home to earn money as well as produce at home. The double burden is hard but profitable when home production is high and wages are good, but it is unendurable when neither is enough to sustain the life of the woman herself or her children.

In homes where both husband and wife work full time, the wife does on average twice the childcare and housework of her husband. When she gets equal pay, her domestic work decreases: she works less than she did – but never as little as him. But a woman who earns more than her husband does more than her fair share of domestic work. As her wages exceed his, her workload at home increases too. Even when the only wage coming in to the household is hers, when the wife is the only one earning – she *still* does the majority of the housework.[76] By 1965, in England, the task of caring at home for the family was increasing. Older women were called on to help young mothers with baby-sitting and child care, as the state closed nurseries and fathers were persistently unavailable. As care for the disabled and the elderly was cut by the government, more women stepped up to look after relatives: 29 per cent of single women and 24 per cent of wives were caring for parents or relatives, but only 16 per cent of men, according to the 1985 household survey. Historian Sheila Rowbotham called women 'the shock absorbers of the economic and social system ... both couples and single mothers were relying increasingly on female relatives, mothers or partner's mothers and grandmothers for sustenance ... Amidst all the talk of expanded choice, familial obligations actually became heavier.'[77]

Women in Authority

The post-war idealisation of a balance of external work and domestic work for women led the queen of England, Elizabeth II, to release photographs and film of her with her family, even washing up at a family barbecue.

The first female prime minister of England, Margaret Thatcher, described running a country like running a house: 'It may just be that many, many women make naturally good managers ... each woman who runs a house is a manager and an organiser. We thought forward each day, and we did it in a routine way, and we were on the job 24 hours a day.'[78]

Women who gained authority post-war tended to pride themselves on their ability to perform all their domestic duties and run their businesses. Journalism and biographies, self-help books and novels all stressed that a successful woman in the world was a successful woman at home. The hugely popular queen and the divisive first woman prime minister modelled wifely obedience and subservience – both promised to 'obey' at their weddings – and middle-class family values of companionate marriage, good child-raising, and an emphasis on religion, patriotism and female modesty. Mrs Thatcher was explicit about her feminine softness combined with feminine authority in a 1976 speech that still makes me feel a little bit queasy: 'I stand before you tonight in my green chiffon evening gown, my face softly made up, my fair hair gently waved. The Iron Lady of the Western World? Me? A cold war warrior? Well, yes – if that is how they wish to interpret my defence of values and freedoms fundamental to our way of life.'[79]

In the 11 years that she was prime minister Thatcher promoted only one other woman to her 22-strong cabinet. With her arrival to power, she believed that the fight was over: 'The battle for women's rights has been largely won. The days when they were demanded and discussed in strident tones should be gone for ever. And I hope they are. I hated those strident tones that you still hear from some Women's Libbers.'[80]

For many women, those who were neither prime minister nor queen, it was hard to see the victory of women's rights. Women were not admitted to the upper House of Parliament, the House of Lords, until 1968. The Earl of Glasgow said frankly: 'Many of us do not want women in this House. We do not want to sit beside them on these Benches, nor do

Princess Elizabeth (1926–2022), a Girl Guide, doing the washing-up in 1944

we want to meet them in the Library. This is a House of men, the House of Lords. We do not wish it to become a House of Lords and Ladies.'[81]

The post-war settlement by the Labour government of 1945–51 was based on the belief that women would marry and wives would stay at home – not seek work and positions of authority. William Beveridge's influential report on state insurance against poverty was rooted in his understanding that wives' work at home was essential to keep their husbands at work for the benefit of the national economy.[82] He wrote, 'Housewives as mothers have vital work to do in ensuring the adequate continuance of the British race and of the British ideal in the world.'[83]

By the 1980s, the ruling party of the Conservatives focused discussion not on women but on the family, which was understood to be a middle-class family, where the man earned a breadwinner wage, and the wife maintained the home, raised children and serviced the needs of her husband.[84] In difficulties, like illness or redundancy, the state was supposed to provide temporary benefits until the family could return to its usual imaginary prosperity.

Trade unions and employers continued to prefer male workers in the late 1960s and just as conditions and wages deteriorated for women, psychologist John Bowlby produced 'attachment theory', the theory that a baby is predisposed to attach to one (only one) parent and will be damaged if this attachment does not successfully take place. Attachment theory was inspired by research with ducklings and 'proved' by research with monkeys.[85] As someone who has raised both babies and ducklings, I am happy to reassure scientists that they are very different.

Attachment theory 'proved' that women needed to be at home because of their innate nature, and babies needed to be with their mothers because of *their* innate nature. Biology triumphed over History – women should not go out to work because to do so was to fly against their own nature. Women staying at home and doing all the housework and caring for the children was not only convenient for men, good for wage control and helpful in keeping an army of workers in reserve till needed – turns out it is essential for the well-being of women and children. *Voila!*

Theories about the nature of women as mothers and guardians of the family spread from the middle classes to every strata. From the World Health Organization to John Bowlby, everyone agreed that the mother should be available to the baby 24/7. Other family members could help only briefly. As Bowlby said: 'The exacting job is scamped at one's peril.'[86]

The failings of poor and unhappy families were increasingly visible both to private do-gooders and to the state and police systems. Successive laws created greater protection for children and increasing intervention into the family until 1989 when children were given a right to inquiry and intervention for their safety.[87] Theorists no longer talked about the 'undeserving poor' but about 'problem families', and 'families' were understood to be 'mothers'. Mothers working outside the home were accused of failing to care for their children: 'latchkey children' were the tragic result of women in work.[88] It was the mother and only the mother who could produce a well-balanced child. Only her constant presence – constantly loving, never rejecting – would make a secure person. Her absence or incompetence would ruin both the child and society.

Women and children who fell outside the model of the imaginary two-parent, breadwinner-father family were punished. The Child Poverty Action Group showed that 3 million children were growing up in poverty in 1970 and quoted the case of a deserted wife with three children, who was refused £12.6s benefit a week, as she owned a washing machine and a television. The lives of working women with young children were made yet more difficult by the 1980 Education Act, which ruled that local authorities were no longer obliged to provide nurseries. When employers did offer workplace nurseries, the Inland Revenue taxed them as a 'perk'.[89] Poor women were further disadvantaged in 1986 when a new law stopped payment of a one-off grant on birth to the 94,000 women who were on income support.

The belief in the traditional family led to changes in the adoption laws to make it easier to create families. Local government officials, guardians, grandparents and parents could all sign adoption orders, so that children could be taken from their mothers and put into new families. Unmarried women were forced into giving up their babies and bullied and belittled. Maternal benefits, food stamps and birth certificates were taken from unmarried mothers, and social workers lied to single mothers, saying that babies were on 'trial' with foster families, when they had been permanently placed. Mothers were declared unfit or confused and their babies taken away.

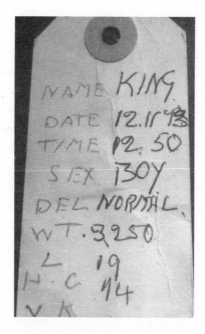

Pat King was 15 years old when forced to give up her illegitimate baby for adoption in 1973. She never saw him again, but kept his name tag all her life

Pat King was a 15-year-old schoolgirl in Whitchurch, Shropshire, when the head teacher at her school told her parents that she believed the girl was hiding her pregnancy. Only three weeks later, Pat gave birth to a boy, and after two weeks of caring for him, she was ordered to hand him over to a social worker. 'My dad was there, quite firmly making sure I didn't make too much fuss. It's one of those things you never forget, just like it was yesterday.'

Pat King said her social worker was 'of the view that you'd committed a sin and this was the best thing, and loving couples out there needed these children. It was almost like that was her goal, to find babies for the parents she'd got on her list; she didn't care about the person giving the child away at all.'

In adult life, Pat looked for her son but never found him.[90]

Not until 1976 were mothers given the right not to be coerced and to have full information before permitting adoption, and the baby had to be more than six weeks old.[91] This decade also saw the ending of 'child migration schemes' that shipped poor, abandoned children and those in foster care to Canada and Australia.

The fashion for encouraging women into the home could not be sustained. In the 1970s, the demand for workers meant women were needed to fill vacancies, while poverty drove many women to work and others demanded a working life. Left-wing feminists insisted on and organised provision for children and called for an end to child poverty, with financial support for children whatever their parent's status. Advice to women as to how to mother their children changed dramatically when the nation needed women workers. In the late 1970s, the emphasis fell on the beneficial educational and socialising effect of nursery and pre-school education for babies and toddlers. Having needed no one but Mother, babies and small children now needed everyone but – and now mothers caused much fake concern about their ill-educated, unsophisticated narrow lives at home, where they were spoiling and overprotecting sheltered children.[92]

Protest

Even during wartime, women protested against the rationing of essential foods. On 16 July 1945, *The British Pathé News* filmed women demonstrating against the government, publicly protesting against austerity. By the end of the war, frustration with austerity and state control had increased, particularly among women who demanded purchasing power and freedom of choice. Meat, bacon, butter, sugar, eggs, tea, cheese, milk, sweets, clothes, petrol were all still restricted.

Women led the protest against the 'national loaf', a new recipe for bread that the government enforced to economise on wheat imports from Canada during wartime. But in 1946, the Labour government introduced bread rationing. Mrs Irene Lovelock of the British Housewives' League led the protest: 'We have put up with the loaf being made smaller, we have put up with it being made darker, but women say here and now that we won't have bread rationing.'[93]

In an extraordinary re-enactment of the medieval food riots, the modern British Housewives' League organised marches with banners that read 'Bread: No Ration.' The women food rioters won and the government took bread off the ration for two years.

As concern increased about the Cold War and damage from radioactive poisoning released by atom bombs, mothers pushing prams led a peace demonstration of 400 marchers to the Russian embassy in 1961. One of the mothers said: 'Up to now women have not had much say in politics ... but we can't just go on cooking food for our families when we know it has been contaminated with radioactive poisons. We know that women all over the world, especially those who have or hope to have children, feel as we do.'[94]

In the fishing port of Hull, Lil Bilocca, a fisherman's wife, set up the Hull Equal Rights Group to support a safety campaign for trawlers, and a year after the Ford strike at Dagenham, women trade unionists established a national campaign for women's equal rights. 'The year of the militant woman' was announced by the magazine *Black Dwarf* in 1969, as women's liberation groups sprang up around the country, picketing the Miss World beauty contests and the Ideal Homes Exhibition.[95] The first women's liberation march took to the streets in London in 1971, calling for equal pay, workplace nurseries, equal representation in the trade unions, free contraception, abortion on demand, and financial help for women and families.

The lack of trade union support for women workers led to a 'mass uprising' in clothing workers at Leeds in 1970, when women workers went around factories calling on other women workers to support a strike for a wage increase, protesting against the employers, the wage council and the trade union that represented them. They elected their own committees.[96] Women also campaigned for wider causes, protecting the environment in Swansea in 1971, blocking the gates of a polluting factory, and campaigned against asbestos dust in 1976.

In 1974, Asian women walked out of the Imperial Typewriter Factory in Leicester because the pace of work had been increased. They faced racial prejudice from employers and even from the trade unionists, who failed to represent them. Two years later, Asian women workers organised a walk-out at a non-union film processing factory at Grunwick, north-west London, demanding improvements to their workplace and better treatment. The women had been forced to raise their hands for permission to go to the bathroom. They joined a union, and their walk-out was widely supported. The government appointed a commission, which reported that the processing plant should be unionised and the striking women should have their jobs back. The company refused, and the Trades Union Congress decided that the strike could not be won and withdrew support. The two-year-old strike by women was broken by a combination of government apathy, employer power and trade union betrayal.[97]

Reclaim the Night marches started in 1978 as part of an international women's demonstration against the threat to women on the street. The first march, in Leeds, was defying police advice that women should stay home after the Yorkshire Ripper attacks. A later march in London brought 2,000 women onto the streets with the slogan 'No curfew for women'.

The internationally famous Greenham Women's Peace campaign began in 1981 with a march of 30 people, mostly women with small children, from Cardiff to Greenham Common, a US base of nuclear missiles. They set up the Greenham Women's camp, leading a national and worldwide protest. A clerk in the Foreign Office, Sarah Tisdall, leaked plans for the arrival of the American Cruise missiles, and was imprisoned for six months, while an MI5 agent, Cathy Massiter, revealed that the Campaign for Nuclear Disarmament was under surveillance as a subversive organisation, along with trade unions and other organisations. The camp lasted for 19 years – itself an extraordinary achievement – and the women appeared in court to defend themselves at almost every level of appeal. In 1991–92 the missiles at Greenham Common were returned to the USA as part of the reduction of the Cold War, and in 1997 Greenham Common was designated a public parkland – returning the common land to the people as women have demanded since 1066.[98]

Striking miners in 1984–85 were out for a year to prevent pit closures under the Margaret Thatcher Conservative government, which was determined to break the power of the big industrial unions. The women who lived in the pit villages defended their homes, their way of life and their family's income in public demonstrations that rallied 50,000 women to London: 'It clearly wasn't any longer about wages or even just jobs it was about who's got the right to decide really how you live,' said protester Jean McCrindle. After the strike was broken, many women moved on to support the 1986 printers' strike against new technology for newspapers at Wapping, London, demonstrations against nuclear power in 1986 and the seafarers strike against new shifts in 1988.[99]

One English-Pakistani woman, Anwar Ditta, fought an almost-solo battle against the English government to regain her children. Ditta was born in Birmingham to Pakistani parents and sent to live with her paternal grandparents in Pakistan when her parents divorced. A marriage was arranged for her there, at the age of 14, and she had two children with her husband, who moved to England, where she joined him, expecting her children to join them later. The Home Office took two years to consider the matter and declared itself unconvinced that the children were hers. Anwar Ditta started her own campaign to be reunited with her children, despite criticism from the Asian community in England. 'They said a woman's place is in the house and not campaigning … I don't give a damn what anyone thinks,' she said.[100]

Anwar Ditta faced racism from the white community, some of whom abused her, pulled her hair and sent hate mail – which she donated to the Ahmed Iqbal Ullah RACE Centre. She was dismissed from her job. Every weekend she campaigned for her children to be admitted to England, taking a bucket for donations and asking for signatures on a petition. She was supported by the Asian Youth Movements in Manchester and Bradford, especially the women's wing of the Asian

Anwar Ditta (1953–2021), born in Britain and with a British passport, had to publicly challenge the Home Office for five years, when it excluded her children from England

Youth Movement at Manchester which worked against the deportation that was dividing families, as well as anti-racist groups. Despite witnesses, sworn depositions and support, Ditta's appeal to the Home Office was rejected in 1980.[101] Her appeal was denied but her campaign became part of a TV documentary, which was shown in March 1981; the Home Office refusal was overturned the following day and Anwar Ditta's children came home to her in Rochdale a month later in April 1981.[102]

Two women of colour became leaders of the immigrant community: Amy Ashwood Garvey (widow of Marcus Garvey, the Jamaican radical) was president of the Association for the Advancement of Coloured People, while Claudia Jones ran the *West Indian Gazette*, which campaigned for women's rights and organised the Caribbean Carnival in Notting Hill, west London.[103]

The 1981 British Nationality Act denied admission to Britain to some British overseas citizens, and women of colour protested deportations and changes to migrant rights. Police violence, especially against young men of colour, radicalised Asian and Black women. In 1986, Shreela Flather, the first Asian mayor of Windsor, said the police were 'sexist and racist and not at all welcoming'.[104]

The marches fizzled out during the 1990s but were revived in 2016 as part of the MeToo movement, and in 2017, 100,000 women marched as a world-wide rebuke to the abuse and repression of women, as Donald Trump – who had admitted assaulting women – was inaugurated as president of the USA. In 2021, after the rape and murder of Sarah Everard by a Metropolitan Police officer, more than 1,000 women gathered in a vigil to mourn her. The vigil – organised by Reclaim These Streets – was banned by the police under coronavirus regulations and the organisers threatened with fines. The demonstration – now declared illegal – went ahead, and many women were forcibly arrested. A hearing by High Court judges said that the police should have allowed the demonstration, and lifted the fines on the organisers.[105] The government called for an independent review of the police, which discovered the London police was failing women and children with 'institutional racism, sexism and homophobia, inside the organisation'.[106]

In the 1990s, women came together for a number of campaigns: for the environment, for the poor, to ban the export of live animals. Debjani Chatterjee from the Bengali Women's Support Group in Sheffield said: 'Many of us would rather not make artificial choices between the individual and the group, between femininity and feminism, and there is a perception that Western feminism has required that such choices be made ... within our sisterhood, there is room for many points of view, and a variety of approaches. Arms are wide.'[107]

Women Divided

Alas, arms were not always wide, as Sheila Rowbotham remembered: 'The 1978 women's liberation conference divided so acrimoniously on the question of inherent male violence that no one was ever prepared to call another one.'[108]

Even women's own causes could be divided when some women felt patronised by protective and safety legislation while others felt that women workers needed specialist protection. The 1960s saw the rise of right-wing women who wanted protection rather than opportunities for women. Mary Whitehouse campaigned against BBC programmes exploring sex and its reporting of war. In 1979 she wrote:

Dear Sir, With ref. to Monday Film BBC1 at 9.25pm Jan. 22nd. The general scenery was superbly photographed, but WHY must you spoil a good film by crudeness and vulgarity. You seem to delight in close-up pictures of …

(i) A young girl putting on her panties.
(ii) A native boy's buttocks.
(iii) A close-up of breasts belonging to a native whilst climbing a tree.
(iv) And please don't tell me it was not done intently: the branches of a tree, photographed in such a way as to resemble the lower part of a woman's body.
(v) The scientist scene, was there a necessity to show a close-up [of] the legs of the woman sitting there?

And you have the cheek to increase our licences! WHAT FOR? To receive rubbish like this in our homes? Yours sincerely.[109]

Margaret Thatcher, prime minister, was more interested in supporting housewives and mothers to stay at home than the rights of women at work, but Labour political star Barbara Castle described feminism as a quest for 'real' equality for poor women struggling with poverty as well as elite women struggling for opportunities: 'To find out what they are, what they want to be and whether they are given the backing of society to lead the lives they want to lead. Equality must go down to the mundane things like – "How do I get enough to live on? Do I or do I not have children? Who will help me to bring them up?"'[110]

The question of free abortion for unwanted pregnancies divided women. Anti-abortionists themselves were divided, some of them wanting to hold men responsible, some to 'protect' the woman from a surgery that she might later regret, some to 'protect' the fetal life. Pro-abortion campaigners were split between those who regarded abortion as an acceptable form of contraception for all women and others who wanted it limited to patients with particular issues.

In 1983, Victoria Gillick, a Roman Catholic mother of ten, petitioned Parliament to ensure that none of her daughters under 16 years old would be given contraception or an abortion without her knowledge. The 'Gillick Competence' test became enshrined in law, ruling that doctors must review a child seeking treatment to confirm they understand the treatment.[111]

Both Conservative-type moral crusaders and feminists campaigned against sex shops. In 1984, the Video Recording Act set up a licensing system for pornography. There was little concern for women in the business of sex. The 1959 Street Offences Act was used against prostitutes, banning them from soliciting on the street (or out of their windows or front doors). The concern was to keep the streets free of soliciting, not to prevent women working as prostitutes, nor to provide them with safe spaces. The 1985 Sexual Offences Act made kerb-crawling (seeking sex in a car from female pedestrians) an offence. Concern about the enslaving of women in England for work, especially sex work, led to an addition to the Sexual Offences Act in 2010 that made it an offence to pay for sexual services from anyone who has been coerced into prostitution.

The Child Support Act of 1991 proved divisive for women as it required a mother to name the father of her child and a government agency to pursue him for payment. Since single mothers carried most of the burden of raising children, this was seen by some women as a positive step. Others resented being forced to name an unwilling man for support, and some second wives bitterly resented the cost of a previous household.[112]

Women were painfully divided by race, as increasing numbers of people were invited to come to England from the former British colonies to undertake hard and dirty work, and join the expanding National Health Service, facing racism at every step.

Immigration

Over 1,000 people from the Caribbean voyaged on the MV *Empire Windrush* in 1948 to dock at Tilbury Docks, London, the first post-war overseas workers invited from the Commonwealth to fill vacancies in Britain. Women on the *Windrush* were required to pay a higher ticket price – the equivalent of half a year's National Assistance – and take a cabin, rather than going steerage like the male immigrants. But 27-year-old dressmaker Evelyn Wauchope stowed away and was discovered mid-voyage. She lived in England for a while before marrying a Bajan man and emigrating to America.[113]

Mona Baptiste was a 21-year-old Trinidadian blues singer, registered as a clerk for the voyage. Six weeks after disembarking, she was singing on the BBC's *Light Programme*, and would go on a successful tour of English theatres and perform on TV shows, including the Ken Dodd show on the BBC. She went on to develop a hugely successful career as a singer in the UK and Germany.[114]

Most of the women were in their mid-thirties, travelling with their families.[115] Although official policy was to welcome volunteers from the Caribbean, there was widespread racism in the Services.[116] Racism towards immigrants prompted the government to impose immigration controls on women, who were banned from bringing husbands and children to England, though incoming men could bring wives and children.

For the next 20 years about 500,000 people of colour from former Commonwealth countries migrated to England. They had permission to stay only if they had both a work permit and proof of a parent or grandparent born in the UK. In 1971, Commonwealth citizens already living

Mona Baptiste (1928–93), internationally successful singer and actress, came to Britain from Trinidad and Tobago on MV *Empire Windrush* in 1948

in the UK were given leave to remain. But migrants who arrived before 1971, and those without parents or grandparents living in the UK, could not prove their right to remain and could not access health services or benefits. Some born in England, or who had lived most of their lives in England, faced deportation. Even at the time of writing, a government apology and compensation scheme has not fully compensated people cruelly treated under this confused and unworkable policy.

Racist injustice from government and British institutions continues to this day in underrepresentation of people of African and Asian descent in institutions, who have worse outcomes than white people in health, education and the justice system.

The people of the Chagos Islands, descended from African people captured as slaves by the French in the seventeenth century, were forcibly evicted from their Indian Ocean homeland by the UK in 1968, to provide the USA with empty islands for a military base on Diego Garcia. The Chagossian people were banned from returning despite multiple appeals under international law. Some people were left without provision in Mauritius and the Seychelles islands, and a few managed to get to England, where they still struggle for permission to either return to their homelands or naturalise in England. A government review recommended that the Chagos people be allowed to return to their homeland; but the naming of the Chagos Island area as a Marine Protected Area – a huge benefit for conservation – is used to continue to keep the people from their homes.

The 1950s also saw increased immigration from India and Pakistan and attacks, verbal and physical, on people of colour, expressing an imaginary belief in white superiority, which continues to this day. Attacks on people of colour and fears about immigration announced in inflammatory language are one of the identifying hallmarks of the English right-wing parties and of those ignorant of demographics or basic manners in the twentieth century.

Health

In 1967, the National Health Service Family Planning Act allowed for contraception to be dispensed for social as well as medical reasons, to married and unmarried women.[117] For the first time, women could reli-

542 / Normal Women

ably control their fertility. Women enjoyed greater sexual freedom, and sexual intercourse before marriage became widely accepted. Some feminists saw this as increasing the exploitation of women – images of women in the media and art became more and more sexualised, and all women (not only poor women, as had been the tradition) were considered potentially available for male sexual gratification.[118]

The use of herbs, fungi and woods to cause abortions or miscarriages, or to 'bring on' reluctant periods, remained part of folk medicine as late as the twentieth century in Norfolk and Lancashire.[119] The debate about abortion increased in the 1950s with growing concern for women who resorted to so-called 'backstreet' abortionists – unregistered, and sometimes fatally incompetent. Abortion was legalised in 1967 if two doctors agreed that it was necessary on grounds of mental or physical health. In the same year, local authorities were allowed to provide contraceptive advice.

There was a pushback, especially from the Catholic Church in the 1970s and large street demonstrations were organised by the Society for the Unborn Child. Women anti-abortionists were themselves divided into those who wanted to support pregnant women so that they could give birth to an unwanted child and those who wanted to encourage births of white babies.[120] Even now, after increased liberalisation and the invention of the morning after pill, there is no general agreement that the woman who is going to carry and birth the child should be the one who chooses to do so.[121]

Abortion is so sensitive because it plays against the imaginary 'nature of women' as maternal or nurturing. The woman seeking an abortion can be cast as deviant, unnatural. It is not seen as a dilemma that any sexually active woman might face since no contraception can be 100 per cent reliable. Instead, it is seen as a failure of the woman to use contraception properly, or at all; or a problem that can only be resolved by a ruling from the House of Commons and the joint advice of two doctors – surely an excessive taxing of medical and legal brains to make a decision that, however painful for the rest of us, surely belongs to the pregnant woman herself.[122]

Sport

Maureen Gardner, a ballerina who took up running to improve her health, won a silver medal in the 80 metre hurdles in the 1948 London Olympics. In 1964, the women's athletics team won a record-breaking five medals in 12 events – the men took 7 from their 24 events. Star of the women's team proved to be Mary Rand, who won gold and broke the world record in the long jump, took silver in the pentathlon and bronze in the 4 x 100 metres relay.[123] Mary Peters won gold and broke the pentathlon world record in the 1972 Olympics, going on to be manager of the British women's team. Tessa Sanderson competed at every Olympics from 1976 to 1996, winning the javelin in 1984 – the first Black British woman to win a gold medal. Sally Gunnell became the only British female athlete to have won Olympic, World, European and Commonwealth titles in the same event – hurdling – and the only woman to have done so over 400 metres.

In 1971, pioneering sportswoman Rachael Heyhoe-Flint set up the first cricket Women's World Cup. She hit the first six in a women's Test match and regularly captained the England international squad. She persuaded Marylebone Cricket Club (MCC) to give women permission to play at the prestigious men-only ground at Lord's, saying: 'Now the mums and the daughters have their own cricket instead of making cucumber sandwiches every weekend.'[124]

Horse-riding remains the only Olympic sport in which men and women compete equally against each other, since women were first allowed into dressage events at the 1952 Olympics, followed in 1956 by showjumping and finally, in 1964, eventing. Britain's Pat Smythe won team bronze for showjumping in 1956, though she had been representing Britain in international competitions since 1947.

The youngest ever British Olympian, ice skater Cecilia Colledge, finished eighth in 1932, aged 11. Four years later she won silver. The first woman skater to perform a double jump, she invented the camel spin and layback spin. During the Second World War, Colledge served as an ambulance driver, before returning to skating and winning the national title for the sixth time.

Football for women reappeared when the Women's FA was formed in 1969 and eventually in 1971 the 50-year-old ban on women's football was reversed. Within three years, the first Women's FA Cup Final and England women's international had been played. In 1993, a Women's Football Committee was established to run the women's game in England. The FA outlined its plans to develop the women's game from grassroots to elite level in 1997 and in the following year appointed Hope Powell as women's national coach.[125]

Women's hockey finally made its way onto the Olympic schedule in 1980 and the British women's team won bronze in 1992. Fencing for women was added to the Olympic schedule in 1924, with Gillian Sheen taking gold in 1952. In 1962, women came first, second and third in the BBC Sports Personality of the Year Award. Swimmer Anita Lonsbrough, who won three gold medals at the Commonwealth Games that year, became the first woman to win the award. Second was sprinter Dorothy Hyman (who would go on to win the following year), and third, swimmer Linda Ludgrove.

Wealth

Women's share of total personal wealth had increased after the 1920s in Britain and the US, to approximately 40 per cent of male wealth in the 1950s. This was probably not caused by women earning more, or families treating boys and girls equally, but that more women were outliving their husbands and transferring the family fortune from his name to theirs.[126]

Women's rights in their own homes were set back in 1969 when a bankrupt husband, Mr Caunce, lost the family home as the bank reclaimed on a loan. His wife, who had contributed to the purchase of the house, had no rights: the judge ruled that the bank was not obliged to discover if she had an interest (in her own home) and that her presence in the house did not establish her right to it. Judge Stamp said from the bench that to enquire into a wife's rights in her home would be an intolerable invasion of privacy.[127]

Mrs Caunce lost her home but a subsequent ruling for Mrs Boland – that houses should be in joint ownership for married couples, and a wife could insist on her right to live in the house – ought to have improved the security of married women in their own homes. It did not. Husbands who had previously obtained loans in secret, now coerced and bullied wives into signing away their rights and allowing their homes to be used for security against a husband's debts. Law historians believe this shows how often women experience pushback: 'Legal reforms that benefit women, are so often followed by renewed efforts by men to maintain the status quo.'[128]

Another Married Women's Property Act in 1964 ruled that women who bought property, or made a profit on the money given them by their husbands, were entitled to half of it on divorce.[129] In 1988, the Finance Act ruled that a wife's earned income should not be included with her husband's earnings for taxation. In effect, this meant that a wife did not have to report to her husband what she earned. It was the last bastion of couverture that had kept women under marital control for 898 years.[130]

In 1969, the Divorce Reform Act allowed couples to divorce after they had been separated for two years (or five years if one of them resisted a divorce). A marriage could be ended if it had irretrievably broken down, and neither partner had to prove 'fault'. But the tradition that wives got 50 per cent of the assets – whoever had earned them – was not established until *White* v *White* in 1996, when the appeal judge ruled that a wife's contribution to the family fortune should be considered as equal to the breadwinner husband's: 'There should be no bias in favour of the money-earner and against the home-maker and the child-carer' – a win for home-making wives but a disadvantage for working wives who also did the domestic work with lesser-earning husbands.[131]

Women Loving Women

The finding by sexologists in the 1950s and 1960s that women's sexual intimacy with women occurred so frequently that it had to be considered a 'normal' expression of desire was widely ignored by doctors and psychologists who only met professionally with women troubled by their feelings – not those who were living happily in loving or sexual relationships with other women.[132]

Lesbians started to speak of themselves as women who choose a particular lifestyle, not identified with homosexual men, and not defined by any particular sexual practice from 1950. They also challenged the convention of heterosexual relationships and traditional female subservience.[133] This linked lesbianism with feminism – which itself was becoming clearer, more coherent and better known.

Observing that the 'breadwinner family' underpaid them at work and made them work for free at home, women began to explore the possibility of a life independent of men. One woman explained: 'If you grew up wanting to be whole as a woman in this society then you have to be a feminist … And once you're a feminist, it's almost impossible to have any kind of whole relationship with a man, because there's all kinds of roles that you're taught, and even if he's really cool, you know, other people lay trips on you, and it's all so ingrained. That's the only way I can see myself going really, from a strong person, to a feminist, to a lesbian. It's just a very logical progression.'[134]

The belief that 'real' sexual intercourse could only be penile penetration with man in dominant position was challenged when lesbians described love-making that satisfied them, without a penis or substitute, without a masculine sex drive and without manly behaviour. While the absence of historical records means that women's experiences in previous centuries can only be imagined, once they began publishing their experiences, they described a range of affectionate, loving and erotic behaviours. Some, in their insistence on lack of sexual contact, would have been familiar to the Ladies of Llangollen and this came to be understood not as modest discretion, hiding a raunchy secret, but as describing a genuine absence of genital sexuality, preferred by some women.

It was difficult for lesbians to speak openly about asexuality, chastity, virginity and frigidity or erotic experimentation without sounding as if they were denying their sexuality. Male sexual rhythms and needs, and male genitals, have dominated discussions about sex for so long that it is hard to know what women might prefer in the absence – not only of men, but also of male ideas about sex.

As late as 1957, the Wolfenden Committee, set up to consider the law on homosexual offences, continued the established silence about lesbianism, since the committee members believed that women did not show the 'libidinous features that characterise sexual acts between males'.[135] In May 1988, one of Margaret Thatcher's most controversial laws came into force. Section 28 prohibited local authorities and schools from promoting homosexuality and prevented councils from funding any lesbian and gay initiatives. Teachers censored their lessons. Librarians removed books from the shelves. Councillors restricted children's services for fear of breaking the law, since 'acceptability of homosexuality as a pretended family relationship' was no longer legal.

One mother claimed that her court hearing about her protection from her violent husband concentrated on the fact that she was a lesbian: 'It was amazing how all the men in the court, whatever their age or their position, were united against lesbianism. My husband and the judge were on the same side.' She was accused of 'feminising' her son, and her husband's violence was seen as justified, and she was banned from having any contact with her woman lover.[136]

In response to the dangerous law, lesbian activists stormed the BBC News studio during the *Six O'Clock News*, believing that the nationwide marches, blockades and protests were being ignored by reporters. Another group abseiled into the House of Lords on knotted washing lines after peers voted in favour of the bill. Scotland repealed the law in 2000 and

Women protesting Section 28 invaded a BBC television news studio. Nicholas Witchell, newsreader, famously sat on one of the protesters

despite several failed attempts, England and Wales finally followed in 2003.

In more open-minded times, lesbians mostly agree that a woman's sexual practice is not what defines her as a lesbian – nor does identifying as a lesbian make any particular sexual practice, or any sex at all, compulsory. One historian of lesbians has written that men who are obsessed with sex are convinced that lesbians are obsessed with sex but 'like any other woman, lesbians are obsessed with love and fidelity ... also strongly interested in independence and having a life's work to do.'[137]

HeteroSex

Even in modern times, the clitoris has proved elusive. It appeared in the 1901 edition of *Gray's Anatomy*, but disappeared in the 1948 edition. Even modern drawings rarely show an accurate image: typically the vagina is shown as an open hole rather than a flexible tube, and the labia are always shown as symmetrical. The size of the clitoris is generally underestimated and the obstacle of the hymen greatly exaggerated.[138] In 1970, mention of the clitoris was becoming 'increasingly taboo' in school education.[139]

Nonetheless, in the 1960s, attitudes towards sexual pleasure for men and women were becoming more liberal. Helen Gurley Brown's bestselling 1962 book *Sex and the Single Girl* described sexual intercourse as a route for a single woman to entice a man into marriage:

You must develop style. Every girl has one ...
Brains are an asset but it doesn't take brainy brains like a nuclear
   physicist's. Whatever it is that keeps you from saying anything
   unkind and keeps you asking bright questions even when you
   don't quite understand the answers will do nicely ...
Your figure can't harbour an ounce of baby fat. It never looked good
   on anybody but babies.
You must cook well. It will serve you faithfully.
You must have a job that interests you, at which you work hard.[140]

Gurley Brown took this attitude to the relaunch of the US magazine *Cosmopolitan* in 1965. Enthusiastic praise in the magazine for heterosexual coupling emphasised a woman's right to an orgasm, but the woman reader was advised to make it her absolute vocation to please a male lover to persuade him into commitment and paying for gifts and treats, and ultimately to support the woman as a wife. In January 1988, *Cosmopolitan* encouraged readers to have sex with HIV-positive men who were carrying the then fatal disease AIDS, wrongly advising that unprotected sex in the 'missionary position' (man dominant) would not transfer the infection.[141] Death itself should not stand between a '*Cosmo* girl's' quest to please a man.

Cosmopolitan financed its global expansion – launching a UK edition in 1972 – with advertising of fashion, beauty and medical goods to young women who were advised to get an education to enable them to appear intelligent, domestic skills that imply future wifehood, and jobs that would put them in environments where aspirational and prosperous men might be found, courted and persuaded into marriage.

The attention to men and sexual generosity was not always reciprocated. The emphasis on female sexuality and female orgasm did not interest all men. In 1965, a male sex advisor, Dr Alexander Lowen, wrote: 'Most men … feel that the need to bring a woman to climax through clitoral stimulation is a burden.' Bringing a woman to orgasm after his own climax is onerous: 'It prevents him from enjoying the relaxation and peace, that are the rewards of sexuality. Most men to whom I have spoken who engaged in this practice resented it.'[142]

Sexual preferences were changing too: the so-called sexual revolution of the 1960s meant that women could experience sexual pleasure without guilt and anxiety. By the 1990s, people could easily access even hardcore pornography on the internet, as media and entertainment became more sexualised. Some women began to ask themselves if they had been freed from conventional modesty and oppressive restraint only so that men could be better served.

The Nature of Twentieth-century Women

Thanks to the improvements in facial reconstructive and other surgery, led by work done on casualties during the Second World War, more could be done to help people who wanted to look more like the sex they felt themselves to be. Charing Cross Hospital believed some individuals should be free to choose their gender and offered sex reassignment surgery to people with so-called 'atypical' genitals. People who declared their unhappiness with their assigned sex, or people like a woman who wanted to transition to be a man so that she could legally marry the woman she loved, were not offered surgery but psychotherapy to try to improve their lives while remaining in their assigned sex.[143]

Women were not only acting out of their assigned nature, but they were dressing to suit themselves. The appearance of women became more varied. They wore men's clothes and styling – some intending to appear like men, some enjoying an androgynous look, some rebelling against the hyper-feminine ideal of the 1950s image.

Female curves went out of fashion, even dresses went out of fashion. According to one historian, 'Not only women but men took to yellow satin flares … men's clothes went over the top … boys adopted feminine signals of allure and even more perplexing, girls appeared in outfits which made them look like Bowie doubles. It was not at all clear who was who.'[144]

Roberta Cowell (1918–2011), racing driver and WW2 pilot, was the first British man to use hormones and surgery – still experimental in 1951 – to become a woman

In 1951, Robert Cowell Marshall, who had driven in the 1939 Antwerp Grand Prix, married and fathered two children, and served heroically during the Second World War as a pilot, chose to undertake experimental genital surgery and officially changed his name to Roberta Cowell on her birth certificate. She became the first person born a man to use surgery and hormones to become a woman, describing herself, in the language of the time, as 'intersex from birth'.

Elizabeth Forbes-Sempill (1912–91) was registered as the youngest daughter of John, Lord Sempill, and was unhappy as a girl, taking a course of medical treatments in Germany and registering as a man, Ewan Forbes-Sempill, in 1952 and marrying a woman. His new identity was challenged by his cousin who was disappointed at the loss of his inheritance to a large estate and loss of the title of 11th Baronet on the arrival of Ewan Forbes-Sempill – a new male heir. The legal challenge took place in secret over three years until the home secretary ruled that Forbes-Sempill was 'intersex' and entitled to inherit as a male heir.

There was confusion at the birth of Georgina Carol Somerset (1923–2013) and she was registered late as a boy named George Edwin Turtle. After training as a dentist, George was called up to serve in the Second World War in the Royal Navy, but in 1957 undertook reassignment surgery and registered as a woman. She married in 1962 and became the first woman to surgically change sex and marry in church.

The word 'transgender' first came into use in England in 1965, and in the late 1960s a gender clinic opened and a conference on gender identity was held in London. People had to convince psychologists, medical doctors and surgeons that they were determined to live as another sex, and only then they could be prescribed experimental drugs and later undergo surgery. Their request had to be framed as if there were two distinct sexes – male or female – and applicants must state that they had always felt that they were born into the wrong one. The not uncommon experience of young girls wanting the freedom and opportunities of boys had to be reinterpreted to a sense of being 'in the wrong body' to satisfy a diagnosis. To be taken seriously by the doctors, there could be no ambivalence about two sexes and how a normal boy or a girl might feel about themselves and their prospects; there could be no genuine enquiry into feelings and hopes and fears. Someone wanting help to transition to a woman was most likely to succeed if they presented in a highly feminine mode. Indeed, a 1968 study in the US found that trans women presented themselves as more comfortable with their femininity than those born as women – a whole new definition of the 'nature of women'. The researchers recorded that the trans women were 'higher in femininity than women … held stereotypical women's jobs and seemed, on the average, to be "better adjusted" to the female role than women were'.[145]

A trans woman could not risk expressing any doubt about the 'nature', prospects or behaviour of the sex she was trying to join. A historian records: 'For a man to be considered for sex change treatment he has to convince the doctors of his femininity. He has to present as "hyper" feminine – and even if he feels it – he is advised not to express the ambivalence and androgyny that birth women experience.'[146]

Ever since the 'nature' of women was defined by the ancient Greek male philosophers, women have struggled or refused to conform to the definition. Now, in order to be accepted as women, people were having to agree to an artificial standard, conform to it and even persuade experts that it exactly described them. This imposition of an imaginary 'nature' upon people desperate to explore their true selves is a new expression of the seventeenth-century conduct books, laying down behaviour for 'ladies' and threatening girls that unless they conformed they would be evidently 'not ladies'.

But it was clear, even to the male doctors who worked with transgender people, that being a woman was not inevitably agreeable. American sex-change doctor Harry Benjamin warned transgender patients hoping to become women: 'So far you have only held a man's job and have drawn a man's salary. Now you have to learn something entirely new. Could you do that? Could you get along with smaller earnings?'[147] It turned out that the nature of women was to be paid less than men – and this was Biology rather than Economics!

April Ashley (1935–2021) was born in Liverpool, one of six children, and christened George. He later said that he prayed every night that he would wake up as a girl. Discharged from the merchant navy he worked as a dancer in a Paris drag club, saving enough money for gender reassignment surgery at a Casablanca clinic.

Ashley registered as a woman and returned to England to a career in acting and modelling as an outstandingly beautiful woman. A tabloid newspaper published her story and she was dropped from her agency and could not find work. She left for the Costa del Sol and married the heir to Lord Rowallan, Arthur Corbett, leaving him almost at once for the

This painting by Thomas Cantrell Dugdale in 1936 shows the indifference of the upper classes of London to the hunger march outside. The hundreds of men, viewed as a mass, are a mild diversion for the modern woman with bobbed hair who holds her string of pearls in one hand and her long cigarette holder in the other. Her partner amuses himself blowing smoke rings and does not even look.

Rotha Lintorn-Orman (1895–1935) formed the British Fascisti, Britain's first fascist organisation. She came from a military family and, having joined the Boy Scouts, had to be persuaded into the Girl Guide organisation. She served in the First World War in the Women's Emergency Corps. Her organisation, the British Fascisti, lost members to the British Union of Fascists under Sir Oswald Mosley.

4 October 1936: Policemen arresting a demonstrator when local people blocked the march of the British Union of Fascists in Cable Street in London's East End.

The Hackett-Lowther all-female Ambulance Unit, which was established in 1917 by Norah Desmond Hackett and May 'Toupie' Lowther. They acquired vehicles and recruited women before departing for the frontline in France. The British army would not use the women's unit, and instead they joined the French Third Army for nearly three years of wartime service.

A member of the Women's Land Army (1915–18) leads a horse out from the stables during the First World War. This photograph is by Horace Nicholls.

WOMEN PRIESTS NOW

12yrs in the ministry – but only the DOG gets the COLLAR !

This 1943 painting by Laura Knight (1877–1970) depicts 21-year-old Ruby Loftus (1921–2004) working at an industrial lathe cutting the screw of a breech-ring for a Bofors anti-aircraft gun. Ruby became an expert in the production of breech-rings in just seven months – something that usually took years. After the war, Ruby and her husband John Green emigrated to Canada and she never worked in a factory or engineering again.

'12 yrs in the ministry – but only the DOG gets the COLLAR!', reads Dr Una Kroll's sign. The Movement for the Ordination of Women (MOW) operated from 1979 to 1994 and was the major organisation to campaign for women to become priests in the Church of England.

heir to the Duke del Infantado. Corbett's request to annul the marriage on the grounds that April was not a woman was heard by Judge Roger Ormrod in 1970.[148]

Mr Ormrod ruled that marriage existed only between men and women, that sex was established at birth or earlier, by so-called 'biological' factors, and that neither medicine nor surgery could create 'a person who is naturally capable of performing the essential role of a woman in marriage'.

In an attempt to create clarity, Mr Ormrod managed to sow confusion: 'naturally', 'capable', 'performing', 'essential', 'role', 'woman' and 'woman in marriage' – every word begged a question. This rather coy definition of womanhood excludes infertile women (if he was referring to conception) and sexless marriages (if he was meaning penile penetration). It says nothing about people who are born with hormonal or genital variations – the very people who were first supposed to be served by medicine or surgery. Not for the last time did it seem easier to pronounce on transgender issues than to think about them. April Ashley married again, worked for Greenpeace and an art gallery, enjoying fame as an early trans woman.

Caroline Cossey (1954–) was born with XXXY syndrome and assigned male sex. She reassigned her sex at Charing Cross Hospital at the age of 20 and went on to become a glamour model, cast as a 'Bond girl' in the 1981 James Bond film *For Your Eyes Only* and appearing in *Playboy* in 1991, concealing her transition throughout. Cossey was recognised as a woman by the European Court of Human Rights and married her husband. A year later, in 1990, the British government appealed and overturned her legal identity as a woman.[149]

A rather bizarre linguistic development in the middle of the nineteenth century came from the widespread understanding of the word 'sex' to mean sexual intercourse (penile penetration with a man on top). Sex as a word was no longer thought adequate to mean not only intercourse but also different sexes: male and female. From the nineteenth century until the middle of the twentieth century, specialists started using the word 'gender' to indicate what had previously been known as 'sexes'. The definition of 'gender' was expanded to cover the male/female roles and behaviours expected, and then to describe identity, then self-identity, until the arrival – around 1980 – of a contradiction between the biological identity of a person (which was now called their 'sex') and their roles, behaviour or identity, which was now called their 'gender'. A

Caroline Cossey became a glamour model, a 'Bond girl' and a *Playboy* star, concealing her transition until 1978, when she was outed by a journalist

discrepancy between the two was pathologised in the 1980s as 'gender disorder', and in 2020 as 'gender dysphoria'.[150] It is hard not to see it as a frantic rearguard action to prevent challenge to rigid definitions of only two sexes, by providing a category that could include multiples and gradations, but which was not 'sex'.

In 1990, the idea of two sexes only was challenged by the work of Anne Fausto Sterling who identified five sexes, which she refined into a theory of gradations of sex on a continuum, and suggested the new term gender/sex to reflect that biology is directly affected by culture since what someone does becomes imprinted on their neuromuscular response, and activity affects sex hormones: gentle nurturing parenting diminishes testosterone in women and men. In this new way of thinking about sex, or gender/sex, the tradition of telling women their nature, requiring them to live up to it, and only defining women as women if they fit the narrow parameters becomes exposed for the circular exercise it always was. In 2007, Eric Vilain, of the Epigenetics, Data and Politics Laboratory at George Washington University, proved that sex was based not only on the genitals, but also on the X and Y chromosomes, and on all the hormones present in the body. Each category – genitals, chromosomes and hormones – has multiple variants. He said, 'An infinite combination of biological genders exists … far more than the five sexes *proposed* … in the 1990s.'[151]

By 2019, the numbers of people reporting to clinics to change sex was booming. The only clinic for children and adolescents reported increases of around 50 per cent of patients year on year since 2010–11, doubling in one year, 2018, from 697 to 1,398 referrals, at a time when the government announced it would hold an inquiry into why so many young women wanted to become male.[152] There has been a 'startling' rise in the number of young women suicides,[153] a trebling of young women reporting self harming between 2000 and 2014,[154] and increased anorexia in girls under 15:[155] 28 per cent of young women have eating disorders.[156] Clearly, for some young women, the 'natural performance of a woman's essential role in marriage' was not an attractive prospect.

In education, women's prospects were improving. In 2015 in the UK, the Higher Education Policy Institute reported that the centuries-old tradition of women being excluded from university had been reversed. Women were 35 per cent more likely to go to university than men, and in 2017, for the first time in its history, Oxford University gave more places to women than men.[157] Girls were outperforming boys in schools and apprenticeships. Hold the phones! Is this the best news for women since women were admitted to higher education? Apparently not – the Higher Education Policy Institute predicted that the situation would only 'get worse'. It said: 'A national determination to tackle the problem is needed.'[158]

Fortunately for national determination, the problem of clever women excelling over men has not yet occurred in business and industry: in the UK, in 2018, 71 per cent of the directors of top companies were men, and 75 per cent of top business boards were men.[159] In 2015, 93 per cent of engineers were men, as were 80 per cent of IT technicians. There was only one female Supreme Court judge among 11 male judges. While 53 per cent of the workforce were men, they constituted 66 per cent of managers, directors and senior officials.[160] The 2012–17 statistics showed women making up to twice the progress of men in entering higher wage brackets (£50,000 to £100,000 per annum), but when it comes to the highest pay, men still dominate. Men earning more than £150,000 outnumbered women by 5 to 1. The ratio was 10 to 1 for £1 million a year.[161]

In a 2018 UK government survey of the top industry boards (FTSE companies), several spokespeople produced a diverse and interesting set of reasons why women are not represented. One said that they 'don't fit comfortably into the board environment'. Another, that there 'aren't that many women with the right credentials and depth of experience to sit on the board – the issues covered are extremely complex.' Apparently, women 'don't want the hassle or pressure of sitting on a board' and competent women executives are amazingly scarce: 'All the "good" women have already been snapped up.'

In direct contradiction, one spokesperson felt certain that women are in excessive supply. He also added: 'We have one woman already on the board, so we are done – it is someone else's turn.'[162]

It seems that when there is a gender imbalance against women this is considered normal and indeed nice; when there is a gender imbalance against men this is a national emergency, and can be read alongside the newly declared 'crisis in masculinity'[163] brought about by the 'feminisation of the workplace'.[164] This 'feminisation of the workplace' is the euphemism given to the modern horror of women getting jobs, getting promotion and getting paid for the work they do. When women did low-paid, unskilled and part-time work, the workplace was apparently just fine. Apparently, when men don't run everything and aren't over-paid for doing so, they don't know what to do. This is probably another national emergency.

What is the nature of women at the close of the twentieth century? Underpaid in wage work, unpaid for domestic work – of which they do the most – making progress in education but usually regarded as less intelligent than men. A 1998 study of male and female intelligence found that men reported themselves as 'significantly brighter than they are' while women's estimates were 'far more modest'.[165]

In 1994, there was one outstanding barrier to female equality – it was in the national church of England. Did women have souls?

Spiritual Equality

In 1950, the Roman Catholic Church ruled that Mary, mother of God, was incorruptible, and that at death she went directly to heaven. Mary (but only Mary) was like a god: 'God's Mother should possess what belongs to her Son.'[166] This made no difference to the priesthood, which continued to be men-only, but it was an extraordinary acknowledgement of the divinity of a woman, a normal woman.

It also made no difference to the other Christian churches, including the national church of England, where there were no figures of women to equal God the father or God the son, or God the Holy Ghost – though the Holy Ghost was sometimes offered, rather grudgingly, as a model for women, though always referred to as 'he'. The Church of England remained resolutely masculine, with only the lowest possible post of deaconess available for women who wanted to serve as priests.

In 1966, the Church of England made a full report on the possibility of women becoming priests – and discovered that it was not possible. The document is a thoughtful, considered repetition of all the reasons that women have not been admitted to profitable or interesting work. It could have been written in previous centuries by any physicians, tailors, weavers or mechanics who decided that a trade was so valuable, or so interesting or of such high status, that only a man should get a shot at it. Being a vicar, concluded the report, is simply too good a job for anyone but a man. The report is an extraordinary document for the 1960s, working patiently through the many reasons that women have not in the past, cannot now, and should not in the future, do well-trained, well-paid high-status work.

First, the report pointed out that women priests went against tradition. If Jesus had wanted a woman apostle, he would have called one. But the Bible tells us he only summoned men. This, the report tells us, is 'just part of the nature of things, in this case of the nature of the Christian Church'.[167]

But Jesus did not just call exclusively men, he had a huge bias towards fishermen. Of his 12 disciples, seven were called to follow him from their fishing. Andrew, Peter, James and John were professional fishermen. Philip, Nathaniel and Thomas were called while fishing. Matthew was a tax collector, Simon was a zealot – probably a revolutionary – and Judas was a thief. The occupations of James, Jesus' cousin, and Nathaniel/ Bartholomew are not described.[168] On this basis, the 'nature of things' would indicate that the ministry should be mostly fishermen, and one twelfth revolutionary, one twelfth clerical and one twelfth criminal.

The report points out that earlier religions tended to have women priests, but later religions that developed monotheism, with a single God, tend to have male priests. To change this would be 'more disruptive of the Christian Church than any heresy or moral deviation'.

The familiar sleight of hand of praising women to justify excluding them is neatly performed by the church report's claims that there is too much maleness in the modern world and that women entering the 'characteristic masculine way of handling life' have made things worse. The solution for society is to maintain the polarity of the sexes. There are only two sexes – and they are completely different: 'There is in fact a masculine and a feminine human nature with some complication from the shadow of the opposite sex in each.' With too much masculinity in society, women should avoid masculine work – and keep out of the church.

Amazingly, in 1966, the church invoked the old concept that a man can represent men and women, but a woman can only represent herself: 'A male priest represents both sexes in a way which a woman does not in organised society and in the Church.'

The report rounds up with a chivalric reason for excluding women from work – the task of being a parish priest is too much for a married woman. A wife might be distracted by pregnancy, a mother by the care of her children. A father presumably need waste little time on the children he has conceived and the woman he has married. A man who found that he was married to a woman who was a priest would face 'considerable complications' in the relationships between husband and wife.

Women, concluded the 1966 report sorrowfully, don't necessarily know what would be best for them. Women have so many opportunities in society that they don't need to enter the church. Regardless of what women say, despite the fact that women felt they were called by God, the church report knew better. The time had passed, the question of women priests was already obsolete. According to the church, no modern women wanted to become a priest – it was an old wish that had been raised and fell unanswered, a generation or more ago.

And finally – a resounding shout-out to the ancient doctrine of separate spheres: 'Women have their own kind of ministry in offering the specific gifts of the feminine sex to the furthering of Christ's work on earth. These opportunities should be extended. Much of their value would be lost if women were drawn into the ordained priesthood.'[169]

It's an extraordinarily complete summary of the reasons men have given over nine centuries of English history (and longer) to keep women from authority, from wealth and from interesting work. It was the last stand of patriarchy on the last hill. Women were not the spiritual equals of men in the eyes of God nor in the view of his church. They could not be priests. They never had been priests – it was not natural. It would ruin the priest business if women were to do it. Women and men are the opposite of each other and cannot do the same work. Women could not be both priest and mother and wife – it would ruin the home, and not even women want this. And finally, women do their own feminine work so beautifully that this work should be improved and extended, and they should do nothing else.

As part of allowing women to extend their role of reading at services, women were allowed to be 'lay readers' in 1969, ten years after it had first been proposed. A bishop assured the debate that it was safe to open the lay readership to women as none would volunteer – young women were too busy with their families to undertake the work. In fact, 44 women found the time in the first year.[170]

In 1975, the Church of England reversed the policy (and presumably 'nature' itself) to announce that, actually, there were no fundamental objections to women being ordained as priests. The motion was promptly rejected the next year – the same year that the Sex Discrimination Act made it illegal to close posts to women. The church gained exemption from the requirement to open posts to men and women and is still (at the time of writing) exempt from sex equality legislation.

Betty Ridley took the chair for the Movement for the Ordination of Women in 1979.[171] Daughter of a bishop, a widow with four children, she had spent her life working for the church in various posts and on committees, and her enthusiasm and that of fellow deaconesses and lay readers won a motion to permit the ordination of women in 1984, which then went into eight years of debate – mainly concerned with how to compensate the male priests who refused to work with women vicars. It was the old problem of opening up a closed shop and paying off disgruntled tradesmen who did not want women in the club. A total of 430 priests resigned from the Church of England rather than see a woman represent God in their church and claimed that their wages should be paid and they compensated for loss of their job and, in many cases, houses. The church estimated that it would cost £24 million to compensate the priests who left. The church paid compensation to priests – even those who stepped straight into a job in the Roman Catholic Church.[172]

Finally, in 1994, the first 32 women priests were ordained in Bristol Cathedral. Twenty years later, in 2014, women were allowed to become bishops, with a simultaneous law to continue allowing churches to refuse female priests and including an amendment to the Equality Act so that it does not apply to the church. This led to some surprising convolutions of logic. For the purposes of the Equality Act, bishops – even archbishops – even those who make the law of the land, sitting in the House of Lords, are said not to 'hold public office', as that would put them under the act.

Despite the rearguard action, despite the closed shop, despite compensating men who will not work beside a woman, the Church of England now ordains women priests. Women have a right to speak as themselves anywhere in England, to anyone in England, even in the national church, even to God. For the first time in the English church, a woman represented God to the congregation, claiming to be made in the image of God, interceding for the congregation to God and telling the word of God to the congregation.

For the first time in England, women were spiritual equals of men in the Christian church, and can claim as part of their 'nature' that normal women are divine.

Afterword

There is no grand conclusion to this book because it is a report of selected real events of 900 years in England, not a condemnation of the past, nor a call to action. There is too much material for a grand conclusion – also, I don't know what you, the reader, will want to take or reject from it, for yourself. But one of the standout ideas for me is the compulsive habit of men, through history, to define the 'Nature of Women'. This completely imaginary label has served as the starting point for laws about women, ways to control women, provide for women, define appropriate work for women, set standards for permitted treatment of women, and even define those who may call themselves a woman. Virginia Woolf tried to kill this imaginary ideal woman: 'Whenever I felt the shadow of her wing or the radiance of her halo upon my page, I took up the inkpot and flung it at her.'[1]

Like a poltergeist summoned by men's imagination, sometimes a warning banshee, sometimes an angel in the corner, this creature calls women to either live up to an unrealistic ideal or rebel against it. Most women queasily worry why, if it is the 'nature' of women, does it feel so unnatural to me? Millions of us have had that sinking feeling of not fitting the mould; in my own life experiences – as a tomboy, an apprentice to a trade, a professional, a scholar, a mother and a feminist – I have often felt completely out of step.

The definition of 'women's nature' has put generations of sportswomen in the stands with the spectators, scientists in the kitchen, scholars in the primary school and politicians in flowery hats behind their husbands: the MPs. Even today, thousands of young girls are so uncomfortable with the nature of adult women looming towards them, like Roberta the T-Rex, that – determined to never grow into *that* – they choose many, sometimes fatal ways to avoid being Her. There has been a 'startling' rise in the number of young women suicides,[2] a trebling of young women reporting self-harming between 2000 and 2014,[3] and increased anorexia in girls under 15.[4] The numbers of young women wanting to transition to men doubled in one year alone, 2022, to 5,000.[5] There are many individual reasons why young women cannot face future life as adult women, and many ways of trying to escape that fate; young women demand another way of being a normal woman than '*that*'.

An artificial distinction of women from men formed part of Pythagoras' dualistic view of the world. The ancient Greek mathematician and philosopher defined a set of ten opposites, which include 'male : female':

Limited : Unlimited
Odd : Even
Unity : Plurality
Right : Left
Male : Female
At Rest : In Motion
Straight : Curved
Light : Darkness
Good : Evil
Square : Oblong[6]

Pythagorean philosophers will tell us (if we let them), how helpful this is in understanding women as the opposite of men; but it was not shared or even agreed by all the ancient Greeks. Aristotle and Plato observed a spectrum of sexuality, from hyper-masculine to hyper-feminine, with hermaphrodites in the middle. Galen (second century CE) believed sexuality to be a spectrum and that an individual's sexuality was determined by many characteristics which could be altered; there was the possibility of biological change from (mostly) female to male, and a third sex of hermaphrodites. The Bible (from about 700 BCE) and early Christian thinkers added yet more characteristics to the definition of women, largely based on Eve: indiscreet, easily tempted, man's only companion but clearly his inferior, her body made from his, her spirit easily tempted and her advice unreliable. The medieval churchmen developed Eve's 'nature' as the prototype for all women: sexual, talkative, argumentative, mistaken. As one commentator says: 'Like all dominant groups, men seek to promote an image of their subordinates' nature that contributes to the preservation of the status quo. For thousands of years, males have seen women not as women could be, but only as males want them to be.'[7]

The twelfth-century stories of courtly love described a new characteristic in men – an overwhelming sex drive that could overcome all obstacles: castle walls, locked doors and even female refusal. A 'perfect knight' would die of desire if he could not get sexual satisfaction. His opposite was the lady – cool to the point of frigidity, the story not her adventure but his. Readers watched him climb the tower, enter the bedroom, pluck the rose. Readers wanted the heroine to resist, but a stand-off is not a satisfactory ending to a narrative – they wanted her to resist, but only for a while. From *The Romance of the Rose*, a courtly love poem, to *Sleeping Beauty*, the happy ending of stories became the hero taking his prize whether or not the woman consented, whether or not she was even awake.

Ideas of what women were, and what they should be, changed again in the fifteenth century, when men pushed back against the rise of women who had taken the opportunities caused by the Great Pestilence. The word 'feminine' in the sense of appropriate for a woman, or typical of a woman, is first used then, as the king's court and the all-male parliament made new laws to set women's pay below that of men and confined women to their home parishes. Guilds and trade associations across the country started to limit entry to men, who might introduce their female dependants.

The Romantic movement from the late 1700s supported the idea that it was 'natural' for men to desire and for women to be cool. Courtly love stories were retold in a new form of novels in which the heroines' 'nature' was to be in a constant state of high arousal (over everything but sex). Women in the novels had faints, nosebleeds and hysterics, and starved themselves to death overstimulated by love of Nature, love of God, maternal love, sisterly love, despair for lack of love or guilt for love. In the real world, qualified doctors assured families that ladies were completely uninterested in sexual intercourse and untroubled by desire, while racked by all other emotions. When women behaved as sexual beings with desires, they faced condemnation and medical and surgical treatments to cure them of sexual arousal, including genital mutilation, hysterectomies and ovariectomies – removal of the ovaries and the womb. Sexual desire was defined as an exclusively male characteristic and since masturbation was said to be as damaging for men as self-restraint, someone had to be found to satisfy elite male lust: 'Every normally constituted man would be a born rapist if the sexual appetite could find no other means of satisfaction.'[8]

Who was going to give elite men the satisfaction they could not be denied? Of course – poor women. Brothels had been allowed since medieval times – in some towns licensed by the local authorities. In the eighteenth century, brothels, clubs and prostitutes were tolerated, only prosecuted if they were disorderly or inconvenient to the elite. Specialist prison hospitals were set up for women with venereal diseases, foundling hospitals provided for bastards, Magdalen houses rescued seduced innocents – aiming not to save sinners, care for fatherless children or cure infected women, but to make it safer and easier for upper-class men to enjoy unprotected sex with women too poor or powerless to refuse. The exploitation of working-class women for sex boomed at the same time as working women found themselves exploited for industrial labour. Both could be justified by the theory of the 'nature' of working-class women: robust, resilient, bawdy, vulgar, venal.

The Victorians revived Aristotle's idea of 'separate spheres' – the home and the public space – and it fitted the two new imaginary 'natures of women'. Elite women were frigid, delicate ladies suited for home and leisure; common women were tough, sexual women suited for assault and overwork in public spaces. The separate sphere was the upper-class home that ladies could develop as a spiritual sanctuary for themselves and as a haven for men returning from exploiting the outer world for profit and working-class women for work and sex. Separate spheres enabled the agonisingly cruel work of women in factories, mines and the streets to take place out of the sight of upper-class women, who also turned a blind eye to their husbands' behaviour. Ladies could be blind, too, to slavery and servitude in England and in invaded lands overseas – where only the resistance of enslaved and persecuted people limited the profits and appetites of colonising men.

As the artificial ladylike standards became more complex, training became more rigorous for both boys and girls. In the medieval world, with a high infant death rate, and no culture of childhood, babies were not defined by sex but swaddled alike and dressed in cut-down adult clothing until the age of around seven, when they would put on adult clothing and enter the adult world. But as the world for men and women became more distinct, children had to be trained up for their future roles. The sex of a baby – and now this was a choice of one of only two options – had to be registered at birth in 1837. Doctors made snap decisions based on the appearance of infant genitals, almost always naming a baby with a small penis as a girl, since it was thought better to be a girl with what looked like a large clitoris than to be a boy with what looked like a small penis.[9] On this simple male vanity, many lives were wrecked. Then, as now, as much as 2 per cent of the population were born 'intersex' and their sex cannot be decided by one of a choice of two by a doctor's quick look at newborn genitals.[10]

Extraordinarily, not all ladies chose to stay in their privileged, airless, protected 'sphere'. From the 1790s, women of the upper classes chose to interrogate the real world about the treatment of women enslaved by the early European empires. Upper- and middle-class women led the campaign against slavery, but failed to see and oppose the racism that was now invented to try to explain enslaving African people. A further gulf opened between white women and women of other races, and another 'nature of women' was created to describe imaginary characteristics of race.

Elite English women learned from the success of the abolition of slavery campaign and in 1850 took their political skills and a dawning sense of feminism to campaign against the Control of Disease laws, designed to manage prostitutes and protect men from disease. Banned from the male campaign because of the fear of shocking their delicate natures, the upper-class women set up their own 'ladies' committee' to stop the curfew, arrest and compulsory treatments of women suspected of prostitution. Later campaigns for the rights of all women, for better work conditions and for the vote drew ladies from sickly luxurious dependence and exposed them to the real world, teaching them political skills and solidarity with women of all classes. Breaking the boundaries of the separate spheres proved an extraordinary step that could only have been taken by women with courage, intellectual curiosity, determination and resilience – all characteristics widely agreed to be absent from 'ladies'.

But physicians, psychologists and educationalists ignored the success of radical and political women and continued to observe innate and 'natural' female inferiority. Nineteenth-century science could be extraordinarily flexible in finding female weakness to explain why women should not be paid a proper wage, or be trusted with power. Charles Darwin himself said that while men were evolving to greater complexity and strength, women were only becoming more fertile.[11]

Female inferiority proved such an ingrained belief that by the time the suffragists demanded the vote at the end of the nineteenth century, there were more women saying that they were not fit to have it than those who wanted it.[12] Only the experience of organising for the vote, violently opposing the government, and then breaking out of the separate sphere into the world of wartime work, persuaded women that they were competent to vote for MPs and to stand for Parliament themselves. But women did not win the vote by their campaigns, nor for their patriotic work. Upper-class women got the vote because it had to be granted to soldiers returning from the trenches of the First World War. Since no working-class man could have anything that an elite woman did not, the vote was allocated to wealthy women so that they should remain – in every way – superior to working men. However disappointing to historians of the suffragettes, this was a decision to maintain the superiority of elite women – not to reward them for their campaign or their war work.

Although some women had the vote and were emerging into society, they were still rigorously coached in appropriate behaviour from babyhood. Babies, previously dressed in white, were now colour-coded, so that even total strangers could cue them appropriately. Unisex rompers went out of fashion, with little boys going into trousers at three or four and girls wearing dresses. A boy would be dressed in pink, as it was a 'strong' colour, while pale blue or pale yellow was suitable for a girl.[13]

In the early twentieth century, sexologists announced four sexes: men, women and two new sexes – men who preferred male lovers and women who preferred women lovers; but after the traumatic evacuations, the destruction of homes and the attack on civilian populations in the Second World War, there was a longing to return to pre-war domestic stereotypes. Media, law and society retreated to the security of the two sexes. Wartime advances in surgery, especially to alter appearance, meant that men wishing to live as women, and women wishing to live as men, could have genital, breast and facial surgery, and they could apply for a legal change in identity. Charing Cross Hospital became a centre for transitions, and those very few people who could afford it made changes to appearance and to legal identity – the transitions sometimes foundered under persecution and challenge.

Awkwardly, psychologists reviewing a man's fitness to transition to his female identity expected patients to conform to the imaginary nature of women – now the 1950s housewife – and male patients learned to express their femininity in stereotypical phrases and a desire for hyper-feminine clothes and goods. Behaviours that women had been challenging for years, such as submissiveness, passivity and emotionalism, had to be exhibited by men wanting to transition, in order to satisfy the doctors. Historians explain: 'For a man to be considered for sex change treatment he has to convince the doctors of his femininity. He has to present as "hyper" feminine – and even if he feels it – he is advised not to express the ambivalence and androgyny that birth women experience.'[14]

The word 'sex' was found inadequate to express the many meanings loaded on to it and in the 1950s – following anthropology and sociology – people started using the word 'genders' in place of 'sexes', to describe a sexual identity which was created by culture. It didn't take long before 'gender' also became defined as strictly one of two and any ambivalence was defined as an ailment: named as a disorder in the authoritative *Diagnostic and Statistical Manual of Mental Disorders* in the 1950s, only softened to 'dysphoria' in 2020 – still insisting that there are only two options and anyone who fails to fit one or the other is at the very least confused, and that so-called experts are better fitted to judge which one of two someone should be – not they themselves.[15]

The post-war housewife was a fantasy beloved not only of the psychologists who should have known better, but of the marketeers who sold goods to the post-war home, the employers who wanted part-time part-paid workers, the men who longed to return from war to an imaginary haven at home, and the politicians and economists who wanted recovery fuelled by free domestic care, cheap part-time labour and domestic consumers. Women themselves fantasised about an imaginary time when a breadwinner wage had been enough to keep a family in a house with a mother at home. As late as 1978, Elspeth Howe, chair of the Equal Opportunities Commission, remained nostalgic for a time that had never existed: 'The traditional single role family where the wife stayed at home and the husband went to work is disappearing. As a society, we are right to worry about what is happening to women, as they struggle to carry the double burden of their traditional duties and their role as workers.'[16]

Pink became a girl's colour, and different toys for boys and for girls began to be relentlessly flogged to the booming consumer market.[17]

'Barbie' the doll was invented in 1959, her first occupation 'teenage fashion model', sporting a body shape that could not sustain life, on legs that would break if they were flesh and bone.[18]

From the 1960s onwards, the booming industries of fashion, make-up and wellness encouraged all women to see themselves as consumers rather than producers. The imaginary '*Cosmo* girl' of the magazines goes to work mainly to display herself and to meet eligible partners; her ideal work is piecework, clerical services or assisting a more important man. She does not craft or make a whole product in her working life; the only thing she produces from first vision to final presentation is her own body: painted, dressed, tattooed, pierced, sometimes abused by dangerous diets or cosmetic surgery, sometimes available for sex, marriage or sale – or a combination of all of those transactions. From the 1960s, women were their own product – commodities – and the arrival of social media in the 1990s meant they could market their own image in their own media campaigns.

Increasingly safe births led parents to announce the sex of a baby even before birth, and the ultrasound scan – developed to diagnose fetal abnormalities – provided highly developed technology to image an unborn child in the womb. Wealthy parents announced their news in 'gender reveal' parties with cannons of pink or blue confetti, a 'reveal' cake and balloons in blue or pink. (Incidentally, this is a misuse of the word 'gender' – but understandable because a 'sex party' would attract a very different sort of guest and dress code.) The popularity of the bigger and bigger reveal party peaked in 2020, when a reveal firework caused the El Dorado wildfire, among the largest in Californian history. The woman who claims to have pioneered the gender reveal party with a pink cake said: 'Could we just stop having these stupid parties?' Her child, whose pink party started the trend, believed (aged 10) that there are many genders.[19] The current science agrees: in 1910, Magnus Hirschfeld calculated 43 million possible combinations of gender and sexuality: 'In each person there is a different mixture of manly and womanly substances, and as we cannot find two leaves alike on a tree, then it is highly unlikely that we will find two humans whose manly and womanly characteristics exactly match in kind and number.'[20] In the 1990s, Anne Fausto-Sterling counted five sexes, and in the twenty-first century Eric Vilain suggested an 'infinite number of biological genders', since chromosomes, gonads, anatomy and hormones all define a person's sexuality, and each one has multiple variants.[21] The current understanding is that 'sex' can be defined by fetal hormones, fetal gonads (which are simultaneously both male and female), adult hormones, adult chromosomes and physical appearance. All of these occur in different combinations, all vary, and all can be altered by behaviour or drugs or surgery – so they are no help in proving an individual to be one gender or another. The current science suggests – as the Greeks believed – a spectrum of sexes, and the possibility of moving through the spectrum as a result of experience and stimuli.

There are no aptitudes, tastes or behaviours exclusive to any particular sex. Modern tests show more difference inside the sexes than between them. Male brains differ more from other male brains than they do from female brains; and, in any case, brains are changeable: education and encouragement mould how they work and how successfully. As sports are discovering, highly trained individuals do not triumph only in their own sexual category. When, in March 2019, cyclist Nicole Hanselmann of Switzerland threatened to overtake male competitors for the first time ever in an elite professional race (at Omloop Het Nieuwsblad), the 'organisers had to intervene because the leader of the women's race was getting too close to the convoy of the men's race'.[22] This endangered the safety of the race, but it was catastrophic for people who wanted to believe in innate male physical superiority. Professional sports troubled by the old categories of male or female, with no reliable way to prove the existence of either, are creating a third 'open' category for athletes in the hopes of preventing trans women from competing with people identified as female at birth.[23]

Strength comes from physique and training, for all the sexes. Aptitude is created by teaching and encouraged by practice. One experiment in the early 1980s found only one highly gifted girl to every 13 highly gifted boys in a programme – supporting a belief in the innate cleverness of boys. Twenty years later, in 2005, after teachers had deliberately encouraged girls, there was one highly gifted girl to two boys.[24] Girls told before a test that male brains have an aptitude for the task do worse than boys. Girls who are not told this perform equally with boys.[25]

The idea that anyone should choose one identity and never change is not supported by scientific research or history. Debates about choice – however violently and passionately expressed – are arguments over two imaginary stereotypes, not about normal women and normal men and all the normal varieties between and beyond. All of the discussion about transitioning from one sex to another relies on the myth that there are only two sexes, that they are quite different from one another, recognisable at a glance, and that it is the task of growing up to choose your team and stick to it.

The diversity and variety of sex discovered by the scientists is reflected in the real world when people are free to identify as they wish. In the 2021 UK census, 30,000 of 45.7 million respondents identified as non-binary (0.06 per cent) and 18,000 (0.04 per cent) replied with what was described on the form as a 'different gender identity'– not one of two.[26] The science, the history and the lived experience suggest that forcing people into one of two categories is as fictional as a 'sorting hat' – we are more diverse and more varied, and more changeable over time, in a richer multiple world than the binary model described. But our varied sexuality has been recruited into a cultural conflict which argues that people should be one of two sexes and that anything else is inauthentic, unbiological and sometimes even dangerous to others.

The safety of everyone in their homes, on the streets, in public bathrooms and in prisons is endangered by badly behaved men, falsely proud of their maleness and the privilege they think it confers on them, who think that they have a right to access women, and to control and abuse them. Very few men abuse and attack women who are unknown to them – most men are violent to women they already know. The problem – as nearly always – is male violence from the minority of violent and abusive men.

At the time of writing there is exaggerated concern about violent men trying to enter female safe spaces using trans women identity as a disguise for their toxic male intentions. In 2019, 76 of the 129 trans women in women's prisons had previously been male sex offenders.[27] Yet even then, there were no reported sexual assaults by the trans women upon women prisoners, and only 4 sexual assaults on women prisoners at all in 2013. Non binary people are most at risk of being a victim of sexual assault – they are not the most dangerous. Also at risk are young people: 9.5 per cent of juvenile prisoners reported sexual abuse in 2012 and 70–80 per cent said they had been assaulted – not by violent prisoners, but by staff.[28] Most at risk are people of colour. The problem is that even spaces designated as 'safe' for women show a lack of care and protection for women. In women prisons, the greatest threat to the lives and well-being of women prisoners is their self-harm and mental illness.

For centuries our societies have trained men to prioritise their needs over others. But the aim of sex training was not to create 'doormat women' – that was an unintended side effect of the real project. The aim was to boost men; making a bully, a winner, a commander out of a sensitive little boy: even if all he can beat are girls, even if all he can command is his wife. Once the tradition was established that inheritance was passed to the boy and not to the most able heir, once authority was vested in men and not in the best candidate, once wealth migrated to male pockets and was not shared among those who had created it, it became essential that the 'nature' of men should be authoritative, powerful and greedy – in order to keep the inheritance, the power and the money. This has been a painful and difficult road for women but also for those good, gentle and kind men who do not want to be overbearing – not even for the rewards they can win.

Defining women as second-rate was not actually designed to oppress women (though it does); it was intended to free men from competition with everyone but other men. It is the fragility of masculinity, the delicacy of patriarchy and the weakness of male candidates that means that our society has to give men the huge advantage of a head start: men only win if we hold women back.

The linking of women to light work, casual work and ill-paid work did not happen because women were defined as having inferior abilities; it was vice versa. Women were forced into light work, casual work and ill-paid work so that challenging, reliable and rewarding labour could go to male candidates. Guilds, professions and universities excluded women so that the feeblest male candidate might get the plum jobs. As a historian makes clear: 'It is fairly clear that this particular working of patriarchy was motivated by fear of female accomplishment.'[29]

A gap between men and women's wages was brought about deliberately as the population recovered from the Great Pestilence, and landlords and employers sought to recoup their losses. Women excluded from making money at home by the enclosure of their shared lands found themselves forced to accept lower rates of pay. Later laws made a pay gap compulsory and men's unions excluded women from craftsmen's work and rates, as professions excluded them from professional fees. Around the middle of the nineteenth century, the 'breadwinner wage' was invented to run alongside the separate spheres argument. Men must be paid enough for two, so that their wives could inhabit the separate sphere of the home and not go out to work. Poor women, desperate to see their husbands earn a living wage, supported the argument for a breadwinner wage, discovering only later that a single woman head of a household with a family to keep did not get a breadwinner wage.

Of course, women will always be paid less than men if half or more of their working life is unpaid. As the commission on wages found to its surprise in 1840, Mrs Sherwin, the weaver's wife, would have earned 4s 7½d a week if her husband had paid her the going rate for winding bobbins for him. But because she worked for her husband for free, she earned only 3s and he earned 6s 6d.[30] Women who work for their husbands as their assistants, supporters or secretaries find that not only are they unpaid, they are unrepresented by anyone but themselves, and have no way of improving their career. A businessman's wife who does the books for him, keeps the wages, and hires and fires at his work, is in effect in management; but she has no title, no career and no salary. No woman sitting with a sick child, or in constant attendance to an elderly parent – even someone else's elderly parent, her husband's elderly parent – expects to receive training, time off, a lunch break, expenses, or proper pay. The GDP figures do not even count her labour as work. Once the nineteenth-century census had ruled that 'ladies' do not work, anything a woman does at home is 'not-work'.

Even when wives and husbands both work full time at paying work outside the home, the wife does on average twice the child care and house-work of her husband.[31] Women aged 26–35 do the most: 34 hours a week. If a woman was paid the current minimum wage of £9.50 for working inside the home for 34 hours and outside the home for 40 hours a week, she would earn a total of £36,556 gross a year. But she is not. She is paid only for the work she does outside the home and so she earns £19,760. By working for free for 34 hours a week, she effectively halves her hourly rate. All this, before she is paid a lesser rate than a man: on average, at the time of writing, a woman earns 90p for every £1 earned by a man – and then zero for the double shift she puts in, on her own, at home.[32]

Those who prefer to mystify relationships between men and women describe this unpaid labour sweetly, as being done 'for love' and, like True Love, this burden lasts forever. Very old and infirm wives still do the bulk of the housework: cooking, cleaning and emotional servicing long after their husband has retired as a breadwinner. The job of being a wife lasts till death: there is no agreed pay, no holidays, no pension and the hours are interminable.

The invisibility of women's work has affected our history. The histories that pluck individuals from obscurity and claim them as heroines do nothing to illuminate the recorded but ignored work of millions, all the invisible women: scientists, inventors and business entrepreneurs whose inventions or patents or fortunes were traditionally registered under their husband or their male partner's name. As recently as 2018, the BBC History page summed up the presence of women in medieval warfare: 'Very little filters out from British history during the next 16 centuries about women at war, though British troops encountered Joan of Arc between 1429–31.'[33]

That's one woman (and she's French!) in 16 centuries of British history? One? You don't have to be raving feminist to say – surely there were more than that? Even present-day media does not reflect women's real lives: in 2019, women were quoted in only 29 per cent of general news stories in the UK – in stories about economics or warfare they are consulted even less.[34]

Design features male biometrics. Technology from mobile phones to seat belts can only be used in comfort by men. Does anybody doubt that self-driving cars will be adjusted for male dimensions and that women drivers will have to pump up the seat to get their eyes to line up with the technology? New drugs are tailored for men and mostly tested on men; the dosage and side effects for women can still be uncertain, even when the drugs are licensed for release.[35] A staggering 80 per cent of drugs withdrawn from the market in the US were causing unacceptable side effects on women.[36]

Women patients suffering from heart attack are more likely to survive if treated by a woman doctor according to an analysis of 580,000 heart attack cases over 19 years in Florida, USA. A total of 13.3 per cent women died under the care of a male doctor, compared with 12 per cent who were cared for by a woman.[37] The only explanation offered for this discrepancy is that male doctors expect to see heart attacks in men but not in women, and women do not present with enough urgency – women have only themselves to blame for not alerting male doctors that they are in the process of dying before them. In a 2022 report, the *Journal of the American Heart Association* reported that women who visited emergency departments with chest pain waited 29 per cent longer than men to see a doctor and were twice as likely to be diagnosed with mental illness than heart disease.[38] Post-traumatic stress disorder is most common and most severe in women who have been raped, but PTSD is most studied in male veterans.[39]

Leaving aside the nature of women – imagined and unknown – women's genitals were invisible to medical men until the late 1500s. Andreas Vesalius, publishing to universal respect in 1543, explained that only 'hermaphrodites' had a clitoris. In the copy of the 1559 edition of Thomas Gemini's *Compendiosa totius anatomie delineatio* held by Cambridge University, the diagram of the female genital area has been deliberately and very neatly cut away, presumably to spare the blushes of clerical students.[40]

In 1559, the clitoris was described as 'the principal seat of women's enjoyment in intercourse',[41] but 18 years later, a description of the vagina copied that of Aristotle, and said it was a mirror image of the male genitals, with ovaries where testes would be, but inverted in the female body, specifically designed to accommodate the penis: 'It is an instrument susceptive, that is to say a thing receiving for taking … the likeness of it as it were a yard reversed or turned inward having testicles likewise aforesaid.'[42] A 1578 text book for surgeons refused altogether to describe female genitalia, as it would be indecent 'to lift up the veil of nature's secrets in woman's shapes'.[43] By the eighteenth century, more physicians and scientists would have seen a flea in the enlarged drawing of Robert Hooke's bestseller, *Micrographia*, in 1665, than would have seen an accurate drawing of female genitalia.[44]

Anxiety about female sexuality and the hopes of eradicating female desire from ladies' lives prompted Isaac Baker Brown to introduce the clitoridectomy in the 1860s, creating a covert fashion for the medically valueless and dangerous operation, now still performed but illegal in England as FGM – female genital mutilation.[45] The clitoris was briefly sighted in the 1901 edition of *Gray's Anatomy*, but disappeared again in the 1948 edition, reappearing later. Today, in otherwise anatomically correct sex dolls made in China (the biggest world producer), the dolls have no clitoris.[46]

Even medical drawings of this century are rarely accurate: most often the vagina is depicted as a wide-open hole rather than a closed flexible tube, and the labia are shown as perfectly symmetrical. The size of the clitoris is generally underestimated[47] and the obstructive nature of the hymen is greatly exaggerated.[48] The clitoris is still frequently described as a small penis, although the internal parts of the clitoris are far bigger than a flaccid penis, connected to a different brain area from that of the penis, and have nothing to do with urination.[49] Even pornographic images of the clitoris and the labia are far from biological accuracy, almost always bald, and sometimes surgically altered, sometimes abused.

Men recorded their mistrust and fear of female genitals very early. The reference to women as 'weaker vessels' in the Tyndale Bible of 1522–35, and the later development of imagery of women as leaking vessels, resonates with the theory of humours that saw women as cold and moist, and the fear of female menstruation and lubrication. As Shakespeare's King Lear says:

> Down from the waist they are centaurs, though women all above.
> But to the girdle do the gods inherit; beneath is all the fiends'.
> There's hell, there's darkness, there's the sulphurous pit –
> burning, scalding, stench, consumption![50]

Girls are taught very young not to touch their genitals anywhere but for washing in the bathroom and in some families they are never correctly named.

Even in our supposedly more liberated times, female genitals are objectified by men: drawn in graffiti and photographed in pornography, and massive advertising budgets are spent on advertising to stimulate anxiety about size, shape, hairiness and scent.[51]

An advert – withdrawn as late as 2021 – described the 'foul sweaty smell' of a healthy vagina, which could be solved by 'female hygiene sprays' for the genital area. One product, in the top 10 on one so-called advice site, advertises that it has an 'exotic kiwi scent'.

(This is a kiwi.)

Even archaeology has been blinded by archaeologists' beliefs that the women of societies thousands of years before ours, in faraway countries, behaved in accordance with the timeless and eternal 'nature' of our imagining, forever dependent on a superior man – 'Men ... become, first, formidable hunters and then, masters of the universe.'[52] Unbelievably this was written in 2004 – a misunderstanding of both evolution and modern-day hunter-gatherer societies.

When a high-ranking Viking warrior, buried with weapons and a war-game board to plan military strategy, was discovered in the Viking graves at Birka, Sweden, in 1878, archaeologists assumed it to be a senior male warrior. As late as 2011, the suggestion that the warrior might have been a woman, as praised in the folklore and ballads about women warriors, was still firmly denied. Six years on, DNA testing proved the warrior was indeed a woman.[53]

There the story might end – with a new understanding of the capacities of women and the honour given to them, even in early Viking society. But in 2020, the professor of archaeology at Uppsala University proposed a new spin: that the warrior was a trans man, as he says 'someone living as a man'.[54] So no Viking woman warrior after all, but a person with female DNA and male gravegoods. Not a fully fledged fighting woman with respect from her Viking comrades – but a woman borrowing male goods? Wearing male clothes? Passing herself off as male? And why is this a more persuasive explanation for a woman buried as a Viking hero than the more obvious suggestion that she was a birth female Viking heroine? And that military success can be won by a woman?

In 2021, at Suontaka Vesitorninmäki, Hattula, in Finland, archaeologists discovered the grave of a Viking warrior, the body wearing female clothes, on a soft feather blanket with trinkets, and two swords. They believe that the person had Klinefelter syndrome, giving rise to XXY chromosomes.[55] This had probably been a person respected in their eleventh-century society, wearing women's clothing, fighting as a warrior, perhaps understood to be one of the many sexes on the huge spectrum of sexual identity that was then known but which we have tried to forget.

Now, archaeologists all over the world are re-examining sites previously defined by experts blinkered by their own beliefs. In 2009, a pair of skeletons, discovered holding hands in a 1,500-year-old tomb in Modena, Italy, were known as 'The Lovers' and assumed to be a man and a woman. In 2019, improved DNA analysis, using tooth enamel, showed

that the hand-clasped pair were actually both male. Other 'lover' archaeology finds are now being explored to see if they too sit outside the
expectations of conventional heterosex – and may also be homosexual or
lesbian lovers – or whether there are other, yet unknown explanations for
a pair of bodies being buried holding hands.[56]

When history is focused only on men, and women are defined as
anything that men are not, we misunderstand so much, and we study so
little. We find what we are looking for, and anything that does not fall
inside our belief system we ignore. We not only lose sight of real women,
but lose sight of what a woman might do, and of the relationships
between women: we don't see daughters, or sisters, beloved friends and
women lovers; we lose sight of what, according to sociologists, is the
strongest relationship in Western family ties: mothers and daughters.[57]
Instead we focus on the relationships women have with men: the dependent relationship of a girl with her father, the constantly criticised life of
the single woman, the desperate search for a breadwinner husband, the
shame of a divorcee, the anxious freedom of a widow. The absence of
interest and records about the mother-daughter bond leaves a vacuum
which is filled with an excessive interest in heterosexual courtship,
marriage and the end of marriage, which becomes the principal topic of
fiction, and the only love in History.

Despite the extraordinary strides that have been made by women
since the nineteenth century, our society is still guided by an ancient
contempt for women. When women workers complain of women bosses
only because they are female, when women critique the behaviour of
other women as inappropriate to their sex, when women oppose
campaigns for women's rights, or mothers are disappointed in the birth
of a girl, we are seeing internalised contempt. When women campaign
to ban abortions, even for women who have been raped: this is internalised contempt, agonisingly exercised on another woman. When women
do not fight for rights and freedoms for independent women, they are
trading their rights for the safety and protection they hope will be given
to them by a dominant husband in a restrictive marriage – and forgetting that the most dangerous place to be a woman is at home with the
man she forgives.

When a woman believes her future happiness and financial security
depend upon her marrying the best partner from a small pool, in the
brief window of her most fertile time, she becomes hypervigilant about

her own appearance and hypercritical of her rivals. She ignores her own desires and ambitions in order to concentrate on the only goal open to her – snagging the best man possible. The 'male gaze' views women as objects, reproducing an unending stream of images, teaching women to watch themselves through male eyes in what has been called an 'inexorable surveillance of women ... internally reinforced by the women themselves'.[58]

When male candidates are favoured for promotion, any woman candidate has a good chance only against another woman. Female colleagues are automatic rivals; quick to criticise, compete and manipulate. There is no chance of networking or sisterhood in these circumstances. The occasional praise of 'exceptional' women feeds the rivalry. When a woman accepts the compliment that she is 'above her sex', she is enjoying individual praise at the price of denigrating her own sex. As Andrea Dworkin writes: 'The token woman carries the stigma of inferiority with her, however much she tries to dissociate herself from the other women of her sex class. In trying to stay singular (not one of them), she grants the inferiority of her sex class, an inferiority for which she is always compensating and from which she is never free.'[59]

Solitary heroines at the top of their business do not encourage other women just by being there. A single woman in a leadership role will have usually got there by being hugely superior to her male colleagues without frightening the bosses – she will have learned to manage her success by conforming to the culture. She may out-man the men – like Elizabeth I sometimes did, calling herself a king – or out-women the women, as Margaret Thatcher liked to do, praising herself for a soft perm and wearing chiffon. Leaders usually recruit in their own likeness – but this is often an impossible task for a woman who has only got to where she is by outdoing other women candidates for the single opportunity to take the token place. A man reaching the top table is among his peers; he will have been assisted upwards by a network of other men. He knows that it is in his interest, and that of his sons, to continue the tradition of patronage – it's called the 'old boy' network. But a woman reaching the solitary chair placed for a woman at the top table may have been helped by no one, indeed she may have got where she is only by fighting the system, male competitors and female rivals. Without warm memories of university networks, mentors and a helpful introduction from someone's aunt, she is not in the mood to help someone's niece.

There is no 'nature' of women, because there are too many versions of women to be encapsulated in one definition. Definitions of women always told them what they could not do; definitions of women are always prohibitions. What I have seen through my research – deliberately focused on women not usually featured in the national history – is not a 'nature of women', which is too beautifully broad and infinitely varied to define. But I have seen some trends. When women are banned from profitable professions they continue their vocations under another title and at less pay – but they hardly ever just disappear. When they are formally banned from education, they teach themselves, or learn alongside brothers, or persuade fathers, husbands or mentors to teach them. Even when women are told they are inferior and hopeless, a few stubbornly persist, survive and succeed. And – most importantly – when women are blocked from open power they work underground, in all sorts of networks, forming communities hidden by acceptable female behaviour, masquerading as social meetings, gaining respectability by drawing on tradition – but women denied power end up taking it.

In the medieval world, women led whenever they could, and whenever they were needed: raising crusades, defending castles, holding towns under siege, setting community standards, conserving the natural world and their access to it, sharing food stores and protecting children. (They also condemned each other, stole, libelled and robbed – that's diversity!) Without training and almost without prompting, some women worked collectively, understanding that their lives, their communities and even the natural world had to be defended against a system that was and still is designed to privatise and profiteer. The medieval food riot which still rides out, in one shape or another, into the modern world, is the great glamorous joust of poor women against the greater strength of the market and the merchants, the bosses and the landlords and their police – the most chivalric and heroic battle that ever was – under-reported, rarely recognised and mostly forgotten. Time and again, working-class women in history rounded themselves up and went out to keep prices fair, food in the village and common lands open.

In the modern world, centuries later, women respond to national emergencies, learning trades and skills and risking their lives and happiness to make their contribution during wartime. They create rent strikes, work strikes, support other women, campaign against war and pollution. Women protest curfews, protest courts' leniency to abusive men, collectively search for missing women and mourn the ones found dead; they open their homes to refugees and staff food banks. Women – with a one in a hundred chance of getting their rapist convicted – still go to the police in the hope of protecting other women, and waive their privacy rights to argue against early release and inadequate sentencing. Women revived 'reclaim the night' marches when they were told they should fear the streets, and spoke up in millions of voices in the MeToo movement, and demanded control of their own fertility worldwide.

Despite assurances that an economically successful future requires poisoned rivers and beaches and cruelty to poor people, homeless people and refugees, despite centuries of being told we are powerless, women still stand up for each other, for children, and for Nature, as we have done since the earliest of times. Sometimes we agree on what really matters to us, sometimes we agree on who we are – and often we don't: and that's because we do not have one male-defined 'nature' but we are diverse and complex.

The history of women is a struggle over identity and inclusion: we are all 'normal' women even when we have been described as exceptional or deviant or inadequate, even when our vanity prompts us to stand apart, or our ambition to compete with each other. This history has only added one voice to the chorus of women who speak up; this history records the everyday heroism of 'normal' women, the extraordinariness of the ordinary, and in a sometimes heartless world, the perennial loving power of sisterhood.

Notes

Introduction

1. George Eliot, *Middlemarch, A Study of Provincial Life*, William Blackwood & Sons, 1871

Part 1: 1066–1348 Doomsday

1. Andrew Bridgeford, *1066: The Hidden History of the Bayeux Tapestry*, Walker and Co., 2005, loc 2366
2. Max Adams, *Unquiet Women*, Head of Zeus, 2018, loc 1928
3. Ibid., loc 1014
4. David Brion Davis, *The Problem of Slavery in Western Culture*, Pelican Books, 1970, p. 53
5. Adams, *Unquiet Women*, loc 1054
6. Ibid., loc 1070
7. P. Stafford, 'Women in Domesday', *Reading Medieval Studies*, Vol. 15, 1989, pp. 75–94 (p. 81)
8. Hudson, 'Women in Anglo-Saxon England'
9. Stafford, 'Women in Domesday'
10. Ibid.
11. Bridgeford, *1066*, loc 3115
12. Ibid.
13. Ibid., loc 2189
14. *Anglo-Saxon Chronicle*, trans. J.A. Giles and J. Ingram, Project Gutenberg, 1996
15. Stafford, 'Women in Domesday', pp. 89 and 90
16. Ibid.
17. Judith A. Green, *The Normans: Power, Conquest and Culture in 11th-Century Europe*, Yale University Press, 2022, loc 3831
18. John Simkin, 'William the Conqueror and the Feudal System', Spartacus Educational, September 1997
19. Bridgeford, *1066*, loc 220
20. Thomas Piketty, *Capitalism in the Twenty-First Century*, Harvard University Press, 2014, p. 344
21. Paul Kingsnorth, 'High House Prices? Inequality? I Blame the Normans', *Guardian*, 17 December 2012
22. 'To the Manor Born: Mapping the Grosvenor Estate', Who Owns England? (online), 17 August 2016
23. H.G. Richardson, 'The Coronation in Medieval England: The Evolution of the Office and the Oath', *Traditio*, Vol. 16, 1960, pp. 111–202
24. Green, *The Normans*, loc 3887
25. Rebecca Abrams, 'The Jewish Journey: 4,000 Years in 22 Objects', Ashmolean Museum, 2017
26. Marty Williams and Anne Echols, *Between Pit and Pedestal: Women in the Middle Ages*, Markus Wiener, 1993, p. 177
27. 'The Rime of King William', Peterborough Chronicle/Laud Manuscript, 1087, Bodleian Library MS Laud Misc. 636, f. 65r
28. Mary Bateson, *Medieval England 1066–1350*, 1903, p. 174
29. Bridgeford, *1066*, loc 2126

30. Adams, *Unquiet Women*, loc 1971

31. Emma Mason, 'Invoking Earl Waltheof', in David Roffe (ed.), *The English and Their Legacy, 900–1200: Essays in Honour of Ann Williams*, Boydell and Brewer, 2012, pp. 185–204

32. Bateson, *Medieval England 1066–1350*, p. 62

33. Henrietta Leyser, *Medieval Women: Social History of Women in England 450–1500*, Weidenfeld & Nicolson, 2013, loc 3373

34. Bateson, *Medieval England 1066–1350*, p. 63

35. Ibid., p. 151

36. Williams and Echols, *Between Pit and Pedestal*, p. 126

37. Leyser, *Medieval Women*, loc 2745

38. Bateson, *Medieval England 1066–1350*, p. 228

39. Caroline Dunn, *Stolen Women in Medieval England*, Cambridge University Press, 2012, loc 4019

40. Williams and Echols, *Between Pit and Pedestal*, p. 123

41. Kaya Burgess, 'Nun Faked Her Death to Pursue Life of Lust', *The Times*, 12 February 2019

42. Barbara A. Hanawalt, *The Ties that Bound: Peasant Families in Medieval England*, Oxford University Press, 1986, p. 130

43. C.M. Woolgar, *The Culture of Food in England 1200–1500*, Yale University Press, 2016, loc 4902

44. Mavis E. Mate, *Daughters, Wives and Widows after the Black Death: Women in Sussex 1350–1535*, Boydell Press, Woodbridge, 1998, p. 42

45. Ian Mortimer, *The Time Traveller's Guide to Elizabethan England*, Bodley Head, 2012, loc 423

46. G.M. Trevelyan, *England Under the Stuarts*, 1904, p. 47

47. Williams and Echols, *Between Pit and Pedestal*, p. 54

48. Frances and Joseph Gies, *Women in the Middle Ages: The Lives of Real Women in a Vibrant Age of Transition*, Thomas Y. Cromwell, 1973, p. 180

49. Ibid.

50. P.J.P. Goldberg, 'For Better, For Worse: Marriage and Economic Opportunity for Women in Town and Country', *Women in Medieval English Society*, ed. P.J.P. Goldberg, Sutton Publishing England, 1992

51. Gies, *Women in the Middle Ages*, p. 177

52. Williams and Echols, *Between Pit and Pedestal*, p. 51

53. Ibid., pp. 51 and 55

54. Gwen Seabourne, *Royal Regulation of Loans and Sales in Medieval England*, Boydell Press, 2003, p. 45

55. Barbara A. Hanawalt, *The Wealth of Wives: Women, Law and Economy in Late Medieval London*, Oxford University Press, 2007, loc 1436

56. Caroline Barron, 'Post Pandemic: How the Years after the Black Death Briefly Became a "Golden Age" for Medieval Women', *History Extra*, 6 July 2021

57. Gies, *Women in the Middle Ages*, p. 180

58. Woolgar, *The Culture of Food in England 1200–1500*, loc 2962

59. Bateson, *Medieval England 1066–1350*, pp. 259–60

60. Barbara J. Harris, *English Aristocratic Women 1450–1550: Marriage and Family, Property and Careers*, Oxford University Press, 2002, loc 116

61. Joseph Strutt, *The Sports and Pastimes of the People of England*, Thomas Tegg, 1845

62. John Marshall Carter, 'Sports and Recreations in Thirteenth-Century England: The Evidence of the Eyre and Coroners' Rolls – A Research Note', *Journal of Sport History*, Vol. 15, No. 2, Summer 1988, pp. 167–73

63. Marilyn Yalom, *Birth of the Chess Queen*, HarperPerennial, 2005

64. Judith M. Bennett, and Amy M. Froide (eds), *Singlewomen in the European Past, 1250–1800*, University of Pennsylvania Press, 1999, pp. 82–105

65. Tracy Borman, 'Matilda, William the Conqueror's Queen', *BBC History Magazine*, October 2011

66. James Michael Illston, '"An Entirely Masculine Activity"? Women and War in the High and Late Middle Ages Reconsidered', University of Canterbury, 2009, p. 61

67. Gies, *Women in the Middle Ages*, p. 105

68. Illston, '"An Entirely Masculine Activity"?', p. 55

69. Rowena Archer, 'How Ladies Who Live on Their Manors …', in Goldberg (ed.), *Women in Medieval English Society*, p. 150

70. Linda Elizabeth Mitchell, *Portraits of Medieval Women: Family, Marriage, and Politics in England 1225–1350*, Palgrave Macmillan, 2003

71. Archer, 'How Ladies Who Live on Their Manors …', p. 151

72. T.D. Fosbroke, 'Abstracts and Extracts of Smyth's Lives of the Berkeleys', London, 1821, p. 152, quoted in Gies, *Women in the Middle Ages*, p. 215

73. Leyser, *Medieval Women*, loc 3609

74. Woolgar, *The Culture of Food in England 1200–1500*, loc 2444

75. Bateson, *Medieval England 1066–1350*, p. 124

76. Leyser, *Medieval Women*, loc 3120

77. Bateson, *Medieval England 1066–1350*, p. 205

78. Magna Carta 1215, Clause 8: The National Archives

79. Williams and Echols, *Between Pit and Pedestal*, p. 146

80. Gies, *Women in the Middle Ages*, p. 161

81. R.H. Maudsley and J.W. Davies, 'The Justice of the Peace in England', *University of Miami Law. Review*, 517, Vol. 18, No. 3, 1964

82. Williams and Echols, *Between Pit and Pedestal*, p. 162

83. Ibid.

84. Helen Barker, *Rape in Early Modern England: Law, History and Criticism*, Palgrave Macmillan, 2021, loc 608

85. Bank of England Inflation Calculator

86. Cheryl Tallan and Suzanne Bartlett, *The Shalvi/Hyman Encyclopedia of Jewish Women*, Jewish Women's Archive, jwa.org

87. Abrams, 'The Jewish Journey'

88. Statute of Jewry, 1275. National Archive ref. E164/9 fol. 31d

89. Lionel B. Abrahams, 'The Expulsion of the Jews from England in 1290 (Continued)', *Jewish Quarterly Review*, Vol. 7, No. 2, January 1895, pp. 236–58, published by University of Pennsylvania Press

90. Bateson, *Medieval England 1066–1350*, p. 260

91. Hanawalt, *The Ties that Bound*, p. 220

92. Ibid., p. 155

93. Ibid., p. 82

94. Eleanor Janega, *The Once and Future Sex: Going Medieval on Women's Roles in Society*, W.W. Norton and Co., 2023, loc 2317

95. Gies, *Women in the Middle Ages*, p. 148

96. Hanawalt, *The Ties that Bound*, p. 225

97. Leyser, *Medieval Women*, loc 2574

98. Williams and Echols, *Between Pit and Pedestal*, p. 177

99. Gies, *Women in the Middle Ages*, p. 159

100. Hanawalt, *The Ties that Bound*, p. 70

101. Mortimer, *The Time Traveller's Guide to Medieval England*, Bodley Head, 2008, loc 3136

102. Woolgar, *The Culture of Food in England 1200–1500*, loc 5341

103. Jane Humphries and Jacob Weisdorf, 'The Wages of Women in England 1260–1850', *Journal of Economic History*, Vol. 75, Issue 2, June 2015, pp. 405–77

104. Ibid.

105. Leyser, *Medieval Women*, loc 2550

106. Gies, *Women in the Middle Ages*, p. 154

107. Hanawalt, *The Wealth of Wives*, loc 2630

108. Bateson, *Medieval England 1066–1350*, p. 34

109. Williams and Echols, *Between Pit and Pedestal*, p. 233
110. Adams, *Unquiet Women*, loc 2156
111. Williams and Echols, *Between Pit and Pedestal*, p. 57
112. Ibid., p. 178
113. Gies, *Women in the Middle Ages*, p. 161
114. Leyser, *Medieval Women*, loc 3181
115. Williams and Echols, *Between Pit and Pedestal*, p. 55
116. Gies, *Women in the Middle Ages*, p. 180
117. Woolgar, *The Culture of Food in England 1200–1500*, loc 1639
118. Williams and Echols, *Between Pit and Pedestal*, p. 60
119. *Smithfield Decretals*, c.1340, British Library (Royal 10 E fol. 581)
120. Bridgeford, *1066*, loc 265
121. Eleanor Parker, 'The Cultured Women of Essex', *History Today*, Vol. 69, Issue 9 September 2019
122. Ibid.
123. Green, *The Normans*, loc 4030
124. Bateson, *Medieval England 1066–1350*, p. 144
125. Ibid., pp. 63, 153, 212, 127, 192, 204
126. Ibid., p. 127
127. Ibid., p. 34
128. Michelle M. Sauer, *Gender in Medieval Culture*, Bloomsbury, 2015, loc 1834
129. Robin L. Gordon, *Searching for the Soror Mystica: The Lives and Science of Women Alchemists*, University Press of America, 2013, p. 3
130. Leyser, *Medieval Women*, loc 2384
131. Bateson, *Medieval England 1066–1350*, p. 184
132. Bernard Capp, *When Gossips Meet: Women, Family, and Neighbourhood in Early Modern England*, Oxford University Press, 2003, loc 3927
133. Carol M. Meale, 'Women's Voices and Roles', in Peter Brown (ed.), *A Companion to Medieval English Literature and Culture c.1350–c.1500*, Blackwell, 2007, pp. 74–90
134. Mortimer, *The Time Traveller's Guide to Medieval England*, loc 1832
135. Katherine Harvey, *The Fires of Lust: Sex in the Middle Ages*, Reaktion Books, 2021, loc 3409
136. Janega, *The Once and Future Sex*, loc 2803
137. Mortimer, *The Time Traveller's Guide to Medieval England*, loc 425
138. Harvey, *The Fires of Lust*, loc 3487
139. Henry Ansgar Kelly, 'Bishop, Prioress, and Bawd in the Stews of Southwark', *Speculum*, Vol. 75, No. 2, April 2000, pp. 342–88
140. Sauer, *Gender in Medieval Culture*, loc 1658
141. Ibid., loc 1661
142. Harvey, *The Fires of Lust*, loc 3430
143. Sauer, *Gender in Medieval Culture*, loc 1678
144. Lindsey McNellis, *Let Her Be Taken: Sexual Violence in Medieval England*, University of Florida, 2008, p. 83
145. Illston, '"An Entirely Masculine Activity"?', p. 53
146. Ibid.
147. T. Blount, *Tenures of land & customs of manors; originally collected by Thomas Blount and republished with large additions and improvements in 1784 and 1815*, Reeves and Turner, 1874, p. 110
148. T. Maddox, *The history and antiquities of the Exchequer of the kings of England, in two periods: to wit, from the Norman conquest, to the end of the reign of K. John; and from the end of the reign of K. John, to the end of the reign of K. Edward II*, W. Owen [etc.], 1769, p. 656
149. Illston, '"An Entirely Masculine Activity"?', p. 96
150. Harris, *English Aristocratic Women 1450–1550*, loc 148
151. Bateson, *Medieval England 1066–1350*, p. 34
152. Illston, '"An Entirely Masculine Activity"?', p. 53
153. Ibid.
154. William Hepworth Dixon, *Royal Windsor*, Vol. 1, 1877, pp. 67–80
155. Agnes Conway, 'The Family of William Longchamp, Bishop of Ely,

Chancellor and Justiciar of England, 1190–1191, *Archeologia Cantiana*, Vol. 36, 1924

156. Catherine Hanley, 'Nicola de la Haye' (online)

157. Illston, '"An Entirely Masculine Activity"?', p. 51

158. Linda Mitchell, *Portrait of Medieval Women, Family, Marriage and Politics in England 1225–1330*, Palgrave Macmillan, 2003, p. 98

159. Illston, '"An Entirely Masculine Activity"?', p. 54

160. Ibid., p. 82

161. Joanna Winfield, 'Female Warriors in the Middle Ages', 2011, Women's History Month (online)

162. Valerie Eads, 'Means, Motive, Opportunity: Medieval Women and the Recourse to Arms', Paper Presented at the Twentieth Barnard Medieval & Renaissance Conference 'War and Peace in the Middle Ages & Renaissance', 2 December 2006

163. Harvey, *The Fires of Lust*, loc 3791

164. Illston, '"An Entirely Masculine Activity"?', p. 72

165. Ibid., p. 73

166. Gies, *Women in the Middle Ages*, p. 177

167. Bateson, *Medieval England 1066–1350*, p. 34

168. Meg Bogin, *The Women Troubadours*, W.W. Norton and Company, 1980, p. 32

169. Illston, '"An Entirely Masculine Activity"?', p. 83

170. Mortimer, *The Time Traveller's Guide to Medieval England*, p. 240

171. Ibid.

172. Janega, *The Once and Future Sex*, loc 2596

173. Hanawalt, *The Ties that Bound*, p. 152

174. Ibid., p. 151

175. Leyser, *Medieval Women*, loc 2638

176. Hanawalt, *The Ties that Bound*, p. 152

177. Janega, *The Once and Future Sex*, loc 2462

178. Mortimer, *The Time Traveller's Guide to Medieval England*, p. 229

179. Bennett and Froide, *Singlewomen of the European Past 1250–1800*, pp. 130 and 134

180. Carole Hough, 'Women and Law in the Anglo-Saxon Period', 2012, Early English Laws (online)

181. Sauer, *Gender in Medieval Culture*, loc 435

182. Ben Levick and Roland Williamson, 'For What It's Worth', Regia Anglorum, 1994, 1999 and 2003

183. Dunn, *Stolen Women in Medieval England*, loc 3040

184. Ibid., loc 145 and 225

185. Ibid., loc 4019

186. Rebecca Frances King, *Rape in England 1600–1800: Trials, Narratives and the Question of Consent*, Theses, 1998, Durham University

187. Sauer, *Gender in Medieval Culture*, loc 450

188. John Marshall Carter, *Rape in Medieval England: An Historical and Sociological Study*, University Press of America, 1985, p. 45

189. Sauer, *Gender in Medieval Culture*, loc 450

190. McNellis, *Let Her Be Taken*, p. 1

191. Ibid., p. 40

192. Dunn, *Stolen Women in Medieval England*, loc 2080

193. McNellis, *Let Her Be Taken*, p. 67

194. Ibid., p. 1

195. Sauer, *Gender in Medieval Culture*, loc 478

196. Dunn, *Stolen Women in Medieval England*, loc 2141

197. Carter, *Rape in Medieval England*, p. 109

198. Ibid., p. 72

199. Ibid., p. 128

200. Sauer, *Gender in Medieval Culture*, loc 1678

201. Carter, *Rape in Medieval England*, p. 130

202. Sauer, *Gender in Medieval Culture*, loc 1491

203. Marilyn Yalom, *A History of the Wife*, HarperCollins, 2001, p. 46

204. Ibid., p. 52

205. Bateson, *Medieval England 1066–1350*, p. 144

206. Mark Searle and Kenneth Stevenson, *Documents of the Marriage Liturgy*, Liturgical Press, 1992, p. 151

207. Abrams, 'The Jewish Journey'

208. Dunn, *Stolen Women in Medieval England*, loc 3461

209. Bennett and Froide, *Singlewomen in the European Past, 1250–1800*, p. 41

210. Leyser, *Medieval Women*, loc 2082

211. Adams, *Unquiet Women*, loc 677

212. Leyser, *Medieval Women*, loc 2169

213. Ibid., loc 1998

214. McNellis, *Let Her Be Taken*, p. 51

215. Leyser, *Medieval Women*, loc 1975

216. Searle and Stevenson, *Documents of the Marriage Liturgy*, p. 163

217. Sauer, *Gender in Medieval Culture*, loc 735

218. Janina Ramirez, *Femina: A New History of the Middle Ages Through the Women Written Out of It*, WH Allen, 2022, p. 188

219. Sauer, *Gender in Medieval Culture*, loc 1758

220. McNellis, *Let Her Be Taken*, p. 57

221. Nicole Rice, '"Temples to Christ's Indwelling": Forms of Chastity in a Barking Abbey Manuscript', *Journal of the History of Sexuality*, Vol. 19, No. 1, January 2010, pp. 115–32

222. Christian D. Knudsen, *Naughty Nuns and Promiscuous Monks: Monastic Sexual Misconduct in Late Medieval England*, PhD thesis, University of Toronto, 2012, p. 69

223. Elizabeth Rapley, *A Social History of the Cloister*, McGill-Queen's University Press, 2001

224. Giles Constable, 'Aelred of Rievaulx and the Nun of Watton: An Episode in the Early History of the Gilbertine Order', *Studies in Church History Subsidia*, Vol. 1, 1978, pp. 205–26

225. Catherine Tideswell, 'How Far Did Medieval Society Recognise Lesbianism in this Period?', medievalists.net (online)

226. Sauer, *Gender in Medieval Culture*, loc 1272–3

227. John Boswell, *Same Sex Unions in Pre-Modern Europe*, Villard Books, 1994, p. 244

228. Kittredge Cherry, 'Hildegard of Bingen and Richardis: Medieval Mystic and the Woman She Loved', Q Spirit, 17 September 2022

229. Norma Giffney, Michelle M. Sauer and Diane Watt (eds), *The Lesbian Premodern*, Palgrave Macmillan, 2011, p. 36

230. St Paul, Romans 1:26–27, 1599 Geneva Bible, Bible Gateway

231. Tideswell, 'How Far Did Medieval Society Recognise Lesbianism in this Period?'

232. Matilda Tomaryn Bruckner, Laurie Shepard and Sarah White, *Songs of the Women Troubadours*, Garland Publishing, 2000

233. Angelica Rieger, 'Was Bieiris de Romans Lesbian?' in Walter D. Paden (ed) *The Voice of the Trobairitz*, University of Pennsylvania Publications, 1989

234. Elizabeth Castelli, '"I Will Make Mary Male": Pieties of the Body and Gender Transformation of Christian Women in Late Antiquity', in Julia Epstein and Kristina Straub (eds), *Bodyguards: The Cultural Politics of Gender Ambiguity*, Routledge, 1991, p. 30

235. Laura Gowing, *Gender Relations in Early Modern England*, Routledge, 2012, p. 9

236. Thomas Laqueur, *Making Sex: Body and Gender from the Greeks to Freud*, Harvard University Press, 1990, loc 242 and 571

237. Gowing, *Gender Relations*, p. 8

238. Sara Middleton and Patricia Crawford, *Women in Early Modern England 1550–1720*, Oxford University Press, 1998, p. 19

239. Ann Rosalind Jones and Peter Stallybrass, 'Fetishizing Gender: Constructing the Hermaphrodite in Renaissance Europe', in Epstein and Straub (eds), *Bodyguards*, p. 81

240. St Paul, Galatians 3:28, Authorised King James Bible

241. Gospel of St Thomas Gospel, translated by Thomas O. Lambdin, v 114

242. Deuteronomy 22:5, and see Debra Haffner, 'Sexuality and Scripture: What Else Does the Bible Have to Say?', *Sex and the Church*, Spring 2006

243. Sauer, *Gender in Medieval Culture*, loc 313

244. Ibid., loc 1954

245. Michael Nolan, 'The Myth of Soulless Women', First Things (online), April 1997

246. St Paul, 1 Corinthians 14:33–35, King James Bible

247. Maayan Sudai, 'Sex Ambiguity in Early Modern Common Law (1629–1787)', *Law & Social Inquiry*, Vol. 47, No. 2, 2022, pp. 478–513

Part 2: 1348–1455 Women Rising

1. Ian Mortimer, *The Time Traveller's Guide to Medieval England*, Bodley Head, 2008, loc 697

2. Ibid.

3. Kate Ravilious, 'Europe's Chill Linked to Disease', BBC, 27 February 2006; William F. Ruddiman, 'The Anthropogenic Greenhouse Era Began Thousands of Years Ago', *Climatic Change*, Vol. 61, No. 3, 2003, pp. 261–93

4. Ralph of Shrewsbury, letter, January 1349, in John Simkin, *Medieval Realms*, Spartacus Educational, 1991, p. 52

5. Christian D. Knudsen, *Naughty Nuns and Promiscuous Monks: Monastic Sexual Misconduct in Late Medieval England*, PhD thesis, University of Toronto, 2012, p. 59

6. C.M. Woolgar, *The Culture of Food in England 1200–1500*, Yale University Press, 2016, loc 3861

7. Mortimer, *The Time Traveller's Guide to Medieval England*, loc 547

8. Lucy Worsley, 'The Survivor, the "Incurable" and the Scapegoat', *History Extra*, 13 June 2022 (online)

9. Helena Graham, '"A Woman's Work …": Labour and Gender in the Late Medieval Countryside', in *Women in Medieval English Society*, ed. P.J.P. Goldberg, Sutton Publishing, 1992, p. 127

10. Henrietta Leyser, *Medieval Women: Social History of Women in England 450–1500*, Weidenfeld & Nicolson, 2013, loc 2615

11. P.J.P. Goldberg, 'For Better, For Worse: Marriage and Economic Opportunity for Women in Town and Country', in Goldberg (ed.), *Women in Medieval English Society*, p. 112

12. Ibid.

13. Caroline Barron, 'Post Pandemic: How the Years after the Black Death Briefly Became a "Golden Age" for Medieval Women', *History Extra*, 6 July 2021 (online)

14. Ibid.

15. Ibid.

16. Ibid.

17. Woolgar, *The Culture of Food in England 1200–1500*, loc 4902

18. Leyser, *Medieval Women*, loc 2817

19. Extract from a deed by Joanna, daughter of Nicholas de Rudyngton and widow of Stephen de Boneye, 29 July 1380, Latin, translated by Kathryn Summerwill in 'Property Ownership', *Wives, Widows and Wimples*, Manuscripts and Special Collections, University of Nottingham, 2010

20. Mavis E. Mate, *Daughters, Wives and Widows after the Black Death: Women in Sussex 1350–1535*, Boydell Press, 1998, p. 11

21. Michelle M. Sauer, *Gender in Medieval Culture*, Bloomsbury, 2015, loc 739/753

22. Leyser, *Medieval Women*, loc 2169

23. Woolgar, *The Culture of Food in England 1200–1500*, loc 5226

24. Eleanor Janega, *The Once and Future Sex: Going Medieval on Women's Roles in Society*, W.W. Norton and Co, 2023, loc 1387

25. Sylvia Federico, 'The Imaginary Society: Women in 1381', *Journal of British Studies*, Vol. 40, No. 2, April 2001, pp. 150–83

26. Sydney Armitage Smith, *John of Gaunt*, Archibald Constable & Co., 1904, p. 247

27. Federico, 'The Imaginary Society: Women in 1381'
28. Ibid.
29. Ibid.
30. Cooper & Cooper, *Annals of Cambridge*, Vol. 1, Warwick & Co., 1842, p. 121
31. Helen Lacey, '"Grace for the Rebels": The Role of the Royal Pardon in the Peasants' Revolt of 1381', *Journal of Medieval History*, Vol. 34, Issue 1, 2008, pp. 36–63
32. Melissa Hogenboom, 'Peasants' Revolt: The Time When Women Took Up Arms', BBC News, 14 June 2012 (online)
33. Federico, 'The Imaginary Society: Women in 1381'
34. Olwen Hufton, *The Prospect Before Her*, Knopf, 1996, p. 473
35. Calendar of the Patent Rolls, Henry VI, Vol. 5, HM Stationery Office, 1909, pp. 338–74
36. Barbara J. Harris, *English Aristocratic Women 1450–1550: Marriage and Family, Property and Careers*, Oxford University Press, 2002, loc 1149
37. Mate, *Daughters, Wives and Widows after the Black Death*, p. 12
38. Leyser, *Medieval Women*, loc 2575
39. Mate, *Daughters, Wives and Widows after the Black Death*, p. 12
40. P.J.P. Goldberg, *Women, Work, and Life Cycle in a Medieval Economy: Women in York and Yorkshire c.1300–1520*, Oxford Academic, 1992, pp. 82–157
41. Maryanne Kowaleski, 'The Demographic Perspective', in Judith M. Bennett and Amy M. Froide (eds), *Singlewomen in the European Past, 1250–1800*, University of Pennsylvania Press, 1990, p. 48
42. Woolgar, *The Culture of Food in England 1200–1500*, loc 2928
43. Goldberg, *Women, Work, and Life Cycle in a Medieval Economy*
44. Leyser, *Medieval Women*, loc 3188
45. Marjorie Keniston McIntosh, *Working Women in English Society 1300–1620*, Cambridge University Press, 2005, p. 30
46. Barron, 'Post Pandemic', *History Extra*
47. Sauer, *Gender in Medieval Culture*, loc 2927
48. Janina Ramirez, *Femina: A New History of the Middle Ages Through the Women Written Out of It*, WH Allen, 2022, p. 320
49. Leyser, *Medieval Women*, loc 3185
50. Barbara A. Hanawalt, *The Wealth of Wives: Women, Law, and Economy in Late Medieval London*, Oxford University Press, 2007, loc 2690
51. Barron, 'Post Pandemic', *History Extra*
52. Marty Williams and Anne Echols, *Between Pit and Pedestal: Women in the Middle Ages*, Markus Wiener, 1993, p. 54
53. Hanawalt, *The Wealth of Wives*, loc 141, 225 and 1601
54. Woolgar, *The Culture of Food in England 1200–1500*, loc 2446
55. Harris, *English Aristocratic Women 1450–1550*, loc 2370
56. McIntosh, *Working Women in English Society 1300–1620*, pp. 38 and 95
57. Leyser, *Medieval Women*, loc 2386
58. Williams and Echols, *Between Pit and Pedestal*, p. 229
59. Ibid.,p. 229
60. Michael Riordan, 'Women at Queen's before 1979', Queen's College, University of Oxford (online)
61. Hanawalt, *The Wealth of Wives*, loc 991, 1470, 581, 591, 684
62. McIntosh, *Working Women in English Society 1300–1620*, p. 241
63. Lucy Davidson, 'What Did People Wear in Medieval England?', History Hit, 26 February 2023 (online)
64. McIntosh, *Working Women in English Society 1300–1620*, p. 241
65. Hanawalt, *The Wealth of Wives*, loc 2724
66. Goldberg, 'For Better, For Worse', p. 112
67. Barbara A. Hanawalt, *The Ties that Bound: Peasant Families in Medieval England*, Oxford University Press, 1986, p. 151

68. Hanawalt, *The Wealth of Wives*, loc 2724

69. Jane Humphries and Jacob Weisdorf, 'Wages of Women in England 1260–1850', *Oxford Economic and Social History Working Papers*, 127, March 2014, p. 16

70. L.R. Poos, 'Sex, Lies, and the Church Courts of Pre-Reformation England', *Journal of Interdisciplinary History*, Vol. 25, No. 4, 1995, pp. 585–607

71. Barron, 'Post Pandemic', *History Extra*

72. Williams and Echols, *Between Pit and Pedestal*, p. 148

73. Anthony Fletcher, *Gender, Sex and Subordination in England 1500–1800*, Yale University Press, 1995, p. 25

74. Rowena Archer, 'How Ladies Who Live on Their Manors …', *Women in Medieval English Society*, ed. P.J.P. Goldberg, Sutton Publishing, 1992, p. 154

75. Hanawalt, *The Ties that Bound*, p. 201

76. Richard Harvey, 'The Work and Mentalité of Lower Orders Elizabethan Women', *Exemplaria*, Vol. 5, Issue 2, 1993, pp. 409–33, p. 427

77. Stéphanie Prevost, 'For a Bunch of Blue Ribbons: Taking a Look at Wife-Selling in the Black Country and the West Midlands', *Blackcountryman Magazine*, Vol. 49, Autumn 2016, pp. 51–7

78. James Bryce, *Studies in History and Jurisprudence, Volume II*, Oxford University Press, 1901, p. 820

79. Simon Payling, 'The Elusiveness of Divorce in Medieval England: The Marital Troubles of the Last Warenne Earl of Surrey (d.1347)', The History of Parliament, 3 August 2021 (online)

80. Ibid.

81. Caroline Dunn, *Stolen Women in Medieval England*, Cambridge University Press, 2012, loc 137

82. Graham, 'A Woman's Work …', p. 127

83. J.B. Post, 'Sir Thomas West and the Statute of Rape 1382', *Institute of Historical Research*, Vol. 53, Issue 127, May 1980, Wiley Online Library

84. Helen Barker, *Rape in Early Modern England: Law, History and Criticism*, Palgrave Macmillan, 2021, loc 1857

85. Ibid., loc 1623

86. Sauer, *Gender in Medieval Culture*, loc 450

87. Dunn, *Stolen Women in Medieval England*, loc 379

88. Ibid., loc 231 and 2090

89. Sauer, *Gender in Medieval Culture*, loc 478

90. Carissa Harris, '800 Years of Rape Culture', *Aeon*, 24 May 2021 (online)

91. Bennett and Froide, *Singlewomen in the European Past, 1250–1800*, p. 2

92. Ruth Mazo Karras, 'Sex and the Singlewoman', in ibid., p. 134

93. Katherine Harvey, *The Fires of Lust: Sex in the Middle Ages*, Reaktion Books, 2021, loc 3529

94. Ibid., loc 3472

95. Leyser, *Medieval Women*, loc 2802–5

96. Harvey, *The Fires of Lust*, loc 3768

97. McIntosh, *Working Women in English Society 1300–1620*, p. 76

98. Harvey, *The Fires of Lust*, loc 3768

99. Karras, 'Sex and the Singlewoman', p. 139

100. Harvey, *The Fires of Lust*, loc 3729

101. Judith M. Bennett, 'Etchingham and Oxenbridge', in Noreen Giffney, Michelle Sauer and Diane Watt (eds), *The Lesbian Premodern*, Palgrave Macmillan, 2011, p. 134

102. The words of Cino da Pistoia quoted in Francesca Canadé Sautman and Pamela Sheingorn, *Same Sex Love and Desire Among Women in the Middle Ages*, Palgrave, 2001, pp. 110 and 111

103. *Knighton's Leicester Chronicle* quoted in Thomas S. Henricks, *Disputed Pleasures: Sport and Society in Preindustrial England*, Greenwood Publishing Group, 1991, p. 53

104. Joanna Winfield, 'Female Warriors in the Middle Ages', 2011, Women's History Month (online)

105. Judith M. Bennett and Shannon McSheffrey, 'Early, Erotic and Alien: Women Dressed as Men in Late

Medieval London', *History Workshop Journal*, Spring 2014, No. 77, pp. 1–25

106. Ibid.

107. Geoffrey Chaucer, 'General Prologue', *The Canterbury Tales*, translated by Larry D. Benson (ed.), *The Riverside Chaucer*, Houghton-Mifflin, 1988

108. Ibid.

109. Janega, *The Once and Future Sex*, loc 1871

110. Geoffrey Chaucer, 'The Wife of Bath', *The Canterbury Tales*

111. Ibid.

112. Ramirez, *Femina*, p. 301

113. Geoffrey Chaucer, 'The Knight's Tale', *The Canterbury Tales*

114. Ibid.

115. Ibid.

116. Leyser, *Medieval Women*, loc 4434

117. Dunn, *Stolen Women in Medieval England*, loc 137

118. Mate, *Daughters, Wives and Widows after the Black Death*, p. 186

119. King's Bench 9/359 m. 67 (1 October 1481), National Archives, translated by Mark Thakkar, University of St Andrews, 2023

Part 3: 1455–1485 Women at War

1. Rowena Archer, 'How Ladies Who Live on Their Manors …', *Women in Medieval English Society*, ed. P.J.P. Goldberg, Sutton Publishing, 1992, p. 161

2. Melissa Snell, 'Life of Margaret Paston', ThoughtCo., 1 March 2019 (online)

3. Philip Payton, Alston Kennerley and Helen Doe (eds), *The Maritime History of Cornwall*, University of Exeter Press, 2014

4. Barbara J. Harris, *English Aristocratic Women 1450–1550: Marriage and Family, Property and Careers*, Oxford University Press, 2002, loc 239

5. Caroline Dunn, *Stolen Women in Medieval England*, Cambridge University Press, 2012, loc 3040

6. Harris, *English Aristocratic Women 1450–1550*, loc 2592

7. Ibid., loc 214

8. Elizabeth Norton, *The Hidden Lives of Tudor Women: A Social History*, Pegasus Books, 2017, loc 1228

9. Miss Evelyn Fox, 'The Diary of an Elizabethan Gentlewoman', *Transactions of the Royal Historical Society*, Vol. 2, 1908, pp. 153–74

10. Eleanor Janega, *The Once and Future Sex: Going Medieval on Women's Roles in Society*, W.W. Norton and Co, 2023, loc 3047

11. Caroline Barron, 'Post Pandemic: How the Years after the Black Death Briefly Became a "Golden Age" for Medieval Women', *History Extra*, 6 July 2021 (online)

12. Jean Donnison, 'A History of the Midwife Profession in the United Kingdom', in *Mayes' Midwifery*, 14th edn, Bailliere Tindall Elsevier, 2011, pp. 13–14

13. Barbara A. Hanawalt, *The Wealth of Wives: Women, Law and Economy in Late Medieval London*, Oxford University Press, 2007, loc 2418 and 2445

14. Davies Gilbert, *The Parochial History of Cornwall, founded on the manuscript of Histories of Mr Hals and Mr Tonkin*, JB Nichols & Sons, 1838, Vol. 4, pp. 132–4

15. Marty Williams and Anne Echols, *Between Pit and Pedestal: Women in the Middle Ages*, Markus Wiener Publishers, 1993, p. 51

16. C.M. Woolgar, *The Culture of Food in England 1200–1500*, Yale University Press, 2016, loc 1631

17. L.R. Poos, 'Sex, Lies, and the Church Courts of Pre-Reformation England', *Journal of Interdisciplinary History*, Vol. 25, No. 4, 1995, pp. 585–607

18. Max Adams, *Unquiet Women*, Head of Zeus, 2018, loc 2422

19. Ibid., loc 2663

20. Ibid., loc 2701

21. Dunn, *Stolen Women in Medieval England*, loc 4019

22. Katherine Harvey, *The Fires of Lust: Sex in the Middle Ages*, Reaktion Books, 2021, loc 3487 and 3729

23. Ibid., loc 3548, 3487, 3548, 3487, 3520

Part 4: 1485–1660 Becoming a Weaker Vessel

1. Christian D. Knudsen, *Naughty Nuns and Promiscuous Monks: Monastic Sexual Misconduct in Late Medieval England*, PhD thesis, University of Toronto, 2012, p. 208
2. Ibid., p. 99
3. Ibid., p. 178, 177 and 118
4. Ibid., p. 105
5. Geoffrey Baskerville, 'The Dispossessed Religious of Surrey', *Surrey Archaeological Collections*, Vol. 47, 1941, pp. 12–28
6. Knudsen, *Naughty Nuns and Promiscuous Monks*, p. 223
7. Stephanie A. Mann, 'More on the Norwich Beguinage', Supremacy and Survival: The English Reformation, 1 June 2013 (online)
8. Knudsen, *Naughty Nuns and Promiscuous Monks*, pp. 223 and 224
9. Ibid., p. 81
10. Norma Giffney, Michelle M. Sauer and Diane Watt (eds), *The Lesbian Premodern*, Palgrave Macmillan, 2011, p. 86
11. Laura Gowing, *Gender Relations in Early Modern England*, Routledge, 2012, p. 52
12. Olwen Hufton, *The Prospect Before Her*, Knopf, 1996, p. 408
13. Madeleine Dodds and Ruth Dodds, *The Pilgrimage of Grace*, London, 1915
14. John Simkin, 'Pilgrimage of Grace', Spartacus Educational, September 1997 (online)
15. Elizabeth Norton, *The Hidden Lives of Tudor Women: A Social History*, Pegasus Books, 2017, pp. 202 and 206
16. Charles Wriothesley, *A Chronicle of England during the Reigns of the Tudors from ad 1485 to 1559*, ed. William Douglas Hamilton, Camden Society, 1875, p. 64
17. Sharon L. Jansen, *Dangerous Talk and Strange Behaviour: Women and Popular Resistance to the Reforms of Henry VIII*, Palgrave Macmillan, 1996, p. 6
18. Norton, *The Hidden Lives of Tudor Women*, loc 2677
19. Robert Hutchinson, *The Last Days of Henry VIII: Conspiracies, Treason and Heresy at the Court of the Dying Tyrant*, Weidenfeld and Nicolson, 2005, pp. 172–3
20. Norton, *The Lives of Tudor Women*, loc 4273
21. Ibid., loc 4282
22. Hufton, *The Prospect Before Her*, p. 407
23. Mary Prior (ed.), *Women in English Society, 1500–1800*, Routledge, 2016, pp. 112–17
24. All the following are from John Foxe: *Foxe's Book of Martyrs, or the Acts and Monuments of the Christian Church; Being a Complete History of the Lives, Sufferings, and Deaths of the Christian Martyrs*, Jas B. Smith & Co., 1856
25. John Morris (ed.), 'Mr John Mush's Life of Margaret Clitherow', *The Troubles of Our Catholic Forefathers related by Themselves*, 1877, pp. 333–440
26. 'Margaret Ward' in David Hugh Farmer, *The Oxford Dictionary of Saints*, 5th edn, Oxford University Press, 2011
27. Gerelyn Hollingsworth, *National Catholic Reporter*, 26 February 2010
28. Cecil Roth, *A History of the Marranos*, Jewish Publication Society of America, 1932, p. 257
29. Barbara Bowen, 'Aemilia Lanyer and the Invention of White Womanhood', in Susan Frye and Karen Robertson (eds), *Maids and Mistresses, Cousins and Queens: Women's Alliances in Early Modern England*, Oxford University Press, 1999
30. Hufton, *The Prospect Before Her*, p. 413
31. Norton, *The Hidden Lives of Tudor Women*, loc 4251
32. Prior (ed.), *Women in English Society, 1500–1800*, pp. 97 and 105
33. Ibid., p. 124

34. James Kelly, '17th-century Nuns on the Run', *History Extra*, 20 March 2012 (online)

35. Hufton, *The Prospect Before Her*, p. 384

36. Lowell Gallagher, 'Mary Ward's "Jesuitresses" and the Construction of a Typological Community', in Frye and Robertson (eds), *Maids and Mistresses, Cousins and Queens*

37. Leyser, *Medieval Women*, loc 4243

38. Roger Hayden, 'Dorothy Hazzard', *Oxford Dictionary of National Biography*

39. Bernard Capp, *When Gossips Meet: Women, Family, and Neighbourhood in Early Modern England*, Oxford University Press, 2003, loc 337

40. Sara Heller Mendelson, *The Mental World of Stuart Women: Three Studies*, Harvester Press, 1987, p. 106

41. Ibid., p. 107

42. Prior (ed.), *Women in English Society, 1500–1800*, p. 96

43. John Wycliffe, Bible, 1382

44. WYC, 1 Peter 3:7, Bible Gateway (online)

45. Ibid.

46. William Tyndale, New Testament, 1525

47. TYN, 1 Peter 3:7, Bible Gateway (online)

48. Anthony Fletcher, *Gender, Sex and Subordination in England 1500–1800*, Yale University Press, 1995, p. 74

49. Marjorie Keniston McIntosh, *Working Women in English Society 1300–1620*, Cambridge University Press, 2005, p. 41

50. 'A Homilie of the State of Matrimony', in *The Second Tome of Homilies*, Edward Allde, 1595

51. Ibid.

52. Ibid.

53. Ibid.

54. Ibid.

55. Fletcher, *Gender, Sex and Subordination in England 1500–1800*, p. 297

56. Ibid., p. 89

57. Mark Searle and Kenneth Stevenson, *Documents of the Marriage Liturgy*, Liturgical Press, 1992, p. 166

58. Robert Burton, *Anatomy of Melancolie*, 1621, quoted by Lisa Picard, *Restoration London: Everyday Life in the 1660s*, Weidenfeld and Nicolson, 1997, loc 3424

59. Anger in Mary Prior (ed.), *Women in English Society, 1500–1800*, p. 172

60. McIntosh, *Working Women in English Society 1300–1620*, p. 41

61. Fletcher, *Gender, Sex and Subordination in England 1500–1800*, p. 70

62. John Knox, *The First Blast of the Trumpet against the Monstrous Regiment of Women*, 1558

63. Clarck Drieshen, 'Lady Jane Grey's Letters from the Tower of London', Medieval Manuscripts blog, British Library (online)

64. Leah S. Marcus, Janet Mueller and Mary Beth Rose (eds), *Elizabeth I: Collected Works*, University of Chicago Press, 2002, p. 97

65. Thomas Laqueur, *Making Sex: Body and Gender from the Greeks to Freud*, Harvard University Press, 1990, loc 2331

66. Retha Warnicke, *Wicked Women of England*, Palgrave Macmillan, 2012, p. 5

67. Ian Mortimer, *The Time Traveller's Guide to Elizabethan England*, Bodley Head, 2012, loc 889

68. A.D. Innes, *A History of the British Nation*, TC and EC Jack, 1912

69. Polydore Vergil, *Three Books of Polydore Vergil*, ed. Henry Ellis, Camden Society, 1844, p. 71

70. Barbara J. Harris, *English Aristocratic Women 1450–1550: Marriage and Family, Property and Careers*, Oxford University Press, 2002, loc 410

71. John Smyth, *The Berkeley Manuscripts 1066–1618, Volume II*, 1883, p. 253. Translation cited by Jorge Castell, Tudor Place (online)

72. Ascham to Sturm, 1550, in Rev. Dr Giles (ed.), *The Whole Works of Roger Ascham*, John Russell Smith, 1865, Vol. 1, p. xiii

73. Harris, *English Aristocratic Women 1450–1550*, loc 2872

74. Mendelson, *The Mental World of Stuart Women*, p. 185
75. Fletcher, *Gender, Sex and Subordination in England 1500–1800*, p. 24
76. Judith M. Bennett and Shannon McSheffrey, 'Early, Erotic and Alien: Women Dressed as Men in Late Medieval London', *History Workshop Journal*, Spring 2014, No. 77, pp. 1–25
77. Mary Wack, 'Women, Work and Plays in an English Medieval Town', in Frye and Robertson (eds), *Maids and Mistresses, Cousins and Queens*
78. Sandra Clark, '"Hic Mulier", "Haec Vir", and the Controversy over Masculine Women', *Studies in Philology*, Vol. 82, No. 2, Spring 1985, pp. 153–83
79. Ibid.
80. Fletcher, *Gender, Sex and Subordination in England 1500–1800*, p. 23
81. Capp, *When Gossips Meet*, loc 4463
82. All the following are from Bennett and McSheffrey, 'Early, Erotic and Alien'
83. Donal Ó Danachair (ed.), *The Newgate Calendar*, Ex-classics Project, 2009, Vol. 1, p. 130
84. Fletcher, *Gender, Sex and Subordination in England 1500–1800*, p. 85
85. Capp, *When Gossips Meet*, loc 4461
86. Mendelson, *The Mental World of Stuart Women*, p. 57
87. Maayan Sudai, 'Sex Ambiguity in Early Modern Common Law (1629–1787)', *Law & Social Inquiry*, Vol. 47, No. 2, 2022, pp. 478–513
88. Ronald Trumbach, 'London's Sapphists', in Julia Epstein and Kristina Straub (eds), *Bodyguards: The Cultural Politics of Gender Ambiguity*, Routledge, 1991, p. 120
89. Susan D. Amussen and David E. Underdown, *Gender, Culture and Politics in England 1560–1640: Turning the World Upside Down*, Bloomsbury, 2017, p. 11
90. Tracy Borman, 'Anne of Denmark: A Killer Queen', *History Extra*, 11 August 2021
91. Amussen and Underdown, *Gender, Culture and Politics in England 1560–1640*, p. 58
92. Borman, 'Anne of Denmark'
93. Amussen and Underdown, *Gender, Culture and Politics in England 1560–1640*, pp. 50 and 59
94. Lisa Gim, '"Fair Eliza's Chaine": Two Female Writers' Literary Links to Queen Elizabeth I', in Frye and Robertson (eds), *Maids and Mistresses, Cousins and Queens*
95. Gallagher, 'Mary Ward's "Jesuitresses" and the Construction of a Typological Community'
96. Diane Dugaw, *Warrior Women and Popular Balladry, 1650–1850*, Chicago Press, 1989, p. 1
97. Mark Stoyle, '"Give mee a Souldier's Coat": Female Cross-Dressing during the English Civil War', *History*, Vol. 103, Issue 354, January 2018, pp. 5–26
98. Kelly Faircloth, 'Searching for the Fighting Women of the English Civil War', *Jezebel*, 3 April 2018
99. Charles Carlton, *Going to the Wars: The Experience of the British Civil War, 1638–1651*, Routledge, 1994, p. 307
100. Rodney Legg, *The Book of Lyme Regis: The Story of Dorset's Western Spa*, Halsgrove 2003, p. 38
101. J.F. Nicholls and John Taylor, *Bristol Past and Present*, J.W. Arrowsmith, 1882
102. Capp, *When Gossips Meet*, loc 3708
103. Ibid., loc 3710
104. Fletcher, *Gender, Sex and Subordination in England 1500–1800*, p. 78
105. Ibid., p. 77
106. Carlton, *Going to the Wars*, p. 178
107. Fletcher, *Gender, Sex and Subordination in England 1500–1800*, p. 78
108. Ibid.
109. Carlton, *Going to the Wars*, pp. 178 and 309

110. Ibid., p. 110
111. Ibid.
112. Ibid., p. 296
113. Ibid., pp. 296–7
114. Ibid., p. 110
115. All the following are taken from: Nadine Akkerman, *Invisible Agents: Women and Espionage in Seventeenth-Century Britain*, Oxford University Press, 2018
116. Tammy M. Proctor, *Female Intelligence: Women and Espionage in the First World War*, New York University Press, 2003, p. 16
117. Peter Rushton and Gwenda Morgan, *Banishment in the Early Atlantic World: Convicts Rebels and Slaves*, Bloomsbury, 2013, p. 12
118. Sara Mendelson and Patricia Crawford, *Women in Early Modern England 1550–1720*, Clarendon Press, 1998, p. 189 and p. 39
119. Gowing, *Gender Relations in Early Modern England*, p. 48
120. Ann Rosalind Jones, 'Maidservants of London: Sisterhoods of Kinship and Labour', in Frye and Robertson (eds), *Maids and Mistresses, Cousins and Queens*
121. Patrick Wallis, 'Apprenticeship in England', in Prak and Wallis (eds), *Apprenticeships in Early Modern Europe*, Cambridge University Press, 2019, pp. 247–81
122. Judith M. Bennett and Amy M. Froide, *Singlewomen in the European Past, 1250–1800*, University of Pennsylvania Press, 1990, p. 241
123. McIntosh, *Working Women in English Society 1300–1620*, p. 132; Bennett and Froide, *Singlewomen in the European Past, 1250–1800*, p. 241
124. Bennett and Froide, *Singlewomen in the European Past*, 1250–1800, p. 241
125. Hufton, *The Prospect Before Her*, p. 273
126. Ibid.
127. Ibid.
128. Anne-Marie Kilday, 'The Archetype of Infanticide in the Early Modern Period', *A History of Infanticide in Britain c. 1600 to the Present*, Palgrave

Macmillan, 2013; Hufton, *The Prospect Before Her*, pp. 274 and 276
129. Alison Wall (ed.), *Two Elizabethan Women: Correspondence of Joan and Mariah Thynne 1575–1611*, Wiltshire Record Society, Devizes, 1983, p. 19
130. Mendelson, *The Mental World of Stuart Women*, p. 42
131. Richard Harvey, 'English Pre-Industrial Ballads on Poverty, 1500–1700', *The Historian*, Vol. 46, No. 4, August 1984, pp. 539–61, p. 553
132. Ibid., p. 559
133. Mendelson and Crawford, *Women in Early Modern England 1550–1720*, p. 44
134. Norton, *The Hidden Lives of Tudor Women*, loc 2342/2347
135. Ibid., p. 11
136. Rebecca Frances King, 'Rape in England 1600–1800: Trials, Narratives and the Question of Consent', Durham theses, 1998, Durham University
137. Helen Barker, *Rape in Early Modern England: Law, History and Criticism*, Palgrave Macmillan, 2021, loc 1623
138. King, 'Rape in England 1600–1800'
139. Capp, *When Gossips Meet*, loc 3050
140. Sauer, *Gender in Medieval Culture*, loc 910
141. Ibid., loc 1721
142. John Frith, 'Syphilis – Its Early History and Treatment until Penicillin and the Debate on Its Origins', *Journal of Military and Veterans' Health*, Vol. 20, No. 4, 2012, pp. 49–58
143. McIntosh, *Working Women in English Society 1300–1620*, p. 77
144. Sauer, *Gender in Medieval Culture*, loc 925
145. Leyser, *Medieval Women*, loc 2811
146. Harvey, *The Fires of Lust*, loc 3487 and 3536
147. Richard Harvey, 'The Work and Mentalité of Lower Orders Elizabethan Women', *Exemplaria*, Vol. 5, Issue 2, 1993, pp. 409–33
148. Miranda Kaufmann, *Black Tudors*, Oneworld, 2017, pp. 220–1

149. Ibid., pp. 15–16
150. Peter Fryer, *Staying Power: The History of Black People in Britain*, Pluto Press, 1984, p. 8
151. Michael Wood, 'Britain's First Black Community in Elizabethan Britain', BBC News, 20 July 2012
152. Fryer, *Staying Power*, p. 8
153. Ibid.
154. Kaufmann, *Black Tudors*, p. 312
155. Ibid., p. 203
156. Ibid., p. 302
157. American Society of Human Genetics, 'ASHG Denounces Attempts to Link Genetics and Racial Supremacy', *American Journal of Human Genetics*, 1 November 2018, p. 636
158. Bowen, 'Aemilia Lanyer and the Invention of White Womanhood', in Frye and Robertson (eds), *Maids and Mistresses, Cousins and Queens*
159. Harris, *English Aristocratic Women 1450–1550*, loc 3380/3387
160. Robert Titler, 'The Feminine Dynamic in Tudor Art: A Reassessment', *British Art Journal*, Vol. 17, No. 1, Spring 2016, pp. 122–30, p. 125
161. 'A Woman, Presumed to Be a Self-Portrait of Susannah-Penelope Rosse', in John Murdoch, *Seventeenth-Century English Miniatures in the Collection of the Victoria & Albert Museum*, The Stationery Office in association with the V&A, 1997
162. Titler, 'The Feminine Dynamic in Tudor Art', p. 122
163. Ibid., p. 124
164. Harris, *English Aristocratic Women 1450–1550*, loc 3468 and 3469
165. C.I. Merton, *Women Who Served Queen Mary and Queen Elizabeth: Ladies, Gentlewomen and Maids of the Privy Chamber 1553–1603*, thesis, University of Cambridge, 1992
166. Elizabeth A. Brown, '"Companion Me with My Mistress": Cleopatra, Elizabeth I and Their Waiting Women', in Frye and Robertson (eds), *Maids and Mistresses, Cousins and Queens*
167. Harris, *English Aristocratic Women 1450–1550*, loc 3419
168. Sarah Laskow, 'A Machine that Made Stockings Helped Kick Off the Industrial Revolution', Atlas Obscura, 19 September 2017 (online)
169. Norton, *The Hidden Lives of Tudor Women*, loc 1918
170. 'Sale of a Lyme Ship', Lyme Regis Museum display board, Lyme Regis visit August 2021
171. Harris, *English Aristocratic Women 1450–1550*, loc 150–75
172. Wall (ed.), *Two Elizabethan Women*, p. 14
173. Hufton, *The Prospect Before Her*, p. 150
174. Mary Lovell, *Bess of Hardwick: First Lady of Chatsworth*, Little, Brown, 2005
175. Heather Delonette, 'Did the Civil War and Its Aftermath to 1660 Offer Any Lasting New Opportunities to Women?', Cromwell Association (online), 2001
176. Mendelson and Crawford, *Women in Early Modern England 1550–1720*, p. 51
177. Warnicke, *Wicked Women of England*, p. 3
178. Capp, *When Gossips Meet*, loc 4093
179. Mendelson and Crawford, *Women in Early Modern England 1550–1720*, p. 58
180. Picard, *Restoration London*, loc 3585
181. Norton, *The Hidden Lives of Tudor Women*, p. 61
182. Leyser, *Medieval Women*, loc 2779
183. Hanawalt, *The Ties that Bound*, p. 151
184. Hufton, *The Prospect Before Her*, p. 153
185. Gowing, *Gender Relations in Early Modern England*, p. 53
186. Mendelson and Crawford, *Women in Early Modern England 1550–1720*, p. 50
187. Capp, *When Gossips Meet*, loc 3805
188. Leyser, *Medieval Women*, loc 2615
189. Wack, 'Women, Work and Plays in an English Medieval Town', in

Frye and Robertson (eds), *Maids and Mistresses, Cousins and Queens*

190. David Kathman, 'Alice Layston and the Cross Keys', *Medieval & Renaissance Drama in England*, Vol. 22, 2009, p. 144

191. Callan Davies, 'Engendering Before Shakespeare: Women and Early English Playhouse Ownership', Engendering the Stage (online)

192. Andrew Gurr, *The Shakespearean Stage 1574–1642*, Cambridge University Press, 1992, 3rd edition, pp. 142 and 45

193. Jones, 'Maidservants of London', in Frye and Robertson (eds), *Maids and Mistresses, Cousins and Queens*

194. Mortimer, *The Time Traveller's Guide to Elizabethan England*, loc 6061 and 5990

195. Leyser, *Medieval Women*, loc 4415

196. Mortimer, *The Time Traveller's Guide to Elizabethan England*, loc 2025 and 1356

197. Harris, *English Aristocratic Women 1450–1550*, loc 424–447, 531–535

198. Mortimer, *The Time Traveller's Guide to Elizabethan England*, loc 6880 and 1356

199. Norton, *The Hidden Lives of Tudor Women*, p. 55

200. Gim, '"Faire Eliza's Chaine"', in Frye and Robertson (eds), *Maids and Mistresses, Cousins and Queens*

201. William J. Thoms (ed.), *Anecdotes and Traditions: Illustrative of Early English History and Literature*, Nichols and Sons, 1839, p. 125

202. Edward Rothstein, 'Authors in Rooms of Their Own', *New York Times*, 23 February 2012

203. Joanna Moody (ed.), *The Private Life of an Elizabethan Lady: The Diary of Lady Margaret Hoby 1599–1605*, Sutton Publishing, 1998, p. xvii

204. Harris, *English Aristocratic Women 1450–1550*, loc 1502 and 499

205. Wall (ed.), *Two Elizabethan Women*, p. 2

206. Norton, *The Hidden Lives of Tudor Women*, loc 1183–1202

207. Fletcher, *Gender, Sex and Subordination in England 1500–1800*, p. 366

208. Moody (ed.), *The Private Life of an Elizabethan Lady*

209. Simon Harcourt's letter to Lady Harcourt, 3 January 1641, in Edward Harcourt (ed.), *The Harcourt Papers*, James Parker & Co, 1876, p. 147

210. Bowen, 'Aemilia Lanyer and the Invention of White Womanhood', in Frye and Robertson (eds), *Maids and Mistresses, Cousins and Queens*

211. Hufton, *The Prospect Before Her*, pp. 431 and 414

212. Mendelson, *The Mental World of Stuart Women*, p. 35

213. Ibid., p. 30

214. Miss Evelyn Fox, 'The Diary of an Elizabethan Gentlewoman', *Transactions of the Royal Historical Society*, Vol. 2 (1908), pp. 153–74, p. 163

215. Norton, *The Hidden Lives of Tudor Women*, loc 5832

216. McIntosh, *Working Women in English Society 1300–1620*, p. 80

217. Mortimer, *The Time Traveller's Guide to Elizabethan England*, loc 1244

218. Ian Mortimer, *The Dying and the Doctors: The Medical Revolution in Seventeenth-Century England*, Boydell Press, 2009, p. 124

219. McIntosh, *Working Women in English Society 1300–1620*, p. 82

220. Norton, *The Hidden Lives of Tudor Women*, loc 513

221. McIntosh, *Working Women in English Society 1300–1620*, p. 84

222. Ibid.

223. Jean Donnison, 'A History of the Midwife Profession in the United Kingdom', in *Mayes' Midwifery*, 14th edition, Bailliere Tindall Elsevier, 2011, pp. 13–14

224. McIntosh, *Working Women in English Society 1300–1620*, p. 83

225. Norton, *The Hidden Lives of Tudor Women*, loc 5332–61

226. J. Loudon, 'Deaths in Childbed from the Eighteenth Century to 1935',

Medical History, Vol. 30, January 1986, pp. 1–41

227. McIntosh, *Working Women in English Society 1300–1620*, p. 83

228. Ibid.

229. Fletcher, *Gender, Sex and Subordination in England 1500–1800*, p. 25

230. Moody (ed.), *The Private Life of an Elizabethan Lady*, p. 7

231. Mortimer, *The Time Traveller's Guide to Elizabethan England*, p. 8

232. Ibid.

233. Malcolm Gaskill, 'Witchcraft and Evidence in Early Modern England', *Past and Present*, Vol. 198, No. 1, 2008, p. 42

234. Hufton, *The Prospect Before Her*, p. 347

235. Charlotte-Rose Millar, *Witchcraft, the Devil, and Emotions in Early Modern England*, Routledge, 2017, p. 153

236. Laura Gowing, 'Pendle Witches Lancashire Witches (*act.* 1612)', *Oxford Dictionary of National Biography*, 2004

237. William E. Burns, *Witch Hunts in Europe and America: An Encyclopedia*, Greenwood Publishing Group, 2003, p. 166

238. Gowing, 'Pendle Witches Lancashire Witches (*act.* 1612)'

239. Ibid.

240. Burns, *Witch Hunts in Europe and America*, p. 166

241. James Sharpe, *Instruments of Darkness: Witchcraft in Early Modern England*, Philadelphia University Press, 1996, p. 129; Gordon Napier, *Maleficium: Witchcraft and Witch Hunting in the West*, Amberley Publishing Ltd, 2017

242. Louise Jackson, 'Witches, Wives and Mothers: Witchcraft Persecution and Women's Confession in Seventeenth-Century England', *Women's History Review*, Vol. 4, Issue 1, pp. 63–84

243. Shannon M. Lundquist, 'Finding the Witch's Mark: Female Participation in the Judicial System during the Hopkins Trials 1645–47', Hamline University, 2014

244. Malcolm Gaskill, 'Introduction', in *English Witchcraft 1560–1736*, ed. James Sharpe, *Vol. 3 The Matthew Hopkins Trials*, Pickering and Chatto, 2003

245. Pip and Joy Wright, *Witches in and around Suffolk*, Pawprint Publishing, 2004

246. Jackson, 'Witches, Wives and Mothers'

247. Gaskill, 'Introduction', in *English Witchcraft 1560–1736*

248. Ivan Bunn and Gilbert Geis, *A Trial of Witches: A Seventeenth Century Witchcraft Prosecution*, Routledge, 2005, p. 81

249. Malcolm Gaskill, 'Witchcraft Trials in England' in Brian P. Levack, *The Oxford Handbook of Witchcraft in Early Modern Europe and Colonial America*, Oxford University Press, 2013, p. 296

250. William Beck and T. Frederick Ball, *The London Friends' Meetings*, 1869, pp. 19–20.

251. Hufton, *The Prospect Before Her*, p. 419

252. Ibid., p. 418

253. Nicholas Blundell (1669–1737), *The Great Diurnal of Nicholas Blundell*, Record Society of Lancashire and Cheshire, 1968, in Peter Radford, 'Picturing Early Women Athletes', Folger Shakespeare Library, 18 February 2022 (online)

254. P. Seddon, *Football Talk: The Language & Folklore of the World's Greatest Game*, Robson, 2004, p. 156

255. McIntosh, *Working Women in English Society 1300–1620*, p. 38

256. Gowing, *Gender Relations in Early Modern England*, p. 44

257. Hanawalt, *The Wealth of Wives*, loc 3172

258. Leyser, *Medieval Women*, loc 2823

259. Norton, *The Hidden Lives of Tudor Women*, loc 1762

260. Ibid.

261. McIntosh, *Working Women in English Society 1300–1620*, p. 135

262. Mortimer, *The Time Traveller's Guide to Elizabethan England*, loc 1244

263. Leyser, *Medieval Women*, loc 2822

264. Norton, *The Hidden Lives of Tudor Women*, loc 1770
265. McIntosh, *Working Women in English Society 1300–1620*, p. 136
266. Ibid.
267. Harvey, 'The Work and Mentalité of Lower Orders Elizabethan Women', p. 428
268. McIntosh, *Working Women in English Society 1300–1620*, pp. 133, 136
269. Wack, 'Women, Work and Plays in an English Medieval Town', in Frye and Robertson (eds), *Maids and Mistresses, Cousins and Queens*
270. McIntosh, *Working Women in English Society 1300–1620*, p. 159
271. Ibid., p. 41
272. Harvey, 'The Work and Mentalité of Lower Orders Elizabethan Women', p. 423
273. McIntosh, *Working Women in English Society 1300–1620*, pp. 99, 107 and 253
274. Ibid., p. 128
275. William C. Baer, 'Early Retailing: London's Shopping Exchanges 1550–1700', *Business History*, Vol. 49, No. 1, January 2007, pp. 29–51
276. Wall (ed.), *Two Elizabethan Women*, p. 16
277. Baer, 'Early Retailing'
278. McIntosh, *Working Women in English Society 1300–1620*, p. 249
279. Baer, 'Early Retailing'
280. Wack, 'Women, Work and Plays in an English Medieval Town', in Frye and Robertson (eds), *Maids and Mistresses, Cousins and Queens*
281. Jane Humphries and Jacob Weisdorf, 'Wages of Women in England 1260–1850', *Oxford Economic and Social History Working Papers*, 127, March 2014, p. 21
282. Ibid.
283. Mendelson and Crawford, *Women in Early Modern England 1550–1720*, p. 103
284. Harvey, 'The Work and Mentalité of Lower Orders Elizabethan Women', p. 428
285. Humphries and Weisdorf, 'Wages of Women in England 1260–1850', p. 15
286. Robert B. Shoemaker, *Gender in English Society 1650–1850: The Emergence of Separate Spheres?* Longman, 1998, loc 3396
287. Humphries and Weisdorf, 'The Wages of Women in England 1260–1850', *Journal of Economic History*, Cambridge University Press, Vol. 75, Issue 2, June 2015, pp. 405–77
288. Mortimer, *The Time Traveller's Guide to Elizabethan England*, loc 491
289. E.P. Thompson, 'The Moral Economy of the English Crowd in the Eighteenth Century', *Past & Present*, No. 50, February 1971, pp. 76–136
290. Andy Wood, 'Subordination, Solidarity and the Limits of Popular Agency in a Yorkshire Valley, c.1596–1615', *Past and Present*, Vol. 193, No. 1, 2006, pp. 41–72
291. Ibid., loc 4051
292. Christina Bosco Langert, 'Hedgerows and Petticoats: Sartorial Subversion and Anti-Enclosure Protest in Seventeenth-Century England', *Early Theatre*, Vol. 12, No. 1, 2009, pp. 119–35
293. Wood, 'Subordination, Solidarity and the Limits of Popular Agency in a Yorkshire Valley, c.1596–1615'
294. William Page and J. W. Willis-Bund (eds), 'Parishes: Castlemorton', A History of the County of Worcester, Vol. 4, Victoria County History, 1924, British History Online, pp. 49–53
295. Langert, 'Hedgerows and Petticoats'
296. Ibid.
297. Ibid.
298. John Walter and Keith Wrightson, 'Dearth and the Social Order in Early Modern England', *Past and Present*, May 1976, No. 71, pp. 22–42
299. Ibid.
300. Mendelson and Crawford, *Women in Early Modern England 1550–1720*, p. 55
301. Lambarde, *Eirenarcha*, p. 180; M. Dalton, *The Countrey Justice: Containing the Practice of the Justices of the Peace out of their Sessions ...*, London, 1622 edn, p. 205

302. Walter and Wrightson, 'Dearth and the Social Order in Early Modern England'
303. Ibid.
304. Ibid.
305. T. Birch, *The Court and Times of Charles the First*, ed. R.F. Williams, 2 vols, London, 1848, Vol. 1, p. 17
306. Acts of the Privy Council, 1629–30, pp. 24–5
307. Walter and Wrightson, 'Dearth and the Social Order'
308. Capp, *When Gossips Meet*, loc 4053
309. Ibid., loc 4035 and 4042
310. Ibid., loc 4051 and 3758
311. Ibid., loc 3758
312. Ibid., loc 4010, 4069
313. Ibid., loc 3978, 3713, 3938
314. Ibid., loc 4016
315. Ibid., loc 4018
316. Ibid., loc 4065, 3971
317. Ibid., loc 1383
318. Martin Ingram, 'Ridings, Rough Music and the "Reform of Popular Culture" in Early Modern England', *Past & Present*, November 1984, No. 105, pp. 79–113
319. Ibid.
320. Ibid.
321. Capp, *When Gossips Meet*, loc 3621, 3638
322. Ibid., loc 1410, 3648
323. Ibid., loc 3972, 3582
324. Mortimer, *The Time Traveller's Guide to Elizabethan England*, loc 6191
325. Capp, *When Gossips Meet*, loc 234, 235 and 237
326. David Underdown, in Hufton, *The Prospect Before Her*, p. 466
327. Capp, *When Gossips Meet*, loc 3448 and 4093
328. Ibid., loc 3713
329. Patricia-Ann Lee, 'Mistress Stagg's Petitioners: February 1642', *The Historian*, Vol. 60, No. 2, Winter 1968, pp. 241–56
330. Ibid.
331. Ibid.
332. Sarah Read, 'A Women's Revolt', *History Today*, Vol. 65, Issue 8, August 2015
333. Ibid.
334. Capp, *When Gossips Meet*, loc 3725
335. Hufton, *The Prospect Before Her*, p. 418
336. Capp, *When Gossips Meet*, loc 3723
337. Prior (ed.), *Women in English Society, 1500–1800*, p. 167
338. Ibid., p. 160
339. Rebecca Abrams, 'The Jewish Journey: 4,000 Years in 22 Objects', Ashmolean Museum, 2017
340. Janet Todd, *The Secret Life of Aphra Behn*, Rutgers University Press, 2006, Chapter 20
341. Ibid.
342. Capp, *When Gossips Meet*, loc 354, 259, 268, 339, 354
343. Christopher Hill, *The World Turn'd Upside Down*, Penguin, 2020
344. Gowing, *Gender Relations in Early Modern England*, p. 33
345. Mendelson, *The Mental World of Stuart Women*, p. 2
346. Harris, *English Aristocratic Women 1450–1550*, loc 911
347. Ibid., loc 930
348. Mendelson, *The Mental World of Stuart Women*, p. 71
349. Wall (ed.), *Two Elizabethan Women*, p. xxvi
350. David Cressy, 'Childbed Attendants', in David Cressy (ed.), Birth, *Marriage*, and *Death: Ritual, Religion, and the Life-cycle in Tudor and Stuart England*, Oxford University Press, 1997, p. 74
351. Harvey, 'The Work and Mentalité of Lower Orders Elizabethan Women', p. 427
352. Capp, *When Gossips Meet*, loc 225
353. M.P. Tilley, *A Dictionary of Proverbs in England, in the Sixteenth and Seventeenth Centuries*, University of Michigan Press, 1950
354. Mendelson and Crawford, *Women in Early Modern England 1550–1720*, p. 128
355. Capp, *When Gossips Meet*, loc 238
356. Fletcher, *Gender, Sex and Subordination in England 1500–1800*, p. 110
357. Frances E. Dolan, 'Home-Rebels and House-Traitors: Murderous

Wives in Early Modern England', *Yale Journal of Law and the Humanities*, Vol. 4, Issue 1, 1992

358. Hanawalt, *The Wealth of Wives*, loc 1963

359. Ian Mortimer, *The Time Traveller's Guide to Medieval England*, Bodley Head, 2008, loc 4359

360. Norton, *The Hidden Lives of Tudor Women*, loc 3154

361. Shoemaker, *Gender in English Society 1650–1850*, loc 2384

362. Harris, *English Aristocratic Women 1450–1550*, loc 1326 and 2038

363. Capp, *When Gossips Meet*, loc 1489

364. Searle and Stevenson, *Documents of the Marriage Liturgy*, pp. 166 and 235

365. Mendelson in Prior quoted here by Fletcher, p. 191

366. Fletcher, *Gender, Sex and Subordination in England 1500–1800*, p. 176

367. Leyser, *Medieval Women*, loc 3004

368. Harris, *English Aristocratic Women 1450–1550*, loc 153

369. Barbara Todd, 'Widowhood in a Market Town: Abingdon, 1540–1720', Oxford University, 1983, pp. 22–8, in Prior, *Women in English Society 1500–1800*

370. Harris, *English Aristocratic Women 1450–1550*, loc 340

371. Wall (ed.), *Two Elizabethan Women*, p. xiv

372. Prior (ed.), *Women in English Society, 1500–1800*, pp. 34, 40, 35

373. Ibid., p. 40

374. Bennett and Froide, *Singlewomen in the European Past, 1250–1800*, p. 242

375. Ibid., p. 246

376. Ibid., p. 5

377. John Boswell, *Same Sex Unions in Pre-Modern Europe*, Villard Books, 1994, p. 262

378. Christian D. Knudsen, *Naughty Nuns and Promiscuous Monks: Monastic Sexual Misconduct in Late Medieval England*, PhD thesis, University of Toronto, 2012, p. 115

Part 5: 1660–1764 Locked Out and Locked In

1. Richard Harvey, 'English Pre-industrial Ballads on Poverty, 1500–1700', *The Historian*, Vol. 46, No. 4, August 1984, pp. 539–61, p. 557

2. John Lawrence, *The Modern Land Steward*, London, 1801, p. 158; Report from the Select Committee on Commons' Inclosure (1844), p. 583 (v), 185

3. Jay Walljasper, 'Stealing the Common from the Goose', *On the Commons*, 18 January 2013 (online)

4. Ian Mortimer, *The Time Traveller's Guide to Restoration Britain*, Bodley Head, 2017, loc 5223

5. Ibid., loc 745 and 1290

6. Jane Humphries and Jacob Weisdorf, 'The Wages of Women in England 1260–1850', *Journal of Economic History*, Vol. 75, Issue 2, June 2015, pp. 405–77

7. E.A. Wrigley, 'Urban Growth and Agricultural Change: England and the Continent in the Early Modern Period', *Journal of Interdisciplinary History*, Vol. 15, No. 4, Spring 1985, pp. 683–728

8. Judith Flanders, 'Slums', British Library (online), 15 May 2014

9. Mortimer, *The Time Traveller's Guide to Restoration Britain*, loc 1698

10. Ibid., loc 1321, 1400

11. Ibid., loc 1072, 1162

12. E.P. Thompson, *Customs in Common*, New Press, 1993, p. 189

13. E.P. Thompson, 'The Moral Economy of the English Crowd in the Eighteenth Century', *Past and Present*, No. 50, 1971, pp. 76–136

14. 'Lyme Rebels', Lyme Regis Museum display board, Lyme Regis visit August 2021

15. Sara Mendelson and Patricia Crawford, *Women in Early Modern England 1550–1720*, Clarendon Press, 1998, p. 427

16. Ned Palmer, *A Cheesemonger's History of the British Isles*, Profile, 2019, pp. 200, 201

17. Donal Ó Danachair (ed.), *The Newgate Calendar*, Ex-classics Project, Vol. 3, p. 143, 2009

18. Olwen Hufton, *The Prospect Before Her*, Knopf, 1996

19. Bernard Capp, *When Gossips Meet: Women, Family, and Neighbourhood in Early Modern England*, Oxford University Press, 2003, loc 4084

20. Robert B. Shoemaker, *Gender in English Society 1650–1850: The Emergence of Separate Spheres?* Longman, 1998, loc 5073

21. Hufton, *The Prospect Before Her*, p. 467

22. Mortimer, *The Time Traveller's Guide to Restoration Britain*, loc 1510

23. Thomas Laqueur, *Making Sex: Body and Gender from the Greeks to Freud*, Harvard University Press, 1990, loc 2860

24. Ibid., loc 285

25. Ronald Trumbach, 'London's Sapphists', in Julia Epstein and Kristina Straub (eds), *Bodyguards: The Cultural Politics of Gender Ambiguity*, Routledge, 1991, p. 112

26. Laqueur, *Making Sex*, loc 178

27. Chris Nyland, 'John Locke and the Social Position of Women', *History of Political Economy*, Vol. 25, 1993, pp. 39–63

28. Anthony Fletcher, *Gender, Sex and Subordination in England 1500–1800*, Yale University Press, 1995, p. 289

29. Ilza Veith, *Hysteria: The History of a Disease*, University of Chicago, 1965, p. 23

30. Marlene LeGates, 'The Cult of Womanhood in Eighteenth-Century Thought', *Eighteenth-Century Studies*, Vol. 10, No. 1, Autumn, 1976, p. 35

31. Mendelson and Crawford, *Women in Early Modern England 1550–1720*, p. 64

32. Richard Allestree, *The Ladies Calling*, 1673, loc 752

33. Mendelson and Crawford, *Women in Early Modern England 1550–1720*, p. 420

34. LeGates, 'The Cult of Womanhood in Eighteenth-Century Thought', p. 39

35. Fletcher, *Gender, Sex and Subordination in England, 1500–1800*, p. 384

36. Allestree, *The Ladies Calling*, loc 278

37. Ibid., loc 1186

38. Ibid., loc 2407

39. Ibid., loc 2470

40. Mendelson and Crawford, *Women in Early Modern England 1550–1720*, p. 418

41. Maureen Bell, 'Elizabeth Calvert', in *Oxford Dictionary of National Biography*, 2004

42. Shoemaker, *Gender in English Society 1650–1850*, loc 5047

43. Mendelson and Crawford, *Women in Early Modern England 1550–1720*, p. 427

44. Capp, *When Gossips Meet*, loc 3758

45. Martin Haile, *Queen Mary of Modena: Her Life and Letters*, J.M. Dent, 1905, p. 139

46. Elizabeth Gaunt, *Mrs Elizabeth Gaunt's Last speech who was burnt at London, Oct. 23. 1685. as it was written by her own hand, & delivered to Capt. Richardson keeper of Newgate*, London, 1685

47. Charles Spencer, *Killers of the King: The Men Who Dared to Execute Charles I*, Bloomsbury, 2014, pp. 300–1

48. Capp, *When Gossips Meet*, loc 4078

49. Ibid., loc 4084

50. John Locke, 1689, in Nyland, 'John Locke and the Social Position of Women', p. 8

51. Laura Gowing, *Gender Relations in Early Modern England*, Routledge, 2012, p. 26

52. *Reports of the Society for bettering the condition and increasing the comforts of the poor* (1798–1808), Vol. 5, p. 84, in Hufton, *The Prospect Before Her*, p. 157

53. Hufton, *The Prospect Before Her*, p. 159

54. Gowing, *Gender Relations in Early Modern England*, pp. 49 and 42

55. Margaret Hunt, 'English Lesbians in the Long Eighteenth Century,' in Judith M. Bennett and Amy M. Froide, *Singlewomen in the European Past, 1250–1800*, University of Pennsylvania Press, 1990, p. 280

56. Amy Louise Erickson, 'Clockmakers, Milliners and Mistresses: Women Trading in the City of London Companies 1700–1750', Letters before the Law conference held at the Clark Library, UCLA, 3–4 October 2008

57. Ibid.

58. Bennett and Froide, *Singlewomen in the European Past, 1250–1800*, p. 250

59. Ibid., p. 251

60. Lisa Picard, *Restoration London: Everyday life in the 1660s*, Weidenfeld and Nicolson, 1997, loc 3576

61. Zara Anishanslin, *Portrait of a Woman in Silk: Hidden Histories of the British Atlantic World*, Yale University Press, 2016, p. 154

62. Ibid., p. 155

63. Ibid., p. 115

64. Ibid., p. 79

65. Mortimer, *The Time Traveller's Guide to Restoration Britain*, loc 3236

66. Ibid., loc 3049

67. Picard, *Restoration London*, loc 530

68. Ibid.

69. Mortimer, *The Time Traveller's Guide to Restoration Britain*, loc 3428

70. William C. Baer, 'Early Retailing, London's Shopping Exchanges, 1550–1700', *Business History*, 2007, Vol. 49, No. 1, p. 32

71. Ibid., p. 34

72. Mortimer, *The Time Traveller's Guide to Restoration Britain*, loc 6585

73. Mark Bridge, 'Prize Fighting Women of Victorian Britain …' *History First*, 12 Jan 2023

74. Mortimer, *The Time Traveller's Guide to Restoration Britain*, loc 7091

75. Betty Rizzo, *Companions Without Vows: Relationships Among Eighteenth-Century British Women*, University of Georgia, 1994, p. 26

76. Anishanslin, *Portrait of a Woman in Silk*, p. 32

77. Gowing, *Gender Relations in Early Modern England*, p. 54

78. Hufton, *The Prospect Before Her*, p. 242

79. Ibid., p. 241

80. W. Henry, 'Hester Hammerton and Women Sextons in Eighteenth- and Nineteenth-Century England', *Gender & History*, Vol. 31, No. 2, July 2019, pp. 404–21

81. Mendelson and Crawford, *Women in Early Modern England 1550–1720*, p. 57

82. National Archive, RG 6/1168D: Quarterly Meeting of London and Middlesex: Burial notes (1785–1794) in Anna Ruth Cusack, *The Marginal Dead of London c.1600–1800*, Thesis, Birkbeck Institutional Research Online, p. 198

83. Mendelson and Crawford, *Women in Early Modern England 1550–1720*, p. 57

84. Ibid.

85. Gowing, *Gender Relations in Early Modern England*, p. 71

86. Mendelson and Crawford, *Women in Early Modern England 1550–1720*, p. 58

87. Gowing, *Gender Relations in Early Modern England*, p. 72

88. Shoemaker, *Gender in English Society 1650–1850*, loc 4959

89. Fletcher, *Gender, Sex and Subordination in England 1500–1800*, p. 367

90. Picard, *Restoration London*, loc 3942

91. Mortimer, *The Time Traveller's Guide to Restoration Britain*, loc 2695

92. Fletcher, *Gender, Sex and Subordination in England 1500–1800*, pp. 365, 367

93. Picard, *Restoration London*, loc 3585

94. Laqueur, *Making Sex*, loc 3695

95. Susie Steinbach, *Women in England 1760–1914: A Social History*, Phoenix Press, 2003, loc 993

96. Rizzo, *Companions Without Vows*, p. 16

97. Amy Erickson, 'Identifying Women's Occupations in Early Modern

London', *History of Population and Social Structure*, University of Cambridge, 1999

98. Mortimer, *The Time Traveller's Guide to Restoration Britain*, loc 1702

99. Ian Mortimer, *The Dying and the Doctors: The Medical Revolution in Seventeenth-Century England*, Boydell Press, 2009, p. 206

100. Max Adams, *Unquiet Women*, Head of Zeus, 2018, loc 3394

101. Ibid.

102. Mortimer, *The Dying and the Doctors*, p. 19

103. Ibid., p. 125

104. Mortimer, *The Time Traveller's Guide to Restoration Britain*, loc 2048

105. David S. Katz, *Philo-Semitism and the Readmission of the Jews to England, 1603–1655*, Clarendon Press, 1982, p. 3

106. Cecil Roth, *The History of the Marranos*, Jewish Publication Society of America, 1932, p. 270

107. N.I. Matar, 'Islam in Interregnum and Restoration England', *The Seventeenth Century*, Vol. 6, Issue 1, 1991, pp. 57–71, p. 64

108. Mortimer, *The Time Traveller's Guide to Restoration Britain*, loc 3236

109. Samuel Pepys, *The Diary of Samuel Pepys*, George Bell & Sons, 1896

110. Helen Smith, '"Print[ing] Your Royal Father Off": Early Modern Female Stationers and the Gendering of the British Book Trades', Vol. 15, 2003, pp. 163–86

111. Hufton, *The Prospect Before Her*, p. 244

112. Bennett and Froide, *Singlewomen in the European Past, 1250–1800*, p. 251

113. Peter Fryer, *Staying Power: The History of Black People in Britain*, Pluto Press, 1984, p. 75

114. Peter Rushton and Gwenda Morgan, *Banishment in the Early Atlantic World: Convicts, Rebels and Slaves*, Bloomsbury, 2013, p. 12

115. Anishanslin, *Portrait of a Woman in Silk*, p. 127

116. Ibid., p. 158

117. Ibid., pp. 155 and 158

118. Mary Prior (ed.), *Women in English Society, 1500–1800*, Routledge, 2016, p. 66

119. Ibid., p. 69

120. Ibid., p. 85

121. Mary Wollstonecraft, *A Vindication of the Rights of Women*, ch 9, 1792

122. Capp, *When Gossips Meet*, loc 342

123. Mortimer, *The Time Traveller's Guide to Restoration Britain*, loc 2103 and 6502

124. Shoemaker, *Gender in English Society 1650–1850*, loc 1674

125. Fletcher, *Gender, Sex and Subordination in England 1500–1800*, p. 343

126. Shoemaker, *Gender in English Society 1650–1850*, loc 1468

127. Fletcher, *Gender, Sex and Subordination in England 1500–1800*, p. 339

128. Laqueur, *Making Sex*, loc 4452

129. Fletcher, *Gender, Sex and Subordination in England 1500–1800*, p. 343

130. Fryer, *Staying Power*, p. 46

131. Dermot Feenan, *The Omitted Page*, 26 September 2021 (online)

132. Fryer, *Staying Power*, p. 59

133. Ibid., p. 228

134. LMA, MJ/SBB 472, p. 41, in Patricia Crawford and Laura Gowing, *Women's Worlds in Seventeenth-Century England: A Sourcebook*, Routledge, 2000, p. 76

135. *Daily Journal*, 8 August 1728, from Runaway Slaves in Britain: Bondage, Freedom and Race in the Eighteenth Century, University of Glasgow (online)

136. *Daily Advertiser*, 29 February 1748, from Runaway Slaves in Britain: Bondage, Freedom and Race in the Eighteenth Century, University of Glasgow (online)

137. Fryer, *Staying Power*, p. 72

138. Ibid., p. 69

139. Robin L. Gordon, *Searching for the Soror Mystica, The Lives and Science of Women Alchemists*, University Press of America, 2013, p. 11

140. 'The Humble Salutation and Faithful Greeting of the Widow Whitrowe to King William', 1690, Special Collections, Birkbeck
141. Prior (ed.), *Women in English Society, 1500–1800*, p. 168
142. Matar, 'Islam in Interregnum and Restoration England'
143. Prior, (ed.), *Women in English Society, 1500–1800*, p. 169
144. Gordon, *Searching for the Soror Mystica*, pp. 127–83
145. Ibid.
146. Hufton, *The Prospect Before Her*, p. 440
147. Prior (ed.), *Women in English Society, 1500–1800*, p. 137
148. Ibid., p. 142
149. Ibid., p. 150
150. Ibid., pp. 146 and 149
151. Warren Chernaik, 'Katherine Philips', *Oxford Dictionary of National Biography*, 2004
152. Ibid.
153. Rizzo, *Companions Without Vows*, p. 5
154. Picard, *Restoration London*, loc 3950
155. Joan Kelly quoted in Shoemaker, *Gender in English Society 1650–1850*, loc 939
156. Shoemaker, *Gender in English Society 1650–1850*, loc 974
157. Hufton, *The Prospect Before Her*, p. 446
158. Ibid., p. 432
159. Ibid., p. 447
160. Shoemaker, *Gender in English Society 1650–1850*, loc 6124
161. Prior (ed.), *Women in English Society, 1500–1800*, p. 172
162. Ibid.
163. Hufton, *The Prospect Before Her*, p. 438
164. Ibid., p. 443
165. Shoemaker, *Gender in English Society 1650–1850*, loc 997
166. Emma Donoghue, *Passions Between Women*, Bello, 2014, p. 137
167. Hufton, *The Prospect Before Her*, p. 443
168. Peter Radford, 'Women as Athletes in Early Modern Britain', *Early Modern Women*, Vol. 10, No. 2, Spring 2016
169. Ibid.
170. Ibid.
171. Christopher Thrasher, 'Disappearance: How Shifting Gendered Boundaries Motivated the Removal of Eighteenth Century Boxing Champion Elizabeth Wilkinson from Historical Memory', *Past Imperfect*, Vol. 18, 2012
172. Radford, 'Women as Athletes in Early Modern Britain'
173. Sarah Murden, '18th Century Female Bruisers', All Things Georgian (online), 21 June 2016
174. From César de Saussure, *A Foreign View of England in the Reigns of George I and George II*, 1902, pp. 277–82, in Radford, 'Women as Athletes in Early Modern Britain'
175. Thrasher, 'Disappearance'
176. Peter Radford, Letter to Editor, *The Times*, 30 July 2021
177. P. Seddon, *Football Talk: The Language & Folklore of the World's Greatest Game*, Robson, 2004, p. 156
178. Janet Todd, *Women's Friendship in Literature*, Columbia University Press, 1980, p. 306
179. LeGates, 'The Cult of Womanhood in Eighteenth-Century Thought', p. 39
180. Ibid., p. 38
181. Ibid.
182. Mendelson and Crawford, *Women in Early Modern England 1550–1720*, p. 68
183. Maxine Berg and Helen Clifford, *Consumers and Luxury: Consumer Culture in Europe 1650–1850*, Manchester University Press, 1999, p. 218
184. Philippa Gregory, *The Popular Fiction of the Eighteenth-Century Commercial Circulating Libraries*, unpublished Phd thesis, Edinburgh, 1984
185. Shoemaker, *Gender in English Society 1650–1850*, loc 2056
186. Marilyn Yalom, *A History of the Wife*, HarperCollins, 2001, p. 111
187. Esther Webber, 'Gretna Green: The Bit of Scotland Where English People

Go to Get Married', BBC News, 19 August 2014

188. Shoemaker, *Gender in English Society 1650–1850*, loc 2126

189. Fletcher, *Gender, Sex and Subordination in England 1500–1800*, pp. 395–6

190. Picard, *Restoration London*, loc 2139

191. Hufton, *The Prospect Before Her*, p. 182

192. Henry Fielding, *The Female Husband*, 1746, p. 51

193. Fletcher, *Gender, Sex and Subordination in England 1500–1800*, p. 394

194. Ibid.

195. Ibid., p. 392

196. Gowing, *Gender Relations in Early Modern England*, p. 52

197. Shoemaker, *Gender in English Society 1650–1850*, loc 2817

198. Ibid., loc 2826

199. Mortimer, *The Time Traveller's Guide to Restoration Britain*, loc 2054 and 2059

200. Hufton, *The Prospect Before Her*, p. 286

201. Mendelson and Crawford, *Women in Early Modern England 1550–1720*, p. 43

202. Shoemaker, *Gender in English Society 1650–1850*, loc 2316 and 2321

203. *Gentleman's Magazine*, 1731, cited in Judy Egerton, 'Mary Edwards', *Oxford Dictionary of National Biography*, 2004

204. Egerton, 'Mary Edwards'

205. Shoemaker, *Gender in English Society 1650–1850*, loc 2334, 2341

206. Mortimer, *The Time Traveller's Guide to Restoration Britain*, loc 2117

207. Harriette Andreadis, 'The Erotics of Female Friendship in Early Modern England', in Susan Frye and Karen Robertson (eds), *Maids and Mistresses, Cousins and Queens: Women's Alliances in Early Modern England*, Oxford University Press, 1999

208. Mendelson and Crawford, *Women in Early Modern England 1550–1720*, p. 235

209. Ibid., p. 242

210. Donoghue, *Passions Between Women*, Bello, 2014. pp. 112, 129

211. Molly McClain, 'Love, Friendship, and Power: Queen Mary II's Letters to Frances Apsley', *Journal of British Studies*, Vol. 47, No. 3, 2008, pp. 505–27

212. Gowing, *Gender Relations in Early Modern England*, p. 21

213. Mendelson and Crawford, *Women in Early Modern England 1550–1720*, p. 246

214. Donoghue, *Passions Between Women*, p. 132

215. Ibid., p. 140

216. Mendelson and Crawford, *Women in Early Modern England 1550–1720*, p. 245

217. Donoghue, *Passions Between Women*, p. 134

218. Ibid., p. 135

219. Todd, *Women's Friendship in Literature*, p. 386

220. Mendelson and Crawford, *Women in Early Modern England 1550–1720*, p. 246

221. Donoghue, *Passions Between Women*, p. 174

222. 'James and Mary Kendall', Westminster Abbey (online)

223. Anishanslin, *Portrait of a Woman in Silk*, p. 67

224. Donoghue, *Passions Between Women*, p. 150

225. Todd, *Women's Friendship in Literature*, p. 364

226. Donoghue, *Passions Between Women*, pp. 4–5

227. Ibid., pp. 291, 162

228. Mendelson and Crawford, *Women in Early Modern England 1550–1720*, p. 247

229. Margaret Hunt, 'English Lesbians in the Long Eighteenth Century,' in Bennett and Froide, *Singlewomen in the European Past, 1250–1800*, p. 282

230. Todd, *Women's Friendship in Literature*, p. 321

231. Fielding, *The Female Husband*, p. 51

232. Patricia Crawford and Sara Mendelson, 'Sexual Identities in Early Modern England: The Marriage of

Two Women in 1680', in *Gender and History*, Vol. 7, No. 3, November 1995, Blackwell, p. 360

233. 'Love in the Royal Court: Arabella Hunt', LGBT+ Royal Histories, Historic Royal Palaces (online)

234. Sara Cunningham deposition quoted in Mendelson and Crawford, 'Sexual Identities in Early Modern England', p. 372

235. Mendelson and Crawford, *Women in Early Modern England 1550–1720*, p. 248

236. Amy Poulter deposition quoted in Mendelson and Crawford, 'Sexual Identities in Early Modern England', p. 373

237. Ibid., p. 367

238. Gowing, *Gender Relations in Early Modern England*, p. 20

239. Ó Danachair (ed.), *The Newgate Calendar*, Vol. 2, p. 100

240. Donoghue, *Passions Between Women*, p. 72

241. Ibid., p. 74

242. Ibid.

243. Ibid., p. 72

244. Ibid., p. 78

245. Ibid., pp. 75–6

246. Fielding, *The Female Husband*, p. 32

247. Ó Danachair (ed.), *The Newgate Calendar*, Vol. 3, p. 35

248. Donoghue, *Passions Between Women*, p. 99

249. Mihoko Suzuki, 'The Case of Mary Carleton: Representing the Female Subject, 1663–73', *Tulsa Studies in Women's Literature*, Vol. 12, No. 1, Spring 1993, pp. 61–83

250. Janet Todd, 'Carleton (née Moders), Mary (nicknamed the German Princess)', *Online Dictionary of National Biography*, 2004

251. Donoghue, *Passions Between Women*, pp. 108, 111, 112

252. Steve Murdoch, 'John Brown: A Black Female Soldier in the Royal African Company', *World History Connected*, Vol. 2, 2004

253. 'The Gentleman's Journal: Or the Monthly Miscellany' [ed. Pierre Antoine Motteux], April 1692,

London, pp. 22–3, quoted in Crawford and Gowing, *Women's Worlds in Seventeenth-Century England*

254. Ibid.

255. Trumbach, 'London's Sapphists', p. 123

256. Donoghue, *Passions Between Women*, pp. 100–8

257. Captain Charles Johnson, *A General History of the Pyrates*, T. Warner, 1724

258. 'Joan Phillips, Highwaywoman', West Bridgford & District Local History Society (online)

259. Shoemaker, *Gender in English Society 1650–1850*, loc 808 and 812

260. Trumbach, 'London's Sapphists', p. 124

261. Fletcher, *Gender, Sex and Subordination in England 1500–1800*, p. 335

262. Ann Rosalind Jones and Peter Stallybrass, 'Fetishizing Gender: Constructing the Hermaphrodite in Renaissance Europe', in Epstein and Straub (eds), *Bodyguards*, p. 101

263. Trumbach, 'London's Sapphists', p. 117

264. Edward Ward, 'Of the Mollies Club', *Satyrical Reflections on Clubs*, Vol. V, J. Phillips, 1710, cited Rictor Norton (ed.), Rictor Norton (online)

265. Fletcher, *Gender, Sex and Subordination in England 1500–1800*, p. 321

266. Susan S. Lanser, 'The Rise of the British Nation and the Production of the Old Maid,' in Bennett and Froide, *Singlewomen in the European Past, 1250–1800*, p. 298

267. Gowing, *Gender Relations in Early Modern England*, p. 50

268. Thomas Newton's 1576 *The Touchstone of Complexions*, cited David Wilson, 'Oat, Sow One's Wild Oats, Feel One's Oats', Word Origins (online), 18 November 2022

269. Lanser, 'The Rise of the British Nation and the Production of the Old Maid', p. 297

270. Donoghue, *Passions Between Women*, p. 136

271. Picard, *Restoration London*, loc 3662
272. Yalom, *A History of the Wife*, p. 114
273. Bennett and Froide, *Singlewomen in the European Past, 1250–1800*, p. 24
274. Rizzo, *Companions Without Vows*, pp. 306, 310
275. Lanser, 'The Rise of the British Nation and the Production of the Old Maid', pp. 310, 314
276. Mortimer, *The Time Traveller's Guide to Restoration Britain*, loc 6137
277. Cusack, *The Marginal Dead of London, c.1600–1800*
278. Ó Danachair (ed.), *The Newgate Calendar*, Vol. 2, p. 239
279. Ibid., p. 239, p. 343
280. Dolan, 'Home-Rebels and House-Traitors'
281. Ó Danachair (ed.), *The Newgate Calendar*, 'Madam Churchill' (online)
282. Ó Danachair (ed.), *The Newgate Calendar* (online)
283. Beattie quoted by Shoemaker, *Gender in English Society 1650–1850*, loc 6435
284. Old Bailey Proceedings Online, 'Trial of Alice Gray, 23 April 1707', v. 7, ref. 17070423-26
285. Ó Danachair (ed.), *The Newgate Calendar*, supplement 3, p. 117.
286. Ibid., Vol. 2, p. 384
287. Ibid., supplement 3, p. 15
288. Mortimer, *The Time Traveller's Guide to Restoration Britain*, loc 6481
289. Picard, *Restoration London*, loc 4976
290. Ibid.
291. Mortimer, *The Time Traveller's Guide to Restoration Britain*, p. 456
292. Elizabeth Gaunt, *Mrs Elizabeth Gaunt's Last speech who was burnt at London, Oct. 23. 1685. as it was written by her own hand, & delivered to Capt. Richardson keeper of Newgate*, London, 1685
293. Mortimer, *The Time Traveller's Guide to Restoration Britain*, loc 1469
294. Ibid., loc 2214, 1436
295. Shoemaker, *Gender in English Society 1650–1850*, loc 6373
296. Jonathan Barry, *Witchcraft and Demonology in South-West England, 1640–1789*, Palgrave Macmillan, 2012, pp. 61–2
297. William E. Burns, *Witch Hunts in Europe and America: An Encyclopedia*, Greenwood Publishing Group, 2003, p. 75
298. Owen Davies, 'Jane Wenham (d. 1730)', *Oxford Dictionary of National Biography*
299. Malcolm Gaskill, 'Witchcraft Trials in England' in Brian P. Levack, *The Oxford Handbook of Witchcraft in Early Modern Europe and Colonial America*, Oxford University Press, 2013, p. 298
300. W. Carnochan, 'Witch-Hunting and Belief in 1751: The Case of Thomas Colley and Ruth Osborne', *Journal of Social History*, Vol. 4, Issue 4, 1971, pp. 389–403
301. William Blackstone, *Commentaries on the Laws of England*, Vol. 1, 1765, pp. 442–5
302. Hufton, *The Prospect Before Her*, p. 291
303. Shoemaker, *Gender in English Society 1650–1850*, loc 2279
304. Ibid., loc 5108 and 2286
305. Ibid., loc 6389
306. Dolan, 'Home-Rebels and House-Traitors'
307. Old Bailey Proceedings Online, 'Trial of Mary Henderson, John Wheeler, Margaret Pendergrass, 1 May 1728', ref. 17280501
308. Rebecca Frances King, 'Rape in England 1600–1800: Trials, Narratives and the Question of Consent', Durham theses, 1998, Durham University
309. Wayne R. LaFave, 'Rape: Overview, Act and Mental State', *Substantive Criminal Law*, 2000, pp. 752–6
310. King, 'Rape in England 1600–1800'
311. Nazife Bashar, published by the London Feminist History Group in 1983, cited in King, 'Rape in England 1600–1800'
312. King, 'Rape in England 1600–1800'
313. Linda E. Merians, 'The London Lock Hospital and the Lock Asylum for Women', in Linda E. Merians (ed.)

The Secret Malady: Venereal Disease in Eighteenth-Century Britain and France, Vol. 128, University Press of Kentucky, 1996, pp. 128–45

314. Mortimer, *The Time Traveller's Guide to Restoration Britain*, loc 5724

315. Ibid., loc 5887

316. Hufton, *The Prospect Before Her*, p. 185

317. J. Loudon, 'Deaths in Childbed from the Eighteenth Century to 1935', *Medical History*, Vol. 30, January 1986, pp. 1–41

318. Mortimer, *The Time Traveller's Guide to Restoration Britain*, loc 5515

319. Ó Danachair (ed.), *The Newgate Calendar*, Vol. 2, p. 295

320. Gowing, *Gender Relations in Early Modern England*, p. 25

321. Fletcher, *Gender, Sex and Subordination in England 1500–1800*, p. 393

322. Ibid.

323. David Pearce, 'Charles Meigs, 1792–1869', General Anaesthesia (online)

324. Hufton, *The Prospect Before Her*, pp. 197–201

Part 6: 1765–1857 Making a Lady

1. 'Lives Remembered: Enslaved People in the 1700s and 1800s', Historic England (online)

2. Stephen Usherwood, 'The Abolitionists' Debt to Lord Mansfield', *History Today*, Vol. 31, 3 March 1981

3. *Daily Courant*, 26 June 1711, from Runaway Slaves in Britain: Bondage, Freedom and Race in the Eighteenth Century, University of Glasgow (online)

4. Sylvester Douglas, *Reports of Cases Argued and Determined in the Court of King's Bench: In the Nineteenth, Twentieth and Twenty-first Years of the Reign of George III, 1778–1785*, Reed and Hunter, 1831, p. 301

5. 'Monk, of the Order of St Francis', *Nocturnal Revels, or the History of King's Place and other Modern Nunneries, comparing their mysteries, devotions and sacrifices*, Vol. II, Goadby, 1779, pp. 75–6

6. Catherine Arnold, *The Sexual History of London*, St Martin's, 2012, Chapter 6

7. Sarah Salih (ed.), *The History of Mary Prince: A West Indian Slave*, first published 1830, Penguin, 2000, p. 5

8. Ibid., p. 28

9. Usherwood, 'The Abolitionists' Debt to Lord Mansfield'

10. Ibid.

11. Peter Fryer, *Staying Power: The History of Black People in Britain*, Pluto Press, 1984, p. 229

12. Roberto C. Ferrari, 'Fanny Eaton', *Oxford Dictionary of National Biography*, 2020

13. Adin Ballou, *Christian Non-Resistance, in All Its Important Bearings, Illustrated and Defended*, J. Miller M'Kim, 1846, p. 119

14. H. Young, H. 'Negotiating Female Property – and Slave-Ownership in the Aristocratic World', *Historical Journal*, Vol. 63, No. 3, 2020, pp. 581–602

15. Mary Seacole, *Wonderful Adventures of Mrs. Seacole in Many Lands*, 1857, p. 79

16. Ibid.

17. Seacole, *Wonderful Adventures of Mrs. Seacole in Many Lands*, pp. 20–1

18. Donal Ó Danachair (ed.), *The Newgate Calendar*, Ex-classics Project, Vol. 4, p. 85, 2009

19. Ibid., p. 53

20. Ibid., Vol. 5, p. 348

21. Ibid., Vol. 6, p. 123

22. *Daily Advertiser*, 17 June 1743, Runaway Slaves in Britain: Bondage, Freedom and Race in the Eighteenth Century, University of Glasgow (online)

23. *Gazetteer and New Daily Advertiser*, 25 March 1765, Runaway Slaves in Britain: Bondage, Freedom and Race in the Eighteenth Century, University of Glasgow (online)

24. Marian Smith Holmes, 'The Great Escape from Slavery', *Smithsonian Magazine*, 16 June 2010

25. Ellen Craft, quoted in Clare Midgley, 'Anti-Slavery and Feminism in

Nineteenth-Century Britain' in *Gender & History*, Vol. 5, No. 3, Autumn 1993, pp. 343–62

26. Midgley, 'Anti-Slavery and Feminism in Nineteenth-Century Britain'

27. Sondra A. O'Neale, 'Phillis Wheatley', Poetry Foundation (online)

28. Debra Michals, 'Phillis Wheatley', US National Women's History Museum, 2015 (online)

29. O'Neale, 'Phillis Wheatley'

30. Fryer, *Staying Power*, p. 60

31. Ibid., p. 95

32. Lawrence, W. Read, 'The Heroines of the British Abolition,' Foundation for Economic Education, 7 August 2019

33. Midgley, 'Anti-Slavery and Feminism in Nineteenth-Century Britain'

34. Anne K. Mellor, 'Sex, Violence, and Slavery: Blake and Wollstonecraft', *Huntington Library Quarterly*, Vol. 58, No. 3/4, 1995, pp. 345–70

35. Erika Rackley and Rosemary Auchmuty, *Women's Legal Landmarks: Celebrating the History of Women and Law in the UK and Ireland*, Bloomsbury, 2018, loc 1601

36. Midgley, 'Anti-Slavery and Feminism in Nineteenth-Century Britain'

37. Robert B. Shoemaker, *Gender in English Society 1650–1850: The Emergence of Separate Spheres?* Longman, 1998, loc 5332

38. A Vindication of Female Anti-Slavery Associations, in Shoemaker, *Gender in English Society 1650–1850*, loc 5393

39. Midgley, 'Anti-Slavery and Feminism in Nineteenth-Century Britain'

40. Ibid.

41. Sarah Ellis, quoted in Thomas Laqueur, *Making Sex: Body and Gender from the Greeks to Freud*, Harvard University Press, 1990, loc 3925

42. Midgley, 'Anti-Slavery and Feminism in Nineteenth-Century Britain'

43. Ryan Hanley, 'Slavery and the Birth of Working-Class Racism in England, 1814–1833: The Alexander Prize Essay', *Transactions of the Royal*

Historical Society, Vol. 26, December 2016, pp. 103–23

44. Robert Harborough Sherard, *The White Slaves of England*, Bowden, 1898, p. 239

45. Fryer, *Staying Power*, p. 210

46. Ibid., p. 209

47. Ibid., p. 71

48. Ibid.

49. Ibid., p. 235

50. Anna Clarke, 'The New Poor Law and the Breadwinner Wage: Contrasting assumptionsAssumptions', *Journal of Social History*, Vol. 34, No. 2, Winter 2000, pp. 261–81

51. W.R. Greg, 'Why Are Women Redundant?', N. Trübner & Co, 1869, pp. 33–4

52. Olwen Hufton, *The Prospect Before Her*, Knopf, 1996, p. 60

53. 'breadwinner', *Online Etymology Dictionary*

54. Joyce Burnette, 'An Investigation of the Female–Male Pay Gap during the Industrial Revolution in Britain', *Economic History Review*, Vol. 50, No. 2, 1997, pp. 257–81

55. Imraan Coovadia, 'A Brief History of Pin-Making', *Politikon South African Journal of Political Studies*, April 2008

56. Ibid.

57. Ibid.

58. 'Address of the Female Political Union of Newcastle', *Northern Star*, 2 February 1839

59. Sheila Rowbotham, *A Century of Women: The History of Women in Britain and the United States*, Viking, 1997, p. 19

60. H. Hartmann, 'Capitalism, Patriarchy, and Job Segregation by Sex', *Signs*, Vol. 1, No. 3, 1976, pp. 137–69, p. 157

61. Sara Mendelson and Patricia Crawford, *Women in Early Modern England 1550–1720*, Clarendon Press, 1998, p. 58

62. Shoemaker, *Gender in English Society 1650–1850*, loc 4317

63. Ibid., loc 3787

64. Grace di Meo, quoted in Mark Bridge, 'Prizefighting Women of

Victorian Britain ...' *History First* (online), 12 January 2023

65. Dorothy George quoted in Shoemaker, *Gender in English Society 1650–1850*, loc 3861

66. Shoemaker, *Gender in English Society 1650–1850*, loc 3644

67. Susie Steinbach, *Women in England 1760–1914: A Social History*, Phoenix Press, 2003, loc 674

68. Shoemaker, *Gender in English Society 1650–1850*, loc 3655

69. Ibid., loc 3644

70. Steinbach, *Women in England 1760–1914*, loc 695

71. Shoemaker, *Gender in English Society 1650–1850*, loc 5453, 5463

72. Ibid., loc 3537 and loc 3713

73. *Women's Trade Union Review*, cited 'Campaigning for a Minimum Wage', The Women Chainmakers' (online)

74. Shoemaker, *Gender in English Society 1650–1850*, loc 3613

75. Henry Mayhew and Christopher Hibbert, *London Characters and Crooks*, Folio Society, 1996, p. 215

76. National Archive, RG 6/1168D: Quarterly Meeting of London and Middlesex: Burial notes (1785–1794) in Anna Ruth Cusack, *The Marginal Dead of London c.1600–1800*. Thesis, Birkbeck Institutional Research Online, p. 198

77. W. Henry, 'Hester Hammerton and Women Sextons in Eighteenth- and Nineteenth-Century England', *Gender & History*, Vol. 31, No. 2, July 2019, pp. 404–21

78. Jon Stobart, The Shopping Streets of Provincial England, 1650–1840, Manchester Metropolitan University, 23 April 2014

79. Simon Rottenberg, 'Legislated Early Shop Closing in Britain', *Journal of Law and Economics*, Vol. 4, October 1981, pp. 118–30

80. Shoemaker, *Gender in English Society 1650–1850*, loc 4268 and 4285

81. Henry Mayhew, quoted in The Flower Girls of 1851, Spitalfields Life (online), 11 October 2010

82. Mayhew and Hibbert, *London Characters and Crooks*, p. 195

83. Shoemaker, *Gender in English Society 1650–1850*, p. 188

84. Ibid., loc 3767

85. Steinbach, *Women in England 1760–1914*, loc 373

86. Shoemaker, *Gender in English Society 1650–1850*, loc 3471

87. The Society of Artists of Great Britain 1760–1791, The Free Society of Artists 1761–1783, *A Complete Dictionary of Contributors and Their Work from the Foundation of the Societies to 1791*, by Algernon Graves, London, 1907, p. 60

88. Lyme Regis Museum, visit August 2021

89. Shoemaker, *Gender in English Society 1650–1850*, p. 187

90. Steinbach, *Women in England 1760–1914*, loc 515

91. Shoemaker, *Gender in English Society 1650–1850*, loc 3822

92. Hufton, *The Prospect Before Her*, pp. 80–1

93. Burnette, 'An Investigation of the Female–Male Pay Gap during the Industrial Revolution in Britain'

94. Steinbach, *Women in England 1760–1914*, loc 1130

95. Davidoff, 'The Rationalization of Housework', in *Dependence and Exploitation in Work and Marriage*, eds Diana Leonard Barker and Sheila Allen, Longman, 1976, p. 132

96. Shoemaker, *Gender in English Society 1650–1850*, loc 4182 and 4197

97. Joanna Major, 'Hannah Norsa, 18th Century Actress: The Intricacies of Relationships Within Her Circle', *Georgian Theatre and Music, Women's History*, 10 February 2014

98. Davidoff, 'The Rationalization of Housework', p. 127; Steinbach, *Women in England 1760–1914*, loc 1000

99. 'Was Pin Money Really for Pins?', *Grammarphobia*, 1 March 2019

100. William Hoke, 'How Women Wove Tax and Suffrage Together', *Tax Notes International*, 14 May 2018

101. Shoemaker, *Gender in English Society 1650–1850*, loc 3917
102. Ibid., loc 4782
103. Steinbach, *Women in England 1760–1914*, loc 3240
104. Ibid., loc 3278
105. Ibid., loc 3292
106. Shoemaker, *Gender in English Society 1650–1850*, loc 4725
107. Fletcher, *Gender, Sex and Subordination in England 1500–1800*, Yale University Press, 1995, p. 373
108. Geoffrey Chamberlain, 'British Maternal Mortality in the 19th and Early 20th Centuries', *Journal of the Royal Society of Medicine*, Vol. 99, No. 11, November 2006, pp. 559–63
109. Thomas Right, 'Working Men's Homes and Wives', *The Great Unwashed*, 1868, quoted in Alison Twells, *British Women's History: A Documentary History from the Enlightenment to World War One*, Bloomsbury, 2007, p. 29
110. Christine Hallett, 'The Attempt to Understand Puerperal Fever in the Eighteenth and Early Nineteenth Centuries: The Influence of Inflammation Theory', *Medical History*, Vol. 49, Issue 1, January 2005, pp. 1–28
111. Chamberlain, 'British Maternal Mortality in the 19th and Early 20th centuries'
112. Druin Burch, 'When Childbirth Was Natural, and Deadly', Live Science, 10 January 2009 (online)
113. Arthur Ashpitel, *Observations on Baths and Wash-Houses*, John Weale, 1852, pp. 2–14
114. Fletcher, *Gender, Sex and Subordination in England 1500–1800*, p. 393
115. Sara Heller Mendelson, *The Mental World of Stuart Women: Three Studies*, Harvester Press, 1987, p. 192
116. Steinbach, *Women in England 1760–1914*, loc 2338
117. Marilyn Yalom, *A History of the Wife*, HarperCollins, 2001, p. 182
118. Shoemaker, *Gender in English Society 1650–1850*, loc 268
119. Ibid., loc 1438
120. Helena Whitbread, *The Secret Diaries of Miss Anne Lister*, Whitbread, 1990, loc 4557
121. Rachel P. Maines, *The Technology of Orgasm: 'Hysteria', the Vibrator and Women's Sexual Satisfaction*, Johns Hopkins Studies in the History of Technology, 1999, loc 548
122. Barbara Ehrenreich and Deirdre English, *For Her Own Good: Two Centuries of the Experts' Advice to Women*, Random House, 2005, loc 2626
123. Conduct book in Shoemaker, *Gender in English Society 1650–1850*, loc 1617
124. 'lovemaking', *Online Etymology Dictionary*
125. Shoemaker, *Gender in English Society 1650–1850*, loc 265
126. Steinbach, *Women in England 1760–1914*, loc 2296, 2308
127. Ibid., loc 993
128. Midgley, 'Anti-Slavery and Feminism in Nineteenth-Century Britain'
129. Shoemaker, *Gender in English Society 1650–1850*, loc 5081
130. 'Am I Not a Woman & a Sister?', Encyclopedia Virginia (online)
131. Mellor, 'Sex, Violence, and Slavery: Blake and Wollstonecraft'
132. Ibid.
133. Steinbach, *Women in England 1760–1914*, loc 3099
134. Sarah Ellis, *Daughters of England*, 1845, quoted in Emma Donoghue, *The Sealed Letter*, Picador, 2011, p. 216
135. Rizzo, *Companions Without Vows*, p. 23
136. Shoemaker, *Gender in English Society 1650–1850*, loc 5150
137. Ibid., loc 5305
138. Midgley, 'Anti-Slavery and Feminism in Nineteenth-Century Britain'
139. 'Orator Hunt and the First Suffrage Petition 1832', UK Parliament (online)
140. Rackley and Auchmuty, *Women's Legal Landmarks*, loc 2395
141. Diggory Bailey, 'Breaking Down Gender Stereotypes in Legal Writing',

Civil Service Blog, GovUK (online), 10 January 2020

142. Janet Smith, 'First Woman Prospective Parliamentary Candidate, Helen Taylor, 1885', in Rackley and Auchmuty, *Women's Legal Landmarks*, loc 2408

143. Lucy Williams and Sandra Waklate, 'Policy Responses to Domestic Violence: The Criminalisation Thesis and "Learning from History"', *Howard Journal*, Vol. 59, No. 3, September 2020, pp. 305–316

144. Henry Fitzroy speaking in Aggravated Assaults Bill, Commons Sitting of 10 March 1853, Series 3, Vol. 124, Hansard Debates, cc 1414

145. Shoemaker, *Gender in English Society 1650–1850*, loc 776

146. Ibid., loc 5270

147. Steinbach, *Women in England 1760–1914*, loc 1284

148. Joanna Bourke, *Rape: A History from 1860 to the Present*, Virago, 2007, loc 2406

149. Shoemaker, *Gender in English Society 1650–1850*, loc 5251–2

150. Adrian Randall, *Riotous Assemblies: Popular Protest in Hanoverian England*, Oxford University Press, 2006, p. 1

151. E.P. Thompson, *Customs in Common*, New Press, 1993, p. 224

152. Randall, *Riotous Assemblies*, p. 100

153. W. Freeman Galpin, *The Grain Supply of England During the Napoleonic Period*, Macmillan, 1925

154. C.R. Fay, 'Corn Prices and the Corn Laws, 1815–1846', *Economic Journal*, Vol. 31, No. 121, March 1921, pp. 17–27

155. Randall, *Riotous Assemblies*, p. 101

156. Derek Benson, 'The Tewkesbury Bread Riot of 1795', *THS Bulletin*, 22 (2013), Tewkesbury History (online)

157. Randall, *Riotous Assemblies*, p. 212

158. Benson, 'The Tewkesbury Bread Riot of 1795'

159. Randall, *Riotous Assemblies*, pp. 224, 232

160. Benson, 'The Tewkesbury Bread Riot of 1795'

161. Randall, *Riotous Assemblies*, p. 215

162. Thompson, *Customs in Common*, p. 192

163. Ibid.

164. Randall, *Riotous Assemblies*, p. 217

165. Thompson, *Customs in Common*, p. 193

166. *Gentleman's Magazine*, 29 September 1795, Vol. 65, Part 2, p. 824

167. Benson, 'The Tewkesbury Bread Riot of 1795'

168. Randall, *Riotous Assemblies*, p. 319

169. Thompson, *Customs in Common*, p. 234

170. Ibid., p. 235

171. Randall, *Riotous Assemblies*, p. 241

172. Shoemaker, *Gender in English Society 1650–1850*, loc 5081

173. Genesis 24, Bible Gateway (online)

174. Shoemaker, *Gender in English Society 1650–1850*, loc 5123

175. Thompson, *Customs in Common*, p. 234

176. Randall, *Riotous Assemblies*, p. 313

177. Shoemaker, *Gender in English Society 1650–1850*, loc 5043

178. Fryer, *Staying Power*, p. 96

179. The Susan Burney Letters Project, Letter 2, 'The Gordon Riots, St Martin's Lane, 8 June 1780', Nottingham University (online)

180. Ibid.

181. George F.E. Rudé, 'The Gordon Riots: A Study of the Rioters and Their Victims: The Alexander Prize Essay', *Transactions of the Royal Historical Society*, Vol. 6, 1956, pp. 93–114

182. The Susan Burney Letters Project, Letter 2, 'The Gordon Riots, St Martin's Lane, 8 June 1780'

183. Shoemaker, *Gender in English Society 1650–1850*, loc 5443, 5218

184. Jo Stanley, 'Luddite Women', Women's History Network, 30 April 2012, Women's History Network (online)

185. Ibid.

186. Bamford in Shoemaker, *Gender in English Society 1650–1850*, loc 5493

187. Emma Speed, '"A Deep-Rooted Abhorrence of Tyranny …": Women

at Peterloo', Red Flag Walks (online), 15 August 2018

188. Ibid.

189. Ibid.

190. Ibid.

191. Robert Poole, 'Peterloo Massacre: How Women's Bravery Helped Change British Politics Forever', The Conversation, 15 August 2019 (online)

192. Speed, '"A Deep-Rooted Abhorrence of Tyranny …"'

193. Bamford, Chapter 34, in Shoemaker, Gender in English Society 1650–1850

194. Poole, 'Peterloo Massacre'

195. Ibid.

196. Richard Carlile quoted in Speed, '"A Deep-Rooted Abhorrence of Tyranny …"'

197. Shoemaker, Gender in English Society 1650–1850, loc 5502

198. Poole, 'Peterloo Massacre'

199. Bamford in Speed, '"A Deep-Rooted Abhorrence of Tyranny …"'

200. Speed, '"A Deep-Rooted Abhorrence of Tyranny …"'

201. Ibid.

202. Shoemaker, Gender in English Society 1650–1850, loc 5515

203. Ibid., loc 5510

204. Shoemaker, Gender in English Society 1650–1850, loc 5562

205. Ibid., loc 819

206. Ibid., loc 5575

207. 'Address of the Female Political Union of Newcastle', Northern Star, 2 February 1839

208. Shoemaker, Gender in English Society 1650–1850, loc 5535

209. David Pickering, Dictionary of Witchcraft, Cassell, 1996

210. 'The Swimming of Witches', Foxearth and District Local History Society (online)

211. Ó Danachair (ed.), The Newgate Calendar, Vol. 5, p. 183

212. Ibid.

213. John Beattie in Shoemaker, Gender in English Society 1650–1850, loc 6349

214. 'Charlotte Walker, c.1754–1806', London Lives 1690 to 1800 (online)

215. Ó Danachair (ed.), The Newgate Calendar, Vol. 4, p. 139

216. Bourke, Rape, loc 1137

217. Bridge, 'Prizefighting women of Victorian Britain …'

218. 'History of Abortion Law in the UK', Abortion Rights (online)

219. Patrick Wilson, Murderess: A Study of the Women Executed in Britain since 1843, Joseph, 1971, pp. 150–3

220. Shoemaker, Gender in English Society 1650–1850, loc 1668, 1701

221. 'Progress of a Woman of Pleasure: Prostitutes in 18th Century London', Jane Austen's World, 24 March 2012 (online)

222. Henry Mayhew, London Labour and London Poor, 1862, p. 476

223. Martha Vicinus, Suffer and Be Still, Methuen, 1980, p. 81

224. Hufton, The Prospect Before Her, p. 312

225. Henry Mayhew, 'Letter XI', Morning Chronicle, 23 November 1849, Victorian London (online)

226. Hallie Rubenhold, Harris's List of Covent Garden Ladies, London, 2005, p. 145

227. Ibid., p. 107

228. Ibid., p. 57

229. Shoemaker, Gender in English Society 1650–1850, loc 1479, 1701

230. J.J. Tobias, Nineteenth-Century Crime: Prevention and Punishment, David & Charles, 1972, p. 62

231. Ó Danachair (ed.), The Newgate Calendar, supplement 2, p. 362

232. Ibid.

233. Rachel Knowles, 'The Magdalen House in Regency London', 6 July 2017, Regency History (online)

234. Ibid.

235. S. Toulalan, '"Is He a Licentious Lewd Sort of a Person?" Constructing the Child Rapist in Early Modern England', Journal of the History of Sexuality, Vol. 23, No. 1, January 2014, pp. 21–52

236. Anthony Simpson, 'Popular Perceptions of Rape as a Capital Crime: The Press and the Trial of Francis Charteris in the Old Bailey',

Law and History Review, Vol. 22, 2004, pp. 27–70

237. Toulalan, '"Is He a Licentious Lewd Sort of a Person?"'

238. J.M. Beattie, *Crime and the Courts in England 1660–1800*, Oxford University Press, 1986, p. 126

239. Ibid., p. 130.

240. A. Clark, *Women's Silence, Men's Violence: Sexual Assault in England 1770–1845*, Pandora, 1987, p. 58

241. G. Walker, 'Rereading Rape and Sexual Violence in Early Modern England', *Gender & History*, Vol. 10, No. 1, 1998, pp. 5–7

242. J. Kermode and G. Walker, 'Introduction', in J. Kermode and G. Walker (eds), *Women, Crime and the Courts in Early Modern England*, University of North Carolina Press, 1994, p. 14

243. Bourke, *Rape*, loc 7738

244. Peter Radford, 'Was the Long Eighteenth Century a Golden Age for Women in Sport?: The Cases of Mme Bunel and Alicia Thornton', *Early Modern Women*, Vol. 12, No. 1, Fall 2017, pp. 183–94

245. Peter Radford, 'Glimpses of Women Athletes in 18th-century England', Folger Shakespeare Library, 11 February 2022

246. P.E.B. Porter in *Around and About Saltash*, 1905, cited S. Baring-Gould, *Cornish Characters and Strange Events*, Bodley Head, 1925, Vol. 2, pp. 289–95

247. Ellis in Shoemaker, *Gender in English Society 1650–1850*, loc 2697

248. Rizzo, *Companions Without Vows*, p. 14

249. Shoemaker, *Gender in English Society 1650–1850*, loc 895, 715

250. Anna Clarke, in ibid., loc 5950

251. Linda, M. Austin, 'Ruskin and the Ideal Woman,' *South Central Review*, Vol. 4, No. 4, Winter, 1987, pp. 28–39

252. Mayhew in Shoemaker, *Gender in English Society 1650–1850*, loc 245 and 533

253. Shoemaker, *Gender in English Society 1650–1850*, p. 120

254. Melanie Renee Ulrich, *Victoria's Feminist Legacy, How Nineteenth-Century Women Imagined the Queen*, unpublished PhD thesis, University of Texas, 2005, p. 42

255. Katherine Margaret Atkinson, *Abduction: The Story of Ellen Turner*, Blenkins Press, 2002, p. 78

256. Shoemaker, *Gender in English Society 1650–1850*, loc 2355

257. Ibid., loc 819

258. Samuel Bamford, 'To Jemima', Poem Hunter (online)

259. Yalom, *A History of the Wife*, pp. 177–8

260. Steinbach, *Women in England 1760–1914*, loc 224

261. Orlando Patterson, *Slavery and Social Death: A Comparative Study*, Harvard University Press, 1990, loc 1356

262. John A. Eisenberg, *The Limits of Reason: Indeterminacy in Law, Education and Morality*, Transaction Publishers, 1992, p. 115

263. Ibid.

264. Ibid.

265. Quoted in Marlene LeGates, 'The Cult of Womanhood in Eighteenth-Century Thought', *Eighteenth-Century Studies*, Vol. 10, No. 1, Autumn 1976, pp. 21–39

266. Yalom, *A History of the Wife*, p. 182

267. Rebecca Jennings, *A Lesbian History of Britain: Love and Sex Between Women Since 1500*, Greenworld Publishing, 2007, p. 51

268. Rizzo, *Companions Without Vows*, p. 6

269. Lawrence Stone, 'Judicial Separation', *Road to Divorce: England 1530–1987*, Oxford, 1990, pp. 183–230

270. For Lord Grosvenor: Stella Tillyard, *A Royal Affair: George III, Random House*, 2010, pp. 169–75; and for Lord Cloncurry: Colin Gibson, *Dissolving Wedlock*, Routledge, 1993, p. 34

271. Kathrin Levitan, 'Redundancy, the "Surplus Woman" Problem, and the British Census, 1851–1861', *Women's History Review*, Vol. 17, No. 3, July

2008, pp. 359–76

272. Eisenberg, *The Limits of Reason*, p. 115

273. Greg, 'Why Are Women Redundant?'

274. Ibid.

275. Ronald Trumbach, 'London's Sapphists', in Julia Epstein and Kristina Straub (eds), *Bodyguards: The Cultural Politics of Gender Ambiguity*, Routledge, 1991, p. 131

276. Ibid., p. 121

277. Ibid.

278. Emma Donoghue, *Passions Between Women*, Bello, 2015, p. 300

279. Helena Whitbread (ed.), *The Secret Diaries of Miss Anne Lister*, Whitbread, 1990, loc 4599 and 4651

280. Ibid., loc 3656

281. Trumbach, 'London's Sapphists', p. 113

282. Ibid., p. 132

283. Donoghue, *Passions Between Women*, p. 163

284. Jennings, *A Lesbian History of Britain*, p. 43

285. Trumbach, 'London's Sapphists', p. 114

286. Lillian Faderman, *Surpassing the Love of Men*, Women's Press, 1985, p. 164

287. Edmund Burke to Eleanor Charlotte Butler and Sarah Ponsonby, Beconsfield, 30 July 1790, Rictor Norton (online)

288. Donoghue, *Passions Between Women*, p. 176

289. Danuta Kean, 'Jane Austen's Lesbianism Is as Fictional as Pride and Prejudice', *Guardian*, 31 May 2017

290. 'LGBTQ+ History', English Heritage (online)

291. Kristina Straub in Epstein and Straub (eds), *Bodyguards*, p. 147

292. Tammy M. Proctor, *Female Intelligence: Women and Espionage in the First World War*, New York University Press, 2003, p. 16

293. Ó Danachair (ed.), *The Newgate Calendar*, Vol. 5, p. 55

294. *The Female Sailor*, undated broadsheet, reproduced in Margaret S. Creighton and Lisa Norling, *Iron Men, Wooden Women: Gender and Seafaring in the Atlantic World, 1700–1920*, JHU Press, 1996, p. 36

295. Grace di Meo, quoted in Bridge, 'Prizefighting Women of Victorian Britain …'

296. Trumbach, 'London's Sapphists', p. 123

297. Rackley and Auchmuty, *Women's Legal Landmarks*, loc 1405

298. Trumbach, 'London's Sapphists', p. 117

299. Donoghue, *Passions Between Women*, p. 69

300. Ibid.

301. Sharon Marcus, *Between Women: Friendship, Desire and Marriage in Victorian England*, Princeton University Press, 2007, loc 4192

302. Rizzo, *Companions Without Vows*, p. 208

303. Donoghue, *Passions Between Women*, p. 78

304. Betty Bennett, *Mary Diana Dods: A Gentleman and a Scholar*, Hopkins University Press, 1995

305. 'Sarah Geals, 18 September 1865', Proceedings of the Old Bailey Online

306. Ibid.

307. Ibid.

308. Gary Kates, 'Gender and Power in 1777', in Epstein and Straub (eds), *Bodyguards*, p. 186

309. L.R. McRobbie, 'The Incredible Chevalier d'Eon, Who Left France as a Male Spy and Returned as a Christian Woman', Atlas Obscura, 29 July 2016

310. Ibid.

311. Jeanne Campan, *Memoirs of the Court of Marie Antoinette, Queen of France*, Floating Press, 2009

312. 'Mrs Bateman', London Remembers (online)

Part 7: 1857–1928 Separate Spheres

1. Erika Rackley and Rosemary Auchmuty, *Women's Legal Landmarks: Celebrating the History of Women and Law in the UK and Ireland*, Bloomsbury, 2018, loc 1875

2. Bodichon in Rackley and Auchmuty, *Women's Legal Landmarks*, loc 1822

3. Ibid., loc 1824
4. 'Cochrane', *The Jurist: Reports of Cases*, S. Sweet, 1840, p. 534
5. Marilyn Yalom, *A History of the Wife*, HarperCollins, 2001, p. 271
6. From Caroline Norton's Submission to parliamentary debate on Matrimonial Causes Act, 1857, in *Yalom, A History of the Wife*, pp. 186–7
7. Yalom, *A History of the Wife*, p. 186
8. Rackley and Auchmuty, *Women's Legal Landmarks*, loc 1993
9. 'Agricultural Labourers' Wages 1850–1914', History of Wages (online)
10. Lacey in Rackley and Auchmuty, *Women's Legal Landmarks*, loc 1986
11. H. Young, 'Negotiating Female Property – and Slave-Ownership in the Aristocratic World', *Historical Journal*, Vol. 63, No. 3, 2020, pp. 581–602
12. Lacey in Rackley and Auchmuty, *Women's Legal Landmarks*, loc 2077
13. G. Frost, 'A Shock to Marriage?: The Clitheroe Case and the Victorians', in G. Robb and N. Erber (eds), *Disorder in the Court*, Palgrave Macmillan, 1999
14. Rackley and Auchmuty, *Women's Legal Landmarks*, loc 3005
15. Ibid., loc 3030
16. Yalom, *A History of the Wife*, p. 270
17. Ibid., p. 271
18. 'The Lanchester Case', *British Medical Journal*, 2 November 1895, 2: 1127
19. 'Edith Lanchester: A Socialist Pioneer Against Patriarchy', Workers Liberty (online), 5 September 2021
20. Rackley and Auchmuty, *Women's Legal Landmarks*, loc 5161, 5266
21. Joanna Bourke, *Rape: A History from 1860 to the Present*, Virago, 2007, loc 6239
22. Kate Woodward, The Story of the Cooperative Women's Guild, Co-operative Heritage Trust (online), 28 May 2020
23. Michael Faraday, *The Times*, 7 July 1855
24. Barbara Ehrenreich and Deirdre English, *Complaints and Disorders: The Sexual Politics of Sickness*, Feminist Press, 2011, loc 920
25. From *Sermon XXXIV. on Matt. XXV. 36.*, published in *The Arminian Magazine* [...]. *Consisting chiefly of Extracts and Original Treatises on Universal Redemption*, Printed by J. Paramore, October 1786
26. Ehrenreich and English, *Complaints and Disorders*, loc 920
27. Susie Steinbach, *Women in England 1760–1914: A Social History*, Phoenix Press, 2003, loc 2000s
28. Quoted in Bourke, *Rape*, loc 2419 and 2427
29. Steinbach, *Women in England 1760–1914*, loc 1409, 1224
30. Deborah Thom, *Nice Girls and Rude Girls: Women Workers in World War One*, Tauris, 2000, p. 107
31. William Acton, *Prostitution, Considered in Its Moral, Social, and Sanitary Aspects*, 1857
32. A woman registered as a prostitute, quoted in Anna Faherty, 'The Prostitute Whose Pox Inspired Feminists', *The Outsiders*, Wellcome Collection, Part 6, 20 July 2017
33. An account of a complaint from a poor woman, in Mrs Butler's third letter, from Kent, *The Shield*, 9 March 1870
34. John Frith, 'Syphilis: Its Early history and Treatment until Penicillin and the Debate on Its Origins', *History*, Vol. 20, No. 4
35. A woman registered as a prostitute, quoted in Faherty, 'The Prostitute Whose Pox Inspired Feminists'
36. J.R. Walkowitz, *Prostitution and Victorian Society: Women, Class, and the State*, Cambridge University Press, 1982, p. 49
37. Steinbach, *Women in England 1760–1914*, loc 2750
38. Faherty, 'The Prostitute Whose Pox Inspired Feminists'
39. Ibid.
40. Steinbach, *Women in England 1760–1914*, loc 5586

41. 'Women's Protest', article published by the LNA in the *Daily News*, 1 January 1870

42. Rafia Zakaria, *Against White Feminism*, Hamish Hamilton, 2021, loc 1773

43. Antoinette M. Burton, *Burdens of History: British Feminists, Indian Women, and Imperial Culture, 1865–1915*, University of North Carolina, 1994, p. 146

44. Rackley and Auchmuty, *Women's Legal Landmarks*, loc 2586

45. Faherty, 'The Prostitute Whose Pox Inspired Feminists'

46. Steinbach, *Women in England 1760–1914*, loc 5342

47. Norton, *Letter to the Queen on Chancellor Cranworth's Marriage and Divorce Bill of 1855*

48. Tessa Boase, *Mrs Pankhurst's Purple Feather*, Aurum Press, 2018, p. 237

49. Steinbach, *Women in England 1760–1914*, loc 5651

50. Eliza Lynn Linton, 'Modern English Women', *London Review*, No. 11, 15 December 1860

51. Boase, *Mrs Pankhurst's Purple Feather*, p. 201

52. Ibid., p. 204

53. Melanie Renee Ulrich, *Victoria's Feminist Legacy: How Nineteenth-Century Women Imagined the Queen*, unpublished PhD thesis, University of Texas, 2005, p. 31

54. Boase, *Mrs Pankhurst's Purple Feather*, p. 203

55. Ulrich, *Victoria's Feminist Legacy*, p. 17

56. Steinbach, *Women in England 1760–1914*, loc 1919

57. Ibid., loc 2369

58. Janet Smith, 'First Woman Prospective Parliamentary Candidate, Helen Taylor, 1885', in Rackley and Auchmuty, *Women's Legal Landmarks*, loc 2386

59. Ibid.

60. Steinbach, *Women in England 1760–1914*, loc 5543

61. 'Women's Suffrage Timeline', British Library (online)

62. 'Who Were the Suffragettes?', Museum of London (online)

63. Miss H, quoted in June Purvis (ed.), *Votes for Women*, Routledge, 2002, p. 139

64. June Purvis, 'Cat and Mouse: Force Feeding the Suffragettes', *BBC History Magazine*, June 2009

65. Julia Bush, *Women Against the Vote: Female Anti-Suffragism in Britain*, Oxford University Press, 2007, p. 3

66. Gail Braybon, *Women Workers in the First World War*, Routledge, 2012

67. Lord Cecil, Debate: Clause 1 (The Capacity of Women to Be Members of Parliament), Hansard, 6 November 1918, Vol. 110 cc 2186-202

68. Lorraine Dowler, 'Amazonian Landscapes: Gender, War and Historical Repetition', in Colin Flint (ed.), *The Geography of War and Peace: From Death Camps to Diplomats*, Oxford University Press, 2004, p 144

69. Nancy Astor on her time as a Member of Parliament, Audio Recording, 2 October 1956, British Library

70. Sheila Jeffreys, *The Spinster and Her Enemies*, Spinifex, 1997, p. 89

71. Melanie Reynolds, 'Ann Ellis and the 1875 Weavers Strike', The Dewsbury Partnership (online)

72. H. Hartmann, 'Capitalism, Patriarchy, and Job Segregation by Sex', *Signs*, Vol. 1, No. 3, 1976, pp. 137–69, p. 156

73. Thom, *Nice Girls and Rude Girls*, p. 107

74. 'Mary MacArthur and the Cradley Heath Women Chainmakers', Strike of 1910', National Education Union (online)

75. Ibid.

76. 'Women and Work: 19th and Early 20th Century', Striking Women (online)

77. T. Thorpe, T. Oliver, G. Cunningham, Reports to the Secretary of State for the Home Department on the Use of Phosphorus in the Manufacture of Lucifer Matches, Her Majesty's Stationery Office, 1899

78. Rackley and Auchmuty, *Women's Legal Landmarks*, loc 2797
79. Louise Raw, 'Women and Protest in Nineteenth-Century Britain', British Online Archives
80. Annie Besant, *The Link*, 14 July 1888, TUC History Online
81. Rackley and Auchmuty, *Women's Legal Landmarks*, loc 2824
82. Ibid., loc 2862
83. Hartmann, 'Capitalism, Patriarchy, and Job Segregation by Sex', p. 157
84. Sheila Rowbotham, *A Century of Women: The History of Women in Britain and the United States*, Viking, 1997, p. 25
85. Ibid., p. 81
86. Steve Humphries and Pamela Gordon, *Forbidden Britain: Our Secret Past 1900–1960*, BBC Books, 1994, pp. 162–3
87. Ken Weller, 'Don't Be a Soldier!', *Journeyman*, 1985, p. 32
88. Rowbotham, *A Century of Women*, p. 129
89. 'A Forgotten Women's Solidarity Campaign: The Women's Committee for the Relief of the Miners' Wives and Children, May 1926 to January 1927', 4 November 2019, Red Flag Walks (online)
90. Sue Bruley, *The Women and Men of 1926: A Gender and Social History of the General Strike and Miners' Lockout in South Wales*, Cardiff University Press, 2010, p. 94
91. Ibid., pp. 95–110
92. Rachelle Saltzman, 'Folklore as Politics in Great Britain: Working-Class Critiques of Upper-Class Strike Breakers in the 1926 General Strike', *Anthropological Quarterly*, Vol. 67, No. 3, Part 2, July 1994, pp. 105–21
93. Ibid.
94. Ibid.
95. Labour Women, 1 August 1926, in 'A Forgotten Women's Solidarity Campaign', Red Flag Walks (online)
96. Virginia Woolf, *A Room of One's Own*, 1929, p. 26
97. John Horgan, 'Darwin Was Sexist, and So Are Many Modern Scientists', *Scientific American*, 18 December 2017
98. Barbara Ehrenreich and Deirdre English, *For Her Own Good: Two Centuries of the Experts' Advice to Women*, Random House, 2005, loc 2291
99. Ibid., loc 2267
100. Shoemaker, *Gender in English Society 1650–1850*, loc 2559
101. G. Stanley Hall, in Ehrenreich and English, *For Her Own Good*, loc 2297
102. Quoted in Ehrenreich, *For Her Own Good*, loc 3560
103. W.R. Greg, 'Why Are Women Redundant?', N. Trübner & Co, 1869, p. 32
104. Jo B. Paoletti, *Pink and Blue: Telling the Boys from the Girls in America*, Indiana University Press, 2012
105. Ibid., Chapter 4
106. Ibid.
107. Denise Winterman, 'History's Weirdest Fad Diets', BBC News, 2 January 2013
108. Kristina Killgrove, 'Here's How Corsets Deformed the Skeletons of Victorian Women', *Forbes*, 16 November 2015
109. Ehrenreich and English, *For Her Own Good*, loc 2095 and 2098
110. Ellis quoted in Thomas Laqueur, *Making Sex: Body and Gender from the Greeks to Freud*, Harvard University Press, 1990, loc 4268
111. Ehrenreich and English, *For Her Own Good*, loc 2116
112. Laqueur, *Making Sex*, loc 4401
113. Steinbach, *Women in England 1760–1914*, loc 2234
114. Loewenfeld in Bourke, *Rape*, loc 6108
115. Lesley A. Hall, 'Sexuality', in Ina Zweiniger-Bargielowska (ed.), *Women in Twentieth-Century Britain*, Routledge, 2001, Section 4
116. Bourke, *Rape*, loc 6223
117. E Sheehan, 'Victorian Clitoridectomy: Isaac Baker Brown and His Harmless Operative Procedure', *Medical Anthropology Newsletter*, Vol. 12, 4, August 1981, pp. 9–15
118. Laqueur, *Making Sex*, loc 3354

119. Ehrenreich and English, *For Her Own Good*, loc 2358

120. Jamie Lovely, 'Women's Mental Health in the 19th Century: An Analysis of Sociocultural Factors Contributing to Oppression of Women as Communicated by Influential Female Authors of the Time', PhD thesis, University of Maine, Spring 2019

121. Ehrenreich and English, *For Her Own Good*, loc 1983

122. Sarah Watling, *Noble Savages: The Olivier Sisters*, Jonathan Cape, 2019, loc 884

123. Maria Cohut, 'The Controversy of "Female Hysteria"', *Medical News Today*, 15 October 2020

124. Ehrenreich and English, *For Her Own Good*, loc 2515

125. Watling, *Noble Savages*, loc 3051

126. Michaela Sharf, translated by Nick Somers, 'Hysteria or Neurasthenia', in 'First World War and the End of the Habsburg Monarchy', Virtual Exhibition, The World of the Habsburgs

127. Ehrenreich and English, *Complaints and Disorders*, loc 327

128. J. Loudon, 'Deaths in Childbed from the Eighteenth Century to 1935', *Medical History*, Vol. 30, January 1986, pp. 1–41

129. Ibid.

130. Rackley and Auchmuty, *Women's Legal Landmarks*, loc 3537

131. Rowbotham, *A Century of Women*, p. 137

132. Sheila Rowbotham, *Dreamers of a New Day: Women Who Invented the 20th Century*, Verso, 2010, p. 103

133. Rowbotham, *A Century of Women*, p. 32

134. Loudon, 'Deaths in Childbed from the Eighteenth Century to 1935'

135. Steinbach, *Women in England 1760–1914*, loc 2508, 2582

136. Rowbotham, *A Century of Women*, p. 140

137. Caroline de Costa, 'The King vs Aleck Bourne', *Medical Journal of Australia*, Vol. 191, No. 4, 17 August 2009

138. Rowbotham, *A Century of Women*, p. 141

139. Chloe Wilson, 'Annie Besant: "[A] Stormy, Public, Much Attacked and Slandered Life"', 4 July 2020, East End Women's Museum (online)

140. Steinbach, *Women in England 1760–1914*, loc 3181

141. 'Surplus Women: A Legacy of World War One?' World War 1 Centenary (online)

142. Steinbach, *Women in England 1760–1914*, loc 2785

143. Rackley and Auchmuty, *Women's Legal Landmarks*, loc 5796

144. Jeffreys, 'On the Birth of the Sex Expert'

145. Edward Carpenter quoted in ibid.

146. Esther Newton, 'The Mythic Mannish Lesbian: Radclyffe Hall and the New Woman', *Signs*, Vol. 9, No. 4, The Lesbian Issue, p. 561

147. Philippa Levine, '"So Few Prizes and So Many Blanks": Marriage and Feminism in Later Nineteenth-Century England', *Journal of British Studies*, Vol. 28, No. 2, April 1989, pp. 150–74, p. 152

148. Ibid., p 158

149. Sharon Marcus, *Between Women: Friendship, Desire and Marriage in Victorian England*, Princeton University Press, 2007, loc 246

150. Ibid., loc 4229, 4254, 1173, 1220

151. Ibid., loc 1098

152. Esther Newton, 'The Mythic Mannish Lesbian'

153. Carpenter quoted in Lillian Faderman, *Surpassing the Love of Men*, Women's Press, 1985, p. 178

154. Faderman, *Surpassing the Love of Men*, p. 214

155. Ibid.

156. Marcus, *Between Women*, loc 1607

157. Ibid., loc 766

158. Minnie Benson, quoted in Faderman, *Surpassing the Love of Men*, p. 208

159. Martha Vicinus, 'Lesbian Perversity and Victorian Marriage: The 1864 Codrington Divorce Trial', *Journal of British Studies*, Vol. 36, No. 1, January 1997, pp. 70–98

160. Ibid.
161. Newton, 'The Mythic Mannish Lesbian'
162. Ibid.
163. Ruth F. Claus, 'Confronting Homosexuality: A Letter from Frances Wilder', *Signs*, Vol. 2, No. 4, 1977, pp. 928–33
164. Steinbach, *Women in England 1760–1914*, loc 1035
165. Newton, 'The Mythic Mannish Lesbian'
166. Ibid.
167. Steinbach, *Women in England 1760–1914*, loc 2770
168. Faderman, *Surpassing the Love of Men*, p. 241
169. Claus, 'Confronting Homosexuality', p. 931
170. Ibid., p. 932
171. Trumbach in Shoemaker, *Gender in English Society 1650–1850*, loc 1786
172. Rowbotham, *A Century of Women*, p. 88
173. Rackley and Auchmuty, *Women's Legal Landmarks*, loc 5495
174. P.E. Szoradova, 'LGBTQ+ History: The Red Rose of Colonel Barker', National Archives Blog, 25 February 2019 (online)
175. Shoemaker, *Gender in English Society 1650–1850*, loc 1773
176. 'Twentieth-Century Trans Histories', Historic England (online)
177. Iwan Bloch in Jeffreys, 'On the Birth of the Sex Expert'
178. Bourke, *Rape*, loc 483, 497
179. Rackley and Auchmuty, *Women's Legal Landmarks*, loc 11539
180. Bourke, *Rape*, loc 6082
181. Ibid., loc 6109
182. Ulrich, *Victoria's Feminist Legacy*, p. 28
183. Steinbach, *Women in England 1760–1914*, loc 977
184. British Library Learning, 'The Campaign for Women's Suffrage: An Introduction', British Library (online), 6 February 2018
185. Ulrich, *Victoria's Feminist Legacy*, p. 110
186. Ibid., p. 112
187. Ibid., p. 81
188. King James Bible, Genesis 3:16
189. Lauren Hubbard, 'What Was Queen Victoria Like as a Mother?', *Town and Country*, 23 May 2022
190. Caroline Norton, Letter to the Queen on Chancellor Cranworth's Marriage and Divorce Bill of 1855, quoted in Ulrich, *Victoria's Feminist Legacy*, p. 17
191. Alexander Walker in Patricia A. Vertinsky, *The Eternally Wounded Women: Women, Doctors, and Exercise in the Late Nineteenth Century*, Manchester University Press, 1989, p. 23
192. James Knowles (ed.), *The Nineteenth Century: A Monthly Review*, Vol. 27 January–June 1890, p. 56
193. Janice Formichella, 'The Victorian Croquet Craze: Crazier Than You Think', Recollections (online), 8 August 2010
194. 'Maud Watson, the "First Lady" of Wimbledon', The All England Club, Wimbledon (online)
195. John Stanley, 'Archery History: The Sport That Pioneered Equality for Women's Participation', World Archery, 10 September 2020
196. Kathleen E. McCrone, 'Gender, and English Women's Sport, c. 1890–1914', *Journal of Sport History*, Vol. 18, No. 1, Spring 1991, Special Issue: Sport and Gender, pp. 159–82
197. M. Evans, 'Women's League Hockey and its Early Development', in D. Day (ed.), *Playing Pasts*, MMU Sport and Leisure History, 2020, pp. 120–36
198. Rafaelle Nicholson, 'The History of Women's Cricket: From England's Greens to the World Stage', Bournemouth University, 5 March 2020
199. Louis Macken and M. Boys (eds), 'Our Lady of the Green, Lawrence and Bullen', 1899, in Vertinsky, *The Eternally Wounded Woman*
200. 'Ladies History', Royal North Devon Golf Club (online)
201. Neil Laird, 'Early Women's Golf', Scottish Golf History (online)

202. Jane George, Joyce Kay and Wray Vamplew, 'Women to the Fore: Gender Accommodation and Resistance at the British Golf Club Before 1914', *Sporting Traditions*, Vol. 23, No. 2, pp. 79–98

203. Laird, 'Early Women's Golf'

204. Miriam Bibby, 'Skittles the Pretty Horsebreaker', Historic UK (online)

205. Erica Munkwitz, 'Vixens of Venery: Women, Sport, and Fox-Hunting in Britain, 1860–1914', *Critical Survey*, Vol. 24, No. 1, 'Sporting Victorians', 2012, pp. 74–87

206. 'Hunting Notes', *The Ladies' Field* 32/405 (16 December 1905): 69, in Munkwitz, 'Vixens of Venery'

207. Alison Matthews David, 'Elegant Amazons: Victorian Riding Habits and the Fashionable Horsewoman', *Victorian Literature and Culture*, Vol. 30, No. 1, 2002, pp. 179–210

208. Andrew Ritchie, 'The Origins of Bicycle Racing in England: Technology, Entertainment, Sponsorship and Advertising in the Early History of the Sport', *Journal of Sport History*, Vol. 26, No. 3, 1999, pp. 489–520

209. Vertinsky, *The Eternally Wounded Woman*, pp. 77–9

210. Jeroen Heijman and Bill Mallon, *Historical Dictionary of Cycling*, Scarecrow Press, 2011, p. xix

211. Suzanne Wrack, 'How the FA Banned Women's Football in 1921 and Tried to Justify It', *Guardian*, 13 June 2022

212. David Day, 'Swimming Natationists, Mistresses, and Matrons: Familial Influences on Female Careers in Victorian Britain', *International Journal of the History of Sport*, Vol. 35, No. 6, 2018, pp. 494–510

213. 'Lucy Morton', Swim England Hall of Fame (online)

214. Marina Dmukhovskaya, 'Look to the Past: Madge Syers, the First Woman to Compete at a Figure Skating World Championships', 15 December 2021, Olympic News (online)

215. 'The Women's Amateur Athletic Association the 1920s', Run Young 50 (online)

216. Gwenda Ward, 'The History of Gender Equity in British Track & Field', *FCN*, 26 April 2022

217. Shoemaker, *Gender in English Society 1650–1850*, loc 2517

218. Leonore Davidoff, 'The Rationalization of Housework', in *Dependence and Exploitation in Work and Marriage*, eds Diana Leonard Barker and Sheila Allen, Longman, 1976, p. 139

219. Steinbach, *Women in England 1760–1914*, loc 349

220. Davidoff, 'The Rationalization of Housework'

221. Ibid.

222. Steinbach, *Women in England 1760–1914*, loc 384

223. Ibid., loc 1110

224. K.E. Gales and P.H. Marks, 'Twentieth-Century Trends in the Work of Women in England and Wales', *Journal of the Royal Statistical Society*, Vol. 137, Issue 1, January 1974, pp. 60–74

225. Ana Muñoz, 'Women in First World War Britain: Exploitation, Revolt and Betrayal', 7 March 2014, In Defence of Marxism (online)

226. Claus, 'Confronting Homosexuality', p. 930

227. McCrone, 'Gender, and English Women's Sport, c. 1890–1914'

228. Greg, 'Why Are Women Redundant?', p. 35

229. Patricia Owen, 'Who Would Be Free, Herself Must Strike the Blow', *History of Education*, Vol. 17, No. 1, 1988, pp. 83–99

230. Rackley and Auchmuty, *Women's Legal Landmarks*, loc 428

231. Watling, *Noble Savages*, loc 4256

232. Rowbotham, *A Century of Women*, p. 22

233. Watling, *Noble Savages*, loc 4215

234. Rackley and Auchmuty, *Women's Legal Landmarks*, loc 455

235. Steinbach, *Women in England 1760–1914*, loc 3136

236. Gloria McAdam, 'Willing Women and the Rise of Convents in

Nineteenth-Century England', *Women's History Review*, Vol. 8, Issue 3, 1999, pp. 411–41

237. Steinbach, *Women in England 1760–1914*, loc 3316

238. Sariya Cheruvallil-Contractor, 'The Forgotten Women Who Helped to Build British Islam', The Conversation, 6 March 2020

239. Steinbach, *Women in England 1760–1914*, loc 3304

240. Rackley and Auchmuty, *Women's Legal Landmarks*, p. 1093

241. B. Heeney, 'Women's Struggle for Professional Work and Status in the Church of England, 1900–1930', *Historical Journal*, Vol. 26, No. 2, 1983, pp. 329–47

242. St Paul, 1 Corinthians 14:34–35

243. Heeney, 'Women's Struggle for Professional Work and Status in the Church of England, 1900–1930'

244. Rowbotham, *A Century of Women*, p. 22

245. Jessica E. Kirwan, 'A Brief History of Women Doctors in the British Empire', *Synapis Journal* (online)

246. Rowbotham, *A Century of Women*, p. 22

247. Steinbach, *Women in England 1760–1914*, loc 877

248. Rowbotham, *A Century of Women*, p. 22

249. Ehrenreich and English, *Complaints and Disorders*, loc 511

250. Mark Bridge, 'Prize Fighting Women of Victorian Britain …', *History First*, 12 January 2023

251. 'Women's Magazines' from article 'Publishing', Britannica (online)

252. Ehrenreich and English, *For Her Own Good*, loc 2858 and 2949

253. Rowbotham, *A Century of Women*, p. 136

254. Rebecca Baumgartner, 'How the Industrial Revolution Played Favourites', 3quarksdaily, 27 June 2022

255. 'The Invention of the Vacuum Cleaner, from Horse-Drawn to High Tech', Science Museum (online), 3 April 2020

256. Rowbotham, *A Century of Women*, p. 66

257. Ibid., p. 65

258. Ibid.

259. 'The History of the Corps', FANY (online)

260. Rowbotham, *A Century of Women*, p. 73

261. Tammy M. Proctor, *Female Intelligence: Women and Espionage in the First World War*, New York University Press, 2003, p. 17

262. Ibid., pp. 1, 19, 27

263. 'Flora Sandes', *Oxford Dictionary of National Biography*

264. Rowbotham, *A Century of Women*, p. 76

265. Thom, *Nice Girls and Rude Girls*, p. 34

266. Quoted in Rowbotham, *A Century of Women*, p. 72

267. Proctor, *Female Intelligence*, pp. 29, 32

268. Ibid., p. 29

269. Ibid., pp. 34, 36

270. Ibid., pp. 20–1, 33

271. Ibid., p. 34

272. Thom, *Nice Girls and Rude Girls*, p. 37

273. Ellen Castelow, 'World War One: Women at War', Historic UK, 20 January 2015

274. Thom, *Nice Girls and Rude Girls*, p. 165

275. Ibid., pp. 125, 128

276. L.K. Yates, *A Woman's Part*, quoted in G. Braybon, *Women Workers in the First World War*, Taylor & Francis, 1981, p. 48

277. Muñoz, 'Women in First World War Britain'

278. Williams, quoted in Braybon, *Women Workers in the First World War*, p. 163

279. J. De Vries, 'Women's Voluntary Organizations in World War I', 2005, in Women, War and Society: Additional Resources, Gale (online)

280. Thom, *Nice Girls and Rude Girls*, p. 44

281. Ibid., p. 194

282. Ibid., p. 144

283. Ibid., p. 187

284. Rackley and Auchmuty, *Women's Legal Landmarks*, loc 3550
285. Watling, *Noble Savages*, loc 4872
286. Thom, *Nice Girls and Rude Girls*, p. 191
287. Rowbotham, *A Century of Women*, p. 87
288. Rackley and Auchmuty, *Women's Legal Landmarks*, loc 4297
289. Rose Staveley-Wadham, 'Policing Pioneers: A Look at the History of the Women's Police Service', British Newspaper Archive, 25 February 2021
290. Thom, *Nice Girls and Rude Girls*, pp. 20 and 40
291. Peter Fryer, *Staying Power: The History of Black People in Britain*, Pluto Press, 1984, p. 302
292. Ibid., pp. 303–4
293. *The Times*, June 1919, quoted in ibid., p. 311
294. Lucy Bland, 'White Women and Men of Colour: Miscegenation Fears in Britain After the Great War', *Gender and History*, Vol. 17, No. 1, July 2005, pp. 29–61
295. Gales and Marks, 'Twentieth-Century Trends in the Work of Women in England and Wales'
296. Rosemary Wall, 'Surplus Women: A Legacy of World War One?', World War 1 Centenary, University of Oxford (online)
297. Rackley and Auchmuty, *Women's Legal Landmarks*, loc 3788
298. Ibid., loc 3857, 3794
299. Hilary Heilbron, 'Women at the Bar: An Historical Perspective', *Counsel*, 31 May 2013
300. Rackley and Auchmuty, *Women's Legal Landmarks*, loc 414
301. Ibid., loc 490 and 498
302. Steinbach, *Women in England 1760–1914*, loc 896
303. Ibid., loc 1486
304. Staveley-Wadham, 'Policing Pioneers'
305. Ibid., loc 1414
306. Rowbotham, *A Century of Women*, p. 18
307. Watling, *Noble Savages*, loc 3943–3951

Part 8: 1928–1945 Into the World
1. Sue Bruley, *The Women and Men of 1926: A Gender and Social History of the General Strike and Miners' Lockout in South Wales*, Cardiff University Press, 2010, p. 17
2. Nora Boswell in 'We'd Been Cowed by the Depression; That's Why We Could Fight the War', *Guardian*, 4 March 2017
3. Sheila Rowbotham, *A Century of Women: The History of Women in Britain and the United States*, Viking 1997, p. 140
4. Jean Edmond, 'No Return to the Thirties: An Eyewitness Warning', *Northern Star*, 5 June 2015
5. Marjorie Broad in 'We'd Been Cowed by the Depression ...'
6. Rowbotham, *A Century of Women*, p. 186
7. Edmond, 'No Return to the Thirties'
8. Stuart Maconie, 'The Jarrow March: The Lasting Legacy of the 1936 Protest', *History Extra*, 5 October 2022
9. Ellen Wilkinson, *The Town That Was Murdered*, Victor Gollancz, 1939, pp. 191–2
10. Nora Boswell in 'We'd Been Cowed by the Depression ...'
11. Rowbotham, *A Century of Women*, p. 176
12. Julie Gottlieb, 'Fascism in Inter-war Britain', British Library (online), 2 November 2021
13. Rowbotham, *A Century of Women*, p. 178
14. *The Blackshirt*, 29 June 1934, quoted in Martin Pugh, 'Why Former Suffragettes Flocked to British Fascism', *Slate*, 14 April 2017
15. Christopher Watson, 'House of Commons Trends: How Many Women Candidates Become MPs?', Commons Library (online), 30 October 2020
16. Pugh, 'Why Former Suffragettes Flocked to British Fascism'
17. Quoted in Sheila Rowbotham, *Hidden from History: 300 Years of*

Women's Oppression and the Fight Against It, Pluto Press, 1973, p. 127

18. Lou Kenton, 'Lou Kenton describes the Battle of Cable Street', Sound Recording, British Library
19. Rowbotham, *A Century of Women*, p. 175
20. Suyin Haynes, 'The Enduring Lessons of the Battle of Cable Street, 80 Years On', *Time* magazine, 3 October 2016
21. 'Women at the Battle of Cable Street', East End Women's Museum, 4 October 2016
22. Ibid.
23. Ibid.
24. Ibid.
25. Haynes, 'The Enduring Lessons of the Battle of Cable Street …'
26. Rowbotham, *A Century of Women*, p. 179
27. Bruley, *The Women and Men of 1926*, p. 18
28. Barbara Ehrenreich and Deirdre English, *For Her Own Good: Two Centuries of the Experts' Advice to Women*, Random House, 2005, loc 3580, 3853
29. Bruley, *The Women and Men of 1926*, p. 17
30. Ehrenreich and English, *For Her Own Good*, loc 3387, 3372
31. Rowbotham, *A Century of Women*, p. 181
32. Erika Rackley and Rosemary Auchmuty, *Women's Legal Landmarks: Celebrating the History of Women and Law in the UK and Ireland*, Bloomsbury, 2018, loc 6744, 6752
33. Ibid., loc 6752
34. Rowbotham, *Hidden from History*, p. 147
35. 'History of Abortion Law in the UK', Abortion Rights (online)
36. J. Loudon, 'Deaths in Childbed from the Eighteenth Century to 1935', *Medical History*, Vol. 30, January 1986, pp. 1–41
37. John Keown, *Abortion, Doctors and the Law*, cited Caroline de Costa, 'The King vs Aleck Bourne', *Medical Journal of Australia*, Vol. 191, No. 4, 17 August 2009

38. Costa, 'The King vs Aleck Bourne'
39. Ibid.
40. Rowbotham, *Hidden from History*, p. 156
41. Stella Browne, submission to the 1937 Committee, in Paul Ewans, 'Stella Browne (1880–1955)', Heritage Humanists (online)
42. G. Jones, 'Women and Eugenics in Britain: The Case of Mary Scharlieb, Elizabeth Sloan Chesser, and Stella Browne', *Annals of Science*, Vol. 52, No. 5, September 1995, pp. 481–502
43. Stella Browne, speech to the 1936 founding conference, in Ewans, 'Stella Browne'
44. Loudon, 'Deaths in Childbed from the Eighteenth Century to 1935'
45. Lillian Faderman, *Surpassing the Love of Men*, Women's Press, 1985, p. 311
46. Esther Newton, 'The Mythic Mannish Lesbian: Radclyffe Hall and the New Woman' in Estelle B. Freedman, Barbara C. Gelpi, Susan L. Johnson and Kathleen M. Weston (eds) *The Lesbian Issue: Essays from SIGNS*, University of Chicago Press, 1985, p. 10
47. Brittain quoted in Faderman, *Surpassing the Love of Men*, p. 310
48. Rowbotham, *A Century of Women*, p. 228
49. P. Summerfield, 'Women, War and Social Change: Women in Britain in World War II', in A. Marwick (ed.), *Total War and Social Change*, Macmillan, 1988, pp. 97–103
50. Carol Harris, 'Women Under Fire in World War Two', BBC, 17 February 2011
51. Rowbotham, *A Century of Women*, p. 228
52. Ministry of Defence, 'The Women of the Second World War', GovUK (online), 16 April 2015
53. Harris, 'Women Under Fire in World War Two'
54. Pearl Patricia Rushton, 'Memoirs', Headley Hampshire UK (online), 16 March 1999

55. The Vital Role of Women in the Second World War, Imperial War Museum (online)

56. Harris, 'Women Under Fire in World War Two'

57. The Vital Role of Women in the Second World War, Imperial War Museum (online)

58. Harris, 'Women Under Fire in World War Two'

59. Jackie Hyams, *The Female Few: Spitfire Heroines*, History Press, 2023, Chapter 5

60. 'Women in the Armed Forces', Royal British Legion (online)

61. Gary Bridson-Daley, 'Stella Rutter: Spitfire Draughtswoman and D-Day Secret Keeper', History Press (online)

62. The Vital Role of Women in the Second World War, Imperial War Museum (online)

63. Ministry of Defence, 'The Women of the Second World War'

64. Mary McKee, 'Women and the Second World War', British Newspaper Archive, 4 May 2020

65. 'Spies, Medics, Soldiers, & Peacemakers: 16 Women Wartime Heroes You Should Know', A Mighty Girl (online), 11 November 2022

66. Ben Macintyre, 'A Princess Turned Spy Wins Her Place in History', *The Times*, 4 April 2020

67. Sally and Lucy Jaffe, 'Chinthe Women: Women's Auxilary Service Burma 1942–1946', Tenter Books

68. Ministry of Defence, 'The Women of the Second World War'

69. The Vital Role of Women in the Second World War, Imperial War Museum (online)

70. Peter Fryer, *Staying Power: The History of Black People in Britain*, Pluto Press, 1984, p. 364

71. The Vital Role of Women in the Second World War, Imperial War Museum (online)

72. Harris, 'Women Under Fire in World War Two'

73. 'World War II: 1939–1945', Striking Women (online)

74. Rackley and Auchmuty, *Women's Legal Landmarks*, loc 6199, 6115

75. Harris, 'Women Under Fire in World War Two'

76. 'War Diary of Nella Last', BBC History (online)

77. Kate Law, '*The Politicization of Food: Women and food queues in the Second World War*, by Charlotte Sendall', Women's History Network, 2 April 2019

78. 'The Evacuation of Children during the Second World War', History Press (online)

79. Richard Morris Titmuss, *Problems of Social Policy*, HMSO, 1950, Chapter VII, Appendix II, pp. 543–9

80. G. Braybon and P. Summerfield, *Out of the Cage: Women's Experiences in Two World Wars*, Taylor & Francis, 2013, p. 215

81. Ibid., p. 216

82. Rowbotham, *A Century of Women*, p. 240

83. Ibid.

84. Lucy Bland and Chamion Caballero, '"Brown Babies": The Children Born to Black GI and White British Women during the Second World War', National Archives (online), 4 January 2021

85. S. Lee, 'A Forgotten Legacy of the Second World War: GI Children in Post-war Britain and Germany', *Contemporary European History*, Vol. 20, No. 2, 2011, pp. 157–81

86. Fryer, *Staying Power*, p. 362

87. National Archives, AIR 2/10673, RAF and WRAF – Homosexual Offences and Abnormal Sexual Tendencies 1950–68, 'Lesbianism in the WRAF', loose minutes from A.P. Doran, Squadron Leader, 13 October 1971, in E. Vickers, 'Same-Sex Desire in the British Armed Forces, 1939–1945', Liverpool John Moores University

88. London Metropolitan Archives PH/ GEN/3/19: Fairfield, 'A Special Problem', 1943

89. Vickers, 'Same-Sex Desire in the British Armed Forces, 1939–1945'

90. RAF Museum, AC 72/17 Box 5, memo on lesbianism from DWAAF to DDWAAF, P and MS, 8 October 1941
91. Vickers, 'Same-Sex Desire in the British Armed Forces, 1939–1945'; RAF Museum, AC 72/17 Box 8, letter from DWAAF to D.P.S., re a case of lesbianism, 2 December 1941
92. Harris, 'Women Under Fire in World War Two'
93. 'Twentieth-Century Trans Histories', Historic England (online)
94. Steven Dryden, 'LGBT Rights in the UK', British Library (online)
95. Rowbotham, *A Century of Women*, pp. 230, 235
96. Elena (Lane) Deamant, 'UK Women Opposing Conscription during WW2', *Peace and Justice News*, Summer 2020
97. Mitzi Bales, 'They said "No" to War: British Women Conscientious Objectors in World War II', War Resisters' International, 22 December 2010
98. Deamant, 'UK Women Opposing Conscription during WW2'
99. Rowbotham, *A Century of Women*, p. 228
100. Ibid.
101. Harris, 'Women Under Fire in World War Two'
102. Ibid.
103. 'Post World War II: 1946–1970', Striking Women (online)
104. Windrush: Arrival 1948 Passenger List
105. Hilary Mantel, 'Unhappy Medium': Essays from the London Review of Books, *Guardian*

Part 9: 1945–1994 A Woman Today
1. Ian Robson, 'Four Weddings, Two Funerals and a Death Sentence – The Story of the Widow of Windy Nook', *Evening Chronicle*, 11 November 2017
2. Lizzie Seal, 'Ruth Ellis and the Hanging that Rocked a Nation', *History Extra*, 10 July 2019 (online)
3. Sheila Rowbotham, *A Century of Women: The History of Women in Britain and the United States*, Viking, 1997, p. 420
4. Karen Ingala Smith, Counting Dead Women (online)
5. 'domestic violence', Collins Dictionary (online)
6. 'Men Still Killing One Woman Every Three Days in UK – It Is Time for "Deeds not Words"', Femicide Census (online)
7. Ingala Smith, 'Counting Dead Women'
8. 'Femicide Census Reveals Half of UK Women Killed by Men Die at Hands of Partner or Ex', 20 February 2020, End Violence Against Women (online)
9. 'Emma' quoted in Pritti Mistry, 'Domestic Abuse Protection Orders "Absolutely Pointless" Say Victims', BBC News, 21 September 2022
10. Ibid.
11. Counter Terrorism Policing, 'Project Starlight: Prevalence of Domestic Abuse Related Incidences within Prevent Referrals', 25 November 2021
12. David Sapsted and Thomas Harding, 'Judge Frees Man Who Strangled His "Nagging" Wife', *Daily Telegraph*, 3 February 2001
13. Erika Rackley and Rosemary Auchmuty, *Women's Legal Landmarks: Celebrating the History of Women and Law in the UK and Ireland*, Bloomsbury, 2018, loc 12104
14. 'Sara Thornton', Justice for Women (online)
15. Rackley and Auchmuty, *Women's Legal Landmarks*, loc 12121
16. Ibid., loc 12153
17. Ibid., loc 12209
18. Heather Carrick, 'Peter Sutcliffe: Who Was Yorkshire Ripper, Who Were Victims, and What Unsolved Crimes Have Been Linked to Him?', *National World*, 23 February 2022
19. Joanna Bourke, *Rape: A History from 1860 to the Present*, Virago, 2007, loc 1522, 2709
20. Ibid., loc 949

21. Julie Bindel, 'The Long Fight to Criminalise Rape in Marriage', Al Jazeera, 15 June 2021

22. Jennifer Brown, Miranda Horvath, Liz Kelly, Nicole Westmorland, 'Has Anything Really Changed? Results of a Comparative Study 1977–2010 on Opinions on Rape', Government Equalities Office Report 2010

23. Bindel, 'The Long Fight to Criminalise Rape in Marriage'

24. Ibid.

25. Bourke, *Rape*, loc 984

26. Ministry of Justice Overview of Sexual Offending in England and Wales 2013, GovUK (online)

27. R. Thiara and S. Roy, 'Reclaiming Voice: Minoritised Women and Sexual Violence Key Findings', Imkaan, March 2020

28. Ibid.

29. Sexual Offences Victim Characteristics, England and Wales: Year Ending March 2020, ONS

30. Bourke, *Rape*, loc 8318

31. Dame Vera Baird, 'The Distressing Truth Is That If You Are Raped in Britain Today Your Chances of Seeing Justice Are Slim', Victims Commissioner (online)

32. Bourke, *Rape*, loc 7869

33. Gaelle Brotto, Grant Sinnamon and Wayne Petherick, 'Victimology and Predicting Victims of Personal Violence', Chapter 3, in *The Psychology of Criminal and Antisocial Behaviour*, eds W. Petherick and G. Sinnamon, Elsevier, 2017

34. Bourke, *Rape*, loc 5869

35. D. Lisak and P. Miller, 'Repeat Rape and Multiple Offending Among Undetected Rapists', *Violence and Victims*, Vol. 17, No. 1, 2002, pp. 73–84

36. Bourke, *Rape*, loc 7697, 7841, 7884, 7697

37. Baird, 'The Distressing Truth …'

38. Bourke, *Rape*, loc 956

39. Ibid., loc 7751

40. Rape Crisis Scotland, False Allegations of Rape: Briefing Paper, September 2013

41. Ibid.

42. Andy Myhill and Jonathan Allen, 'Rape and Sexual Assault of Women: The Extent and Nature of the Problem, Findings from the British Crime Survey', Home Office Research Study 237

43. Bourke, *Rape*, loc 6025

44. Ibid., note 36 loc 6306, 6460, 6326

45. Ibid., loc 4219, 4187, 4394, 4436

46. Brotto, Sinnamon and Petherick, 'Victimology and Predicting Victims of Personal Violence'

47. Ministry of Justice, Freedom of Information Act (FOIA) Request – 201123016, 'Sexual assaults in prison by sexual identity of victim', December 2020

48. Ministry of Justice, HM Prison and Probation Service, New Transgender Prisoner Policy Comes into Force, 27 February 2023

49. Richard Wheeler, 'Minister: No Sexual Assaults by Trans Inmates in Women's Prisons since Reforms', *Independent*, 21 February 2023

50. Ministry of Justice, 'Women and the Criminal Justice System 2021', 24 November 2022

51. 'Black and Mixed Ethnicity Women More Than Twice as Likely to Face Arrest', Prison Reform Trust, 31 August 2017

52. Rackley and Auchmuty, *Women's Legal Landmarks*, loc 8013

53. Rowbotham, *A Century of Women*, p. 245

54. 'The Marriage Bar', *Spectator*, 23 August 1946

55. Rackley and Auchmuty, *Women's Legal Landmarks*, p. 526

56. Robin Lloyd, 'Rosalind Franklin and DNA: How Wronged Was She?', *Scientific American*, 3 November 2010

57. Rowbotham, *A Century of Women*, p. 350

58. Ibid.

59. Susie Steinbach, *Women in England 1760–1914: A Social History*, Phoenix Press, 2003, loc 909

60. 'Diane Abbott', Britannica

61. Rowbotham, *A Century of Women*, p. 495

62. Evelyn Kerslake, '"They Have Had to Come Down to the Women for Help!": Numerical Feminization and the Characteristics of Women's Library Employment in England, 1871–1974', *Library History*, Vol. 23, No. 1, 2007, pp. 17–40

63. Rackley and Auchmuty, *Women's Legal Landmarks*, loc 3702

64. Ibid., loc 4402

65. The Baroness Casey Review, Met Police UK, March 2023

66. Rowbotham, *A Century of Women*, p. 413

67. 'The Grunwick Dispute', Striking Women (online)

68. Rowbotham, *A Century of Women*, p. 488

69. Christina quoted in ibid., p. 488

70. Rowbotham, *A Century of Women*, p. 291

71. Emily Hope, Mary Kennedy and Anne de Winter, 'Homeworkers in North London', in *Dependence and Exploitation in Work and Marriage*, eds Diana Leonard Barker and Sheila Allen, Longman, 1976, p. 89

72. National Minimum Wage and National Living Wage: Rates and Overview

73. Rowbotham, *A Century of Women*, p. 558

74. Hope, Kennedy and de Winter, 'Homeworkers in North London', p. 97

75. Rowbotham, *A Century of Women*, p. 406

76. Cordelia Fine, *Delusions of Gender: The Real Science Behind Sex Differences*, Icon Books, 2010, p. 80

77. Rowbotham, *A Century of Women*, p. 501

78. Ibid., p. 473

79. Margaret Thatcher, speech to Finchley Conservatives, 31 January 1976

80. Margaret Thatcher, speech on Women in a Changing World (1st Dame Margery Corbett-Ashby Memorial Lecture), 26 July 1982

81. Rackley and Auchmuty, *Women's Legal Landmarks*, loc 6979

82. Rowbotham, *A Century of Women*, p. 246

83. Ibid., p. 247

84. Ibid., p. 473

85. Saul Mcleod, 'John Bowlby's Attachment Theory', Simply Psychology, 16 June 2023

86. Rowbotham, *A Century of Women*, p. 293

87. David Batty, 'Timeline: A History of Child Protection', *Guardian*, 18 May 2005

88. Rowbotham, *A Century of Women*, p. 421

89. Ibid., pp. 419 and 498

90. 'Unmarried Mothers Whose Babies Were Taken Away and Never Seen Again', ITV News, 26 July 2022

91. 'The Violation of Family Life: Adoption of Children of Unmarried Women 1949–1976', Human Rights (Joint Committee), HC270/HL43, published 15 July 2022, p. 33

92. Rowbotham, *A Century of Women*, p. 421

93. Lovelock quoted in Louise Peterkin, 'Bread Rationing: A Surprising and Timely Subject', HCA Librarian, University of Edinburgh, 27 October 2020

94. Rowbotham, *A Century of Women*, p. 344

95. Ibid., p. 348

96. Ibid., p. 406

97. 'The Grunwick Dispute', Striking Women

98. Rackley and Auchmuty, *Women's Legal Landmarks*, loc 9978, 10038

99. Rowbotham, *A Century of Women*, pp. 484, 485

100. Anwar Ditta obituary, *The Times*, 3 December 2021

101. Anandi Ramamurthy, 'Families Divided: The Campaign for Anwar Ditta and Her Children', Our Migration Story (online)

102. Anwar Ditta obituary, *The Times*, 3 December 2021

103. Rowbotham, *A Century of Women*, p. 302
104. Ibid., p. 484
105. Lizzie Dearden, 'Sarah Everard Vigil organisers Win Legal Challenge Against Metropolitan Police after "Rights Breached"', *Independent*, 11 March 2022
106. The Baroness Casey Review
107. Ibid., p. 573
108. Ibid., p. 407
109. Mary Whitehouse, 24 January 1979, in Ben Thompson, *Ban This Filth: Letters from Mary Whitehouse*, Faber, 2012
110. Rowbotham, *A Century of Women*, pp. 473 and 341
111. Rackley and Auchmuty, *Women's Legal Landmarks*, loc 10979
112. Rowbotham, *A Century of Women*, pp. 507 and 553
113. 'What Became of the Windrush Stowaway, Evelyn Wauchope?', Historycal Roots (online)
114. 'Mona Baptiste', Historycal Roots (online)
115. Jo Stanley, 'Women of Windrush: Britain's Adventurous Arrivals That History Forgot', *New Statesman*, 22 June 2018
116. Rowbotham, *A Century of Women*, p. 228
117. Rackley and Auchmuty, *Women's Legal Landmarks*, loc 7887
118. Ibid., loc 7860
119. Olwen Hufton, *The Prospect Before Her*, Knopf, New York, 1995, p. 183
120. Rowbotham, *A Century of Women*, p. 430
121. Rackley and Auchmuty, *Women's Legal Landmarks*, loc 7610
122. Ibid., loc 7614
123. 'Great British Female Olympians Down the Decades', Team GB (online)
124. Rachael Heyhoe-Flint obituary, *Wisden Almanack*, John Wisden & Co, 2017
125. 'The Story of Women's Football in England', Football Association (online)
126. C. Deere and C. Doss, 'The Gender Asset Gap: What Do We Know and Why Does It Matter?', *Feminist Economics*, Vol. 12, Issues 1–2, 2006, pp. 1–50
127. Rackley and Auchmuty, *Women's Legal Landmarks*, loc 9771
128. Ibid., loc 9858
129. Married Women's Property Act 1964, Women's Legal Landmarks (online)
130. Rackley and Auchmuty, *Women's Legal Landmarks*, loc 11245
131. Lord Nicholas of Birkenhead, White v White, Conjoined Appeals Judgment, House of Lords, Parliament UK (online), 26 October 2000
132. Lillian Faderman, *Surpassing the Love of Men*, Women's Press, 1985, p. 330
133. Ibid., p. 385
134. Quoted in ibid., p. 391
135. Rackley and Auchmuty, *Women's Legal Landmarks*, loc 5773
136. *Guardian*, 25 April 1988, Section 28 LAIC Subject File, in Kelly McGhee, 'The Destruction Caused by Clause 28', Glasgow Women's Library (online)
137. Faderman, *Surpassing the Love of Men*, p. 329
138. Suzannah Weiss, '"Fear of the Clit": A Brief History of Medical Books Erasing Women's Genitalia', *Vice*, 3 May 2017
139. Rowbotham, *A Century of Women*, p. 510
140. Helen Gurley Brown, *Sex and the Single Girl: The Unmarried Woman's Guide to Men*, Bernard Geis, 1962, p. 18
141. 'AIDS in New York: A Biography', *New York Magazine*, 26 May 2006
142. Rachel P. Maines, *The Technology of Orgasm: 'Hysteria,' the Vibrator and Women's Sexual Satisfaction*, Johns Hopkins University Press, 1998, loc 1358, 1362
143. D. Griffiths, 'Diagnosing Sex: Intersex Surgery and "Sex Change" in Britain 1930–1955', *Sexualities*, Vol. 21, Issue 3, 2018
144. Rowbotham, *A Century of Women*, p. 422

145. Judith Shapiro in Julia Epstein and Kristina Straub (eds) *Bodyguards: The Cultural Politics of Gender Ambiguity*, Routledge, 1991, p. 253

146. Ibid.

147. Ibid., p. 255.

148. Veronica Horwell, 'April Ashley Obituary', *Guardian*, 19 January 2022

149. James Michael Nichols, 'Trans Supermodel Shares How Hugh Hefner Fought For Her When No One Else Would', HuffPost, 2 October 2017

150. Anne Fausto Sterling, 'Gender/Sex and the Body', Psychology Podcast, YouTube

151. Philippe Testard-Vaillant, 'How Many Sexes Are There?', CNRS News, 8 January 2016

152. Kate Lyons, 'Gender Identity Clinic Services Under Strain as Referral Rates Soar', *Guardian*, 10 July 2016

153. From 2.5 deaths to 3.6 per 100,000 in 2021, 'Suicides in England and Wales: 2021 Registrations', ONS, in 'ONS Report Shows Alarming Rise in Suicide Rates among Young Women', Mental Health Innovations, 7 September 2022

154. 6·5 per cent in 2000 to 19·7 per cent in 2014, Sally McManus et al., 'Prevalence of Non-Suicidal Self-Harm and Service Contact, 2000–2014', *Lancet Psychiatry*, Vol. 6, pp. 573–81, 4 June 2019

155. Annelies E. van Eeden, Daphne van Hoeken and Hans W. Hoek, 'Incidence, Prevalence and Mortality of Anorexia Nervosa and Bulimia Nervosa', *Current Opinion in Psychiatry*, Vol. 34, No. 6, November 2021, pp. 515–24

156. 'Nearly One in Five Women Screened for Possible Eating Disorder', NHS, 15 December 2020

157. Richard Adams, 'Oxford University Admits More Women Than Men for First Time – Ucas', *Guardian*, 26 January 2018

158. Mary Curnock Cook, 'Foreword' in Nick Hillman and Nicholas Robinson, 'Boys to Men: The Underachievement of Young Men in Higher Education – and How to Start Tackling It', Higher Education Policy Institute Report 84, 2016

159. 'Record Number of Women on FTSE 100 Boards', GovUK (online), 8 March 2018

160. Working Futures 2010–2020, Evidence Report 41, UK Commission for Employment and Skills, August 2012

161. Nicholas Hellen, Rosamund Urwin and Rosa Ellis, 'Men Earning over £150,000 Outnumber Women 5–1', *Sunday Times*, 7 April 2019

162. Kevin Rawlinson, 'FTSE Firms' Excuses for Lack of Women in Boardrooms "Pitiful and Patronising"', *Guardian*, 31 May 2018

163. Ross Raisin, 'Men or Mice: Is Masculinity in Crisis?', *Guardian*, 6 October 2017

164. Ibid.

165. David Reilly, 'Men Think They're Brighter Than They Are and Women Underestimate Their IQ. Why?', The Conversation, 14 March 2022

166. Catechism of the Catholic Church – The sacrament of Holy Orders, The Vatican

167. The Case Against the Ordination of Women to the Priesthood, Being the Report of a Commission Appointed by the Archbishops of Canterbury and York, Church Information Office, December 1966, Chapter 5, in Women Priests (online)

168. Erin Martise, 'What Were the Professions of the Twelve Apostles?', The Classroom (online)

169. The Case Against the Ordination of Women to the Priesthood, Being the Report of a Commission Appointed by the Archbishops of Canterbury and York

170. 'Sex is Irrelevant to This Office', *Church Times*, 3 May 2019

171. Margaret Duggan, Dame Betty Ridley obituary, *Guardian*, 4 August 2005

172. Sophie Goodchild, 'Church Pays Millions to Clergy Who Walked Out Over Women Priests', *Independent*, 10 March 2002

Afterword

1. Virginia Woolf, 'Professions for Women', lecture, January 1931, in *The Death of a Moth*, Harcourt Brace, 1974, p. 238
2. From 2.5 deaths to 3.6 per 100,000 in 2021, 'Suicides in England and Wales: 2021 Registrations', ONS, in 'ONS Report Shows Alarming Rise in Suicide Rates among Young Women', Mental Health Innovations, 7 September 2022
3. 6.5 per cent in 2000 to 19.7 per cent in 2014, Sally McManus et al, 'Prevalence of Non-Suicidal Self-Harm and Service Contact, 2000–2014', *Lancet Psychiatry*, Vol. 6, pp. 573–81, 4 June 2019
4. Annelies E. van Eeden, Daphne van Hoeken and Hans W. Hoek, 'Incidence, Prevalence and Mortality of Anorexia Nervosa and Bulimia Nervosa', *Current Opinion in Psychiatry*, Vol. 34, No. 6, November 2021, pp. 515–24
5. Amelia Gentleman, '"An Explosion": What Is Behind the Rise in Girls Questioning Their Gender Identity?', *Guardian*, 24 November 2022
6. 'Table of Opposites', Britannica (online)
7. Marvin Harris, quoted in Christopher Ryan and Cacilda Jetha, *Sex at Dawn: How We Mate, Why We Stray, and What it Means for Modern Relationships*, Harper, 2010, loc 3661
8. Willem Adriaan Bonger, quoted by Joanna Bourke, *Rape: A History from 1860 to the Present*, Virago, 2007, loc 1872
9. Nina Brochmann, Ellen Stokken Dahl and Lucy Moffatt, *The Wonder Down Under: A User's Guide to the Vagina*, Quercus, 2018
10. Jo B. Paoletti, *Pink and Blue: Telling the Boys from the Girls in America*, Indiana University Press, 2012
11. John Horgan, 'Darwin Was Sexist, and So Are Many Modern Scientists', *Scientific American*, 18 December 2017
12. Julia Bush, 'The Anti-Suffrage Movement', 5 March 2018
13. Paoletti, *Pink and Blue*
14. Judith Shapiro in Julia Epstein and Kristina Straub (eds), *Bodyguards: The Cultural Politics of Gender Ambiguity*, Routledge, 1991, p. 253
15. Anne Fausto Sterling, 'Gender/Sex and the Body', Psychology Podcast, YouTube
16. Sheila Rowbotham, *A Century of Women: The History of Women in Britain and the United States*, Viking, 1997, p. 406
17. Paoletti, *Pink and Blue*
18. Priyanka Aribindi, '13 Fascinating Careers You Never Knew Barbie Had', *Time*, 30 July 2015
19. 'Stupid Gender Parties', *The Times*, 9 September 2020
20. Soma Sara, *Everyone's Invited*, Gallery Books, 2023, p. 23
21. Philippe Testard-Vaillant, 'How Many Sexes Are There?', CNRS News, 8 January 2016
22. Charles Bremner, 'Let Me Race Against Men, Says Top Female Cyclist', *The Times*, 19 March 2019
23. 'UK Athletics Want to Prevent Transgender Athletes from Competing in Women's Category', Reuters, 3 February 2023
24. Cordelia Fine, *Delusions of Gender: The Real Science Behind Sex Differences*, Icon Books, 2010
25. Ibid.
26. First Census Estimates on Gender Identity and Sexual Orientation, Census 2021, ONS, 6 January 2023
27. Comparisons of official Ministry of Justice statistics from March/April 2019 (the most recent official count of transgender prisoners): Written evidence submitted by Rosa Freedman, Kathleen Stock and Alice Sullivan, 'Evidence and Data on Trans Women's Offending

Rates', GRA 2021, Parliament UK, November 2020

28. 'Coercive Sex in Prison: Briefing Paper 3', Commission on Sex in Prison, Howard League for Penal Reform, 2014

29. Michelle M. Sauer, *Gender in Medieval Culture*, Bloomsbury, 2015, loc 3431

30. Joyce Burnette, 'An Investigation of the Female–Male Pay Gap during the Industrial Revolution in Britain', *Economic History Review*, Vol. 50, No. 2, 1997, pp. 257–81

31. Fine, *Delusions of Gender*, p. 80

32. Pamela Duncan, 'UK Gender Gap: Women Paid 90p for £1 Earned by Men', *Guardian*, 6 April 2022

33. Peter Craddick-Adams, 'Women at War: "She-Soldiers" Through the Ages', BBC History

34. Susan Byrnes, 'Missing Perspectives: How Women Are Left Out of the News', Bill and Melinda Gates Foundation, 2 December 2020

35. Leslie Young, 'Drugs Aren't Tested on Women Like They Are on Men, and It Could Have Deadly Consequences', Global News, 2 November 2016

36. Alyson McGregor, 'Why Medicine Often Has Dangerous Side Effects for Women', TED Talk, 5 November 2015

37. 'Women Doctors "Best for Female Heart Patients"', BBC News, 7 August 2018

38. Lindsey Bever, 'From Heart Disease to IUDs: How Doctors Dismiss Women's Pain', *Washington Post*, 13 December 2022

39. David Morris, *The Evil Hours*, quoted in Rebecca Solnit, *The Mother of All Questions: Further Feminist Essays*, Haymarket Books, 2017, loc 467

40. Suzannah Weiss, '"Fear of the Clit": A Brief History of Medical Books Erasing Women's Genitalia', *Vice*, 3 May 2017

41. Rebecca Jennings, *A Lesbian History of Britain: Love and Sex Between Women since 1500*, Greenwood Publishing, 2007, p. 15

42. Anthony Fletcher, *Gender, Sex and Subordination in England 1500–1800*, Yale University Press, 1995, p. 35

43. Ibid.

44. Patri J. Pugliese, 'Robert Hooke', *Oxford Dictionary of National Biography*

45. Barbara Ehrenreich and Deirdre English, *For Her Own Good: Two Centuries of the Experts' Advice to Women*, Random House, 2005, loc 2369

46. Jeanette Winterson in *The Times*, 21 August 2019

47. Weiss, '"Fear of the Clit"'

48. Brochmann et al., *The Wonder Down Under: A User's Guide to the Vagina*, Quercus, 2018

49. Weiss, '"Fear of the Clit"'

50. William Shakespeare, *King Lear*, Act IV, scene 6

51. Daisy Payling, 'Selling Shame: Feminine Hygiene Advertising and the Boundaries of Permissiveness in 1970s Britain', *Gender and History*, Wiley Online, 2023

52. Leonard Shlain, *Sex, Time, and Power: How Women's Sexuality Shaped Human Evolution*, 2004, p. 182

53. Ben Panko, 'This High-Ranking Viking Warrior Was a Woman', *Smithsonian Magazine*, 11 September 2017

54. Rosamund Urwin, 'Odin's Beard! Transgender Vikings May Have Played a Key Role in Pillage Life', *Sunday Times*, 16 August 2020

55. Nadia Brooks, 'DNA Tests Solve Mystery of Finnish Warrior Buried in Women's Clothes', *The Times*, 2 August 2021

56. Ida Emilie Steinmark, 'Archaeology's Sexual Revolution', *Observer*, 16 January 2022

57. Olwen Hufton, *The Prospect Before Her*, Knopf, 1996, p. 219

58. Sara, *Everyone's Invited*, loc 919

59. Andrea Dworkin, *Right-Wing Women*, Perigee Books, 1982, p. 215

Acknowledgements

I am so grateful to the very many people who have helped me research, think about, and write this book. Especially I should like to thank Zahra Glibbery, for research, especially anything about horses, marathon copy edits, and her meticulous work on the detail of footnotes and captions, Victoria Atkins and Anna Cusack for research, Karen Ingala Smith for her unique and valuable list of women killed in domestic violence, Arabella Pike for being such an encouraging editor, Iain Hunt for such care and thought, Julian Humphries for listening to my idea and producing an image both symbolic and beautiful, Charlie Redmayne for understanding at once what I was trying to do with such an ambitious project and bringing in the entire HarperCollins team who have all been so enthusiastic and helpful from day one – including the audio books team Molly Robinson, Fionnuala Barrett and Caroline Friend, the children's Farshore team, Emily Lamm, Melissa Fairley and Harriett Rogers. and those, at the time of writing, that I have yet to meet and work with as this project goes from one edition to another.

I would not have embarked on such a huge book without the encouragement of friends: Christopher Cook, Stella Tillyard, Malcolm Gaskill, Kirk Moore, Anna Whitelock, Diane Purkiss, Michael Jones, Gareth Russell, Jennie McNamara, my sister Tina Ryan, and some wonderful teachers whose loss I have felt acutely when writing about their particular interests: Geoffrey Carnall, Alun Howkins and Maurice Hutt.

I owe such a debt of gratitude to the inspiring thinkers who wrote the books that I have read and re-read. Their dedication to the history and progress of women has made it possible for me to write here a longer, wider story, without losing the detail of the past. Only a very few of their books are listed in the bibliography due to lack of space. And I thank also, those wonderful men and women who campaigned so effectively for the education of women, that there was a place for women at universities, and those women who directly encouraged or funded my study: Elaine Gregory, Mary Wedd, a Cambridge graduate, and Winifred Leonard, who graduated at Oxford before women were awarded degrees. I was indeed blessed in Aunts. Thanks also to Butter, the Irish setter – who has accompanied me on many thoughtful walks – and Bob-Bob, the tawny owl who showed me how to fly free.

List of Illustrations

175: John Phillips, 'The examination and confession of certaine wytches at Chensforde', Willyam Powell for Wyllyam Pickeringe, 1566 (*Granger/Bridgeman Images*)

176 and cover: 'Sathan' in ibid. (*Public domain*)

181 and cover: Frontispiece, *Annalia Dubrensia*, 1636 (*Public domain*)

225: Halfpenny token of Mary Long at the sign of the Rose in Russell Street, Covent Garden, 1669 (*Folger Shakespeare Library*)

260 and cover: The monument to Mary Kendall and Lady Catherine Jones, 1710, St John the Baptist Chapel, Westminster Abbey (*Dean and Chapter of Westminster*)

270 and cover: Kit Cavanagh from *The Girl's Own Annual*, 1 October 1904 (*duncan1890/Getty Images*)

272 and cover: Anne Bonny from Captain Charles Johnson, *A General History of the Robberies and Murders of the Most Notorious Pyrates*, T. Warner, 1724 (*The Picture Art Collection/Alamy*)

273 and cover: Mary Read from Charles Ellms, *The Pirates Own Book*, Sanborn & Carter, 1837 (*Science History Images/Alamy*)

274 and cover: Hannah Snell, painted by R. Phelps, engraved by J. Young, 1750, British Museum (*Public domain*)

293: A Monk of the Order of St Francis, *Nocturnal Revels*, M. Goadby, 1779 (*The History Collection/Alamy*)

299: Mary Seacole in a collection by Ely Duodecimus Wigram, discovered by Dr Geoffrey Day at Winchester College (*Winchester College/Mary Seacole Trust/Mary Evans*)

300: Florence Nightingale by William Edward Kilburn, *c.*1856, Royal Collection Trust (*Alpha Historica/Alamy*)

305 and cover: Phillis Wheatley, possibly based on a portrait by Scipio Moorhead from Phillis Wheatley, *Poems on Various Subjects, Religious and Moral*, Archibald Bell, 1773 (*Stock Montage/Getty Images*)

317 and cover: 'A *drawer*' pulling a coal tub, originally published in the Children's Employment Commission (Mines) 1842 report (*Classic Image/Alamy*)

322: South Bank Lion by William F. Woodington, 24 May 1837, photographed by anon (*Michael Wald/Alamy*)

325 and cover: Hannah Norsa by R. Clamp, after Bernard Lens III stipple engraving, 1794 (*National Portrait Gallery, London*)

451: Nettie Honeyball, photograph by unknown in *The Sketch magazine*, 6 February 1895 (*Chronicle/Alamy*)

452: Dick, Kerr & Co factory team, official team photo by unknown photographer, *c.*1921 (*Bob Thomas/Popperfoto/Getty Images*)

463 and cover: May 'Toupie' Lowther from Martinho Botelho's *Revista Moderna*, 1899 (*Chronicle/Alamy*)

465: Flora Sandes, unknown photographer, *c.*1919 (*GL Archive/Alamy Stock Photo*)

469: 'These Women Are Doing Their Bit, Learn to Make Munitions', wartime recruiting poster, 1916 (*Hulton Deutsch/Getty Images*)

477: 'What do the Tea Leaves Say?', Conservative Party poster, 1929 (*Public domain*)

480 and cover: Ellen Wilkinson by unknown photographer, Hyde Park, 1 November 1936 (*Daily Herald Archive/Getty Images*)

486: 'What Are the Wild Waves Saying?', Beecham's Pills advertisement, late nineteenth century (*Chronicle/Alamy*)

490: ATS plotters by War Office official photographer, Coastal Artillery Headquarters in Dover, 1942 (*Imperial War Museum*)

491 and cover: Jackie Moggridge by unknown photographer, Gloucestershire, 5 October 1949 (*TopFoto*)

493 and cover: Noor Inayat Khan, unknown photographer,1943 (*IanDagnall Computing/Alamy*)

499: Mark Weston, photograph published in *Western Morning News*, 1936 (*Public domain*)

503: Mary Elizabeth Wilson by unknown photographer, *c.*1957 (*Popperfoto/Getty Images*)

529 and cover: Princess Elizabeth as a Girl Guide, in Windsor, Berkshire, 25 July 1944 (*Paul Popper/Popperfoto/Getty Images*)

531: Pat King's baby's name tag from 1973, personal archive (*Courtesy of Pat King*)

536: Anwar Ditta with her daughter Samera Shuja by John Sturrock, 1981 (*John Sturrock/Report digital*)

540: Mona Baptiste in Hamburg by unknown photographer, 13 September 1956 (*Keystone/Getty Images*)

547: Women protesting Section 28, front page of the *Daily Mirror*, 24 May 1988 (*Daily Mirror/Mirrorpix*)

550: Roberta Cowell, from *Picture Post*, 27 March 1954 (*Maurice Ambler/Getty Images*)

554: Caroline Cossey by Kent Gavin, May 1990 (*Mirrorpix/Getty Images*)

575: Kiwi bird (*GlobalP/Getty*)

First Plate Section

One of the five women pictured in the Bayeux Tapestry, *c.*1070, Musée de la Tapisserie de Bayeux (*Ancient Art and Architecture/Alamy*)

One of the 93 penises in the Bayeux Tapestry, *c.*1070, Musée de la Tapisserie de Bayeux (*Paul Williams/Alamy*)

[And cover] Acrobat balancing on sword tips, from the *Smithfield Decretals*, *c.*1340 (*British Library Board/Bridgeman Images*)

[And cover] 'Sin of the mouth' illumination in the *Bible moralisée*, *c.*1220 (*Austrian National Library/Interfoto/Alamy*)

[And cover] 'A garden of pleasure' illustration by unknown artist, Guillaume de Lorris, *The Romance of the Rose*, Biblioteca universitaria (*Public domain*)

Graph of the mean wages in pence per day of unskilled men and women, based on data from Humphries, Jane, and Weisdorf, Jacob, 'The Wages of Women in England 1260–1850', *Journal of Economic History*, Cambridge University Press, Vol. 75. Issue 2, June 2015 (*Martin Brown*)

Second Plate Section

The Execution of Lady Jane Grey by Paul Delaroche, 1833, National Gallery (*IanDagnall Computing/Alamy*)

[And cover] *Miss Mary Edwards* by William Hogarth, 1742, Frick Collection (*Fine Art/Getty Images*)

Arabella Hunt Playing a Lute by Sir Godfrey Kneller, 1692, Government Art Collection (*Government Art Collection*)

[And cover] *The Fencing-Match between the Chevalier de Saint-George and the Chevalier d'Eon* by Alexandre-Auguste Robineau, *c.*1787/9, Royal Collection (*Royal Collection Trust/© His Majesty King Charles III 2023*)

[And cover] *Portrait of Dido Elizabeth Belle Lindsay and Lady Elizabeth Murray* by David Martin,1779, Scone Palace (*Art Reserve/Alamy*)

Saartjie Baartman or 'La Belle Hottentote' by Louis François Charon, 1815 (*National Library of France*)

Third Plate Section

[And cover] *Mary Anning* by Benjamin John Merifield Donne, 1850, Sedgwick Museum (*Public domain*)

The Rt. Honble. Lady Eleanor Butler & Miss Ponsonby, 'The Ladies of Llangollen' by James Henry Lynch, 1880s, Welsh Portrait Collection (*Maidun Collection/Alamy*)

[And cover] *Portrait of Ada, Countess of Lovelace* by Alfred Edward Chalon, 1840, Science Museum Group Collection (*Public domain*)

Mrs Fanny Eaton by Walter Fryer Stocks, 1859, Princeton University Art Museum (*Public domain*)

Henry Fawcett; Dame Millicent Fawcett by Ford Madox Brown, 1872, National Portrait Gallery (*National Portrait Gallery, London*)

[And cover] Countess Markievicz photographed by Keogh Brothers Ltd photographers, 1915, National Library of Ireland (*Public domain*)

[And cover] Maud Allan as Salome in 'The Vision of Salome' photographed by Foulsham & Banfield, 1908 (*Chronicle/Alamy*)

Fourth Plate Section

[And cover] *The Arrival of the Jarrow Marchers in London, Viewed from an Interior* by Thomas Dugdale, 1936, Museum of the Home (*Public domain*)

Rotha Beryl Lintorn Lintorn-Orman photographed by Bassano Ltd, 22 August 1916, National Portrait Gallery (*National Portrait Gallery, London*)

[And cover] Policemen arresting a demonstrator, unknown photographer, 4 October 1936 (*Topical Press Agency/Getty Images*)

The Hackett-Lowther all-female Ambulance Unit by Jacques Ridel, 1918 (*ECPAD/Défense*)

A member of the Women's Land Army by Horace Nicholls, *c.*1915–18 (*Imperial War Museum*)

[And cover] *Ruby Loftus Screwing a Breech-Ring* by Laura Knight, 1943, Imperial War Museum (*Imperial War Museum*)

Dr Una Kroll, unknown photographer, LSE Women's Library (4/17) (*LSE Library*)

Select Bibliography

Abraham, Keshia N., and Woolf, John, *Black Victorians*, 2022

Adams, Max, *Unquiet Women: From the Dusk of the Roman Empire to the Dawn of the Enlightenment*, 2018

Akkerman, Nadine, *Invisible Agents: Women and Espionage in Seventeenth-Century Britain*, 2018

Allestree, Richard, *The Ladies Calling: In Two Parts* (1673), 2017

Amt, Emilie (ed.), *Women's Lives in Medieval Europe, a Sourcebook*, 1993

Amtower, Laurel, and Kehler, Dorothea, *The Single Woman in Medieval and Early Modern England: Her Life and Representation*, 2003

Amussen, Susan D., and Underdown, David E., *Gender, Culture and Politics in England 1560–1640: Turning the World Upside Down*, 2017

Anishanslin, Zara, *Portrait of a Woman in Silk: Hidden Histories of the British Atlantic World*, 2016

Appignanesi, Lisa, *Mad, Bad and Sad: A History of Women and the Mind Doctors, from 1800 to the Present*, 2007

Baer, William C., 'Early Retailing: London's Shopping Exchanges 1550–1700', *Business History*, Vol. 49, No. 1, January 2007, pp. 29–51

Baird, Dame Vera, 'Annual Report by the Victim's Commissioner, 2021–2022', published online at https://victimscommissioner.org.uk/document/annual-report-of-the-victims-commissioner-2021-to-2022/

Barker, Diana Leonard, and Allen, Sheila (eds), *Dependence and Exploitation in Work and Marriage*, 1976

Barker, Helen, *Rape in Early Modern England: Law, History and Criticism*, 2021

Barret-Ducrocq, Françoise, *Love in the Time of Victoria*, 1991

Bartley, Paula, *Queen Victoria*, 2016

Bates, Laura, *Everyday Sexism*, 2014

Bateson, Mary, *Medieval England 1066–1350*, 1903

Baumgarten, Elisheva, *Mothers and Children: Jewish Family Life in Medieval Europe*, 2000

Bennett, Judith M., and Froide, Amy M. (eds), *Singlewomen in the European Past 1250–1800*, 1999

Bennett, Judith M., and Karras, Ruth Mazo, *The Oxford Handbook of Women and Gender in Medieval Europe*, 2013

Bennett, Judith M. and McSheffrey, Shannon, 'Early, Erotic and Alien: Women Dressed as Men in Late Medieval London', *History Workshop Journal*, Spring 2014, No. 77, pp. 1–25

Biberman, Matthew, *Masculinity, Anti-Semitism and Early Modern English Literature*, 2004

Boase, Tessa, *Mrs Pankhurst's Purple Feather: Fashion, Fury and Feminism – Women's Fight for Change*, 2018

Bogin, Meg, *The Woman Troubadours*, 1976

Boswell, John, *Same Sex Unions in Pre-Modern Europe*, 1994

Bourke, Joanna, *Rape: A History from 1860 to the Present*, 2007

Braybon, G., and Summerfield, P., *Out of the Cage: Women's Experiences in Two World Wars*, 2013

Bridgeford, Andrew, *1066: The Hidden History of the Bayeux Tapestry*, 2006

Brochmann, Nina, and Støkken Dahl, Ellen, *The Wonder Down Under: A User's Guide to the Vagina*, 1998

Bruley, Sue, *The Women and Men of 1926: A Gender and Social History of the General Strike and Miners' Lockout in South Wales*, 2010

Brunskill-Evans, Heather (ed.), *The Sexualized Body and the Medical Authority of Pornography: Performing Sexual Liberation*, 2016

Burns, Christine (ed.), *Trans Britain: Our Journey from the Shadows*, 2018

Burns, William E., *Witch Hunts in Europe and America: An Encyclopedia*, 2003

Butler, Judith, *Gender Trouble: Feminism and the Subversion of Identity*, 1990

Capp, Bernard, *When Gossips Meet: Women, Family, and Neighbourhood in Early Modern England*, 2003

Carter, John Marshall, *Rape in Medieval England: An Historical and Sociological Study*, 1985

Castor, Helen, *She Wolves: The Women Who Ruled England before Elizabeth*, 2010

Clark, Alice, *The Working Life of Women in the Seventeenth Century*, 1968

Davidoff, Leonore, *Family Fortunes: Men and Women of the English Middle Class 1780 to 1850*, 1987

De Costa, C.M., 'The King versus Aleck Bourne', *Medical Journal of Australia*, Vol. 191, No. 4, August 2009, pp. 230–1

De Pisan, Christine, *A Medieval Woman's Mirror of Honour: The Treasury of the City of Ladies*, 1989

Delphy, Christine, *Close to Home: A Materialist Analysis of Women's Oppression*, 2016

Donoghue, Emma, *Passions Between Women*, 2014

Dunn, Caroline, *Stolen Women in Medieval England: Rape, Abduction and Adultery, 1100–1500*, 2013

Dworkin, Andrea, *Right-Wing Women*, 1978

Dworkin, Andrea, *Woman Hating*, 1974

Earle, Peter, *The Making of the English Middle Class*, 1989

Ehrenreich, Barbara, and English, Deirdre, *Complaints and Disorders: The Sexual Politics of Sickness*, 1973

Ehrenreich, Barbara, and English, Deirdre, *For Her Own Good: Two Centuries of the Experts' Advice to Women*, 2005

Epstein, Julia, and Straub, Kristina (eds), *Bodyguards: The Cultural Politics of Gender Ambiguity*, 1991

Erickson, Amy Louise, *Women and Property in Early Modern England*, 1993

Faderman, Lillian, *Surpassing the Love of Men: Romantic Friendship and Love Between Women from the Renaissance to the Present*, 1985

Federico, Sylvia, 'The Imaginary Society: Women in 1381', *Journal of British Studies*, Vol. 40, No. 2, April 2001, pp. 150–83

Fine, Cordelia, *Delusions of Gender: The Real Science Behind Sex Differences*, 2010

Fine, Cordelia, *Testosterone Rex: Unmaking the Myths of our Gendered Minds*, 2017

Fisher, Elizabeth, *Woman's Creation*, 1979

Fletcher, Anthony, *Gender, Sex and Subordination in England 1500–1800*, 1999

Freedman, Estelle B., Gelpi, Barbara C., Johnson, Susan L., and Weston, Kathleen M. (eds), *'The Lesbian Issue': Essays from SIGNS*, 1985

Frye, Susan, and Robertson, Karen (eds), *Maids and Mistresses, Cousins and Queens: Women's Alliances in Early Modern England*, 1999

Fryer, Peter, *Staying Power: The History of Black People in Britain*, 1984

Gaskill, Malcolm, *Witchfinders: A Seventeenth-Century English Tragedy*, 2005

Gies, Joseph, and Gies, Frances, *Women in the Middle Ages: The Lives of Real Women in a Vibrant Age of Transition*, 1978

Giffney, Noreen, Sauer, Michelle M., and Watt, Diane (eds), *The Lesbian Premodern*, 2011

Goldberg, P.J.P. (ed.), *Women in Medieval English Society*, 1992

Goldin, Simha, *Jewish Women in Europe in the Middle Ages*, 2011

Gordon, Robin L., *Searching for the Soror Mystica: The Lives and Science of Women Alchemists*, 2013

Gowing, Laura, *Domestic Dangers: Women, Words and Sex in Early Modern London*, 1996

Gowing, Laura, *Gender Relations in Early Modern England*, 2012

Green, Judith A., *The Normans: Power, Conquest and Culture in 11th-Century Europe*, 2022

Greg, W.R., 'Why Are Women Redundant?', 1869

Hanawalt, Barbara A., *The Ties that Bound: Peasant Families in Medieval England*, 1986

Hanawalt, Barbara A., *The Wealth of Wives: Women, Law and Economy in Late Medieval London*, 2007

Harris, Barbara J., *English Aristocratic Women 1450–1550: Marriage and Family, Property and Careers*, 2002

Harvey, Katherine, *The Fires of Lust: Sex in the Middle Ages*, 2021

Harvey, Richard, 'English Pre-Industrial Ballads on Poverty, 1500–1700', *The Historian*, Vol. 46, No. 4, August 1984, pp. 539–61

Harvey, Richard, 'The Work and Mentalité of Lower Orders Elizabethan Women', *Exemplaria*, Vol. 5, Issue 2, 1993, pp. 409–33

Haynes, Alan, *Sex in Elizabethan England*, 1997

Hays, Mary, *Appeal to the Men of Great Britain in Behalf of Women*, 1798

Hodgkin, Katharine (ed.), *Women, Madness and Sin in Early Modern England: The Autobiographical Writings of Dionys Fitzherbert*, 2010

Houlbrooke, Ralph A., *The English Family 1450–1700*, 1984

Hufton, Olwen, *The Prospect Before Her: A History of Women in Western Europe, 1500–1800*, 1995

Hughes, Ann, *Gender and the English Revolution*, 2012

Humphries, Jane, and Weisdorf, Jacob, 'The Wages of Women in England 1260–1850', *Journal of Economic History*, Vol. 75, Issue 2, June 2015, pp. 405–77

Hunter, Clare, *Threads of life: A History of the World Through the Eye of a Needle*, 2019

Illston, James Michael, '"An Entirely Masculine Activity"? Women and War in the High and Late Middle Ages Reconsidered', MA Thesis, University of Canterbury, 2009

Jaleel, Rana M., *The Work of Rape*, 2021

Jennings, Rebecca, *A Lesbian History of Britain: Love and Sex Between Women Since 1500*, 2007

Jones, Vivien (ed.), *Women in the Eighteenth Century: Constructions of Femininity*, 1990

Karras, Ruth Mazo, *Sexuality in Medieval Europe: Doing Unto Others*, 2005

Kaufmann, Miranda, *Black Tudors: The Untold Story*, 2017

Kermode, Jenny, and Walker, Garthine (eds), *Women, Crime and the Courts in Early Modern England*, 1994

Kingsley, Kent Susan, *Gender and Power in Britain 1640–1990*, 1999

Knudsen, Christian D., *Naughty Nuns and Promiscuous Monks: Monastic Sexual Misconduct in Late Medieval England*, PhD Thesis, University of Toronto, 2012

Laqueur, Thomas, *Making Sex: Body and Gender from the Greeks to Freud*, 1990

Lee, Patricia-Ann, 'Mistress Stagg's Petitioners, February 1642', *The Historian*, 1968, Vol. 60, No. 2, Winter 1968, pp. 241–56

LeGates, Marlene 'The Cult of Womanhood in Eighteenth-Century Thought', *Eighteenth-Century Studies*, Vol. 10, No. 1, Autumn 1976, pp. 21–39

Lewis, C.S., *The Allegory of Love*, 1936

Leyser, Henrietta, *Medieval Women: Social History of Women in England 450–1500*, 2013

Loudon, J., 'Deaths in Childbed from the Eighteenth century to 1935', *Medical History*, 1986, Vol. 30, No. 1, pp. 1–41

Macfarlane, Alan, *Marriage and Love in England 1300–1840*, 1986

Marcal, Katrine, *Who Cooked Adam Smith's Dinner? – A Story of Women and Economics*, 2012

Marcus, Sharon, *Between Women: Friendship, Desire and Marriage in Victorian England*, 2007

Mate, Mavis E, *Daughters, Wives and Widows after the Black Death: Women in Sussex 1350–1535*, 1998

Mayhew, Henry, *London Characters and Crooks*, ed. Hibbert, Christopher, 1996

McGregory, Alyson J., *Sex Matters: How Male-Centric Medicine Endangers Women's Health and What We Can Do About It*, 2020

McIntosh, Marjorie Keniston, *Poor Relief in England, 1350–1600*, 2012

McIntosh, Marjorie Keniston, *Working Women in English Society 1300–1620*, 2005

McNellis, Lindsey, *Let Her Be Taken: Sexual Violence in Medieval England*, MA Thesis, University of Florida, 2008

Mellor, Anne K., 'Sex, Violence, and Slavery: Blake and Wollstonecraft', *Huntington Library Quarterly*, Vol. 58, No. 3/4, 1995, pp. 345–70

Mendelson, Sara, and Crawford, Patricia, *Women in Early Modern England 1550–1720*, 1998

Mendelson, Sara Heller, *The Mental World of Stuart Women: Three Studies*, 1987

Midgley, Clare, 'Anti-Slavery and Feminism in Nineteenth-Century Britain', *Gender & History*, Vol. 5, No. 3, Autumn 1993, pp. 343–62

Moody, Joanna (ed.), *The Private Life of an Elizabethan Lady: The Diary of Lady Margaret Hoby, 1599–1605*, 1998

Mortimer, Ian, *The Dying and the Doctors: The Medical Revolution in Seventeenth-Century England*, 2009

Mortimer, Ian, *The Time Traveller's Guides (4 Volumes)*: 2009–2020

Mosse, Kate, *Warrior Queens and Quiet Revolutionaries: How Women (Also) Built the World*, 2022

Murray, Jenni, *A History of Britain in 21 Women: A Personal Selection*, 2016

Norton, Elizabeth, *The Hidden Lives of Tudor Women: A Social History*, 2017

O'Donnell, Katherine, and O'Rourke, Michael (eds), *Queer Masculinities, 1550–1800: Siting Same-Sex Desire in the Early Modern World*, 2006

O'Donoghue, Bernard, *The Courtly Love Tradition*, 1982

Oakley, Anne, *Housewife*, 1974

Olusoga, David, *Black and British: A Forgotten History*, 2016

Orme, Nicolas, *Going to Church in Medieval England*, 2021

Palmer, Gabrielle, *The Politics of Breastfeeding: When Breasts Are Bad for Business*, 1988

Paoletti, Jo B., *Pink and Blue: Telling the Boys from the Girls in America*, 2012

Perez, Caroline Criado, *Invisible Women: Exposing Data Bias in a World Designed for Men*, 2019

Phillips, Kim M. (ed.), *The Cultural History of Women in the Middle Ages*, 2013

Phillips, Kim M., *Young Women and Gender in England 1270–1540*, 2003

Picard, Lisa, *Restoration London: Everyday Life in the 1660s*, 2013

Plowden, Alison, *All on Fire: The Women of the English Civil War*, 1998

Power, Nina, *One-dimensional Woman*, 2009

Power, Nina, *What Do Men Want?: Masculinity and Its Discontents*, 2022

Prince, Mary, *The History of Mary Prince (1831)*, 2000

Prior, Mary (ed.), *Women in English Society, 1500–1800*, 1985

Proctor, Tammy M., *Female Intelligence: Women and Espionage in the First World War*, 2003

Purkiss, Diane, *The English Civil Wars: A People's History*, 2006

Rackley, Erika, and Auchmuty, Rosemary, *Women's Legal Landmarks: Celebrating the History of Women and Law in the UK and Ireland*, 2018

Ramirez, Janina, *Femina: A New History of the Middle Ages Through the Women Written Out of It*, 2022

Randall, Adrian, *Riotous Assemblies: Popular Protest in Hanoverian England*, 2006

Read, Sara, *Maids, Wives, Widows: Exploring Early Modern Women's Lives 1540–1740*, 2015

Rich, Adrienne, *Compulsory Heterosexuality and Lesbian Existence*, 1981

Rizzo, Betty, *Companions Without Vows: Relationships among Eighteenth-Century British Women*, 1994

Rose, June, *Marie Stopes and the Sexual Revolution*, 1992

Rowbotham, Sheila, *A Century of Women: The History of Women in Britain and the United States*, 1997

Rowbotham, Sheila, *Hidden from History: 300 Years of Women's Oppression and the Fight Against It*, 1977

Rowbotham, Sheila, *Woman's Consciousness, Man's World*, 1973

Rubenhold, Hallie (ed.), *Harris's List*, 2012

Saini, Angela, *Inferior: How Science Got Women Wrong, and the New Research That's Rewriting the Story*, 2017

Sanyal, Mithu, *Rape*, 2016

Sauer, Michelle M., *Gender in Medieval Culture*, 2015

Sautman, Francesca Canadé, and Sheingorn, Pamela (eds), *Same Sex Love and Desire among Women in the Middle Ages*, 2001

Scott, Linda, *The Cost of Sexism: How the Economy Is Built for Men and Why We Must Reshape It*, 2020

Searle, Mark, and Stevenson, Kenneth W., *Documents of the Marriage Liturgy*, 1992

Shoemaker, Robert B., *Gender in English Society 1650–1850: The Emergence of Separate Spheres?*, 1998

Showalter, Elaine, *The Female Malady: Women, Madness and English Culture, 1830–1980*, 1987

Smith, Geoffrey, *Royalist Agents, Conspirators and Spies*, 2011

Smith, Joan, *Homegrown: How Domestic Violence Turns Men into Terrorists*, 2019

Soma, Sara, *Everyone's Invited*, 2023

Steinbach, Susie, *Women in England 1760–1914: A Social History*, 2003

Stone, Laurence, *The Family, Sex and Marriage in England, 1500–1800*, 1977

Stonehouse, Julia, *Father's Seed, Mother's Sorrow: How the Wrong 'Facts of Life' Gave Men Control of the World*, 2016

Tabori, Paul, *The Social History of Rape*, 1971

Thom, Deborah, *Nice Girls and Rude Girls: Women Workers in World War One*, 1998

Thompson, E.P., *Customs in Common: Studies in Popular Culture*, 1993

Thompson, E.P., *The Making of the English Working Class*, 1963

Todd, Janet, *Women's Friendship in Literature*, 1980

Traub, Valerie, *The Renaissance of Lesbianism in Early Modern England Cambridge*, 2002

Tsjeng, Zing, *Forgotten Women*, 4 vols, 2018

Tuchman, Barbara W., *A Distant Mirror: The Calamitous 14th Century*, 2014

Twells, Alison, *British Women's History: A Documentary History from the Enlightenment to World War One*, 2007

Ulrich, Laurel Thatcher, *Well-Behaved Women Seldom Make History*, 1998

Ulrich, Melanie Renee, *Victoria's Feminist Legacy: How Nineteenth-Century Women Imagined the Queen*, PhD thesis, University of Texas, 2005

Vickery, Amanda, *The Gentleman's Daughter: Women's Lives in Georgian England*, 1999

Wall, Alison D. (ed.), *Two Elizabethan Women: Correspondence of Joan and Mariah Thynne 1575–1611*, 1983

Ward, Jennifer, *Women in Medieval Europe 1200–1500*, 2002

Warnicke, Retha, *Wicked Women of England: Queens, Aristocrats, Commoners*, 2012

Whitbread, Helena (ed.), *The Secret Diaries of Anne Lister*, 2 vols, 2010

Whitelock, Anna, *Elizabeth's Bedfellows: An Intimate History of the Queen's Court*, 2013

Williams, Marty, and Echols, Anne, *Between Pit and Pedestal: Women in the Middle Ages*, 1995

Wollock, Jennifer G., *Rethinking Chivalry and Courtly Love*, 2011

Woolgar, C.M., *The Culture of Food in England, 1200–1500*, 2016

Yalom, Marilyn, *A History of the Wife*, 2001

Yalom, Marilyn, *The Amorous Heart: An Unconventional History of Love*, 2018

Zakira, Rafia, *Against White Feminism*, 2022

Index

abbeys/convents/nunneries: female hermits (anchoresses), 3, 14, 16, 56; women escaping to safety of, 8, 14; and Waltheof, Earl of Northumbria, 12; pilgrim ways, 13; elite/powerful women in, 14–16, 111; as centres of learning/scholarship, 15–16, 36, 111, 121, 228; escaping nuns, 16–17, 53, 106; textile departments, 31; nuns and sex, 60–1, 106, 109–10, 206; women loving women in, 61, 206; impact of Black Death, 68; mismanagement and abuse in, 109–10; Henry VIII's *Compendium Compertorum*, 109; loss of in Reformation, 110–12, 205; Mary Ward's convent at York, 228; nuns in Victorian era, 457

Abbott, Diane, 524
abortion, 287, 361, 485–7, 538, 542, 578; folk traditions, 287, 428, 485, 542
Addison, Joseph, 385
adoption laws, 531–2
Ælfgifu (wife of King Cnut), 5
Aelred of Rievaulx, 16, 61
Æthelflæd (daughter of Wynflæd), 6
agriculture/rural life: in medieval/feudal era, 9–10, 11, 13, 17, 28–31, 67, 68–9, 70, 71, 79, 82; women farm labourers, 9–10, 17, 319; empty land ('waste'), 11, 13; market towns, 13, 17, 35; small-scale industry, 13, 17, 31; wild animals, 13; great famine (1315–18), 17; women's casual work, 30, 31; impact of Black Death, 67, 68–9, 70, 71; women farmers, 69, 70, 82, 321; country estates, 124, 168, 321; impact of post-Restoration land-grab, 207–11; mechanisation of,

321, 349, 442; courtship traditions, 334–5; childbirth in, 428; Women's Land Army, 467–8, 494, 501 *see also* common land
Ahluwalia, Kiranjit, 516
Air Transport Auxiliary (ATA), 491, *491*
Albert, Prince, 370–1, 373–4, 442, 443
Aliens Restriction Act (1914), 466
Alkyn, Joan ('Parliament Joan'), 146
Allan, Maud, 438, 466
Allestree, Richard, 215–16
Americas, first nations in, 298
Anger, Jane, 128
Anglo-Saxon England, 5, 6–9, 36, 52
Anne, Queen, 221, 232, 238, 245, 257–8, 287
Anne of Denmark, 139, 140
Anning, Mary, 329
apprenticeships, 18–19, 30, 148, 233–4, 301–2; female apprentices, 20, 39, 69, 70, 80, 182–3, 222, 223; women training apprentices, 35, 37, 70, 223
Aquinas, Thomas, 42, 60
archaeology, 576–7
archery, 446–7
architecture, 15, 69–70, 111
Argyll, Archibald Campbell, Earl of, 217–18
Aristotle, 54, 63, 253, 562, 564, 574
art: female artists, 15, 31–2, 56, 157–8, 223–4, 225, 298, 322, *322*, 379–80; and nunneries, 15; textile artists, 31–2, 56, 223–4; female patrons, 37, 80; courtly love tradition, 64–6, 87, 93, 95–8, 128, 216; botanical artists, 223; portraits of slaves and owners, 296–7; slaves as artist's